Communism in Italy and France

Communism in Italy and France

Edited by Donald L. M. Blackmer
and Sidney Tarrow

PRINCETON, NEW JERSEY
PRINCETON UNIVERSITY PRESS

Copyright © 1975 by Princeton University Press
Published by Princeton University Press, Princeton, New Jersey
In the U.K.: Princeton University Press, Guildford, Surrey

ALL RIGHTS RESERVED

ISBN 0-691-10054-3 (Limited Paperback Edition)
ISBN 0-691-08724-5 (hardcover edition)

*Library of Congress Cataloging in Publication Data
will be found on the last printed page of this book*

This book has been composed in Linotype Caledonia

*Printed in the United States of America
by Princeton University Press, Princeton, N.J.*

First Limited Paperback Edition printing,
with new Preface, 1977

Preface

This book has been germinating longer than most. In retrospect it is clear that the seeds were sown more than a decade ago, in Rome, when the editors first met to trade ideas about the research they were pursuing on Italian communism. It was a stimulating exchange, in part because we were approaching our common topic with substantially different intellectual interests and backgrounds. One of us was investigating the Communist party in the south of Italy using insights acquired in the study of comparative politics and problems of development, the other was trying to understand the party's international behavior from a perspective largely derived from the study of Soviet policy and international Communist relationships. To some degree we talked past each other, and yet we also came to recognize that in an important sense we were interested in much the same thing. By our quite different routes we had been led to ask the same basic question: how were we to comprehend and communicate the dual and ambivalent reality of a party that was, on the one hand, avowedly *Communist* in ideology, in organizational style, in international loyalties, and on the other hand, most obviously *Italian* as well?

Continued exchanges of view over the intervening years helped make each of us less certain of his own verities and more receptive to the other's insights and criticisms, until it was no longer certain to either of us where a particular idea had originated or what had happened to it as it passed back and forth between us. For better or for worse, the entire structure of this book, as well as the introductory and concluding chapters, reflect this mode of collaboration.

But the book is a collaborative venture in far more than this sense. Anyone who has experienced the satisfactions and frustrations of putting together a volume based on a conference knows that the organizers and editors must rely on the indispensable assistance of a host of persons, visible and invisible, at every stage of the way.

The book owes its existence, first of all, to the initiative of the

Planning Group on Comparative Communist Studies, which was sponsored during the seven years of its existence by the American Council of Learned Societies by means of a grant from the Carnegie Corporation of New York. In 1969 the Planning Group, then under the chairmanship of Alexander Dallin, established a subcommittee on nonruling Communist parties which held a small conference at Columbia University's Arden House to discuss the status of research on these parties and to test the feasibility of a larger international gathering. The discussion, taking off from Joseph LaPalombara's stimulating agenda paper, convinced most of us that the time was not yet ripe for global comparative studies in this field. It also generated great enthusiasm for the idea of a conference devoted to the French and Italian parties, as is explained more fully in the Introduction. The Planning Group agreed to this proposal, and in accordance with its usual practice delegated to one of its members—in this instance, Donald Blackmer—principal responsibility for organizing the conference. He promptly coopted Sidney Tarrow, and in due course the conference took shape. We are most grateful to the ACLS, represented by its vice-president Gordon B. Turner, to the Planning Group as a whole, and particularly to its last two chairmen, Robert Tucker and Richard Burks, for the encouragement and the intellectual and financial support we have received throughout this enterprise.

The conference was held at M.I.T.'s Endicott House in Dedham, Massachusetts, in October 1972. The contributors to this volume made up the largest number of participants, but a number of others contributed in major ways to the debate and helped the authors to hone their ideas against the judgments of a sharp, but not abrasive audience. These participants, many of whom presided over panels as well, have our special thanks. They are Suzanne Berger, Piero Bolchini, Peter Gourevitch, Thomas Greene, Stanley Hoffmann, Juan Linz, Alessandro Pizzorno, Jean Ranger, and Nicholas Wahl.

The editing of conference papers into a reasonably coherent whole, intellectually and stylistically, is no simple task. The first steps were taken by Judith Chubb, who converted her feverishly written conference notes, along with those made by Robert Berrier and Alan Posner, into a useful record to guide the editors in assisting the participants with their revisions and in preparing the introductory and concluding chapters. Susan Tarrow labored to translate the distinctive, but different French prose styles of Annie Kriegel and Georges Lavau into something like the same English. Ellen Offner did a masterful job of editing each of the revised papers, raising sharp substantive questions as well as putting order into a diversity of styles and usages. At Princeton University Press, Polly Hanford has been unfailingly helpful and courteous in seeing the volume through the publication process. Always ready to help in ways large and small, Judith Chubb stepped into the breach once again to prepare the index and the list of abbreviations. And throughout the process, Lisa Martin has been indispensable as coordinator of a complicated communications network, impeccable proofreader, typist of semi-legible manuscripts, and much more. We are greatly in the debt of all these people.

More time than we like to recall has passed between the presentation of the papers to the Endicott House Conference and the publication of this volume. In part, there were the usual delays due to publisher's readers and publication schedules. Equally important, however, were the editors' ambitious expectations for revisions and each contributor's dedication to stylistic or substantive perfection. That the revised papers collected here will justify that effort is not for us to judge, although we heartily hope so. In any event our last and greatest debt is to the colleagues and friends who collaborated with us in this enterprise. Working with them has been one of the greatest pleasures of our professional lives, and we thank them for their hard work, their insight, and for the patience required of them in awaiting publication of their work.

DONALD L. M. BLACKMER
SIDNEY TARROW
Cambridge, Massachusetts
Ithaca, New York
April 1975

Preface to the Paperback Edition

Since the original edition of this book went to press, less than two years ago, the pace of change in Western Europe has been unusually rapid. The French and Italian Communist parties have been substantially affected by national and international developments and have themselves contributed to the general sense of movement by the important changes they have undergone.

In the early 1970s, it appeared that both parties, along with their respective political systems, had for the time being settled into a stable and unexciting state, a period of recuperation after the traumatic years of student unrest, labor strife, and conservative backlash. By mid-1975, however, everything was in motion again. To the domestic economic strains touched off by the industrial conflicts of the late 1960s were added an international economic crisis and a rampant inflation, especially in Italy where the inflation rate jumped to 20 percent or more. In both countries a severe fiscal crisis threatened the survival of the extensive systems of social welfare erected over the past thirty years. These economic and environmental shocks had important political counterparts, especially in Italy.

The divorce referendum of 1974 and the regional elections of June 1975 were the first tangible signs that the Italian political stalemate might be on the way to being broken. The electoral and social support of the Democrazia Cristiana (DC) appeared to be declining, along with the religious allegiance that had replaced many voters' ideological or programmatic party loyalty. The DC's decline was especially marked among younger voters frustrated by its failure to introduce reforms, cope with corruption in government, or take substantial measures to meet the economic crisis. Conversely, the patient and moderate policies of the Partito Comunista Italiano (PCI) seemed finally to have overcome the barriers of anti-Communist sentiment in the electorate. National elections in 1976 consolidated PCI gains in many important cities and regions and made it clear that the party had at last become not only a possible but an almost inevitable *partito di governo.* Since the 1976 elections, the PCI has become part of a curious "government by abstention," counselling and practicing restraint and cooperation in a situation that is tolerable only because the currently visible alternatives appear worse to all concerned.

Not surprisingly, the Italian party's international strategy has been revised to reinforce its domestic gains. Earlier, the PCI's identification with pro-Soviet and anti-American positions had provided an unanswerable argument to those seeking to prevent its entrance into the government. Particularly constraining at a time when "historic compromise" was the slogan of the day was the party's long-standing opposition to the Atlantic Alliance and its call for Italy's withdrawal from NATO. In a significant reversal of policy, therefore, the PCI announced in 1976 that it would respect Italy's alliances, and that unilateral Italian withdrawal from NATO would upset the strategic balance between the two competing blocs and threaten detente. In its relations with the USSR, the PCI has continued to voice forcefully its unorthodox views, using even the XXVI Congress of the Soviet Party in March 1976 as a forum in which to dissent from certain aspects of Soviet ideology and practice. And in increasingly open ways, the PCI has tried to open lines of communication with the United States, which—along with West Germany—remains the strongest external constraint on its future entry into an Italian government.

The recent outspokenness of the PCI toward Moscow should not be attributed exclusively to its strengthened domestic position. A significant change has also occurred within European Communism generally, in directions distinctly favorable to the Italians. The revolutionary tactics of the Portuguese Communists failed, much to the PCI's relief; the transition to a post-Franco regime brought into prominence a Spanish CP that was verbally as democratic and pluralist as the Italian and even more outspokenly critical of the Russians; and most surprising of all, despite its reversion to type in supporting the aggressive Cunhal strategy in Portugal, the French party began to voice essentially "Italian" positions with respect to a number of domestic and international issues. In late June of 1976, at the long-delayed Conference of European Communist parties, these three Western parties, in company with the Yugoslavs and Rumanians, obliged the Soviet leaders in substantial measure to recognize and accept their terms concerning future relations among European Communist parties.

What are we to make of the recent changes in the French party? It would have been rash to suppose, much before mid-1975, that the French Communists would soon publicly disavow the classic slogan of the "dictatorship of the proletariat" and proclaim a "Socialisme aux couleurs de la France" which seemed to borrow substantially in spirit from their more innovative Italian comrades. The French took another leaf from the Italian book when they criticized the Soviet party about forced labor camps and other issues of civil rights under "socialist democracy."

A number of internal developments have accompanied the French party's recent change in policy line. Both the number and the composition of its membership have changed rapidly, with a far greater middle class component and an increased appeal to young people and women. But the basic reason for the party's recent organizational adaptation is external: the very real threat to its position represented by the rapid growth in influence of the French Socialists. Given the dynamic leadership and enhanced popular support of the Parti Socialiste, in fact, a victory of the French Left seems at this point more likely to be a Socialist than a Communist triumph. A new image for French communism—in terms of program, ideology, and organization—seems a prerequisite, though by no means a guarantee, of a successful PCF response to the Socialist challenge.

But the changes in the PCF, though they appear dramatic and far-reaching when compared to its relative orthodoxy in the 1960s, may still lack a solid substratum in the attitudes and habits of party militants at all levels. In contrast to the comparable PCI adaptations, which were preceded by two decades of internal and programmatic evolution and have become firmly rooted in party practice, those so far found in the PCF are recent and largely symbolic—as was the formal denunciation of the dictatorship of the proletariat—and thus far have had little impact on the way the French party operates internally. Further changes in internal orientation are not to be excluded, but caution should be exercised in assuming that the PCF can, in only a few years, travel a route that the PCI took two decades to traverse.

Our purpose in mentioning the recent changes in both Communist parties is twofold. First, we wish to signal that some important developments have occurred in recent months which are not reflected in the body of the book. Had they been given the opportunity, some of our authors (certainly the editors themselves) would have chosen to bring a few references up to date and modify or rephrase certain judgments. Most importantly, however, we wish to express the belief that our fundamental observations and analyses remain valid, despite the changes that have taken place.

Our approach has been to avoid global generalizations about these two parties, emphasizing instead what we called in the introduction "the critical differential impact of national environmental conditions" as well as the complex interactions among each party's political strategy, its international relationships, its organization and membership, and its various local and regional expressions. The recent changes in European politics have led many journalists, and at least some scholars, to accept the global formula of "Euro-Communism" as an adequate shorthand for explaining the current situation. Certainly, the overall strategic situations of the French, Italian, and Spanish Communist parties have much in common, inclining them to respond similarly, in certain ways and at certain times, to the pressures of domestic and international politics. Moreover, the sense of being relatively close to a share of governmental power seems almost certain to induce each of these long-time opposition parties to accentuate its potential for domestic political alliances and to increase its distance from the USSR.

But is there some underlying uniformity which seems likely to determine the emergence in the near future of a common strategy for these parties, with their very different histories and political-institutional settings? We think not, and we continue to resist interpretations and generalizations which in our view give insufficient weight to differences of history, party composition, the nature and alignment of political forces, and other important environmental circumstances. We do not believe that it will help us much in interpreting the recent past, or in intelligently anticipating the near future, to speak of the French party as becoming "Italianized" or of the Iberian ones becoming "Westernized." As the strategy of the Portuguese party in the 1974-75 period showed, national differences and internal party traditions can be decisive.

To illustrate this point, three essential differences in the situations of the French and Italian Communist parties can be cited.

First, since Italy and France bear a different relationship to the western alliance and to the center of Western Europe, international changes are bound to affect their Communist parties differently. The impact of this is clear in the continued greater "nationalism" of the PCF vis-à-vis the greater support for European integration found in the PCI. Secondly, despite the economic and social trends of the past few years, France still has a stronger and more compact bourgeoisie, which implies that the forces opposing Communist entry into government are certain to be greater there than in Italy. Third, the basic strategic difference in the two parties' search for power has, if anything, widened with the ripening of the PCI's historic compromise strategy. While the PCF continues to count on what is essentially a Popular Front strategy, the PCI hopes with increasing credibility to enter a government alongside its Christian Democratic opponents. The effect of these international, class, and strategic differences will best be understood through sustained close analysis of each party's internal life, its domestic alliances, and its international strategy. It is this approach that we and our co-authors have tried to follow in this book.

DONALD L. M. BLACKMER
SIDNEY TARROW
Cambridge, Massachusetts
Ithaca, New York
December 1976

Contents

List of Abbreviations

ACLI	Associazioni Cristiane dei Lavoratori Italiani
APB	Artigianato Provinciale Bolognese
ARCI	Associazione Ricreativa Culturale Italiana
CC	Comitato Centrale
CERES	Centre d'Etudes et d'Education Socialiste
CFDT	Confédération Française Démocratique du Travail
CFTC	Confédération Française des Travailleurs Chrétiens
CGIL	Confederazione Generale Italiana del Lavoro
CGT	Confédération Générale du Travail
CGTU	Confédération Générale du Travail Unitaire
CI	Commissione Interna
CIR	Convention des Institutions Républicaines
CISER	Centro Italiano di Studi e Ricerche
CISL	Confederazione Italiana Sindacati Lavoratori
CLN	Comitato di Liberazione Nazionale
CNJA	Confédération Nationale des Jeunes Agriculteurs
CNR	Conseil National de la Résistance
CPSU	Communist Party of the Soviet Union
CUB	Comitati Unificati di Base
DC	Democrazia Cristiana
EEC	European Economic Community
EGF	Electricité et Gaz de France
ERIS	Etudes, Recherches et Information Socialiste
ESI	Editrice Sindacale Italiana
FEN	Fédération de l'Education Nationale
FFI	Forces Françaises de l'Intérieur
FGCI	Federazione Giovanile Comunista Italiana
FGDS	Fédération de la Gauche Démocrate et Socialiste
FIM	Federazione Italiana Metalmeccanici
FIOM	Federazione Impiegati Operai Metallurgici
FLN	Front de Libération Nationale
FN	Front Nationale
FO	Force Ouvrière
GAM	Groupes d'Action Municipale

KPD	Kommunistische Partei Deutschlands
MLN	Mouvement de Libération Nationale
MODEF	Mouvement de Défense des Exploitants Familiaux
MPL	Movimento Politico dei Lavoratori
MRP	Mouvement Républicain Populaire
MSI	Movimento Sociale Italiano
NATO	North Atlantic Treaty Organization
OURS	Office Universitaire de Recherches Socialistes
PCF	Parti Communiste Français
PCI	Partito Comunista Italiano
PDIUM	Partito Democratico Italiano di Unità Monarchica
PDM	Progrès et Démocratie Moderne
PLI	Partito Liberale Italiano
PNM	Partito Nazionale Monarchico
PR	Proportional Representation
PRI	Partito Repubblicano Italiano
PS	Parti Socialiste
PSDI	Partito Socialista Democratico Italiano
PSI	Partito Socialista Italiano
PSIUP	Partito Socialista Italiano di Unità Proletaria
PSU	Parti Socialiste Unifié
PSU	Partito Socialista Unificato
RPF	Rassemblement du Peuple Français
SFIO	Section Française de l'Internationale Ouvrière
TVA	Taxe sur valeur ajoutée
UDI	Unione Donne Italiane
UDR	Union des Démocrates pour la République; 1968— Union pour la Défense de la République
UFD	Union des Forces Démocratiques
UFF	Union des Femmes Françaises
UIL	Unione Italiana del Lavoro
UNEF	Union Nationale des Etudiants Français
UNR	Union pour la Nouvelle République
WFTU	World Federation of Trade Unions

Communism in Italy and France

Introduction

DONALD L. M. BLACKMER

This volume was conceived during a conference held several years ago at Arden House under the auspices of the Planning Group on Comparative Communist Studies. The conference had been called to test the proposition that a group of specialists on the world's nonruling Communist parties could design a framework for research on this group of parties, as had been earlier attempted, with some success, for the Communist parties in power.[1] In terms of that goal, the Arden House conference was a failure—stimulating and thoroughly enjoyable, but a failure. By and large the participants went home prepared to agree that we had neither adequate conceptual tools nor sufficient empirical data for effective comparative analysis of even the major types of nonruling Communist parties.

Difficult though it is to compare Communist parties governing political systems at widely varying stages of development, with quite different cultural and political heritages, one can at least make some reasonable assumptions about the similar functions that parties in power must perform in any system. It became clear at Arden House that not even this much could safely be said about the Communist parties out of power. Despite similarities in rhetoric, there seemed no convincing reason to suppose that they shared or meant the same thing by such apparently obvious goals as "coming to power," "modernization," or "radical social and economic change." It was clear, moreover, that there existed a serious data problem. Research on the nonruling parties was sparse and uneven in quantity and quality, concerned more with doctrinal matters and interparty relations than with the more essential questions of party organization and strategy.

A more modest approach to the problem was then proposed. Why not begin by looking comparatively at the French and Ital-

[1] The results of that summer study have been published in Chalmers Johnson (ed.), *Change in Communist Systems* (Stanford, Calif.: Stanford University Press, 1970).

ian parties? No two Communist parties were likely to be any more comparable than these, and the amount of research already carried out, or then under way, on these two parties was substantial. Under the Planning Group's auspices once again, a three-day conference accordingly took place at M.I.T.'s Endicott House in October 1972. This volume contains revised or completely rewritten versions of most of the papers presented there, plus the concluding comparative chapter and one new contribution stimulated by the discussions.

As we planned the conference and the book, we had three broad purposes in mind. The most straightforward of these was to make more widely available the results of a number of empirical investigations we knew had recently been carried out on the Italian and French parties. These studies seemed to us not only to provide valuable evidence about what was happening to and within these parties but also to demonstrate convincingly that Communist parties, contrary to general belief, could in fact be studied as effectively, and with many of the same techniques, as other political parties. It would in itself be useful, we believed, to challenge the assumption of inaccessibility that may have restrained many from exploring the nonruling Communist parties at all and that may have limited others to microscopic analyses of what *was* readily accessible—their doctrinal and other public statements.

A second purpose was to make as much progress as we could toward careful comparative analysis of the two parties. This proved to be more difficult than we had expected. First, we succeeded in finding virtually no one who had actually worked on both parties and who could be persuaded to undertake a directly comparative study. Second, we had less success than we had anticipated in uncovering parallel, directly comparable pieces of research by different authors. Given the limited number of studies on the two parties, this should probably not have been surprising. It was revealing, however, to discover that researchers on the two parties had generally gravitated toward different topics, a circumstance no doubt reflecting intrinsic differences between the parties as well as their relative accessibility to study. We responded to the situation by commissioning papers that would, we hoped, be as nearly comparable as possible. We then organized the discussion at the conference itself to emphasize comparisons and browbeat our authors (with occasional success) to revise their papers in a more explicitly comparative mode. What we have learned on this score is primarily to be found in the concluding chapter, where Tarrow (with Blackmer acting as critic-collaborator-sounding board) has attempted to develop a framework for comparative analysis of the two parties.

Our third general purpose was to explore a particular theme. Like most of those who come to grips with the issues of working-class politics, we have been fascinated—and frustrated—by the classical dilemma faced by the Communist and Socialist parties in Europe. Can they somehow remain "revolutionary," in at least the minimal sense of working effectively for the economic, social, and political transformation of their societies, or are they fated to become (if this has not happened already) largely or totally integrated into those societies, adapting to existing institutions and values rather than seriously challenging them? This was of course the central issue underlying the great debate over revisionism at the beginning of the century, and for Social Democracy the conclusive answer has long since been given, with minor variations from country to country. But will the European Communist parties follow the same path? The historical analogy is tempting, and developments over the past fifteen years or so have persuaded many analysts that the Communist parties of Europe are far along the road toward a definitive abandonment of the Leninist and Stalinist heritage that has kept them for so long outside the mainstream of politics in their respective countries.

We found ourselves troubled by prevailing treatments of this issue. First, there seemed to be emerging too easy and simplistic a consensus on what struck us as a complex and many-sided problem. To counter conservatives who, whether out of conviction or political expediency, continued to argue that the Communist parties still represented a serious revolutionary or radical threat, many analysts quickly leaped to the opposite conclusion— that complete assimilation and deradicalization were just around the corner. But assimilation to what and deradicalization along which dimensions? In political systems as fragmented and conflictual as the French and Italian ones, few scholars would be so bold as to declare a certain knowledge of what rules of the game constitute "the system" to which the Communist parties are supposedly assimilating. The "deradicalization" issue is even more complex; a party may revise its ideology on an issue that is becoming less important at the same time it is adopting more radical stands on newer and more relevant problems.

A number of considerations led us to feel that there was no obvious or easy way to respond to such broad questions—and that the "answer" was not so likely to lie at one or the other pole as in some ambiguous, intermediate realm located somewhere between the alternatives of radical change and complete assimilation. For one thing, the French and Italian parties themselves seemed to differ considerably in important and relevant respects, casting some doubt as to whether any single set of generalizations about the past or speculations about the future could effectively be applied to both parties. The Parti Communiste Français (PCF) had always appeared to most observers more dogmatic, more sectarian, more closely tied to the industrial working class, more dependent on the Soviet Union—in sum, less open than the Partito Comunista Italiano (PCI) to the pressures and influences of the bourgeois society surrounding it. Was this really true and if so, what were the implications of these differences?

Second, it did not seem enough to look at these parties as homogeneous national entities: the degree and nature of their assimilation, or lack of it, might be expected to vary greatly according to level of organization, geographical region, and functional or other differentiation within the party. To speak of the way "the" Communist party responds to "its" environment is almost meaningless unless one can take into account not only the great diversity that exists within each party, but also the varying quality of relationships between party headquarters in Rome and Paris and the local organizations.

Third, we believed that a large area of ambiguity about the behavior and ideology of these parties persists even at the national level. In some respects they appear to have adapted almost entirely to the norms of their societies, while in others they appear to retain and to value attributes deriving from their Communist heritage that distinguish them clearly from other parties operating in these societies. We felt that this confrontation and coexistence of Communist values and practices with the attitudes and behaviors resulting from long participation in industrially developed, parliamentary societies might well be leading to the emergence of distinctly new value patterns and modes of integration, quite different from those associated with the classical patterns of Socialist and Social Democratic parties.

For many years after the Second World War such questions as these were not raised. In the strong consensus of the Cold War years, there was never any doubt that the Communist revolutionary threat in Europe should be taken seriously. The radical Communist rhetoric and intransigent style were made convincing by the insistence of the parties on Leninist qualities of superior organization and disciplined obedience that not only appeared antidemocratic but suggested an almost infinite capacity for mobilization of the masses behind party goals. An image was generated of the European Communist parties as being so apart from—and so hostile to—the values and institutions of the societies in which they functioned that the notion of an eventual assimilation could hardly arise. The Communist parties might be defeated—they were not likely to be absorbed.

For that matter, it hardly seemed revelant to test the revolutionary intent of the Communist parties by examining their domestic records. There had never been much doubt—either for Party members or for anyone else—that the Communist parties of Western Europe were in the last analysis responsive not so much to their domestic needs as to the interests of the Soviet party. Sophisticated research was not required to demonstrate that the sudden shift of the French and Italian parties to militant tactics in the fall of 1947 was undertaken at Moscow's direct command. This vivid demonstration of loyalty, recalling others in years past, tended to make any careful empirical examination of actual party behavior seem quite beside the point. What did it matter exactly what the parties said or did, since they said and did whatever the Russians asked? One should look to Stalin for enlightenment, not to Togliatti or Thorez. And by and large, that is just what students of communism and other political analysts did. During the 1950s and well into the next decade, a quantity of literature appeared on the Soviet Union, while virtually nothing was published on the nonruling parties aside from personal accounts of former party members and historical studies of the prewar period. Most of what did appear bore the imprint of the "totalitarian model" then almost universally current among Western students of communism. The nonruling Communist parties were seen as flexible and devious in their tactics but undeviating in their pursuit of long-range revolutionary goals and monolithic in their organization.[2] Given this appreciation of their qualities, the notion that they might be significantly influenced by their participation in the parliamentary systems of capitalist societies did not readily come to mind. Consideration of the French and Italian parties during those years was by and large dominated by the view that they were a menace to "free societies" and an appendage of Soviet foreign policy.[3]

Toward the end of the 1950s this consensus about the European Communist parties began to be undermined, not in consequence of empirical study of the parties themselves but as a by-product of attempts to understand the nature and meaning of certain broader historical developments which appeared to be affecting Europe as a whole. One set of events had to do with the radical transformation occurring in the international Communist movement, and in the Soviet Union itself, following Stalin's death. A second set, more gradual and more difficult to perceive and understand, had to do with the rapid pace of economic change in Western Europe and the social and political consequences associated with that change. Each of these major sources of change for the European political scene were before long seen to have potentially decisive implications for the nonruling Communist parties. These implications came to be expressed through two theories, neither very clearly or fully developed, to which we can give shorthand labels: the "revisionist" and "integration" theories. Although they approached the problem from quite different perspectives and employed wholly different data, the two ap-

[2] A partial exception to these generalizations is Gabriel Almond's *The Appeals of Communism* (Princeton, N.J.: Princeton University Press, 1954), which sensitively explored attitudinal data gathered from interviews with former Communist party members in England, the United States, France, and Italy. Almond's insistence that "we are not dealing with a homogeneous phenomenon"—that "we must talk of types of appeals, to various types of persons, in different kinds of situations"—is particularly refreshing in its contrast with most other writing of the time. (Quotation on p. 185.)

[3] One of the few book-length studies of the European Communist parties during this period, and the standard work for many years, was *Communism in Western Europe* by Mario Einaudi, Jean-Marie Domenach, and Aldo Garosci. (Originally published by Cornell University Press in 1951 and long out of print, it was reprinted in 1971 by Archon Books, Hamden, Conn.) Its analyses of French and Italian party organization and strategy in the late 1940s have value even today, but the interpretation lies firmly within the interpretive context just described. For example, "Since 1947 Western European communism has been deprived of all participation in national governments and has been exposed as the agent of the aggressive aims of the Soviet Union" (p. 6).

proaches arrived at similar and complementary conclusions which departed substantially from the Cold War consensus described above. Let us first look briefly at the revisionist theory.

As should be plain to anyone moderately well versed in the history of the Communist movement, the term "revisionist" represents anything but a coherent set of ideas and political strategies. The original revisionist controversy around the turn of the century did in fact center on intellectual and political issues still relevant to Western European Communists today. The great debate between the self-styled orthodox Marxists and the revisionist followers of Eduard Bernstein, occurring as it did at a time when socialism had not yet come to power anywhere, had to do with the nature and likely evolution of the capitalist system and the appropriate strategy for the working class seeking power. The Communist parties of Western Europe are still confronting these issues, and doing so, moreover, in the same basic parliamentary setting that had proved to be a prime source of classical revisionist theory and practice. It is understandable, then, that revisionism should come to mind as a suggestive historical analogy. If the critical fact about revisionist Social Democracy in Germany and other European countries is that it came to terms with the capitalist, democratic system—that it became reformist rather than revolutionary—then the analogy suggests watching for a similar process to occur in European Communist parties today. Thus Kevin Devlin, in "Prospects for Communism in Western Europe," can start his essay with the ironic phrase, "There is a specter haunting West European Communism; it is the specter of Eduard Bernstein," and can summarize his argument as follows:

> . . . it seems altogether likely that the trends of revisionist adaptation outlined earlier will continue to characterize West European Communism as a whole. This would mean further emphasis on electoralism, on seeking popular support through calls for gradualist reforms, on winning the collaboration of other left-wing forces even at the cost of doctrinal and political concessions, and on building up the party's image as a progressive, responsible force operating *within* the existing system, which it wishes to transform but not to overthrow.[4]

[4] In R. V. Burks (ed.), *The Future of Communism in Europe* (Detroit: Wayne State University Press, 1968), p. 60. Italics in the original. For a stimulating critique of Devlin's article, from a perspective close to that of

9

The point we wish to make is not that such predictions or characterizations are necessarily wrong, for they do indeed catch important aspects of the behavior of West European Communist parties today. The point is that they are at best partial, that they grasp only one dimension of a complex reality, and not necessarily the most important part at that. To focus our attention centrally on "revisionist adaptation," understood as an historical analogy with the classical revisionism of German Social Democracy, is beside the mark and does not help greatly to understand the nature of the dilemma facing the Communist parties today.

If revisionism means anything today, it is not primarily with reference to the issues that were being debated within the Second International between 1890 and 1914. These issues, having to do with the correct interpretation of the Marxian ideological and political heritage, are no longer particularly salient. From this perspective, the Italian and French Communist parties became revisionist some time ago, and for that matter so did the Soviet Union itself. Flexible, neo-Marxist interpretations of capitalism, adherence to reformist strategies, participation in elections and in bourgeois parliaments—all these "heresies" have long since become orthodoxies. To refer to the European parties as "revisionist" in this sense is not wrong, it is simply banal and unhelpful as a distinguishing characteristic of their current reality.[5]

"Revisionism" was revived as a polemical term following Stalin's death. It arose with reference to tendencies in the Communist movement in Eastern rather than Western Europe and it

---

the present authors, see Kenneth T. Jowitt, "The Changing Character of European Communism," *Studies in Comparative Communism* 2, nos. 3-4 (July/October 1969): 386-403; a reply by R. V. Burks to Jowitt's review is in the same issue, pp. 383-385.

[5] Tucker has made a stimulating effort to introduce the term "deradicalization" as a way of conceptualizing the secular change in Marxist movements. Analysis of the German Social Democratic movement caused him to suggest that "the process of deradicalization has a certain inner 'dialectic.' For deepseated reasons, theory and practice diverge. The movement intensifies its theoretical adherence to revolutionary goals at the very time when in practice it moves down the path of reformism." This generalization applies at best weakly to the French Communist party and not at all to the Italian. The lack of fit—which relates directly to the much lower salience of traditional doctrinal issues—illustrates the difficulty of drawing lessons for today from the German experience. See Robert C. Tucker, "The Deradicalization of Marxist Movements," in his *The Marxian Revolutionary Idea* (New York: Norton, 1969), pp. 172-214. (Quotation on p. 192.)

had little substantively to do with classical revisionism. Whereas Bernstein was "revising" Marx, the Eastern European Marxists were "revising"—or more accurately, repudiating—centrally important dimensions of Leninist and Stalinist ideas and political practices.[6] After Stalin's death the issue that counted most in the Communist world was the legitimacy of the domestic and international systems created by Lenin and Stalin and of their supporting ideology. This was obviously the central issue with respect to Eastern Europe, as the long series of rebellions and interventions since 1953 demonstrates; it was only somewhat less obviously salient with respect to the Western European parties.

It is instructive to think back for a moment to 1956, that year of crisis when revisionism became once again the devil theory of the Communist movement. When the Italian party attacked a prominent internal critic such as Antonio Giolitti, it did so by branding him a revisionist and making his reformist approach to the party's economic and political strategy the main explicit target of attack. In reality, Giolitti's ideas on these subjects were hardly more than a vigorous restatement of the party's own position, and the charge of revisionism with respect to strategic questions was largely an ideological smokescreen. Far more serious was Giolitti's insistence on democracy within the party, on the importance of democratic liberties in a socialist society, and on the errors of the Soviet approach to building socialism. His unpardonable deviation lay in these realms, in his challenge to Leninist and Stalinist views about the party, not in his ostensibly revisionist views about capitalist society. Similarly, when the French party at about the same time attacked the Italian party as revisionist, its critical comments were addressed primarily to the PCI's propensity for economic and social reform programs to be implemented by parliamentary action. The more urgent issue, however, had to do with the PCI's alleged underestimation of the role of the Communist party in building socialism and the permissiveness with which it treated dissenting views on the Soviet handling of the Hungarian revolution. Palmiro Togliatti proved his legitimacy to Soviet and other Communist leaders not

[6] For a useful collection of essays, see Leopold Labedz (ed.), *Revisionism: Essays on the History of Marxist Ideas* (New York: Praeger, 1962). Especially relevant are Karl Reyman and Herman Singer, "The Origins and Significance of East European Revisionism," pp. 215-222, and William E. Griffith, "The Decline and Fall of Revisionism in Eastern Europe," pp. 223-238.

by repudiating his party's domestic strategy but by reaffirming his loyalty to the Soviet Union, by supporting its actions in Hungary, and by acting with proper Leninist toughness against the dissenters in his own party. By these, the crucial tests of the post-Stalin era, Togliatti was no revisionist.[7]

To demonstrate in this fashion the several connotations the term has taken on in conjunction with the political and ideological conflicts of the Communist movement should adequately suggest the weakness of revisionism as an explanatory or analytical concept. Current realities cannot adequately be expressed or explained by a term which arose toward the end of the last century in a particular historical context and which has more recently, during the ideological battles of the feuding Communist powers, acquired quite different connotations.

This is not to deny the attractiveness and plausibility of a rough analogy between the pressures that led to the "classical" revisionism of Lenin's day and the forces making for change in Communist parties today. Indeed, beginning in the late 1950s much the same point was independently being made, in quite different language, by a number of leading political scientists and sociologists interested in Europe who were then exploring one or another aspect of what has come to be known as the "end of ideology" argument. Giuseppe Di Palma has constructed a useful composite summary of the central trends perceived by the analysts associated with this view; the following excerpts from his summary are especially relevant here:

> There has been a blurring of traditional economic and social class lines as a result of the increasing pervasiveness, complexity, and efficiency of production and organization in industrial societies. Living standards have improved for all. Mass education, mass production, and mass consumption have helped close the gaps among classes by stimulating social mobility or by equalizing life styles. . . .
>
> Hence there has been a decline in the strength of political parties that base their appeal on class, language, ethnicity, or religion, and a growth of heterogeneous parties appealing to various constituencies and interests. Also, most parties, irre-

---

[7] A detailed analysis of this period may be found in Donald L. M. Blackmer, *Unity in Diversity: Italian Communism and the Communist World* (Cambridge, Mass.: The M.I.T. Press, 1968), Chapters 3-5.

spective of their original ideologies, have become more convergent in their appeals and more diversified in their clientele in order to gain support and to vie more effectively for uncommitted voters and marginal gains.

As a concomitant of such developments, total ideologies have been weakened or have become marginal, and the politics of intransigent, ideological confrontation among social groups has increasingly given way to a politics of bargaining, with basic agreements on many issues that once sharply separated the political Left from the political Right. . . .[8]

The central implications of such an analysis for the Communist parties of France and Italy were not that far distant from those addressed in Bernstein's original argument to the Social Democratic party of Germany: the economic, social, and political changes occurring in Europe are such as to reduce the intensity of class conflict and lead working-class parties toward electoral and reformist activities; integration rather than revolution has become the unacknowledged real objective of these parties. Sophisticated contemporary analysts, armed with theories of social change based essentially on assumptions about the impact of economic and technological development, thus seemed to have arrived at prognoses not all that dissimilar from those put forward by Bernstein a half century earlier. "Integration" went hand in hand with "revisionism" as the convenient shorthand labels adopted by many scholars—and, naturally, by left-wing adversaries of communism—to identify and explain the major trend of Communist party evolution in Western Europe.

This is not the place for a critical review of the "end of ideology" and "integration" theses; only a few general points need to be made. First, the general validity of these ideas has been called into question on both empirical and theoretical grounds: class and other cleavages have in fact shown surprising persistence in Europe despite rising levels of affluence, leading to a suspicion that the implications of social change for political life have as yet been inadequately understood. Second, the evidence that "most parties have become more convergent in their appeals" is mixed, at best, and the correlation claimed by the "end of ideology" the-

[8] *The Study of Conflict in Western Society: A Critique of the End of Ideology,* pamphlet (Morristown, N.J.: General Learning Press, 1973), p. 2. This excellent essay includes an extensive bibliography of books and articles on the subject.

orists between economic development and ideological convergence has found little solid empirical support.[9] Third, the "end of ideology" argument, with its implications as to the weakening of the class parties and/or their "integration" into the existing system, was never really linked by its proponents to empirical research on the Communist parties. The thesis was essentially deterministic in spirit: it was assumed or asserted, with little evidence offered, that the Communist parties would sooner or later be subject to the same basic pressures from the economic realm as were perceived to be affecting other parties and groups.[10]

It was granted that the Communists, in contrast to their Socialist predecessors, did not yet fit the model, and efforts were made to explain the lag. Otto Kirchheimer noted their superior organizational capacity to withstand environmental pressures but nevertheless argued that the Communist parties were having difficulty recruiting members and keeping them actively involved and that they were tending, like other mass parties, to evolve into electorally oriented "catch-all" parties.[11] Seymour M. Lipset, in a passage headed "Communism Resists the Trend," pointed to two explanatory factors. He observed first that "the nations with large Communist movements are on the whole among the less developed" of the European nations, leaving the implication that further progress toward modernization would, all else being equal, tend to erode Communist strength.[12] He then went on to state, in effect, that all else was *not* equal, that the Communist parties were different because they had been subject to the intervening influence of the Soviet Union. "There is little doubt," he concluded, "that if the various European Communist parties had

[9] See Sidney Tarrow, "Economic Development and the Transformation of the Italian Party System," *Comparative Politics* 1, no. 2 (January 1969): 161-183.

[10] I am indebted to Peter M. Lange's analysis of the integration thesis in an unpublished manuscript, "The Italian and French Communist Parties: A Comparative Analysis of Postwar Evolution."

[11] "The Transformation of Western European Party Systems," in Joseph LaPalombara and Myron Weiner (eds.), *Political Parties and Political Development* (Princeton, N.J.: Princeton University Press, 1966), pp. 177-200 (on p. 191).

[12] "The Modernization of Contemporary European Politics," in his *Revolution and Counter-revolution: Change and Persistence in Social Structures*, rev. ed. (Garden City, N.Y.: Doubleday, 1970), p. 292. This essay was first published in the Winter 1964 issue of *Daedalus* under the title of "The Changing Class Structure and Contemporary European Politics" and was used without substantive changes in the later book.

14

been genuine national parties—that is, if their behavior had been largely determined by experiences within their own countries— they would have evolved in much the same way as the European socialist parties."[13] (One is reminded of Lenin's effort to explain the failure of Marx's predictions about the evolution of capitalism by reference to the countervailing impact of imperialism.)

The theorists of "integration" have undeniably drawn attention to important social and political phenomena that deserve further detailed exploration. We have not found, however, that our understanding of the French and Italian Communist parties can be much advanced by asking whether these parties are, or are not, "integrated" into their respective political systems. (By the same token, we find the question of whether they are "inside" or "outside" the system beside the point.)[14] We assume that of course they are integrated: to argue otherwise would be to overlook the fact of their continued organizational survival and electoral success—almost unbroken, in the case of the French party, for over fifty years. Similarly, there seems little point in attempting to measure relative degrees of integration of the two parties, given the variety of measures of integration one might choose to look at and the variety of meanings that could be attached to them.

For example, either larger or smaller party membership and organizational size could be cited as representing a successful adaptation to the environment, according to the circumstances in each country and one's assumptions about their meaning. Greater or lesser policy activity in parliament or local government might, similarly, be used either to show that the nonruling party is carrying out its historical function or abandoning it, depending on its overall strategic choices. Electoral success would on the face of it seem to be at least a neutral indicator of integration. Even here, however, there are difficulties of interpretation. A high and steady quotient of electoral success might signify that a party has reached the upper limits of its popularity and lacks a margin for action, while a lower or more volatile vote might be a clue that it has a potential for future success. More interesting for us than the *degree* of integration of nonruling parties are their *patterns* of adaptation to different national settings, pat-

---

[13] Ibid., p. 295.

[14] Giovanni Sartori, "European Political Parties: The Case of Polarized Pluralism," in LaPalombara and Weiner (eds.), *Political Parties and Political Development.*

terns that can best be understood by looking at the contours of the party's internal life, its relation to the international movement, and its place among the different forces in the political system of which it is a part.

We do not attempt in this book to advance a new general theory about the processes of change affecting the Communist parties of Western Europe. Indeed, in the present state of knowledge, we feel little confidence in the possibility of isolating the determinants of party behavior. In our view, attempts to explain the behavior of the nonruling parties have tended to fall into one or more of the following errors: (1) they have too readily assumed that one could generalize about these parties, lumping them together and thus underestimating what we regard as the critical differential impact of national environmental conditions on party behavior; (2) they have been insufficiently historical in perspective, thereby overlooking the considerable degree of continuity in the behavior over time of each party; (3) they have tended to treat "the party" as a monolithic structure, ignoring the significance of local and regional differences in composition and in implementation of party policies; (4) they have failed to examine in a serious way the interactions among such critical sectors of party activity as political strategy, international relationships, organizational styles and constraints, ideologies and belief systems. We have been impressed, in short, with the great complexity of the problem and with the need for a conceptually more sophisticated and empirically richer understanding of it.

In this volume we have tried to present some evidence of this complexity and partially correct some of the deficiencies just mentioned. We have, for example, put unusual emphasis on party activities at the local and provincial level in the hope of illustrating the great and probably growing diversity that exists. We have attempted to provide a reasonable balance between broad interpretive essays and detailed empirical studies of particular problems and situations. We have, in addition, put particular stress on the question of social and political alliances—believing them to be crucially important to the future of both parties—and have attempted to suggest some of the ways in which alliance strategies have influenced, and been influenced by, the parties' organizational strengths and weaknesses.

The concluding chapter attempts to identify the characteristic patterns of action that have emerged in different sectors of party activity in response to international, domestic, and organizational factors and to show how they have tended to complement and reinforce one another so as to become the dominant strategic models for each party's behavior. These strategic models are then used to suggest differences in the patterns of change that are evident in the two parties' behavior, even now, when they are closer together than they have been for many years.

We have not tried to provide an "answer" to the ultimate question of where these parties may be heading, because in the last analysis their futures appear to us inextricably linked to far larger and even less soluble questions about the evolution of the domestic and international environments in which they are functioning. Their activism, their official optimism, and their self-conscious attention to matters of strategy and organization create a sense that the French and Italian Communist parties are somehow more nearly masters of their fate than other parties. In some ways this may be true. At the very least they have shown a remarkable capacity for survival, for retaining political and organizational vitality under circumstances that might well have seen them wither away, and yet we must recognize that their autonomy is and will remain sharply limited by factors, domestic and international, over which they have little or no control. We hope that in this volume we have conveyed a richer sense of the dynamic internal reality of each of these parties and of their interaction with the wider environment around them.

PART ONE

Change and Continuity

I.

Continuity and Change in Postwar Italian Communism

DONALD L. M. BLACKMER

This volume approaches in different ways the evolution and adaptation of the French and Italian Communist parties. Many of the essays report the results of recent empirical research on party organizations and cadres operating in a variety of geographical and institutional settings. Others, including this one, approach the problem from the broader perspective of how the parties as a whole have acted—that is to say, how their leaders have responded to the infinite variety of signals that reach them from the party organization, from the domestic political arena, from the economic and labor fronts, from the international scene. The behavior of top party elites represents, in effect, their net judgment about which of the manifold aspects of a complex environment should, at a given moment, be given the greatest weight. What do they tend to listen to? To what extent do the two parties today listen to the same signals they did over twenty-five years ago when they were "reborn" after the Second World War as mass parties centrally involved in the politics of their respective countries?

My own inclination with regard to the Italian party is to put rather greater weight on elements of continuity than of change. An endless number of relevant changes have of course occurred, in the party itself, in the Italian economy and society, in international affairs. These seem to me of secondary importance, however, compared to certain structural factors that have remained constant throughout the postwar years. The most obvious and decisive of these factors has certainly been the Christian Democratic and Catholic predominance that has kept the Partito Comunista Italiano (PCI) in a permanent minority position, both politically and socially. Hardly less important has been an international context that, despite significant recent changes in international alignments, has found the Italian government a consistent supporter of the United States and the PCI an equally consistent ally of the USSR. These structural continuities have been powerful enough to set fairly rigid boundaries on the degree of choice or of change open to the PCI, given the basic interests it has sought to protect and promote.

The heart of the issue lies in this last phrase. Can we, without too gross a simplification, identify certain patterns of behavior clear and persistent enough to be designated as basic or permanent interests of the party? I will propose such an interpretive framework and illustrate it from the party's behavior during the postwar era. The illustrative material can be nowhere adequately detailed, but will be more fully developed for the early than for the later years, for two reasons. First, the 1943-1948 period seems to me more crucial for understanding the party's development than is often realized, in that a pattern was established which has in many respects continued down to the present. Second, since the contributions to this book concentrate largely on recent events, it seems especially necessary to draw attention to this critical earlier period.

By the concept of "permanent interests" I intend to convey something a good deal broader than is normally implied by words such as "goals" or "strategies." To discuss a Communist party's evolution in terms of changing goals seems to me a fruitless endeavor, largely because the problem of distinguishing ends from means is virtually insoluble. The distinction turns out to be an essentially subjective one, not open to empirical tests. Debates about whether a party has or has not become "revisionist," that is, whether it has consistently pursued its original goals or has "betrayed" them, can never be resolved since they rest on an appraisal of the intentions of party leaders: in Leninist terms one may make compromises without becoming an opportunist as long as one does not lose sight of the longer-term objectives behind present actions. Strategies are more readily identified than goals, but have too narrow a connotation: they generally refer to the choice of means and ends designed to influence over a period of time the environment in which the party operates. Strategy has an active, positive connotation about it, within which it is difficult to encompass many of the passive or reactive dimensions of party behavior. When the PCI in 1956 supports the Soviet invasion of Hungary, is this best regarded as an aspect of its "strategy"? I find it more useful to think of such behavior as a response designed to protect certain basic party interests, of which domestic strategy, in the conventional sense, is only one.

I will suggest, then, that the PCI's behavior during the postwar period can be understood in terms of its pursuit of three basic interests: (1) development and maintenance of the Communist party itself and its influence over other organizations and groups; (2) search for the political and social alliances that constitute the core of the *via italiana al socialismo*; and (3) maintenance of a close link with the Soviet Union and the international Communist movement as a whole.

This set of interests comprises three aspects of party behavior —organization, domestic strategy, and international relations— that are generally dealt with under separate headings and only loosely linked to each other. It seems to me analytically advantageous to consider all three aspects within the same framework. Such an approach encourages attention to interactions among the three and to changes over time in their content and relative salience for the party. I am unwilling to argue that any one of these interests has a clear general priority over the others. I do not believe, for example, as some hold to be the case for both the PCI and the Parti Communiste Français (PCF), that allegiance to Soviet interests is in the last analysis the party's top priority. (For a contrasting view, see Annie Kriegel, Chapter 2 in this volume.) Nor can I accept the opposite contention that the PCI's evident conflicts of interest with the USSR imply that the requirements of its domestic strategy have come to predominate over its international allegiances.

My conception, in general, is that the art of leadership in the PCI has consisted in maintaining a working balance among these three permanent interests and in modifying their content in response to changing external conditions. The most comfortable and productive periods for the party have been those during which there has existed a basic compatibility among these interests—when, that is, they have tended to reinforce rather than conflict with each other. The most difficult and sterile periods have been the ones in which the party was obliged to choose among them, to sacrifice substantially in one realm in order to protect its interests in others. The necessity of maintaining a balance—of never sacrificing *completely* any one of its basic interests—has also meant that no one of them could be developed to

23

the fullest possible extent. Loyalty to the Soviet Union has been genuine but limited, just as the party's real and serious pursuit of domestic alliances has been constrained by its international ties. As has often been noted, the interplay of such internal tensions or "contradictions" as these has resulted in a political style in which apparent decisiveness has masked an underlying ambiguity of purpose.

I will try to elaborate on this design by looking at the ways in which these interests of the party were expressed and how they interacted in each of the three basic periods of the party's postwar evolution. These periods will for convenience be labeled the phases of *participation* (1943-1948), of *confrontation* (1948-1956), and of *opposition within the system* (1956-present).

The Phase of Participation (1943-1948)

It would be difficult to exaggerate the importance of the Resistance and early postwar years for the PCI. Despite the striking changes that have taken place in Italy and on the international scene, the behavior pattern established by the party at that time has shown remarkable vitality. The choices made between 1943 and 1948 have proved in most important respects to be fundamental strategic choices, not merely tactical responses to a specific set of environmental conditions.[1] The specific content of party behavior has of course changed in important ways; but a pattern of basic values was revealed during this period that seems to me largely valid even today.

During this period both the international and the internal political situations were dominated by a dual alliance: on one level that of the Allied powers with the Soviet Union, and on the other that of domestic anti-Fascist (or national democratic) forces, in the "people's democracies" as well as in Western Europe. Within this context, PCI strategy—until shattered by the

---

[1] It is more conventional to consider 1944 (Togliatti's return to Italy) and 1947 (the PCI's exclusion from the government) as the boundary dates for this period. While these are certainly the decisive events, it seems to me more accurate to see the period as beginning with a series of triumphs for the PCI in 1943-1944 (strikes in the factory centers of the north, the fall of Mussolini, the insurrection against the Germans, the entry of the PCI into the government) and ending with a series of disasters during 1947-1948 (ouster from the government, creation of the Cominform, deepening of the Cold War, the electoral defeat of 1948, etc.).

24

elections of 1948—was entirely consistent. Since an objectively revolutionary situation did not exist, the party's immediate objective was not socialism but a "progressive democracy" which, by destroying the political and economic vestiges of fascism and introducing structural reforms which would ensure the participation of the masses in the direction of the country, could open the way for a gradual and democratic transition to socialism. The keystone of party strategy was national unity—collaboration between political parties and social classes—for the purpose first of military victory over the Germans and then of economic reconstruction and creation of a democratic political order. The strategy gave first priority to democratization of political life and was premised on Communist participation in government as the legitimate representative of working-class interests.

Within the above strategic context, the PCI sought to maximize three potential sources of strength, all of which had been created or greatly strengthened as a result of its participation in the Resistance movement. These resources were: (1) *a capacity for political alliances*—the experience of the Resistance and the imperative of close collaboration among anti-Fascist forces of all political shades which it engendered gave PCI leaders and militants a capacity for alliances with forces outside the working class which they had largely lacked before; (2) the *party* itself, no longer conceived as a semiclandestine cadre organization but rather as the core of a mass following initially attracted by the PCI's organizational capacity and prestige during the Resistance; (3) a strong *link to the USSR*, one which had always existed but which emerged strengthened from the war as a result of the decisive Soviet contribution to the war effort and the impact of the Stalin myth, then at its apex.

These assets, which came into being in a very specific historical context, would gradually be transformed into what I have termed the permanent interests of the party. For a brief time, as we shall see, all three resources pulled in the same direction and reinforced each other. Then as a result of circumstances that the PCI could do nothing to influence, they began to pull in conflicting directions, creating a state of inner tension that has been a source both of difficulty and of vitality for the party ever since. If the PCI is to attain even its intermediate goal of regaining a share of governmental power, it must discover and exploit a way to allow its three basic assets once again to work in harmony.

25

It will be necessary first to examine the nature of these three basic party interests as they emerged in the war and early postwar context. I hope at the same time to give some sense of how these interests were rooted in the party's earlier experiences in the difficult years under the Fascist regime.

The Strategy of Alliances

The strategy of collaboration and national unity announced by Togliatti in 1944 implied as a condition for its success the need to construct a system of alliances with other political parties and social groups. Acutely aware of its weaknesses as a minority party in a Catholic, agrarian country with a strong socialist, but democratic, tradition among the relatively small working class, the PCI leadership was constantly preoccupied with the danger of isolation and the need to avoid it by extending political and social alliances beyond the working class. That the urgency of this problem was understood by the leadership even before Togliatti's return from Moscow is clear from Luigi Longo's admonition in September 1943 concerning party policy toward the Committees of National Liberation (CLN), in which a wide range of political groups collaborated: "It is clear . . . that all our actions must follow from the necessity of maintaining the unity of the CLN, especially if a break would mean our isolation."[2]

Such an outlook was by no means new to the PCI. The strong subordination of the party's domestic interests to those of the Soviet Union and the consequent acceptance of periodic shifts in the party line had not prevented the gradual development of a preference for a strategy of alliance-building. Since the ouster of Bordiga in 1924, the PCI leadership had tended to favor the goal of working with other socialist and democratic forces toward a transitional democratic system to replace fascism. The alternative objective of working directly for a socialist revolution without passing, at least briefly, through the stage of a bourgeois democratic republic was advanced only reluctantly, under Soviet pressure, and was dropped whenever circumstances allowed. Because his political career came to an end with his arrest in 1926, before the Comintern turned to the left, Gramsci was never obliged to accommodate his own subtle and somewhat ambigu-

[2] Ernesto Ragionieri, "Il partito comunista," in Leo Valiani, Gianfranco Bianchi, and Ernesto Ragionieri, *Azionisti, cattolici e comunisti nella Resistenza* (Milan: Franco Angeli Editore, 1971), p. 326.

ous views on this issue to the radical formulas emanating from Moscow. Togliatti was not so fortunate in that respect, but the pattern of his relations with the Comintern and the USSR left no doubt as to his position; he was under severe attack in 1929 and again in 1937, when the major shifts to the left were accomplished, and he reached the pinnacle of his Comintern career between 1934 and 1936, the years of the Popular Front and the Spanish Civil War, in which interclass alliances and united front governments were being sought as transition stages to the proletarian revolution.[3]

Its experience with fascism strongly influenced the postwar strategy of the PCI. In its analyses, the party emphasized the role that division among working-class and democratic forces had played in the advent of fascism and insisted on the importance of fascism as a *mass* phenomenon and on the significance of middle-class support as one of the bases for the survival of the Fascist regime.[4] These perceptions underlined the need for cooperation not only with Socialists, but above all with Christian Democrats and Catholics in the anti-Fascist struggle and the construction of a postwar democracy. Having matured politically in the heroic but futile battle against fascism, the PCI leadership learned much about the dangers of isolation in Italian politics and the need for compromise and cooperation among all "democratic" forces.

Given this prewar heritage, it should not have been so surprising as it then seemed that Togliatti's first political act upon his return to Italy was to reverse existing party policy and to reject the so-called *pregiudiziale repubblicana* (in the name of which the Communists, Socialists, and Actionists had insisted upon the abdication of the monarchy, deeply compromised by its involvement with the Fascist regime, as the condition for participation in any government coalition). From the day in April 1944 when Togliatti proclaimed the *svolta di Salerno*, by which the PCI agreed to enter a coalition of national unity under the king and Marshal Badoglio, to the day three years later when the party was removed by De Gasperi from the governing coalition, party strategy was dominated by one overriding motive: to avoid isola-

[3] See Joan Barth Urban, "Moscow and the Italian Communist Party: 1926-1945" (Ph.D. dissertation, Harvard University, 1967), Chapters 4 and 6.

[4] See Palmiro Togliatti, *Lezioni sul fascismo* (Rome: Editori Riuniti, 1970).

tion and to participate in the government, in collaboration with other anti-Fascist forces. The *svolta* itself, and every other major tactical decision the party made, was consistent with that strategic objective.

The decision to assume the role and the attitudes of a government party was initially explained in terms of the overwhelming need for national unity to win the war of liberation and to lay the foundations for democratic political structures. The priority assigned to these *immediate* objectives was absolute, and the party leadership took great pains to avoid actions which might jeopardize collaboration with other groups, both by excluding from party statements all references to class struggle or socialist revolution and by refusing even to consider any discussion of postwar institutional arrangements which might provoke dissent within anti-Fascist ranks and thereby impede the war effort:

> To linger today over discussions about future programs, about what the government of Italy will be and will do after the war, to condition today's struggle by what will be done tomorrow when the war is over, this would mean to remain on the Aventine, to play a passive waiting game, it would mean slowing down and weakening the struggle.[5]

The only essential condition that Togliatti laid down was that a Constituent Assembly based on universal suffrage be elected once the war was over to decide the future institutional structure of the country. This was the minimum condition necessary to guarantee the possibility of future influence for the PCI and the working class as a whole. The significance of Togliatti's *svolta*, however, is not merely that the PCI and other parties were persuaded to lay aside their differences temporarily in the broader national interest of pursuing the war effort. Although it could not be clear at the time—there was, indeed, considerable difference of opinion on the point among party leaders and widespread skepticism among ordinary members—the *svolta* in fact represented a long-term strategic decision. The effort to collaborate— politically, socially, and economically as well as militarily— would be the dominant motif in the party's postwar strategy.

The strategy applied above all to the Christian Democratic party and the Catholic Church. The PCI hoped to extend the uni-

[5] *La nostra lotta*, May 1944, quoted by Pietro Secchia, "I CLN al potere in un dibattito della sinistra," *Critica marxista* 3, no. 2 (March-April 1965).

tary experience of the CLN well beyond the close of the war and to this end proposed to the Democrazia Cristiana (DC) a "pact of common action, which looks forward to the struggle of the broad Catholic masses for a common program of economic, political, and social regeneration."[6] While recognizing the dual nature of the DC, the Communists accentuated the populist side of that party's character and the essentially peasant nature of its mass support, in contrast to its emerging role as the representative of the Italian bourgeoisie. The PCI was deeply concerned with the problem of constructing close ties with the Catholic masses, especially the peasants, but hoped to achieve this critically important *social* alliance through the *political* strategy of collaboration with the DC. The sympathy of many Christian Democrats for proposals for land and other structural reforms nourished PCI illusions about the prospects for a "progressive" development of the party, in which its "mass" base would prevail over its more reactionary elements. Optimism about the possibility of substantial agreement between the two parties led the PCI leadership to regard the tripartite governmental collaboration of 1944-1947 as a long-range prospect of constructive cooperation—a "bloc of forces historically and politically determined":[7]

> If we want the government and its action to be in conformity with the democratic will of the majority, the mass parties of the left and the Christian Democratic party must collaborate, and collaborate not in a temporary way, reserving the right to attack and destroy each other at the first opportunity, but in a permanent way, with a long prospect of common reconstructive activity.[8]

These hopes had been reinforced by the results of the 1946 elections for the Constituent Assembly in which the relative strengths of the three mass parties (Communists and Socialists, 39.6 percent; DC, 35.2 percent) gave the PCI reason to believe that the "democratic" forces in the country would indeed prevail.

Policy toward the Church was a central issue for the PCI from the outset, inseparable as it was from the problem of the peas-

[6] Palmiro Togliatti, *Politica comunista: l'Unità* (Rome, 1945), p. 84; cited in Livio Maitan, *PCI 1945-1969: Stalinismo e opportunismo* (Rome: Samonà e Savelli, 1969), p. 21n.

[7] Palmiro Togliatti, *Discorsi alla costituente* (Rome: Editori Riuniti, 1958), p. 155.

[8] "Crisi democristiana," *Rinascita* 4 (January-February 1947): 2.

29

antry and of class alliances more generally in a country where large sectors of the working classes and *ceti medi* remained strongly under the influence of the Vatican. Recognizing the crucial function which the Catholic masses would necessarily play in the construction of a democratic and later a socialist society, the leaders of the PCI had long accepted the necessity of coming to some workable compromise with the Church. As Gramsci had written in 1920: "In Italy, in Rome, there is the Vatican and the Pope; as the liberal state had to find a system of equilibrium with the spiritual power of the Church, so also will the workers' state have to find a system of equilibrium."[9] Thus when, at the time of the debates over the Constitution, the party was faced with the potentially explosive issue of the Church's position in the new Republic, Togliatti subordinated all other considerations to the urgent need for national unity. Reaffirming the party's respect for the religious convictions of the people and presenting a new image of the PCI as a defender of religious liberty, he not only gave full support to Constitutional guarantees of freedom of conscience and of religious propaganda and organization, but also cast the decisive votes of the party in favor of including in the Constitution the 1929 Lateran Pacts which perpetuated the Church's special status in the state. This preoccupation with avoiding religious controversy that might isolate the Communists by dividing the country along religious lines remains as much a part of PCI strategy today as it was in 1947.

PCI strategy toward the middle classes is most clearly illustrated by the party's postwar economic policy, which was shaped in accordance with the search for party and class collaboration. Accepting the necessity of working within the framework of a capitalist economic system, the party limited its declared objectives to general reforms such as economic planning, nationalization of large monopolies, and land redistribution which would strike at the sources of power of those groups and institutions which had supported the Fascist regime. At the same time care was taken not to alienate the broader middle-class groups that had provided the mass base for fascism. Togliatti's "progressive democracy" thus attempted to appeal to the broadest possible spectrum of Italian society—everyone, including small and

[9] Antonio Gramsci, quoted in Palmiro Togliatti, *Comunisti e cattolici* (Rome: Editori Riuniti, 1965), cited in introduction by Luciano Gruppi, p. 14.

medium-sized entrepreneurs, who might in any way identify their interests with the working class against the common enemy, monopoly capitalism. So deeply rooted was this strategic orientation that even in the electoral campaign of 1948, when the lines of opposition were clearly drawn, the PCI attempted to revive the unitary tradition of the CLN in the form of the *Fronte Democratico*, appealing for support among all categories of workers, the petty bourgeoisie, and small industry.[10]

The party's economic policy within the government was based on a *politica produttivistica* which undertook to curtail labor agitation (acceptance of a wage truce, a moratorium on political strikes) and to maintain discipline in the factory as the necessary price for the resumption of productive activity and the reconstruction of the economy—national goals in the name of which the party subordinated the immediate interests of the working class, thereby providing a demonstration of its "national and constructive spirit." No independent or potentially threatening economic program was put forward, the party having temporarily renounced any action which might be construed as an attempt to alter economic or property relationships. The PCI line was so eminently moderate and its apparent willingness to compromise with the capitalist system so complete, that even De Gasperi, during the 1948 election campaign, was compelled to acknowledge its reasonableness: "We are not fighting the Communist party because of its economic program, with regard to which an agreement might be possible, up to a certain point."[11]

Constructive PCI participation in the government for the realization of "progressive democracy" and economic reconstruction had its natural complement in class collaboration at the factory level as well, the most striking example being the *Consigli di Gestione*. These Management Councils were an outgrowth of the factory CLN established during the Resistance as de facto organs of workers' self-government and of working-class leadership in the restoration of production, not for the purpose of imposing a class regime, however, but because the majority of the capitalists had deserted the factories. Instead of exploiting this temporary

[10] For a full analysis of PCI policies and attitudes toward the middle classes, see Stephen Hellman, Chapter 10 in this volume.

[11] Alcide De Gasperi, quoted in Mario Einaudi and François Goguel, *Christian Democracy in Italy and France* (Hamden, Conn.: Archon Books, 1969), p. 52.

31

hegemony, the CLN appealed to the capitalists to resume their reponsibilities, posing as a condition for their return not nationalization but only democratic control from below through the Councils and the introduction of national economic planning. The original conception of the Councils was dual in nature: on the one hand, they were created as organs of technical collaboration, of constructive coresponsibility by labor and management for the direction of the factory, symbolizing the renunciation of class conflict and the "policy of alliance between the working class and the productive bourgeoisie for the reconstruction of the country";[12] on the other, representing as they did the assumption by the working class of direct and responsible participation in the running of the factory, they could equally be conceived as potential instruments for an eventual replacement of the *padroni* by the workers.

The party's priorities in this period required the effective subordination of this potential for mass mobilization to the need for unity. The failure to fight for a dual power structure in the factory had left the Councils at the mercy of the prevailing balance of forces within the enterprise. Once the owners' willingness to cooperate disappeared, the Councils were relegated either to sterile ineffectiveness or to a duplication of the tasks of the union. Only a victory by the Left in the 1948 elections could have restored to them an autonomous and meaningful function on the terrain for which they were created. Defeat condemned them to futility and made their elimination only a matter of time.

The PCI's early postwar strategy of party and class collaboration, both in the government and in the country at large, can best be understood as a combination of two complementary instincts: an "offensive" desire to exploit the resources generated by the leading role of the PCI in the Resistance and by its new "national" image, and an equally strong "defensive" desire to avoid isolation. This combination of the party's effort to maximize its unique strengths and minimize its weaknesses gave rise to one overriding objective: to stay in the government and to exert influence from within. It is in terms of this goal and of the absolute priority assigned to it that all party choices during this period must be viewed. The PCI acted from the beginning as a *partito di governo*, relying in practice almost entirely on top-level inter-

[12] Aris Accornero, "La classe operaia protagonista della ripresa," *Rinascita* 22 (April 24, 1965): 5.

party collaboration and on the instruments of government for the enactment of its program of progressive democracy and structural reforms. Its dependence on the power of institutional arrangements led the PCI to see its own presence in the government as a sufficient guarantee of democratic control over the political and economic development of the country. Thus, so long as power was kept out of the hands of the monopolies and mass participation guaranteed by democratic institutions, compromise on immediate objectives could be justified for the sake of unity: "The vigilant presence in the government [of the PCI] made acceptable to the workers the return of the capitalists, the demobilization of the workers, and the sacrifice of certain wage increases."[13]

Little serious consideration seems to have been given to an alternative strategy, that is, to using the party's organizational resources as instruments of internal opposition. Little effort was made to mobilize mass pressure to force concessions from coalition partners in favor of PCI positions. While emphasizing in its own propaganda the need to supplement political activity at the summit with mass initiatives and social alliances from below, the PCI seems in practice to have largely ignored its own doctrine as to the intimate link between the political and social aspects of strategy. It depended almost completely on an elite-level approach, utilizing its mass resources for electoral purposes only. The experiences of the CLN, the *Consigli di Gestione*, and the *Fronte Democratico* are instructive examples in this regard: in each case the party leadership explicitly recognized their potential as organs of base-level mobilization and of pressure on the DC through the participation of Catholic workers, and in each case sacrificed this potential either to formal unity or to an exclusively electoral perspective. Party spokesmen writing about this period today often implicitly acknowledge that the policy of those years may have been excessively one-sided. Alessandro Natta, for instance, raises this question:

Was our interpretation of the unity policy perhaps too concerned about possible ruptures, about a split between north and south, a split with Christian Democracy? And more basically, was it a limit of our policy or a fact imposed on us by reality, that is, the idea already in effect in November-Decem-

[13] Ibid.

33

ber 1945 that the game would from then on be played out essentially on the terrain of the basic institutional choice of the Constituent Assembly, of relations among the large mass parties, rather than on that of the development of democratic organization from below (the question of the CLN) and the struggle for social reforms?[14]

There is room for legitimate debate about the party's wisdom in putting so many of its eggs in one basket, but it can hardly be argued that the outcome would have been significantly different. The game was in fact being played out essentially on an international plane, and so far as Italy was concerned, it was the DC, not the PCI, which was responsible for the failure of the collaboration effort. It is clear, however, that PCI expectations were so centered about the prospect of long-term governmental collaboration that the leadership failed to prepare the base of the party for the break of 1947 and, given the widespread faith in electoral victory in 1948, for the future of permanent opposition which awaited it.

Building the "partito nuovo"

Perhaps the most powerful "lessons" learned by the PCI in the prewar period had to do with the party itself. On the positive side there was pride and satisfaction in the power of ideology and of organization to create and maintain a clandestine party in the face of Fascist repression. Leninism had proved itself viable in at least that minimal sense. Coupled with that, however, was the powerful and frustrating realization of the party's ineffectualness as long as it remained a tiny group of embattled leaders and activists. If it were to matter, politically, it would have to develop a well-organized mass base. Putting together these positive and negative lessons led to the model of the *partito nuovo* that emerged toward the end of the war, a model that sought to combine the virtues of a cadre party and a mass party.

While there is no doubt that the struggle against fascism and the Germans helped enormously to strengthen the organizational

[14] "La resistenza e la formazione del 'partito nuovo,'" in Paolo Spriano et al., *Problemi di storia del Partito Comunista Italiano* (Rome: Editori Riuniti, 1971), pp. 77-78. See also the similar comments by Giorgio Amendola, "Lotta di classe e sviluppo economico dopo la liberazione," in Istituto Gramsci, *Tendenze del capitalismo italiano*, 2 vols. (Rome: Editori Riuniti, 1962), 1: 164-172.

34

and leadership capacities of the party and thus to lay the bases for its rebirth as a "mass" party, its incredibly rapid growth during the Resistance was in part a spontaneous phenomenon, an instinctive response of many workers and intellectuals to the PCI's leading role in the Resistance and to its association with the symbols of national and international socialism. From a membership of a few thousand at the start of the war, the party grew to about half a million in 1944, a million seven hundred thousand a year later, and about two and a quarter million in 1947.[15] Although the initial process may well have been an unexpected windfall, the party quickly moved to transform it into a permanent asset. It should be kept in mind that this was not a self-evident response on the part of party cadres brought up in the tight conspiratorial world of the underground and exile party under the Fascist dictatorship. It took strong prodding by Togliatti to persuade many of the PCI organizers that the strategy of national unity he proclaimed in 1944 had its organizational counterpart in the *partito nuovo*:

> . . . our party must today become a great mass party; and this is why we say to the old comrades, who might have a tendency to remain a small group, the group of those who have remained pure, faithful to the ideals and to the thought, we say to them: "You are wrong, you will be a leading group to the degree that you will be able to make of our party a great mass party, a great organization which has in its own ranks all the elements necessary to establish contacts with all categories of the Italian people and to direct them all toward the goals that we are proposing to achieve."[16]

The PCI must be accounted to have succeeded remarkably well in achieving this first goal of building and maintaining a strong mass party. Whatever might be said about the decline in membership from the peak of nearly two and a half million in 1954 to the plateau of about 1.6 million in recent years, or about the declining levels of active participation in the party's affairs, it must still be acknowledged that the original calculation was a

[15] Giordano Sivini, "Le Parti communiste: Structure et fonctionnement," in *Le Communisme en Italie*, Fondation Nationale des Sciences Politiques (Paris: A. Colin, 1974), p. 4.

[16] Palmiro Togliatti, "I compiti del partito nella situazione attuale," speech at Florence, October 3, 1944; reprinted in *Critica marxista* 1, nos. 5-6 (September-December 1963): 336.

sound one: the party's mass base has been the key to its electoral success over the years and the basis for its less consistent but still impressive capacity to organize demonstrations and other activities of mass protest. The PCI failed, however, in its effort to stretch the mass party to the maximum possible dimensions by merging with the Socialist party. Between 1944 and 1946 the PCI did its best to translate the Unity of Action pact made with the Socialists in 1934 and renewed in September 1943 into an arrangement for "organic unity." The "new party," it was proclaimed, must now become the "single party of the Italian working class."[17] Although this ambition at times seemed realizable, it could not survive the differences of tradition and outlook between the two parties, the cross-pressure of left and right wings within the PSI, nor the intimidating effect of the PCI's own organizational achievements. Italian postwar political history would be one of splits, not fusions.

The *partito nuovo* was to be not merely a mass party in the sense of membership or electoral support, but the center of a network of semiautonomous working-class organizations, springing from and in everyday contact with the masses (the most important being the trade unions, but including also the *Lega Cooperativa*, the *Comitati della Terra*, youth and women's organizations, etc.). This goes back to Gramsci's concept of hegemony and his emphasis on the necessity for PCI *presence* in every aspect of Italian society as an essential precondition of the party's capacity for mass mobilization. Such a conception of the party's role in society directly reflected its new "national" character and implied extending its reach beyond a strictly Leninist alliance of workers and peasants. Togliatti spoke of the "Party's task to gather round itself all the productive forces in the country" and defined the "nation" which the PCI must strive to represent as not only the working class per se, but "the peasantry, the masses of intellectuals, the masses of all those who work with their brain as well as those who work with their arms—professional men, technicians, clerks," excluding only "those egotistic groups, those property-owning reactionary classes whose policy is incapable of rising above considerations of their own narrow interests or of

---

[17] See, for example, Ruggiero Grieco, "Socialisti e comunisti," *Rinascita* 2 (January 1945): 3-4; and Celeste Negarville, "L'Unità organica della classe operaia," *Rinascita* 3 (January-February 1946): 7-10.

putting these below the general interests of the people of their country."[18]

In the immediate postwar period, a primary focus of PCI efforts to construct mass-based organizations was the trade-union movement. The widespread feeling that divisions within the working class had contributed to the advent of fascism, coupled with the party's constant reiteration of the themes of national unity and constructive collaboration, gave the prospect of union unity great power and appeal. By the time of the signing of the Pact of Rome on June 3, 1944, by means of which the representatives of the three "mass" parties—DC, PCI, and the Partito Socialista Italiano di Unità Proletaria (PSIUP)—formally created a single union, the Confederazione Generale Italiana del Lavoro (CGIL), to represent all Italian workers, unity had in fact already been the practice among the clandestine labor organizations of the north. Although Communist influence was dominant in the CGIL from the beginning (owing to the prevalence of Marxist attitudes among the rank-and-file workers, the organizational capacity and prestige of the PCI in the Resistance, and the quality of Communist union leadership), the founding agreement and the subsequent organizational congress revolved about the theme of unity. The new union was to be based on the principles of absolute equality of representation for the three *correnti* in all executive organs, the avoidance of ideological conflict, and the independence of the union from all political parties, although it reserved the right to take a stand on political issues affecting the interests of the working class.

Given their relative positions of strength vis-à-vis the membership (at the CGIL National Congress in Florence in 1947, the Communists received 57.8 percent of the votes, the Socialists 22.6 percent, and the Catholics 13.4 percent), it may seem surprising that the Socialists and Catholics ever agreed to enter a unified union within which the real, as opposed to the formal, power balance placed them at such an obvious disadvantage. The experience of the unitary CGIL (1944-1948) makes sense only in the context of the broad political collaboration, first in the CLN and then in the national government, of which it was a logical expression. Furthermore, the policy pursued by the Communist leadership in the union was fully consistent with the constructive pos-

---

[18] "I compiti del partito," pp. 333, 335.

ture adopted by the PCI within the government. Priority was unequivocally given to one goal—the restoration of production and its corollary, the curbing of inflation—objectives to which little opposition could be found in any but extreme left-wing segments of Italian political opinion. The PCI thus relied upon the moderate line of the union and its overall conciliatory posture toward the government and toward management, combined with the symbolic appeal of unity among the workers, to maintain the unitary structure of the union movement and to make de facto Communist domination tolerable to the DC and other minority groups (the Socialists remained tightly bound to the Communists through the Unity of Action pact).

For the purpose of mass mobilization, the unitary CGIL was an ideal instrument in the implementation of PCI strategy. Within a framework of party and class cooperation and a formally nonpartisan structure, it gave the PCI, by virtue of its superior organizational and leadership capabilities, an opportunity to politicize the workers, to extend its influence, and to establish a positive reputation as a defender of working-class interests among Catholic-oriented sectors of the working class. This *mano tesa* to the Catholic workers was potentially two-sided, skillfully combining collaboration and competition. Through the CGIL, the PCI tried both to mobilize the workers under its own banner and, at the same time, to extend its political reach by an alliance with the Catholic sector of the labor movement.

Union unity thus cannot be considered merely a facade, promoted by the Communists to camouflage their own domination of the labor movement. It was an integral part of the policy of collaboration and national unity common to all parties in the immediate postwar years, and its symbolic significance was such that, despite the onset of the Cold War and increasingly bitter conflict among the opposed *correnti*, the formal veneer of unity survived for over a year after the expulsion of the Communists and Socialists from the government in 1947. When the split finally occurred in 1948, it meant the loss to the PCI of any influence over the Catholic workers; but since collaboration with the Socialists continued, a critical part of the purpose of the unity strategy was salvaged.

The mass party which the PCI was striving to construct in these years might have been used in a very different way, as party strategy after 1948 illustrates. The crucial point to be made about the earlier period is that the party was not conceived by the leadership as a potential insurrectionary force, nor even as an instrument of internal mass opposition to the system or of pressure on the government majority for enactment of specific policies and reforms. On the contrary, Togliatti warned against the sectarianism of those who viewed the party's role solely in terms of propaganda and opposition. The new circumstances created by the war and the Resistance meant that the party must now participate in the government and in national life in a positive and constructive way, not limiting itself to criticism but taking an active and responsible role in the solution of the grave political and economic problems facing the country.

The leaders of the PCI were thus seeking to use the party organization as an effective instrument for the realization of party strategy. In this basic sense the two interests of the party complemented each other well: the search for alliances was being materially aided by the building of a great mass party with a broad social and regional base. There were, however, at least two important sources of tension between the two objectives. First, Communist success in building a large and cohesive organization to gain influence among groups whose allegiance was being sought by other political parties was bound to generate a reaction. The Christian Democrats, using the channels of the Church, were not long in constructing an organizational network at least as powerful as that of the PCI. This was merely one of the difficulties inherent in a strategy of competitive coexistence, of collaboration with one's principal long-run opponent.

The second source of tension was within the party itself. Even during the Resistance, and more strongly thereafter, many of the most dedicated party cadres and members—the ones on whom the party had to rely to carry out its policies at the grass-roots level—simply could not accept at face value the strategy of collaboration. They regarded it as only a tactical necessity, to be abandoned once the war was over, and were relieved when domestic and international circumstances combined to overturn it.[19] This underlying tension at the base suggests the difficulty of trying to use an ostensibly revolutionary organization, constructed in the Bolshevik tradition, for nonrevolutionary purposes. The

[19] For some vivid illustrations of such attitudes, taken from Party Archives of the Resistance period, see Ragionieri, "Il partito comunista," in Valiani et al., *Azionisti*, pp. 410-414.

way out of that dilemma—the creation of a mass rather than a cadre party—only raised the opposite question of whether the party should continue to merit the label of a "revolutionary" or a "Leninist" organization.

The Role of the Soviet Union

The fact that our attention has thus far focused on the domestic bases of the PCI's policy is not intended to imply that the policy was an entirely autonomous one, developed without regard for—or only coincidentally in harmony with—the interests of the Soviet Union. On the contrary, the policy was certainly meant to promote the Soviet cause as well as that of the PCI. The salient point is that during this brief period a situation existed that would not occur in so full a degree again: both the PCI and the USSR felt that their interests were in essential harmony.

There can be no ambiguity whatever about the legacy of the past in regard to relations between the two. The PCI, like the other Communist parties created at this time, was formally a section of the Communist International and fully accepted—although it often chafed under—the Comintern's authority to determine its domestic strategy and designate its leadership. Those who could not accept the basic premise that their party's fortunes were irrevocably tied to the power and the ideology of the Soviet Union were weeded out along the way, during the crises of the twenties and thirties. The rest, Palmiro Togliatti first among them, made their peace with the situation. Whatever misgivings they may have had about the consequences of Stalinism for the Soviet Union and the Communist International would very likely have been dissolved by the triumphs of the Second World War: the successes of Soviet industry and Soviet arms in beating back the German invaders must have overcome any latent doubts and reinforced their sense of the legitimacy of Stalin's rule and of Soviet command of the Communist movement. Under the circumstances, it would have been almost inconceivable for the leaders of the PCI to have followed a strategic line in 1944 that was not fully and explicitly endorsed by Stalin.

The historical record leaves no doubt, moreover, that Togliatti's famous *svolta di Salerno* was intended directly to further Soviet diplomatic interests. Early in March of 1944, after conversations begun some weeks before, the Italian Foreign Ministry announced its acceptance of a Soviet offer to restore diplomatic relations, a move intended to strengthen the king's position and weaken the opposition of the reviving political parties (including the Communists) to military collaboration with the monarchy against the Germans.[20] When Togliatti shortly thereafter proclaimed his party's readiness to enter a government coalition under the king and Marshal Badoglio, he certainly meant to reinforce the Soviet move. His initiative, in fact, could hardly have succeeded, given the resistance to it within the PCI and the other parties, without Soviet prestige to back it up.

This policy of collaboration was the first concrete illustration of a basic Communist strategy in Italy which reflected the Soviet Union's broader stance toward Europe. Beyond the essential goal of securing the widest possible support for the war effort, Stalin's primary concern was to guarantee the future security of the Soviet Union's western border. On the basis of bitter experience, he believed that such security could be achieved only by creating a zone of satellite states in central Europe, backed up by substantial Soviet forces. As a corollary, he perceived the continued presence of American troops in Europe as a potential threat to these interests; the encouragement of rapid American disengagement was thus another important goal of Soviet foreign policy.

Although many of Stalin's actions tended in fact to defeat such an end (in Poland, for example), an overall appraisal of Soviet foreign policy in the early postwar years reveals a prudent assessment of the USSR's vital interests and a consequent effort not to arouse unnecessarily the suspicions of the Western powers either by indiscriminate expansionary efforts or by encouragement of revolutionary activity, especially in Europe. Stalin appears to have accepted quite explicitly the Yalta division of spheres of influence among the Great Powers and to have given clear priority to strengthening the Soviet position in Eastern Europe. Not wishing to jeopardize Soviet gains in that area, he withdrew Soviet troops from northern Iran after Western protests and denied support to the guerrilla movement in Greece. This concern to avoid where possible direct provocation of the Western powers, coupled with the disposition of Allied forces at the war's end, made it inevitable that revolution in Western Europe would be subordinated to the consolidation of Soviet interests in the East. It was on the basis of a highly realistic assess-

[20] C.R.S. Harris, *Allied Military Administration of Italy, 1943-45* (London: Her Majesty's Stationery Office, 1957), pp. 141-143.

41

ment of Soviet interests and of the prevailing balance of forces, then, that Stalin formulated his strategic guidelines for the French and Italian parties: the wartime alliance of the Soviet Union with the Allied powers must continue to find expression in postwar political collaboration at the domestic level.

PCI leaders fully shared Stalin's perspective. They had no illusions that Italy, occupied by Allied armies, would emerge from the war outside the Anglo-American sphere of influence. This consideration was reinforced by others, of a domestic nature, which convinced the party leadership of the impossibility of utilizing the Resistance movement as a springboard for socialist revolution. In the first place, the Resistance was entirely a northern phenomenon; in the south, the old bureaucratic state apparatus had already been fully restored, under the protection of American troops. Not only would any attempt to establish a socialist state in the north have in all likelihood provoked Allied intervention, but, given this division between north and south, even a successful revolution would have meant the sacrifice of national unity and the permanent occupation of the rest of the country by the Western powers. Moreover, despite the prominence of the Communists and the socialist inclinations of many of the partisans, the Resistance had very real limits—it was a *national*, not a class, movement and its revolutionary component was only a minority. In this period, then, Togliatti's and Stalin's assessments of the balance of domestic and international forces in postwar Europe and of the basic strategic line to be followed were in complete agreement: as the objective situation was not a revolutionary one, the order of the day was participation in coalitions of national unity for winning the war and for the construction of postwar democratic regimes.

Although PCI leaders were entirely realistic on this plane, it does seem possible that they were suffering from other serious illusions. There seem to have been two significant miscalculations, or false hopes. The first of these was the apparent expectation that the international coalition against the Germans would last much longer than it did. Far from considering this alliance as a short-term hypothesis (a sort of "popular front" in the sphere of international relations), the party leadership appears to have seen it as the essential external framework for the development of their postwar domestic strategy. While still in Moscow (1942), Togliatti had warned against "the error of considering the current alliance with the democratic and sincerely anti-Fascist forces of the West, such as England, France, and the United States, as something transitory and of brief duration. . . . This alliance is not a trick; it corresponds to the deepest needs of the working class."[21] This long-term international perspective helps explain the extent of PCI collaboration at the national level and its willingness to accept far-reaching compromise with the DC in order to preserve unity. Despite his Leninist training, with its instrumental attitude toward alliances, Togliatti may well have entertained some of the same sorts of illusions about the postwar world as other Western politicians.[22]

The second miscalculation concerned Soviet policy toward the Communist movement. It seems reasonable to suppose that the dissolution of the Comintern in 1943 was regarded by the party leadership as an implicit declaration of intent to loosen Soviet control and to allow greater autonomy to individual Communist parties. In fact, the directives of the Seventh Congress of the Comintern for the formation of popular fronts and the transferral of the anti-Fascist struggle to the national plane, along with the new responsibilities such a line placed on member parties, had contained the seeds of its future dissolution. A strategic line based on popular frontism and national unity resurrected the issue of the role of "national peculiarities" in the struggle for socialism. Any policy posed in these terms demanded at least limited autonomy for each party to adapt general policy to the particular conditions it faced in its own country. Given the continuity of Togliatti's thought on this subject from as early as the 1920s (see his analysis of the national characteristics of fascism) and his leading role in the elaboration of the theses for the Seventh Congress, it is entirely consistent that he should have regarded the dissolution of the Comintern as a significant opportunity for further accentuation of the *national* character of the party and for development of the "polycentrism" which he would later articulate.[23]

Such an expectation would have been reinforced by the evolution of the "people's democracies" in Eastern Europe during this

---

[21] Quoted in Ragionieri, "Il partito comunista," pp. 308-309.

[22] This is the judgment of Ragionieri, one of the PCI's most eminent historians; see ibid., pp. 385-386.

[23] See "Un discorso inedito di Togliatti ai comunisti napoletani (June 1944)," *Rinascita* 28 (January 29, 1971): 21.

same period. Until 1947 the political and institutional situation in these countries remained fluid and Soviet policy cautious. As in France and Italy, the Communists participated in broad democratic coalitions dedicated to the goals of democratization of the political life of the country, economic reconstruction, and the enactment of structural reforms. Declaring that the presence of the working class in the government assured a "progressive democracy," the Communist parties advocated reform from within and eschewed explicit class measures in favor of progressive reforms supported by a broad spectrum of democratic forces.

The theoretical justification for this new state form, neither classical bourgeois democracy nor yet a dictatorship of the proletariat, emphasized, much as did the PCI in Italy, the absence of an objectively revolutionary situation and the consequent need for a transitional period of "progressive democracy." For the moment, then, the task of the Communist parties was to carry out national democratic rather than socialist revolutions. Especially for parties participating in government, this required a substantial degree of flexibility in dealing with the "national peculiarities" which shaped every specific situation. The wide range of diversity within the people's democracies, the scope reserved for the autonomous judgment of individual parties, and finally the apparent acceptance of democratic government and gradual change may well have led Togliatti, here as well, to overestimate the durability of this transitional phase and the extent to which Stalin was prepared to grant meaningful autonomy to other Communist parties.

Despite these false hopes, PCI and Soviet policies were until 1947 in essential harmony. This conformity of fundamental interests was a tremendous advantage for the PCI in dealing with its own members. The persistent tension at the base of the party with regard to the strategy of collaboration could be dealt with not only by pointing out the realism of the position, given the existing balance of forces, but also by stressing the fact that this was Soviet policy as well. In this period perhaps more than any other, the link of the PCI to the USSR—to the immensely strengthened myth of Stalin and the prestige of the Soviet Union as a world power in the wake of Stalingrad and the victorious Russian armies—was a powerful asset and one of the reasons for the party's extraordinarily rapid expansion.

This point demonstrates once more how complete, during this

period, was the harmony among *all three* basic interests of the PCI: loyalty to the demands of Soviet policy, domestic strategy, and party-building. For perhaps the first and last time, party leaders were not constrained to make difficult choices nor to assign priority to one or another of these interests: in the implementation of the party's strategic line, the demands of each were mutually reinforcing. Soviet and domestic policy, identical in their basic lines, required the construction of a new national, mass-based party, whose growth was in turn stimulated by the policy it was designed to serve. Never again would the coincidence of these diverse and potentially contradictory claims on the party be so complete.

The Phase of Confrontation: The Cold War Years (*1948–1956*)

During the course of 1947 and 1948 the PCI was forced into an abrupt reversal of its previous policies. The first blow was struck by the party's would-be collaborator Alcide De Gasperi who, by the spring of 1947, had discovered the combination of domestic and international support necessary to govern without the participation of the Communist and their Socialist allies. Dismissal from the government did not result in an immediate change in the party's line: the work of the Constituent Assembly, on which the party placed the highest importance, was still only half-finished and in any case the defeat was not regarded as definitive —the leaders of the PCI were not in a mood to believe that power could be removed from their grasp for the next quarter-century and more.[24] Not until the elections of 1948, when the Christian Democrats won the impressive total of 48 percent of the vote as against the 31 percent of the Communist-Socialist Popular Front, did the magnitude and likely permanence of the disaster become plain.

But another crucial fact had intervened well before the election defeat. In September 1947, at the founding meeting of the Cominform, the Soviet leaders and their colleagues in the East European parties had lowered the boom on the French and Italian parties. A new era of harsh confrontation between the "peace-loving democratic states" and their erstwhile capitalist allies was

[24] See Gian Carlo Pajetta's rueful comment to this effect in Spriano et al., *Problemi di storia*, p. 102.

proclaimed, and the West European parties were summoned to play their part in the drama. With the Yugoslav leaders Kardelj and Djilas serving as Zhdanov's principal spokesmen, the PCF and the PCI were mocked for their foolish and opportunistic policies of collaboration. As recorded in the notes of Eugenio Reale, Kardelj opened the attack:

> The Italian Communists praised De Gasperi as an honest man and his party as a mass party and did not unmask this party as a servant of the Vatican. When they did this, the plot to chase them from the government was already under way. . . . Popular democracy does not begin with the participation of Communists in a bourgeois government. Can it be said that the PCI or the PCF had taken clear positions? No. With their theory of popular democracy they disarmed the masses. [Take] the slogan of a national policy and the national role of the Communist party. Certainly, there is no other party that can call itself national as the Communist party can. But a national party is one thing and nationalism another. The PCI saw too late the real meaning of American policy. That explains the slogan: Neither London, nor Washington, nor Moscow. But it is clear that without Moscow there is neither liberty nor independence.[25]

Zhdanov himself put the seal on the matter: interrupting Duclos, who was attempting to explain why his party had continued even after its removal from the government to call itself a "party of government," he sarcastically commented that the people might have understood the PCF better if only it had begun to call itself an opposition party; but neither Duclos nor Thorez had used the phrase. And to Longo, Zhdanov made it clear that the PCI could not get off lightly with only minor self-criticism: what was called for was a radical change of its political line.[26]

It was hardly conceivable, especially given the depressing direction in which domestic events were moving, that this assault could be resisted. The Russians, in their usual brutal style, were only drawing conclusions that were by then almost self-evident. Once the disaster of the 1948 election had occurred, and the PCI's hopes for returning to the government had been definitive-

[25] *Nascita del Cominform* (Verona: Arnoldo Mondadori Editore, 1958), p. 119.
[26] Ibid., pp. 139, 149.

46

ly shattered, the illusions of the recent past were officially held up to scorn, just as though it had not been the party's foremost leaders who had so assiduously fostered them:

> In the democratic political and social euphoria of the last months of the war and of the early postwar it might have seemed to some that a period was opening up in which traditional political and class conflicts deriving from the very structure of capitalist society were being attenuated to the point of permitting a permanent collaboration between political forces profoundly different in nature, *operai* and *lavoratori socialisti* on the one hand, conservative bourgeois members of capitalist society on the other. To others it might have seemed possible, generalizing from a transitory experience of a parliamentary type, that these conflicts, although continuing to exist, might be overcome through a *system* of compromises.[27]

The party's language reverted to classical themes of class struggle and confrontation with capitalists, Christian Democrats, and the Church, and to a degree the party's behavior followed suit: those were the years of peasant mobilizations for land reform, strikes by agricultural and industrial workers in response to the layoffs and economic reorganization which followed the DC's political victory, and mass demonstrations against NATO and the Marshall Plan. The response of the government to such attempts at mass mobilization was in most cases immediate and brutal. It has been estimated that the years 1948-1954 saw 75 dead and 5,104 wounded as a result of police intervention against such protest; there could no longer be any question that a climate of confrontation and repression had definitively replaced the constructive collaboration of a few short years before.[28]

It seems less important, however, to evoke the well-remembered confrontations of the Cold War years than to recall that beneath this aggressive facade the PCI was in fact struggling to keep alive the essence of its earlier strategy. The party was obliged to attack parliamentary illusions and foolish hopes of political alliances with nonsocialist parties, but this hardly represented a viable strategic outlook. When it came to defining its

---

[27] "Sulla nostra politica," *Rinascita* 5 (September-October 1948): 331.

[28] Renzo Del Carria, *Proletari senza rivoluzione: Storia delle classi subalterne italiane dal 1860 al 1950*, 2 vols. (Milan: Edizioni oriente, 1966), 2: 399.

47

basic political line, the party could do no better than to assert the continued validity of the struggle for peace and independence, for the application of the Constitution, and for defense of the national economy and of the workers' standard of living.[29]

Despite the climate of intense hostility and confrontation, and the PCI's isolation from all political groups except the PSI, the party continued in important respects to act *as though* the strategy of participation were still in effect. In Parliament, for example, even in 1948-1953 at the height of the Cold War, PCI deputies voted against government proposals only one-third of the time.[30] The extent to which the PCI had renounced a purely "obstructionist" strategy in Parliament in favor of continued cooperation emerges even more vividly from an analysis of Communist behavior in legislative committees. Noting that about three-quarters of all laws approved by Parliament are passed directly in committee without ever reaching the floor, Giorgio Galli has shown that the rigid ideological hostility manifested by the Communists in floor debates was complemented by a surprising willingness to compromise in legislative committees: throughout the first legislature the proportion of laws passed in committee either by unanimous vote or with only sporadic individual dissent was consistently greater than 50 percent.[31] Although passage of the majority of these laws was dictated either by local interests or by the technical nature of the bill, the Communist attitude was clearly one of constructive contribution to the effective functioning of Parliament.

On the labor front, the major proposal made by the CGIL under the leadership of Di Vittorio called for a national plan to increase productivity and employment, with the workers accepting certain sacrifices—in the form of a wage truce—for the sake of this national goal. It is particularly striking that this *Piano del lavoro* was presented in 1949-1950, years in which the *controffensiva padronale* in the factory was well under way and workers

[29] Risoluzione del Comitato Centrale, "Per il migliore orientamento politico e per il rafforzamento ideologico del Partito," in *VII Congresso nazionale del Partito Comunista Italiano. Documenti politici del Comitato Centrale, della Direzione e della Segreteria* (Rome: Editori Riuniti, 1951), p. 69.

[30] Franco Cazzola, "Consenso e opposizione nel parlamento italiano: Il ruolo del PCI dalla I alla IV legislatura," *Rivista italiana di scienza politica* 2, no. 1 (April 1972): 84.

[31] *Il bipartitismo imperfetto: Comunisti e democristiani in Italia* (Bologna: Società Editrice Il Mulino, 1966), pp. 310-314.

were increasingly threatened with demotions and loss of jobs as the price for affiliation with left-wing parties and political activity in the factory. Even in the one case where the party moved decisively to lead the most radical movement in postwar Italy— the occupation of the land—it soon muted its radical appeal to *braccianti* and landless peasants in favor of a more general line (the rebirth of the Mezzogiorno) intended to attract a broader spectrum of southern society—small landholders, artisans and shopkeepers, the middle classes and professionals, in addition to the poor peasantry. This search for more inclusive alliances around general programs of economic and social reform obliged the party to restrain the more extreme and violent aspects of the peasant land occupations.[32]

The moderation—and realism—of the party's strategy is illustrated further by its position on the agrarian reform bill enacted by the DC in 1950; in the debate on the bill the PCI consistently supported the formation of small peasant properties rather than distribution of the land in the form of cooperatives (the position of the Left DC), realizing that its alliance strategy in the south depended on support of the landowning interest of the vast majority of the population.[33] Thus even, or perhaps especially, in this period of most harsh confrontation on both the domestic and international levels, the PCI tacitly recognized its status as a minority party in both a political and a social sense and accepted the constraints which this imposed on its strategic options. Despite the apparent futility of its actions in these years, the party's only chance for power within the system continued to lie in the construction of broad political and social alliances—a narrow class line would mean permanent isolation.

What vision of the future did this sequence of events leave open? The party's alliance strategy survived, but only as an aspiration, a potential for some future day. Its ties to the Soviet Union had been reconfirmed, but at the price of encouraging the assumption—deeply ingrained in many of the party's own militants as well as its most ardent foes—that the PCI's only real expectation of coming to power was through an insurrection backed by Soviet bayonets. There remained to the party one vital interest to protect, one asset to cultivate: the organization of the

[32] Sidney Tarrow, *Peasant Communism in Southern Italy* (New Haven and London: Yale University Press, 1967), pp. 284–290.
[33] Ibid., p. 365.

party itself and its capacity to penetrate into the fabric of Italian society. For the next years, until the strategic reversal of 1956, the party devoted its energies above all to organizational matters. It is indicative of the shift in priorities that at the Seventh Congress in 1951 the Political Resolution could be reported in only eight pages of text, whereas the corresponding document on organization was twice the length.

One concern was to strengthen the compactness and effectiveness of the party itself. The earlier stress on numerical growth yielded to qualitative concerns: recruitment was focused on geographical areas and social strata where the party was weak, and primary emphasis was put on raising the ideological level and activism of members and, above all, of cadres.[34] Was the party simply turning inward, lavishing attention on internal matters because it saw no way to make a significant dent on the world outside? In part this was so, and by far the greatest proportion of cadre time was devoted to questions of institutional maintenance —to collection of dues, distribution of newspapers, indoctrination of members, maintaining the vitality of social and political life within the cells and sections of the party. Sivini is certainly right in asserting that the strong emphasis given to the network of dues collectors between 1948 and 1955 "is characteristic of a phase in the party's life during which administration and routine work replace political action and mobilization of the base and during which the image of the faithful and active Communist is exalted, taking no account of his capacity for political initiative."[35]

But this is not the whole story. During this same period, particularly in the earlier years, the party leadership struggled to direct the organization outward, to transform it into a strategic asset in the society at large. Over and over, at party congresses and in its organizational documents, the refrain appears that "our task is not only to organize the party well but to organize the masses and their struggles."[36] What this meant, in concrete terms, was to channel the energies and organizational talents of party members into the mass associations representing the social, occu-

[34] C. Ghini, "Problemi attuali della edificazione del Partito," *Rinascita* 5 (July 1948): 275-278.

[35] "Le parti communiste," p. 13.

[36] "Organizzare l'attività dei comunisti nelle associazioni di massa," in *VII Congresso nazionale del Partito Comunista Italiano*, p. 333.

pational, and interest groupings of Italian society—the trade unions, cooperatives, youth and women's groups, veterans, sporting and cultural associations that had been re-created or established after the war. Through its presence in these organizations the party would seek to establish its hegemony in the society at large. This required persistent, organized effort: "The coordination of this activity should take place in different ways, but it cannot be left to spontaneity."[37] *Comitati di corrente* of the best Communists in each organization were expected to orient and direct the action of other party members and to maintain working links with the relevant sector of the party organization.

By developing to the maximum possible extent its organizational skills, in order to acquire power at the roots of Italian society, the party tried to compensate for its weakness at the summit. Having been denied the resources of governmental power, it sought, in other words, to substitute a social for a political strategy. In large measure this effort failed. The party's cadres, chosen for their qualities of loyalty and their ability to carry out the routine operations of internal party life, were for the most part poorly adapted to administer the more subtle operations required to gain influence within the mass organizations. Even if they had been better suited to the task, however, the political cleavages of Italian society after 1948 were simply too strong to permit the party to make headway among groups where its influence was not already dominant. Catholic organizations of a nominally social or cultural nature (the most important being Catholic Action and its various divisions—men's and women's unions, youth movement, etc.) were already deeply rooted in the prewar era and constituted important sources of strength for the Christian Democrats. To these must be added the economic organizations—Confederazione Italiana dei Sindacati dei Lavoratori (CISL), Associazioni Cristiane dei Lavoratori Italiani (ACLI), Coldiretti, Confederazione Cooperativa—which were created in the immediate postwar years in response to the Communist challenge for control of the working class. By contrast, the mass organizations of the PCI (with the partial exception of the CGIL) largely failed in their purpose of extending the influence

[37] "Risoluzioni organizzative del VII Congresso del Partito Comunista Italiano," in *Documenti politici del Comitato Centrale, della Direzione e della Segreteria. IV Conferenza nazionale del Partito Comunista Italiano* (Rome: Editori Riuniti, 1954), p. 33.

51

of the party into broader sectors of the population, since the membership in party-sponsored mass organizations for the most part coincided with those already enrolled in the party itself:

> In practice the PCI actively promoted a vast network of supporting organizations according to the models of traditional Communist organization, but the new organisms created did not in fact succeed in extending more than marginally the zone of influence of the party, already equipped to carry out by itself and in quite large zones of Italian society the functions and tasks of the supporting movements.[38]

The party's organizational effort was by no means only a failure, however. It may not have succeeded in its positive aspect of expanding the party's influence into new sectors of society, but it did perform other vital functions well. Through its control over the mass organizations, the party achieved an impressive capacity for mobilization that enabled it not only to conduct campaigns on behalf of Soviet international policies but also to defend its own most vital domestic interests. The narrow defeat in 1953 of the so-called *legge truffa* by which the Christian Democrats sought to give themselves a permanent parliamentary majority through a change in the electoral law was certainly a critical victory for the PCI, and one that depended heavily on its capacity to mobilize broad and strong support around the country. This victory showed that the party still retained a capacity for alliance with the non-Communist Left, at least when the issues were of an institutional rather than an economic and social character. Recalling the defeat of the *legge truffa*, and the party's similar success in mobilizing opposition to a right-wing government during the crisis of 1960, Togliatti pointed to the critically important defensive function of the party organization:

> In every situation, our line of conduct was always that of calling the masses to action and, with the thrust of their movement, confronting even the gravest perils. This close and unbroken bond with the masses has always been considered by us as, and is in fact, the preparation that enables us to confront successfully any attempt at reactionary adventure.[39]

[38] Istituto di Studi e Ricerche "Carlo Cattaneo," *La presenza sociale della DC e del PCI* (Bologna: Società Editrice Il Mulino, 1968), p. 178.
[39] "Relazione di Palmiro Togliatti," in X Congresso del Partito Comunista Italiano: Atti e risoluzioni (Rome: Editori Riuniti, 1963), p. 34.

In summary, the "phase of confrontation" was one in which the party's strategic interest in domestic alliance-building, though by no means forgotten, was largely subordinated to its international and organizational interests. These latter interests strongly reinforced each other in that they both rested upon a reassertion of classical Communist ideological principles. It was not an easy matter for the party to overcome the shock of the abrupt and total collapse of its strategy and of the hopes that had nurtured it. The crisis was surmounted by a vigorous return to orthodoxy which enabled the party to capitalize fully on the deepest instincts of its cadres and members—faith in Stalin and the Soviet Union, hostility to political, class, and religious enemies at home, solidarity with the party and the working class. For the great mass of party members, these attitudes—not those required to advance the party's alliance strategy—were what being a Communist was all about.

The Phase of Opposition within the System (1956 to the Present)

Like its predecessors, the third phase in the PCI's postwar history was largely set in motion by events and decisions that took place in Moscow, not Rome. The most influential factors in the watershed year of 1956 were the strategic innovations proclaimed at the Twentieth Congress of the Soviet party, Khrushchev's attack on Stalin, and the Soviet invasion of Hungary. These events, and others that flowed from them, would in the space of a few years radically transform the character of relationships among Communist states and parties. For the Italian party they were essential prerequisites, in both a psychological and a political sense, for its gradual but persistent evolution since that time.[40]

[40] It is tempting to suggest that this phase came to an end in 1968. A case could be made that the party's response to developments such as the invasion of Czechoslovakia, student and labor agitation, the failure of Socialist reunification following the 1968 elections, and the Manifesto challenge cumulatively amounted to a qualitative change in its overall pattern of behavior. In my view, however, these undoubtedly important events essentially served to confirm and highlight trends already well established in the party. The passage of time, moreover, has tended to show that the events of 1968-1969, suggestive though they were, did not produce the changes either in the party or in the society at large that many observers—particularly those on the left—believed they would.

53

It is important to recall, however, that internal signs of crisis had been mounting for some time. Many in the party sensed that a dead end had been reached, that the party had begun to lose ground in certain critical respects. Although the Unity of Action pact signed in 1947 with the Socialists was still nominally in effect, ties with the PSI were visibly eroding and talk of a possible reunification of the Nenni and Saragat wings of the old Socialist movement was beginning to be heard. The PCI was even more tangibly losing ground in the labor movement, as the CGIL's competitive position weakened in the face of political discrimination and the union's own slowness to adapt to changing conditions in industry; a particularly disastrous defeat was suffered in the spring of 1955 in elections at the Fiat plants in Turin. Even electoral trends, although in general the brightest side of the picture for the PCI, were showing disquieting signs, especially in northern industrial centers. And most worrisome of all to party leaders who had come to measure success heavily in terms of organizational strength, membership figures were steadily declining in the north and, after 1954, in the country as a whole. The loss of members was but one indication of what appeared to be a general decline in organizational vitality. The conception of the *partito nuovo* as one in which every member was an activist seemed increasingly far from realization, and at the end of 1954 Pietro Secchia, the party leader most closely identified with the "bolshevization" of the party, was removed from his post as secretary responsible for organizational matters.

To have overcome this highly unfavorable situation of the mid-1950s must be considered a major achievement for the PCI—second only to the initial feat of consolidating its wartime assets into a permanent position as the second political force in the country. In 1956, under the lash of difficult circumstances, the party began to pass from the phase of isolation and frontal opposition into the phase of "opposition within the system." This expression may be misleading in that the PCI has in fact acted throughout the postwar period as the major opposition party, while accepting the basic institutions and procedures of the political system. What I mean to stress is that only during this most recent period has the PCI gradually come to accept its role of within-system opposition in an explicit and fully conscious manner and to act accordingly. In the immediate postwar years the party tried, against the instincts of many of its cadres and members and contrary to the dominant political and social realities of the country, to act as though it were part of a "new majority," and not an opposition party at all. During the Cold War years the party's rhetoric, the attitudes of its members and cadres, and many aspects of its behavior went to the opposite extreme and appeared to deny the possibility of anything but all-out opposition to the system. Since 1956 the PCI has consistently acknowledged the possibility of working as an opposition party to transform the system, and in the process has accepted the legitimacy of many of its features. Equally significantly, its opponents and public opinion more generally have come increasingly to accept the party's own legitimacy. The PCI's goal, still far from realization but no longer as implausible as it seemed a few years back, is to use its assets as an opposition party in order to re-create the situation of the early postwar years and win acceptance once again as a collaborator in government.

As the PCI has tried to respond to the events of the past fifteen years, it has had to confront in a changed context the same three fundamental issues as in the past: How can it maintain and promote the political and social alliances necessary to acquire a share of governmental power? How can it use the party organization itself as an effective instrument to realize this political objective? How can it build alliances and move toward participation in government while at the same time maintaining its ties with the Soviet Union and its commitment to proletarian internationalism? The PCI's most basic interests—political, organizational, and international—continue to be expressed in terms of such questions. Constraints of time and space prevent me from exploring them fully. Two prime considerations lead me to concentrate almost exclusively in this last section on the international component of the party's life: first, this is the area in which by far the greatest change has occurred, and second, other contributions to this volume will deal in greater detail with questions of PCI strategy and organization. (See especially Chapters 7 and 10 by Peter Lange and Stephen Hellman.) Before turning to international questions, however, I would like to make a few brief comments on strategic and organizational matters.

Little will be said at this point about the party's domestic strategy because it has, in my view, remained basically unchanged. As in the past, the heart of the strategy lies in the effort to develop the political and social alliances necessary to win a share of power. This strategy has two essential components, the first of which is the specific political goal of keeping alive the potential for collaboration with the Socialist party. The PSI continues to represent the best guarantee against Communist political isolation in periods like the present, when the Italian political balance shifts to the right, and a potential bridge into the government if the balance should move again to the left. The PCI can contend with Christian Democracy, whether in opposition or in collaboration, only by working with and through the Socialists, not in opposition to them. In short, the structure of political parties and social forces in Italy is such that the alliance potential for the Communist party lies almost exclusively to its right. The PCI's essentially conservative posture toward the radical movements of 1968-1969—notwithstanding an attitude of flexibility and openness that distinguished it sharply from the French Communist party—confirmed the party's commitment to this interpretation of Italian politics. Moreover, the subsequent electoral and organizational failure of the left-wing groups—Manifesto group, Movimento Politico dei Lavoratori (MPL), PSIUP, ACLI—that had sought to capitalize on the radical mood of those years suggests that the Communist perception of the political scene has been not only prudent but basically correct. This point needs no further elaboration, but the conclusion is evident: Communist strategy will continue to be strongly conditioned in a conservative direction by the desire to preserve the potential for alliance with the PSI.

The second and equally persistent component of the alliance strategy is the search for reforms. It cannot be denied that the party has taken enormous strides in the past decade in developing a broad and concrete program of specific social and economic reforms: the highly generic and vague character of its proposals in the early postwar years, and in 1956 as well, when the reform strategy was brought back to life, has been translated into far more concrete proposals that the party has tried to implement through action in Parliament and outside, most notably in cooperation with the trade unions. Reinforcing its more serious and constructive reform proposals have been important modifications of doctrine with respect to the nature of the state and of modern capitalism. These doctrinal innovations have tried to legitimize the party's reform strategy in the eyes of its own militants and of others on the left, and at the same time to persuade potential allies that its commitment to reforms is genuine, by stressing one central point: that reforms within the framework of a capitalist society, even modest and partial reforms, can represent significant steps toward the construction of a socialist society. It is by invoking this argument that the party justifies its parliamentary support of economic and social reform measures that it acknowledges are grossly inadequate to the problems at hand.[41]

An important question of interpretation arises at this point. If the PCI leaders believed literally in the value of reforms for their own sake, as steppingstones toward the gradual realization of socialism, they would indeed merit the reformist label pinned on them by the radical Left. The relevant question is not whether the PCI does or does not genuinely desire reforms—it clearly does. The question is *for what purpose* it wants them. I cannot here defend but only assert my belief that the PCI should not be regarded as an essentially reformist party because, in the last analysis, it looks upon reforms in an *instrumental* way. First and foremost, reforms are seen as a way to build political alliances and win electoral support by creating a sense of common interest with other parties and social groups. The PCI is profoundly aware of its limitations as a reformist party. The logic of its political position obliges it to back only moderate reforms likely to attract substantial support from other quarters; the best it can do is to find issues, like regional reform, that are not immediately threatening to vested political or economic interests but whose implementation could over time result in a substantial shift in the balance of power. The party understands all too well that those who hold power in the state, the economy, and the Church can block or fail to implement reforms that seriously undermine their dominance. Despite their rhetoric about the intrinsic value of reforms, party leaders almost surely believe that significant transformations of the system cannot take place unless and until the PCI obtains a share of governmental power. Reforms accomplished without PCI participation would only isolate the party and greatly damage its prospects—this was the ultimate threat, so far groundless, of the Center-Left. A reform coalition led by the PCI, whether successful or not in the short run, remains the essential road to power.

[41] For a fuller analysis of recent PCI reform strategy, see Donald L. M. Blackmer, "Italian Communism: Strategy for the 1970's," *Problems of Communism* 21, no. 3 (May-June 1972): 41-56.

In this general context, what can be said about party organization? It seems clear that many of the traditional organizational characteristics of the party remain fully as relevant to the success of its political strategy as in the past. For instance: the mass character of the party remains a vitally important electoral asset in maintaining and extending the Communist vote; the mobilizational capacity of the party is still highly valuable in creating temporary coalitions around certain types of issues, especially those with an anti-Fascist content; the disciplined and hierarchical nature of the party is an enormous advantage in resisting the tendencies to factionalism that are bound continually to emerge in response to the PCI's inescapably complex and ambivalent strategy. For these and other reasons the party will continue to put great energy into maintaining the vitality of its organization at all levels and resisting trends toward a decline in active participation.

A good deal more interesting, however, than such traditional uses of party organization is the question of whether the party can somehow adapt its organizational structures and functions to strategic needs that are not narrowly political or electoral. Since 1968 the party has been giving increasing verbal attention to the need for more effective ways to reach out to social and economic groups beyond its traditional constituency—that is, to different sectors of a growing and heterogeneous middle class. To do this requires more than making broad reform proposals at the national level. It means working on very specific issues with people in regional, city, and local governments and with those who wish to influence these governments. It means grass-roots politics of a different kind, aimed at different groups, than has been characteristic of the PCI and other Communists parties. It demands active participation in party-sponsored activities by different kinds of militants than have staffed party organizations in the past—younger, better informed and more concerned about the issues, less susceptible to party guidance and discipline. It means new kinds of relationships with mass movements such as have been developing with the trade unions.

Is there more than verbal evidence, through the party's organizational behavior at all levels, that it takes this problem seriously? Is it likely to be able to develop the new organizational styles and the new cadres necessary to pursue a serious social-alliance strategy that can supplement and reinforce its parliamentary strategy of political alliances? Can the PCI, in short, somehow use its "organizational weapon" in a new way to give fresh content to its role as an opposition party? Here I can do no more than to raise such questions—which are addressed more seriously by other contributors to this volume—and to suggest that the answers are as yet far from obvious.

The PCI's International Policy

The international dimension of party policy has undergone far more change in the postwar period than domestic strategy and party organization. Since 1956, particularly during the 1960s, a new and apparently stable pattern of international interests and policy preferences has been developed by the PCI. One major consequence of international developments in these years has been to reduce significantly the tension that characterized the Cold War era between the PCI's need for domestic alliances and its need for friendly relations with the Soviet Union. Although this "contradiction" still exists, the two interests are now more nearly compatible than at any time since 1947. And where the two interests do conflict, the PCI has been able to minimize the danger to its domestic position by expressing its dissent in an open and explicit manner. While the most dramatic change in relations between the two parties has undoubtedly been this emergence of open conflict on certain issues, it would be one-sided to focus exclusively, as many have tended to do, on the elements of PCI dissent without also stressing its concurrent and unequivocal reassertions of fundamental solidarity with the Soviet Union and loyalty to the principle of proletarian internationalism. My interest here is to indicate how these two attitudes toward the international movement coexist and how the international dimension as a whole relates to other basic party interests.

The point of strongest and most obvious mutual interest between the PCI and the USSR concerns the overall tendency of Soviet foreign policy, which since the Twentieth Party Congress has by and large emphasized détente and peaceful coexistence. It requires little imagination to perceive the Italian party's preference for a Soviet Union that appears as a benevolent and constructive force and for an international environment free of direct confrontation between the two great powers. In such a world ideological barriers begin to fade, anti-Communist campaigns lose their vitality, the potential for alliances with Catholic

59

and other nonsocialist groups is enhanced. A climate of détente is crucial to realization of the party's aspirations and is thus one of the strongest bases for its continued allegiance to the USSR.

The second major plank in the PCI's foreign policy, however, has involved it in direct and serious disagreement with the Soviet Union. The PCI has been one of the most persistent advocates of the view that each Communist party, because it confronts political, social, and economic conditions peculiar to it, must be responsible for working out its own destiny within some broad limits prescribed by Marxist-Leninist tradition. Ever since 1956 the PCI has enthusiastically welcomed every Soviet affirmation of this principle. More importantly, it has—at first only indirectly and then with increasing vigor and explicitness—resisted the perennial Soviet attempts to insist anew on the validity of certain universal laws of socialist construction. No party is the depository of absolute truth, the PCI has insisted, and no single model of socialism can possibly apply to parties and states functioning under enormously diverse internal and international conditions. As Enrico Berlinguer proclaimed at the Moscow conference of Communist parties in 1969:

> We reject the idea that there can be a single model of socialist society valid for all situations. It is not only a question of national peculiarities which must be considered in the context of the general laws of the development of the socialist revolution and of the building of socialist society. In fact, these general laws of the development of society, these essential and universal traits of the socialist revolution, never exist in the pure state, but always and only in particular circumstances, historically determined and unrepeatable.[42]

The Soviet leadership, while in some circumstances willing to accept this point in the abstract, has been anything but prepared to accept the political corollary that each Communist party and state must be fully autonomous, free from external intervention. Perhaps the best measure of change in the PCI's international posture is its evolution on this point. In 1956, despite heavy political costs, Togliatti summoned his party to support Soviet

[42] "La posizione del Partito Comunista Italiano sui problemi in discussione alla Conferenza," speech of Enrico Berlinguer at the International Conference of Communist Workers' Parties in Moscow, reported in *L'Unità*, June 12, 1969, p. 5.

armed intervention in Hungary, insisting that the obligation of solidarity to international socialism must be met and that non-intervention of one state in the affairs of another could not be accepted as an absolute principle. In 1968, Togliatti's successors denounced the Soviet invasion of Czechoslovakia and rejected un-equivocally the "Brezhnev doctrine" by which the Soviet leaders justified their action. Their position this time left no room for ambiguity; it was expressed in perhaps its most explicit form in response to subsequent developments in the Czech situation: "We do not admit that the sovereignty of a socialist country can be in conflict with its 'class and internationalist' character. Sovereignty is an inalienable right. For us, this is not an abstract in-terpretation but a value which we cannot renounce."[43]

There were of course substantial objective differences between the two cases which help explain the sharp contrast in the PCI's response. The critical point, however, is that by 1968 the PCI no longer hesitated to challenge the Soviet Union publicly on a mat-ter of vital national interest. The possibility of reprisal by the Soviets, or of a disruptive internal challenge from pro-Soviet groups inside the party, was no longer sufficiently threatening to deter the leadership from this step. The PCI had thus gone a long way toward overcoming one of its most serious weaknesses: it had insulated itself against the disastrous consequences of being obliged, at some future time, to associate itself with an aggressive act of Soviet diplomacy. It was now to some extent even able to derive credit from such occasions, as it did in 1968, by demon-strating to potential allies its autonomy from the Soviet Union.

The Italian position, however, goes well beyond a simple as-sertion of the need for autonomy, whether its own or that of other parties and states. Hardly less sensitive from the Soviet point of view is the PCI's increasingly open concern with political institutions and processes in the Soviet Union and Eastern Eu-rope. Khrushchev's criticisms of Stalin at the Twentieth and Twenty-Second Congresses had a decisive political and psycho-logical impact on the PCI, for they made possible—indeed neces-sary—a confrontation between the USSR as a symbol of socialism and the USSR as a social and political reality. Togliatti himself began the process by his cautious suggestions, in 1956, that the abuses denounced by Khrushchev should not be attributed only

[43] *L'Unità*, January 15, 1971, p. 12.

to Stalin's "personality cult" but also to broader factors having to do with the evolution of the Soviet system as a whole. It is true that the PCI has not developed its criticisms of the Soviet system very fully. Despite repeated assertions about the need to examine the roots of unspecified "violations of democratic principles and of socialist legality," the party has been outspokenly critical only on rare occasions, generally when Soviet attacks on literary and cultural freedom were in the news. The balance of PCI comment on the Soviet Union, moreover, has remained positive, dominated by strong praise of the economic and social achievements of the pioneer state of socialism. Nevertheless, these undeniable limits on the scope of PCI public criticism of the USSR should not obscure the fact that the party has in many respects explicitly rejected the USSR as a desirable model of socialist society.

It was of course the experience of Czechoslovakia that brought out far more strongly than ever before the PCI's antipathy for the Soviet model, focusing attention for the first time on the most sensitive issue of all: the role of the Communist party. The enthusiasm of the PCI leadership for the Czech experiment was unquestionably genuine. At last a type of democratic socialism seemed to be emerging, and in a country whose level of economic development and experience with parliamentary democracy was similar enough to Italy's to hope that it might serve as a positive point of reference for a broad spectrum of the Italian Left. Party commentary focused particularly on three aspects of the Czech experiment, often explicitly contrasting these with Soviet practice: (1) the attempt to overcome the absolute identification of party and state and to permit more than a single party to function freely; (2) the insistence on the need for democracy, and dissent, within the party; and (3) the need for mass social organizations such as trade unions to be independent of the party and to make an autonomous contribution to national decision-making. The single theme most commonly stressed was the need to overcome bureaucratic and authoritarian tendencies through decentralization of power and the development of new modes of participation by the masses in the decison-making process.

How important are these endorsements of a kind of socialist society in which social groups are broadly represented and actively participate in the management of state and society? One view would be that the PCI, having extracted the right of dissent from the ruins of the once-monolithic Communist movement,

now has little to lose internationally and much to gain domestically by lending verbal support to democratic principles in the
hope of improving its image among Italian politicians and the
general public. True as far as it goes, this is too shallow and cynical a view of the PCI's interests and perspectives. The party's
leaders have learned much—first from the experience of fascism
and more importantly from their disillusionment with the failures
of socialism in the Soviet Union and the East European states—
about the dangers of the highly centralized one-party state. They
are profoundly aware, moreover, that for them the road to power
can lie only in alliances with other parties and social groups.
More self-consciously than other Italian parties they have attempted to reckon with the diversity of interests and social forces
in Italy and have built their entire strategy around this awareness. They have deeply absorbed the single most important lesson that Togliatti taught: that to succeed they must *fare politica*,
"be political," precisely in the sense of building a coalition out of
diverse forces. If I am right, the attitudes that emerged most
clearly during the Czech crisis represent basic political instincts,
not transient tactics.

Given the PCI's dissent from the Soviet handling of relations
with its neighbor socialist states and its distaste for the quality of
Soviet political life, is it then possible that the party might one
day take the final step of renouncing its fundamental loyalty to
the USSR and to the concept of proletarian internationalism? It
could persuasively be argued that a PCI proclamation of neutrality in foreign affairs, at the right time, might be the decisive ges-
ture required to overcome the barriers to Communist participation in an Italian government. Such a move seems to me unlikely,
however, for two principal reasons.

The first of these has to do with the links the PCI leadership
perceives between international relations and domestic policy.
The PCI's reaffirmation of the party's profound commitment to
the solidarity of the international movement, despite its increasingly open criticism of Soviet policies within the Communist
movement and of political and social structures within the socialist camp, is rooted in part in a conviction about the direct and intimate relationship between domestic strategy and the balance
of international forces. This perspective seems especially valid
for a country such as Italy, subordinate both politically and economically to international forces largely outside its control.

63

While accepting the reality of European integration, the PCI can thus plausibly denounce the sacrifice of Italian interests within the Common Market to those of stronger nations such as Germany. More generally, it attacks the increasing power of multinational monopolies and international bureaucracies at the expense of national sovereignty and democratic processes. Strategically, the PCI sees Italy as a mere puppet of United States political and military interests within the NATO alliance, an instrument of a policy of containment and confrontation in the Mediterranean and the Middle East and of support for military and repressive regimes. This posture is seen as alien to Italy's true interests of peace in the Mediterranean and solidarity with the Arab nations.

The PCI feels, not without reason, that the ultimate guarantee of DC hegemony in Italy is the backing it receives—economically, politically, militarily, ideologically—from the United States, and that the crucial barrier to the accession to power of the Communists is likely to be American resistance. Party leaders appear convinced that in a showdown the United States would use its power to preserve the political and economic interests of the NATO alliance, even at the cost of a right-wing government which would liquidate the prospects for democratic progress and internal reform in Italy. In this situation the only means of neutralizing the power of the United States, NATO, and the Common Market lies in continued identification with the one force which represents a challenge to American predominance in Europe—the Soviet Union and the socialist camp. The party perceives this as a choice profoundly in the Italian national interest, since the domestic changes it deems essential are dependent on the future shape of Europe.

The PCI's insistence that Italy's adherence to NATO prevents effective national autonomy on the domestic as well as the international level has led the party to a broader criticism of the logic of bloc politics in general. While accepting in principle Soviet arguments about the objectively different nature of the two opposed blocs, the PCI tends to emphasize that in practice the effects of Great Power hegemony on the autonomy of the member states are identical. This point ties in directly with the party's evaluation of the Czech events. Far from being merely a "tragic error" in an otherwise correct Soviet strategy of coexistence and détente, the intervention has been seen as a logical consequence

of an international strategy which remains tied to a static conception of the division of Europe and the world into two opposing
political-military systems. This conception is regarded by the PCI
as a concession to imperialist notions of spheres of influence
which inevitably subordinates the sovereignty of the Eastern
European states and the free interplay of political and social
forces within these societies to the demands of bloc politics.[44] For
the PCI, the development of democratic and socialist forces, in
Western and Eastern Europe alike, is fundamentally linked to
the eventual dissolution of both blocs and to the construction of
a general system of all-European security and collaboration. PCI
dissent from Soviet actions within the international Communist
movement thus goes far beyond tactical questions of domestic
political advantage to touch basic issues of principle and deeply
rooted convictions regarding the nature of international relations. This dissent does not, however, in part for the reasons suggested above, acquire an anti-Soviet or even a genuinely neutral-
ist connotation.

The second set of considerations that make highly unlikely an
explicit PCI repudiation of loyalty to the Soviet Union concerns
the potentially damaging consequences for the party itself. The
danger lies in at least two directions. The most obvious consequence of a break with the USSR would be to create the possibility of a Soviet-supported split inside the party which might seriously compromise its unity and strength. Although there are
virtually no Soviet loyalists in influential positions in the party
any longer, and a rapidly declining number of older militants at
lower levels who retain the memories and emotional attachments
of earlier years, there remain many thousands of loyal party
members who would find it next to impossible to swallow a general repudiation of ties to the USSR and the international movement. The Czech affair brought back into party section meetings
hundreds of older members, inactive for some years, to protest
the party's anti-Soviet stance. A broader policy of PCI dissent
would arouse even stronger resistance from some quarters of the
party.

The political risk of alienating the Stalinist fringe within the

[44] See, for example, Achille Occhetto, "Forze rivoluzionarie e lotta per il
socialismo nell'Europa capitalistica," *Rinascita* 25 (September 6, 1968):
3-4; and Luca Pavolini, "Le frontiere della rivoluzione," *Rinascita* 25 (September 20, 1968): 5-6.

party seems a good deal less serious, however, than the more subtle long-term danger of undermining at a vital point the party's entire ideological structure. The PCI's link to the Soviet Union and to the socialist world more generally has always been a central component of the belief system promoted by the party. Whereas this aspect of ideology is no longer related in a positive sense to the party's domestic strategy (its search for allies and its conceptions of the road to a socialist society), it can hardly be separated from other beliefs concerning the nature of the party itself. The PCI would find it difficult to maintain the viability of its self-image as a *Leninist* party—that is, as a disciplined, centralized party able to maintain unity and effectiveness while taking difficult decisions—if it were to cut itself off from the Soviet party that best represents the continuity and force of this political tradition. Too severe a break with the USSR and with the traditions of proletarian internationalism would not merely arouse the substantive opposition of many in the party, but would also tend to legitimize the very principle of opposition by weakening belief in the basic concept of democratic centralism.

The more general point to be made in this connection is one that could best be supported by sensitive empirical examination of the beliefs of party members: namely, that there is a reasonably coherent set of beliefs that together determine the loyalty of members to the party as a whole and to its leadership. The legitimacy of the leadership depends in part on its success in adapting party strategy and organization to meet changing circumstances, but it also depends on maintaining the continuity and vitality of its heritage. A strong awareness of this latter need is very likely what has led Giorgio Amendola, in some contexts the strongest and most consistent innovator among the party leaders, to take in recent years the conservative stance of arguing the imperative need to defend the *patrimonio* of the party, including its associations with the Soviet Union.[45] For all its effort to forge alliances by demonstrating its ability to cooperate with other parties in solving commonly recognized social and economic problems, the party's appeal to its own membership and to its electorate lies in being and offering something *different* from other parties. The more its domestic politics and programs

[45] See particularly Giorgio Amendola, "La crisi della societa' italiana e il Partito comunista," *Critica marxista* 7, no. 2 (March-April 1969): 17-52.

come to resemble those of other groups, the more important it may be that it continue to offer a distinctly different international perspective and a different understanding of the nature and role of a political party.

If this seems paradoxical, it is because the PCI has equally deep roots in Communist tradition and in the soil of its native Italy. The question is whether the party's ambivalence will in the end prove a fatal weakness or a source of strength. The weakness is obvious: the party's alienation from some of the central dimensions of Italian politics (e.g., Catholicism and a pro-American bias in foreign policy) may keep it indefinitely at the margins of political power. The strength is less easy to define, but relates to a certain vitality stemming from the tensions inherent in its situation: there is a constant dialectic between the external pressures of Italian domestic politics and the internal pressures emanating from the party itself, from the traditions and values shared by the leadership and the base. The PCI must labor constantly to stay abreast of changing developments in Italy and at the same time to avoid the pitfalls of a modern-day "revisionism." In the Italian context being "revisionist" has little or nothing to do with violating Marxian or Leninist precepts about the economic and social development of capitalist society or the party's role in confronting them: from that standpoint the PCI has long since ceased to be orthodox. The Leninist tradition remains relevant and vital, however, with respect to the party's internationalism and its self-image, attitudes closely related to each other and not easily abandoned without repudiating the PCI's own past and its reason for being.

From the PCI's point of view, therefore, two converging sets of calculations dictate the maintenance of its alliance with the Soviet Union: one springing from a rational consideration of the effects of the international balance of power on Italian politics, the other deeply rooted in Communist ideology and tradition and in the party's internal needs. It may bear repeating that different considerations—notably those having to do with carrying out an effective strategy of political and social alliances—similarly oblige the party to avoid too close an identification with Soviet international and domestic policies.

In this context, too, as in others we have touched upon, the ambiguities and "contradictions" in the behavior of the Italian

DONALD L. M. BLACKMER

Communist party can be clarified by understanding its persistent effort to pursue simultaneously three not always compatible interests: reinforcement of the unity and strength of the party itself, maintenance of its links with the Soviet Union and the international Communist movement, and promotion of the political and social alliances that might one day bring it again a share of governmental power.

II.

The French Communist Party
and the Fifth Republic

ANNIE KRIEGEL

COMMUNIST LOGIC

The Parti Communiste Français *and* the Fifth Republic: not the
PCF *within the framework* of the Fifth Republic, nor even the
PCF in relation to the Fifth Republic; for the fundamental guiding
principle for any analysis of Communist party policy in a particular period must be a recognition of the singular nature of the
Communist phenomenon in France: its necessary allegiance,
from the outset, to two distinct entities or camps.

1. *The international Communist movement,* a multidimensional
system of states, parties, and alliances subject to a central point
of reference, allegiance to the Soviet Union—in other words, the
Soviet version of Leninism. We use a term which is sometimes
mistakenly construed only in its territorial sense, the term "socialist camp."

2. *The French political system.* The results of this dual allegiance are twofold. It is a mistake to study the PCF merely
as one part, one section, one element of the French political
system, a tendency peculiar to those specialists whose vision is
strictly limited to the French hexagon; and it is equally incorrect to view it as one element or section of the international Communist movement, an error made by "run-of-the-mill anti-Communists." We should rather place the PCF at the crossroads of the
two groups in which it plays a role. This definition is not wholly
satisfactory, however. In the study of any political phenomenon,
it is an extremely complex task to try to give equal weight to
the effects and influences of domestic and international politics;
and in trying to analyze Communist policy, it is just as difficult to
keep the French context and that of international socialism
simultaneously in mind. One must therefore establish a temporal
and spatial scale of the influence exerted respectively by these

69

two spheres on their common offspring, the PCF. The problems involved are the following.

For any Communist party, membership in the international Communist movement is basic to its existence. It is the practical corollary to its major goal—world-wide proletarian revolution. It therefore enjoys an absolute priority which, viewed in the central unifying perspective of world revolution, results in turn in the primacy of foreign policy in the decision-making processes of the PCF. One might go so far as to say that the relative amount of attention the PCF pays to issues of international politics (measured, for example, by the percentage of Central Committee meetings, parades, or demonstrations dedicated within a certain period to international issues) could serve as a useful criterion in dividing the history of French communism into periods: the periods in which the PCF has been forced to retreat from the field of French politics have also been those in which foreign policy dominates its activities. The "white trials" which occurred in France in the 1950s, and which were related to the big political trials in the popular democracies, mark the highest level reached in this process of withdrawal from the field of French politics, and absorption in the international Communist movement.

But by reaffirming the necessity of the PCF's allegiance to the international Communist movement, we have not resolved the problems raised by the party's peculiar position at the crossroads of two distinct entities. There are four major problems.

The first problem is the unequal distance separating the French Communists from the two systems that spawned them. Moreover, this distance varies unequally depending on which level of the French movement we are discussing. *Geographic* proximity, which means that the PCF is territorially integrated in the national framework, constitutes one factor, even though the new media are supposedly wiping out geographic distance. A more effective factor, however, is *cultural* proximity, which means that the PCF is basically a product of the grafting of Leninism on the body of pre-1914 French socialism, and thus preserves elements of the latter in its genetic heritage. Consequently, in an effort to maintain its dual identity, the PCF has had to set up a whole ideological and organizational apparatus designed to correct and compensate for the weight of its proximity to the French political system. This set of rules, designed to foster openly its fundamental ambiguity, has succeeded in preventing its essential Frenchness from progressively overwhelming its other component and absorbing it completely.

The second problem is that once we acknowledge the primary importance of the PCF's ties to the international Communist movement, we should also define precisely what obligations these ties entail. For although the "touchstone" of all Communist policy is the defense of the vital interests of the international Communist movement, two further points should be considered.

"Self-interest" is not necessarily peculiar to the socialist camp, but is just as evident elsewhere, as in Western society, for instance. Communists too are troubled by the ambivalence inherent in life and history. It would be both naive and non-Marxist to expect Marxism to be able to deduce from its first principles the one "true" response to any concrete problem.

The socialist camp should not be construed as the pure logical projection of its doctrine. It is a heterogeneous product of its own history. In fact it brands its own "impurities" as the vestiges of its capitalist forebears. However, the fact of the matter is that the socialist camp is ridden with cleavages (social, ethnic, national, provincial, cultural, and generational), cleavages which arise from sociocultural spheres alien to the socialist system, yet which nonetheless interfere with the one creative cleavage in socialist logic, that of class (transposed here into the dichotomy: socialist camp/imperialism).

The third problem is that the PCF's primary allegiance to the international Communist movement plays the same role in the political domain as the determining character of the economic infrastructure plays in the theoretical domain: "a last instance." But unfortunately, from a historical point of view, there is no "last instance." "Last" is a word that literally has no meaning, so to take a certain level or moment and designate it the "last" is an inevitably arbitrary choice.

The fourth problem, the well-known phenomenon of "delayed consciousness," is another factor in the socialist world. For instance, the near monopoly that the Leninist-Stalinist brand of Marxism exercised in the marketplace of revolutionary ideologies was profoundly shaken in 1956 with the Twentieth Congress of the Soviet Communist party and the Khrushchev Report. But the agitation that gradually reached into every level and sector of the socialist camp did not invoke a major crisis until 1960, the year

71

of the Sino-Soviet confrontation. And it was not until 1965, five years later, that the Sino-Soviet split was recognized as an insurmountable reality that must be included as a permanent variable on the worldwide socialist scene. And five more years were to follow before, in the early seventies, the main thrust of the Sino-Soviet rupture was felt—that is, a generally acceptable conversion from the old bipolar system of international relations to a new system involving three or five major powers—a system that required a new set of rules. This "delayed consciousness" has had other curious ramifications. Certain disturbances at work far below the surface of French society have not been acknowledged and dealt with by the party until much time had passed.

These problems serve to underline the dangers of applying the principle of "dual allegiance," however well founded it may be. It is easy to discuss it in the abstract, but much harder to deal with in concrete terms. It is this principle of sorts, however, that justifies the constant use of a *two-stage process* in any analysis of French Communist politics.

The first stage can be divided into two parts: (1) concrete analysis of the current political situation in the international Communist movement (position, circumstances, plans, strength, intermediate goals, and so forth); (2) evaluation of the current French political situation. It is well known, too, that Communist documents themselves (reports to congresses, to the Central Committee, and even indictments by the Public Prosecutor at major political trials) are usually based on this two-part analysis. Thus we have two variables that, provisionally at least, seem mutually exclusive.

But *a second stage* consists of putting these variables side by side to see how they can mesh. Any number of possible combinations will finally lead us to two major types of case. (1) In the first case the two loyalties of the PCF are not in opposition. That is to say, the interests of the socialist camp do not contradict French interests—either because their interests converge and reinforce each other (as was the case, for example, in the period 1941-1944); or because their interests, though separate, do not interfere with one another (in a way this was true during the height of the Cold War period). (2) In the second case the two camps are antagonists. Of course, this is the "normal" state of affairs, as it corresponds to the fundamental gap indicated by the capitalism/socialism dichotomy.

But the nature, cause, level, or form of this gap can give rise to a great number of variations that call for a different approach. Thus when we analyze some of the PCF's theoretical and political activity, we should bear in mind that the Communists are trying to juggle and reconcile the conflicting signals they receive from their two parent systems, in an effort to adapt as best they can to both sets of interests without being split down the middle. We should also take into account the fact that the international Communist movement, by the interpretation it puts on its vital interests, places strictly defined limits on how far the French Communists may go in their search for a maximum degree of harmony between two basic incompatibilities.

COMMUNIST LOGIC APPLIED TO GAULLISM

First Period: A System of Controlled Mutual Aggression

The PCF views the Gaullist phenomenon from *two opposing angles*. Inasmuch as it represents a "certain conception" of contemporary France, Gaullism is the political expression of "monopolistic capitalism." Whatever process the Communists may use to justify the connection they have established between variables belonging to two different spheres—politics and economics—it is important that they succeed in making clear their *negative* attitude to Gaullism on this point. But insofar as it represents a particular view of international relations in the world today, the Gaullist phenomenon is viewed as a positive expression of the contradictions that assail and weaken the imperialist camp.

It is worth noting that this Communist portrayal of the Gaullist phenomenon is stable and of long standing. After 1943, and certainly after the summer of 1944, Stalin and Thorez, after intense discussions in Moscow, came to an agreement on this evaluation. And in the Casanova-Servin affair of 1961, at least in its strategic aspects (there were other aspects, more obvious but in fact secondary), it was precisely the rejection or support of this evaluation that was at stake. At this time the insurgent group led by Casanova and Servin championed the idea of continuing and even stepping up the stand against Gaullism. From the Soviet point of view, this "affair" forced Thorez to return to a position of strict orthodoxy—with respect to the overriding interests of the socialist camp—at a time when (ever since 1956) he had been cherishing hopes of somehow escaping its rigors. He consoled himself by showering verbal abuse on the group that had briefly been the torchbearers of orthodoxy, and he had his revenge in due course when, to the quiet surprise of people in the know, he chose Waldeck Rochet as his successor.

Thus this permanent factor, the fundamental ambiguity of the PCF's relationship with the French establishment, was further accentuated after May 1958 by a specific factor: the Communists' ambivalent portrayal of Gaullism. The consequence—that is, the Communist response to Gaullism—is necessarily complex and blurred. After a period of groping between 1958 and 1962, it was agreed that the PCF constituted an *opposing force* without being an *alternative*. Communists and Gaullists opposed but complemented each other; it was a controlled system of mutual aggression. This may explain the feeling of sham abounding in French political life at the time; the hostility which the two adversaries harbored for each other was by no means a pretense, but they were also aware of the need to contain their conflict within the boundaries of the rules of the game.

Second Period: The Balance Shifts (1962-1968)

But this delicate balance of interacting forces, subtle and complex in its details but firmly established in principle, began to falter. Why?

The Communists have not altered their opinion of Gaullist foreign policy, as their constant use of the term "realist" will attest. In Communist parlance, a policy termed "realist" is one which, although carried out by a "class adversary," is nevertheless "on the right track." This is because the old and once narrowly conceived theme of a Franco-Soviet rapprochement has expanded into a worldwide policy. On the one hand stress is laid on the fact that Europe, from the Atlantic to the Urals, can avoid any internal tension that might threaten peace in the region, that she can disengage from any alliance that might drag her into conflicts where she has no vital interests. On the other hand, Vietnam and the Middle East are areas where the convergence of French and Soviet policy is evident.

The substance of this policy is no innovation in Gaullist thinking. For some time the main design of General de Gaulle's foreign policy, according to Michel Tatu's interpretation, was to break up "the double hegemony of the superpowers."[1] Feeling victimized by one of them, he turned directly to the opposite camp under the banner of "détente, entente, and cooperation."

He still depended on favorable conditions to advance his policy beyond the stage of projection and symbolism, but from that time on these conditions did in fact materialize; the settlement in Algeria, economic growth, the strengthening of the franc on the one hand and American escalation in Vietnam on the other, increased Europe's ability to realize her aspirations for independence from the United States. These favorable conditions resulted in renewed diplomatic activity; the calendar was filled with comings and goings, from Giscard d'Estaing's visit to the USSR in 1964 to the "triumphal" year of 1966 when General de Gaulle went to Moscow in June and Kosygin came to Paris to December.

Admittedly, despite the tenacity with which General de Gaulle followed his lodestar, he achieved only slim results abroad. France did not really become a third party in the dialogue between the two superpowers, and the USSR found much more in common with Germany. Tatu in fact suggests that these meager achievements were merely the inevitable consequence of a mistaken first premise; Gaullist strategy was based on the conviction that a rapprochement or even a dialogue between the Soviet Union and the United States was absolutely out of the question.

But at least on the home front, Gaullist foreign policy worked wonders. As early as 1947, de Gaulle regarded the Communists as "separatists" and the Communists branded the postwar Gaullist party *Rassemblement du Peuple Français* as the "American party," without this diverting them in any way from their major common target—the third force. After General de Gaulle's return to power, even though the Gaullists demonstrated their ability to draw 1.5 million votes from the Communist party, de Gaulle denounced "totalitarian communism," and the Communists for their part cursed "one-man rule" and the "power of monopolies." Nevertheless the "positive aspects" of his foreign policy allowed the president to believe that he held such sway over those "who give prior service to a foreign power" that he no longer had to consider them a threat. This plan actually worked well for quite a time because the Communists, loyal to the idea of primary al-

[1] Michel Tatu, *The Great Power Triangle—Washington, Moscow, Peking* (Paris: Atlantic Institute, 1970).

legiance to the interests of the socialist camp, behaved in such a way as to avoid embarrassment for the Fifth Republic right up to 1964. To put it bluntly, the pro-Soviet policy carried out by de Gaulle was France's best guarantee against communism.

But the tenure of Waldeck Rochet (1964-1969) unexpectedly upset this balance, to the extent that it constituted a heterodox attempt to reverse the classic order of priorities from which Communist plans are usually derived. During his tenure, Waldeck Rochet in fact made a series of specific and long-range decisions which, when taken in concert, reveal a three-pronged approach.

An international dimension: France's position in the international Communist movement had to be modulated in such a way that by drawing closer to the Italian position, it would aim to stand as a force for political negotiation and broader contacts between all the members; no member should be privileged in any way, not even the Soviet Communist party, which should relinquish both in theory and in practice its old role as "polestar of the movement."

A national dimension: The PCF had to advance resolutely into virgin territory and work out a doctrinal response to those both within and outside its ranks who were uneasy about the possible repetition of a Leninist-type "dictatorship of the proletariat," should socialist forces ever take power in France. Whence the hypothesis of a pluralist democracy not only *during* but also *after* the establishment of a socialist regime.

A third dimension was a link between the first two. It aimed at breaking away from the situation that had arisen as a result of the relationship established between Gaullism and communism after the Liberation, which made them so-called objective allies.

The striking proof that Waldeck Rochet was inching his way toward heterodoxy—perhaps not fully aware himself that he was steering his party out of its Stalinist mold—was his support of François Mitterrand's candidacy in the presidential elections of 1965. This absolutely personal decision of Maurice Thorez' successor, which marked the zenith of his authority, in fact meant that the PCF intended to become an active and determined partner in a real opposition. In short, he placed the interests of the French Left before those of the socialist camp. In these aspects, Waldeck Rochet's leadership can be seen as the French equivalent of Khrushchev's venture in Russia and Dubcek's moves in Czechoslovakia, with the variations and nuances inherent in the differences between the men, the times, and the current situation in the countries concerned.

Waldeck Rochet failed just as Khrushchev and Dubcek failed. One reason, of course, was the "French May" of 1968 which intruded on the slow but promising process that Rochet and Mitterrand had set in motion to overthrow the Gaullist majority by peaceful means. In retrospect, it is obvious that Waldeck Rochet was the major victim of the *gauchiste* short-circuit, and sustained more permanent damage than Mitterrand. The paradox can be elucidated thus: when orthodoxy is challenged and shaken from within, the rebel currents that bring pressure upon it rely on the same source of power, and combine to provoke an unstable and explosive situation that can further their common desire for change and renewal; but at the same time they each march to a different drummer, and struggle to impose their own particular solution. From this angle, since the secretary-general of the PCF failed to check in time the anticipated *gauchiste* breakthrough on the other wing of the general process of de-Stalinization, May 1968 may be considered the proof that the route Waldeck Rochet chose to de-Stalinize the French Communist movement would not work.

But Waldeck Rochet's failure was due not so much to an inopportune French event as to the fundamental hostility that any such step arouses in the international Communist movement. It was at this point that the predictable limitations of the liberalization of the Khrushchev era came into play. Khrushchev recognized the need to de-Stalinize the Soviet party and state apparatus, but refused to extend the benefits of the operation to fraternal parties and to the socialist camp. He gave a brutal demonstration of this policy in Budapest in 1956, and his successors followed his example in Prague in 1968. Because the Russians decided to intervene in Czechoslovakia, Waldeck Rochet became the indirect victim in the West of a Red Army which by its mere presence in Prague could put the secretary-general of the French Communist party out of action—a new version of a political demise perpetrated by remote control on a man beyond physical reach.

Third Period: Will the Picture Change (1967-197—)?

The picture was merely out of balance, will it now change? Two contributory factors are converging to effect such a change. While the PCF is returning to a strictly orthodox line, will the

77

uncertain trends of French foreign policy lead the party to review the type of relations it originally established with de Gaulle?

The first factor is the return of the PCF to strict orthodoxy. After August 1968, when the Russians' show of force made an example of the unfortunate Czechs, the Brezhnev brand of neo-Stalinism won the day and asserted its sway over the whole socialist camp. For more than four years, the Russians had been hoping to organize an international Communist conference in Moscow, aimed at reconstituting the socialist bloc without China; but they were forced by the subtle tricks of Communist parties both in and out of power to accept a whole string of disappointing "preparatory meetings." In the spring of 1969, however, they achieved their aim. A combination of bargaining and tests of strength finally proved successful, and paved the way for a new ordering of affairs whereby nearly all the world Communist forces, with the exception of China, remained loyal to the Soviet Union, albeit with some duly accepted nuances.

The PCF did not escape the effects of this reestablished order. Its return to the orthodox fold was heralded first by a change in leadership. Although Waldeck Rochet was protected from the Russians by the French bourgeois legal system, his subsequent illness afforded sufficient punishment for the audacity of his thought and actions—an old man struck down with a Shakespearean malady, he is lost in the mists of his destiny. The reins have passed to Georges Marchais; the selection and training of this man have been assiduously controlled, particularly during the course of bilateral and multilateral meetings, discussions, conferences, and so forth in which he participated, as representative of the French party, with the delegates of other fraternal parties and of course the Soviet party.

The PCF's return to orthodoxy has also been marked by a decisive clarification of its strategy with regard to *gauchisme*. Once the internal crisis in the international Communist movement had been cleared up, the PCF really had no common cause with *gauchisme*, which drew its strength from the crisis of the Soviet model. Even though in May 1968 the relations between the party and *gauchisme* were those of fierce competition within the *framework* of concomitant aims and activities, by the autumn of the same year the only ambition they had in common was mutual destruction. And at the same time *gauchisme* moved away from its original point of departure. It henceforth was portrayed as an attempt to *replace* Leninism with a new type of socialist revolution, rather than an attempt to *correct* the weaknesses and faulty concepts with which the Stalinist version of Leninism had been imbued.

Finally, the PCF's return to orthodoxy was reflected by a return to the classical system of priorities. Whereas the Communists' decision to support François Mitterrand as the presidential candidate in 1965 was a heterodox decision that served as a prelude to an eventual basic change in the PCF, their abstention in the second round of the presidential elections of 1969 was a logical outcome of the necessary primacy accorded to foreign policy. And Duclos' famous quip about "*blanc bonnet*" being the same thing as "*bonnet blanc*" (with reference to Georges Pompidou and Alain Poher) emphasizes that if a politician is credited with pro-European ideas on foreign policy this cancels out any profit the Communists might see in supporting a left-wing domestic policy.

The second factor is the Communists' suspicion that post-de Gaulle Gaullism might revert to a certain degree of loyalty to NATO as was suggested by Pompidou's meeting with Nixon in the Azores in October 1971. It is not relevant here to debate whether the foreign policy of the Fifth Republic under President Pompidou is in fact subject to change. What is relevant is whether the Communists think it will change. There is no doubt that after October 1971 the Communists, along with the international Communist movement, began to question the favorable construction they had always put on Gaullist foreign policy; at the very least they felt the need, on their own behalf or on behalf of the socialist camp, to voice aloud their fears and suspicions, even if only as a preventive measure.

Since they understood the reasoning that had led General de Gaulle to define his foreign policy—to keep France as far removed as possible from the site of any nuclear conflict—the Communists were in a position to realize that the changeover from a bipolar to a tripartite system of international relations would inevitably lead to a shift in French foreign policy, since the area then most likely to witness a nuclear conflict would no longer be the area between the United States and the USSR, but in Asia, and more precisely between the USSR and China. Thus the same reckoning that once inspired de Gaulle to lean toward a kind of

79

neutrality, or even a European version of Finnish' neutrality, might encourage President Pompidou to urge the countries of Western Europe to stand aloof from the Soviet Union in the event of a possible conflict in the Far East.

The PCF Hedges Its Bets

Of course, the point of no return has not yet been reached, either in French foreign policy or in the Communists' construction of it. Therefore the French Communists take care not to speak out plainly, lay any bets, or put all their eggs in one basket, but are forced to play their cards one by one, so that whatever the contingency, they can support a French foreign policy that best suits the point of view of the socialist camp.

This is extremely well illustrated by the negative Communist vote at the referendum on Europe (April 1972). It had nothing to do with its domestic policy—the arguments of this kind that it made were merely a buttress or pure camouflage; the Communist *non* was a literal one and responded frankly to the question of the referendum.

In fact, the French Communists' response to Pompidou's challenge was doubly effective because it was coherent, a logical derivative of Communist parties' allegiance to the Soviet Union. First, it served to reiterate the fact that French political reality is deeply divided, and partly subject to traditional themes of conflict, not all of which correspond to the overall cleavages in political opinion. The issue of Europe clearly proved that a certain type of configuration of opinion conflict which one associated with the Fourth Republic was still operative. Even though in the days leading up to the referendum President Pompidou managed to prove that the chasm separating Communist and Socialist foreign policy had not been bridged, on the other hand the results of the referendum proved that the Communists, by their negative vote, could still reactivate their old alliance with the nationalist factions in the Gaullist party—exactly the kind of alliance that a quarter of a century before had assured the defeat of the European Defense Community plan.

Of course, one can support the concept of Europe for different and often contradictory reasons, just as the idea of national independence can derive from different or even opposing motives. It is clear that the Communist demand for national independence, which in the past was deployed against German fascism (after the turning point of 1941), and then against the American Marshall Plan and the Atlantic Alliance, is given prominence today to prevent the nations of Western Europe from building up an economic, political, and possibly military community. For obviously the socialist camp would scarcely benefit from the presence of a European bloc flanking the bloc of socialist states of central and eastern Europe. The nationalists in the Gaullist movement cling to the old slogan of "France alone." But differences in motives and ultimate goals have not prevented an actual coalition and alliance which, at least for the time being, engenders and strengthens a "political sensitivity."

The striking show of force that the Communist *non* achieved seems to have been clearly understood by the party in power. It cannot be categorically stated that it was the Communist shepherd's reply to the Gaullist shepherdess that caused a chauvinist reaction in French diplomacy (and a change in the government), but it is no exaggeration to assert that, ever since the mediocre results of the referendum and probably up to the next elections, the present government is displaying some caution, and is busily blurring the outlines of its European policy. So in any event, General de Gaulle's heirs have retained their overall power position, while the Communists for the moment maintain a position where they have considerable leverage on French foreign policy; for by exerting pressure on the nationalist wing of the party in power, they can separate it still further from the pro-European wing.

Second, far from spoiling the chance of an agreement with the Parti Socialiste (PS), the Communists' negative vote in the referendum turned out to be the decisive stage in the "long march"—to all appearances a period of marking time—that has faced the PCF since that day in 1962 when it defined and made public its major short-term objective: to work out a common Communist-Socialist platform. The Communists' *non* clarified the points the Communists regarded as nonnegotiable, and thus made the Socialists realize just what price they would have to pay if they wanted to reach an agreement, whether it be merely electoral or a program of government, on a short- or long-term basis. In fact, the Socialists ended up even more eager for an agreement than the Communists, because they had no other irons in the fire and were anxious to form an alliance with the Communists or anyone else.

And the Socialists of their own accord employed a tactic the Communists have always used in the framework of a frontal strategy—that of blocking the right flank of the Socialist party so as to cause a major swing to its left. This is one consequence—positive from the Communist point of view—of the general radicalization of the French Left since 1968. It is this process, marked by a return to a certain Marxist tone in the Socialists' program (witness the vocabulary of their recent motions, resolutions, and statements) that gives the helm to the Communists. Even though they consider the Socialists' rhetoric either insufficient or excessive, the important point is that they can set themselves up as a judge. Furthermore, this radicalization has encouraged the renovation of the Socialist apparatus (in only a limited way despite the heated clamor of its activist fringe), for any attempt to overhaul a left-wing party (even though it may fail) is traditionally a task of the Left.

Ever since the Socialists forswore any alliance on their right (at least provisionally), the Communists have known that negotiations would be advantageous to them, whether the Socialists liked it or not.

From this point of view, it is unhelpful and may even be erroneous to take the program of government put out respectively by the PCF and the PS and compare them with the program they negotiated and adopted jointly, and to draw up a detailed list of the mutual "concessions" consented to by the two parties. To point out by this means who "won" and who "lost" is a parlor game fraught with pitfalls. On the one hand, the substance of each "concession" may be weighed in different terms depending on the reference points employed by each party, whether explicitly or implicitly; on the other hand, it reduces a party's strategy to the sum of its specific policies. Thus the Communists can cheerfully include recognition of the existence of the Common Market (even though their ulterior motive may be to paralyze and destroy it from within under the guise of democratization) in the list of "concessions" granted to the vestiges of European attachment among their Socialist partners. For them, accepting the recognition of a "reality" (in the sense that a certain Europe, not the geographical Europe, in fact exists) is concession enough, since to them the first step in a Marxist analysis of the capitalist world is the rejection of this reality.

A more sound project in this early stage is to measure the profound differences between the type of plan that lay behind Waldeck Rochet's support of Mitterrand's candidacy in 1965 and that which inspired the common governmental program in 1972. One need only set up a list of the problems that in each case initiated the most arduous discussions, exchanges, and negotiations.

What were the Communists talking about in 1965? They were discussing what stage in history would be reached with the establishment of a "new democracy" (it was called "true democracy" and, after 1968, "advanced democracy"). Was it to be merely an *intermediate* stage *following* the collapse of "personal power" (linked to "monopolistic state capitalism") but *preceding* the setting up of "socialism," after the manner and conceptions that evolved in the 1930s of the "United Front" and then of the "Popular Front," and the "popular democracies" in the late 1940s? Or was it to be something else—perhaps a point of no return, but one which would not be followed by any revolution or assumption of power—the peaceful path to socialism by means of a long, slow transition? These debates challenged the very foundations of the Leninist theory of the conquest and exercise of power. The dictatorship of the proletariat, the party system, even the type of party required by the working class of an industrially advanced country—such were the themes that were discussed time and again in the open dialogue between Communists and Socialists. Waldeck Rochet's hesitancy, his fearful withdrawals in the face of theoretical modifications, were clear proof that the stakes were fundamental: to retain or abandon the Soviet model of revolution and socialist society.

These themes have more or less disappeared today, buried beneath a purely formal rhetoric of successive proposals that are either without substance or calmly contradict one another, so that, like the prophecies of the Delphic oracle, all interpretations of them are equally valid. This is true for example of the formula adopted for the key question, that of "alternation in power."

In contrast, what subjects are pursued most relentlessly today? Europe, defense policy, nationalization. Should one then interpret the 1972 approach as a more "realistic" approach, since it implies neither revolution nor even power? This is suggested by those observers who are convinced of the Communists' "reformist degeneration," and of their definitive lack of taste or ambition for revolution. In fact, we should remember that the Socialists and Communists do not occupy the same position in relation to pow-

83

er. The Socialist party, like any political party, becomes rigid and weak in opposition. Not so the French Communists for they are not merely in opposition. As members of the international Communist movement they have a share in the power established worldwide by the socialist camp.

Furthermore, once the Communists have returned to the orthodox neo-Stalinist fold, they need no longer worry about the new type of revolutionary power and postrevolutionary society they would have to build if given the means. For it is useless and even harmful for them to play overconfidently with the idea of taking and exercising power before the subject actually figures on the day's agenda. Taking power is not a question of "will," but the result of setting up the machinery which, once in motion, even its creators could not escape. And the point of the governmental agreement of 1972 is set up this machinery. What exactly does it involve? It means attempting to reach a new stage which, following the eventual victory of the allied parties (at the next elections or at a later date), would serve to reorient French policy in such a way that it would not merely remain aloof from the "imperialist camp" and thus be neutralized, as was the case with Gaullism, but would begin to adapt itself to the operational norms that govern the socialist camp.

From this point of view, the subject of nationalization is very enlightening. Despite all appearances, it is only marginally dependent on domestic economic policy. Moreover, the Communists opposed nationalization in 1936 and were reticent on the subject in Chile in 1972; for they know better than anyone that a nationalized economy cannot alone resolve the problems of growth—the experience of Eastern European countries has made that abundantly clear. The subject of nationalization does not depend on domestic policy, either. The Communists would be happy to see a new link established between political power and the economy, but this is not one of their central preoccupations, since the time is not yet ripe for them to tackle the question of power. This is not to say that they view nationalization as a mere slogan for mobilizing the masses. In fact, for them nationalization, by strengthening the politico-economic power of the nation-state, would tend (1) to hinder the integration of the French economy into the European market, and the political unification of Europe where the role of each state would be necessarily reduced, and (2) to favor closer links between a nationalized

84

French market and the equally state-controlled economies of the socialist countries.

So the Communist line continues to evolve. In a period of relative uncertainty as to which French political alignment will win, the Communists are careful to cover all contingencies. In the event that the Gaullists remain in power, they mean to exert intense pressure to prevent French foreign policy from leaning further toward the United States or even toward Europe. If the alliance with the Socialists should lead to a "government" or "popular front" type of situation, the Communists have planned ahead of time to hem in their partners in a carefully selected network of obligations which in themselves delineate the type of system and society they would establish together, whether the Socialists like it or not—at least for a while.

For the common governmental program, firmly established as it is now, cannot be guaranteed, in the long run, against the dreams of treachery that may surface once the initial charms of union have faded. Indeed, both parties already know that the breakup of their alliance is not only an inescapable fact, founded as it was on contradictions and ulterior motives, but also a desirable fact. They differ, of course, as to when this breakup should occur and as to what should follow. For the Communists the rupture should coincide with taking power, while for the Socialists it should coincide with a return to the center and a reestablishment of a Center-Left majority.

Are these prospects merely political fantasy, or a gloomy reminder of past actions? It is unwise to speculate in this domain. It is interesting nevertheless to note the importance the Communists attach to the new perspective opened by the signing of the joint program. It can be measured by the declaration put out by the PCF on July 28, 1972, on the political trials of the overly loyal partisans of "socialism with a human face" in Czechoslovakia. It would be superficial to view it as merely a timid and sheepish reiteration of the condemnation they launched on August 21, 1968, against the Soviet military intervention, for such a view misses the main point. The first text was specifically addressed to the Soviet Communist party, while the second pretended that the Czech leaders had complete autonomy to make their own decisions, without any interference from the Soviet occupation forces.

85

How can we ignore the fact that this second text was published the day after a congress of the twenty-seven European Communist parties, including the Soviet party, had met in Paris at the headquarters of the French Central Committee? It was obvious that, even though the official object of the meeting was to "reiterate their solidarity with the people of Vietnam," the Soviet delegates in Paris, Boris Ponomarev and Vadim Zagladin (the former an expert on international Communist affairs with the political bureau of the Soviet party, and the latter the assistant head of the international section of the Soviet Central Committee), had been consulted about the French initiative and had given it prior approval. We can draw only one conclusion from this: if changes have occurred in the Communist world, they are not limited to the French Communist party, whose transformation has been spurred by events in France and by its Socialist allies; of equal importance is the fact that the whole international Communist movement is once more secure enough in its fundamental homogeneity to tolerate relative differences of strategy applied to a local situation. Thus, as in the 1930s, the Soviets hold up the strategy of the PCF as an example to the Communist parties of Europe who are not in power in their country.

III.

The PCF, the State, and the Revolution: An Analysis of Party Policies, Communications, and Popular Culture

GEORGES LAVAU

For a long time many sincere people believed—and many still believe—that the French Communist party constitutes a serious threat to the French political system. This fear, alive since at least 1928, has often come to a head: in 1936 after the electoral triumph of the Popular Front and the wave of strikes and factory occupations that followed; in June 1940 when General Weygand announced to one of the last Councils of Ministers of the Third Republic: "Thorez is installed in the Elysée Palace . . ."; in 1944-1945 when the Parti Communiste Français (PCF) seemed to hold all the trump cards for taking power; from late 1947 to 1952 when the leaders of the "third force" really believed that they and their American allies had saved France from the fate of becoming a popular democracy; and in May 1968 when Georges Séguy and Waldeck Rochet were largely responsible for the return to work of millions of strikers. In fact, even though the French political system over the past forty-five years has obviously not always been sturdy and solid enough to discourage the PCF from attempts to upset or overthrow it, this political system has to all appearances never really been at the mercy of the Communist party.

Neither in 1936, in 1944-1945, nor even in May 1968 did the party try to exploit a situation that to some observers contained "revolutionary possibilities"; one might even go so far as to say that on these occasions it lent some support to the legal authorities of the period and to the restoration of order. In the autumn of 1939, party militants and leaders either offered little resistance to their trial and imprisonment or went into hiding. In 1958, 1960, and 1961, the party volunteered to defend the republican government against the "Committees of Public Safety," the Al-

87

giers rebels, and the putschist generals. True, from October 1947 to late 1952, the PCF's attacks on those in power in the Fourth Republic often assumed a violent and quasi-insurgent form; nevertheless in retrospect (and despite the lack of historians of this ambiguous period) it really seems that the PCF's objectives were not so much to destroy the institutions and system of government of the Fourth Republic as to come to power within the framework of this system; not so much to make France a popular democracy as to break up the American alliance.

The arguments outlined above will never convince those who believe in the "danger" of the PCF. They raise two objections: that on each of these occasions, the party was either too weak or encountered such determined opposition that with its perennial pragmatism it preferred to back down rather than lose all; and that in any case, the party is concealing its hand and biding its time; whatever changes it may have made, whatever new faces may come and go, and whatever statements it may make, it remains a Bolshevik party—"not like the others"—still as determined as ever to destroy the political system.

The various currents artificially grouped under the title *gauchiste* maintain the opposite argument. Their position is not based on the premise of the "political system" of democracy and of the government, nor even of "democratic socialism," but on that of class struggle, revolution, and Marxist theory. From this viewpoint, the most common criticisms are well known. The PCF is *in* the system, it collaborates with it and supports it. It is a party that has ceased to be a party of revolution and class struggle. Since it has become "revisionist," it defuses the real class issues and tries to channel them toward fruitless electoral battles for vaguely reformist programs and broad "leftist" electoral coalitions. The PCF's goal is now merely an electoral victory that will more or less maintain the same state and the same society. No longer the vanguard of the revolution, it has become a party of management and order. It clings to the defense of established petit-bourgeois values, those of the majority of the voters, and it seeks their support without attempting to transform their views. It constantly seeks to prove its respectability and its "sense of responsibility."

There is no lack of evidence to support this argument: it can be derived from an analysis of Communist communications (its press, posters, electoral programs, and fêtes) and an analysis of the party's action (its distrust of certain types of conflict and strikes, its denunciation of *gauchiste* factions, its caution).

Thus we are faced with two points of view, each one supported by a variety of arguments, some less convincing than others but each one plausible. However, both are ideological in the sense that they are based implicitly, and sometimes explicitly, on what their respective partisans consider *should be*: what the PCF should be to qualify as a "normal" party within the system, or what it should be to qualify as a "revolutionary" and Marxist party.

We should try to rid ourselves of this normative assumption before attempting any analysis. Three other precautions should also be taken. First, we should not confuse political analysis with political or moral judgments. We shall not examine here the degree of sincerity behind the PCF's "conversion" to a pluralistic party system and to the idea of reaching socialism by electoral and democratic means.

Secondly, whether we are analyzing the theory or the practice of the PCF, we should distinguish between different levels of significance. Of course, *all* the party's texts and *all* its actions are both important and significant. Nevertheless, articles appearing in the daily *L'Humanité, France nouvelle,* and *Cahiers du communisme* commit the party much more deeply and represent its position more precisely than those published in *L'Humanité-Dimanche,* an illustrated weekly that is aimed at a wide sector of sympathizers of different degrees of commitment. Propositions adopted at the end of a congress, a manifesto adopted by the Central Committee, or a report presented to this Committee are much more significant than the speech of a Communist deputy in the National Assembly or a statement from the Communist mayor of a big city, even though he may be a member of the Central Committee. A statement or a text from the party leadership that expresses the party's position in its own name is much more meaningful than a text of "alliance," that is, a text drawn up by the PCF together with other non-Communist organizations, or a text drafted by party members that aims to set up a platform or program in which many other organizations are invited to participate. No one can fail to be impressed by the gap that exists between the theoretical positions of the PCF and the cultural and ideological content of the annual fête that *L'Humanité* has organized for several years now, a combination of annual village fair and circus parade. But even when we have taken account of

89

these different levels of significance there remains another problem: does the amount of time, resources, and effort that the PCF devotes to these occasional statements, these secondary activities, and to this "popular communism" not progressively *contaminate* the revolutionary nature of the party? Although this problem can perhaps not be resolved with any certainty, we cannot ignore it.

The third and final precaution will define the plan of this chapter. The PCF calls itself a "revolutionary" party, and in its program it declares that if it should come to power, its aim is to overturn the current political and social system. But on the other hand it is a major legal party, with important roles at almost every level of the political system today; it is one of the principal— if not *the* principal—spokesmen in open opposition to the government and its representatives, as well as to management. Thus the PCF finds itself between two poles, and its decisions must be determined by whichever one appears to hold out some hope of success. So we must look at the situation from both these vantage points in order to analyze the PCF.

From the point of view of the political system, we must ask whether the net result of the PCF's activity, regardless of its intentions and theory, is to deprive this system of a vital portion of its legitimacy, or rather indirectly to bring millions of French people to accept the legitimacy of *certain elements* of this system, people who, *without the Communist party*, might be much more negative and unstable in their attitudes. We should also consider the fact that the political system can derive a certain degree of security from this dual activity of the PCF, which consists on the one hand of posing as the great defender of the underdog, and on the other hand of channeling all these protest movements into organized and orderly mass demonstrations and into an opposition vote at election time. This could indeed reduce the frequency and magnitude of violent and disorganized movements, as well as the boomerang effect of their suppression. In short, has the PCF not paradoxically contributed, in two different ways at two stages in its history, to the survival of the political system? The first time, the PCF presented a plan for an alternative system so closely copied from the Soviet model, so far removed from French traditions and political culture, it proposed such unrealistic measures, and engaged in activities that made any alliance with it so difficult and suspect, that its opponents found it easier than ever to defend the system, its institutions, and its govern-

90

ments, even during periods of weakness, and easier to rally others to their side. The second time, by accepting many principles and rules of the political system, by forming alliances with political organizations which themselves accept the essentials of the French political system, by a daily manifestation of its hostility to disorder and violence, and by showing that it is becoming capable of a relatively critical stance with regard to the Soviet Union, the PCF indicates to a growing sector of opinion that it can be associated with a profound change of policy that would not palpably alter the nature of the French political system.

If we now examine the matter from the opposite pole, from the point of view of revolution and of the "alternative" system, we must ask quite different questions. First of all, does the PCF of the 1960s and 1970s still seem to *want* revolution? Even supposing that the answer to this question is more or less positive, we must also ask, *what kind* of revolution does it want? What is the "alternative" system that takes shape through the discussions and activities of the PCF? And finally, by mitigating its differences with respect to its non-Communist environment, by proposing an alternative system that no longer seems radically opposed to the established system, by increasing the number of speeches, demonstrations, and activities aimed at rallying the greatest possible number of people, by assiduously emphasizing the distance between themselves and the *gauchistes*, and by cultivating an image of "responsibility," are they not underestimating the influence of the *dominant ideology*—a dominant ideology to which the party makes considerable concessions, even though it may view them as purely tactical ones? And at the same time, does it not overestimate the inevitable effects, in destroying capitalist and bourgeois hegemony, of taking political power, and still more, of its own participation? In Gramsci's words, even if the PCF has abandoned none of its desire to overturn *political* society, may it not in fact have abandoned the fight against the *civil* society of the capitalist mode of production?

The Communist Party's Contribution to the Political System

Has the overall activity of the PCF, particularly in the last fifteen or twenty years, been of benefit to the French political system? To put the problem in these terms is to say that its activity has encountered certain "functional needs" in the system and has *in fact* satisfied them, at least to a certain extent and in ways that perhaps were not deliberate or envisaged by the PCF, nor even by those in control of the system. In most cases, of course, it is a question of *latent* functions, except where the PCF states openly that it accepts and upholds certain elements of this system.

Although we shall be using a functional type of analysis at this point, it will depart from functionalism proper in many aspects.[1] First of all, we shall maintain that *no* party, however progovernment it may be and however many historical links it may have to a political system, is totally "functional" for the political system in which it plays a role, with the possible exception of the Soviet Communist party. This is all the more true of a party such as the PCF.

Secondly, we shall not attempt to evaluate the PCF's contribution to every "functional need" of a political system. Moreover, when one enumerates such functional needs as value maintenance, integration, problem solving, adaptation and survival of the system, one compiles a list of such general "needs" that they embrace a multitude of "functions." We shall confine ourselves to a limited number of "functional needs" that take into account the peculiarities of the political history of *this* concrete system, of its social cleavages and its political culture, without claiming that they correspond in any way to the requirements that are absolute and universal for all political systems in all places at all times.

Finally, when most functionalist writers define "functional needs," they look at the political system as a complex of stable mechanisms and working rules, of integration and self-preservation. We think a political system is certainly that, but *not only that*: it is also, and particularly in a pluralistic and liberal political system, a complex of mechanisms and institutions that allows people to challenge and—within certain limits and under certain conditions—to *change* societal trends and existing social relationships.

---

[1] I am presenting here, in a completely new way and with some basic modifications, some ideas developed in two of my earlier studies: "Le Parti communiste dans le système politique français," in *Le Communisme en France*, Cahiers de la Fondation Nationale des Sciences Politiques, no. 175 (Paris: A. Colin, 1970), pp. 7-81; "Partis et systèmes politiques: Interactions et fonctions," *Canadian Journal of Political Science* 1 (1969), 18-44.

Having made these clarifications, we can now look at the problem in the following way. In a country like France, whose political history has included so many revolutions and long-drawn-out confrontations between opposing camps, the political system needs a large political force with radical views in opposition, one that can persuade its partisans to accept and respect certain basic factors of the system: the general principles of the regime, some essential rules of the game, respect for law and order. This is what we shall call the "function of *legitimation*."

In a country like France, where objective class conflicts are perhaps no deeper than elsewhere, but where class-consciousness is widespread, where the traditions of the working-class movement lead to conflict rather than to negotiation and contractual relations, and where the overcentralized state and an often distrustful management are generally neither inclined nor apt to negotiate or accept compromise, there must be a large organized and centralized force to act as "tribune of the people" and to divert waves of discontent and the class struggle toward the safer ground of legal political conflict. This is what we shall call the function of "tribune of the people."[2]

Finally, in France as in any other democratic and pluralistic political system, there must be an opposition. But *what* opposition? There are societies in which various historical factors have resulted in the major opposition parties being only slightly differentiated from the ruling parties, and their criticism of the existing order is limited to mere details, particularly if they have frequently been in power themselves and have thus contributed to this order. As long as these societies actually maintain such mild social and political divisions, such an opposition is probably beneficial. If, however, serious cleavages appear, another kind of much more radical opposition will probably develop; but since the position of political opposition is already filled, the new opposition will be driven to stay on the fringes, perhaps remaining powerless, but dangerous nevertheless. We are presenting the hypothesis that, in societies such as these, it can in the long run be healthy for the political system that criticism voiced by the

[2] This terminology has been criticized. I have been accused of inventing it just to describe certain activities of the PCF, and that it could not be applied to any other party except perhaps the PCI. I disagree. However, I accept that the "function of tribune of the people" is merely a particular means of fulfilling another more general function, that of "representation."

major opposition force be radical, proposing a truly "alternative" society, but at the same time that it be regarded by a large percentage of opinion as a *tolerable* alternative. We shall call this the function of political opposition.

Has the PCF satisfied these "needs"?

Legitimation

It is an irrefutable fact that after some early difficulties, the PCF was organized from about 1928 onward along the lines of the Leninist and Bolshevik model; that is to say, many aspects of its organization, recruitment, and its way of functioning stand in the way of its total absorption in the political system, which is not true for the majority of European Social Democratic parties. This is probably still the case today, at least in part. But we find equal evidence to support the view that since the Popular Front[3] the PCF has not attempted to remain outside the system, even during the periods between September 1939 and June 1941, and again between 1948 and 1952, when it was ostracized because of its activities; on the contrary, its energies have been and still are directed increasingly toward an acceptance of certain elements of the political system.

Naturally, we are talking only of a partial and ambivalent type of legitimation. First of all, the PCF has never seen its mission as simply bringing the most politically self-conscious elements of the working class to power "only to manage the affairs of the great capitalist bourgeoisie."[4] What is more, although the PCF still claims to be the only "revolutionary party in the true sense of the word,"[5] it seems to cling to the idea that the French political system is unacceptable and must be destroyed. This paradoxical contribution that the PCF makes to the legitimation of the system should be examined with respect to its three component parts: the national community, the political regime, and the political élite.

One of the numerous contradictions inherent in the PCF is that on the one hand its nationalism is often acknowledged, and denounced by some as a blemish, while on the other hand it is often

[3] Particularly since the Eighth Congress at Villeurbanne in January 1936.
[4] A formula used by Waldeck Rochet at the Central Committee meeting at Argenteuil, March 13, 1966.
[5] Waldeck Rochet, *Qu'est-ce qu'un révolutionnaire dans la France de notre temps?* (Paris: Editions Sociales, 1967).

94

reproached for being a "foreign national party," and for "giving too much weight to Soviet interests in its decisions."[6]

There are many arguments on either side. But we should base our judgment on a few indisputable indications, even if their scope is limited. During the 1920s and 1930s, the PCF supported all the regionalist and autonomist movements in France, particularly in Alsace, to a lesser extent in the German-speaking region of Lorraine,[7] and in Britanny.[8] But for a long time (certainly since 1944), there has been no trace of any such attitude on the part of the PCF: not only does it refuse to support such movements, even though some of them have undergone a significant revival in recent years, but it condemns them unequivocally. In this respect, the "national Jacobinism" of the party is spotless. It does not even mention the different "federalist" currents, even the most moderate ones. With respect to movements for national independence in Indochina, Madagascar, North Africa, or in the French Antilles, the PCF has taken positions that vary according to the period, the local situation, and the political trends of these different movements.

Although it is still forbidden to read the party press in French army barracks, the PCF is not hostile to the army nor to military service. Up until the time conscientious objection was legally recognized, the party opposed objector status; now it merely demands strict adherence to these new regulations without having changed its basic opinion, and declares that conscientious objection is not the real solution, which can only be achieved by a democratization of the army and a redefinition of its purpose. It was much more outspoken, particularly during the Algerian war, in its condemnation of military insubordination and desertion.

These indicators have limited importance when compared with the PCF's unswerving attachment to the Soviet Union, "homeland

[6] According to a SOFRES survey in February 1968, 44 percent of French people agreed with this view, 20 percent disagreed, and 36 percent had no opinion. (See the analysis of this survey by A. Lancelot and P. Weill in *Le Communisme en France*, p. 287.)

[7] Serge Bonnet, *Sociologie politique et religieuse de la Lorraine* (Paris: A. Colin, 1972), pp. 335-337.

[8] In 1933, Marcel Cachin lent support to the action of Yann Sohnier, the leader of the Parti National Breton. On this occasion *L'Humanité* denounced "the crushing of Celtic civilization by France, and the cultural desert in which the ruling French government has left Brittany" (quoted by Morvan Lebesque in *Comment peut-on être Breton?* [Paris: Seuil, 1970], p. 170).

95

of socialism." Since the end of the Cold War, no French Communist leader has had occasion to assert, as Maurice Thorez once did, that under no circumstances would French workers agree to fight against the Soviet Union: but no one can be sure that this is no longer the PCF's position, should such circumstances ever occur. Even though the PCF openly disapproved of the intervention of Warsaw Pact forces in Czechoslovakia, even though the most official spokesmen of the party make no bones about their disapproval of Soviet restrictions on literary and artistic freedom of expression, the Communist party is nevertheless very sensitive in its reactions to anything it construes as an "anti-Soviet" campaign.

So the basic problem is to ascertain whether—and how—the PCF manages to reconcile its attachment to the French nation and its attachment to the socialist homeland. Here again, the ground is fraught with endless debate. One relatively certain fact is that the East-West rapprochement and the policy of détente with the East that the Fifth Republic has pursued, and the relatively loose realignment of Communist parties in the international Communist movement, have both helped the PCF to effect this reconciliation.

It is possible that a vigorous campaign run on the theme of the PCF's allegiance to Moscow might solidify voters who are hostile to the Communists anyway, but for another sector of opinion that is more susceptible to "popular communism,"[9] this theme is not particularly unsettling. For this sector, the PCF is the party of the Fourteenth of July and the First of May, of the *Marseillaise* and the *Internationale*, of the Resistance and the peace movement. The PCF is no longer the "French section of the Communist International"; in contrast to its practice in 1934, it no longer refers to "French soviets"; its press and its official organs no longer refer to the Soviet model when they outline the "alternative system" that the party is proposing for France.[10]

We find the same ambivalence in the PCF toward the legitimation of the political regime. However, we feel that on the whole the PCF has contributed, and more specifically since 1936, to a partial legitimation of the Third, Fourth, and even Fifth Republics; this seems to hold true at any level of the regime—its general values and principles, its ground rules, its institutions.

[9] This expression comes from Bonnet, *Sociologie*.
[10] These points will be developed in the second half of this chapter.

At the level of principles and values, since November 1934 the party has adopted in full the cult of the values and symbols of the Jacobin secular republic. Until quite recently, however, there remained some weaknesses: the "personality cult" of the Soviet model, the idea of the single party in the Socialist phase, and the necessity of a temporary dictatorship of the proletariat. Now, as the Twentieth Congress of the Soviet Communist party demonstrated, the personality cult "represented a violation of Socialist principles."[11] Thus the party is not contradicting itself when it denounces "personal power" in France. The idea of the single party was rejected by the Seventeenth Congress. The necessity of the dictatorship of the proletariat, which was still being discreetly upheld at the Central Committee meeting at Argenteuil in 1966, seems in recent years to have been reduced to a vague set of control measures to be taken after the advent of "advanced democracy" to prevent reactionaries from sabotaging structural reforms.

The party does not merely adhere to the gamut of values and principles of the political system. It adds something to them and accepts them on condition that they be "developed." To the panoply of Republican principles it adds socialism, and the role of the working class as protagonist in the class struggle. But are these values in fact foreign to the French political system? Were they not those of Jaurès, Léon Blum, and many others who no longer figure as elements foreign to the values of the system? For the PCF, whose doctrine on this point does not differ from that of the Socialist party, the "development" of the principles of the Republic and of political democracy demands a different economic and social regime. As far back as the Tenth Party Congress of June 1945, Maurice Thorez declared that "democracy is a sustained act of creation," a concept that has become more and more synonymous with the idea that any progress in the field of political democracy cannot fail to involve a natural step forward toward socialism.[12] As to what the PCF now considers an authentic

[11] Waldeck Rochet in a speech before the Central Committee at Argenteuil, March 1966.

[12] See the pamphlet published by the Institut Maurice Thorez, *La Marche de la France au socialisme* (Paris: Editions Sociales, 1966): "French Communists set out from the premise that, under the conditions of state monopolistic capitalism, any democratic movement evolves *naturally and normally* into a Socialist movement, any true democratic conquest is *simultaneously* a step forward toward socialism" (p. 77, emphasis added).

97

democratic conquest, it is above all the creation of a democratic government of popular union with the participation of Communist ministers. Of course, such a government would have to take certain measures to initiate progressive steps to socialism and thus to a change in the economic system. Nonetheless, in defending the values and principles of the political system, the PCF clearly dissociates the political regime from the economic system: these principles are sound in themselves, even under a capitalist regime.

What are the rules of the game that the party objects to? Not the principle of free elections with universal suffrage, not an electoral system that assures fair popular representation, not the representative system, not Parliament's control over the government, not the independence of the judicial branch, not the power of civil authorities over the military, not the political neutrality of the Civil Service, not the principle of majority rule, nor the decentralized management of local communities. The party complains about the ways in which the rules of the game are actually applied in practice by the Gaullists, but it no longer demands the abrogation of the Constitution of 1958, and it no longer even seems to object to the election of the president of the Republic by universal suffrage.

For a long time there was a marked contrast between this meticulous defense of the rules of the game and the totally different rules the PCF applied to its own internal operation. But since the Seventeenth Congress passed a modification of the statutes dealing with the secret vote for the election of the *bureau politique*, this argument has lost some of its force.

No one is naive enough to suppose that this respect for the rules of the game is without underlying motives or that one should take it for gospel truth. There is just one point to be made: this respect that the party has proclaimed for so many years for the rules of the game is the *only* point of view that reaches the public. Is it not then highly probable that—even unintentionally—the PCF has legitimated and rehabilitated these rules for the majority of its voters, both sympathizers and militants? As for the hard core of party workers, can we be so sure, as Annie Kriegel asserts, that Communist education has such a total hold over them that they can feign respect for years without ending up with a certain emotional attachment to an attitude they have continually voiced?

As regards the *institutions and mechanisms* of the regime, legitimation seems an indisputable fact from many angles. First, the PCF respects the electoral system very highly, and it has encouraged its followers to take an interest in it, to expect much from it, and to participate in it seriously, even if there is little hope of success: *every* election is an important event in the activity of Communist militants. It was in fact the Communist militants who fought most forcefully against the idea that the electoral system is a "trap," and that the only worthwhile struggles are those undertaken in the factory or on the "front line of the class struggle."[13]

No political role is scorned or minimized by the PCF: voter, local candidate, mayor, deputy, minister, member of a parliamentary commission, or member of a board or assembly. The time is long past when Communist members of Parliament used the podium to agitate and shout abuse; their speeches and motions are carefully prepared, they use the rule of amendment and oral questions cleverly and seriously. This behavior obviously reaps benefits; but does it not also contribute indirectly to the stabilization and legitimation of these political roles?

Lastly, the PCF, which in 1971 controlled more than 1,000 municipalities, including about 46 towns of more than 30,000 inhabitants, manages these communes well and on the whole appears to hold scrupulously to the letter of the law, even while attempting to direct its administration in favor of working-class needs. In any event, the PCF declines to turn towns with a Communist administration into "red bases," and in March 1971 it refused to draw up a joint list with the Parti Socialiste Unifié (PSU) for the municipal elections because, among other things, the PSU wanted to develop the campaign theme of "municipal power," which smelled of *gauchisme* to the Communists: for one of the fundamentals of French public law is that there is no such thing as "local power," only the power of the indivisible Republic.

[13] Immediately after General de Gaulle's speech of May 30, 1968, in which he announced the forthcoming elections, the PCF opened its campaign and decided it should do nothing to impede the course of those elections. We should also mention the attitude of the Communists in the Côtes-du-Nord during the long strike and occupation of the factory of *Joint Français* at Saint Brieuc in 1972; as soon as the campaign for the referendum on Britain's entry into the Common Market began, hardly any further mention was made of the strike in the departmental Communist federations' leaflets, even though the situation had entered an acute phase.

99

The legitimation of the political élite calls for little comment. For political reasons, the PCF is combative and abusive toward some governments, politicians, and political parties, but there are different gradations to this hostility and not all are subject to criticism. The political élite do not come into disfavor on principle merely because they happen to serve a bourgeois regime. Previously, under Léon Blum's first government in 1936, even though the party did not participate in it, party leaders met with the Premier or with his close associates every week.

The PCF is certainly not in favor of technocrats nor of the higher civil service, but it is willing to argue with the technocrats without any undue ill-feeling, and it has never advocated the abolition of the Ecole Nationale d'Administration.[14] With respect to the political authorities, the PCF engages in political combat, sometimes harshly, but rarely resorting to insults, personal attacks, or provocation. This "responsible" behavior certainly stands the party in good stead, except with the "ultra-Left," but of course it does no disservice to the authorities either.

The Function of Tribune of the People

The word *defense*, associated with "workers" or the "laboring classes," is one of the most frequently used in the Communist party's vocabulary. Whether it is referring to its social policy, agricultural policy,[15] nationalization, local authorities, or the educational system, themes of the defense of so-called democratic conquests are always in the forefront. These themes take up a far greater proportion of Communist speeches than real proposals for reform.

Therefore, it is not surprising that public opinion usually associates this image of the "defender" with the PCF.[16] The party is perceived much less as a party desirous of revolution and the

[14] François Billoux, in his work *Quand nous étions ministres* (Paris: Editions Sociales, 1971) likes to remind us that in 1944-1947, Communist ministers had good relations with higher civil servants and that they in return had been loyal friends.

[15] The group of farmworkers most influenced by the Communists is called "Mouvement pour la *défense* de l'exploitation familiale."

[16] According to IFOP surveys in 1966, the problems most frequently associated with the image of the PCF are "wage demands," "fair distribution of taxes," "defense of secular schools," and not such topics as "France's role in the world," "economic expansion," and so on. (See the analysis of these surveys by M. and R. Fichelet, G. Michelat, and M. Simon, in *Le Communisme en France*, pp. 268-271.)

establishment of a Communist regime than as a party that represents and transmits grievances, and that constitutes a useful opposition force; and this is true even for those who vote for the PCF.[17]

If the importance attached to these themes of defense has caused the PCF to be accused of promoting a facile exploitation of popular demands and of representing a left-wing version of Poujadisme, it is because the party has been generally unselective in its choice of social and economic groups to be defended. More precisely, it seems that only two criteria are required for a group to be defended by the PCF: being one of the "little guys" and being a voter. This allows the party—when one of these groups feels threatened or makes claims—to take up the cudgels for small farmers, artisans, small businessmen, small manufacturers, managers and technicians in industry, civil servants, teachers and students, small investors, and so on. This activity in defense of innumerable social and economic groups is also promoted by the activity of the Confédération Générale du Travail (CGT) and of numerous other specialized mass organizations; militants and lifelong members of the party working within these organizations are generally under party control. It is still easier in the Communist-run municipalities, and can reap more concrete benefits for all concerned; here, the party has solid means at its disposal which can testify to its interest and solicitude for certain social groups, particularly artisans, shopkeepers, retired people, large families, schoolchildren, and teachers.

It is this aspect of the PCF's activity that has earned it the most sarcastic comments and accusations of electoralist demagogy, in particular the accusation that it has failed to use its vast resources to raise the level of political consciousness among the masses. One thing is clear. If the PCF devotes so much energy and so many resources to this role of "tribune of the people," it is because, apart from two brief periods, it has always been in opposition; not only has it not had governmental responsibilities, but it has sometimes been the victim of such ostracism that the majorities in Parliament made sure that the party's motions were systematically rejected. As a result, the PCF, rightly or wrongly,

[17] See the responses found in the surveys of 1966 and 1968, quoted in my article "Le Parti Communiste dans le système politique français," in Le Communisme en France, pp. 23, 30.

may consider itself justified in not proposing "constructive" measures, in showing no understanding for the policy-makers, in refusing to arbitrate between two grievances that to them symbolize the failure of government policy. What is more, the PCF is to a certain extent circumscribed by its extraordinary success at the polls after the Liberation, particularly by its victories in lightly industrialized and rural areas, or with clienteles that were formerly sympathetic to the Section Française de l'Internationale Ouvrière (SFIO) and the Radical party: any noticeable decrease in votes in these areas and among these groups would have been interpreted as a decline, would have benefited its opponents and deprived it of resources. So the party took pains to champion those social groups that over the years would inevitably fall victim to the modernization of the economy.[18]

It is true that there are demagogic and electoralist aspects to this practice of defending almost any category of malcontent, and that the PCF has not been particularly imaginative in proposing radical measures for reform based on a truly sound economic policy. But we should give the picture more balance. First, however solicitous the PCF may have been toward small businessmen and artisans, for example,[19] or toward small farmers and diverse other categories, it is the industrial workers and lowest-paid white-collar workers who receive the most concrete attention; in towns with a Communist administration these groups benefit most from the Communists' local government policies on housing, social and family welfare, and leisure. Secondly, if the PCF's aim is to convert all the malcontents it has championed into Communist voters, it cannot cherish too many illusions on this score and it cannot ignore the meager return on its investment. The Communist electorate today has the highest proportion of both active wage-earners and factory workers; these categories con-

[18] This point is illustrated by Waldeck Rochet's statement on agricultural policy: "Our role as Communists is not to help capitalism in its expropriation measures, but to denounce its misdeeds and defend its victims, in order to make them allies of the working class in the struggle for progress and for socialism." Speech of Waldeck Rochet at the *Journées d'études sur le travail du parti à la campagne,* Aubervilliers, November 13-15, 1964, in a pamphlet entitled *Les Communistes et les paysans* (1964), p. 49.

[19] Initially, the Communists favored the protest movement launched by Pierre Poujade on behalf of small businessmen and artisans in 1955, and some of their militants took part in its organization (UDCA). Pierre Poujade himself put an end to this collaboration by stripping the Communists of all responsibilities in the organization.

stitute the majority of its voters. Its electorate also has the lowest percentage of higher socio-professional categories of any French party. Since 1958, the PCF has consistently lost ground in most of the rural areas with an old left-wing tradition, while it has consolidated and improved its position in industrial areas, even in those where it had hitherto achieved only modest results.[20]

As for the positive aspects of this role of "tribune of the people," they are not limited to the fact that the PCF has long been the sole party to take consistent action on behalf of wage-earners and underprivileged groups. It must be stressed that the party organizes, controls, and politicizes protest. Since 1936 it has never encouraged direct action, desperate or violent acts of rebellion; it has never even incited groups with the most pressing grievances to take the law into their own hands. By placing its elected members and officials at the head of protest marches, demonstrations, and processions, it can marshal them, control them, and make sure that the affair does not degenerate into violence. The PCF has been criticized for its taste for big solemn demonstrations that are too well organized, with practically the same scenario and staging every time. But apart from reflecting its own style, this organization serves specific purposes. The party shies away from improvisation and spontaneity. It tries to impart a feeling of its own power to those it gathers together (it is the powerful champion of the oppressed), and a feeling of the *people*'s power, thus encouraging them not to give up hope and abandon their goal. The party provides *political slogans* for each defensive or protest action, both to inhibit other political groups from using this discontent for their own purposes, and also to ensure that the protests are not limited to the professional or social sphere that spawned them.

On the whole, this function of "tribune of the people" has been beneficial to the PCF. Aware of its inability to take power, the party has been able to make substantial electoral gains, to remain the "party of the working class" while building up sympathy and clienteles in many other social spheres, to create a favorable image as the tireless champion of the "little man," to be a pres-

---

[20] The best studies of this subject are by Jean Ranger: "L'Évolution du vote communiste en France depuis 1945," in *Le Communisme en France*, pp. 211-279, and "L'Électorat communiste dans l'élection présidentielle de 1969," *Revue française de science politique* 20, no. 2 (April 1970): 282-311.

ence among the "masses." This activity has also had its negative effects, however: it has alienated certain intellectual circles from the party, it prevents it from modifying or abandoning positions that economic evolution has made obsolete, and it uses up a degree of resources and militant activity that is not fully compensated by subsequent gains at the polls.

As regards the political system, the results of this activity of the PCF have perhaps been less damaging than we were wont to think. Of course, the government is hindered in its efforts to effect a policy of economic modernization and rationalization, of productivity, of financial and monetary reform, by finding itself constantly confronted with a large party which exploits and magnifies grievances and which is able not only to lure voters away from parties associated with these policies, but to incite strikes and disruptions. Sometimes the other parties are loath to allow the PCF alone to exploit this "left-wing Poujadisme." From this point of view, however, the task of the government and the majority party has been eased by the enormous resources bestowed on them by the Constitution of the Fifth Republic.

Aside from these drawbacks, the political system has derived some indirect benefits. First, in a country without an Ombudsman, in which trade-union and professional organizations are (with a few exceptions) relatively weak and split into rival groups, where the other left-wing parties are less well equipped than the PCF to learn the needs of the exploited masses, the party's activity of defense and protest has often served as a "warning light" and has compelled governments and administrators to examine more closely the social consequences of their policies. It is perhaps an exaggeration to say that the PCF has improved their access to information; it has certainly increased the amount of information they receive.

Of greater consequence is the indirect benefit drawn from the manner in which the PCF organizes, controls, and politicizes protest: this activity, which in the short term can be embarrassing for the government, is in the long run beneficial for the political system. The Communist party strives to turn simple protesters into *political actors in the political system*, and to stress the effectiveness of *political means* rather than *direct action*.

The Function of Political Opposition

If one believes that it can be "healthy" for a political system to have a political movement that expresses a radical criticism of societal trends, the political regime, and social relationships, then the Communist party seems to fulfill this role to perfection. Of course, from some points of view, the churches, intellectuals, prophetic movements, small ultra-radical political groups could perform this function even better, particularly where very specific goals are involved; but then, by virtue of their very nature, their action would be restricted to the fringes of the political system and, save for exceptional cases, would exert no direct influence on its operation. Intransigent observers will object that the PCF's criticism is radical only on the surface: first, because it relies too much on defensive themes; second, because its criticism is cautious and traditional, generally avoiding delicate issues (abortion until quite recently, women's liberation, drugs, migrant workers, prison conditions, the death penalty) and taking care not to offend popular prejudices; and finally, because it insists that the origin of all perplexing problems, such as the frustrations of regional minorities or youthful malaise, lies in the phenomenon of "capitalist exploitation." One might even add that it sometimes ends up defending what it once criticized: thus, for example, it now defends such undemocratic institutions as the departmental *Conseils Généraux* and the Senate.

Nonetheless, all through the Fourth Republic and under the Fifth Republic, the PCF has been the only *major* party to furnish this radical criticism. Even if the new Socialist party of 1971-1973 now voices a qualitatively comparable criticism, it does not have the means to develop and popularize it to the same degree as the PCF. Other political organizations, such as the PSU or the Trotskyite *Ligue Communiste*, have just as high a rate of militancy and organizational capacity and their criticism is more radical; but they are very small organizations, and their effective presence is unevenly distributed.

On the other hand, whatever censure one may direct at the style and content of PCF criticism, the masses seem to perceive it as a truly radical criticism, not merely because it reaches into every sector of the government's policy and that of its allies, but because it is also a criticism of values and ideologies, of social structures and economic relations. Even though the party has softened its tone considerably, it is still quick to declare itself revolutionary and to celebrate the October Revolution. It tries, of course, to maintain its image as a responsible party, but not as a pragmatic party—and why should it, in a country where political culture does not make of pragmatism a cardinal virtue?

But of what use is it to a political system that a large party criticize it in a radical and coherent manner if, either because its "radicalism" oversteps the bounds of tolerance of majority opinion, or because the majority of the country, irrespective of its own radical nature, spontaneously rejects this party as a legitimate contender for power?

As for the excessive "radicalism" of the PCF, there was once a time when the party was open to this reproach. Since the days of the Popular Front, its language has been considerably moderated, but for a sizable sector of opinion, part of this criticism is still unacceptable. However, it seems that even those who avowedly reject Communist party themes because they are too revolutionary, do so in fact because they have no confidence in this party.[21] The reasons for this lack of confidence are too obvious to merit a long exposition. The sincerity of party programs is in doubt. People suspect that if the party came to power, it would take advantage of the situation to exercise sole power and to hold its opponents hostage. Finally, they think that its solidarity with the Soviet Communist party governs all its actions, and that it would not break away if it came to power.

Whether these convictions are justified or not, they are shared by the majority of the French electorate, with the result that even if the PCF respects legality and upholds order, even if it is "responsible," even if its proposals are not wildly revolutionary, it

---

[21] The Socialist party, with a program that is now just as radical as that of the PCF, and which has formed an alliance with it, encounters much less negative reaction. Another indication is to be found in the very different responses to two apparently similar questions posed in different terms. These were part of surveys run by IFOP in December 1966 and by SOFRES in February 1968:

IFOP—*1966*

Do you consider the Communist party above all as:
—the party of the working class	41%	
—the party that wants revolution	7	(1% among PCF voters)
—2 other descriptions	44%	
—no answer	9	

SOFRES—*1968*

Do you agree or disagree with the following statement:
"If conditions appeared favorable to the Communist party, would it be ready to cause a revolution to take power?"
—agree	27%
—disagree	36
—no opinion	37

has not yet succeeded in portraying itself as an acceptable "alternative" or a genuine opposition. It is in this sense—and this sense alone—that one can apply to the PCF the comment that Giovanni Sartori made on the Italian Communist party: "The PCI would constitute an excellent opposition if it were an opposition, that is, a possible alternative government."[22]

In these circumstances we can understand the importance of all the steps the PCF has taken in recent years to prove its sincerity, its attachment to the rules of liberal and pluralistic democracy, its internal democratization, its independence from the Communist party of the Soviet Union, and its desire to avoid dominance over its political allies.

In its attempt to dissipate the suspicions surrounding it, the party has obviously gained from the alliances contracted with "respectable" partners like the Socialist party and the left-wing Radicals, particularly since the results of the March 1973 elections show that Socialist and Radical voters were not scared away by this alliance, and that an overwhelming proportion of them did not hesitate to vote for the Communist candidate in the second ballot when the Socialist and Radical candidates had withdrawn. On the other hand, the PCF has been extremely embarrassed by such events as the invasion of Czechoslovakia in 1968 and any event that shows that de-Stalinization in Russia has not put an end to the violations of personal liberty and to the police state.

In order to break away from its image as a "Moscow-dominated" party, the PCF first, on the occasion of the Czech affair and despite pressure against it from the Communist parties of Eastern Europe, asserted in most categorical terms its right to criticize and be independent, even though it recognized that the Soviet Communist party plays a decisive role in the international Communist working-class movement.[23] On the subject of the lack of freedom of expression in the USSR, the most official voices in the PCF have stated clearly: we do not approve, but what happens in the Soviet Union has nothing to do with what would hap-

[22] "European Political Parties: The Case of Polarized Pluralism," in Joseph LaPalombara and Myron Weiner (eds.), *Political Parties and Political Development* (Princeton, N.J.: Princeton University Press, 1966).

[23] A Central Committee meeting held at Ivry, October 20-21, 1968, was devoted to this problem. Most important were the statement by Gaston Plissonnier, and the speech by Waldeck Rochet (full text in *L'Humanité*, October 23, 1968; extracts quoted in my "Le Parti communiste," pp. 77-81).

pen in France if the Communists came to power. In contrast to its policy of a few years ago, the PCF is now careful not to level frenzied insults at those of its members who champion the cause of freedom for Russian writers, artists, and opponents of the regime. But since the PCF cannot remain in a defensive position on this matter, and because it must take care that its Socialist partners do not use these facts as a pretext for breaking up the alliance or for making excessive demands, it counterattacks by asserting that any systematic anti-Soviet campaign is in fact a campaign orchestrated against "socialism" in France.

If we wondered, particularly during the Cold War period, whether the PCF really wanted to take power, or perhaps preferred to create agitation and wait for a major crisis, there is no doubt that since 1962-1964 it has pursued this aim. All its actions tend in this direction, and the progressive weakening of solidarity between the Socialist party and the various Center parties at the heart of a "third force" have given the Communists an added boost.

To reach its goal, the PCF can be aggressive, and it constantly attacks the current majority and those among its allies who have been lukewarm in their attitude toward the Common Platform; and it can be cautious, for it knows it must win over and reconcile the middle classes, and on this score, the failure of the Chilean experiment of Popular Unity has strengthened this conviction. It also realizes that its ability to govern will seem credible only when it stops proposing accommodating programs full of hollow slogans. Therefore, during the past four years it has been more circumspect in its support of malcontents, regardless of their problems. The resolution passed by the Central Committee at Argenteuil in March 1966 that invited Communist intellectuals to give free rein to their creative abilities also seems to have borne fruit; and for a while now economic research has been more widely dealt with in specialized party publications, and it even seems to be reflected in the official positions and analyses of the party.

If a left-wing coalition came to power, the Communists would obviously claim the right to ministerial responsibilities.[24] By presenting Jacques Duclos as their candidate in the 1969 presidential

[24] This is clearly stated by Georges Marchais, especially in his preface to Billoux's *Quand nous étions ministres.*

election, and by assiduously omitting to say that it might allow a Socialist to be the sole representative of the Left at the next elections, the PCF clearly wanted to offset the widely held opinion—current even among a significant segment of its own voters—that it might if pressed fill some ministerial posts, but that a Communist certainly could not take over the responsibilities of the president of the Republic.[25]

It would be presumptuous to speculate on whether the majority of French opinion today believes basically that the PCF—or more precisely, an alliance in which this party would play a predominant role—would constitute a possible, normal alternative without posing a real threat to the political system. The mere fact that there might be some doubt and that opinion is divided on this point is the sign of ambivalence. On the one hand, the PCF seems to have almost managed to make itself acceptable as a useful and necessary element in the political system; on the other hand, it still has the kind of reputation that means that this system does not quite consider it a tolerable element. And it is the *only major party* in France to find itself in this situation.

In any event, even accepting the proposition that since 1936 or 1944 the Communist party has made a partly positive contribution to the French political system, what does it prove? Merely this: first, that it is not a *frontal* or *clandestine*[26] assailant of the system, second, that it has been forced for a variety of reasons to make some compromises, and finally, that it is not a foreign body in the political system. But the possibility remains that this desire for integration in the system is the result of a very deliberate tactical choice made when the PCF realized—first in 1935-1937 and then again after the Resistance—that it has much more to gain from being *inside* the system, respected and respectable, than by remaining outside, impotent and violent. In consequence, despite this tactical choice, perhaps it has in no way abandoned its revolutionary will and its goal of taking power. But it is a distinct pos-

---

[25] According to the SOFRES survey of February 1968, 54 percent of the French people opposed the idea of a Communist president of the Republic, 14 percent approved, and 32 percent had no opinion (see *Le Communisme en France*, p. 297 for complete tables).

[26] Certain writers like to stress the clandestine aspects of the party's activities. Naturally the PCF has some clandestine areas, but they relate to some aspects of its internal organization and its relations with the international Communist movement.

sibility that, even if this situation is neither comfortable nor permanent, the party currently has a foot in each camp, in that of the political system and that of revolution—at least of a *certain type* of revolution.

THE PCF, REVOLUTION, AND THE DOMINANT IDEOLOGY

The Party Continues to Call Itself "Revolutionary"

The following section is an analysis of Communist themes and programs. Even though we shall restrict ourselves to those texts issued by the leading organs of the party, the analysis on its own is far from conclusive; it will be rounded out by an analysis of party activities in the latter portion of this chapter.

In its most recent documents, the PCF has continued to assert in the most categorical terms its revolutionary nature, its desire to bring about socialism and the "radical transformation of the relations of production"[27] in the near future. See, for example, such publications as the pamphlet of the Institut Maurice Thorez, "France's Progress toward Socialism" (1966), or that of Waldeck Rochet, "What Is a Revolutionary in France Today?" (1967), or the Champigny Manifesto, "For an Advanced Democracy, for a Socialist France" (December 1968).[28]

It is true, however, that the way in which this revolutionary nature is proclaimed is geared to the current situation and to tactical necessities. So, for example, while Waldeck Rochet's rather colorless 1967 pamphlet deliberately stressed that his party was revolutionary "in the good sense of the word" and most of his content was aimed at refuting the true revolutionary character of the Chinese Communists and their imitators, as well as other *gauchistes*, the Champigny Manifesto is remarkable for its more decisive and less discreet tone;[29] it was adopted by the Central

[27] *Manifeste* adopted by the Central Committee at Champigny, December 5-6, 1968, published under the title *Pour une démocratie avancée, pour une France socialiste*. This juxtaposition of the two "stages" in the title of the Manifesto, with the time lapse symbolized by an enigmatic comma, is very typical of the party's style.

[28] This is also ceremoniously repeated in the *Thèses* adopted by the Nineteenth Congress at Nanterre, February 4-8, 1970, Thesis 44 (*Cahiers du communisme*, nos. 2-3 [February-March 1970]: 449).

[29] *Manifeste de Champigny.* In this document we find a reintroduction of the idea of the dictatorship of the proletariat, and of the idea that the use of violence to attain socialism cannot be excluded, even though in France today neither seems necessary or likely.

110

Committee after the storms of May-June 1968, when the party was forced to admit that a real revolutionary current had developed to its left and that it would not disappear overnight.

It is also true that the tone of these revolutionary pronouncements has changed considerably in comparison with the old days. At the end of 1934, when the PCF reached a major turning point, it made no attempt to hide the fact, either in texts to be distributed to its allies or in those for internal consumption, that the revolution it aimed for was destined to destroy the bourgeois state completely, and was to be derived strictly from the Soviet model.

A comparison of the two texts quoted below shows that things have changed a good deal in the 1970s. This comparison is particularly enlightening because it deals with two texts of the same type thirty-six years apart, both strictly for internal consumption and a perfect expression of the party catechism, since they are taken from course manuals used in the party's elementary schools in 1934 and 1970.[30] We have selected portions that deal with the following points: the problem of the transition to revolution, civil war and violence, winning over a majority through elections, the use of democratic institutions, and the nature of the state today. By comparing these fragments, we find that in 1934 the PCF stood firm on several counts: a cautious reminder of the dictatorship of the proletariat ("defense of Socialist victories"), and the assertion that the state apparatus under capitalism remains an apparatus of coercion and domination that serves the ruling class. On the other hand, the PCF of 1970 avoids calling the current state "bourgeois," it excludes revolution through "civil war," it no longer talks of "revolutionary violence," and to be reassuring, it claims that once advanced democracy comes into being, the bourgeoisie will no longer be able to unleash a civil war; the party will no longer have to be content, as in 1970, to win over "the majority of the working class" but indeed, by popular union, it must win over the majority of the *nation.*

[30] For 1934: *Que veulent les Communistes? Quatre cours élémentaires,* 2d ed. rev. and corr. (Paris: Bureau d'éditions, 1934). For 1970: *Supplément au bulletin de propagande et d'information no. 7, Octobre 1970,* édité par le Comité Central. (Four pamphlets entitled: "La Lutte des classes et l'évolution de l'Humanité"; "L'Exploitation capitaliste, l'unité ouvrière et l'union des forces démocratiques"; "La Démocratie avancée, le socialisme"; "Le Parti communiste français.")

111

1934   *1970*

VIOLENCE

". . . the bureaucracy does not allow us to win the majority of the working class over to our party's influence by peaceful means; from now on it will use violence to prevent us. Therefore the workers must defend themselves by any means at their disposal. . . ."

". . . the proletariat can only take power and free itself from exploitation by revolutionary violence" (p. 18).

". . . the defense of Socialist victories against hostile acts by the former exploiters and imperialist reaction is a necessary function of the Socialist state. The capitalists will not be allowed to reestablish capitalism" (Pamphlet no. 3, p. 28).

"It is impossible to say by which path we shall achieve socialism in France, but the Communist party for its part calls for the peaceful path without civil war" (Ibid., p. 21).

CIVIL WAR

"The victory of the proletariat is not the beginning of a period of peace between the classes, but of a desperate civil war" (p. 22).

"It would be suicidal to allow the enemies of the proletariat the freedom to agitate and to organize during this period" (Ibid.).

"Contrary to statements by the bourgeoisie and *gauchiste* groups, the Revolution is not synonymous with civil war" (Ibid., p. 21).

"Under the conditions of advanced democracy, the enfeebled bourgeoisie would not be in a position to resort to civil war" (Ibid.).

THE CURRENT STATE

"This bourgeois state is an instrument of oppression with its police, its tribunals, its parliament, etc." (p. 15).

"The state apparatus (institutions and instruments): all together they form an apparatus of constraint, coercion and

112

1934	*1970*

"The emancipation of the working class and the setting up of socialism can only be realized by the struggle against the bourgeois state, a struggle that will end with the destruction of this state and the setting up of the proletarian dictatorship" (p. 16).

"This state must be destroyed, and on its ruins we must build the proletarian state . . ." (p. 19).

domination in favor of the ruling class" (Ibid., p. 6).

"The Socialist state guarantees and extends the liberties, rights, and institutions won by the people in the course of their history. It perfects them and creates new ones" (Ibid., p. 28).

THE CONQUEST OF THE MAJORITY

"We are struggling for the conquest of the majority of the working class. This is not the same thing as waiting for the time when the majority of the proletariat will vote for the Communist party" (p. 18).

"Should we not direct all our efforts to gaining a majority in Parliament, which would then allow us to set up socialism peacefully by democratic means? Experience proves the falsity of this reformist teaching. In the class struggle, it is not parliamentary power that counts, but real power" (p. 17).

"The party is winning over the largest segments of our population to its ideas and its policy . . ." (Pamphlet no. 4, p. 18).

"At the present stage, the aim is to achieve agreement between the parties of the Left on a common program of struggle and government to overcome the forces in power and construct the advanced democracy" (Pamphlet no. 2, p. 23).

Enlightening though this comparison may be, it is not definitive. In fact the undeniable changes made by the party in its pronouncements on the revolution—regardless of whether these

113

changes are sincere or tactical—could be interpreted as a simple adaptation. After all, no one speaks in the same way today as he did in 1934; furthermore, everyone agrees that from 1936 onward, the PCF dropped its sectarian behavior, and thus also the vocabulary and syntax of a sectarian language. In short, a major party does not express itself like a minor sectarian group. On the other hand, on such essential articles of faith as the revolution, socialism, nationalization of major industries, the party still teaches the same lesson to its militants.

Political Society and the State

In December 1934 when negotiations were under way between the parties of the Left on the formation of what was destined to be the Popular Front, the Central Committee of the PCF defined thus its *own* program with regard to the state: "The state as it now is, the bourgeois state, the minion of the Bank and Big Industry, and of the big landowners, will be shattered in all its components because they serve only to crush the wage-earners; the Prefects will be dismissed, the corrupt police force will be replaced by the judiciary of the workers and peasants. In place of the present state and its organs will be substituted the organs of a true democracy of workers, peasants and soldiers, the *French soviets*. From bottom to top, from the local level and the factory to the department or the region, right up to the workers' and peasants' government, *all power* will belong to councils elected by the wage-earners, *both legislative power and executive power*."[31] From 1935 on, the PCF was never again to write anything like this statement.

Naturally, no official PCF document ever contains even the most surreptitious allusion to the withering of the state under the socialism to be engendered in France, nor to French "soviets," nor to the popular judiciary,[32] nor to the transfer of power to elected councils, even at the local level or in the factory.

An analysis of current Communist parlance[33] would probably

[31] Letter of December 9, 1934, from the Central Committee to the Permanent Administrative Commission of the SFIO (*Cahiers du communisme*, no. 11 [November 1959], pp. 1172-1181).

[32] The party has always been hostile to the "Russell Tribunal"; in 1970-1972, when certain *gauchiste* organizations set up "tribunals" to give symbolic judgments on various causes, the party disapproved strongly.

[33] This study is in fact being undertaken now for a doctoral dissertation under my direction by Dominique Labbé.

114

show that the word "state" is one of those in least frequent use, with sometimes pejorative connotations—"state monopolistic capitalism"—and sometimes positive connotations—"Socialist state." But the state, either as an abstract political form or a concrete political form of present-day French society, is never contested as such, and its legitimacy is never denied.[34] The PCF often calls for its "defense," desires an extension of its powers, and considers that "public service"—an idea central to French public law—is the best form of social and economic organization.[35]

It would be hard to find in official PCF texts and in its theoretical writings any precise indications that in failing to reject the state, it has in mind a *state of a different kind*, with a different internal organization and different relationships between its institutions, individuals, and groups. The proposal for a Constitution for the Fourth Republic that the Communist group submitted to the first Constituent Assembly in 1945 was more than anything a proposal full of historical reminiscences, for in its general structure, it was basically the same as the old so-called Jacobin Constitution of 1793, which never came into effect and was therefore largely symbolic—a constitution that would establish a centralized state, very democratic, and outstanding for the absolute authority of a single Assembly. Since then—and particularly since the constitutional regime established by the Fifth Republic makes it yearn for those of the Third and Fourth Republics—the Communist party has accepted the Senate, now makes only intermittent and half-hearted demands for the suppression of the prefectoral system, has no proposal for a fundamental reorganization of the administration, the judiciary, or the army (and greets any such proposals with great suspicion), and now seems in fact to place little weight on a change in the structure of the state. Such texts as the Champigny Manifesto (December 1968) or the theses adopted by the Nineteenth Congress (Nanterre, February 4-8, 1970), both of which contained material for a party platform, make no reference to any of those fundamental transformations of the state.

If the PCF does not question the existence of a centralized

[34] See Moreau de Bellaing, "Paternalisme politique, transfert de pouvoir et contestation de l'autorité," *Communications* (November-December 1968), p. 66.

[35] Lucien Nizard, "A propos de l'Etat, d'une mythologie à l'autre," *La Pensée*, no. 175 (June 1974).

state, all-powerful with ever-increasing jurisdiction, it is because it is sticking to the idea—derived from a highly simplified Marxism—that the end of economic exploitation and the suppression of the power of the "big monopolies" will lead automatically to the transformation of the nature and goals of the state. Should we interpret this as a sign that as far as the party is concerned, there is no independent influence of a society's institutional and ideological superstructures? Knowing how suspicious the PCF is toward Gramsci's analyses, this interpretation may be justified.

The sole transformation of the state and state organizations demanded by the PCF is always expressed by the same word— "democratization"—of the state, the vote, the administration, the judiciary, the army, education, the treasury, etc. What does the term mean? First, in its most technical sense, it calls for several well-known reforms: the reestablishment of proportional representation for political elections and a fairer division of electoral districts, financial and material aid such as scholarships and study grants to allow a less bourgeois recruitment into the administration, and removal of the social barriers that prevent access to higher education and culture. Many of these "reformist" proposals are useful and carefully thought out. In a less technical sense, "democratization" of the state demands that the working class play a more important, if not leading, role in it. But since the PCF has consistently stressed the slogan, "the Communist party *is* the party of the working class,"[36] "democratization" takes on a much more precise meaning: the state will be "democratic" as long as the PCF has its "rightful" place in the government. This is the import of François Billoux's pamphlet *When We Were Ministers* (1972), and of its preface by Georges Marchais; this is also the criterion used by the party to classify different political regimes in the world on a scale of "democracy."[37]

In any event, it is certain that "democratization" will not involve the diminution of the state's supremacy in political relations, nor its dismemberment by distributing some of its power either to regional or municipal authorities or to "autonomous

[36] *Manifeste de Champigny.* The same theme appears in Thesis 23 adopted at the Nineteenth Congress: The working class "has in the Communist party an authentically revolutionary party which bases its activity on a scientific doctrine of struggle, Marxism-Leninism" (p. 435).

[37] For more on this subject, see the excellent study by Frédéric Bon, "Structure de l'idéologie communiste," in *Le Communisme en France*, p. 143.

counter authorities." For several years now the party has been hostile to any proposal of this kind, as it has to the idea of self-management, not only because these proposals were issued by groups or parties it distrusts (political clubs, the Confédération Française Democratique du Travail [CFDT], the PSU), but much more basically because it considered them injurious. The Communist party rejects anything that smells even faintly of anarchism, anarcho-syndicalism,[38] or federalism, and it takes a very rigid stand on the priority of *political* power and of the *parties* in deciding what general directions to give society and the masses.

In the classical Marxist distinction between the economic and the political struggle, the PCF considers that economic struggles —even when, as in May 1968, they constitute "a powerful popular movement of a magnitude unequaled in our history"[39]—are only a preparation. Economic struggles can exert pressure on those in power, but they remain exposed to countermeasures from this power if they are not protected by political struggles capable of giving them a political opening, that is to say, a victory or an advance of the "working-class and democratic forces," and *thus* a democratic transformation of the state. This political struggle is the party's province.

This pattern of thought lies at the heart of the controversies in 1971 and 1972 between the PCF and the CGT on the one hand, and the CFDT on the other. The CFDT, in a resolution adopted by its National Council at the end of October 1971, defended the proposition that no group takes precedence in the political struggle, and that, depending on the situation, the trade unions are just as qualified as the parties to take a leading role in it. As a whole the document questioned all the classic "democratic" concepts: elections and universal suffrage are no more democratic means than actual struggles at the place of work, and true socialism must necessarily pass through forms of self-management of social and economic organizations, without which the simple collective appropriation of the major means of production and exchange will not alter social relationships.

One of the members of the Political Bureau of the PCF, who was also federal secretary of the CGT, fiercely refuted these

[38] One of the oldest expressions in the party language is the coupling of "anarchism-petit bourgeois."

[39] *Manifeste de Champigny*, p. 123.

117

arguments of the CFDT in a series of articles in *Vie ouvrière*.[40] "By their very nature," asserted Henri Krasucki, "the parties have a vocation to govern. . . . It will fall to the parties that desire socialism to direct the state and consequently take the lead in building up socialism on the basis of confidence shown in them by the electorate" (p. 57). The idea of autonomous power centers is rejected in the name of vital unity of the state and of a suitable central power.[41] As for the idea of self-management, it too is the object of sarcastic comment.[42]

So the PCF sticks firmly to a classic position where everything depends ultimately on the state. As one of its more brilliant intellectuals said at the Nineteenth Congress: "The stake of all political struggle is to know who is going to hold power in the state";[43] economic struggles merely serve to make possible a *political* victory. As for imagining that before taking this power over the state and destroying the power of the monopolies, the Left could take action to try to change social attitudes and relationships, "that," replies Krasucki, "is quite simply impossible, because people have no other choice than to live within the dictates of the system" (p. 23).

The Transition to Socialism: "Take Care!"

Three times in the course of its history, the PCF has refused to exploit opportunities because it adjudged the situation less than revolutionary: in May-June 1936, during the major strikes when factories were occupied, and when the Popular Front government was being set up; in early autumn 1944, when the provisional government still seemed weak and the party had armed partisans at its disposal; and at the end of May 1968 when the government seemed to have lost all its trump cards. In all three

[40] These articles appear together in a pamphlet by Henri Krasucki, *Syndicats et socialisme* (Paris: Editions Sociales, 1972), from which I am quoting.

[41] "France is still one nation. She constitutes an entity whose unity must be safeguarded. There is just one national economy, one polity, one culture. . . . To want a democratic structure for a Socialist state should not lead us to neglect the need for this state and its essential role, and the need for an appropriate central power, nor should we regard the idea itself with suspicion . . ." (ibid., p. 37). On the subject of self-management, after some heavy sarcasm, Krasucki fulminates: "this would lead to a disruption of the economy, it would fall apart. . . . The economy is a serious thing . . . it is not something you play around with" (ibid., pp. 23, 31).

[42] Ibid., pp. 29-32.

[43] Michel Simon, Speech at the Nineteenth Congress, 1970 (*Cahiers du Communisme*, nos. 2-3 [February-March, 1970], p. 243).

118

cases the party dedicated its efforts either to trying to manipulate the government's weak points to obtain material benefits for the strikers (1968), or to secure a return to work (1936, 1968), or to consolidate its own political position by preparing for the coming elections (1944, 1968).

This recurring behavior is not necessarily a precedent for the future. It is still possible to imagine that in more favorable circumstances, the party could at some future time consider the situation revolutionary.[44] It is improbable, however. In Leninist thinking, the concept of a "revolutionary situation" is closely linked both with the idea of active minorities and with the idea that only a majority of the *working* class—albeit a minority of the populace—could be won over to the revolution. Today the PCF and the Communist parties loyal to Moscow have a plan of historical development that makes any recourse to the concept of a revolutionary situation unnecessary and even dangerous.

This plan, unchanged for twenty years, is based on the doctrine of the generalized crisis of capitalism (derived from *Imperialism, the ultimate stage of capitalism*), which is destined to crumble but remains dangerous as long as it lasts. This crisis supposedly entered a new phase after 1950 with the strengthening of the socialist camp, the emancipation of colonized peoples and the "class struggle that is developing on a world-wide scale with increasing volume and intensity."[45] Capitalism is, of course, trying to survive in the form of state monopolistic capitalism which appears on the international scene as a strengthening of imperialism dominated by the United States, and on the domestic scene as the dominance of the monopolies who impose a more authoritarian political regime. But "the relation of forces is and *will remain* in favor of socialism,"[46] for on the international scene the socialist camp already has the strength to cause the retreat of imperialism (which continues to make new enemies), and on the domestic scene, "broader and broader strata of wage-earners and

---

[44] In 1936, the PCF was still weak; if it had wanted to "exploit" the strikes and make trouble for Léon Blum, it would obviously have lost the advantage of a still young Popular Front, which had won the election by only a narrow margin, and which in the months to come was to bring it waves of new members. In 1944, the PCF was certainly much stronger than in 1936, but it was still too close to the events of September 1939 to risk being once more alienated from French opinion; furthermore, the country was occupied by very popular allied armies.

[45] Nineteenth Congress, Thesis 2, p. 417.

[46] Thesis 4, p. 420.

middle-class people" are becoming aware of their exploitation and of class conflicts. Thus "there is a greater possibility of winning them over to the cause of an advanced democracy that would open up the path to socialism."[47] So the important thing is that the party and the forces of progress remain mobilized, and work for union and the victory of an "advanced democracy." For once this stage has been reached, it will be unnecessary to debate over a long period of time whether a given situation is "revolutionary": the transition to socialism will be very brief. In fact, since the Fifteenth Congress in June 1959, Maurice Thorez' words have been repeated practically verbatim: "In our times there are no longer any long historical intervals between democratic transformations and Socialist transformations."[48]

What is involved in this plan of historical development is once again this concept of the continuing creation of socialism, of an indefinite and inevitable expansion of past experience, victories, and revolutions. This is not a totally new concept. The seeds of it are to be found in Engels' 1895 preface to Marx's *The Class Struggles in France 1848-1850.*[49] For the German Socialist party in 1895 as for the PCF of the 1960s and 1970s, success at the polls (and in France the prospects of alliance with the Socialist party) allowed them to hope that they could attain their goal without "disruption" (as Engels said), without an armed uprising, and without violence.

Under these circumstances, it is more important than ever to exercise caution. This was one of Engels' preoccupations: "And if we are not crazy enough to allow ourselves to be pushed into street battles for the convenience of the bourgeois authorities, they will ultimately have no choice but to break this law themselves." The same preoccupation was apparent when a member of the Central Committee declared in March 1972: "With a view to a future that could now be close at hand if no mistakes are made, we show the true perspective of political and social change."[50]

[47] Thesis 14, pp. 427-428.

[48] *Oeuvres Choisies*, 3: 162. See also, Institut Maurice Thorez, *La Marche de la France*, p. 77; Nineteenth Congress, Thesis 19, p. 433.

[49] Preface to Karl Marx, *Les Luttes de classes en France* (1848-1850) (Paris: Editions Sociales, 1970), p. 35.

[50] Pierre Juquin, "Les Manipuleurs," *L'Humanité*, March 16, 1972. The article attacks the "collusion" between *gauchiste* "provocateurs" and those in the government.

Avoiding any rash moves, what does this mean? It means first of all, to resist being drawn into discussions on compromising subjects, and with allies who are overly fond of "revolutionary language" during negotiations on electoral alliances and common platforms. It also means making sure that a demonstration or parade organized by the PCF or the CGT, or one in which they take part, should have only slogans agreed upon in advance, should follow a set route announced to the police, with enough marshals to contain the demonstrators. For the CGT, it means remaining attentive and circumspect over wage demands and workers' conflicts when the movement originates in a spontaneous group or in another trade-union organization renowned for its "recklessness." For both the CGT and the PCF, it means attempting to put an end to social unrest and to end strikes when the wage-earners are obliged to mobilize for a political battle.[51] But above all, this preoccupation with caution is one of the major reasons why the PCF has attacked the *gauchistes* so relentlessly since May 1968.[52]

The PCF has never accepted the idea of being outflanked on its left. Even during periods when its cautious and reformist actions (1936, 1944-1947, the Algerian war) might favor this outflanking on the left by ultra-radical groups, in particular by Trotskyites, it has always been able to avert the danger by a combination of extreme brutality and cunning. But in May 1968 it was well and truly outflanked, and since then, even though many *gauchiste* groups are now on the wane, there remains an extreme-Left current which, despite its internal divisions, manages to harass the PCF and the CGT through its press, its demonstrations, and most of all by the active presence of its militants in the factories or at their gates. They attack the party in the two areas that it has always considered its own preserve: activity in industry and Marxist theory. On this latter point, their work is intensive and well diffused by a good publishing network. The PCF cannot accept that.

[51] See n. 13 above.

[52] Two examples: an article published in *L'Humanité-Dimanche* of May 26, 1968, the day after the night of rioting in Paris (reproduced in *Le Communisme en France*, pp. 70-73); an article by Georges Séguy, "Gauchisme, opportunisme et luttes de classe," *L'Humanité*, March 14, 1972, dealing with the serious incidents at the Renault plants. See also Waldeck Rochet, "Le Danger le plus pressant est aujourd'hui le gauchisme," in *Les Enseignements de mai et juin 1968* (Paris: Éditions Sociales, 1969), p. 88.

121

Why is *gauchisme* so dangerous to the PCF? To our way of thinking, the main reason is quite simply the one that the PCF itself offers: *gauchisme* could compromise the chances of victory for the Popular Front coalition, and thus the Communist party's chances of coming to power. When the PCF accuses those *gauchiste* agitators responsible for spectacular disorders or verbal and physical acts of violence, of being "provocateurs," when it denounces a "plot" between *gauchiste* groups and the government, it does not really believe that there has been collusion. These are purely polemical devices at which the party is very adept. It merely means that the consequence of *gauchiste* actions benefits the government because it is detrimental to PCF strategy.[53] For the PCF is still traumatized by the results of May 1968. Just when its alliance with the Fédération de la Gauche Démocratique et Socialiste (FGDS) had won over many deputies and had succeeded in placing the government majority in a critical position, when it had just signed a joint declaration with the Socialists, Radicals, and *Conventionnels* in the FGDS on February 24, 1968, which sowed the seeds of a Common Platform after the elections of June 23, 1968, it found itself with fewer elected members, with weakened alliances, and confronting a majority that had won an unprecedented electoral victory; and on top of that, during the whole campaign it had been represented as the group mainly responsible for the disorders that had paralyzed the country!

The PCF, like other Communist parties the world over, has repeatedly had to face the fact that public opinion still views communism with so much reserve, fear, and suspicion that any climate of disorder and violence is detrimental to it, even if it had nothing to do with the events, and is used against it by those trying to reestablish order. The party is aware that this suspicion and fear are present even in those who agree to form an alliance with it.

This is why the PCF has taken such care, since its Champigny Manifesto (December 5-6, 1968) to give its own interpretation

---

[53] G. Marchais dealt with this very explicitly at the time of the incidents at the Renault factory in March 1972: "We have never seen the plot as an affair organized by Geismar and Marcellin. . . . The *gauchiste* groups are instrumental to the government's purposes of creating a climate of violence, fear, and civil war. . . . [In 1968] the government exploited this climate of fear to get the UDR and its allies elected to the National Assembly in large numbers" (*L'Humanité*, March 21, 1972).

of the May 1968 movement, an interpretation that prudently strips this movement of any romantic aura or revolutionary significance.[54] This attempt to rewrite history is of great importance. Since it cannot undo what is done, the party declares that we should forget all its insurgent aspects.

The PCF regards *gauchisme* rather as the USSR regards China: the one on the French domestic scene, the other on the international scene, they constitute a tinderbox that, once ignited, might spark off an opportunity for the monopolies in France and the imperialist "hawks" to stop all progress toward socialism. Peaceful coexistence for the international scene, and the imperceptible transition "without any long historical interval" from advanced democracy to socialism for the domestic scene, spring from the same plan and involve the same prerequisites: a great deal of caution and intense vigilance over "inflamed elements." For the PCF, this need to bolt the door to the Left and to the Right ("struggle against leftist opportunism and rightist opportunism") is designed to prevent their Socialist allies from turning to a third-force strategy as they did between 1947 and 1962, which would once more leave the PCF in isolation and unable to attain power.

We always return to this theme—coming to power in a popular front with the support of the majority of the nation. In trying to prove that power is not indispensable to the party, it is quite wrong to stress the "Bolshevik" nature of the PCF, and its ability, which stems from its hard core of bolshevism, to remain healthy during a long period in opposition. Even if the party can continue undamaged in opposition for an indefinite period, all its actions since 1962, all the theoretical concessions it has made have convinced this writer that its fundamental goal is to take power, and to take power by the means it has stated.

Does this mean that, to achieve its goal, the party no longer wants to fight? Or, for instance, that it puts the brakes on the CGT and its most aggressive militants? It certainly does not seek out physical confrontations, whereas in the past its militants proved they knew how to go about it and were always in the thick of any battles. In social conflicts, the militants of the party and of the CGT certainly give priority to well-organized actions run by the trade unions over actions called in demand for con-

[54] Thesis 14, pp. 427-428.

crete monetary claims, which take place without violence and according to long-established working-class practice. They regard with great suspicion any actions that resist trade-union organization, that are connected with adventurist qualitative claims, or that go outside the bounds of the place of work and involve locking out managers and bosses. They are frankly opposed to any intervention in conflicts involving the agitation of elements from outside the factory and particularly outside the working-class sphere.[55] Certain of the most active *gauchiste* groups, certain militants from the PSU or the CFDT are perhaps correct in their assertion that in such and such a case they were more pugnacious than those of the PCF and the CGT, and that this lack of involvement stemmed from the directives of their organizations. Does this prove that the only battle the PCF wants to wage is the electoral battle? We think not. It is clear, however, that the electoral battle is its main concern and all others are subordinate to it.

One might conclude from all this that the PCF is no longer a *truly* revolutionary party. But as we said earlier, we shall not make any assertions on this point because there is no universally accepted definition of a "true" revolutionary party.

There is, moreover, another objection that cannot be ignored. After all, it may be said, the PCF may well have changed not at all since 1932, whatever its public theory and practice. Perhaps it still wants "French soviets," a "workers' and peasants' judiciary" to take power by force if necessary, to totally destroy the bourgeois state. But if it did, why should it proclaim its aims from the rooftops as it did in 1934, noisily publicize its sympathy for the *gauchiste* commandos, warn possible future allies, management, the police, and foreign embassies that it intends to foster general disorder as soon as the opportunity arises, and to take power with or without the help of the Red Army? There is only one answer to this objection: it is absurd. The police force and intelligence services are efficient enough so that, if these were indeed the PCF's goals (goals which could not fail to leave some

[55] In May-June 1968, when those students who wanted to "unify working class and student struggles" tried to join forces with the strikers occupying the factories, the CGT and the PCF expressed their opposition. In many of the other conflicts that have arisen in recent years, the PCF and the CGT always react very strongly when PSU or CFDT militants try to support militant action on the premises by people who are not employed there and have no trade union backing.

124

trace in the wastepaper basket or on a magnetic tape), many governments would have been only too pleased to unmask it. No such thing has occurred.[56]

Victory—to What End?

The most complete statement of the policy the Communist party would like to put into effect if it came to power is the "governmental program for a democratic government of popular union" which the Central Committee adopted on October 9, 1971,[57] and which was used as a basis for negotiation in working out the Common Platform with the Socialist party. This text does not hide the fact that it is only proposing "reforms" (but not, as Georges Marchais makes clear in his preface, "pseudo-reforms"), to prepare for the stage of "advanced democracy" and not that of socialism.

According to one's political opinions, one can see positive or negative aspects in the content of this program. In any event, it is a collection of coherent measures, carefully studied, proving that the party has made good use of the experience and technical knowledge of its militants, and has taken into account the work of its experts. In many cases, it deals with measures that are quite feasible. Many of them, if put into operation, undoubtedly represent a policy radically different from that employed by the successive governments of the Fifth Republic, and would bring about substantial improvements for the least privileged classes. There is a design for a left-wing policy within the framework of existing political and administrative institutions and social structures, with only slight modifications. And the reforms proposed by the PCF would be apt to gradually create the conditions for more basic social and political change.

But a *program*—and particularly a program designed in preparation for an alliance pact—is only a program. Whether one reproaches the PCF for no longer being socialist and revolutionary, or whether one reproaches it for concealing much more radical aims beneath reformist rhetoric, one can regard this program as devoid of any real significance. One should try to evaluate the PCF on the basis of its practice rather than on its theory.

[56] It is interesting to note the farcical incident of the pigeon found on the seat of J. Duclos's car in 1952, which people thought at first was a carrier pigeon carrying secret messages, but was in fact his lunch.

[57] Subtitled *"Changer de cap"* (Paris: Editions Sociales, 1971).

But what practice? Apart from its role in social struggles at the place of work, in which the CGT is much more active than the PCF, there are only two spheres where the French Communists *have exercised power* and on which we can base any judgment of what they *might* do if they came to power. One is their participation in power from 1944 to 1947, and the other is their activity in localities where they have absolute municipal control. Both have limited scope and significance.

No serious in-depth study has been made either of the conditions under which the Communists carried out their political, governmental, and administrative responsibilities from 1944 until their eviction from power at the beginning of May 1947, or of the balance-sheet of their tenure. We know little beyond the slightly anecdotal aspects (the apparently smug satisfaction that Communist ministers experienced in power), or facts that are widely known (the suspect patriotism, unresisting acceptance of the dissolution of patriotic militia, the battle waged for the development of production and for wage controls, support for the "nationalist" policies of Georges Bidault, the mobilization of members of the old Resistance movements, the display of *démocratisme*, and so on).

It is true that we have an *indirect* means of forming an opinion: that is, the way in which the PCF sees this experience of power, or rather wants it to be seen. We can find this view expressed by François Billoux (who was in the government from April 1944 to May 1947).[58] On many points we find simply a confirmation of well-known facts. On others, we find some interesting facts: for instance the very direct reassertion of the opinion that at the time of the Liberation, "internal and external conditions had not been fulfilled for establishing a Socialist regime in France,"[59] the assertion that the PCF has "no desire to return to the Constitution of 1946,"[60] or slightly sheepish explanations in defense of its attitude at that time toward France's relations with its overseas possessions.[61] On the whole, however, quite apart from its intrinsic mediocrity, this work is of little use. It is by no means either a historical work nor even an eyewitness account of history; it is an official party document obviously designed to serve as an illustration—as Georges Marchais frankly states in his preface (p. 11)—of the governmental *Programme* of October 9,

[58] *Quand nous étions ministres,* preface by G. Marchais.
[59] Ibid. [60] Ibid., p. 72. [61] Ibid., pp. 96, 174.

126

1971. With its didactic tone of self-vindication, the whole work tries to prove that as "a responsible party, a democratic party, a national party, a party of government" (p. 184), the PCF "has a constructive, not a negative attitude" (p. 183), that no one has suffered because of "the activity of Communist ministers except for traitors . . . speculators, parasites, and profiteers" (p. 178), and all this leads to the conclusion that "to claim a democratic government without the Communists is a delusion" (p. 182).

Let us look now at their municipal activities. Obviously, it is not within this geographically narrow framework that a party, even if its initiatives were not thwarted by other parties associated with it in the municipality, can make a "small local revolution" nor even carry out a policy radically different from that generally exercised in comparable conditions by "bourgeois" municipalities. Having stressed the very limited nature of this local Communist activity, we should nevertheless search for some telltale signs of the revolutionary, socialist, or radical character of the PCF.[62]

One initial point in its favor is that between the 1965 municipal elections, which went well for the party, and those of 1971, the PCF lost none of the large towns (over 30,000 inhabitants) it held, and it won six more; this may be the result of general satisfaction with its administration. Admittedly, this success can also be explained—and the two explanations are by no means contradictory—by the fact that, in these communes more than anywhere else, the party disposes of considerable energy and funds both for its current electoral activities, and for its "tribune" activities on behalf of its long-term electoral interests. And municipal power in these towns also gives it other means not otherwise available (financial means, meeting places, poster displays, militants with communal appointments).

No one seriously denies that these communes are administered with great care, with a real respect for legality, administrative regulations, and fiscal honesty, and that rarely are there any

[62] Many of these towns are situated in the immediate vicinity of large agglomerations, and follow belatedly the same demographic evolution as the city-centers: the working class population tends to go down as the white collar and management classes increase. Working class occupations also tend to decrease, except for nonskilled jobs and menial jobs that are filled more and more by immigrant workers whom the Communist communes have to receive. Despite these often unfavorable factors, the number of Communist voters in these communes, *particularly* in municipal elections, is not going down.

scandals involving their municipal officers and employees. Everything points to the fact that, despite this prudent and lawful administration, their efforts to resolve the problems that confront
the underprivileged classes in particular (low-income housing,
town planning, urban transport, schools, family and social welfare services, old age pensions, and so on) are more fruitful than
those generally undertaken by other communes, thanks to an
excellent organization of general services set up by the party
for its municipalities,[63] and sometimes involve quite heavy
expenditure.

Differences with non-Communist communes are equally noticeable with regard to political personnel. Many mayors and
councilors elected on the ticket of other parties quickly become
local notables who are relatively independent of their party and
play a personal and autonomous political role. The Communist
officials, whatever their ability or their local popularity, remain
under the control of the party's local apparatus and that of the
Federation; their political clout, like that of the parliamentarians,
is weak in the party; thus it is really the party that, through its directive bodies, in fact directs the trend of municipal government.

Finally, even if the exact number of members (the true tally of
political militancy) and the levels of cell activity are lower than
we imagine or than the party would like, the PCF, without any
real political competition in these areas, bombards the population
with an unceasing flow of propaganda, thanks to the thousands
of tracts distributed, to the local cells' newsletters, to the door-
to-door distribution of *L'Humanité-Dimanche*, to public meetings, and to speeches outside the factories. Whatever one's opinion may be of the quality of these messages, they are always
political messages which deal with peace, foreign policy, national
elections, economic policy, general problems in national education, and so on. In no other communes do the municipal authorities engage in such political education, nor are the people so encouraged to take an interest in politics.

We can find much to criticize in the way the Communists handle municipal power. Criticism from the Right: the Communists'
administration is too one-sided, they do not provide municipal
channels for the expression of non-Communist ideas, they keep mu-

[63] The party has been responsible for the creation of private (or cooperative) ventures such as urban study groups, construction businesses, city
planning agencies, and credit bureaus.

nicipal jobs for their own militants, as well as housing assigned by the Habitations Loyers Modérés (HLM) offices. The political climate is stifling because Communist propaganda holds a monopoly—"one might be living in a popular democracy." Criticism from the Left: Communist municipal activity falls into what the PCF itself once called "municipal cretinism," a mixture of prudent management and demagogy. What is more, this administration is authoritarian and paternalistic: it is totally under the auspices of the party, which has sovereign power; the "informational" meetings it organizes are in fact nothing but meetings to explain and justify their actions after the event before audiences posing no opposition, and they make no real attempt to bring the population into decision-making processes, and still less to delegate responsibilities. It has also been observed that in many of these communes, militancy is more and more the job of people who are party employees, officials of their mass organizations, or of the communes they administer; that party membership denotes less and less a deep personal commitment but rather a token of sympathy that they dare not refuse in view of the "benevolent" and "devoted" aura of communism that surrounds them.[64]

Can the PCF presume to call itself an "authentically revolutionary party" with these men, with this experience of power, with these references? As regards the revolution, its municipal activity, like its governmental activity from 1944 to 1947, proves nothing. The PCF *says* it wants revolution. What it has done and what it is doing offer no proof of this, but nevertheless suggest that if one strips the word "revolution" of any insurgent connotation and any reference to historical events that Marxists themselves usually call "revolutions," the PCF perhaps wants a *certain kind* of revolution. For the moment, one thing is certain, that it wants to be in power. That is all we can say for sure.

"Civil Society" and the Dominant Ideology

Return to power, formation of a democratic government of popular union, application of the Common Platform (or a modi-

---

[64] In these circumstances, where in each housing block the non-Communist is engulfed in a Communist environment, people become members "to be nice." Often one member of the family becomes a member in the name of the whole family; this bears witness to the family's gratitude to the Communists in the town, but it does not imply a personal involvement or commitment on the part of the cardholder.

fied version of it), realization of "advanced democracy," then a "transition to socialism"—all this has to do only with *political* society. There remains the question of *civil* society.

If the French Communist party has retained any links with Marxist theory, it cannot be unaware that the "dominant ideas" of a mode of production, that is, theoretically speaking, the ideology of the dominant class, eventually permeate the subject classes who thus, despite their active social struggle, cannot break free as long as they remain prisoners of the dominant ideology. According to certain interpretations of Marxism at least, this struggle against the dominant ideology to attain self-consciousness can be carried forward only if the proletariat is concentrated in a distinct "party." According to these interpretations, Communist parties—the party "of the working class"—are the instruments of this struggle against the dominant ideology.

From this standpoint—that is, from the standpoint of *its own theory*—where does the PCF stand and what is it doing? Here we may recall very briefly Gramsci's notion that the basic task of a Communist party is to accomplish with the help of Marxist "philosophy" an "intellectual and moral" reform for the popular masses to fight against the *sens commun* of a bourgeois society.[65] This is a difficult task, not only because it demands at the outset "a transcendence of earlier and present modes of thought,"[66] but also because it requires the party to remain in contact with the masses and to understand popular sentiment. Gramsci writes: "The philosophy of *praxis* does not aim to keep simple people confined to a primitive philosophy at the level of the *sens commun*, but on the contrary to lead them to a higher concept of life. If it asserts the need for contact between intellectuals and simple folk, it is not in order to lower the level of scientific activity or to maintain unity at the low level of the masses, but expressly to build up an intellectual-moral bloc that makes intellectual progress politically possible for the masses and not just for small intellectual groups."[67]

There is no doubt that in some respects the PCF has fulfilled and continues to fulfill the mission thus defined by Gramsci. The PCF has shown its understanding of the importance of creating

---

[65] These themes are developed mainly in two works by Gramsci: *Il materialismo storico e la filosofia di Benedetto Croce* (Turin: Einaudi, 1954); and *Letteratura e vita nazionale* (Turin: Einaudi, 1954).

[66] *Il materialismo storico*, p. 9.   [67] Ibid., p. 2.

130

its own ideological apparatus to offset the dominant ideas and the *sens commun* of a bourgeois society by forming its own mass organizations and assigning its own militants to them, by making special efforts to have its own press and to assure its widespread distribution; it has encouraged its intellectuals to participate in running radio and television media, it has created its own chain of publishing houses, bookstores, and record shops, it has organized the distribution of political films in its own cinemas by skillfully making use of *maisons de la culture* and *maisons de la jeunesse*, it has named streets and school buildings in its communes with names of symbolic French and foreign revolutionary heroes, it has constantly organized demonstrations to commemorate great revolutionary events such as the Paris Commune and the October Revolution. The Communist party also reiterates that "despite the growing penetration of Marxism-Leninism," "bourgeois ideology remains the dominant ideology" and that fighting it "constitutes the essential task in the ideological struggle."[68]

Nor can we fault the party of Communist intellectuals for having failed in their struggle against "bourgeois" philosophy, the most concrete expression of the dominant ideology: idealism, Freudianism, Hegelianism, existentialism, phenomenology, neo-Marxism, and many other currents have been unmasked by the dozen, and condemned with that polemical vigor in which the party excels. In response, the Communists have made an effort to create their own reviews and their own philosophical circles.[69] All the same, up to the time of a renaissance of Marxist philosophy among the *party* intellectuals, which did not begin until 1960 and only then in publications for intellectual readers, this criticism of "bourgeois" philosophy took the exclusive form of unmotivated censure, invective, and purely political arguments. Despite the resolution dealing with ideological problems[70] that was adopted by the Central Committee at Argenteuil in March 1966, and despite a current renewal of creative activity among Communist philosophers to develop *Marxism*, the criticism of other philosophies, at the level of *official* party documents, is still marked either by the same tone of summary censure or—more serious—by a political opportunism which allows some indul-

[68] Nineteenth Congress, Thesis 36, p. 443.
[69] On all these problems, see the excellent article by Nicole Racine, "Le Parti Communiste Français devant les problèmes idéologiques et culturels," in *Le Communisme en France*, pp. 141-182.
[70] Ibid.

gence to a particular current because it is useful in the fight against imperialism and the power of the monopolies. In the field of literature and the plastic arts, the PCF leaders have only recently discarded their official support of a "populist" classical and conventional form of art that copied official Soviet art, which was supposed to correspond to the taste of the masses and to working-class morals and aesthetics. Now in party publications and at the *fête de l'Humanité* people can exhibit and evaluate what was anathema only a short time ago.

But it is not at the level of philosophy, or artistic and literary creativity that the most important element of the ideological struggle lies for a party that claims to be the educator of the masses and the party "of the working class"; it is rather at the level of the *sens commun* and popular beliefs. At this level, the struggle is important from two points of view that themselves reflect the two communisms existing in France—party communism and popular communism. By "popular communism," a form of communism which can continue to permeate the mentality of many militants despite party schooling, we mean a propaganda closely related to the problems of the "little man" in their least political dimensions,[71] an ideological patriotic-republican-working-class syncretism, a sentimental and shallow attachment encouraged by a warm ambiance and by frequent celebrations (the First of May, the *fête de l'Humanité*, and of local Communist newspapers, the annual renewal of party cards in the cells, and so on). Is this popular communism—which is prospering so well on the former territory of popular Catholicism, doubtless because they have the same scope and function—so different from the "religion of the people," that is, from the *sens commun*? And has not "party communism"—the communism of responsible party leaders—been engulfed in this *sens commun* by very reason of the priority accorded by the party to electoral victories, to rallying the "wider segments of society," to the "union of working-class and democratic forces?"

These two related questions should first be examined at the level of the ideological apparatus of the dominant ideology and

[71] On this subject, I refer once more to Bonnet's extremely penetrating analyses in his *Sociologie*, especially pp. 394-427. For a very different approach (using an analysis of interviews) see also Guy Michelat and Michel Simon, "Catholiques déclarés et irreligieux communisants: Vision du monde et perception du champ politique," *Archives de sociologie des religions* 35 (1972): 57-111.

the counterapparatus mounted by the PCF. The mass organizations that are controlled and encouraged by the party are part of this counterapparatus. Some of them are weak or have lost ground, and often have influence only in communes with a Communist administration, where they find plenty of facilities available to them. But it is not true of all these organizations, and although they are less numerous than in Italy, they are sufficient in number to exert widespread influence. But for many of them, their activity is so closely linked and subordinate to the *immediate political tasks* of the party that they are only fully mobilized to serve as an amplifier and a sound-box for the party's political campaigns (for example against the cost of living, against subsidies for parochial schools, or for the Common Platform), and much less as the leaders of the ideological struggle against the *sens commun*, popular prejudices, old beliefs, and "folklore."[72] In these mass organizations, Communist militants really try to explain "popular passions," as Gramsci suggested, "by relating them dialectically to the laws of history, to a scientifically molded concept of the world." Unfortunately, the "laws of history" boil down to something very simple: "France's progress to socialism" thanks to the "powerful party of the working class"; and the "concept of the world" is interpreted by the perennial theory of capitalist exploitation.

Publications like *L'Humanité-Dimanche*, or *Nous, les garçons et les filles* (for adolescent consumption), or the children's weekly magazines are naturally not as significant as newspapers and documents that state the party's position on different issues; the same is true of an event like the *fête de l'Humanité*. Nonetheless at the level of the struggle against the dominant ideology and the *sens commun*, their function as an ideological counterapparatus is basic, since the party daily, its scholarly magazines, and the publications of the Maurice Thorez Institute or the Marxist Research and Study Group are not aimed at popular communism and concern only a limited segment of party communism. These publications and demonstrations aimed at the general public have

[72] It seems to me excessive to accuse the PCF of fostering racism and popular xenophobia. In a moment of crisis (May 1968), it admittedly placed too much emphasis on the German nationality of the *gauchiste* leader Cohn-Bendit. And it is often placed in a difficult situation by the reaction of its voters to the overcrowding of immigrant workers in Communist towns. But it succeeds in resolving most of these problems, and to my knowledge its officials have rarely been faulted on this issue.

to correspond to the current tastes and reflect the current culture of the widest segments of society. So in a modern society, where all the old forms of authentic popular culture and real folklore have disappeared, the sources of this present-day "popular" culture are of necessity the big mass-media mills, which reflect the *sens commun* and the various mass consumption mythologies, or which snap up all the aspects of underground cultures that seem like a good commercial proposition. Here we must proceed with caution, because the real problem lies in determining by precise means, with sufficiently full and diversified data, the mixture of *sens commun* and non-*sens commun* elements in a PCF mass circulation medium.[73]

We do have more data on two other spheres of ideological influence: the *family* and the *school*. Ever since the early days, Marxist theoreticians (Engels, Bebel, Lenin, Clara Zetkin) have been interested in the family and in relationships between men and women. The PCF and the mass organization it created in 1945, the Union des Femmes Françaises (UFF) have followed in their footsteps, albeit with great caution and traditionalism.[74] One indication of these attitudes is the fact that it is always the women on the Central Committee who are responsible for questions relating to the family and women (Jeannette Vermeersch, Marie-Claude Vaillant-couturier, Mireille Bertrand, Madeleine Vincent), and they rarely intervene in other matters. The PCF and the UFF are very well informed on economic conditions and the financial problems of working women or wives in working-class families, and they use this information in an intelligent way to show up the processes of economic exploitation, and to propose social measures to rectify injustices, particularly in the case of large families; but even though the PCF is not against women working, it also wants to win over unemployed housewives, so it explains that women work because their husband's salary is insufficient, and that women do not work because women's salaries

[73] In 1971, one of the most popular stands was the information stand: "Homage to science or a concession to a modern idolatry?" In such a varied event as the *fête de l'Humanité*, one section is given over to the singers, painters, and artists who represent social criticism and revolt, while another is the domain of the singers who represent the big popular "naive" successes—neither group has exclusive rights.

[74] I am using data from Pierre Bréchon and Marie-Louise Strapazzon, "*L'Idéologie du Parti Communiste Français sur la famille,*" mimeographed (Institut d'Etudes Politiques de Grenoble, 1972).

134

and family allowances are insufficient. Once more, the theory of capitalist exploitation brings the analysis to a full stop. The word "woman" is invariably associated with three attributes: "laboring," "citizen," and "mother"—another example of the set phrases of Communist parlance. As "mothers," women should mobilize for peace, and as "mothers and citizens" they should mobilize in political battles to defend their children's future.

The tone and the terms used to exploit maternal love in the political struggle often appeal to the most elemental "popular passions," particularly by Jeannette Vermeersch in the years between 1949 and 1956. Only quite recently have family problems ceased to be considered exclusively in terms of the woman as mother, and one now sees other protagonists involved: the man and the couple. Relations between men and women are never presented as antagonistic, nor are those between young people and adults; antagonism exists only between the classes, and it is only capitalism that exploits women. It is superfluous to recall how strenuously the PCF fought for so many years against legal contraception: here again the demise of exploitation was to resolve the problems of unwanted pregnancies.

Aside from these anecdotal aspects, we are concerned with the Marxist theory on which the party claims to be based. The PCF has branded "superstructures" as infamous, but rather than producing analysis of the dominant ideology and popular forms of consciousness, it has exploited them loosely and indiscriminately for its own "tribune" activities, and itself makes use of the most traditional social images. If one compares the ideological content of Communist statements on the family with those of left-wing intellectual circles or, better still, of feminist movements or certain *gauchiste* organizations, this accusation holds. If, on the other hand, we compare it with the ideological content of the statements of popular Catholicism, then the PCF, particularly since 1965, seems to have made some headway in categorizing the various groups of beliefs and traditional images.[75]

[75] According to an unpublished survey by SOFRES (September 13-17, 1973) on pornography, people claiming to be "close to the PCF" gave consistently more liberal answers to each of the questions than people who claimed to be close to the other major political groups. We had rather different results in a study we organized on political alienation (November 1972) among a sample of young people between the ages of 16 and 34 in the Paris suburbs, where *gauchiste* tendencies were much more strongly represented than in the SOFRES survey; individuals close to the PCF were

135

The educational institution is a field to which the PCF has long given special attention and which its intellectuals have been able to analyze with slightly more freedom. The party has always seen the public school as one of the most precious heritages of the Republic, both because of its general function of transmitting knowledge and because it serves the common people. It has always defended it, and thus followed the tradition of all left-wing parties, and at the same time it has always wanted to reform it.[76] Numerous Communist militants are active within the *Ligue de l'Enseignement*, the oldest defender of the public schools, as well as in the big Fédération de l'Education Nationale (FEN) which includes the vast majority of the teachers. Their positions are expressed in a well-written journal called *L'École et la nation*.

The PCF's interest in national education has not been limited to defending the teachers' interests, nor to defending public schools vis-à-vis private schools, nor to demanding a larger proportion of the national budget, nor even to working toward a democratization of the educational system. It has been equally involved in problems that have longer-range electoral returns— reforms in teaching methods, school psychology, and so forth. Communist teachers, in their professional activities, are not credited with being passive and indifferent toward the ideological content of the schools' message.

All the same, particularly since May 1968, the party reacts in a cautiously scandalized way to the criticisms leveled at the schools by those who want either to limit its function as a transmitter of knowledge, or to oppose it as a vehicle of bourgeois ideology. In 1972, the education commission of the Central Committee officially spelled out the party's dissociation from what it calls "crisis ideologies" and "fundamental questioning of the school system itself."[77] At the same time, the intellectuals' journal *La Nouvelle Critique* also voiced a clear condemnation of advanced educational ideas such as those propounded by Ivan

---

more repressive on issues of sexual freedom. See Janine Mossuz, "Radicalisme politique et permissivité sexuelle," *Revue française de science politique* 24, no. 1 (February 1974).

[76] See, for example, the plan for the democratic reform of education worked out in 1946 under the direction of two Communist intellectuals, Paul Langevin and Henri Wallon.

[77] Entitled "Crise de la société, crise de l'enseignement," *L'Humanité*, March 17, 1972.

Illich.[78] Authors inspired by Marxism and especially by the concept of a "state ideological apparatus" made fashionable by Louis Althusser are not spared either.[79]

Perhaps we have in its attitude to educational questions one of the PCF's main stumbling blocks. Where certain aspects of the sacred heritage of the Republic are concerned, those aspects which have benefited all the French people—communal schools, the 30,000 little communes each with their own council, their own mayor, and their meager powers, republican principles—the party no longer dares to advance an ideological criticism of them. There is another reason for the PCF's scandalized reaction to attacks on the school system. In France as elsewhere, for the most disadvantaged social strata who face so many obstacles to advancement, the school and its diplomas—the object of so much sacrifice, so much effort—represent a *rare* social and economic prize. These people have no sympathy for anyone who wants to "burn down the school." In May 1968, the Communist militants reminded the "wild ones" that the workers' children needed to take their examinations.

But we should do more than merely examine how the PCF, through its countermeasures, tries to neutralize and offset the ideological apparatus of the dominant class and the insidious power of the *sens commun*. Does the party produce *another* philosophy, *another sens commun*, other "popular beliefs" that would constitute an effective alternative? Actually this question deals with the relationship between the PCF and Marxism, which is too vast a subject to be dealt with here and which in any case is outside our province. We shall merely make these comments.

To this very day, the PCF has never been *led* by intellectuals, and it is proud of the fact that it is run by "workers." The few intellectuals who worked in the Political Bureau were hardly well-known Marxist theoreticians and had little influence. The Central Committee, a larger body, which for some years now seems to have been playing a more important role in the political leadership of the party, certainly includes some intellectuals, but few of them could be considered theoreticians. Not only party leaders but also Marxist research and study groups have given scant attention to Gramsci and other outstanding Marxist theoreticians.

[78] Ibid.
[79] Aimé Guedj and François Hincker, "Le Malaise des enseignants. Faut-il brûler l'école?" *La Nouvelle Critique*, no. 49 (January 1972): 7-19.

Perhaps in the past, and even today, this attitude has held certain advantages for the PCF by maintaining its image as a proletarian party, by helping to preserve its unity, and by avoiding too great a gap between "popular communism" and "party communism." It is not clear, however, that there have been no negative consequences. Although in recent years Communist intellectuals have felt free to express more audacious opinions in specialized *party* journals, the way the party works at the top has not changed. Its leaders always ignore or brush aside theoretical analyses, preferring to pursue short-term political objectives and to continue to subscribe to the classical deterministic model of exploitation. In addition, for some years now other political organizations have been producing radical criticisms of the dominant ideology.

The party pays great attention to certain Marxist concepts inherent in what it takes for theoretical analysis, and particularly in this model of exploitation: the development of the forces of production,[80] property relations, surplus value and capital; but despite its abundant use of the word "ideological," it pays much less attention to other aspects such as social relationships between people, superstructures, and ideologies.

The "ideological work" of the party always seems to fluctuate between two poles. At one extreme is the justification both of the party's power in French society and of its cautious short-term political activity. The other pole states the rules of an ideology of "guardianship": it is forbidden to threaten our heritage, to be Utopian or anarchist, to be "irresponsible," to "insult the working class," or to offend popular sentiments and the *sens commun*.

One can find many justifications for the patient and cautious strategy for "taking power" over political society which the PCF seems to support: no use of force, no violence, but alliances, electoral victory, and an "advanced democracy." It is a strategy that can lead to dead ends, but there is no guarantee that other measures might be more successful. On the other hand, its strategy for transforming civil society and for combating dominant ideas is more puzzling. But perhaps this latter strategy pays the price for the success of the former.

[80] PCF texts abound with declarations of admiration for the development of technology, for science's contributions to production (see, for example, Nineteenth Congress, Thesis 48). One of the reproaches always leveled at capitalism is that it wastes productive forces without developing them to their utmost.

In his excellent book, *Sociologie politique et religieuse de la Lorraine*, Serge Bonnet demonstrates with great shrewdness the aspects that "popular communism" and popular Catholicism have in common in this region. With centuries of history behind it and the Last Judgment as its horizon, the Catholic Church must have often thought, like Henri Krasucki, that people "cannot live in any way but in that imposed by the system."[81] Therefore it has continually debaptized and rebaptized the old holy places and the pagan festivals, it has incorporated rather than uprooted the old pagan religions, popular beliefs, and superstitions, and has placed the popular heroes of modern mythologies in its churches and its minor ceremonies. This religion for the masses has probably done more for its power than all the martyrs and theologians.

However, the parallel has its limitations. Can the Communist party, like the Catholic Church, function for so long a period of time? Another fundamental difference is that since Constantine the Great, the Church—at least in the West—has been on the side of the political and social powers, it is not in conflict with them (or not always), its ideological apparatus has been helped, defended, often funded by these powers and has collaborated with the apparatus of the state and other major social groups. In these circumstances, why should it sacrifice these means of power to an uncompromising struggle to purge all faith of its popular superstitions and semipagan folklore? After all, in spite of these advantages (which the PCF does not have), the Church has not been spared its Reform, its schisms, or the desertion of many of its disciples.

Such is the situation of the PCF today—not quite, but almost, inside the political system. And it remains to be seen whether it can continue much longer as it is without some modifications in one direction or another.

[81] See Krasucki, p. 23. What is implied in a phrase such as this is an "economist" version of Marxism.

PART TWO

The Communist Politician

IV.

Party Activists in Public Office: Comparisons at the Local Level in Italy and France

SIDNEY TARROW

When the reigning orthodoxy among students of comparative communism began to give way, after 1956, to the admission that the Communist world could be less than monolithic, it was inevitable that, sooner or later, students of nonruling Communist parties would begin to ask: "How do Communist activists in Western parliamentary systems mediate between their primary roles as party loyalists and their roles in the political system as a whole?" At the local level, the problem could be approached through an analysis of a Communist party's policies: Did such policies aim to advance the interests of the working class or, rather, to unite local communities behind the party, thereby making it more "respectable" and efficient?[1] The problem could also be looked at from the point of view of the party's performance in local administration: does it aim at the creation of enclaves of "municipal socialism" through a great deal of investment in public services, or does it run the communities it controls with a "business as usual," budget-balancing mentality?[2]

Neither the policy-oriented nor the performance approach, however, comes to grips with the most important question about the adaptation of Communist militants to political life in parliamentary systems. That is, to what extent is this participation ever likely to lead to an erosion of the party's monolithic structure and discipline and to its increased capacity to play a legitimate role in the game of democratic politics? Such questions have most fre-

[1] See, for example, the PCF local platforms reproduced in Jean-Pierre Hoss, *Communes en banlieue: Argenteuil et Bezons* (Paris: A. Colin, 1969), Chapter 3, and the PCI's campaign tactics in Bologna, described by Robert Evans, *Coexistence: Communism and its Practice in Bologna, 1945-1965* (Notre Dame, Ind.: University of Notre Dame Press, 1967), Chapter 3.

[2] Jean-Claude Ducros, "Politique et finances locales," *Analyse et prévision* (July-August 1966): 499-518 and Robert Fried, "Communism, Urban Budgets and the Two Italies," *Journal of Politics* 33 (December 1971): 1008-1051.

quently been asked at the national level, but in recent years, both the French and Italian parties have placed increased stress on the "democratization" of *local* government. In the Partito Comunista Italiano (PCI), this had taken the form of the creation of neighborhood councils and the development of networks of contacts with citizens' groups of all kinds.[3] In the French case, the emphasis has been on more formal consultation,[4] with some recent evidence of a greater willingness to experiment with more spontaneous forms of participation.[5] In both countries, however, an important question remains: To what extent does the reality of Communist practice at the local level reflect this verbal policy of democratization?

Many students of Communist practice in non-Communist systems have focused on the "sincerity" of the Communist commitment to democratic norms of political practice. Our concern is more limited and, perhaps for that reason, more practical. We wish to understand the *capacity* of each party at the local level for applying, in practice, the goals of openness, flexibility, and broad popular participation that both parties have recently proclaimed to be their goal at the level of ideology. We shall argue that this potential for local democratization varies, both as a function of the different circumstances in which the two parties find themselves, and as a function of differences in the nature of grass-roots partisan involvement within them.

The usefulness of the local level for such a comparison is threefold. First, it is sufficiently distant from the centers of decision-making in the party to give local leaders a reasonable chance to develop their own mechanisms of adaptation and operation; second, it is sufficiently visible to the public for the party to be concerned about the impression that is made by its local representatives; third, in such highly centralized political systems, it is sufficiently interlocked with the state to force Communists in local office to come to grips with the problem of their relationship to public authority in the bourgeois state.

---

[3] For examples, see Peter Lange, Chapter 7 in this volume, and the sources he cites therein; in particular, see *Decentramento urbano: burocrazia o partecipazione* (Milan: C.S.L., 1970).

[4] A description of the panoply of the new modes of participation used by a Communist-run municipality in the elections of 1971 is found in François Hincker, "Une Municipalité dans la lutte politique: Givors," *La Nouvelle Critique* 42 (March 1971): 14-18.

[5] The most advanced statement of the PCF's more open line is found in Michel Simon, "Le Centralisme démocratique, pourquoi, comment?" *L'Humanité*, June 22, 1973, p. 8.

144

These three factors—the party, the public, and the state—intersect in the roles played by local activists of the PCI and the Parti Communiste Français (PCF) who find themselves in public office. We shall try to analyze how such local officials reconcile the three different roles of party activist, elected representative of the people, and administrative official, and how the roles they play as public officials qualify or disqualify them to lead Communist practice at the local level toward greater participation, inventiveness, and democratization.

The analysis will be based both on some general considerations drawn from the literature on French and Italian local communism, and from an interview survey of 250 French and Italian mayors carried out between 1969 and 1971 in matched samples of municipalities from 500 to 50,000 populations in four regions of each country.[6] The number of Communist mayors interviewed in each country (21 out of 117 mayors in France and 30 out of 133 in Italy) was modest, but the information gathered about their relationships with the party, the state, and the public was extensive, and reveals a consistent pattern of differences between the two groups that suggests a totally different model of Communist adaptation to local politics in each country. Turning, first, to their relationship to the party, second, to their response to the electorate and to electoral activity and, third, to their relationship to the state, we shall turn, finally, to a consideration of the potential of each party, at the local level, to carry out a strategy of advanced socialism that is not only new, but also open and democratic.

[6] The mayors were chosen according to an identical quota system based upon population size and electoral coloration of the communities in each of twelve French departments and Italian provinces. Note that, because the object was to compare communities of similar size and complexity, the larger number of miniscule communes in France are undersampled, as are the larger number of more heavily populated communes in Italy. The regions were, for France: the valley of the Loire, the east (Lorraine), the Midi-provençal, and the southwest (the areas of the Tarn and the Limousin); for Italy: the northwest (Piedmont), the northeast (the Veneto), the center (contiguous provinces within Tuscany, the Marches, and the Romagna) and the south (Campania). The interviews used a combination of directive and semidirective techniques and each took between one and one-half and three and one-half hours. After an initial attempt at recording them proved to constrain some of the mayors, they were recorded by typewriter after the interview was completed. Details of the larger study will be found in my forthcoming work tentatively entitled "Integration at the Periphery: Grassroots Politics in Italy and France."

Involvement in the Party Subculture

Why should Communists in public office interest us more than activists from other political parties? The answer, of course, lies in the deeper integration of the Communist into a political subculture organized around the party nerve center. Writers on Italian politics sometimes refer to the "organizational network" which encapsulates the Communist militant and insulates him against competing ideological currents,[7] while French writers are more familiar with the concept of the left-wing "political family," which has almost the same connotation.[8] How does involvement in the party subculture color the activist's dedication to the goals of public office, the use he makes of it, and the programs he advocates? After immersion in the private life of a party in which ideological purity and class or party interests come first, how can we expect the Communist activist in public life to deal pragmatically with representatives of other parties, with the general public, and with the state?

That Communist mayors are more involved in the life of their parties than other French and Italian local officials can be easily illustrated. The Communist mayors interviewed in both countries report having had a greater length of party organizational experience, more party offices above the local level, and a greater proportion of party-dominated group memberships than the non-Communist mayors. These comparisons, which are documented in Table 1, verify what we would suspect from the embracing nature of Communist party membership, compared to affiliation with less militant and less extreme political organizations.

But Table 1 also leads to a second set of considerations, one that is closer to the heart of our problem. While the degree of organizational involvement is equally asymmetrical in each country, the magnitude of the *Italian* Communists' advantage over their competitors is much greater than that of the PCF mayors. That is, not only is the organizational involvement of the Italian Communists greater than that of their non-Communist Italian

[7] Giovanni Sartori, "European Political Parties: The Case of Polarized Pluralism," in J. LaPalombara and M. Weiner (eds.), *Parties and Political Development* (Princeton: Princeton University Press, 1966), pp. 134-177.

[8] E. Deutsch et al., *Les Familles politiques aujourd'hui en France* (Paris: Minuit, 1966).

146

counterparts; it is also greater than that of their PCF comrades. This can be succinctly illustrated by the scores of the two groups of Communist mayors on an additive index of partisan experience which was constructed out of a number of questionnaire items on the mayors' partisan involvements.[9] More than 75 per-

TABLE 1. ORGANIZATIONAL ASPECTS OF PARTISAN INVOLVEMENT BY COUNTRY AND PARTY*

	FRANCE				ITALY		
		Non-Communist				Non-Communist	
Percent:	PCF	Left	Center	Right	PCI	Left	Right
Having held two or more party jobs	24	14	4	8	69	32	34
Holding party job at provincial or national level	15	32	30	8	31	9	3
Whose group memberships are all party dominated	58	44	22	5	86	43	48
(N =)	(21)	(25)	(30)	(29)	(30)	(22)	(78)

*Nonparty identifiers excluded.

cent of the Italian Communists scored "high" on this index, when the results were trichotomized, compared to only 45 percent of the French Communists. French Communists have an overall level of party organizational experience only slightly greater than that of their Socialist competitors, while more than twice as many Italian Communists score higher on this measure than their opponents on the non-Communist left.

TABLE 2. PARTISAN INVOLVEMENT BY COUNTRY AND PARTY

Percent Scoring "High" on Index of Partisan Involvement:	Communists	Non-Communist Left	Center	Right
France	45	38	15	3
Italy	76	29	—	30

[9] For a description of the index and its construction, see my "Partnership and Political Exchange in French and Italian Local Politics," Sage Publications, Professional Papers in *Contemporary Political Sociology*, 1974.

In effect, then, the PCI emerges as the only party at the local level in either country whose organization reaches into the local governing class. One PCI mayor's responses were typical. "Now I am a member of the 'permanent cadre' of the party at C—. Before I was mayor, I was a member of its 'disciplinary cadre.'" Another PCI mayor contrasted membership in his party with membership in the Partito Socialista Italiano (PSI), a party which had originally attracted him. "When I returned from the war," he said, "I was undecided for a while. . . . I even thought of the PSI, which was then a different party than it is now. . . . But then I decided 'If I'm going to put myself inside, I'll put myself inside all the way (*fin in fondo*),' I said to myself, and that was how I joined the party." A third Communist mayor also contrasted his party with the PSI. "I was in the Resistance," he said. "Returning home, I was asked to join the PSI. But I preferred the Communists because—and the facts have borne me out—it seemed to be a more serious and more coherent party."

The French Communist mayors had much less experience in the party organization than their Italian comrades. More than 40 percent had never held a party office higher than that of secretary of a cell or section, and almost 30 percent reported holding no party offices at all. In their comments during the interviews, PCF mayors were vigorous in their denials that they were deeply involved in the party organization. "I have never been anything but a simple militant," one of them proudly remarked.[10] It is not that organization was *un*important to the PCF mayors, with their Leninist training and instincts. One of them observed that his party's greatest success had been "developing thousands upon thousands of militants, whether they are mayors or not, who strive to improve the lot of the working class." But the PCF mayors themselves were less integrated into the party organization than their Italian comrades.

Part of the reason for this difference undoubtedly relates to underlying differences in French and Italian political culture. In Italy, especially since the end of fascism, party membership has become inextricably interwoven with social and economic activities of all kinds, and activity in a party organization is often an

[10] The same statement, in almost the same words, turns up in several of the Communist interviews carried out by Denis Lacorne in two other French regions. I am grateful to him for the chance to consult his original materials.

148

essential way station to high office in the community, or a stepping-stone to success outside the community.[11] In France, especially since the beginning of the Fifth Republic, party activity has been in disrepute, and the party organizations—never strong at the grass roots—have shrunk in many communities into informal cliques of notables and public officeholders.[12] Public indifference to party activity also plays a role. A city councilor in a southern French village said, "For the French, sitting around a table and discussing a problem seems useless." In Italy, as one study showed, the party activist is "the most lively animator and the most political one, of discussions in the town square, of meetings for the most diverse groups of citizens."[13]

If political cultural differences are part of the reason for the variations we have observed, the strategic paths of each Communist party since the war are no less important. Emerging from the Fascist experience with no effective organizational tradition, the Italian party's instinctive response was mass, often very unselective, recruitment, and the rapid construction of a vast network of party cells, sections, and federations. With a large number of unpaid or poorly paid organizational jobs to be filled, it was natural that the party should call upon its public officeholders to double as party organizers and vice versa. This led to a relatively high degree of interpenetration between public and organizational roles and—one may suppose—a greater ease of communication between the apparatus at the local and provincial level and the officeholders who are the party's most visible representatives. The Italian Communist mayors are not only deeply involved in the party organization at the local level; they reveal a relatively high degree of integration *between* the organization and the party's public representatives at that level.

For the PCF, with an organizational tradition that was practically unbroken since the 1920s, recruitment after 1945 was more deliberate. Once the first blush of enthusiasm of the 1944-1947 period was over, mobility upward in the party organization was

[11] For a community study which illustrates the manifold connections of political parties with Italian community life, see Alessandro Pizzorno's *Comunità e razionalizzazione* (Turin: Einaudi, 1960), Chapter 11.

[12] Mark Kesselman, "The Recruitment of Rival Party Activists in France: Party Cleavages and Cultural Differentiation," *Journal of Politics* 35 (January 1973): 2-44.

[13] F. Alberoni et al., *L'attivista di partito* (Bologna: Società Editrice Il Mulino, 1967), p. 309.

slower and more cautious than in Italy.[14] As one Communist mayor pointed out, "You never ask a guy to join the party; it is he who has to come in of his own volition." A correlate was the maintenance of a greater separation between organizational roles and public officeholding, with the former considered the repository of party authority and the latter seen more in terms of public relations.[15] With a smaller, and more streamlined, organization, the PCF was seldom forced, as was the Italian party, to draw local *élus* at all deeply into the apparatus, and integration between the two sectors of party activity was weaker than in Italy.

But if the number of organizational posts held by the PCF mayors is much lower than in the PCI, the *quality* of partisan involvement is no less intense and, from one point of view, it may be more faithful and dependable. This is because: (1) PCF mayors were likely to have entered the party in response to class and economic issues; (2) they are part of an insulated system of political communication that is central to the party's survival as a subculture; and (3) despite their less extensive involvement in the party organization, they have fewer ties with non-Communist political leaders. These characteristics of the relationship of the PCF mayors to their party leads to a less open quality of public activity than we can observe in the case of the PCI, as we shall see below.

Socialization into Politics

The PCF entered the postwar period with a model of the class struggle that had been determined in Moscow and given a French accent during the economic struggles of the 1930s; in the same way, almost half of the Communist local officials we interviewed in France had entered politics during the 1920s or 1930s, when economic and social issues were of overwhelming importance in French life. Forty percent of these mayors referred to economic, social, or occupational group motivations in bringing them into the party. One mayor said, "I entered it [the party] not on the basis of an ideology, but because of their politics of de-

---

[14] Thomas Greene, "The Communist Parties of Italy and France: A Study in Comparative Communism," *World Politics* 21 (October 1968): 1-38.

[15] See the support for this point found in a study of the Haute-Vienne by Alain Savy, "Recherches sur le personal politique en Haute-Vienne, 1945-1965" (Unpublished memoir, Faculté de Droit et de Sciences Economiques, Poitiers, 1965).

fending the working class." Another PCF mayor spoke of the injustice he had suffered while working as an apprentice for 60 or 70 hours a week. "After that," he said, "I took to communism naturally, like a duck takes to water."

Only 7 percent of the Italian mayors stressed such social and economic motives in discussing their party initiation, a finding, incidentally, which parallels Gabriel Almond's much earlier one in *The Appeals of Communism*, that family economic suffering and labor disorders were much less important as pathways to partisanship in Italy than in France.[16] And just as Almond found in 1954 that it had been the struggle against fascism and enemy occupation that brought the largest group of activists to the PCI, the bulk of the PCI mayors we interviewed had entered politics during the 1940s, most of them during the anti-Fascist resistance or during the period of popular unity which immediately followed. Moreover, over half of the Italians stressed predominantly ideological paths to communism, as opposed to only 25 percent of the PCF mayors. The importance of antifascism was particularly clear in the case of one PCI mayor who had been a prisoner of the Russians. "I was formed in Russia," he said, "as a prisoner of war, by reading things and just by looking around me."

The importance of the anti-Fascist resistance in the formation of the PCI's postwar strategic model has been stressed by more than one author.[17] This is not to deny the contribution that the PCF made to the French Resistance—although its extent is still a matter of dispute. But for the Italians, fascism had been a longer and more profound trauma, and antifascism was a primordial experience for most of its militants. What they gained from it was an elemental desire for political *unity* that goes far deeper than the Leninist instinct for protective social alliances. Their orientations to politics were formed in the context of a national interclass struggle for liberation, an experience which could not fail to mark their political activity later on. For the PCF, in contrast, the Resistance was only a layer of experience over the characteristics it had developed during the bolshevization of the 1920s and the class struggles of the 1930s. As one PCF mayor said, the

[16] In *The Appeals of Communism* (Princeton: Princeton University Press, 1954), p. 198.

[17] See Chapters 10 and 15 in this volume and Stephen Hellman, "Organization and Ideology in Four Italian Communist Federations" (Ph.D. Dissertation, Yale University, 1973), p. 77.

151

party's greatest success was "the constancy of its path, always being there."

The Intensity of Partisan Commitment

Many students of communism have remarked on the party's capacity to maintain itself as a counterculture of zealots, even, or especially, in the face of unfavorable political conditions. For a variety of reasons, this capacity has been more marked in the PCF than in the PCI. Possessed of a myth of natural hegemony over the proletariat that was practically unbroken since 1920, and with the prevalent image of the Communist activist as the antithesis of French bourgeois society,[18] the PCF had more chance to sustain such a tradition than the PCI, which dwelt underground for most of the Fascist period and emerged from the Resistance animated more by an ideology of national solidarity than by a myth of proletarian hegemony.[19] The rapid and chaotic expansion of the Italian party during the early postwar years then helped to dissipate a primary tie which could bind the activist into an intense spiritual community, leading ultimately to what one group of researchers has called "a kind of emancipation from a primary type of integration in the party."[20]

Although local officials are far from a typical cadre of Communist activists, we nevertheless find greater evidence of an intense pattern of commitment among the French Communist mayors than among the Italian ones. This is evident, first of all, in the more stylized character of the PCF mayors' responses. A tendency to give textbook answers to certain questions about the functions of local government was matched by a tendency to perceive their personal political development in stereotyped deterministic language. For example, in discussing his own recruitment, one mayor said: "Everything is conditioned, nothing is accidental." The Italians placed more emphasis on individual will or personal influence in bringing them to the party. As one mayor said: "It was during the partisan war that I was formed. Our best leaders were all Communists and they were examples for all of us. It was there that they explained to me and there that I began to understand."

[18] The best studies of the French Communist counterculture are found in Annie Kriegel's *Les Communistes français* (Paris: Seuil, 1968) and Ronald Tiersky's *Le Mouvement communiste en France: 1920-1970* (Paris: Fayard, 1973), Chapter 10.

[19] See, for the development of this point, Chapter 15 in this volume.

[20] Alberoni, *L'attivista*, p. 318.

When they spoke of their party's most important success, the French Communists were more likely to talk about the defense of the working class or the strength of the party's internal life. For example, a PCF mayor from eastern France saw the party's greatest success in "the formation of thousands upon thousands of militants . . . who strove to ameliorate the conditions of the workers." Another mayor said simply: "Our greatest success? De Gaulle is gone and we are still here." And a third mayor said, "It is the best organized party. . . . There is fraternal solidarity from the base to the summit."

Responding to the same question, the majority of Italian Communists spoke of the PCI's contributions to the Italian political *system*. For example, one PCI mayor thought the party's greatest success was "being in touch with the real problems of the masses, and having elaborated an original, Italian route to socialism." And another mayor said, "Having carried out a policy of unity which has permitted us to avoid being isolated and has inserted us into the center of Italian social life." A third mayor said, "Having given a determining contribution to the struggle for the affirmation of democracy and for structural reform in our country."

The PCI's concern with its contribution to the Italian political system has been seen by some as a betrayal of socialist values, and by others as an expression of anxiety—especially over the past few years—lest the country sink back into reaction.[21] Whatever the reason, when Italian Communists speak about their party, it is more frequently an outward-looking pride that emerges; when French Communists talk with pride about the PCF, it is more often in terms of its internal life or its organic links with the proletariat. Only 14 percent of the French Communists spoke of their party's contribution to the country, compared to 62 percent of the Italians. (These differences can be seen in the left-hand column of Table 3.)

Non-Communist Contacts and Communications

If the PCI mayors have a more outward-looking attitude to politics than their PCF comrades they are also more thoroughly exposed to non-Communist channels of communication. These differences are also revealed in Table 3, where we compare the

[21] For the former view see Carl E. Boggs, Jr., "The Transformation of Italian Communism" (Ph.D. Dissertation, University of California at Berkeley, 1970).

aspects of political involvement that *transcend* party boundaries for the Communist mayors in each country. First of all, when asked to list the newspapers or magazines they regularly read, two-thirds of the PCF mayors named only Communist or Communist-inspired sources, compared to one-quarter of the Italians. The PCI mayors were more likely to mention media sources of more than one ideological hue, or a number of newspapers, some partisan and others nonpartisan. Over two-thirds of the Italians fell into this combined category, compared to only two-fifths of the Frenchmen.

TABLE 3. Aspects of Political Involvement that Transcend Party Boundaries, by Party

	Perception of Party's Success as Contribution to the Country (%)	Exposure to Both Communist and Non-Communist Press (%)	Contacts with Leaders of all Local Parties (%)	Contacts with National Legislators from Other Parties (%)
PCF (21)	14	39	5	35
PCI (30)	62	69	80	73

It is surprising that, in so literate a country as France, the PCF mayors claimed to be doing so little reading. Many said their reading consisted entirely of *L'Humanité, L'Humanité-Dimanche, La Terre* or left-wing regional papers like *L'Écho du centre* or the *Marseillaise.* The Italian mayors almost all mentioned the party daily, *L'Unità,* but also frequently mentioned were other journals on the left and various non-Communist regional newspapers.[22] To some French Communists, the reading of the party press appeared to be almost a sacred rite. Several recalled the very year they had begun to subscribe to *L'Humanité,* while others said pointedly, "I do not buy any non-Communist newspapers." The Italian mayors named more newspapers, of a wider ideological provenance, and seemed to regard their reading in a more casual and less ritualized fashion.

Second, in terms of their local political contacts, a large majority of the PCI mayors reported regular contacts with representatives of the other parties, while the PCF mayors more commonly asserted that they see only their own party leaders, the

[22] The Italian findings are supported by Alberoni, *L'attivista,* p. 289.

leaders of ideologically neighboring groups or *no party leaders at all* (this latter response came mostly from isolated villages). Five percent of the PCF mayors, compared to 80 percent in Italy, claimed to have contacts with representatives of all the local political parties. We cannot tell much from these findings about the *quality* of interaction between PCI mayors and local representatives of non-Communist parties. Their "contacts" may consist of pragmatic political exchange or of shouting matches in which no goal other than propaganda is served.[23] But it is reasonable to suppose that interparty contact of whatever kind implies the possibility of accommodation at the level of local problems on which Communists and non-Communists may find common ground.

Paradoxically, observers have found that, as the political climate heats up, interparty contacts tend to increase for the PCI and to decrease even further for the PCF. The reason lies in the primordial anti-Fascist vocation of the PCI, and in the corporate working-class instincts of the PCF. When tension increases in Italy, the PCI instinctively calls up the symbol of interparty anti-Fascist resistance as a model for political action, even when the issues involved are economic and not fundamentally constitutional.[24] The PCF, in contrast, tends to meet both economic and constitutional crises in a class-oriented way, alienating possible allies on the non-Communist left as well as the bourgeoisie.

Third, the PCI mayors claimed a higher level of contact with national legislators from the non-Communist parties as well. Many PCI mayors cited evidence of their aggressive efforts to get help from non-Communist deputies, senators, and provincial councilors. One man said, "We never let any possibility escape us, and, when it is necessary, we take every possible avenue, even when this makes it difficult to tell who gave you the help that really counted in the long run." Over 70 percent of the Italian Communists interviewed said they had good relations with elected representatives of other parties. Of course, they preferred to use their own party's representatives to get help from Rome, but many referred to Socialists and others who had proved helpful. One mayor said, "To get 70 million lire for my

[23] The latter seemed to have been quite frequent in the municipal council "dialogue" described by Alan Stern in his "Local Political Elites and Economic Change" (Ph.D. Dissertation, Yale University, 1970).

[24] On the continuing anti-Fascist vocation of the PCI, see Chapter 15 in this volume.

community, I had the help of two Christian Democratic deputies. If I got the money right away, it was thanks to their interest." Another PCI mayor, admittedly a single case, went even further. He said, "When it's a question of getting to a minister or some other high personality in the government, we do it through the local priests, who have better access to certain Christian Democratic personalities than the deputies do."

Only a third of the French Communists said they had contacts with representatives from other political parties and, of these, several spoke not of the representative's goodwill but of the political harm they could do him if he refused to help. "They [the deputies] have no interest in having the municipality fail to work properly," said one. "In that case we would show the population whose fault it was and organize demonstrations against them." The majority of the PCF mayors said that their opponents could not, or would not, help them in Paris. One mayor said, "I wouldn't ask them, because then they would say that everything had been done because of their help." On the other hand, PCF mayors frequently claimed to get help from their canton's general councilor, whose membership in the *Conseil Général* of the department gives him privileged access to the prefect and to other departmental notables.

These contrasts reveal, once again, how the complex interaction between the properties of the French and Italian political systems and the characteristics of each Communist party produce different patterns of political involvement at the local level. If the PCF mayors are more deeply insulated by the communications subculture of their own party, this expresses, in part, the greater survival of a proletarian counterculture in the PCF but it also reflects the greater cleavages within the Left in France than in Italy. If the Italian mayors have more extensive contacts with the representatives of other parties than the French, it is owing to their more open partisan posture, but it is also because the other Italian parties are more open to local collaboration with them than in France. Institutional differences play a role, too. The majority-list electoral system in French local elections was designed to encourage anti-Communist coalitions and to limit the role of organized parties in local administration, while the Italian proportional system in communes of over 5,000 population reflects more of the true strength of the PCI in the electorate.

In their ties with national politicians, the Communist mayors

156

are also at the intersection between forces within their own parties and in the political system in general. If the PCF mayors are more diffident about contacts with non-Communist legislators, it is as much owing to the weakness of the legislative institutions of the Fifth Republic and to the hostility of potential allies in Paris as to their own sectarian insulation and political closure. And if the French Communists perceive their party's successes more in terms of the maintenance of a counterculture than in terms of its contributions to the political system, this reflects not only the more sectarian orientations of the PCF, but also the fact that its failures in the political system have been all too obvious. In other words, while the differences between these two groups of mayors are clear and important ones, they inevitably reflect both the general strategic directions of each party and the different objective conditions in which each one operates.

The more important question lies not in the origins of the differences we have sketched, but in their consequences. If the Italian Communists have a more outward-looking notion of their party's function, a broader exposure to non-Communist communications, and a wider range of party contacts than their PCF comrades, this cannot fail to have important results for their integration into the political system as a whole and, not incidentally, for their ability to capture resources from it for their communities. It is perhaps for this reason that, of the more than 8,000 Italian communes, about 800, or 10 percent of the total, have Communist-run administrations. In France, in contrast, only about 3 percent of the more than 37,000 communes have Communist mayors, a figure that is dramatically lower than the proportion of adult Frenchmen who vote for the PCF in national elections.[25] The Gaullist electoral system and the hostility of the non-Communist parties in France no doubt account for some of the local weakness of the PCF. But it seems a plausible hypothesis that the political closure, the surviving myth of proletarian hegemony and the resistance to political contacts of the PCF local elite also account for some of these differences. This will be illustrated dramatically when we turn to the public aspects of the French and Italian Communist mayors' roles, and especially their relationship to the electorate.

[25] The Italian data are from PCI, *Dati sulla organizzazione del partito* (Rome: PCI, 1971), p. 125; the figures on the number of French Communist administrations are from *Est et ouest* 7 (March 1-15, 1971): 123.

157

Representative and Electoral Roles

Despite their Leninist provenance, both the PCI and the PCF have taken on the burden of election campaigns with great energy. Even in districts in which there is little hope of success, Communist lists can usually be found and, even in the most apolitical villages, Communist candidates hold election meetings—sometimes to empty halls. This can have an extremely positive function for the local democratic process; if not for the Communists stimulating debate and criticizing the incumbent administration, many small communes in both countries might soon give up local election campaigns altogether and sink into the uncontested hegemony of the incumbent administration, whatever its political coloration.

But when we turn to the attitudes of the Communist mayors toward election campaigns, we quickly observe some fundamental differences in the gusto with which the French and Italians approach the electoral contest. The PCF mayors give the impression of turning from administration and party work to campaign activity mostly as a duty. Only 40 percent of the French Communists said they enjoyed election campaigns "a great deal." Several complained that campaigns "get the people all worked up," and one mayor said that during the campaign "all kinds of shots are permitted." A third complained that as a candidate he was forced to drink too much; and a fourth, that elections embarrass him in his relations with non-Communist friends. "I cannot say that I run after election campaigns," said a fifth PCF mayor.

The reasons given for disliking election campaigns were various, but generally turned on their lack of relevance to the problems of local administration. "The campaign," said one PCF mayor, "should be carried on during the six years of an administration's mandate—that's the best campaign." Another complained of television, which takes the people's interest out of local politics. Even the PCF mayors who claimed to enjoy campaigning sounded more like classical Leninist combatants than seasoned politicians. When asked why he liked election campaigns, one French Communist answered: "Because it's hot. You fight against the others, there are enormous numbers of people around you. You discuss, the crowd bubbles over, everybody is disputing. When there is opposition, it's better then, for you can win.

158

. . . But when there is no opposition, it's still hot, you can still struggle."

In the Italian interviews, 70 percent of the mayors claimed to like electoral campaigns a great deal. Some simply liked mingling with the voters. One PCI mayor said: "Going door to door, factory to factory, you get to touch reality like it really is; to understand and to feel the real problems of the people." Others spoke of the feeling of interaction with opponents. "We go to the homes of people who think differently than we do," said one, "and we are always well received there."

However, most of the Italian Communists felt positively about campaigning for essentially *systemic* reasons. One PCI mayor said: "They [elections] are an element of confrontation between different positions and of verification before the citizens and before the other political forces." Another Italian put the same point more abstractly. "Electoral campaigns," he said, "are a continuing sign of democratic maturity, because they give scope to a free exchange of ideas in which it can be shown that there is no longer the degree of intolerance that there once was for the ideas of your opponents." As another Italian Communist said, "People just don't follow political life very closely. It's therefore essential that they be activated at least during the forty days of the election campaign." There can be no greater contrast to the PCF mayors, who felt that local election campaigns were not useful because people are not interested.

Is it simply electioneering that the PCI mayors seem to enjoy, or is it contact with the public in general? When asked about the meetings they hold for their constituents *apart from* electoral campaigns, more than half of the Italian Communists claimed to have organized three or more meetings over the past year, and very few said they had organized no meetings at all. In France, in contrast, only 10 percent of the mayors claimed to have organized three or more nonelectoral meetings over the past year, while 40 percent said they had organized no meetings at all. Communication with constituents appeared to be more formalized and impersonal than in Italy. As one PCF mayor said: "We put out a municipal bulletin, with not too much information in it. If we organized meetings, very few people would come."

In both countries, reporting on past activities and consulting the people with respect to new ones were the major reasons given

159

for organizing meetings. And, in both countries, great stress was placed on bringing the people into the decision-making process. This was more common on the Italian side, however, where the mayors more frequently spoke of organizing people in individual neighborhoods on a permanent basis, and of using these meetings to "escape" the bureaucratic atmosphere of the *municipio*. As one Italian mayor said, "I stay in this office as little as possible, and I'm glad we're pushing for a policy of administrative decentralization. My contacts with the citizens, and the meetings and assemblies we hold, get me out of the city hall fairly frequently." The French mayors also spoke of the party's policies of bringing the people into local government. That this has not been an easy task is reflected in the comments of one PCF mayor in an interview in the Communist press. "Democracy is tiring," he said. "It is much easier to sit in your office. . . . It's tiring, but it is necessary."[26]

The Italian mayors appeared to enjoy their contacts with the public during *and* between elections and both inside and outside the party. "During the campaign," said one mayor, "there is a climate of festivity, like a public outing. The contact with the people, the warmth, the human relations are all like a party, favored by the fact that in our country there is a great civilization, even among our opponents." Internal party relationships were not neglected either. For instance, one mayor said, "My personal experiences and satisfactions are united with those of the party." But, more commonly for the PCI mayors, the goals of the party were combined with the satisfactions of contact with the public. For example, when asked to talk about his most satisfying personal experience, one PCI mayor said, "That of being mayor . . . because it allows me to be in a continuous dialectical relation to the masses, continually being judged by them and, at the same time, it permits me to be useful to the party."

The French mayors, in contrast, were diffident to interpersonal contacts *outside* the party, but this diffidence was not at all evident with respect to internal party relationships. Indeed, when discussing intraparty contacts, the French Communists would often warm to the theme. In the PCF, said one mayor, "there is a fraternal entente from the summit to the base." Another said, "I have never felt so free as within my party. I think that that's

[26] Hincker, "Une Municipalité," p. 18.

where liberty is." A PCF municipal councilor, denying that the party was a kind of isolated political ghetto, rejoined, "No, it's the fellow who *thinks* of himself as a Communist, who *declares* himself to be a Communist, but who fails to militate within its ranks, who is enclosed in a kind of a ghetto." When they spoke of contact with the public, the PCF mayors were far less enthusiastic. One mayor said, "It is hard to make everyone happy, and it's often among your own followers that you are most disappointed." Another said his greatest disappointment had been seeing that "the love one has for the public good is not sufficiently felt by the citizens." "Politics," said another PCF mayor, "it is not a beautiful thing."

In part, we may be sure, these differences in orientation to contact with the public result from the contrasting nature of French and Italian society. In France—especially in small towns—people mix socially far less than in Italy, where a more verbal, interpersonal culture persists. In France, private ideological conviction and written forms of political communication often take the place of the stroll in the town square, the frequent meetings in bars, and the generally more vocal character of community life in Italy. But, in large part, the cause must also lie in the divergent social strategies of the two parties. The PCI has made the linchpin of its strategy a *presence* throughout the structures of Italian society, while the PCF—with its myth of proletarian hegemony and more classbound organization—has evolved a more selective social presence.

Once again, it is the consequences of the differences we have outlined that seem most important. The more positive orientation of the Italian mayors toward public contacts and election campaigns may be largely a function of the character of Italian political culture; but it certainly cannot hurt a mass party of the Left that wishes to transform from within the institutions of an advanced capitalist society. Conversely, the PCF may well reflect some of the peculiarities of French culture when its militants show little inclination to organize public meetings or to campaign enthusiastically for office. But regardless of its origins, this factor may have retarded the emergence of the PCF as a modern, truly mass party of the Left. The PCF may be entirely sincere in its desire to transform itself into a vital, flexible, democratic organization. What our evidence points to is a weakness in the

161

potential of some of its local officeholders to implement this strategy and make it work for the party at the local level. These differences in what we may now call the potential for a new politics of the two Communist parties can best be illustrated by the roles the two groups of local officials take with respect to the state.

The Claims of Public Office

The roles of a local public official are complex.[27] On the one hand, he may be part of a partisan subculture, and we have seen that—whatever the differences—this is the fundamental allegiance of both French and Italian Communist mayors. Secondly, he relates to the electorate and to the rest of the political class through public activities that are more or less oriented to success in the political arena. These orientations and allegiances, as we have seen, are more fully developed among the Italian Communists and mesh more completely with both the nature of the PCI partisan subculture and the free-wheeling character of Italian political life in general. It is when we turn to their roles in public offices that we begin to understand more fully the contours of the French Communists' orientations to their roles. The PCF mayors appear, along every dimension, more experienced at their jobs, more fully committed to local administration, and more accepting of the norms of local administration that are established by the state and reinforced by the agencies of French field administration than the Italians.

The evidence for this difference is remarkably clear. We saw earlier that the Italian Communists had longer and more diversified experience in the party organization than their French comrades. The French, in contrast, reported longer and more specialized experience in local government. Sixty-five percent had been elected to the city council before 1958, compared to only 30 percent in Italy. Many had had additional experience as cantonal general councilors, a position which gives a French mayor direct access to the allocation of resources at the departmental

[27] For the most elaborate treatment to date of the complexity of roles and commitments of local public officials in America, see Heinz Eulau and Kenneth Prewitt, *Labyrinths of Democracy: Adaptations, Linkages, Representation, and Policies in Urban Politics* (Indianapolis: Bobbs-Merrill, 1973).

level. The more politically active Italians did not have this concerted kind of experience in local and provincial administration. For example, only 25 percent of the PCI mayors reported maintaining at least moderately frequent relations with administrative officials at the provincial level (prefects, prefectoral officials, agents of the central ministries), compared to 40 percent in France. As one French mayor said, "One could not say that our contacts with members of the administration were bad. They are representatives of the state . . . but they don't create any obstructions." Another PCF mayor said of administrators: "There is no systematic opposition on their part, but they are forced by the government to apply the orders they get."

Not only were the PCF mayors more experienced in local administration than the Italians; they appeared to be as aggressive in their demands on administrators as the Italians had been in their contacts with non-Communist politicians. For instance, one French mayor said, "We have good relations with the prefect to the extent that we fight and get the population to go along with us. If we stuck to the letter of the law, the present policies of the government would not favor us. The best we can do is to collect petitions and go to the Prefecture or to the ministries." Another PCF mayor said of potential disagreements between local leaders and state functionaries: "It is the mayor who wins because he is willing to struggle." One French Communist told of having threatened a minister with resignation if he was not helped in his plans for his community, and another told of threatening legal action if his request for funds was not processed at once. The PCI mayors appeared to be more cynical and pessimistic about the possibility of getting cooperation from the state. Their attitude was not so much critical of particular personalities in the bureaucracy as of the bureaucratic system as a whole. As one Italian Communist said: "The prefecture is only the wheel of a cart that travels with rusty axles."

Third, PCF mayors who were interviewed had more positive attitudes toward their role in local administration than their PCI counterparts, as could be seen in their remarks on their most agreeable political experiences. Whereas half the Italian Communists spoke of satisfying experiences they had had in party life (only one-fifth in France), half the French mayors spoke of agreeable experiences in local administration (compared to one-

163

third in Italy). An extreme, but not unrepresentative, French example follows:

> Q. What was your most agreeable political experience?
> A. The meeting of the Council when I was elected mayor. I was so surprised, I was so happy. . . . And then my daughter came home from school saying, "Papa, they say in the village that you are the new mayor. Is it true?" . . . For me it was something historic.

For this French Communist, becoming mayor had been the most important event in his life.

A more typical response, in France, emphasized particular policy successes or initiatives the mayor had taken in local government. One mayor said: "My satisfactions have been at the level of the projects I have initiated." Another said he had been most pleased by "putting in installations that will be appreciated by the people; street lights to begin with." A third tried to combine his Marxist formation with his administrative preferences. When asked what had been his most satisfying experience in public life, he said, "I like the material aspects of the work because I am a materialist. Things like getting sidewalks put in."

It could not be said that the Italian Communists had anything like this kind of appreciation of the joys of administration. For example, in discussing their most disagreeable political experiences, *half* the PCI mayors mentioned aspects of their work as mayors, compared to less than one-tenth in France. One Italian mayor said: "As a mayor, I have had perhaps only one negative experience—having succeeded in finding out about the system, and having discovered the existence of so many walls that can't be penetrated." Another said: "Being inside this administrative machine, you see so much corruption." A third said his most unhappy experience had been learning about "the bureaucratic routine you have to follow as mayor. . . . You fill out and send off the application today, but they build your road three years from now."

There were many French Communists who expressed distaste for the administrative routine as well. But the comparison is instructive; the Italians more often show a *general* dissatisfaction with administration and, particularly, with their failure to realize their party's goals through local public office. A forceful example is the following PCI mayor's response:

Q. What has been your most disagreeable political experience?

A. Seeing all that needs to be done and being unable to do anything. Because you are only a little reality. Because the state suffocates your autonomy. Being fooled by continual promises that are not kept, and you can't solve the people's problems because you don't have the money. Seeing the people leaving the countryside; watching them emigrate because you, as mayor, as a municipality, are little and you can't do anything.

The French mayors who spoke negatively about administration most often mentioned the failure of a specific project, a personal attack against themselves, or a disappointment with some specific aspect of administration. They give the impression of being willing administrators who wish they could administer under better conditions. "We do not suffer from being a Communist commune," said one, "but from being a French commune."

Third, the PCF mayors appeared to accept—or at least to respect—the norms of *apolitisme* and good apolitical management that are widespread among non-Communist French local officials.[28] The Italian Communist mayors are totally part of the partisan subculture of Italian life, and are affected very little by the normative culture of local administration. The French Communists, with their more specialized careers in local government, give the impression of sharing with other French mayors the norms of a dense administrative subculture alongside the values of party loyalty and militance that they share with other Communists.

A distinction of this kind is difficult to document, but some evidence for it comes from the mayors' perceptions of the causes of the most important changes in their communes during the past few years. Like good Marxists, many of the Communist mayors assigned the responsibility for such changes to underlying social or economic forces. However, this kind of response was almost three times as frequent in Italy (43 percent) as in France (15 percent). Forty percent of the French mayors saw the agent of change in the state (only 20 percent in Italy) and 35 percent saw

---

[28] The most incisive treatment of the culture of *apolitisme* in French local administration is Mark Kesselman's *The Ambiguous Consensus* (New York: Knopf, 1967).

165

it in the actions of their administrations (against 23 percent in Italy). In their emphasis on the importance of the state, the French mayors are simply registering a reality—the reality of France's stronger administrative tradition—but it is also possible that they are more deeply involved in an administrative subculture that directs their attention toward the state superstructure rather than toward the economic base or the structures of civil society.

In some ways, the PCF mayors sounded much like the non-Communist mayors who were interviewed in France. They placed a great emphasis on their concrete administrative achievements, and very little on gaining political benefits from their activity. For example, when asked what he liked about the job of mayor, a French Communist said, "I like everything about the work. . . . You struggle and you can see the results of the work that you accomplish." Many contrasted this with the kind of work a deputy does. Other French Communists stressed the impartiality necessary to being a good local administrator. In response to a question about the most important attributes of a good mayor, the French Communists said:

. . . loving administration;

. . . being faithful to your word . . . being an administrator for everybody;

. . . not being sectarian; accepting everybody. . . . He must be the mayor of the whole population;

. . . avoiding every particularism, not making any distinctions among the voters.

One PCF mayor even recalled that a local aristocrat had personally recognized his honesty and impartiality after the Liberation, when the mayor distributed a precious stock of gasoline impartially and fairly. " 'You are honest and straight,' the baron said to me," he reported.

In answer to the same question, the Italian Communists often mentioned personal characteristics also, but they were more likely to turn to the implementation of their party's programs. For example, in response to the question about the aspect of the job he liked best, one PCI mayor said: "It's a way of occupying

166

myself actively in politics, because it permits me to make clear with my acts and my choices my conception, and that of my party, of how to direct the commune." Another Italian Communist said he liked his job because "in that way I can contribute in a useful way to bringing my party closer to the masses. For me, being mayor is also a political struggle." And while personal qualities like honesty, seriousness, perseverance, good will, and a spirit of sacrifice were mentioned by several PCI mayors, the emphasis on impartial administrative qualities that we observed in France was seldom found in the Italian interviews.

Underlying these contrasts are some obvious differences in French and Italian politics which may help to explain them. Just as the Italian Communists' stress on political exchange with voters and other political groups has to be seen in the context of a party system that is more locally vital and more bound up in the life of the community, the French Communists' stronger orientation to public office cannot be separated from France's stronger administrative tradition, and from a state which has greater influence over local government, the economy, and private associations. If the Italian Communists are more attuned to the game of local compromise and alliances, that may simply be necessary to capture resources for their communities in an administrative system characterized by personalism and shady practices, while the French mayors are more integrated in the norms and activities of the administrative subculture in France for the very same motivations. The patterns of adaptation differ; the motives for adaptation may be the same.

But it would be wrong to regard these differing patterns of adaptation in wholly instrumental terms. After all, the French party system—and the Communist party more than most—is profoundly influenced by the French Jacobin heritage, one which, if it accords no legitimacy to the present regime, is nevertheless deeply instilled with the values of central control of the administration. In Italy, the Left has little historical dedication to the values of centralization, if only because the revolutionary moments in Italian life have all been provincial or autonomist in inspiration. These contrasts can be seen in the different attitudes of the PCF and the PCI toward regional government. The Italian Communists share with their political opponents an enthusiasm for regional devolution of almost any sort; the French Commu-

167

nists are far more circumspect.[29] As Peter Gourevitch writes, "In Italy, the existence of an anti-Roman, localist tradition on the Left facilitates the development of a locally-oriented strategy in the postwar period when objective conditions encouraged it. In France, the historical-ideological identification of the Left with centralization discourages the development of such a strategy."[30]

Moreover, and this is the important point, whether adaptation to these different patterns of local political and administrative life is instrumental or ideological, it could only with difficulty be maintained over a period of years without bringing about an *institutional* adaptation of each party's local representatives that goes far beyond the traditional tactic of *noyautage*. The two groups of Communist local activists whom we have studied in this chapter have both adapted to the bourgeois political system in which they operate, but the Italians have adapted almost as political entrepreneurs, wheeling and dealing among their non-Communist counterparts, and, it would seem, in close touch with the electorate, while their PCF comrades have adapted primarily to administrative roles which stress concrete achievements and contacts with administrators, and tend to play down the role of the broader public between the party and the state.

Administrative and Partisan Roles: Some Convergences and Contradictions

The consequences of these differences in partisan and administrative roles are many, but, in closing, several may be stressed that are particularly close to the themes that have been canvassed during this analysis.

First, the PCF local official—to the extent that our interviews are a valid guide—has a simpler set of roles and commitments to reconcile than the Italian. His specialization in local public office puts him, particularly in smaller communities, only infrequently in touch with the party organization. He gets his general ideological signals from the party press and—where one exists—from

[29] For a more detailed discussion of this point, see my "Local Constraints on Regional Reform: A Comparison of Italy and France," in *Comparative Politics* 7 (October 1974).

[30] "Reforming the Napoleonic State: The Creation of Regional Government in France and Italy" (Cambridge, Mass.: West European Studies Working Paper no. 16, February 1973). I am grateful to the author for allowing me to quote from this unpublished paper.

the local party section,[31] and he lacks the involvement in the party organization that might create conflicts between his role as a man of the apparatus and an unbiased representative of the local general will.

But the same pattern of specialization creates a gap between the PCF mayor's partisan commitment—which, as we have seen, is sectarian and inward-looking—and his orientations to public office, which are heavily influenced by the administrative subculture in which he is engaged. This creates the danger that local public office may be used only to show that the party is impartial and efficient, while its local policy goals are honored only in the abstract. Indeed, despite their more sectarian pattern of partisan involvement, it was the French mayors who stressed local projects which would distribute benefits more or less evenly among the population. They seldom spoke of far-reaching structural reforms at the local level, nor were they enthusiastic about cooperating with other municipalities in their region to overcome the subservience of local government to the state.

But if there seems to be a contradiction here between sectarian partisan involvement and apolitical administration, it is not one which often impinges on the actual political behavior of the French mayors. The reason, of course, lies in the centralization of French Communist decision-making, and in the minimal role that the party's strategy assigns to a widespread social and political presence at the community level. The French Communist mayor can be both a sectarian partisan and an apolitical administrator because local political creativity and initiative have played so unimportant a role in his party's strategy, at least until the very recent past.

This is the great challenge of the French party's recent policy of cautious *ouverture* at the local level; if it involves its militants in a network of self-generating relationships with non-Communists and encourages them to express their policy preferences in local government, the contradiction between sectarian partisanship and apolitical administration will become more meaningful, as local activists begin to seek a more important role. As long as party leaders succeed in dealing with such episodes through a determined "explanatory pedagogy,"[32] the danger may

[31] For the linkages between local officials and party sections at the local level, see Denis Lacorne, Chapter 8 in this volume.
[32] Ibid., pp. 315-320.

169

not be great, but, then, neither will the amount of change in the cloistered inner life of the PCF.

The Italian Communists have a broader network of roles and commitments to reconcile than their French comrades. They are at once party activists, organizational officials, public figures, and political entrepreneurs who must manipulate a number of potential sources of support—both party and nonparty—to capture resources for their communes. There is no doubt that they manage to extract more than their share of resources from the state. For example, a larger proportion of the Italian Communist municipalities' revenues come from loans and grants received from the state for capital investment than was the case in the Communist-run communities in France. The PCF mayors may be more integrated into the administrative subculture of France; the PCI mayors appear to invest more heavily in administrative infrastructure and to prefer projects with more potential to change the life of the community. As one PCI mayor said, "Any functionary can get public works constructed—to do so is only to use your power on behalf of the state. What interests me is . . . local administration as a center of popular power."

But it follows that the Italian Communists' need to reconcile public and partisan commitments creates a greater sense of contradiction between their partisan and their public involvements. Many PCI mayors spoke of their discomfort and personal anguish at the contradictions involved in holding both partisan and administrative roles. One PCI mayor shouted, in frustration, when asked about the aspect of his job that he liked least: "We are forced to administer poverty!" Another said, "The drama, for a mayor, is to receive people in your office who don't even have enough to eat . . . and for these people you can only provide charity, that is, if you are lucky." Several mayors even showed distaste for their own offices, and one pointed to the "lack of human warmth that there is in this office." Another PCI mayor confided: "I have even gotten to the point of not coming to my office sometimes, so that I won't have to say to somebody, 'I'm sorry.'" Another Italian Communist spoke of the difficulty, for a PCI officeholder, of "preserving above all the characteristic of being a man apart—that is, the representative of a working-class party, being a part of the working class."

It is perhaps owing to the frustrations of this dual commitment —to the party organization which has nourished him and to the public office he holds on its behalf—that the PCI mayor turns with more passion than his French comrade to the world of electoral politics and to contact with the public as a whole. Throughout the interviews, the Italian Communists stressed over and over the importance of interpersonal contacts in making a heavily bureaucratic system work. One mayor said the most important aspect of his job was "keeping open continuous contacts with everyone—the population, the *giunta*, the city council." Others spoke of the warmth of contacts with the public, in sharp contrast to the gray and passionless world of the bureaucracy. The French mayors also frequently spoke of the need to maintain contacts with the population, but they spoke more often of contacts within the official parameters of their office, and of the concrete achievements they could offer to the people. One PCF mayor said: "To be mayor so that I can preside over banquets? No. To be mayor so that I can do something for the people? Yes!"

This takes us back to the question posed at the outset. In recent years, both the French and the Italian parties have stressed the opening up of the party's life at the base, the deconcentration of national governmental authority to the provinces, and the decentralization of local government from the city hall to the people. In both countries, conscious efforts have been made to implement this more "participationist" line of action. But we have found some differences in the two groups of local officials, differences which affect the capacity of a party to carry out a policy of grass-roots democratization at the base. Very few PCF mayors spoke with any fervor of the pleasures or benefits of electoral consultation—except as a verification of administrative successes already enjoyed; almost none spoke of the desire to decentralize local administration; and, during a period which had recently seen the defeat of the Gaullist referendum on the regions, none at all urged the creation of new regional institutions that would break the iron grip of the prefecture over French local life. In Italy, in contrast, the passion of the PCI mayors for broad political contacts with the people was in marked contrast to their displeasure with their administrative responsibilities. Their enthusiasm for deconcentration of the national state and neighborhood decentralization of local government appeared as the desire to escape from administrative roles that allowed little scope for creativity or for the realization of their party's programs within existing local institutions.

171

Of course, the desire for broader political contacts and the experimentation with new modes of participation that has marked the Italian party at the local level during the past few years are also supported by what we know of the PCI's strategy as a whole: more outward-looking and flexible, and less marked by a "totalistic" model of individual involvement than seems to have been the case in the past. Both the open quality of political involvement in the PCI and the character of the Italian bureaucratic system of local administration combine, from either side, to encourage the Italian Communist mayors to develop their contacts with non-Communist politicians and to stimulate the participation at the base that is less a part of the French Communist mayors' desires and potentialities. The contradictions between the PCI mayors' greater involvement in the party subculture and their repulsion from their public roles finds its outlet in the role of the mayor as representative of the people and as a member of a highly entrepreneurial and active local political class.

But these characteristics of the PCI mayors' roles—so formidable a tool in the party's policy of stimulating new modes of participation at the base—are not without disadvantages. As is the case throughout the network of Italian Communist presence in Italian society, the PCI mayor must utilize a large range of contacts and influences just to achieve meager administrative successes that he would be able to achieve through the ordinary mechanisms of the state administration were these to function efficiently. The PCF mayor, whose greater adaptation to the norms of local administration we have stressed above, can use the resources of the state—however unwilling they are proffered —to service the community he administers, while the PCI mayor must use a considerable portion of his time and energy developing contacts and mobilizing the public to achieve the same result. Thus, the PCI must use its local resources to their capacity in its day-to-day routine activities, while the PCF can conserve its resources for some future historical confrontation, which, it goes without saying, may never arrive.

V.

The Italian Communist Politician

ROBERT D. PUTNAM

Students of European radicalism in this century have been mesmerized by two events that bracketed the First World War: the decision of the German Social Democrats in 1914 to vote credits to finance the Kaiser's war, thus formalizing the domestication of Marxism that had been occurring in Western Europe during the previous several decades; and the seizure of power by Lenin's Bolsheviks in 1917, consummating a violent revolution led by a sectarian, "vanguard" party. Throughout the subsequent decades our interpretations of radical politicians have oscillated between the two poles symbolized by these events. Activists and leaders claiming to want revolutionary social change have been forced into one or the other of two conceptual boxes. The first, labeled "Social Democrats," is peopled by politicians whose revolutionary fervor has cooled to the merely verbal level and whose commitment to "the system" is no longer in question. The second, labeled "Bolsheviks," contains those who, while awaiting a propitious moment for violently subverting the institutions of bourgeois democracy, remain closed within a conspiratorial community of true believers.

In most discussions of the changing characteristics of parties and politicians of the European Left these two ideal types—the Bolshevik and the Social Democrat—have anchored the ends of a single dimension of "revisionism." As suggested in Figure 1, a common view has been that there is a strong tendency over time for radicals to slide or sidle from the Bolshevik pole toward the Social Democratic pole, in a process of integration into the constitutional regimes in which these politicians and parties are operating. There has been much dispute about the location along this dimension of particular parties or politicians at particular times, but nearly all the disputants have accepted this unilinear theoretical framework as a basis for interpreting both continuity and change.

173

FIG. 1. Varieties of Radicalism: A One-Dimensional View

"Bolsheviks"   "Social Democrat"

(revolutionary)   (reformist)

My argument here will be instead that however well these conceptual categories may have served to sort out the varieties of
radicals who have thronged through the first half of this century,
they will do no longer. The orthodox interpretive framework obscures certain crucial distinctions and hence hampers efforts to
understand the realities of contemporary European radicalism.
The idea of a single dimension stretching from the fanatic, revolutionary Leninists to the reformist, domesticated Social Democrats obscures the distinction between socioeconomic values,
goals, and policies, on the one hand, and political values, procedures, and habits, on the other.

FIG. 2. Varieties of Radicalism: A Two-Dimensional View

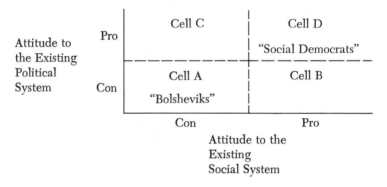

Figure 2 offers a tentative two-dimensional interpretation
based on this distinction between orientations to the socioeconomic system and orientations to the political system.[1] In Cell A

---

[1] For the sake of simplicity of exposition in this introductory formulation
I treat these dimensions as if they were dichotomous, "either-or" variables,
although in fact both the orthodox view and my alternative proposal should
properly be phrased in continuous, "more-or-less" terms.

Pio Uliassi offers an analogous distinction between "the 'transfer' and the
'goal' cultures of revolutionary movements—the code of conduct or grand

are the "Bolsheviks," hostile both to any form of capitalism and to the norms of constitutional democracy. In Cell D are the "Social Democrats," fundamentally committed both to the existing socioeconomic order and to the existing political order. The orthodox interpretation sketched in earlier paragraphs assumes that only these two cells are populated, that—in the language of statistics—political values and socioeconomic values are perfectly correlated. But whereas there may be some empirical correlation of this sort, it is dangerous to make this a logical or definitional assumption, for such an assumption would blind us to the possibility that politicians and parties might be radical on one of these dimensions but not on the other. For example, the orthodox view excludes by definition the possibility that Cell C might be occupied, that is, that parties or politicians could be committed to genuinely radical socioeconomic change within the framework of constitutional politics. An analyst using the orthodox model would systematically misinterpret "constitutional radicals" of this variety. Labeling them "Social Democrats" would obscure the sweeping character of their socioeconomic objectives, while labeling them "Bolsheviks" would obscure the conventionalism of their politics. That all socioeconomic radicals are political revolutionaries and that all nonrevolutionaries are merely reformist in terms of socioeconomic policy ought to be, at best, an empirical discovery rather than a definitional assumption.

My immediate objective in this chapter is to sketch an empirically based composite portrait of Communist politicians in Italy. Doing justice to the subject requires us to move from the one-dimensional world of Figure 1 toward the more complex world of Figure 2. In the conclusion, I will consider some of the broader implications of these findings for our understanding of communism in contemporary Italy.

The evidence in this chapter comes from several related studies I have conducted over the last several years on various elements in the Italian political class. The first of these studies (and for our present purposes the most useful) was based on intensive interviews conducted in 1968 with a random sample of 83 members of the Chamber of Deputies, including 20 members of

---

strategy designed to change a social system and the utopian image of what is to replace the established social order," in his "Communism in Western Europe," in Dan N. Jacobs (ed.), *The New Communisms* (New York: Harper & Row, 1969), p. 283.

the Partito Comunista Italiano (PCI). (Methodological details of this study are available elsewhere, and I shall not repeat them here.)[2] A second sample of 58 *deputati* (including 11 Communists) was interviewed in 1970. In the same year we interviewed a sample of 109 regional councilors (including 30 Communists) in Lombardia, Emilia-Romagna, Lazio, Puglia, and Basilicata. We have not yet completed analysis of the open-ended, or conversational, parts of these last two sets of interviews, but in this chapter I shall draw occasionally on responses to written questionnaires completed during the interviews.

All these respondents were, formally speaking, legislators, but the studies did not deal with legislative behavior in a strict sense. Rather, they focused on how these men and women conceive the world of politics and their own role in it. Nor were the original studies aimed primarily at understanding communism in Italy. Hence, certain themes of special interest to students of communism were touched only in passing. Thus, for example, our evidence on party discipline, decision-making within the party, and attitudes to international affairs is not extensive. On the other hand, the fact that data are available for both Communist and non-Communist politicians makes this evidence particularly useful. For if we are to understand how (and, indeed, whether) the PCI is really a party *sui generis,* as some have claimed, we must distinguish between those characteristics unique to the Communists and those they share with other Italian politicians.[3]

---

[2] See my "Studying Elite Political Culture: The Case of 'Ideology,'" *American Political Science Review* 65 (1971): 651-681, and *The Beliefs of Politicians: Ideology, Conflict, and Democracy in Britain and Italy* (New Haven: Yale University Press, 1973). I have at several points in this paper paraphrased arguments made in the latter.

[3] For studies of the legislative behavior of Italian Communists, see Giorgio Galli and Alfonso Prandi, *Patterns of Political Participation in Italy* (New Haven: Yale University Press, 1970), pp. 255-301, and Franco Cazzola, "Consenso e opposizione nel parlamento italiano: Il ruolo del PCI," *Rivista italiana di scienza politica* 2 (1971). The inferential leap from my parliamentary samples to the leadership of the PCI as a whole is less hazardous than one might think, for there is considerable overlap in membership between the *gruppo parlamentare* and the leadership of the party organization. Slightly more than half of all members of the Central Committee since 1945 have been members of one house of Parliament or the other, in most cases the Chamber of Deputies. Fully 88 percent of the members of the *Direzione* have been members of Parliament as well. Looked at the other way around, over half the deputies in my samples have held major national or regional posts in the party organization. See F. Cervellati Cantelli et al., *L'Organizzazione partitica del PCI e della DC* (Bologna: Società Editrice

Motivation: The Zeal of Missionaries

To begin with motivations, the Communists seem more committed to a life of political activity and more comfortable in the world of politics. At the outset of each interview we asked, "What do you find most satisfying about your political activity? What would you miss most if you left politics today?" "It isn't an easy question," said one young working-class Communist, "I can't imagine an existence without being interested in political problems." "For me politics is a profession, it's life itself," said one of his colleagues from the Red Belt. "I'm not in politics to play games. I have dedicated my whole life to politics." "I believe that the most attractive aspect of politics lies precisely in considering it not a career, but a mission," explained a third.

As contrasted with non-Communists of both Left and Right, Communists define their satisfactions more often in terms of commitment to broad ideals and goals, less often in terms of opportunity for personal influence. And when asked about their dissatisfactions, Communists refer less frequently than others to the constraints of party discipline or to the climate of hostility and suspicion that envelops Italian public life. Rather, the Communists are more frustrated by the unproductiveness and inefficiency of the Italian Parliament and by the slowness of the pace of social reform.[4] One of the leaders of the *gruppo parlamentare* put this point quite clearly.

Il Mulino, 1968), p. 516, and Giovanni Sartori, *Il parlamento Italiano* (Napoli: Edizioni Scientifiche Italiane, 1963), p. 132. In order to make clear what characteristics of our Italian Communists are genuinely distinctive and what characteristics they share with other leftist politicians, I have usually presented relevant statistics broken down between the non-Communist Left and the Center/Right. In the case of the two 1970 studies it has not yet been practical to separate Christian Democrats into the left and right wings; hence, for those studies the non-Communists are divided into Socialists (of the Partito Socialista Italiano [PSI] and the Partito Socialista Italiano di Unità Proletaria [PSIUP]) and all others.

[4] I shall not provide detailed statistical evidence for each of the generalizations made in the text, although each is in fact based on quantitative analysis of our interviews. For example, 50 percent of the Communists specifically mentioned a life commitment to politics as contrasted to 10-15 percent in the other parties. Fifty-five percent of the Communists mentioned among their dissatisfactions the frustrations of not making progress toward solving social problems, whereas only 30 percent of the non-Communists made such a reference. On the other hand, 35 percent of the non-Communists complained about party discipline and 31 percent about the moral

177

Well, the least attractive aspect [of politics], I think, is represented by the great difficulties that one encounters in the political struggle as it is organized in Italy today—the effort that is necessary to reach even very modest results. . . . I don't deny, indeed I affirm that we've achieved—I'm speaking now not just as a Communist, but in general as a democratic citizen—we've achieved some important results, in the sense of the transformation of the country. . . . There have been results, measurable even from the individual point of view, that is, the improvement of the standard of living or, on another plane, the conservation and expansion of individual liberties. But certainly the general picture has not changed. . . . Sometimes one is inclined to reflect how difficult and sometimes even disappointing is this engagement that does not always yield results.

Yet despite these frustrations and despite their generally critical stance toward the existing institutions of Italian society, these Communists are, as we will see again later, more optimistic and less cynical about Italian politics than are their opponents. For four out of five of our Communist deputies the satisfactions of politics clearly outweigh the disappointments; among non-Communists the ratio is barely two out of five. In motivational terms Italian Communist politicians are men and women with a mission, frustrated by delays but content with their calling.

Marxist Ideologues in a Neocapitalist Society

In one important respect Communists and non-Communists share a common assessment of the problems of contemporary Italian society. For at both the national and the regional level there is broad agreement about what problems ought to be on the public agenda and even about their relative priority. Asked in 1968 to list "the three or four most important problems facing Italy today," deputies from all parties concurred in citing reform of the state, development of the Mezzogiorno, and the need to raise the standard of living of the poorer classes. Two years later we asked the newly elected regional councilors to rank the urgency of a series of public problems. There was, of course, some variation from region to region, and even within each

climate of Italian politics, whereas among the twenty Communists none cited the former as a source of dissatisfaction and only one cited the latter.

party. But across the sample as a whole the ranking by Communists was virtually identical to that by their opponents. Employment and economic development came at the top of the list, followed by education, health and hospital services, agricultural improvements, and housing. Environmental protection and urban transportation were ranked next, with crime and public order rated last.

Hardly less important than this basic agreement about the ills of the nation, however, is the fundamental difference between the diagnoses offered by Communists and non-Communists. PCI legislators systematically conceive these public problems in broader terms than their opponents and propose more radical solutions. One way of describing this contrast is in terms of differing styles of political analysis.

As I have discussed elsewhere, politicians differ systematically in the way they analyze policy problems.[5] These differences cluster along two principal dimensions. The first dimension, tapped in our data by an Ideological Style Index (ISI), reflects the fact that some politicians tend to discuss issues in abstract and deductive terms, referring with some frequency to specific doctrines and to more or less coherent social goals, whereas others "particularize" their discussions, reasoning inductively and concentrating on specific details of the immediate policy problem. The second dimension of political style, measured in these data in terms of an Index of Partisan Style (IPS), captures the fact that some politicians "moralize" their discussions of issues—attributing blame for the problems to specific groups or individuals—and defend their proposed solutions in terms of benefits or losses that will flow to specific social categories, whereas others refer instead to more "objective" criteria, such as technical practicality or administrative efficiency.

On these dimensions the style of Communist politicians is sharply more ideological and partisan than that of their opponents. Of the Communist deputies in the 1968 study, 85 percent

[5] See my "Studying Elite Political Culture." Each respondent's discussion of two specific issues was analyzed in terms of twelve "stylistic characteristics," such as the use of a historical context, inductive vs. deductive thinking, moralization, and reference to group benefits. Ratings of these stylistic characteristics are found to cluster in intelligible ways, and the Ideological Style Index and the Index of Partisan Style are based on the respondents' scores on the two dominant factors that emerge from a factor analysis of the intercorrelations among the stylistic characteristics.

rank above the national median on the ISI, as contrasted with 41 percent of the non-Communist Left and 37 percent of the Center and Right. Ninety percent of the Communists rank above the national average on the IPS, as compared to 26 percent of the non-Communist Left and 25 percent of the Center and Right. These statistics reflect the fact that when discussing concrete problems of public policy, deputies from the PCI employ the language and logic of Marxist analysis and adopt the stance of fervent defenders of the interests of the less privileged sections of Italian society. Communists are not blind to the details and peculiarities of such problems as urban transportation or regional poverty, but they see them not as technical problems of social management but as matters of underlying social structure and fundamental political choice.

One self-described revolutionary, a member of the party since 1924, recounted in painful detail his struggles with the Roman bureaucracy to gain military pensions for some of his constituents. "What are the causes of this problem?" I asked. "The origins are distant, but there is one fundamental reason—that those who have until now dominated social, economic, and political life in Italy have an interest in maintaining a State of this sort." Later when I raised the issue of urban transportation, he described the fiscal difficulties of Italian cities and the lack of controls over land speculation.

> In my city, land which was worth twenty or thirty thousand lire per square meter was sold two years ago for a million lire per square meter. As far as I am concerned, this corresponds to the fact that military pensions [from World War II] will [according to the Minister] not be completely settled until 1997. These are all aspects of the same reality. The problems you're asking me about—no matter where you begin, they're all the same. . . . These are not technical problems. They are political problems.

If "ideological" is understood in the limited sense of intense commitment to a social philosophy and a political program, then most Italian Communist politicians are ideologues. Their programmatic commitment and their rejection of a technocratic approach to social problems are captured by a number of items in the 1970 questionnaires. Table 1 shows that Communists are consistently more likely than other Italian politicians to reject a merely possibilist, short-run approach to policy-making, to discount the view that the right answer to public problems usually lies in the middle, to stress a Government's program and not merely its strength and efficiency, and to emphasize political factors over technical considerations.[6]

TABLE 1. COMMITMENT TO A PROGRAMMATIC ORIENTATION TO POLITICS, 1970

		PCI	PSI & PSIUP	Other
		(percentage agreement)		
1. Politics is the "art of the possible," and therefore the leaders of the country should worry more about what can be done in the short run than about ambitious ideals and long-run plans.	Councilors Deputies	24 11	45 50	59 61
2. Generally, in political controversies one should avoid extreme positions because the proper solution usually lies in the middle.	Councilors Deputies	5 36	55 40	82 97
3. The strength and efficiency of a government are more important than its specific programs.	Councilors Deputies	11 20	36 40	68 63
4. In contemporary social and economic affairs it is essential that technical considerations have greater weight than political factors.	Councilors Deputies	0 18	8 10	48 42
(N =)	Councilors Deputies	18 11	11 10	44 32

This approach to politics is closely linked to a pervasive Communist suspicion of experts, a suspicion that surfaced repeatedly in our interviews with the regional councilors. When we asked about the importance of various influences on the councilors' decisions on policy matters, only 24 percent of the Communists gave a high rating to "the opinions of experts and authorities," as contrasted to 62 percent of the Socialist councilors and 78 percent of the other respondents. Asked about the most urgent tasks facing the newly elected councils, 47 percent of the Socialists and 57 percent of the respondents from the other parties assigned

[6] Responses to closed questionnaire items are never in themselves probative, particularly when dealing with political elites. In the absence of a fuller exploration of the open-ended sections of the 1970 interviews, however, I shall use these closed-ended data to supplement and confirm evidence from the richer 1968 interviews.

181

a high priority to establishing a staff of technicians and experts at the service of the council; only 27 percent of the Communists stressed this.

The sources of this antipathy to experts are complex. In part it probably reflects a contingent fact of political strategy in today's Italy: calling in so-called experts may shift the balance of power toward the Communists' opponents. In part the hostility to experts is linked to the radical populism that, as I will later show, is characteristic of PCI politicians. But in substantial part this disparagement of expertise is a corollary of the Communists' consistently more political style of policy analysis.

The programmatic commitment of the Communist councilors does not imply a lack of concern with the concrete problems of their regions. Indeed, Communists were less likely than others to agree with the statement that "carrying out an idealistic political struggle is more important than worrying about the individual problems of the region"; only 22 percent of the Communists agreed, as contrasted with 58 percent of the Socialists, and 64 percent of the councilors from the other parties. It is not that the Communists put program or ideology before practical problems, but rather that they interpret those practical problems in more programmatic or ideological terms. They even seem to project their own programmatic concerns onto the electorate at large. Asked about the motivations of voters in their region, 85 percent stressed the regional party platform, as compared with 42 percent of the Socialists and 19 percent of the others. (The non-Communists put more stress instead on traditional party attachments and the candidate's attractiveness.)

The substance of the program to which these Communist politicians are so committed is fairly familiar to students of Italian communism and requires no extended treatment here. These are no mere social democrats, content to tinker with the surface manifestations of what they see as fundamental social injustice. The distinctiveness of their ideals for Italian society became clear in responses to a 1968 question about "the kind of society you would like to see for your children and grandchildren." To be sure, in broad terms many of the desires mentioned at this point —greater social justice, greater personal freedom, more secure democracy, and so on—were shared by Communists and non-Communists alike. But as these visions of a better Italy were spelled out in more detail, fundamental differences appeared. The Communists stressed the need to overcome poverty and unemployment and the importance of public control of economic enterprises, whereas non-Communists emphasized technical and economic progress, citizen maturity and morality, and social consensus.[7] The Communists emphasized changes in society, while their opponents gave more attention to changes in the individual. The Communists stressed social justice, while their opponents stressed social equilibrium.

The philosophical roots of the Communists' visions of the future were often made explicit in the interviews.

> The society I'd like to see is one in which each man is the equal of his fellows and has no *capo* who stands over him and commands him—an egalitarian society, perhaps the society of Rousseau. But how can we reach this society? Simply eliminating the dominion of man over man. How do we eliminate the dominion of man over man? . . . If we eliminate the possession of capital, if we socialize capital, then we will have eliminated the dominion of man over man.

After reading each interview carefully and completely, the coders of our 1968 interviews were asked to assess the respondents' "general attitude to the existing socioeconomic order," using the scale shown in Table 2. While there might be marginal disagreements about the placement of individual respondents, the broad outlines of the results reflect the stance of most Italian Communists as hostile critics of Italy's present socioeconomic system. All this suggests that historical analogies to the social democratic politicians of northern Europe are misleading and, at the very least, premature. In this sense—though, as we will see later, not in all senses—the PCI remains an antisystem party.

CONFLICT AND COMPROMISE: THE PRACTICE OF PLURALIST POLITICS

A fundamental tenet of classical Marxist social theory is that "the history of all societies up to the present is the history of class

---

[7] The statistical evidence for these generalizations is as follows: Respondents mentioning more jobs—PCI, 50 percent; Other, 18 percent; Respondents mentioning a socialist economy—PCI, 65 percent; Other, 10 percent; Respondents mentioning technical and economic progress—PCI, 15 percent; Other, 50 percent; Respondents mentioning citizen maturity and morality— PCI, 0 percent; Other, 40 percent; Respondents mentioning social consensus —PCI, 0 percent; Other, 24 percent.

183

struggles," and that "every class struggle is a political struggle."[8] Much of politicians' behavior is dependent on whether their implicit social philosophies predispose them to perceive conflicting or common interests in public affairs.[9] And Communist politicians in Italy share Marx's view that conflict and discord are at the heart of politics.

"Some people say that there is always bound to be conflict among various groups in society and politics, while others say

TABLE 2. Attitudes to the Existing Socioeconomic Order, 1968

	PCI	Non-Communist Left* (in percentages)	Center & Right
1. Total rejection, destruction proposed	15	4	0
2. Rejected, but ameliorative reforms proposed	70	15	0
3. Accepted, but ameliorative reforms proposed	15	81	61
4. Accepted, no important reforms proposed	0	0	39
	100	100	100
	(N = 20)	(N = 27)	(N = 36)

*Non-Communist Left is composed of deputies from the PSI, the PSIUP, and the left-wing of the DC.
NOTE: The intercoder reliability of this judgment is tau-beta = .60; only 2 percent of the respondents were placed more than one point apart by the two independent coders.

that most groups have a great deal in common and share basically the same interests. What do you think about this?" I asked respondents in the 1968 study. Ninety-five percent of the PCI politicians stressed social conflict rather than social harmony, and 60 percent argued that this conflict was difficult, if not impossi-

[8] Karl Marx and Frederick Engels, *Selected Works*, 2 vols. (Moscow: Foreign Languages Publishing House, 1962), 1: 34, 43. The citations are from the *Communist Manifesto*.

[9] See my *Beliefs of Politicians*, pp. 93-128 and 150-156. Detailed evidence is offered there showing the impact of broad social philosophy on more specific political attitudes, perceptions, and behavior.

184

ble, to reconcile. The comparable figures for the non-Communist Left were 78 percent and 33 percent, while for the parties of the Center and Right, the figures were 67 percent and 6 percent.

Nor is this stress on conflict merely a matter of abstract social philosophy. In their analyses of concrete public problems Communists were much more likely than non-Communists to perceive a clash of opposing interests. For example, the problem of urban transportation, seen by most non-Communists as a technical problem of coordination and technological innovation, was interpreted as follows by one Communist deputy, a specialist in urban affairs.

> For the causes you must always go back to the fact that transport policy is very strongly influenced by the virtually complete monopoly by FIAT of the automobile industry. FIAT needs to produce and sell cars, trucks, vehicles of all sorts. . . . The problem is one of interests that clash, of conflict. If you don't enter into conflict with these [monopolistic] groups, obviously they will pursue their own interests. If I were in Agnelli's position, I'd probably do the same. But if I were in the position of the State, I'd pursue the interests of the vast majority of the population.

An older Communist from the Mezzogiorno made the same point when discussing economic planning. "The problem is not economic planning, yes or no," he commented. "It isn't that anymore. It is which type of planning, that is, in whose interest are we going to plan?"

These mental images of society and public affairs clearly affect political behavior. For example, the marked tendency we noted earlier for Communist politicians to adopt a more political view of policy-making, their suspicion of so-called experts, and their strongly partisan style of policy analysis are all linked to their assumptions about the structure of interests underlying public problems.

In contrast to the views of many non-Communist Italians, the pedigree of the Communists' perspectives on social conflict is Marxist, not Hobbesian. The Communists' emphasis on social discord is not linked to misanthropy and distrust of "the generalized other." On the contrary, respondents from the PCI are consistently *less* likely than non-Communists to endorse such assertions as, "If you don't watch yourself, people will take

185

advantage of you" or "No one is going to care much what happens to you when you get right down to it." There is even some evidence from the study of regional councilors that this generalized faith in other people spills over into the political arena. Sixty-one percent of the Communist councilors agreed that "normally in politics one can trust others," as contrasted with 27 percent of the members of other parties. The Communists' sense of the ubiquity of conflicting interests is seldom personalized.

One might expect, however, that one consequence of the Communists' emphasis on social conflict would be firm resistance to compromise and to the give-and-take typical of pluralist politics. An important aspect of the image of sectarian militant normally used to interpret the behavior of Communist politicians is an uncompromising defense of ideological purity and of the interests of the proletariat. Our evidence, however, speaks strongly against this view.

Several indicators of attitudes toward compromise are available in our data. For example, each of our samples was asked to agree or disagree with the proposition that "compromising with one's political opponents is dangerous because it usually leads to the betrayal of one's own side." In each case the Communists are no more hostile to the principle of compromise than are other Italian politicians. Indeed, with the consistent exception of the Socialists, the Communists are more open to compromise than are any of their opponents. For example, in the survey of regional councilors, 56 percent of the PCI rejected the proposition that compromising is dangerous, as contrasted to 46 percent of the non-Communist councilors. Grouping together the two samples of deputies, the comparable figures are 78 percent for the PCI and 52 percent for the non-Communists.

Richer, fully consistent evidence is available from the open-ended questions of the 1968 study. "Are there ever situations in which what is politically feasible must take precedence over what is ideally desirable?" I asked. Most politicians, Communists and non-Communists alike, agreed that such situations arise, but unlike many of their opponents, Communist respondents typically stressed the positive rather than the negative aspects of adjusting to political realities.

You're referring to political compromise? I would say that that is the daily bread of any politician whom one would respect, because obviously even for those who want to arrive at a new society, as we do, it is clear that you can't pursue that objective following the old canons of anarchism. This intransigence about objectives, which is [only] verbal, of course, works to the detriment of concrete results. This applies not just to discussing long-term prospects, but also to resolving all the immediate problems of the country. As far as I am concerned, this is the rule.

Communist respondents frequently added the qualification that the proposed compromise must not violate fundamental principles and must open possibilities for later progress. For example, a Communist leader in the Chamber of Deputies said:

Certainly there are moments, which I would say occur almost every day in politics, in which faced with a more general ideal vision, one limits oneself to pushing for more limited demands, but always on the assumption that these demands leave open the possibility of a still more ideal development. After all, politics is the art of the possible. [*Is that to be regretted, in your opinion?*] It's not a matter of regretting these possibilities. Perhaps one should regret certain opportunities which have been lost because one did not see what perhaps was possible in a more limited way at a certain moment, which instead was lost in the long run by not knowing how to make use of what was possible, even if in a more limited way at that point.

One deputy who had had long experience in legislative politics gave an eloquent defense of the art of compromise.

Look, politics is the art of possibilities, it isn't the achievement of ideals which might be beautiful, but are still abstract. As far as I'm concerned, even solutions [which are appropriate] from a scientific point of view, but which are not yet ripe from the point of view of political consciousness and even in terms of the harmonization of certain interests, become a bit utopian. You engage in battles, [but] you risk not even being understood by the country. Hence, certain compromises that salvage the substance of the things and achieve a real step forward toward the achievement of an objective which as yet appears rather theoretical—certain compromises are always useful. Otherwise everyone would always remain fixed to his own ideas, and in Parliament you would never find the synthesis, the solution of any problem.

There were exceptions, of course. One hard-liner argued, "There is just no possibility at all of any halfway meeting between our side—the forces of socialism—and the great monopolies. There is no possible reconciliation of such divergent interests. I believe in coexistence, but coexistence doesn't mean compromise and meeting halfway. Coexistence means struggle." But hard-liners can be found on all sides in Italian politics. Only this one Communist among those interviewed in 1968 (5 percent) viewed political feasibility primarily in unfavorable terms, as compared to 11 percent of the non-Communist Left and 24 percent of the Center and Right.

For neither Communist nor non-Communist does a willingness to entertain the possibility of compromise imply that compromises will always be found. Whether a politician accepts compromise in a given case depends in part on the circumstances. Even a person relatively open to compromise in general might be unwilling to accept a particularly disadvantageous proposal, and even someone generally reluctant to compromise might in some circumstances be willing to reach an accommodation. But some politicians are relatively more inclined than others to cooperate and compromise with their adversaries; their cooperation threshold is lower. There is no evidence in our data that the cooperation thresholds of Communists are typically higher than those of less radical politicians.

The explanation for these findings is not to be sought in some innate softheartedness of Italian Communists. Any permanent minority wishing to exert real influence on policy-making must be prepared to compromise some of its principles, at least in the short run. One deputy made this argument explicit, in response to a question about interparty collaboration.

For anyone who concerns himself with public affairs, this is an everyday problem. Even when—as in my province, for example—the Communist party has an absolute majority, one acts so as to take into account what the others want. In fact, the greater the majority, the more the opinion of the others is sought. In Parliament, of course, where the Communist party doesn't have this absolute majority, collaborating with others is an everyday matter. Otherwise, we would be simply engaging in deceptive wishful thinking (*azioni velleitarie*), and the Communist party, I believe, has always forced itself not to be that kind of party, but to be a concrete party seeking to solve concrete problems.

This, of course, is the fundamental significance of the *via italiana*, and the general endorsement of compromise by PCI politicians is at least in part the result of a systematic effort to remove sectarian, hard-line elements from the party cadres and the party image. But the success of this campaign is perhaps even greater than the party leadership recognizes, with probably irreversible results. For many Italian Communists openness to collaboration and compromise has become a central element of their identity as politicians.

One former shipyard worker knew personally the meaning of class conflict.

It isn't possible to live without conflict, as I see it. Wouldn't it be lovely to find a boss or a Confindustria who said, "Fine, let's share. We've made this much; you take a little and I'll take a little." It's a little unlikely! It's not for nothing that class parties were born.

But later, talking about compromise, a different aspect of his outlook became apparent.

Conflicts always end up with a compromise. You certainly can't always make war. Even with a strike it's the way. . . . I remember once we were striking, we held out for seventy days. But afterwards we arrived at a compromise. An agreement is a compromise between the two sides. It doesn't satisfy anyone, doesn't satisfy either the one side or the other side—it's a compromise. It's like husband and wife. Either one dominates or the other dominates, or by compromising, you live together. Are you married? [*My bachelor assistant: "No!"*] Beh, you'll learn.

His choice of simile suggests, I think, the extent to which this Communist politician has internalized the principle of political compromise. The PCI's strategic choice of the *via italiana* helps to explain our findings, but it does not explain them away.

Italian Communist politicians by no means see their role exclusively as impartial brokers among a plurality of equally legitimate interests. On the contrary, our PCI respondents clearly interpret their responsibilities as tribunes for the neglected interests of the underprivileged.

Defining the boundaries of the underprivileged constituency for which they wish to speak has created dialectical difficulties, to be sure. To the industrial proletariat of orthodox Marxism have been added both the intelligentsia and the peasantry. In their more expansive moments Italian Communists speak as well of including artisans and independent farmers and even small businessmen within their fold. All this requires brokerage skills of a fairly high order, as many of our respondents are frank to admit. One parliamentary leader used language reminiscent of functionalist political science in describing this process of interest aggregation within the parties.

> Look, in my view the role of parties should be precisely that . . . of being able to balance their programmatic position, taking into account the interests, the aspirations, the pressures which emerge from the reality of the country, and therefore having a function of overcoming sectoral or corporative pressures, elevating the sectoral impulses, the group pressures into a more general view of the economic needs of the country.

But most Italian Communists strenuously resist being cast in the role of oil-can bearers for capitalist society. We asked the regional councilors whether or not they agreed that "the principal role of the politician is to mediate the divergent interests in society." Only 15 percent of the Communists accepted this view, as compared to 25 percent of the Socialists and 93 percent of the other respondents. Similarly, when offered a series of descriptions of the job of regional councilor, the Communists were much less likely than other respondents to select "mediating the conflicting requests of the various groups of the region," and were much more likely to endorse such alternatives as "defending the interests of the less protected sectors of society," or "aiding individual citizens in their dealings with the public administration." Whether this tribune-like stance would survive an experience of sharing national governing responsibility is a matter of conjecture. But at least for the moment the Communists' willingness to bargain and compromise does not mean a renunciation of their self-assigned role as partisans for the underprivileged.

As the discussion to this point would suggest, the attitudes of Communist politicians toward their partisan opponents are

190

mixed. Some see party politics as essentially a morality play, a struggle between good and evil. Asked about interparty differences, one young working-class militant responded.

> What difference is there between the class of the exploiters and the class of the exploited? . . . Between the Communists and the Christian Democrats, between the Communists and the Liberals, between the Communists and the neo-Fascists, it's the same difference between the class which has the power in its hands, which dominates the class that instead is dominated.

More typical, however, are more modulated attitudes. In the 1968 interviews Socialists of the PSI were generally characterized as lost brethren, fundamentally committed to Marxist socialism, but having made a strategic miscalculation about the pliability of neocapitalism in Italy. The Democrazia Cristiana party (DC) was recognized as an extremely variegated composite of conflicting tendencies: "They've got a little bit of everything in there," said one Communist deputy. Most criticism of the DC was directed not at the party as such, but rather at the current leadership, seen as the principal defenders of the Communists' *bête noire*, monopoly capitalism. Even at that, most members of the PCI did not contest the Christian Democrats' commitment to the Constitution of the Republic; we will see later how important a touchstone this is for most Communists. The Liberals and Social Democrats were generally treated as irredeemably reactionary, but again their loyalty to the Republic was seldom questioned. Only the neo-Fascists were the objects of unrelieved and indiscriminate hostility. In most respects the Communists' mental map of the Italian party system was remarkably like that of other Italian politicians on the left.[10] Like most other Italians, Communists see considerable differences among the parties, though they also share with most of their opponents a sense that the barriers of distrust and hostility have been lowered somewhat over the last two decades.

From the responses to several open-ended questions in the 1968 study, an Index of Partisan Hostility was constructed, meas-

[10] The regional councilors in 1970 were asked to rate each national party on a left-right scale from 0 to 100. The only significant difference in the placements made by Communists and non-Communist leftists was a slight tendency for the Communists to place the PCI itself a bit further to the left than other respondents thought appropriate.

uring the extent to which respondents displayed intolerance toward opposing ideologies, engaged in dichotomous, black-and-white thinking, and attributed evil or insidious motives to their opponents.[11] Forty-two percent of the Communists rank above the national mean on this Index, as contrasted with 15 percent of the non-Communist Left and 62 percent of the remaining respondents. These statistics neatly summarize one's general impression that while the Communists are more sectarian than their colleagues on the left, they are considerably more open in their partisanship than their opponents on the center and right. These findings at the elite level are precisely parallel to the conclusions of Gabriel A. Almond and Sidney Verba about patterns of partisanship at the mass level.[12]

The relatively high level of interparty hostility characteristic of Italian politics may be undergoing a secular decline. As I have reported elsewhere,[13] levels of suspicion and resistance to collaboration are much lower among the younger cohorts of Italian politicians. These generational differences are greatest within the PCI.[14]

Italian experience with pluralist politics is still short, and the impact of the Fascist regime on political tolerance and trust is slow to fade. Perhaps the most sensitive analysis of the reasons for the greater interparty tolerance of younger Italian politicians was offered by an older Communist militant in our 1968 sample.

> We had a twenty-year period in which the more active anti-Fascists were constrained to work in France or work clandestinely with the specter of the special tribunal always hanging over their heads. The others made a passive resistance, not concerning themselves with politics. . . . The young people today, who were just kids during the Fascist period—or perhaps not even born yet—don't have this heredity to cope with, a monk's habit to have to change, and therefore, they are the bearers of new ideas. The older classes, the older men, still have much of the heredity—even involuntarily at times, even

[11] See my "Studying Elite Political Culture," pp. 669-671.
[12] See *The Civic Culture* (Princeton: Princeton University Press, 1963), p. 160.
[13] "Studying Elite Political Culture," pp. 673-677.
[14] For similar evidence from a sample of local activists, see Galli and Prandi, *Patterns*, p. 144, and (in much greater detail) Francesco Alberoni et al., *L'Attivista di partito* (Bologna: Società Editrice Il Mulino, 1967), pp. 340-387.

without knowing it—have much of the mentality of a regime which dominated absolutely for twenty years.

Both in their continuing tendency to distrust political opponents and in their growing acceptance of genuine interparty collaboration, PCI politicians betray their integration into the broader Italian political culture. Their firm commitment to Marxist social philosophy and political analysis does not preclude an equal commitment to an open, bargaining style of practical politics. This seeming paradox will assume broader dimensions as we examine the Communist politicians' attitudes to the Italian political system.

RADICAL POPULISTS IN A LIBERAL DEMOCRACY

One of the most perplexing features of political discourse in Italy is the frequency with which politicians resort to the word "democracy." On nearly all sides faith is pledged to democracy and demands are made for strengthening and extending democratic institutions in Italy. Yet with equal intensity charges of lack of commitment to "genuine" democracy are exchanged, and a bewildering jumble of lines is drawn separating the supposedly democratic forces from the enemies of democracy. The only constant in this frenzy of demarcation is that the speaker and his party always end up on the "democratic" side of whatever line is drawn.

One cynical interpretation of this is that Italians are masters of the politician's art of using language to impugn others' motives while concealing one's own. But a more productive approach is to try to understand just what it is that each side seems to mean by democracy. As I have shown elsewhere, it is possible to identify a limited number of distinctive conceptions of democracy used by politicians in Italy and Britain.[15] If we are to assess Italian Communists' commitment to democracy, we should begin by asking them what they mean by the term.

A deputy who had been a member of the PCI since 1924 recalled:

When I was younger, I used to say that democracy was the worker with a rifle on his shoulder . . . . Since then there have been profound changes in the world. But I think that democracy is that form where the citizen participates in as broad a

---

[15] *Beliefs of Politicians*, pp. 166-181.

way as possible in all the problems of society, not just called to vote once every five years and then he minds his own business and others act for him. . . . He must have the possibility of not just following with some attention the activities of those to whom he has delegated authority, but also of making them change their positions. In the end democracy is the participation of everyone in all problems. In this sense the gravest thing for us Communists was the Stalinist period, because Stalin tried to substitute for this infinite initiative and participation his own authority and the authority of a group of leaders, who were capable and strong, but who could never substitute for millions of men.

A younger Communist lawyer, strikingly conversant with and even sympathetic to Anglo-American political philosophy, summed up the central elements in the Communists' conception of democracy.

The essential elements of a democracy are these. The greatest diffusion among the members of the possibility for each to decide, after you've assured economic and political points of departure such that on the basis of those points of departure no one is able to prevail over the others. That is, equality which is not only political, but also economic, in the context of real economic equality, so that there are no bosses and dependents, or "exploited," as we say, using an old-fashioned word. Within this context democracy must be as wide as possible— not restricted to individual groups, but extended as far as possible to everyone.

In terms I have employed elsewhere, Italian Communists employ almost exclusively classical and socioeconomic conceptions of democracy. Only rarely do they stress elements of liberal or polyarchal democracy—free speech, the rule of law, limited government, political competition, and so on. Not Locke and Schumpeter but Marx and Rousseau are their intellectual forebears.

It is not surprising, therefore, that when Communists are asked for proposals for "making Italy more democratic," their suggestions center on ways for increasing the ability of ordinary citizens to participate more actively in politics and government, and that in particular they are concerned to stress socioeconomic equality as well as political equality. Table 3 summarizes the prescriptions offered by our 1968 respondents for the role of ordinary citizens in politics and government. The commitment of Communist politicians to participatory democracy is displayed quite clearly.

A number of items on the written questionnaires given each of our three samples seem to tap the intensity of their support for

TABLE 3. ATTITUDES TO THE PUBLIC'S ROLE IN POLITICS, 1968

Question: "What do you think should be the role of ordinary citizens in politics and government?"

	PCI	Non-Communist Left* (in percentages)	Center & Right
Voting or less	0	0	21
Interest in politics and/or communication to representatives	0	52	56
More direct involvement (in parties, associations, local government, etc.)	100	48	24
	100	100	101
	(N = 20)	(N = 27)	(N = 34)

*See Table 2 for explanation of this category.

political equality. In 1968 seven of these items were grouped to form an Index of Political Egalitarianism. Ratings on this index confirm that the most passionate advocates of political equality were the members of the PCI (see Table 4). An analogous Index of Opposition to Elitism (composed of some of the same items as the Index of Political Egalitarianism) has been calculated for the 1970 samples. Once again (as shown in Table 4) the Communist respondents scored considerably higher. All the available evidence supports the conclusion that if advocacy of mass participation in politics and hostility to elitism in government be the only criteria, the Communists are the most democratic force in Italy. Their concept of the state and of the political process, so far from being authoritarian, as Giorgio Galli and Alfonso Prandi claim, is essentially populist.[16]

[16] Patterns, p. 306. For empirical evidence and conclusions consistent with mine, see Timothy M. Hennessey, "Democratic Attitudinal Configurations Among Italian Youth," Midwest Journal of Politcial Science 13 (1969): 169-193. By "populist" here I mean a political philosophy that stresses an active political role for ordinary citizens and that locates ultimate political authority with the people. I do not use the term in the occasional European sense that refers to the lower classes—simple, unsophisticated, and unspoiled

195

TABLE 4. INDICES OF SUPPORT FOR POLITICAL EQUALITY

I. *Index of Political Egalitarianism, 1968*

1. Every citizen should have an equal chance to influence government policy.
°2. It will always be necessary to have a few strong, able people actually running everything.
°3. Certain people are better qualified to run this country because of their traditions and family background.
4. People ought to be allowed to vote even if they cannot do so intelligently.
°5. In this complicated world the only way we can know what is going on is to rely on leaders or experts who can be trusted.
°6. Few people really know what is in their best interests in the long run.
°7. A few strong leaders would do more for this country than all the laws and talk.

	PCI	Non-Communist Left†	Center & Right
Percentage scoring above the national median	90	45	23
(N =)	10	20	26

II. *Index of Opposition to Elitism, 1970*

°1. Certain people are better qualified to lead this country because of their traditions and family background.
°2. In a world as complicated as the modern one it doesn't make sense to speak of increased control by ordinary citizens over governmental affairs.
°3. It will always be necessary to have a few strong, able individuals who know how to take charge.
4. People should be allowed to vote even if they cannot do so intelligently.
°5. Few people know what is in their real interest in the long run.
6. All citizens should have the same chance of influencing government policy.

		PCI	PSI & PSIUP	Other
Percentage scoring above national median	Councilors	83	75	32
	Deputies	100	70	33
(N =)	Councilors	18	12	44
	Deputies	11	10	33

° The starred items were reversed for scoring in the calculations.
†See Table 2 for an explanation of this category.

---

by modernity—as the distinctive repository of truth. Marx's own theory of democracy was quite close to that I have termed classical or populist democracy. For two otherwise very divergent interpretations, which nevertheless agree on this point, see Giovanni Sartori, *Democratic Theory* (New York: Praeger, 1965), pp. 416-419, and Paul M. Sweezy, in Richard McKeon (ed.), *Democracy in a World of Tensions* (Chicago: University of Chicago Press, 1951), pp. 391-424.

196

However, as we have already noted, political competition and civic freedoms are less central to the Communists' interpretation of democracy. Wishing to test support for political liberty and anticipating widespread verbal endorsement of this value, I tried in the 1968 study to make it as easy as possible for respondents to express reservations about complete freedom for political agitation and propaganda. I began by asking, "Some people say that there are certain political groups that engage in tactics that are unfair, or illegitimate, or even dangerous to the country's welfare. How do you feel about this—do you think there ought to be more careful controls over any activities of this sort?" If—as was fairly common—the respondent hesitated or denied knowledge of any dangerous groups, I went on to ask about the activities of extremists at the opposite end of the ideological spectrum from the respondent himself. This series of questions was designed to push support for civic freedoms to the breaking point, since from the respondent's point of view I was virtually asking if he thought subversives should go uncontrolled. Nevertheless, the technique gives us some sense of the tensile strength of support for political liberties among Italian politicians.

Communist deputies responding to this question were in a rather special position, for the party's official line calls for the implementation of the clause of the Italian Constitution which prohibits the formation of a neo-Fascist party. Many simply wrapped themselves in the Constitution and demanded that the Movimento Sociale Italiano (MSI)—widely acknowledged to be in fact a neo-Fascist party—be dissolved. One Communist respondent said:

> In this case it doesn't seem to us to create a limit to the freedom of expression, because in effect it is the Constitution which proposes to limit the liberty of acting contrary to it. Other than that, we are opposed to limitations of political liberty.

Some Communists, however, were more reluctant to take the drastic action of outlawing a party.

> You could say that the Constitution should be faithfully applied. [*And therefore the MSI should be forbidden, you think?*] Oh, I wouldn't forbid the idea of any organization, of any party, because I am for the maximum of democracy and liberty. . . . What is forbidden is the old Fascist party. But if

197

you call yourself MSI, and want to be a party of the Right, carry out your activities, you're free to do so. We will confront our ideas, make clear our conflicts of class interest, fine. But the introduction of the method of violence, however, is excluded; that isn't admissible.

As shown in Table 5 the Communists, taken as a group, appear to be less staunch supporters of political liberties than are the non-Communist politicians of the Left; on the other hand, the Communists seem no more eager to restrict freedom of speech and association than do Italian politicians of the Center and Right. (For comparative purposes, the responses of a similar sample of British politicians are included in Table 5. These data

TABLE 5. Support for Political Liberties, 1968

Question: "Some people say that certain organizations engage in activities that are unfair, or illegitimate, or even dangerous to the country's welfare. . . . Do you think there ought to be more careful controls over any activities of this sort?"

	PCI	Non-Communist Left†	Center & Right	British MP's
			(in percentages)	
Respondent is willing to impose certain limits	31	6	45	0
Respondent is willing to impose limits, though reluctantly	46	61	28	10
Respondent unwilling to impose any limits, but makes no explicit reference to political liberty	15	11	7	36
Respondent unwilling to impose any limits, and refers explicitly to political liberty	8	22	21	54
	100	100	101	100
	(N = 13)	(N = 18)	(N = 29)	(N = 62)

†See Table 2 for an explanation of this category.

198

show that, relative to British sentiment, support for civil liberties is fragile in all Italian parties.)

In 1970 both the regional councilors and the national deputies were presented with the proposition that "the freedom to make political propaganda is not an absolute freedom and the state should carefully regulate its use." Every one of the Communist councilors and deputies disagreed with this statement, as compared to disagreement rates of 83 and 100 percent for Socialist councilors and deputies, respectively, and 57 and 58 percent for councilors and deputies from the parties of the Center and Right. A more cautious conclusion about the Communists' attitudes to political competition, however, is suggested by responses to another item on the regional questionnaire: "In a true democracy the power must from time to time pass from one party to the others." Only 72 percent of the Communist councilors agreed, as contrasted to 100 percent of the Socialists and 91 percent of the councilors from the remaining parties.[17]

The most reasonable summary of these findings is that Italian Communists are not uniformly firm advocates of political liberty, and that alternation of parties in power is not a salient feature of their conception of democracy, but that on the other hand, their willingness to tolerate opposition is not, on balance, notably lower than that of the other Italian parties. Italian Communist politicians are not so firmly civil libertarians as, say, British Members of Parliament, but then neither are non-Communist Italian politicians.

During the interviews Communists often protested their commitment to a multiparty system and to the free expression of divergent views. For some this commitment to political pluralism stems from a genuine concern for political liberty, but for others it reflects a simple recognition of the realities of Italian politics. For many members of the PCI (as for many of their opponents on the other side of the political spectrum), dissent is tolerated less because tolerance is thought morally right than because it is thought politically necessary.

[17] In comparison to the non-Communists' responses, it is appropriate to say "only 72 percent" of the Communists agree with this statement, but in the light of traditional Leninist views about the "dictatorship of the proletariat," one might equally well emphasize that nearly three-quarters of the Communists endorse rotation in power as a necessary condition for democracy.

199

Sometimes the instrumental character of the commitment to the freedoms of what the Communists call formal democracy was transparent. I asked one deputy close to the national leadership of the PCI to what extent he would be willing to sacrifice formal democracy in order to attain the more substantial democracy of a socialist society.

> I think that here in the West, even if we are scarcely enthusiastic about formal democracy, nevertheless it is a point that cannot be renounced. And I would not risk paying prices for a substantial democracy if it was at the expense of formal democracy. If necessary, you just have to have patience; the road will be long. You have to wait, to do things more slowly. But in order to do things securely, well, you can't abandon the terrain of formal democracy. . . . Here, for us, no—it would be too dangerous. [*Too dangerous? You're referring to the international context?*] No, no—to our internal situation.

The transition from instrumental to intrinsic commitment is a familiar pattern in the evolution of norms. Religious freedom in the Anglo-American nations was a necessity several centuries before it was a right. A similar process may well be occurring with respect to political freedom in Italy. Communists who protest their commitment to free speech initially for tactical reasons may come to have a functionally autonomous commitment to this value, just as conservatives who have tolerated Communist political activity merely to avoid revolutionary discontent may come to accept the moral imperative of tolerance.

Turning from these fundamental issues of political philosophy to judgments about the existing Italian political system, we find, not surprisingly, that Communist politicians are sharply critical. Consistent with their Marxist analysis of society and politics, they stress the power that (as they see it) conservative economic forces currently have to thwart the will of political organs and in particular, the will of *le forze popolari*. When asked what changes ought to be made in the current pattern of power in Italy, the Communists were unanimous in suggesting substantial reforms, although few of the changes seem to deserve the label "revolutionary."

The most common proposals from PCI deputies were for facilitation of popular participation in politics and government, decentralization of power, particularly to the regions, increased parliamentary control over the executive branch of government, and, of course, reduction in the power of big business interests. Similarly, the Communist regional councilors stressed the need for citizen involvement in the decision-making process, for close supervision of the regional executive by the council, and for a high degree of regional autonomy from the central government. (Communists were unanimous that the prefectural system should be abolished, but they were joined in this view by a majority of non-Communist councilors.)

All these reforms are, of course, consistent with the PCI's own strategic strengths and weaknesses in Italian politics, which are concentrated at the mass level and in the legislative branch of government. But with the exception of the proposals for strengthening the Parliament, the suggested reforms are also consistent with the Communists' fundamental populism. It would be difficult, perhaps impossible, to disentangle the relative importance of normative and contingent motives behind these proposals.

The Communists' attitudes to the institution of Parliament are interestingly ambivalent. For many of the older and more orthodox among them, service in Parliament represents merely a tour of duty in one of the several sites of the party's struggle for power. As one long-time functionary in the national party organization put it:

> Really, my parliamentary activity is not an exclusive activity, because my origin is an origin as a professional revolutionary, as we say, and mine is essentially a party career. Hence, all the parliamentary activity which I have had to undertake is merely complementary. . . . In my political life the principal part and the most attractive part has been and still is that of the party itself.

On the other hand, many of those I spoke with seemed completely integrated into the affairs of Parliament and at ease with the normal methods of parliamentary politics. As others have argued, the postwar record of the PCI in the Italian Parliament is essentially one of constructive collaboration within the limits set by the rigidities of the party system.[18] The experience of these Communist deputies in living out the PCI's parliamentary strategy has, it seems, led many of them to value the parliamentary institutions for their own sake.

[18] See n. 3 above.

Indeed, there were repeated illustrations in our interviews that the Constitution of the Republic has become virtually an object of veneration for Italian Communists. Many of their most heated attacks on the parties of the majority are phrased in terms of failure of those parties to implement the Constitution that emerged out of the unity forged during the Resistance. One deputy with considerable legal training argued:

> After the fall of Fascism and after the Resistance struggle, we created for ourselves a Constitution which is among the most advanced constitutions in the world. The gravest fraud [perpetrated by] the ruling parties, above all by the Christian Democratic party, was to accept this Constitution at a time when they feared there might be an earthquake, and then later to default. The regions were to have been established within a year of the enactment of the Constitution, and yet from 1949 until today we're still discussing how to implement the regions—and so on for many other institutions. For me, democracy begins with an honest, fair application of the Constitution.

A still more striking illustration of incipient Constitution-worship comes from an interview with a deputy widely reputed to be one of the party's leading unreconstructed Stalinists. I began by asking him about "the most important problems facing Italy."

> Well, really the most important problem . . . is that of carrying out the Constitution. . . . The Parliament should be developed in correspondence to the vision of the Constitution. Sure, the Constitution claims to conserve the fundamental bases of the present society from the economic point of view. But the Constitution also anticipates a development of this society in the direction of greater social justice, of greater defense of labor, and of greater involvement of the people in the affairs of state and therefore of the Parliament. But this isn't happening. Parliament has stopped in midstream. . . . Why? There is strong pressure from the past, from past laws, past conceptions, and there is strong pressure from the groups with economic power who influence various parties, and in particular, the Christian Democrats, who accept verbally the idea of the implementation of the Constitution, but in fact always put on the brakes, delay, keep us from going ahead. We have a crisis of the Par-

liament, yes, and of the State, but it is a crisis of immobility. [Later, speaking of his attitude to the Christian Democratic party:] It isn't really that we have things in common with the Christian Democratic party. But we did make this Republic in common and we did create the Constitution together.

As this man fully recognizes, the verbal agreement on the Constitution barely hides deep disagreement over how it ought to be implemented. But the fact that his disagreement is framed in terms of the constitutional mandate (as he sees it) for social change suggests how misleading are facile descriptions of the PCI as an antisystem party.

One can in fact find considerable evidence that PCI politicians are more at home in the bustle of pluralist politics than many of their adversaries. For example, more than most non-Communist Italian politicians, Communists are sympathetic to the role played by parties and pressure groups in modern society. In all three surveys Communists were more likely to agree that "citizens have a perfect right to exert pressure for legislation which would benefit them personally," and they were much more likely to disagree with assertions that "the general welfare of the country is seriously endangered by the continual strife between particularistic interest groups," and that "although parties play an important role in a democracy, often they uselessly exacerbate political conflicts."

Communist politicians are also less subject than many of their non-Communist counterparts to the virtually untranslatable Italian vice of *qualunquismo*, that is, an indiscriminate and cynical alienation from the game of democratic politics and a preference for authoritarian government. As I have noted earlier, Communists consistently score higher on measures of social and political trust. In the 1970 studies Communist respondents were twice as likely as non-Communists to reject the view that "often those who enter politics think less about the welfare of the citizen than about their own welfare or that of their party" or that "in politics today there is a notable discrepancy between what is said and what is really meant to be done."[19]

---

[19] Only 25 percent of the Communist deputies and councilors agreed with the first assertion, as compared to 60 percent of the non-Communists. Only 42 percent of the Communists agreed with the second statement, as compared to 84 percent of the non-Communists.

Italian Communists are, like most other observers, critical of many of the institutions and processes of contemporary Italian politics. But the impression that emerges from these data is not one of fundamental alienation from pluralism or parliamentary democracy. In political terms the Communists seem to be radical reformers, but hardly revolutionaries, not even in the attenuated sense of wishing basic, though nonviolent, changes in the rules of the game. In Table 6 are shown the coders' judgments about

TABLE 6. Attitudes to the Existing Political Order, 1968

	PCI	Non-Communist Left* (in percentages)	Center & Right
1. Total rejection, destruction proposed	5	0	0
2. Rejected, but ameliorative reforms proposed	30	4	17
3. Accepted, but ameliorative reforms proposed	65	93	61
4. Accepted, no important reforms proposed	0	4	22
	100	100	100
	(N = 20)	(N = 27)	(N = 36)

*See Table 2 for an explanation of this category.

Note: The intercoder reliability of this judgment is tau-beta = .70; none of the respondents was placed more than one point apart by the two independent coders.

the attitudes of our 1968 respondents toward the existing political order. As in the case of the analogous judgments about attitudes to the socioeconomic system (see Table 2), there was some room for disagreement about the proper placement of individual respondents, though the intercoder reliability was quite high. In any event the broad outlines are clear and striking; only one of the twenty Communist respondents was judged by the coders to be openly hostile to the system of parliamentary democracy. Equally interesting is the comparison between Tables 2 and 6, for whereas 85 percent of the Communists seem to be essentially alienated from the Italian socioeconomic system, only 35 percent of them seem equally estranged from the political system. This is the fundamental sense in which the PCI is not an antisystem party.

THE PARTY: DISCIPLINE OR SELF-DISCIPLINE?

Communist politicians in Italy identify much more closely with their party than do non-Communists. One pervasive sign of this identification is the use of the personal pronoun: Communists normally use "we" in talking about their political views, whereas non-Communists use "I." But the identification is more than verbal. PCI deputies are much less disturbed than other politicians by the ubiquity of party discipline in the Chamber. Describing his decision-making on issues, the Communist regional councilor gives much greater weight to his party's position than does the typical non-Communist. Only 47 percent of the PCI councilors (compared to 75 percent of the non-Communists) agree that "in the final analysis, loyalty to one's fellow citizens is more important than faithfulness to the party." Only 3 percent of the Communists (compared to 29 percent of the Socialists and 47 percent of the other parties) could imagine taking a regional line in conflict with national party policy. Party discipline may well become more flexible as the regions gain more autonomy, but the infrequency of public dissent from the party line continues to distinguish Communists sharply from other Italian politicians.

This party loyalty is not necessarily uncritical. Some Communists are rather outspoken on the subject of the party's authority. One commented:

> I am a rationalist. I believe in reason. I would prefer to die the day on which I had to conclude that reason must succumb. . . . The highest thing is not even, as some among us say, the party —"The party is always right." The highest thing is reason, which must prevail in the party.

Nevertheless, party plays a much greater role in the lives of Communist politicians than for non-Communists.

The Italian Communists' deference is to the party as an institution, rather than to the leaders of the party as individuals. When I asked deputies in 1968 about the role of the party leader and about the balance of rights and duties between leaders and fol-

205

lowers, the Communists were no more likely than non-Communists to stress the obligations of the followers. Indeed, Italian Communists are often very sensitive to the implicit accusation of Stalinism when discussing intraparty affairs.

> We have had an experience at the international level of the cult of personality. But we can say that within Italy this problem has never existed in those terms, in the sense that the Italian party is a party which has always been able to think. It has had its troubles, its disputes—this, I would say, is the daily bread of a political struggle.

For older party members who can remember the days of clandestine struggle, the question of leader-follower relations has a much more personal aspect.

> It's a relationship of trust that is born out of years of work. . . . Friendships, sympathies are created. There are certain principles that everyone shares, and out of all this is created the personality of the leader with respect to the party. Togliatti was undisputed precisely because we had all known him since '21.

When describing the role of the party leader, a number of our respondents stressed the importance of maintaining democratic relationships within the party.

> [The leader] must not close himself within himself. He must know how to make internal democracy work in the party, because every party has its own internal dialectic. It's unthinkable that a leader would say, "Let's do this today," and let it go at that. He can convince me that it is right to do something, and I'll do it; but I'll do it, not because he told me, but because I am convinced that it is right. It is in the extent to which a party leader knows how to develop this sort of mechanism that he shows that he is a real leader.

If, as I am arguing, the deference of the Communist politician in Italy is not to the orders of the leader, but rather to the consensus within the party as an organization, then our judgment about the likelihood of sharp strategic shifts must be modified accordingly. Consensus-building must be a major and continuing preoccupation of the leadership of any large organization, and the burden of proof would seem to lie on those who would argue that the PCI is uniquely immune from this organizational imperative. My argument here buttresses the case that the commitment of the PCI to the *via italiana* within the confines of the Republican Constitution could not be lightly discarded. It is in this sense, I think, that we should understand Sidney Tarrow's reference to "the institutionalization of tactics."[20]

If we assume that discipline in the PCI is based on organizational consensus, then it becomes very important to know how this consensus is created. Unfortunately, it is on precisely that point that my own evidence is most scant. The few comments offered by our respondents are equivocal on this point. A leader of the *gruppo parlamentare* gave one interpretation.

> We periodically call a meeting of the *gruppo*. We submit various legislative problems to the assembly, the choices which have to be made, whether to vote one way or another. There are discussions and in the end a decision is reached. Naturally, sometimes you might not be in agreement on certain decisions taken by the majority. The important thing is that there be a majority which makes them, and hence that the individual in this case, after having fought his battle, defers to the decision of the majority. What is important in a situation like this is the search for consensus, the broadest possible discussion, even the longest, until all sides of the problem have been exhausted.

This description has much about it that is familiar to anyone who has ever taken part in committee discussions. On the other hand, a deputy who was later to leave the party to join the Manifesto group was less sanguine about the efficacy of intraparty debate.

> Leaders don't ever like to be controlled. Hence, a supporter must have faith and a sense of discipline, but in my view he must never do anything without being at ease with himself. He must always control in a real, genuine way. This is the problem of democracy inside a political organization. There is always a vanguard. What is the relationship between the vanguard and the rest? The vanguard always tends to reply that the relationship is a relationship of consensus—of debate, not a "blank-check" consensus. This is a great problem that has al-

[20] See *Peasant Communism in Southern Italy* (New Haven: Yale University Press, 1967), pp. 155-161. For a comparable analysis of party discipline in the French Communist party, see Denis Lacorne, Chapter 8 in this volume.

most never worked in our case. There's a reason, of course. It depends on the fact that when a party is a party in battle against the rest of society, it's a little like an army. And an army is never the best example of a democratic dialectic.

Which of these two views is really more accurate cannot be determined without much more evidence on the nature of policy-making within the party than is now available. Nevertheless, in their descriptions of the role of a good party leader Communists lay exceptional stress on the ability to keep in touch with the feelings of *la base*, the base of the party, and through it, with the population. Along with the more instrumental qualities demanded of leaders in all Italian parties—organizational ability, decisiveness, intellectual stature, and so on—Communists, more than others, see the party leaders as the servant and custodian of the party's traditions and ideals.

The subject of authority relations within the PCI is very complex. The attitude toward authority held by individual members, even the relatively senior members interviewed in these studies, is certainly not the only relevant factor. Organizations have power and inertia. Structures of incentives and sanctions affect the behavior of individuals quite apart from their private desires. But the evidence discussed here should at least call into question the simple-minded notion that Italian Communists typically are personally authoritarian.

Since one important characteristic of Communist parties is their link to an international movement, I should perhaps close with a few words about the attitudes toward international affairs revealed in our interviews. First, international affairs seem much more salient for Communist than for non-Communist politicians. Although my opening question in the 1968 study about "the most important problems facing Italy" did not refer to foreign policy, 63 percent of the PCI respondents began by talking about international affairs, as contrasted with only 9 percent of the non-Communist deputies. Part of the explanation, of course, lies in the Communists' keen sense of being part of an international movement. But perhaps equally important is their awareness that patterns of domestic politics in Italy are very dependent on trends in world politics. They often argue that the PCI's hopes for a share of political power in Italy depend on continuing relaxation of Cold War tensions in Europe. I asked one Communist

208

deputy in 1968 if he were optimistic or pessimistic about the chances of reaching the kind of society he wanted for his children.

I'm neither optimistic nor pessimistic. You have to look carefully at the situations. Certainly, for example, if there could be a relaxation of world tensions, if the boil of Vietnam could be extirpated, if the discourse on peaceful coexistence could be begun again, then even these things I have been calling dreams could become reality in the not too distant future. [*And how about the domestic situation in Italy?*] I *am* talking about the domestic situation, because the domestic situation and the relations between the parties are dependent on all this.

But despite the salience of international relations in the Communists' view of politics, it is striking that the USSR and the socialist bloc are rarely referred to in their discussions of Italian politics, and almost never are held up as models of what socialism and the workers' state should be. In fact, comments critical of the Soviet Union or disparagements of the relevance of the Soviet experience to Italian affairs are more common than admiring statements. Nor can this be attributed simply to reticence in the presence of an American, for few of the Communists I spoke with made any effort to hide their repugnance for United States foreign policy or their rejection of American society as fundamentally corrupt. Even in the pre-Prague spring of 1968 there was much more viewing the West with alarm than pointing with pride to the East.

Conclusions: Italian Communists as Constitutional Radicals

To sharpen the image of Italian Communist politicians that emerges from these studies, let me set down in schematic form the summary judgments most consistent with our evidence.

1. *Italian Communist politicians are radical, programmatic, and ideologically committed Marxists.* Their mission is more than the mere amelioration of the worst features of neocapitalism. They reject the view that the problems of modern society are essentially technical, requiring expertise rather than political engagement. They share with non-Communists a sense of what

209

Italy's problems are, but their diagnoses are consistently and fundamentally Marxist, and their prescriptions typically more drastic.

2. *Italian Communist politicians are populists.* They are committed to a version of political democracy that has a recognizable pedigree in Western Europe, one that stresses maximum equality and participation. They are less fully committed to the values of liberal democracy, but that is a characteristic they share with many members of the parties now governing Italy.

3. *Italian Communist politicians are at home in the world of constitutional, pluralist politics.* They are sensitive to the need to bargain and compromise, they are less alienated from the realities of Italian political life than many of their fellows, and they are committed to the Republican Constitution, which, as Tarrow rightly says, "the PCI considers its greatest achievement and the condition of its legal and political survival."[21]

4. *Italian Communist politicians are disciplined members of the party, but there is little evidence that they are either authoritarian in personality or dogmatic in their orientation to the world movement.*

Most Italian Communist politicians seem to have accepted the political values of their environment, but continue to reject prevailing socioeconomic values. For this reason they do not fit comfortably at *any* point along the orthodox dimension from Bolshevism to Social Democracy. I can illustrate this paradox by using the summary assessments of our 1968 respondents' political and socioeconomic attitudes (see Tables 2 and 6) to array these respondents simultaneously along the two analytic dimensions I postulated in Figure 2.[22] Table 7 presents the joint distribution of our twenty Communist deputies in this two-dimensional space. Two conclusions flow from this array. First, there is—as assumed by the orthodox interpretation—a modest positive correlation between socioeconomic radicalism and political radicalism. The

[21] See his "Le PCI et la société italienne," in *Le Communisme en Italie,* Fondation Nationale des Sciences Politiques (Paris: A. Colin, 1974).

[22] It is not my assumption that these variables accurately capture all the distinctions and nuances that are needed to assess a politician's outlook or even all the dimensions of attitude and value discussed in this study. For example, the respondents' orientation to compromise is only partly reflected in the "political" variable used here. Nonetheless, these two variables do seem to measure much of what I have been discussing, and Tables 7 and 8 illustrate my argument, though they do not prove it.

Communist politicians in our sample who are most alienated from the existing social system are also the most likely to be hostile to the existing political system. But, secondly, this correlation is far from perfect, for fully half the respondents fall in the off-diagonal cell containing those whom I earlier labeled "constitutional radicals."[23] This is precisely the variety of radicalism that the orthodox one-dimensional theory is prone to misinterpret.

TABLE 7. VARIETIES OF RADICALISM IN THE PCI, 1968

		Attitude to the Existing Social System†		
		Rejects	Accepts	Total
Attitude to the	Accepts	10	3	13
Existing	Rejects	7	0	7
Political System°	Total	17	3	20

°See Table 6 for fuller presentation.
†See Table 2 for fuller presentation.

I have so far avoided the issue of whether and how the PCI's orientations have changed or are likely to change over time. On general historical grounds one could plausibly defend opposing views. On the one hand, it seems likely that with increasing involvement in the practice of constitutional politics, Communist politicians ought to become increasingly committed to the system in a political sense, though not necessarily in terms of their socio-economic values. On the other hand, a sensitive history of the PCI might reveal that the commitment to a gradualist, pluralist political strategy predates the PCI's postwar parliamentary experience.

Comparison of the attitudes of different age cohorts within the party may cast some light on this question, particularly if, as evidence in other contexts suggests, one's basic political attitudes and values are set in the first two or three decades of life and are thereafter less susceptible to modification.[24] Dividing our 1968

[23] Not surprisingly, none of the Communists rejected the political system while accepting the social system. Indeed, only five respondents among our 83 deputies in the 1968 sample fell into the fourth cell; all of them were from the extreme right of the political spectrum.

[24] See my *Beliefs of Politicians*, pp. 140-142 and the sources cited there.

sample of Communist deputies into those over fifty and those under fifty segregates two groups with markedly different socialization experiences. The average member of the older group, thirty-three years old at the fall of Fascism in 1943, was first exposed to the world of politics (and, I am assuming, formed his basic political orientations) before the Republican Constitution was ever written. The average member of the younger group, only nineteen years old in 1943, almost certainly first entered politics in the postwar period of parliamentary democracy. Table 8 shows how each of these two cohorts is distributed in the two-dimensional framework I have proposed for interpreting contemporary radicalism.

TABLE 8. VARIETIES OF RADICALISM AND POLITICAL GENERATIONS IN THE PCI, 1968

| | | Attitude to the Existing Social System | | |
		Rejects	Accepts	Total
	Deputies Aged 50 and over			
Attitude to the	Accepts	3	2	5
Existing	Rejects	5	0	5
Political System	Total	8	2	10

| | | Attitude to the Existing Social System | | |
		Rejects	Accepts	Total
	Deputies Aged 49 and under			
Attitude to the	Accepts	7	1	8
Existing	Rejects	2	0	2
Political System	Total	9	1	10

Each cohort displays the modest positive correlation between the two basic variables, but each also reveals that the relationship is less than perfect. More important, there are several significant differences between the figures for the two cohorts. The younger group is much less radical than the older group along the political dimension, but the younger group, is, if anything, slightly more radical than the older group along the socioeconomic dimension. The corollary: Whereas less than one-third of the older group falls in the category of constitutional radicals, more than two-thirds of the younger group are in that anomalous cell.[25] The political significance of these differences is highlighted by the fact that while 70 percent of the younger cohort were subsequently reelected to Parliament, only 30 percent of the older cohort served after 1968. If these suggestive differences do in fact reflect enduring generational phenomena, it may become increasingly difficult to interpret the PCI within the one-dimensional world implied by orthodox discussions of revisionism and adaptation.

One qualification must be noted. Even if these data do reflect a genuine historical trend, the nature of that trend may not be as simple as the data seem to imply. That is, we may have merely glimpsed in mid-course a longer process of change. Perhaps as a radical party adapts to a nonrevolutionary society, political values are the first to change, followed eventually by socioeconomic values, so that (in terms of Figure 2) Cell C ("constitutional radicals") is simply a way station on the passage from Cell A ("Bolsheviks") to Cell D ("Social Democrats"). Perhaps the PCI will eventually move back onto the orthodox diagonal, and the predominance of "constitutional radicals" that we have noted will—in the perspective of history—be seen as merely a transitional phase. In any event, while waiting for the future to reveal the answer to this conundrum, analysts ought to recognize that the PCI today represents a quite anomalous brand of radicalism.

[25] Despite the low N's the difference in the proportion of "constitutional radicals" in the two cohorts is statistically significant at the .09 level, using a one-tailed chi square test corrected for continuity. This means that there is less than one chance in ten that this difference could be due purely to chance. A more detailed analysis suggests that a number of generational differences common to all Italian parties are particularly sharp within the PCI. The younger Communist cohort shows strikingly lower levels of partisan hostility, political and social distrust, and resistance to compromise. These findings are consistent with the generational differences Stephen Hellman found within the Communist party apparatus; see his "Generational Differences in the Federal Apparatus of the Italian Communist Party: Origins and Implications" (Paper delivered at the Sixty-eighth Annual Meeting of the American Political Science Association, Washington, D.C., September 1972).

In this paper I have focused almost exclusively on the attitudes and values that, I have argued, guide and inform the behavior of Italian Communist politicians. This focus is, of course, not the only possible perspective from which one might try to predict political behavior. In particular, one theoretical alternative, which we might appropriately term the Machiavellian approach, emphasizes the strategic and tactical calculus of political man as power-seeker. It may be useful to compare, if only briefly, my results with the implications of such a strategic analysis. This comparison is particularly urgent for two related reasons.

First of all, the image I have drawn of the PCI as a party of constitutional radicals is admittedly a congenial one from the point of view of the party itself. The party would like to believe —and would like others to believe—that it seeks radical socioeconomic change by constitutional means. Just why this is so, we shall see in a moment. Secondly, the image I have drawn of the party's value structure may seem to contain a possible strategic inconsistency. It might be simply impossible to attain radical socioeconomic goals without using radical political means, that is, violent revolution. Perhaps under the pressure of events this inconsistency would have to be reconciled, either by limiting the goals (and thus becoming real Social Democrats) or by removing limits on the means (and thus becoming real Bolsheviks).

To explain why these inconsistencies between my value analysis and the Machiavellian analysis are largely illusory, I need to borrow from Juan Linz's suggestive explication of the strategic situation of radical parties in pluralist democracies.[26] The strategic problem for such a party is that pluralist democratic procedures, stressing negotiation, compromise, and consent, do not facilitate major social revolution, particularly if the radical party does not have an absolute majority of the votes or parliamentary seats. For a party like the PCI, gaining power is risky, and gaining power against the united opposition of powerful enemies is riskier still. If radical social change must be sought with the support (or at least the acquiescence) of non-Communists, the party

[26] Linz presented the outline of this analysis at the Conference on French and Italian Communism at which this chapter was first presented. I have taken some liberties in my formulation of Linz's argument, and hence the reader should in fairness attribute the insights here to Linz and the obfuscations to me. Some of the ideas that follow are also drawn from some very stimulating conversations with Professor Alessandro Pizzorno, although Pizzorno would probably not accept my argument as here presented.

must gain the confidence and reduce the fears of its opponents.[27] At the same time, the party must strive to remain true to its maximalist socioeconomic goals, because of the expectations of its constituents, the demands of its organizational activists, and the ideological commitments of the leaders themselves.

FIG. 3. RADICAL STRATEGIES IN A PLURALIST POLITY

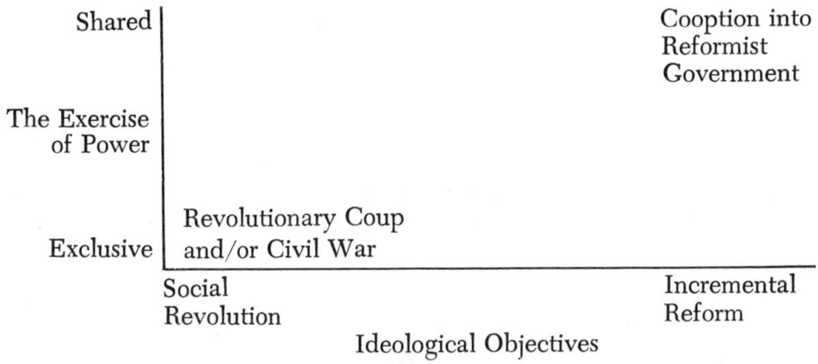

```
Shared   |                          Cooption into
         |                          Reformist
         |                          Government
The Exercise
of Power |
         |
         |  Revolutionary Coup
Exclusive|  and/or Civil War
         |_____
          Social                   Incremental
          Revolution               Reform
                 Ideological Objectives
```

Linz has proposed a diagram similar to Figure 3 to explicate this problem. The horizontal axis refers to the ideological objectives of the party, ranging from radical socioeconomic change to marginal reforms. The vertical axis refers to the ways power might be exercised to attain those goals, ranging from shared power to exclusive power. Accession to power in the lower-left quadrant implies violent, thoroughgoing revolution—the Bolsheviks' dictatorship of the proletariat. Accession to power in the upper-right quadrant implies cooptation of the radical party into a merely reformist (Social Democratic) government. Either of these alternatives is costly for a radical party in a pluralist system. Positions at the right on the horizontal axis imply limited objectives and thus create internal organizational and ideological difficulties. Positions low on the vertical axis are difficult to sustain because of the fearful reactions of other actors in the system. There seems to be an iron law linking greater (internal) aspirations and greater (external) opposition. To talk a maximalist line internally and a minimalist line externally does not work for a

[27] As has often been pointed out, the historical experience of the PCI from 1921 to 1947 left the party and its leaders with a keen sense both of the costs that can be incurred by frightening opponents and of the benefits that can be obtained by collaborating with non-Communist progressives.

215

mass party in an open society, for supporters become confused and opponents warier still.

This strategic dilemma cannot easily be resolved. One important element in the equation, of course, is the reaction of the non-Communists in the system. Hence, a strategic analysis of the PCI's role in Italian politics is incomplete without a thorough investigation of the interests, objectives, and attitudes of non-Communist elites and masses. But to judge by their public and private statements (including those in my interviews with non-Communists in the larger study from which this paper draws), the fears of non-Communists seem to concern primarily political values, whereas our evidence here is that the aspirations of the PCI concern primarily socioeconomic policy. Neither of these sets of preferences is absolute, of course. The PCI would like to make political changes, not just socioeconomic ones, while the non-Communists (or at least some of them) fear socioeconomic changes, not just political ones. But at the margins the strategic calculus would seem to suggest that the PCI adapt to the institutions of parliamentary democracy, while continuing to press for radical socioeconomic change. Moreover, if this scheme is really to work, Communist activists and supporters must be persuaded that it is strategically and ideologically sound, not just momentarily convenient; otherwise their aspirations may outstrip the party's ability to deliver. And, as I have already argued, that process of persuasion itself makes a change in strategy increasingly difficult.

Thus, in terms of Figure 3 the optimal strategy would seem to lie in the upper-left quadrant—acceptance of the political values of pluralist democracy, but rejection of the socioeconomic values of neocapitalism. This conclusion (and the associated logic) matches precisely the image that emerges from my analysis of the outlook of contemporary PCI politicians, particularly those who have come of age politically in the postwar period.

There are, as one of my Communist respondents pointed out to me, no guarantees in the business of politics. There is no assurance that the party's supporters will be satisfied with the socioeconomic concessions it can win, nor that the party's opponents will be satisfied with its political concessions. The entrance of the PCI into some future government of Italy will place great strain on both the party's political values and its socioeconomic values. How great will depend in large part on the reaction of the other relevant actors, both domestic and foreign. But both my analysis of party leaders' values and this abbreviated strategic analysis imply that the main efforts of the PCI leadership in such a situation would be directed at socioeconomic change rather than political-constitutional change. It is, of course, consistent with both my value analysis and the strategic analysis to suppose that the PCI would try to implement specific socioeconomic reforms—such as the nationalization of certain industries—that would weaken the structural power of their opponents. But it is also consistent with both the value analysis and the strategic analysis to suppose that the PCI would assign low priority to attempts to monopolize political power, limit political debate, or modify the Constitution.

The "constitutional radicalism" of the PCI may create ideological inconsistencies and organizational tensions. But it may also equip the PCI better than most other radical parties for adapting to its changing environment, for these Italian Communist politicians are probably less exposed than most to the twin dangers of sectarianism and parliamentarism. In their stress on participatory democracy Italian Communists have a closer affinity to the Maoist "mass line" than to the Leninist "vanguard" party. In their commitment to fundamental change in the social structure of Italy they are visibly to the left of all the European social democratic parties. Analysts should beware of interpreting radical politics of the late twentieth century in terms of concepts and models drawn from the late nineteenth century. As one of my respondents said to me at the end of a long and thoughtful interview, "*Siamo dei curiosi comunisti!*"—"We're peculiar Communists!"

PART THREE

Communist Parties in Local Politics

VI.

Political Legitimacy in Local Politics: The Communist Party in Northeastern Italy

ALAN STERN

A generally successful adaptability that is marred by serious regional failures has been the hallmark of the Partito Comunista Italiano (PCI) throughout the postwar period. The strategy of the PCI, perhaps more strikingly than for any other nonruling Communist party, requires it to adapt to its social environment, and often leads observers to mistakenly label it revisionist. Such an evaluation is inappropriate, for where its political strategies have been successful, the PCI has stimulated desired changes in the environment in which it operated. Successful adaptation is not passive capitulation, but complex manipulation of social forces. Yet an inept attempt to interact with local social arrangements, or still worse, having its local branches forced to assume configurations set out for the Communists by the opposition, leaves a party such as the PCI severely hampered. Our principal concern here is an analysis over time of an instance of relatively weak PCI adaptation.

Successful Communist adaptation in any locality is greatly facilitated by popular acceptance of the PCI as a legitimate contender for political power. Without this perception among members of the community, the PCI is deprived of essential resources and is likely to be permanently relegated to a rather rigidly defined minority status.

The most notable example of positive adaptation where legitimacy has been attained is provided by the party in the provinces of central Italy. There electoral hegemony and social organization combine to yield strong political subcultures and regional administrative power.[1] At the other pole, the best known and

[1] The PCI in the central regions of Italy is illuminated by sections of the following books in the landmark Società Editrice Il Mulino series: Francesco Alberoni, V. Capecchi, A. Manoukian, F. Olivetti, and A. Tosi, *L'Attivista di*

most carefully studied example of relative failure is the case of the PCI in the undeveloped south.[2] But here, the development and utilization of local legitimacy does not seem to be a central question. In comparison, a rather massive and significant demonstration of PCI inability to grapple successfully with local social arrangements is provided by the areas of traditionally staunch Catholic religiosity, especially in the northeastern areas of Italy.[3] An analysis of PCI weakness in this dependable reservoir of Christian Democratic votes seems particularly well suited to the investigation of political legitimacy as a partisan resource.

A study of northeastern Italy helps us in the larger task of assessing the prospects for the attainment of what appears to be a central instrumental goal of the PCI as a whole: gaining acceptance as a rightful partner in the exercise of power at the highest levels of government. The achievement of this goal depends upon two related developments: first, increased electoral support and second, the wider diffusion of a sentiment among non-Communist voters, that the PCI is entitled to, and can be trusted to help govern the nation. The two fundamental questions of party growth and party legitimacy are intimately related, because it is

---

partito (Bologna, 1967); Luciano Brunelli, Umberto Canullo, Gianluigi Degli Esposti, Giorgio Galli, Anna Lena, Agopik Manoukian, Luciana Pepa, Antonio Picchi, Alfonso Prandi, Alberto Mario Rossi, Bruno Scatassa, Ada Sivini Cavazzani, and Luigi Turco, *La presenza sociale del PCI e della DC* (Bologna, 1968); and Franca Cervellati Cantelli, Vittorio Cioni Polacchini, Paola de Vito Piscicelli, Stefania Guarino Cappello, Gianfranco Poggi, Giacomo Sani, Giordano Sivini, and Ada Sivini Cavazzani, *L'Organizzazione partitica del PCI e della DC* (Bologna, 1968). Robert Evans, *Coexistence: Communism and Its Practice in Bologna, 1945-1965* (South Bend, Ind.: University of Notre Dame Press, 1967) and G. Degli Esposti, *Bologna PCI* (Bologna: Società Editrice Il Mulino, 1966) offer case studies of the largest Communist-dominated city, Bologna. Consult Alessandro Pizzorno, "Introduzione allo studio della partecipazione politica," *Quaderni di sociologia* 15 (July-December 1966) for a discussion of political subcultures.

[2] See Sidney Tarrow's *Peasant Communism in Southern Italy* (New Haven: Yale University Press, 1967) and his recent analysis of the last decade, "The Political Economy of Stagnation: Communism in Southern Italy, 1960-1970," *Journal of Politics* 34 (February 1972): 93-124. One must be careful to accent *relative* failure, for the percent of PCI strength has grown steadily in the south since 1946.

[3] The northeast is not the only minimally Communist, staunchly Catholic area, merely the most distinct, extensive, and important of these zones. For example, the Catholic world seems very entrenched in parts of Abruzzi-Molise.

not likely that a weaker PCI will be accepted as a coalition partner, nor are the prospects for significant electoral expansion good
without broader popular acceptance.

PCI electoral support in the northeast has some potential for
growth in the midst of continuing social change. The work force
and the social structure of the Veneto have become increasingly
complex, differentiated, commercialized, and industrial. This oc-
cupationally more diverse population, however, is still over-
whelmingly loyal to the Democrazia Cristiana (DC), which is
supported by the Catholic Church. Since it must continue to base
a capacity to grow upon a system of broad social alliances, the
PCI can no longer afford to ignore the Catholic masses, who are
among the last potential sources of sizable new electoral growth.
But no significant electoral development can take place if the PCI
does not penetrate the wall of exclusive legitimacy that the DC
has managed to maintain in areas like the Veneto. Without that
achievement, where the Catholic Church, the only truly national
Italian institution, is strongest, the Italian Communists will continue to encounter great difficulty in being accepted as an un-
tainted participant in political forums.

A detailed comparative study of Catholic grass-roots political
hegemony initially built on a foundation of preindustrial legitimacy, but maintained in the environment of social change, may
help direct attention to some of the theoretical dimensions of political dominance. The focus of this study is an investigation of
the character of Christian Democratic hegemony as the exercise
of such dominance poses problems for the Communist minority.

A historical framework is utilized to accent the evolution of
two very different forms of political hegemony, each with distinct
characteristics that necessitate sharply contrasting forms of maintenance. The Christian Democratic variety that flourishes in
northeastern Italy is fueled efficiently by a stable social organization that deemphasizes the place of politics in community life. In
comparison the Communist variant thriving in central Italy, and
utilized in this study for contrast, accents the urgent attention
that political matters should command among the local citizenry
and thereby constantly reaffirms the relatively recent sense of
legitimacy that underlies PCI political control.

According to Weber's classic definition, traditional dominance
inheres in the belief in everyday routine as inviolable norms of

223

conduct.[4] In two of the four communities on which this study is based—the two DC strongholds—this traditionally established resource, with its political power undiminished, has developed into political hegemonies based on less rigid, but nonetheless distinct, publicly acknowledged perceptions of "oughtness" or moral appropriateness that citizens ascribe to a particular political regime or political organization.

Gradually the DC acquired legitimacy as influence and authority was successfully transferred from the nonpolitical to the partisan realm.[5] In this transfer and the subsequent process of maintenance, the manipulation of traditional symbols is critical. Intangible rewards, expressed symbolically, serve as secondary reinforcements of exclusive political legitimacy, thus reducing the number of concrete benefits, or primary reinforcements, the party and the regime it controls must dispense.[6] Adopting Edelman's vocabulary, we shall refer to synthetic representations of past tradition as "condensation symbols."[7] Throughout our discussion we shall pay special attention to the local social structures that facilitate, tolerate, or inhibit the development, maintenance, and defense of monopolistic political legitimacy. The ultimate concern is an evaluation of the prospects of the PCI in what has long been a hostile environment.

Data are drawn from interviews collected in a comparative study of four communities, two dominanted by the Christian

[4] For Weber's definition see H. H. Gerth and C. Wright Mills, *From Max Weber: Essays in Sociology* (New York: Oxford University Press, 1958), p. 296. Reinhard Bendix analyzes the Weber discussion of traditional domination in *Max Weber: An Intellectual Portrait* (Garden City, N.Y.: Anchor-Doubleday, 1962), pp. 331-384.

Good modern discussions of legitimacy include Richard Merelman, "Learning and Legitimacy," *American Political Science Review* 60 (September 1966); David Easton, *A Systems Analysis of Political Life* (New York: John Wiley and Sons, Inc., 1965); Seymour Martin Lipset, *Political Man* (New York: Doubleday, 1963); Peter Berger and Thomas Luckmann, *The Social Construction of Reality* (London: Penguin, 1969). For a criticism of legitimacy conceptualized in terms of opinion patterns, see John Schaar, "Legitimacy in the Modern State," in P. Green and S. Levinson (eds.), *Power and Community* (New York: Random House, 1970), pp. 276-328.

[5] A clear introductory analysis to these questions is provided in Jean Blondel, *Comparative Government* (New York: Praeger, 1969), Chapter 3.

[6] For an application of learning-theory concepts to the analysis of legitimacy, see Merelman, "Learning and Legitimacy."

[7] Murray Edelman, *The Symbolic Uses of Politics* (Urbana, Ill.: University of Illinois Press, 1964), p. 6, adapts the term from psychoanalytic theory.

224

Democrats and two dominated by the Communists. The material from the two Communist-dominated central Italian towns allows comparison with a nontraditional form of dominance and seems especially important in the historical section of the study which traces the origins of different forms of hegemonic legitimacy.[8]

THE ESTABLISHMENT OF MONOPOLISTIC LEGITIMACY: THE DC IN NORTHEASTERN ITALY

What are the origins of the legitimacy that sustains long-term political domination? More particularly, what is the origin of the enduring ties between the Catholic Church and Christian Democracy where that tie is best developed? What are the means of transfer from a pure type of traditional dominance to a more modern variety of hegemonic political legitimacy?

Christian Democratic political hegemony in the Veneto depends upon the widely diffused popular acceptance of the exclusive title to legitimate exercise of public authority bestowed on the party by the Catholic Church. This traditional political dominance developed easily and unobtrusively in the northeast. In the Veneto, a socially aware clerical hierarchy, when forced to react to rapid political change after Italian unification, maintained its preunification position as the keystone and regulator of proper social behavior.

Enduring clerical vitality was not determined by the social structure of the region. However, there is no doubt that in the preindustrial era, an economy based upon the small independent farmer, renter, or owner facilitated this clerical success.[9]

The Venetian clergy skillfully utilized its unique position in the community in the period of political chaos that characterized the transition from Hapsburg rule to solidify its tie with the citi-

[8] The larger study upon which this paper draws is Alan J. Stern, "Local Political Elites and Economic Change" (Ph.D. Dissertation, Yale University, 1971). Some complementary data are drawn from the report of the Cattaneo Research in a town cited as Community B. See Francesco Alberoni et al., *L'Attivista di partito* (Bologna: Società Editrice Il Mulino, 1967), esp. pp. 153-159.

[9] The historical discussion in this section deals primarily with the partisan loyalties formed in the period from the Italian unification (1860-1870) until the banning of democratic party politics in the mid-1920s under fascism. In this section both of the Veneto towns and both of the central Italian communities are dealt with as units, since their preindustrial patterns do not differ substantially.

zenry, by rendering material service and, perhaps even more important, by providing a sense of, and symbols for, social continuity and security. Clergy in other areas of Italy, notably the central regions where the PCI came to flourish, squandered considerable, if less extensive, social resources by failing to act in an effective fashion.

In spite of the fact that the Vatican bitterly opposed Italian unification, when the process was complete only the Church among national institutions was, in some areas with richly articulated organizations that penetrated to the community level, in a position to influence political attitudes as they formed among the citizens of the fragile new nation. A common identification as Catholics, regardless of their enthusiasm for the label, represented one of the few organic ties that bound together citizens of the new Italian state. This old "bond of allegiance," to use Blondel's phrase, by its very uniqueness gave the Church special advantages.[10]

It is common to accent the remarkable resiliency of clerical political influence in the northeast, yet the truly exceptional situation may be that of central Italy where local Church policies seem to have almost forced anticlerical feelings. By comparing the interaction between Church and society at the local level in the Veneto and Tuscany, we may gather insight, from the Veneto, into the sources of enduring monopolistic legitimacy and, by comparing it with the central Italian record, the way in which a hallowed, institutionalized tradition loses its social influence.[11]

There can be no doubt that the Church enjoyed advantages in the Veneto. Before discussing the social structure in which it operated, the autonomy that accrued to the clergy under the last period of Austrian rule (1815-1870) should be accented. Until the Concordat of 1855, the Austro-Hungarian administration was content to allow the local Venetian clergy almost total responsibility for all local administrative matters, save taxation.[12] Many

[10] Jean Blondel, *Comparative Government* (New York: Praeger, 1969), p. 63.

[11] One of the few preliminary attempts to deal with the interplay of church and land tenure systems is Mattei Dogan, "Political Cleavage and Social Stratification in France and Italy," in *Party Systems and Voter Alignments: Cross National Perspectives*, Seymour Martin Lipset and Stein Rokkan (eds.) (New York: Free Press, 1967), p. 184.

[12] Gabriele de Rosa, *Giuseppe Sacchetti e la Pieta Veneta* (Roma: Editrice Studium, 1968), p. 221.

of these Church-related activities, like the rite of unction, were deliberately collective, physical reminders of the organic, intimate tie to the Church.[13] After 1855, some centralization at the bishopric level was established, but unlike their colleagues in central Italy, who were closely tied to the Vatican, the Venetian clergy were relatively independent.

The opportunity to preserve its central role in regional affairs was enhanced by the social structure of the northeast. The earliest indications of the structure of the land-tenure system in northeastern Italy after unification indicate a great mass of independent farmers. Though the figures may be only approximate, Morpurgo, drawing on census material from 1878 and 1883, estimates 516,000 independent farmers in a population of 2,800,000 within the regions we know as the Three Venices: Trento Alto Adige, Veneto, and Friuli Venezia Giulia. Undoubtedly, the sale of ecclesiastical property after 1870 contributed to this fractionalization of farmland. According to the best available figures the average size of a purchase of Church property in the Veneto was two and one-half hectares, compared with an average purchase of more than fifteen hectares in Tuscany.[14] The pattern of small holdings was almost uniform in the extensive mountainous area of the subalpine zones, somewhat less so in the plains. In those few zones where very large holdings were found, the big farms were characterized neither by extensive capitalization, nor by the sharecrop system. Instead a wide variety of rental arrangements prevailed.[15]

Ecological studies of national Italian electoral behavior from 1946 to 1963 find a strong positive correlation between the percent of independent farmers in the work force and DC vote.[16] It would be incorrect to interpret this material as simple affirmation of inevitable conservatism among small farmers who zealously defend even minimally productive properties.

The social relationships typical of the life pattern of the independent farmer tolerate established arrangements, even those that place the farmer at minimal advantage. This toleration is

[13] Ibid., p. 217.
[14] Agricultural statistics and local historical studies are collected and cited in ibid., pp. 188-189.
[15] Ibid., p. 190.
[16] Vittorio Capecchi, Vittoria Cioni Polacchini, Giorgio Galli, and Giordano Sivini, Il Comportamento elettorale in Italia (Bologna: Società Editrice Il Mulino, 1968), p. 240.

227

possible first when institutions that lie at the heart of the historical social order are at least minimally useful to the ordinary citizenry; second, when individuals responsible for local economic
difficulties are anonymous in the sense that they are outside the
world of personal experience; third, when the local social structure does not consistently remind the farmer of inferiority and
abject dependence on others.

The contrast between the *mezzadria* (sharecrop) system of central Italy and the independent farm framework of the northeast
is sharp. In this respect, the Tuscan sharecrop system was a form
of family-sized tenancy.[17] This form of land tenure separates individuals into two polar groups with widely divergent life patterns. The landowners (*padroni*) usually maintained a local residence and closely supervised operations, but virtually never
engaged in any actual labor. The sharecrop family was not
invariably poor; in fact, there is scattered evidence to indicate
that peasants in central Italy rarely suffered the severe impoverishment common in the Veneto.[18] Braga concludes that the
social tensions that were manifest in the region, especially after
unification, were created not by poverty, but by the certainty
that there could be no social mobility and by the constant threat
that the sharecrop peasant might at any time lose whatever social
and economic position he had secured. Dovring similarly calls
attention to the impact of the decision-making structure of the
sharecrop system upon social and political life.[19] As practiced in
central Italy, the *mezzadria* system involved regular contact and
close association between landowner and *mezzadro*. While some
pieces of land passed from generation to generation, there was
uncertainty each year.[20]

And the annual need for renewal of contract was only one

---

[17] For a detailed helpful discussion of the sharecrop system in central
Italy, see the work by anthropologist Sydel Silverman, "Agricultural Organization, Social Structure and Values in Italy: Amoral Familism Reconsidered," *American Anthropologist* 70 (February 1968): 1-20.

[18] See Arthur L. Stinchcombe, "Agricultural Enterprise and Rural Class
Relations," *American Journal of Sociology* 67 (September 1961): 165-176.

[19] Giorgio Braga, *Sociologia elettorale della Toscana* (Rome: Edizione
Cinque Lune, 1963) and Folke Dovring, *Land and Labor in Europe, 1900-
1950* (The Hague: Nijhoff, 1956), p. 149.

[20] Many respondents reported family crises at renewal time. For example,
Interview #47.

traumatic event. There were opportunities for others. The allocation of authority, more than the standard of living, embittered the *mezzadri* against the landowners.[21] One should not ignore the fact that the *mezzadro* could and did benefit occasionally from the presence of landowner families. But gifts and favors were marred by the humiliating manner in which they were distributed.[22]

Some sharecrop families could enjoy communal cultural facilities built by the wealthy *padroni*, that many Venetian towns were unable to support. But again the personal social costs were high. In one Tuscan town, the distance between *padroni* and *mezzadri* was flamboyantly emphasized in the public theater. The *piazza* and *cafe* at the entrance were reserved for landowners and their special guests, who from the heights could literally look down on the sharecrop majority.[23]

The personal insecurity and regular humiliation involved in the authority system when fulfilling the sharecrop role embittered the *mezzadri* against the recognizable set of oppressors, the landowning caste. Such a social structure undoubtedly furnished fertile ground for political radicalism, but even under those unusual circumstances a revolt against traditional religious institutions and practices would not, I believe, have taken place had not the local clergy egregiously alienated their peasant congregations.

The Tuscan clergy badly mismanaged its situation. The clergy had to function within a local economy dominated by the share-

---

[21] Sharecropping is perhaps the most conflict ridden of all forms of farm tenure. In outright ownership, the individual is his own boss. In tenancy, a contract is made with the landlord and after that the tenant is his own boss. But in sharecropping, there are grounds for continuous landlord-lessee conflict. What to plant, and how much on the individual's own plot, the time and conditions of harvest, the responsibility for mistakes in judgment are all recurring issues. The most important cause for conflict is division of the crops.

The statement is from an unpublished manuscript by Juan Linz, cited by Richard Hamilton, *Affluence and the French Worker in the Fourth Republic* (Princeton, N.J.: Princeton University Press, 1967), p. 129n.

[22] One ex-*mezzadro* remembers getting bread and wine at Easter time, but he remembers more vividly having to bow before his *padrone* when receiving the gifts. Another recalls the prepension-days' custom of *sabatare*, the Saturday journey of elderly sharecroppers from door to door dependably collecting small coins from which to subsist until the next week. The coins helped make life easier; the begging engendered a sense of anger.

[23] This tale was recounted in Interview #47.

cropping system.[24] Yet the local priests personally alienated the majority of the population by ostensibly lending clerical sanction to that land-tenure system. Understaffed and poorly financed, the older generations of clergymen did not probe popular opinions, if they saw full churches on Sunday. A clergyman noted, "The old good priests, good men, were content with exteriors; they saw the Church full and were content."[25]

After the integration of Tuscany into the new Italian Republic, the local Church suffered financial catastrophe. Before the 1860s, the central Italian clergy was extremely prosperous. Its large annual income came from leasing extensive Church-owned lands according to the *canone* system. During the *risorgimento*, the state confiscated Church lands. In a short period, the Tuscan Church lost its capital, as well as its income.

Faced with this crisis, clergymen faced personal penury. Most Tuscan churchmen, especially parish priests, came from modest social backgrounds. No longer could they rely on the Church hierarchy for adequate living allowances. Of course, the clergy could have literally followed the vows of poverty; but most of them willingly accepted the generosity of the rich landowners, reciprocating that patronage with a tolerance of practices that deeply embittered the sharecrop majority.

The head of the community parishes (the *arciprete*) explained:

> Where I served as a country *parroco*, the priest used to be tied to the landowner, because the *padrone* gave the priest wood, bread, oil. He gave wine and then often extended invitations for dinner. The peasant saw them together and the *padrone* would say "get to work." And the priest was silent, he said nothing. . . .

> The peasants for the most part went to mass because, fundamentally, they were religious. And in the first row sat the *padrone*. [After the service] the *padrone* stationed himself at the door of the church and when the peasant walked out of the church, he said, "now to work." And the priest was silent. . . .

[24] There are a few places in Tuscany where direct cultivators, not sharecroppers, prevailed. In these areas, for example, in the Province of Lucca, Christian Democratic allegiances are pronounced and the Church is vigorous. For statistics on the agricultural population in Tuscany, see Corrado Barberis, *Le migrazioni rurali in Italia* (Milan: Feltrinelli, 1960), p. 118.

[25] Interview #93.

230

Then the moment came when the Communists said to the peasants, and no one had said it 'til then, "You are the equal of the *padrone*, you are people like him." The peasant put the priest in the same box as the landowner.[26]

The priests may not have realized that by depriving the sharecroppers of a respite from a social structure that constantly reminded them of their inferiority, it was inevitable that the clergy and the landowner would be thought of together as part of the same authority system.

It is remarkable that so many Tuscan respondents, clergymen, PCI leaders, and DC leaders alike see strong attachments to the Church still characteristic of the population.[27] The sociologist of religion, Burgalassi, himself a Tuscan clergyman, reports that of every thousand marriages performed, only sixteen were civil ceremonies, compared with the national average of thirty.[28]

In Tuscany a strong anticlerical rebellion against all churchmen and Church practice never developed. Instead, the clergy lost any influence in community affairs that *did not directly concern* religious life.[29] It lost the ability to transfer the mantle of unique political legitimacy to a chosen political organization. The Tuscan clergy was not in a position of strength from which it could declare radical Left political ideas alien and inappropriate for community citizens. By the time Socialist, and later Communist, political organizers came to central Italy, the majority of the people had turned away from the Church for social and political guidance.

[26] Interview #96.

[27] Eleven of the eighteen Communist leaders in Tuscany who answered a mailed questionnaire said they thought local religious traditions were strong. Four of the nine DC Tuscan respondents answered similarly. Clergymen report that in recent years the local population has afforded them great respect. One man remembers being pushed in the streets during the 1948 election campaign, but calls it an isolated incident. A PCI section secretary told me that the population is extremely tied to Church ritual. Men rarely attend masses, but many women do. According to the Communist leaders, virtually all the families in the commune have their children baptized, receive Easter blessings, build a Christmas creche, and are married and buried according to the Catholic ritual.

[28] Silvano Burgalassi, *Il comportamento religioso degli Italiani* (Florence: Vallecchi, 1968), p. 39. Data come from a 1960 survey.

[29] This interpretation may help explain the puzzling contradiction Burgalassi (p. 41) cannot understand. He found both religious observance and Communist voting pronounced in the provinces of Umbria, Lazio, Basilicata, Toscana, and Puglia.

No similar events took place in the Veneto. The Venetian clergy made the best of a good situation. Not only did it retain its traditional legitimacy and social influence, but emerged from a period of trial, first having to cope with the laws of the new secular state and then having to counter Socialist appeals, with a virtually unchallenged right to define the proper political values for its congregants, and therefore to bestow monopolistic political legitimacy on the party of its choice.

First, and most obviously, the northeastern Catholic Church was not involved with an oppressive class system. This form of relationship simply could not exist in an economy dominated by small farmers. Instead of catering to a small group of wealthy patrons, the local clergy in the Veneto provided many minor but important services for the community. As one of few local men with some education and with ties outside the community, the priest was a natural center of activity.[30] Key members of the local elites interviewed furnish illustrative supporting contemporary testimonies.[31]

The parish priest is, and was, the most important person in each town. . . .[32]

Many times clergymen supply a letter of recommendation.[33]

Here in our community, the Church still remains the *social church*. . . . Consider an outlying village? The priest represents the whole place. If the town councilors need to do something, they talk with the priest.[34]

Intimate involvement with the local peasantry was maintained in the Veneto even as the clergy and their allies organized strong units of the Catholic Congresses in 1874 to battle, in rather intransigent fashion, for the restoration of Vatican rights. In fact, in the 1870s and 1880s, the Venetian Congress units were simultaneously and energetically responding to both the secularism of the new liberal state and the equalitarianism that was the inspiration of the early Socialist movement. Leaders of the Congress movement were the first to organize large-scale popularly oriented programs. First, some relief to the poor and sick was provided

[30] De Rosa, *Giuseppe Sacchetti*, p. 221.
[31] Key members of the elite refer to the mayors, and local political party secretaries.
[32] Interview #23. [33] Interview #20. [34] Interview #26.

throughout local sections of the *Leghe Bianche*.[35] Then, in the cultural domain, simplified versions of the new work of Christian sociologists, especially Toniolo, were offered in church class-rooms.[36] And most important, efforts were made to help small farmers cope with crises stimulated by unification. The Congress units established the first low-cost credit institutions in the area. *La Banca Cattolica del Veneto* is remembered in one community, at least, as saving local farmers from usury and even in some cases making some capital available to smallholders, so that they could purchase minor tracts of ecclesiastical property.[37]

Another major accomplishment of the Congress Movement was the establishment of the multipurpose agricultural centers, the *Casse Rurali*. Cooperative efforts facilitated the production, mar-keting, and purchase of some farm machinery. What the Church demonstrated by actively supporting the *Casse* in the Veneto was not radicalism, for the Church was and remains basically con-servative, but an ability to modernize and revitalize its long-standing close ties to the rural majority. Much of this behavior in the Veneto preceded Pope Leo's famous encyclical of 1891, *Rerum Novarum*, which officially urged social activism on the Catholic hierarchy.

To be sure, those who accent the paternalism inherent in the pattern of clerical social concern are correct.[38] But this paternal-ism would not necessarily offend recipients, as would the de-meaning paternalism of the clergy and landlords in the central provinces. In the northeast, relationships between the clergy and the population, and even between the bourgeois landowners and the renting farmers, were not strained.[39] Catholics of the Veneto

[35] For some discussion of White Leagues, see Gabriele de Rosa, *Il partito popolare italiano* (Bari: Laterza, 1969); Giuseppe Are, *I Cattolici e la ques-tione sociale in Italia, 1894-1904* (Milan: Feltrinelli, 1963); and Richard A. Webster, *The Cross and the Fasces* (Stanford, Cal.: Stanford University Press, 1960). For a discussion of Bianchindustria history, see Interview #13.

[36] Are's discussion and excerption from Toniolo is very helpful, *I Cattolici*.

[37] Interview #13. Theoretically, the Church lands were to be sold in small portions even in terms of deferred payment to small farmers. But, in reality, save in extraordinary instances, such as took place in some parts of the Veneto, peasants could not secure loans. The private credit companies pre-ferred direct investment in the land themselves. See Denis Mack Smith, *Italy: A Modern History* (Ann Arbor, Mich.: University of Michigan Press, 1959), pp. 87-88.

[38] For example, Webster, *The Cross*.

[39] There is little documentation of the small farmers' relationship with the bourgeoisie. De Rosa's observations in *Giuseppe Sacchetti* are cautiously stated.

remember the assistance the Church provided as a rightful, appropriate outcome of loyalty to the clergy and the Catholic creed.

Even as the more progressive *Partito Popolare*, the early DC, supplanted the Congress leadership and led the Catholic masses slowly into the electoral arena in the late 1890s, the Venetian clergy maintained its leverage. Its ability to use advisory powers to exploit its unique position as intermediary between citizenry and political organizations, is demonstrated in electoral statistics. In local administrative elections when the Church encouraged participation by loyal Catholics, the turnout of eligible voters was high, in contrast to the remarkably low levels of voting in the national parliamentary elections that the Church continued to boycott for some years. Venetian voters turned out at the polls in national elections only when the Church hierarchy despaired of fighting parliamentary government in Rome. This clerical ability to regulate voter turnout was not characteristic in other regions of Italy. In the south, for example, turnout in legislative elections even in the first republican elections was considerably higher than was the case in local contests.[40]

The bond of allegiance between local clergymen and their constituencies was strengthened when Church leaders emphasized civil tranquillity, serenity, solidarity, dependability, and order, as opposed to the salvation of the heavenly realm. Venetian political elites even today like to contrast the familiar unostentatious, flexible rituals of their Venetian Church with the overly abstract, mystical, elaborate ceremonies they believe are observed elsewhere in Italy.[41] The symbols tying the northeastern farmer to his Church are familiar, not awe-inspiring. They are symbols that mostly "condense" around the notion of the trustworthiness of the parish priest as an individual rather than in the abstractions of theological principles.

The transfer of legitimacy from Catholic Church to Catholic political parties, first in local elections and then, with the end of the Papal prohibition of national political participation, to parliamentary candidates, was uncomplicated. But transfer may be a misleading term. The clergy urged loyal Catholics to support the Catholic party, but the primary ties of the population remained religious, not political. Every contemporary local politi-

---

[40] Capecchi, et al., *Il comportamento elettorale* and local archives.
[41] Interviews #16, #91.

cian in the Veneto went out of his way to make this point. DC leaders were candid. One said, "Here most of the people are still convinced that the Church is Christian Democracy."[42] Another explained voter psychology in this way: "In this area, the people are trustworthy. They see the priest as an example of altruism and generosity, who has continued a tradition. Therefore, it is a vote of trust."[43]

The few empirical studies of the sociology of religion in Italy offer some evidence of the survival of the centrality of the Catholic identification in the northeast. The people of the Venetian provinces remain more closely tied to the Church than the population of any other area. In fact, Venetians have the lowest percentage of civil marriages, the highest percentage of Easter communions, and the highest rates of attendance at Sunday mass in all of Italy. Only five Venetian marriages out of a thousand employed a civil ceremony, compared with an Italian average of thirty. Ninety percent of the population in the Venetian dioceses receive Easter communion, compared with an Italian national average of 61 percent. While only 37 percent of Italians attend Sunday mass, according to the best figures available, 80 percent of those in the Venetian dioceses are regular Sunday worshipers.[44]

Remarkable among clerics of any denomination, Venetian clergymen express satisfaction with the level of financial support the townspeople offer the Church:

> There is money that circulates and here the people are very generous. There is an extreme cordiality. There was a committee of families that went to the Bishop, it wanted to create a new parish, it wanted a new Church. There is a committee for the Church that functions marvelously.[45]

Traditional respect for the clergy erodes only under unusual circumstances such as those provided by the social structure of the central provinces during the period following the unification of Italy. The extraordinary enduring social and political influence of the Veneto clergy can be traced first to a helpful but not determinant agricultural economy, and secondly to the uncommon sensitivity of the northeastern clergy to community welfare.

42 Interview #21.   43 Interview #11.
44 Burgalassi, *Il comportamento religioso*, Chapter 2 presents 1960 data.
45 Interview #91.

CHALLENGE TO HEGEMONY: THE PCI IN NORTHEASTERN ITALY

How has the Communist party in an inhospitable environment challenged the hegemonic Christian Democrats? How does monopolistic legitimacy respond to political challenge? Even skillful management of traditional resources carried out within a supportive social structure cannot eliminate dissent. Our task in this section is to analyze the interaction between the Communist opposition to Christian Democratic hegemony and the strategy which has allowed the DC to maintain its remarkable strength.

First, it should be clear that within this region only the PCI seriously attempts political challenge. The Partito Socialista Italiano (PSI) preceded the Communists as an organized presence in the area. And, in the communities examined, the PSI polls almost as many votes. But the political activities of the Socialists are, at best, sporadic. Today, as in the late nineteenth century when the local branches of the party were established, the PSI in the Veneto is led by a handful of middle-class citizens, many of them merchants, who seem absolutely reconciled to DC predominance, content with the civic visibility of seats on the town council, reserving their bursts of vigor for criticisms of factional schisms within their own party.[46]

In discussing the PCI in the Veneto, it is necessary to distinguish between farm areas and industrial centers. The communities on which this report is based allow us to make that contrast. In agricultural Pianbianco, the PCI is largely a party of the *braccianti*, the agricultural day laborers. Strength among the *braccianti* has eroded through continuing emigration. While most of the party membership came from that group, none of the activists are day laborers. Not one of the PCI representatives on the town council, nor the secretary of the party section is a day laborer. To keep the PCI section alive in decaying Pianbianco external support is required. The real leader of Pianbianco's band of PCI activists is a full-time Federation official who, as one of his many duties, supervises activities in the farm town and serves as *capo gruppo* (party leader) of the four PCI councilmen. His chief support comes from a former resident who now

---

[46] Ineffective, stable, mainly middle-class Socialist minorities were observed in each of the four communities studied. The PSI at the local level, appear to have difficulty mounting a serious challenge to either Catholic or Communist dominance.

works as an artisan in a provincial center more than a half-hour away.

Towns like Pianbianco that cannot attract factories seem doomed to increasing decay. The Communists seem to have reconciled themselves to this situation and maintain an organized presence in such places mostly as a means of preserving the dependable, if small, electoral support the town yields and to visibly accent its widespread presence.

In the dwindling farm areas, even in the decade of the 1960s, monopolistic political legitimacy rests more on a purely traditional foundation. Modernization has not been forced by the opposition, nor by the needs of a more complex local population, nor by elements of loyal Catholic clerical or lay leadership. The DC hegemony has few challenges. In fact, in the decaying farm areas of the Veneto almost no effort is made to disguise the primacy of Church over party. The secretary of the DC zone committee sees his job as less the recruitment of party members and the sponsorship of party activities and more a matter of coordinating ties among parish priests.[47] Talking about the depopulated farm region he supervises, the secretary candidly notes, "If we ever have the active support of the Church torn from us, the party will be sabotaged."[48] The DC does not even bother to maintain distinct party headquarters, merely using the parish house when meetings are scheduled. The current deputy mayor of Pianbianco, one of the handful of elementary school teachers who are key DC activists, stated succinctly, "The political party [DC] exists inasmuch as the parish organization exists."[49]

This has not been the case in the industrial communities of the area that are representative of ever wider sectors of the region.[50] Here monopolistic legitimacy has had to adapt to a more sustained and substantial minority opposition and to a new social climate. In Bianchindustria, the local PCI draws almost all its strength from workers in the older, sizable industrial facilities in the area, and from the Confederazione Generale Italiana del Lavoro (CGIL) union organization that developed among left-wing employees.[51]

[47] Interview #23. [48] Ibid. [49] Interview #26.
[50] For a discussion of diffusion of industry in the northeast, see Calogero Muscara, *La Geografia dello Sviluppo* (Milan: Edizioni di Comunità, 1967) and the transformation matrices in Capecchi et al., *Il comportamento elettorale.*
[51] Interviews #39, #40, #41, #42, #43.

237

We must probe more deeply into the strategies that monopolistic legitimators use to ward off and forestall challenge. Three main alternatives that we may paraphrase as elimination, preemption, and domestication have been prominent.[52] The post-World War II political history of the area illustrates each of the defensive postures, although the clergy and most DC leaders of the Veneto today prefer a variant of the third strategy.

Elimination

The active harassment of Communist militants by the Church and the newly organized DC party units in the period that began during the election campaign of 1948 and continued until the mid-1950s was a break with tradition, and from many points of view a culturally uncongenial choice for the hegemonic Catholics. This was the response of a Church and party convinced, for a short time, that they had to fight desperately for existence. Therefore, a campaign of elimination, utilizing new symbols, was launched. The social and economic discrimination so common during 1948-1955 yielded to a more subtle defense of legitimacy, which most of the clergy and many DC party leaders found more congenial.

Even so, a brief review of the events of the 1948-1955 era demonstrates vividly the enormous resources of the culturally entrenched, uniquely legitimate Catholic hegemony, when fully utilizing its resources. Instead of invoking the positive symbols of a Catholic society: the good priest, the concerned Church, the tranquil life style, the Christian principles of the DC; the hegemonic Christian Democrats propagated symbols that stressed the evil, sacrilegious dimensions of the combined 1948 Socialist-Communist opposition.

Invoking fears of the takeover of Czechoslovakia, and of the PCI's friendship for the Soviet Union, the DC and the openly partisan organized clergy depicted the opposition as tainted with atheism. DC party posters depicted the PCI as depriving poor Italians of bread from Marshall Plan programs and, though the public statements of the Left Alliances promised otherwise, the campaigners of the DC assured the largely rural population that confiscation of even small properties would follow a victory of the United Left.

The priests refused the sacraments to known Communists, go-

---

[52] Berger and Luckmann, *Social Construction*, p. 139.

ing so far as to have party spokesmen excommunicated by higher Church officials. Traditional religious rituals, such as the Easter blessing of the home were denied to all Communists.[53] Moreover, the definition of a Communist was broad; union veterans remember that for years priests refused to absolve CGIL members at confession.[54] And the children of Communists were often shunned in school. One bitter PCI activist remembered "fifteen or twenty years ago, when someone in this town saw a Communist, he saw a leper."[55]

Perhaps more injurious still were the economic sanctions Communists in the DC stronghold had to endure. Every member of the PCI minorities who was not self-employed was fired at least once during the period from 1948 to 1956.[56] The willingness of the Church to work hand-in-glove with factory owners who cared mostly about maintaining a nonunionized work force to ensure low wages was not congruent with the established local clerical tradition of some concern for the mass of the population. The air of national crisis or the hope of permanently eliminating all political opposition, or a combination of these emotions, came to dominate clerical thinking at the time.

The harsh strategy of elimination that involved cooperation with the exploitative capitalistic owners was gradually abandoned by the Venetian Church. Elements of the DC leadership candidly acknowledge a nostalgia for a Church that actively intervenes in politics, impugning the moral integrity of Communists.[57] But a combination of national Church directives after the ascendance of John XXIII to the Papacy and wide dissent within local clerical and party ranks emanating mostly from younger militants helped return the dominant Catholics to a more fruitful, positive, benevolent defense of their monopolistic legitimacy.

As a result of a strategy of elimination, even after its official demise, the DC has been rather successful in discouraging wideranging relationships of PCI partisans. Social isolation and insulating activities characterize the PCI minority party groups. In the Veneto, both in the industrial communities as well as in the decaying redoubts of traditional DC hegemony, the PCI organizations continue to draw both leaders and followers from single

[53] This was the uniform experience of all PCI militants interviewed in the Veneto. No clergyman denied the incidence of such events.

[54] Interview #105.   [55] Interview #72.

[56] Interviews #39, #40, #41, #42, #43.

[57] Interview #16.

social strata. In striking contrast, in central Italian communities, where local Communist groups are strongest, the interclass nature of support is especially impressive. In both of the industrial sites discussed here, the PCI and the affiliated CGIL union branch flourish almost exclusively in a handful of industrial establishments. Unwittingly, the very concentration of PCI supporters aids the hegemonic opposition in its chosen task of containing and insulating Communist sympathizers.

In Bianchindustria, with a 1968 population of 19,200, the PCI is led by five principal activists. Every one of the five has a working-class background. Four of these individuals hold seats on the town council; the fifth serves as secretary to the local PCI party section. Not only do most of the 165 dues-paying party members work in the same large factory, but all four key male elite members work there too. The collective effect of these circumstances is the isolation of party members.

Insulation in the work place is reinforced by the tendency for membership to run in families. Three of the militants, including the sole female member of the council, the PCI council spokesman, and the secretary of the section are married to Communist party members. Without noting anything unusual, militants routinely report that family social activities are closely attuned to PCI events. Local leaders readily admit that both their personal social lives and party activities are relatively closed and even use the word sectarian to describe them.[58]

The limited boundaries of the local PCI world are paradoxically accented by political efforts hypothetically designed to extend, and not just to reinforce, support. For when describing major efforts such as newspaper sales, meetings, and campaigning, the activists make it plain that they solicit help only among families they know to be potentially sympathetic.

The persistence of a rather circumscribed world of working-class families allied to the CGIL where primary group ties prevail is striking. Both the ingenious tactics of the Catholic opposition and the local PCI's choice of inappropriate targets help to account for this situation.

Preemption

The hegemonic Christian Democrats emphasize a policy program determined to produce concrete benefits for broad seg-

[58] Interviews #39, #40, #41, #42, #43.

240

ments of the community. In this evolution of strategy, the DC elite has never directly incorporated any Marxist ideological positions, although leaders frankly admit they understand the mass appeal of broadly redistributive programs. Rather than trying to adopt uncongenial and perhaps dishonest radical rhetoric, the ruling leaders rather flamboyantly shun and deride any insignia of extreme conservatism. For this purpose, the tiny local unit of the openly capitalistic Partito Liberale Italiano (PLI) serves them well. The dominant Catholic politicians often condemn what they like to call the "socially irresponsible" positions of the few factory owners who are conspicuous in local Liberal ranks. Socially responsible policies are exemplified in projects such as a new hospital, schools in the outlying hamlets, a technical institute for industrial job training, a new city hall, and an expanded central plaza.

The productive administrative record of the DC is regularly extolled in an ostensibly nonpolitical quarterly magazine controlled by leaders of the party. In the periodical, clerical and civic accomplishments are deliberately mixed together. Prominent members of the Catholic hierarchy alternate with bigwigs in the Christian Democratic elite in filling the feature-story sections.[59]

By interweaving the reinforcements of customary Catholic loyalty with the support engendered by helpful new projects, the hegemonic leadership is skillfully preparing the ground for a modernized version of legitimacy maintenance.[60] As traditional Church intervention in political life becomes less frequent and, even where practiced, less absolutely dependable, the DC Veneto elite seems to be supplanting sources of traditional legitimation with the fruits of government patronage.[61]

Key local leaders enjoy excellent ties with some of the most important members of the *Doroteo* faction of the Christian Democratic party. This moderate group is currently the largest in the national party and has many ties to state corporations. There is ample evidence that some of the proud project accomplishments partly enumerated above had central government assistance.

---

[59] Each issue of the monthly magazine, started in 1961, was carefully read. Not one article was devoted to explicit partisan appeals. On the other hand, each issue heralded some achievement of the DC local government.

[60] Merelman, "Learning and Legitimacy."

[61] For a discussion of the skillful usage of government patronage by DC politicians in another region, see Tarrow, *Peasant Communism*, Chapter 12.

Having accepted the inevitability, indeed the desirability of local industrialization, the DC seems to have the resources to retain legitimacy in a changing social environment. The Christian Democrats are not abandoning traditional strategies. Rather they are partially substituting resources. The DC now utilizes government aid to local industry to buttress a diminished clerical ability to shape political loyalties.

Domestication

The contemporary version of monopolistic Christian Democratic political legitimacy relies on domesticating and segregating the opposition as a party, as it extends measured toleration to known Communists, as individuals. The governing Catholic forces, in sharp contrast to ensconced central Italian Communists, work to minimize the proper role of partisan politics in community life. The DC elites promote the impression that outspoken Communist opposition is not evil, but meaningless and out of place in the community.

Here it is instructive to compare the two Veneto communities with a similar pair of towns long controlled by PCI administrations in central Italy. In the northeastern communities, though there is some variation even between the farm and industrial centers, town council meetings are held infrequently: in Pianbianco two or three times a year, in Bianchindustria five or six times a year. By contrast, council meetings are held at least monthly in the PCI towns. A single meeting may be adjourned and may stretch over several evenings and special sessions are frequently invoked.

The tone and content of the meetings offer vivid differences. In the Veneto, the dominant DC leaders work quickly and quietly through a short agenda. In the Communist towns, there is a deliberate effort to accent and dramatize the significance of all political discussion. Especially prominent in the heated, politicized discussions in central Italian council meetings are the themes of international politics. By focusing on areas outside the community and Italy, the PCI has ample material with which to portray itself as a dynamic left-wing party dedicated to militant goals. The dominant DC politicians localize their discussion because their claim to exclusive political legitimacy lies in the claim to special virtue for the established customs of the area. One might reemphasize here that the DC variety of legitimacy can be bolstered by a relatively relaxed political operation. In sharp contrast, where PCI legitimacy is established, it must be continuously refueled by Communist party activities that impress the population with their meaning. DC legitimacy has historical justification; the PCI has not yet engineered this kind of cultural acceptance. Militants in central Italy intent upon maintaining lopsided hegemonies seem correct in their preoccupation with a highly visible local social presence.

Though they work hard to minimize the role of partisan politics, the flexible Catholic manipulators of an established legitimacy no longer suppress the opposition: they smother them with slightly patronizing forbearance. When PCI spokesmen do manage to talk of fascism in Greece, the DC majority listens quietly, refuses to respond, and then moves on to another issue.

The change in clerical attitudes toward the local PCI militants is instructive. By the late 1960s, the clergy had, in the developing Veneto town, abandoned political sermons and ritual exclusion as "out of place" in modern settings.[62] The chief clergyman of the community, the *arciprete*, and several of his conservative colleagues in hamlets surrounding the main town center, talked of Communists as a special, mild, home-grown variety of radical. Said the *arciprete*, we have "white" communism here. "It is like a vegetable that has an unpleasant red skin and tender white meat, not like harsh fanatics of Emilia."[63] One parish priest talked of "'my Communists' who insist upon voting PCI, but regularly attend Church and seek my advice on all important matters."[64] While I do not want to push the analogy too far, such language reminded me of a mother scolding incorrigible but "basically good" children, who are not to be taken seriously by adults but who, with proper guidance, will mature. The clergy probably have little expectation of altering the loyalties of the PCI minority. The clergy's main hope is to help persuade the majority of townspeople to perceive the Communists as silly rather than as a serious alternative or a dangerous threat.

Protecting monopolistic political legitimacy through domestication and segregation imposes costs on the majority. At times, cooperation with the vigorous dedicated Communist minority would undoubtedly benefit the community. Situations like fighting natural disasters or opposing the impending shutdown of a

[62] Interview #90.   [63] Interview #90.   [64] Interview #89.

major industrial facility, or even routine matters like the efficient supervision of public works projects, are tasks that require as much grass-roots leadership and organization as possible. Openly acknowledging the energy and discipline of PCI militants, the hegemonic Catholics seem to have evolved a formula. They eschew any cooperation with the PCI. However, clergy, PCI activists, and DC elites all relate instances of *personal* cooperation. For example, when road construction contracts are inexpertly fulfilled in Bianchindustria, the complaints of a knowledgeable PCI town councilor are immediately accepted. But when that councilor's party *as a group* wants to help supervise a public works operation, the whole question is quickly tabled.[65] To pose another somewhat fanciful analogy, the parallels between the DC-clerical interaction with local Communists resembles the relationship of some United States southern whites with blacks in the precivil rights era: limited private acceptance and strict public distance, thereby preserving the symbolism and ceremony that surrounded the accepted legitimate definition of monopolistic political power.

The Communist response to this strategy of domestication has, in the past, been ineffective. On one level, the PCI leaders have stated their undoubtedly sincere belief that "the DC vote is an act of religion" and they have angrily denounced the pervasive influence of the Church in the political life of the community. They dispute the Catholic theology abstractly. Yet on another level, that of day-to-day social interaction, the Communist minority has largely assumed the role the hegemonic majority defined for it. In part, the preservation of Catholic hegemony is thus buttressed by the minority. By valuing the rewards of some individual recognition and social integration, Communists are apt to accept public definition of their political group as alien. The majority maneuvered the minority PCI leadership into a position where the PCI grass-roots elite have some stake in conserving the status quo. One implicit Communist rationalization for this mode of behavior is a citation of the impossibility of combating such a solidly entrenched party.

What emerges from this curious mixture is the retreatist, rather unaggressive political pattern the Veneto Communists maintain. The local PCI unit is a kind of bastion or fortress. And in recent years, it is an unbeleaguered fortress, for this arrange-

[65] Interview #42 and council records.

244

ment suits the DC majority. The Communist minority helps seg-regate itself politically and from this isolation is in no position to challenge a flexibly managed (or manipulated) sense of legiti-macy among most of the population. Indeed, to the present, de-fense—that is, preservation of the small group of activists and their dependable 12-15 percent of local voters—rather than ex-pansion seems to have served as the primary PCI goal.

The Vulnerabilities of Monopolistic Legitimacy

What are the prospects for a decline in hegemonic Catholic legit-imacy and alternatively for the evolution of a publicly accepted Communist party? More particularly, what are the strategic al-ternatives for the minority Communists as the northeast under-goes alterations in its economic base and social structure?

Many prominent theories link, in one way or another, a popu-lation experiencing industrialization with both the erosion of tra-ditionalism and the development of radical attitudes and behavior. Many writers have reevaluated Marx's pessimistic assessments of the prospects for the development of radical self-awareness among recent immigrants from the countryside. Mod-ern authors have stressed that farm people who find it necessary to leave the land for unfamiliar, unhealthy factory employment and urban ghetto residential quarters are ripe to rebel against the capitalistic system and those who support it. Some discussions stress the strong possibility of a sense of alienation among new factory workers whose exertions in the factory are devoid of meaning and intrinsic satisfactions.[66]

Earlier, this report emphasized the concentration of Commu-nist support in a few established Veneto factories. Moreover, the overall pattern of remarkably stable voting patterns has been repeatedly underlined. Our task in this section is to explore the possibility that the multiplication of factories and the reaction of new workers to the rigors and complexities of industrial employ-ment will alter partisan preferences and thereby affect the socio-political relationship between dominant Christian Democrats and their Communist opponents.

[66] For a reassessment of Marxian hypotheses, see John C. Leggett, "Up-rootedness and Working Class Consciousness," *American Journal of Sociology* 58 (May 1963): 682-694, and the Chinese and American research cited in nn. 5 and 6 of his article.

To investigate the possibility that an erosion of traditional DC legitimacy will occur as greater numbers of farmers enter factories, I interviewed a group of twenty-six peasants born in Bianchindustria who decided to become industrial employees.[67] When asked whether they had changed any of their political ideas, since beginning factory work, a very small number of respondents answered positively. Only four (15 percent) of the twenty-six *peasant-workers*[68] said they had altered any of their political ideas. Twenty-two respondents (85 percent) reported no reorganization of political attitudes, even when this question was followed by careful probes.

The new workers appear to be apolitical. On first inspection the data on party identifications indicate that the response group is remarkably nonpolitical: only seven clearly support the dominant party in the community. The Socialist and Communist parties each claim one worker; seventeen workers declare no party identification at all.

Yet a closer examination of the interview transcripts does reveal a political dimension in what the respondents articulate as a religious identification. Two men who are registered Christian Democrats reveal this information, immediately and proudly, only when asked whether they are members of a Catholic association. Earlier in the interview these same men had denied any interest in politics and any connection with a political party. Fourteen of the fifteen nonparty identifiers among the respondents report regular church attendance, a custom they share with everyone else in the sample save the lone Communist loyalist. I think that if I had put the question, "What do you think the duties of a Catholic include?" rather than asking only about

[67] Local archives demonstrated that most of the limited migration to Bianchindustria is from the neighboring countryside. Interviews with immigrants from other regions would be unrepresentative. Therefore, I selected, randomly, males listed in the town registry as locally born, but who had changed their predominant occupational status from farmer to factory worker. The set of interviews with the new factory workers is not strictly random. Because the town registry maintained many mistaken occupational categorizations, it was necessary to check a list of fifty male electors listed as factory workers who had changed their occupational categories before the twenty-six interviews could be collected. Five refused to be interviewed. The talks in Bianchindustria were conducted by a student assistant recommended by Italian academics. He used a prepared questionnaire. With two exceptions, the interviews were tape-recorded.

[68] I have adopted a literal translation of the Italian *contadini-operai* because I think the expression is precise.

church attendance and formal membership in church groups, I would have elicited many statements of Christian Democratic loyalty among the ostensible nonparty identifiers. This small set of interviews supports the discussion in the first section of this chapter that stresses the development of an inconspicuous, persistent, clerically defined traditional political hegemony.

The Catholic world demonstrates a capacity, within its own spectrum, to retain loyalists even as they experience change in life styles. Of the four peasant-workers who do report a change in their political perspectives, three retain an affiliation with the Christian Democrats. For example, one man is careful to point out that he is an anti-Communist. He attributes his improved understanding of politics to membership in the Associazioni Cristiane dei Lavoratori Italiani (ACLI), a group affiliated with the left wing of the DC.[69] Another says that until he was forty-five years old, he did not realize a person could work through politics to help himself. This new consciousness resulted in multiple memberships in the Catholic Union, the Confederazione Italiana Sindacati Lavoratori (CISL); the Christian Democratic party; and *Azione Cattolica*, a Church association.[70] A broadly articulated Catholic organizational structure may have some problems in cohesiveness, but its range can accommodate some movement to the political left internally.

Only one man of the twenty-six interviewed reacted to the factory environment in a manner that led him to join the Communist-affiliated union, the CGIL, and support the Communist party. "One sees with one's eyes that there is no justice," he said. "The owners take everything."[71] The respondent traced his new understanding of politics to the first strikes organized in the tannery where he works. He was a new activist and broke with the Church. He is the only respondent who maintained that he had changed his ideas about religion. "Priests," he said, "have no interest in the problems of factory workers."[72] The respondent stopped going to church regularly. Profound political change seems to require the alteration of church allegiance. So fundamental is the Church—its clergy, social activities, and religious ritual—to the population of Bianchindustria that only an intense

[69] Peasant-worker Interview #26.
[70] Peasant-worker Interview #5.
[71] Peasant-worker Interview #12.
[72] Ibid.

247

interest in a political party radically different from the one they have long supported will stimulate factory laborers to reorient their perceptions drastically.[73]

A sizable shift of new factory workers to the Communists appears to be unlikely in the Veneto. The intelligent invocation of Catholic identity by Christian Democratic elites within the setting of a social structure that remains capable of supporting conservative politics, blocks a mass migration to the radical Left. Strategies of maintenance were analyzed in the last section. Here we need to devote some attention to conditions of the local social structure. The PCI depends in the Veneto upon the support, albeit minority support, of full-time factory workers in large plants concentrated in urban centers. Yet gradual industrialization in the northeast often involves employees who are part-time farmers, working in small plants diffused around the periphery of an urban center.[74]

Research in societies as diverse as the United States, Germany, and Japan testifies to the conservative effect of lingering ties to rural life.[75] The objective economic advantages of such an arrangement that might retard salary dissatisfaction are manifest: substantial savings on food and housing costs. Typical, I suspect, are the small vineyards, truck vegetable gardens, and stock-raising farms that Bianchindustria peasant-workers often maintained. Perhaps even more significant, from the perspective of preserved political ties, is the availability of industrial jobs in the immediate area, obviating the need for uprooting unstable family life. Migration is rarely necessary and the peasant-worker can

[73] Using French data, Hamilton, *Affluence and the French Worker*, p. 274, argues that religion has a very great moderating effect on those workers who have maintained a commitment to the Church.

At least in northeastern Italy, we do not find the "de-Christianization" of the working class which Frank M. Myers, "Social Class and Political Change in Western Industrial Systems," *Comparative Politics* 2 (April 1970), argues accompanied European industrialization, thus freeing workers from strong conservative influence, rendering them "potentially responsive to radical ideologies," p. 397.

[74] See Muscara, *La Geografia* for indicative data. To my knowledge, this complex social ph. .omenon has been minimally investigated.

[75] See S. H. Franklin, *The European Peasantry: The Final Phase* (London: Methuen, 1969); Bruce L. Melvin, "The Place of the Part-Time Farmer," *Rural Sociology* 19 (1954): 281-286; Glenn Fuguitt, "A Typology of Part-Time Farming, *Rural Sociology* (1962), and the *New York Times* feature on the southeast, "Industry in Rural South Sets U.S. Pace in Growth," July 2, 1973, pp. 1 and 18.

often arrange for family members, often his wife, to earn extra funds, when there is a seasonal workload in the factory.[76] Especially when the industrial outlets are located outside major urban concentrations—and this is increasingly common as road and power infrastructure improves—daily, even twice daily, commuting is not an onerous chore.

From one perspective, then, the emergence of the little-investigated peasant-worker class can serve as a mechanism that facilitates the transition from a farm to an industrial-capitalist society. Mass migration from the countryside is avoided, but at the same time, more factory employment frees land to be grouped in larger, more efficient agricultural units.[77]

But there is another perspective to be considered. A rapid increase in the proportion of the labor force involved in some form of factory labor necessarily complicates social arrangements. In Bianchindustria, for example, in the years between the 1950 and 1960 censuses, the industrial work force increased by 61.1 percent and local figures indicate only a slightly slower growth in the following decade. During this relatively smooth period of social change, unions acquired a new prominence, workingmen's recreational clubs were formed, as were commuters' clubs. The Church itself, ever alert, helped establish other groups: some daycare facilities for children of working mothers and an expanded ACLI (Catholic Workers) quarters among them. Does this tendency to multiply group life have any political implication? Jean Blondel, for one, has hypothesized that it does. Blondel argues that the capacity for the transfer of legitimacy weakens as individuals multiply their associational ties and are subject to more complex group pressures.[78] The observer may correctly reply that in the Veneto, the Church itself has helped foster some of these new associations. Certainly this is the case, but part of the sponsorship has been reluctant and, importantly, the new groups strengthen a less conservative sector of the local clergy. Moreover, even though the Church may lend assistance to selected groups, the ability to politically lead the individuals joining those associations may decrease.

Consider the union situation. More than half the new worker

---

[76] A similar pattern seems to be developing in southern Italy. See Tarrow, "Political Economy," p. 107.

[77] S. H. Franklin, *The European Peasantry*, p. 22.

[78] Blondel, *Comparative Government*, p. 70.

249

group have joined: eleven, the CISL; two, the CGIL; one, the Unione Italiana del Lavoro (UIL). Others express lively interest. Several frankly admit that they derive full benefits of contract agreements without paying membership fees. The full-time union organizer, who simultaneously heads the Catholic ACLI and CISL units, reports steadily increasing interest in his organizations. He notes that as the peasant-workers spend some time at their industrial jobs, which in Bianchindustria are mostly in small and medium-sized tanneries, the trend will accelerate. While the small numbers are obviously only indicative, it seems significant that a much larger group of the respondents thinks it important to join unions, rather than political parties. Of the group of 26, only 5 hold party membership cards: four Christian Democrats and one Socialist.

Yet neither increasing union membership nor deep economic dissatisfactions yield significant partisan change. The peasant-workers report fundamental complaints. Neither the extra benefits they can derive from supplementary farm activity, nor the fact that 24 of the 26 acknowledge the family finances are significantly improved, prevent fully 87 percent (22) of the peasant-workers from being unhappy about the levels of their salaries or the practices frequently employed to exploit inexperienced employees. They consistently note that salary zones, which at the time of the research regulated wage structures of industrial categories in different parts of Italy, provided unjustly low rates in the Veneto, as compared with Lombardy and Tuscany. Similarly, they condemn the common practice of employing underage apprentices and the extension of the trainee period beyond legal limits. In contrast to Fiat workers, 81 percent preferred full farm labor, if it paid as well as industrial employment.[79]

The apparent paradox of minor political change and major complaints is deepened by the knowledge that only 4 of the 26 peasant-workers in the sample believe Italy is a democracy. Most of the respondents say a "real" democracy would do more for poor people, for workers, for old people, in short phrases we recognize as standards of Communist party programs. Yet of this group of peasant-workers who conceive of democracy in terms

[79] The study of Fiat workers of rural background is presented by Paolo Ammassari, "The Italian Blue-Collar Worker," in N. F. Dufty (ed.), *The Sociology of the Blue-Collar Worker* (London: Brill, 1969), esp. pp. 16-18.

of the social benefits, only one is a Communist voter and another a moderate Socialist.

Although admittedly hampered by some structural conditions and the extensive range of the Catholic organizational spectrum, the PCI still seems in the decade of the 1960s to have underutilized some opportunities available to it, for many new workers are broadly dissatisfied. No suggestion is made that the Veneto Communists could have made broad gains. Yet it would appear that especially among the new workers policy positions that on the one hand accented higher wages and better working conditions in tanneries and on the other hand avoided any denunciation of local clergymen would have achieved some growth in electoral support, while, perhaps even more crucially, injecting a sense of innovative vitality into local PCI activities. It may be that the Communist minority overly simplified its vision of its opposition and chose to denounce openly the least vulnerable aspect of the DC-Catholic legitimacy, namely, traditional religious leadership.

More recent strategic thinking indicates that the local PCI is considering accepting the social primacy of the Veneto Catholic Church. As it accepts the centrality of the clerical role, it attempts to link or at least color some of its own activities and major local personnel with the symbols of Catholic legitimacy. Similarly, the Communists are experimenting with the abandonment of long-term originally defensive propaganda denouncing the intimate tie between the local clergy and the community Christian Democratic organization, that only seemed to infuriate most local residents and reinforce PCI isolation. Instead the PCI is working toward expanding the scope of political life that is accepted in the area. This goal requires that Communist militants disregard the inequities of the past and work to publicize and demonstrate flexibility.

There is some evidence of initial developments in this direction. The most important of them has been stimulated by the indisputable growing autonomy of local unions, especially since the rash of national militancy during 1968-1969. As more united trade-union organizations press for social change, it seems clear that as a party the PCI stands most to gain from a cooperative union movement in the long run. Yet in the short term, the Communist party must not reverse their contemporary position of up-

251

holding a genuine independence on the part of union allies they effectively controlled in the past.[80] Viewed at the grass roots, the developing union autonomy will continue to require special forbearance by the minority PCI sections, like that of Bianchindustria. Funding, recruiting willing militants, and securing physical facilities will be even harder. Yet precisely where they find themselves a marginal, tolerated minority, the PCI stands most to gain eventually from encouraging CGIL autonomy and interunion cooperation. For the CGIL within the context of the union movement, and not the Communist party per se, has the best chance of breaking the barrier of illegitimacy that surrounds radical political life. The PCI might then step through the breach in the wall of isolation.

In Bianchindustria, the CGIL organizer is making candid efforts to solidify the separate, non-PCI identity he has begun to establish for his group. He notes that he would like to have a headquarters apart from the *Casa del Popolo* because, "although they are mistaken, workers are reluctant to enter the building, because they assume they are walking into Communist party headquarters."[81] The official specifically notes the advantages accruing to the union from the distinction the Church is now willing to make between CGIL and PCI.[82]

Discussions with the leader of the CISL, the DC-affiliated union, confirm the local appearance of increased interunion cooperation. In fact, so convinced is the CISL leader that unions must be distinct from political parties that he probably will not stand for reelection as a Christian Democratic delegate to the town council for fear that CISL members will confuse his trade-union and partisan political roles. Both CGIL and CISL local leaders readily acknowledge that the emerging cooperation would have been quite unthinkable as late as the mid-1960s, and impossible without tacit Church toleration, if not encouragement.

The industrial sphere that attracts most cooperative effort is the one which has grown fastest and has no entrenched union organization, namely, the tannery industry where peasant-workers are most prominent. Both union leaders acknowledge some difficulty in reconciling the interests of part-time farmers with

---

[80] For a recent view of party-union relationships, see D.L.M. Blackmer, "Italian Communism: Strategy for the 1970's," *Problems of Communism* 21 (May-June 1972): pp. 50-52.

[81] Interview #105.   [82] Ibid.

factory employees living in urban centers. But the leaders believe that low salary scales and unsanitary conditions of the tanneries will bring the peasant-workers into the trade-union movement. Both leaders argue that their tasks will be made easier if partisan politics are minimized, since the peasant-workers, they note, are particularly uninterested in partisan appeals.[83]

Allowing, indeed encouraging, CGIL autonomy and interunion unity, may in the short run cost the PCI some dependable militants and valued opportunities for politicization. Prospects for long-term gain lie in the ability to call upon the support of the unionized worker, even if enrolled in another party, for social change the party favors, and the achievement of a diffused perception of the party as a fully accepted participant in local political life.

Both goals may be best stimulated by the PCI's decision not to sabotage the growing strength of the left-wing factions of the Christian Democratic party. Certainly, in Bianchindustria, and it would appear in other parts of the northeast as well, the growth of the Catholic labor movement swells the power of the Church-oriented workers' associations, such as ACLI, at the expense of the various components of Catholic Action long dominant among clerical associations in the area and closely allied with the most conservative elements in the regional Church hierarchy.[84] For the PCI, this gradual shift of influence within the hegemonic party, still predominantly conservative, makes instances of public cooperation more likely and statements aimed at reminding the population of a Communist's doubtful morality less common.

Another significant indication of PCI willingness to forgo both immediate small gain in votes among new workers and perhaps even a risk of short-term loss of militants is the effort to inspire some dialogue with willing members of the local clergy. The goal is a strengthening of the emerging moderates in the parishes of the Veneto. Carrying out these intentions has proved difficult. For the lone newly elected deputy Communist from the large Veneto constituency, dialogue on any terms appears more useful than rhetorical denunciation, which, in fact, helps the opposing

[83] Interviews #105, #14.

[84] For a discussion of the various associational groups tied to the church and their ideological tendencies, see Brunelli et al., *La presenza sociale*, esp. pp. 340-344.

253

majority keep the PCI isolated. During the 1963 parliamentary election, he engaged in a series of unprecedented public discussions with a young priest interested in exploring the common ground between Marxism and Catholicism. As long as these dialogues remained relatively inconspicuous, they were tolerated by the local hierarchy in spite of Christian Democratic objections. However, when the Communist leader appeared as an invited speaker before a group of Catholic youth and the priest in question talked of toleration in a sermon, the highest officials in the diocese forbade further public interactions.[85] Instead of openly denouncing this ban, the PCI activist has resolved to continue his clerical contacts on a personal level. His hope and the hope of his party in the region is that any dialogue with clergymen who believe they can find common ground with the PCI may aid in driving a wedge between the Church and the present key incumbents in the Christian Democratic regime.

Such a choice has much to recommend it, for the great strength of the Catholic cultural hegemony in the area focused around the personal qualities of parish priests. If growing numbers of such revered "condensation symbols" of monopolistic legitimacy find it useful to talk and work with Communists, the taint of immorality attached to the PCI can wear thin. The investment of legitimacy in social roles rather than abstractions made the Catholic-DC hegemony especially strong, but also builds in special vulnerabilities that the PCI is only beginning to exploit.

Some sign of public disapproval, by even a handful of clergymen, of the policies of the upper-middle-class notables who control the local DC section is very beneficial for the PCI.[86] First, it demonstrates divisions within a party that prided itself on unity. Second, it reintroduces political conflict into community affairs without heaping opprobrium for such an act on the minority PCI. Naturally, the sacral source of the conflict makes it harder to brand manifestation of political hostility as inappropriate and illegitimate. Once again, in this operation, there is a good prob-

[85] Interviews #40, #91.

[86] A social background analysis of the dominant Christian Democratic local elite documents this assertion. One-third of the Bianchindustria elite is professional or industrialist; another 50 percent are public or private middle-class white collar workers. And the key leaders including the Mayor are all from this group. This tendency for DC areas to be controlled by a rather small group of notables is also reported by *L'Attivista* researchers, Alberoni et al.

ability that working people who desert the oligarchic DC notables will move to support moderate clerics and the Left faction of the DC these priests prefer.

However, a critically important antecedent of such an intraparty shift of allegiance, analogous to a new preference for progressive instead of conservative priests, would be a reasoned reevaluation of traditional norms that were interpreted almost as moral strictures. Movement within the broadly defined Catholic world may encourage ordinary citizens to examine critically the monopolistic political legitimacy they have long upheld. The potentially significant side effects for any party challenging that legitimacy would obviously be great.

In several ways, the pattern of social allegiances that the PCI minority may attempt to consolidate, in an effort to exploit emerging vulnerabilities in the monopolistic DC legitimacy, is both difficult to execute and uncertain in yield. Execution is more complex because the minority PCI sections must allow the progressive forces among the organized Catholics in the CISL union, in the ACLI workingmen's club, in the Church itself to set the pace. The results of such alliances are more than usually unclear. It is possible that the Christian Democratic Left will, for the foreseeable future, have usurped the space on the political left that the PCI presently occupies in the northeast, just as more working-class citizens are attracted to that political stance.

But in other dimensions, the prospective PCI alliances are similar to the strategies of successful party adaptation elsewhere in Italy, especially in the central provinces: they seek to build upon, and do not oppose, the long-established legitimate cultural heritage of the region. While it certainly was easier for the PCI groups in central Italy to link their efforts to established Socialist and Anarchist traditions which after all emphasize the need to alter the status quo and especially the structure of authority, it is no less important for the minority Communists of the Veneto to work in concert with some aspects of the area's Catholic heritage.

CONCLUSION

This analysis has focused upon the complex relationships among three leadership groups as it examined the Italian Communist party in the northeast: the Communist party minority militants,

255

their opponents in the dominant Christian Democratic party, and the Catholic clergy who form the region's traditionally endowed legitimate leadership that had long been associated with the DC and inflexibly opposed to the PCI. The interactions of these three sets of organized local elites over time are discussed as they unfold within the context of a social structure that is changing rather rapidly to a factory economy after being dominated by small farm enterprises. Some summary observations are offered below.

In the Veneto, and in central Italy where community comparisons were made, the regional social structure never impinged so directly on political life as to determine political arrangements. In the Veneto an evolving society was tolerant of a variety of basically conservative political leaders. This was possible as long as the traditional Church leaders stood behind their preferred partisan activities and, as clergy, demonstrated some degree of sensitive personal concern for the ordinary citizen. To be sure, in the central regions some structures, such as the sharecrop system, as contrasted with independent farming or part-time farming, dispose those who live within them to a rejection of the system and hence to radical political alternatives. Yet even in this rather extreme situation, egregious errors on the part of the clerical elite were a prerequisite of radical politicization. Political leaders, especially those who can draw upon the resources of traditional legitimacy, have much flexibility. They can exercise considerable discretion before they approach the limits imposed on their political influence by the social structure.

Helpful concrete programs sponsored by the hegemonic legitimate elites not surprisingly reinforce their dominance. Less obvious is the importance accruing from the symbolic expression of benevolence attached to exclusive legitimacy. In the northeast, the parish priest was invested with the mantle of legitimacy that was his as an individual, not the Church's as an organization, to bestow on the political party of his personal choice. But consistent DC strength in changing environments required the body of parish priests to be united in opposition to the Communist minority. Any division in the local clergy would indicate to an essentially Catholic electorate that some other political choice was consistent with their sacral obligations. The PCI was slow to work hard for such visible divisions.

But we have identified the beginnings of a shift in PCI local strategy. The minority PCI's decision to seek legitimacy and votes indirectly is of both practical and theoretical interest. The Communist activists are experimenting with support, and not contestation, of the sympathetic moderate clergymen. Such experiments may have been stimulated by the growing diversity in the local social structure which is dominated by an industrial working class, itself divided between full-time and part-time factory workers.

A series of tacit PCI social alliances with the Catholic Left has worked to strengthen those factions' power in the Catholic trade union, workingmen's clubs, and the Church itself. If adhered to for any length of time and in many localities, this strategy commits the party to a patient wait for delayed gratification in a two-step transition toward the political left outside the boundaries of what was long the exclusively appropriate political patterns.

Adaptation as conceptualized in this report focuses on the capacity of the PCI minority in northeastern Italy to cope reasonably yet advantageously with its environment. Adaptation is seen as encompassing both active and passive components, and should be distinguished from adjustment, which is viewed here as an essentially passive phenomenon.[87] From this perspective the PCI in the Veneto has begun to move from adjustment to adaptation. It has begun to move from building a political strategy based on an acceptance of the monolithic linkage of the local clergy and the Christian Democratic party to a strategy that attempts to encourage division among the pillars of Catholic culture.

Certainly it is fair to note that in the past the possibilities to effect such cleavages were minimal and, to a considerable degree, in the northeast the PCI is still rather dependent upon the opportunities that the stronger elite groups present to the Communist opposition. But it also seems fair to say that in the past the Veneto PCI did not try to stimulate conditions that would precipitate DC-clerical disengagement. On the contrary, repeated impassioned Communist denunciations of Church-DC alliances helped cement these ties. More recently, even if their decisions involve risks of temporary setbacks, the PCI in the Veneto is not

[87] The perspective on adaptation utilized in this paper is drawn from the work of Heinz Hartmann, *Ego Psychology and the Problem of Adaptation* (New York: International Universities Press, 1958), Chapters 2 and 3. See also Burness E. Moore and Bernard D. Fine (eds.), A *Glossary of Psychoanalytic Terms and Concepts* (New York: The American Psychoanalytic Association, 1971), pp. 17-18.

emphasizing immediate marginal electoral gains. Rather, the Communists work to strengthen indirectly the clerical moderates and activists of the DC Left who may reinforce Church-party autonomy as they encourage trade-union cooperation. Such developments offer the Communists in the northeast prospects of considerable long-term growth and even the possibility of securing local legitimacy.

VII.

The PCI at the Local Level: A Study of Strategic Performance

PETER LANGE

The strategy of most political parties is shaped in part by a determination to share or control national political power, and formulations of strategy are made in terms of the national political, economic, and social context. What alliances should a party seek? What activities and policies should it pursue? How should the party organization function? The answers to all these questions will be based on the party leadership's understanding of what is necessary in order to shift, or maintain, the national balance of power in the party's favor. In many cases, however, implementation of the strategy depends heavily on lower units in the party hierarchy which are to perform tasks contributing to the achievement of general strategic goals. Thus, in order to succeed, nationally conceived strategy must be implemented in local contexts which often differ substantially from the composite national one. A tension may therefore result between the tasks established by the central party administration and the pressures on lower units created by the local conditions in which they must operate. Where such a tension exists, one can expect to find adaptation of the nationally determined goals.

To the degree this problem is a real one, it should certainly be visible in the operations of the *Partito Comunista Italiano* (PCI). The PCI is a mass party whose strategy relies heavily on the ability of its grass-roots organizations to activate a large number of volunteer members on a fairly continuous basis. Much of the responsibility for strategic implementation, therefore, rests with the sections at the base of the party's organizational structure, which must perform many strategically determined tasks. The party statute describes the role of the section as follows:

> The section should tend to have a permanent headquarters which should be the meeting and activity center for the Com-

259

munists and a hub of political, cultural, educational, recreational, and assistential life for all the workers of the locality.

It should promote, direct, and coordinate the activity of the Communists in every aspect of mass political action in the centers of productive, cultural, and associative life which exists in the territory under its jurisdiction.[1]

This broad set of goals and accompanying strategic tasks represent the ideal of how a party section should function if the PCI's strategy is to be carried out effectively. They are both the expression of the party's overall strategy as it involves the grass roots and a standard by which party officials, as well as outside observers, can measure section performance. To the degree that sections are not carrying out their tasks as prescribed, adaptation is occurring.

How common is such adaptation in the PCI? Does the highly centralized, and supposedly highly disciplined, character of the party assure conformity irrespective of local conditions? Does, in fact, the PCI fit the image of the classical Leninist party?[2] The characteristics of the sections lead us to believe that there may be considerable adaptation. While the higher levels of the party organization are staffed by full-time paid functionaries, section leaders and members are almost exclusively part-time volunteers.[3] In addition, the sections, as contrasted with the traditional cells which have now largely disappeared,[4] are rather large and do not permit the intensive face-to-face relationships among all members which in the past seem to have encouraged rigid discipline. As a result, section leaders are unlikely to be well insulated from the outside world and can be expected to be influenced by local socioeconomic and political conditions. And the sections are

[1] "Statuto del Partito Comunista Italiano" (PCI internal document: Rome, 1969), p. 12.

[2] For arguments that it does not see Sidney G. Tarrow, *Peasant Communism in Southern Italy* (New Haven: Yale University Press, 1967), especially pp. 97-101, as well as several of the chapters in this volume.

[3] In my study of a random sample of 41 party sections in the province of Milan I encountered no section secretaries who were full-time employees of the party and officials of the Milan Federation told me that there were few exceptions to this rule.

[4] With the exception of the "red" regions, the neighborhood or territorial cell structure has almost entirely disappeared since its point of maximum strength in the mid-1950s. There continues to be an active factory cell system, but such cells will not be considered in this study, which looks only at party units defined territorially.

260

likely to adapt the PCI's strategic goals and methods to suit their local context.

The following analysis of section behavior will show some varieties of adaptation at the section level resulting from contextual factors. The presentation is divided into two principal parts. First, I will describe the specific tasks the party establishes for the sections. This will provide us with a general standard by which to judge performance. Second, I will examine the actual implementation of the tasks by a sample of sections in the province of Milan.

STRATEGIC DIMENSIONS AND TASKS

The PCI's strategy, and consequently the tasks it establishes for the sections, is extremely complex and reflects the character of postwar Italian society and the difficulties inherent in trying to break through the deep social and political cleavages which block the Communists' access to national power. I do not intend here to dwell at length on the multiple aspects of the strategy or to present the process of postwar evolution which has led to its current formulation. Rather, in the following pages I will simply outline the principal dimensions of the strategy when analyzed as a formula for achieving a shift in the national balance of power and will present the specific section tasks which give operational meaning to each of the dimensions. This will give us a picture of the ideal party section as an operating unit and thus will provide a standard in terms of which we can examine section adaptation. By linking this picture to the basic dimensions of the strategy, furthermore, we should be able to gain some impression of the "strategic costs" of poor performance by sections of any particular task.

Both the dimensions and the tasks associated with them are analytical categories developed on the basis of the party's own discussion of its strategic perspective and intended to organize loosely all the aspects of the party's activity. They do not represent ironclad compartments into which any individual section activity can be fitted but rather functions and subfunctions; any single activity will usually contribute to more than one of them. In fact, particularly successful activities are those which simultaneously contribute to the achievement of several tasks.

In order to understand the dimensions and tasks of PCI strat-

261

egy, we need to review briefly the national context in which the strategy is designed to operate. Since early in the postwar period, the PCI has been in a position of what Donald Blackmer has called "strategic inferiority" in relation to its principal opponent, the Democrazia Cristiana (DC).[5] This inferiority has had both political and social manifestations. Politically, it has resulted in the PCI's seemingly permanent status as a minority party and its resultant inability to be an initiating force in the national Parliament and in national politics in general. At no time since 1948 has the party had the realistic prospect of coming to power electorally. Its vote has never exceeded 28 percent of the national total, and its increments have been small. Even an electoral alliance with the party's traditional ally, the Partito Socialista Italiano (PSI), has held little hope. The increase in the Communist vote in the postwar period has been accompanied by a similar decline in the PSI's. Although there is no hard evidence that Socialist electors have been shifting to the PCI, it is clear that the electoral "space" occupied by the Left has grown only slightly in the last twenty-five years.[6] Thus the DC's preeminent role in the determination of the national governing coalition seems electorally secure and, given the nature of the Italian party system, that position of dominance also assures the DC its role as prime initiator of almost all national policy.

The seeming permanence of the PCI's subordinate political position is undoubtedly strongly related to its strategic inferiority at the social level. The pervasive effects of the traditional religious cleavage between Catholics and the Marxist Left have cut the Communists off from many of those citizens and social groups whom the party would consider its "natural" supporters. As a party of the working class, the PCI has been able to gain the backing of only about half of the working-class electorate. The DC has dominated the remainder as well as being the principal force among other social categories.[7] These electoral data merely

[5] Donald L. M. Blackmer, "Italian Communism: Strategy for the 1970's," *Problems of Communism* 21 (May-June 1972): 43.

[6] For a discussion of the PCI's postwar vote and its relation to the overall vote of the Left and the DC, see Giorgio Galli, ed., *Il comportamento elettorale in Italia* (Bologna: Società Editrice Il Mulino, 1968), parts 1 and 2.

[7] Ibid., part 3; see also Mattei Dogan, "Un fenomeno di atassia politica," in Mattei Dogan and Orazio Petracca, eds., *Partiti politici e strutture sociali in Italia* (Milan: Edizioni di Comunità, 1968), pp. 465-480.

reflect the commanding position of the DC and its traditional social ally, the Catholic Church, in the society at large. Through their cultural predominance and through a broad range of social institutions like Catholic Action, the Catholic trade unions and cooperatives, they have been able to isolate the PCI and the socialist subculture from many potential sources of mass support. Thus the PCI finds itself politically weak in relation to the DC and culturally and institutionally blocked from many of the social groups whose backing would be necessary in order to alter the relationship between the two parties.

The dimensions of the PCI strategy represent the party's response to this position of strategic inferiority.[8] Three distinct dimensions can be identified. Two, the political and the social, are designed to increase the party's influence with political and social actors—other parties, interest groups, social categories, individuals—outside the party and eventually to permit the party to develop coalitions with some of these targets. The third dimension, reinforcement, is designed to maintain and strengthen the party's own organization. Each of these dimensions is intended to increase the party's capacity to break out of its inferior strategic status and each establishes specific tasks which the sections are to perform if the maximum strategic effectiveness is to be achieved. Let us look briefly at these dimensions and tasks.

The *political alliance dimension* refers to the party's attempts to maintain and extend its influence with the leadership of other parties. It includes work in Parliament, local governments and other state institutions, and in elections. This effort, which the Communists often refer to as being *di vertice* ("at the top," i.e., with political leadership groups and about narrowly political relationships) is primarily directed toward two parties, the PSI and the DC. Communist intentions toward the Socialists can be interpreted as a desire to restore, or at least prevent further deterioration of, relations with a former consort.[9]

---

[8] The best contemporary PCI description of its strategy is contained in the conclusions of then Vice-Secretary Enrico Berlinguer to the Twelfth Party Congress; see PCI, *XII Congresso del Partito comunista italiano* (Rome: Editori Riuniti, 1969), pp. 746-777. Berlinguer has since become general secretary of the party.

[9] For an excellent discussion of the PCI's postwar relation to the PSI prior to 1964 and particularly after the crisis of 1956, see Donald L. M. Blackmer, *Unity in Diversity: Italian Communism and the Communist World* (Cambridge and London: M.I.T. Press, 1968), esp. Chapters 2, 7, and 8.

Through cooperation on progressive legislation, an open policy of collaboration with the PSI at the local governmental level, restrained criticism of Socialist activity in the national government and only limited electoral competition, the Communists seek to assure that the Socialists will always remain a potential national coalition partner for them and will not participate in a DC effort further to isolate the party from the rest of the polity.

With the DC the political alliance effort is more of an adversary process. The Communists conceive of the DC as an "interclassist" party, one which through the glue of religious sentiment holds together under one banner two basically incompatible interests, that of monopoly capital and that of the Italian working populace. DC national policy is conservative and yet the factions which supposedly represent the DC's popular base remain loyal to the party, thereby betraying the "real" interests of their constitutents. PCI intentions are to make explicit this basic contradiction and thus to force the leaders of the Left factions to chose either party loyalty and submission to the conservative majority, or alliance with the PCI (and PSI) and effective representation of their mass of followers.[10] To do this the Communists seek to embarrass the DC by sponsoring reform legislation differing from that of the governing coalition and, more generally, by trying to show that "without the PCI there can be no reform."[11] In addition, the party has a highly competitive electoral relationship with the DC, hoping to make the latter pay at the polls for its legislative conservatism.

[10] It has always been unclear whether the PCI hopes for a scission in the DC with the left wing breaking off to join in a coalition with the Communists and Socialists or whether the hope has been to shift the balance within the DC to a degree sufficient to permit the formation of a coalition including the PCI, PSI, and most or all of the Catholic party. The slogan of the *compromesso storico* between Communists and Catholics launched by Berlinguer in the last two years supports the latter of these two interpretations in the present period. It should be evident that this version is much more threatening to the Socialists, who may have much to fear if caught in the middle of such a "grand coalition." The attempt to build an alliance with all of the DC also suggests that the PCI would prefer any split in that party to occur on the right rather than the left.

[11] This slogan has been popular in PCI propaganda in recent years and especially after 1969. The proof cited by the party is that several pieces of recent reform legislation, e.g., the reform of the land rent system, were passed because of PCI support or abstention when the right-wing factions of the DC withdrew their backing.

Within the general framework of the attempt to build political alliances, two critical tasks for the sections can be identified. First, they must vigorously pursue the party's electoral policy, seeking always to maximize the Communist vote, particularly at the expense of the DC. Second, they must utilize the opportunities afforded by participation in local political institutions, especially the town council, to maintain and/or extend alliances with the PSI and the DC. One set of questions to pursue when we turn to the actual practice of party sections concerns the degree to which the sections carry out each of these tasks with respect to each of the target parties.

If the PCI concentrated all its activity on implementing the tasks of the political alliance dimension, it would be little different from any other opposition party in a modern democratic polity.[12] Furthermore, given the nature of the DC's institutionalized political and social support, such a policy would have little prospect of enabling the Communists to escape their strategic inferiority. It is in this light that the social alliance dimension of the strategy is absolutely central to the prospects for the party's eventual success.

The *social alliance dimension* refers to the Communists' effort to use the party program of "structural reform" to build a reform movement (whose structural base the party conceives of as a "social bloc" of forces) which cuts across cleavages of religion and class and which can create continual and broad-based pressure for a shift in political alliances which will allow the PCI to share in national power.[13] From the standpoint of its implications for the sections, the social alliance dimension has two features of particular importance. First, the attempt to maintain and extend the party's influence is to be directed toward an extremely broad array of targets. Almost no interest group or social category is excluded with the exception of the monopoly capitalists; peasants, urban and rural wage laborers, small businessmen and shopkeepers, white-collar workers, technical personnel, even small and medium industrialists are all supposedly potential par-

[12] The party acknowledges this and points both to the social alliance dimension of its strategy and to its mass organization as signs that the party is *diverso dagli altri*.

[13] For a concise statement of the social alliance dimension and its relation to Communist traditions and experience see Enrico Berlinguer, "Classe operaia e blocco sociale," *Rinascita* 28 (January 15, 1971): 5-6.

265

ticipants in the social bloc.[14] In actual fact, however, it appears that the PCI's intentions vary depending on the character of the target. Put schematically, it would seem that the greater any individual's probable receptiveness to the structural reform program (i.e., someone in the working class and/or already identifying with the socialist subculture), the more the party is seeking to involve him actively in the reform movement. As such probable receptiveness declines, the effort tends increasingly to be directed toward "neutralizing" opposition to the reformist thrust and its political implications by making the target recognize the legitimacy of the PCI as an actor in the Italian political system.

Second, the social alliances created through the reformist effort are not to remain simply sentiments of solidarity. Rather, the movement is to be activated in order to put pressure on the political sphere. Through various activities the party hopes to use the movement to show other political forces that significant reforms must be undertaken and that such reforms are impossible without the inclusion of the PCI in the area of national governance. The party's intention, in other words, is to create not only an extremely broad movement but also one which will be active in developing intensive pressure on the political parties for social and political change.

At this point it should be noted that the coexistence of these two emphases within the social alliance dimension may create a difficult problem for the sections. In theory the efforts to extend the party's social alliances and to create intense pressure for social and political change may be compatible. Both are certainly necessary if the party is to come to national power. But, in practical terms the two emphases would seem to contain a possible contradiction. Attempts by the sections to organize activities which will create significant political pressure may be precisely the kinds of undertakings which will alienate some of the party's potential allies and convince those already hostile to the party that it is not a legitimate actor in the system. Building a tenant alliance cutting across religious barriers and then occupying a new housing development to dramatize the need for housing re-

[14] The concept of "social bloc" (*blocco sociale*) is used prominently in previously cited conclusions of Berlinguer at the Twelfth Congress. It represents an explicit attempt to link current party strategy to the theoretical work of Antonio Gramsci. For an early statement of the breadth of the party's social alliance aspirations, see Palmiro Togliatti, "Ceto Medio e Emilia Rossa," in *Il Partito* (Rome: Editori Riuniti, 1964).

form, for instance, may create some pressure for change in housing policy and for inclusion of the PCI in the deliberations about the outlines of such policy, but it may also convince some that the PCI is unwilling to work through the system.[15] To the extent that this tension exists, the sections are faced with a difficult dilemma.

Three distinct tasks for the sections can be identified with respect to the social alliance dimension. The first is the information task, that is, the dissemination of materials informing the public about the party program, the nature of the reforms sought, and how these reforms might be achieved. While the activities associated with this task are obvious, two things should be noted: (1) the degree to which a section is actually performing this task can, in part, be measured by how much information work it does outside of electoral periods. To the degree that such activity is confined to elections, the section would be failing to do the kind of continual alliance-building necessary in order to carry out the social alliance dimension of the strategy; (2) information activities require nothing from the target of such activities. The party is active, but the recipients of the information being disseminated can remain wholly passive.

The second task is mobilization—the generation of mass activity around specific public issues in order to apply pressure on political institutions and to increase the salience of those issues among the nonmobilized public. Activities included under the mobilization task include such things as public meetings, demonstrations, and occupations of buildings. In contrast to the information task, successful mobilization requires active participation by individuals outside the party, though the commitment implied by such participation will vary considerably depending on the character of the specific activity.

The third social alliance task is institutionalization, that is, the development and/or maintenance of nonparty organizations and participation in them. The degree to which such organizations have an explicitly political content varies considerably; some, such as local cultural or recreational *circoli*, have little manifest political content; they serve social and subcultural functions.

---

[15] This tension would seem to represent a more limited version of the more general "contradiction" in postwar PCI strategy discussed by Tarrow, *Peasant Communism*, esp. Chapters 5, 10-13. Tarrow argues that Togliatti and the postwar PCI have had an "additive" approach to alliances (p. 116) and that this represents a limitation on the intensity with which the part can organize the mobilization of particular social groups or classes.

267

Others, such as organizations of tenants or artisans, are explicitly intended to be organs for the expression of the economic interests of a specific social group to the relevant political authorities. Institutionalization also requires some active participation or commitment on the part of the target individuals or groups.

Effective prosecution of the political and social alliance dimensions of the strategy requires a strong and active party organization.[16] The *reinforcement dimension,* i.e., the effort to maintain and increase party membership and to make members active agents working for the achievement of party goals, is intended to meet this requirement as well as to assure that even without extensive alliances the PCI will be a force to reckon with in Italian society. Three tasks for the sections can be identified under this dimension. The first is maintenance, that is, the administration of section life including renewal of memberships, collection of dues and other funds, and recruitment. These are the minimal activities necessary to assure the viability of the organization. If reinforcement work is confined to such activities, however, the section is clearly failing in its strategic responsibilities, for it is not generating the active participation by members necessary in order to undertake the manifold tasks of the other strategic dimensions. A second reinforcement task, therefore, the participation task, involves the effort to increase member activism and thereby to expand the pool of human resources available for other activities. As should be evident, however, not all members will be active and a third reinforcement task falling to the sections is that of assuring that as many as possible of those members who are not highly active in section initiatives are informed about the character of the party's strategy, the Communist position on specific issues which arise at the national or local level, and what stance is expected of party members. This socialization task is important to the section's overall success not only because it makes reenlistment of the nonactive easier and increases the possibility that some of the less participant members will eventually become more heavily involved in section affairs but also because it is the only way the party can assure that each member

[16] The best recent discussion of the role of the sections is Ugo Pecchioli, *Un Partito Comunista rinnovato e rafforzato per le esigenze nuove della societa italiana: relazione al Comitato centrale,* January 14, 1970, published by the party in 1970. A good analytical organizational history of the party is Giordano Sivini, "Le parti communiste: Structure et fonctionnement" (unpublished paper).

will be a representative of the PCI in the spheres of his daily life. In this manner the party seeks to extend its "diffuse presence"[17] even into those areas in which it has no organized influence.

The tasks described represent a standard against which the strategic performance of sections can be measured. The effectiveness of any section as an instrument of PCI strategy can be loosely gauged by how well it performs the various tasks. Different patterns of task performance (i.e., the degree and manner in which tasks are undertaken) indicate varieties of adaptation of party goals to the local environment. What form does such adaptation take? Which tasks are performed well, which poorly? This study is too limited to attempt to develop definitive answers, but I want to describe some aspects of the process of adaptation I observed in a sample of party sections in the province of Milan. The essay focuses on the relationship between certain features of the social and organizational structure of the environment and the character of the sections' operations.

THE LOCUS OF THE STUDY

In order to introduce the environments in which I examined strategic task performance by the sections, a word of introduction is necessary about my use of the term "environment." PCI sections are assigned responsibility for the organization of party life and activity within a certain territorial jurisdiction determined by the provincial party federation.[18] The size and character of these jurisdictions vary markedly: some are as small and quiet as a commune with fewer than a thousand residents, others as large and dynamic as a neighborhood with 15,000 or more inhabitants in a large commune or city. The term "environment" as used in this study refers to these jurisdictional areas. Given the

---

[17] This concept was at the heart of Togliatti's vision, developed in 1944, of the postwar PCI as a *partito nuovo* which would avoid the sectarianism and isolation which had characterized party behavior in its formative years. In this connection see Togliatti, *La politica di Salerno* (Rome: Editori Riuniti, 1969) and Alessandro Natta, "La Resistenza e la formazione del 'partito nuovo'" in Paulo Spriano et al., *Problemi di storia del Partito comunista italiano* (Rome: Editori Riuniti, 1971).

[18] These jurisdictions are often more the product of historical precedent than rational calculation of organizational needs and possibilities. Thus a town which in 1945 had 5,000 inhabitants and one section may today have 25,000 residents but still only one section.

269

great diversity of environments, I sought to identify certain types each of which shared certain social and political characteristics that might produce particular patterns of section adaptation. My purpose in adopting such a procedure was clearly not to identify specific variables which would lead to particular patterns of task performance but rather to try to identify broad differences in such performance as they coincided with major differences in the type of environment the section operated in.

The choice of the province of Milan was based on two criteria. First, the province is one in which neither the DC nor the PCI has political hegemony and in which both the Catholic and the socialist subcultures have strong institutional roots. In other words, the province is neither "red" nor "white" but rather has a political relationship between the DC and the PCI which somewhat resembles that of the nation as a whole.[19] The selection of such a "nondominance" area seemed appropriate both because there had been little study of grass-roots Communist operations under such conditions[20] and because the party's strategy seemed particularly designed to shift the balance of political power in such areas.

The second criterion was socioeconomic. The province of Milan traditionally has been in the vanguard of Italian industrialization and today is the most highly industrialized province in the nation.[21] As such it provides an excellent site for the evaluation of the extent to which the PCI is able to implement its strategy under the conditions of social change accompanying the later stages of capitalist industrial development.

[19] For a detailed discussion of electoral relationships in the province and their relation to postwar demographic change, see Vincenzo Tomeo, *Mutamento sociale e scelta politica* (Milan: Giuffre Editore, 1967). On p. 177 Tomeo states: "From the general point of view, one can observe, first of all, that the electoral dimension and structure of the Milanese party system does not significantly differ from the national one."

[20] Two excellent studies of party operations at the federation and local level are those of Stephen Hellman, "Ideology and Organization in Four Italian Communist Federations" (Ph.D. Dissertation, Yale University, 1973), and Alan Stern, "Local Political Elites and Economic Change: A Comparative Study of Four Italian Communities" (Ph.D. Dissertation, Yale University, 1971). Both studies, however, concentrate most of their attention on party operations in "red" and "white" areas rather than in areas where party competition resembles the national situation.

[21] For an extremely detailed historical and contemporary account of the socioeconomic development of the province see Etienne Dalmasso, *Milan: Capitale Economique de l'Italie* (Paris: Editions Ophrys, 1971). See also Tomeo, *Mutamento*, Chapter 3.

270

Even in its advanced form the development process has not created a uniformity of environments throughout the province. Rather, the impact of postwar industrialization on the preexisting social and economic demography has produced considerable variation between different areas. It was possible, using criteria which I have described at length in another work,[22] to identify three distinct types of environments into which a large majority of the jurisdictions of the PCI sections in the province could be classified. Each of these three types: the stagnant peripheral town, the dynamic suburb, the urban, has been affected differently by the postwar development process and each would seem to present different problems for party sections seeking to meet their strategic responsibilities. The following are the most salient characteristics of the three environmental types:

1. The urban environment—the section jurisdictions (all with populations over 12,000) in the city of Milan. The population is heterogeneous but increasingly dominated by the middle-class and white-collar workers. Both these groups are pushing the proletariat out of the traditional working-class neighborhoods and into new housing on the city periphery or in the suburbs. Factories as well are concentrated on the periphery, and the urban center is becoming increasingly a business and leisure-time area. Owing to enormous shifts in population and the easy availability of alternative sources of entertainment, social life in the city is no longer heavily influenced by the subcultural institutions which were quite prominent before the war.[23]

2. The dynamic suburban environment—environments with populations ranging from 10,000 to a little more than 100,000 found almost exclusively in a circle around the city of Milan commonly referred to as the "hinterland."[24] These environments usu-

[22] "Continuity and Change in the Italian Communist Party: A Study of Strategy and Organization" (Ph.D. Dissertation, M.I.T., 1974).

[23] On the development of the city and its neighborhoods see Alessandro Buzzi-Donato, "Note sullo sviluppo di Milano negli ultimi cento anni" in *Quaderni di documentazione e studio* (Milan: Comune di Milano, 1969), pp. 1-132; Luciano Cavalli, *La città divisa* (Milan: Guiffre Editore, 1965); Alberto Magnaghi et al., *La città fabbrica* (Milan: Clup, 1970); M. Boffi et al., *Città e conflitto sociale* (Milan: Feltinelli, 1972); Domenico De Masi e Giuseppe Pranzo, "Ricambio demografico e risultati elettorale in un polo d'attrazione" in Dogan and Petracca, eds., *Partiti politici*, pp. 353-407; and an unpublished five-volume study by Alessandro Pizzorno and a group of other scholars.

[24] The specific criteria for the selection of these towns was that they had a population over 10,000 in 1969 and that there was a population increase

ally have several large factories and their populations, though far more heavily working class than those of the city, are somewhat heterogeneous. These are the most rapidly growing environments in the province and have absorbed the large majority of immigrants who have come to Milan from other parts of Italy in the last fifteen years. They therefore have a relatively dynamic social structure. They are also areas which most sharply display the social problems accompanying rapid social change—health, transportation, and housing. Social life in these towns, while certainly not determined solely by old subcultural institutions, is heavily influenced by these, in part because other outlets for social activity have been slow to develop. Organizations such as trade unions, with a certain autonomy from the PCI and the Church, are extremely prominent, particularly in recent years when they have begun to spearhead drives for social reform.

3. The stagnant peripheral town environment—small communes (population under 10,000) which comprise the vast majority of all communes in the province.[25] These environments have little autonomous economic life and their population is largely lower class with a small *petite bourgeoisie* of shopkeepers and almost no real middle class. These are primarily former agricultural towns whose population now commutes to Milan or the hinterland to work in factories. They have a rather static social structure with little population growth or change, and social life tends to be dominated by the subcultural institutions of the Left and the Church.

Before analyzing section performance in these three types of environments, let me briefly describe my data. First, and most prominently, I will be using information collected through interviews with the leaders of a random sample of 41 of the 380 territorial sections of the PCI in the province: 9 of these sections are

of more than 50 percent (the provincial mean) from 1951 to 1969. Sixty-four of the 248 communes in the province met these criteria. It should also be noted that 75 of the 88 factories with more than 500 employees in the province (1967) were in these towns, as were all the factories with more than 1,000 employees. All these environments are within what Tomeo (*Mutamento*) calls the "area of agglomeration" (Chapter 3). See also Dalmasso, *Milan*, parts 3 and 4.

25 The criteria for this category were that the towns had less than 10,000 inhabitants in 1969 and that their rate of population growth from 1951 to 1969 was less than the provincial mean of 50 percent. For further discussion of these towns see Tomeo, *Mutamento*, Chapter 3.

urban, 14 are in the dynamic suburbs, and 18 in the peripheral towns. These interviews were conducted with the cooperation of the Milan federation of the PCI and would have been impossible without the aid afforded me by numerous party officials.[26] The interviews were designed to use the section leaders as sources of information about the activities of the sections. Given the obvious dangers involved in the use of this methodology, corroborative data from other sources were sought whenever possible. Such data include party records furnished to me by the federation and my own observations of a large number of section and other party meetings.[27]

The analysis is organized in terms of a series of questions which emerged from the discussion of the three strategic dimensions and of the tasks those dimensions create for the sections. Because of length limitations I shall present one or two indicators of performance relating to the various questions. Even in this impressionistic approach, three rather distinct patterns of section performance and three different adaptations of nationally defined strategic performance goals to specific local conditions will emerge.

SECTION PERFORMANCE OF STRATEGIC TASKS

The Political Alliance Dimension

To what degree do the sections concentrate their attention and activity on the town council? How important is electoral activity in the overall profile of section activity? To what degree do the sections seek to maintain and/or extend their ties to the PSI and the DC?

Use of the political institutional framework to advance party positions is a cardinal principle of PCI strategy. When we look at section performance, however, we find significant differences

[26] I want to express my gratitude to party officials at the national and federation levels for their willingness to aid me in gaining access to the sections for the interviews and for observations of meetings. I am also deeply indebted to the leaders of the sample sections who were willing to give two or more hours of their scarce leisure time to tell me about life in their sections and to observe their section meetings and operations. Their full cooperation and frank responses to my questions were more than I could have anticipated or expected. All interviews and observations took place in the twelve-month period from July 1970 to June 1971.

[27] I was able to attend more than sixty party meetings of various kinds.

between the sections operating in the urban environment and those outside the city. Activity in the town council was a dominant theme in the work of both groups of nonurban sections. In the interviews, section leaders were asked: What initiatives has the section taken in recent months? Twenty-eight of the thirty-two responses of the nonurban leaders cited proposals or actions undertaken in the town council among such initiatives; in 4 cases, all in the peripheral towns, such initiatives were the only ones, apart from meetings of the section itself, which the respondents could cite. A further sign of the importance of local council matters, and undoubtedly one of the reasons why they played such a large role, is that there was a great deal of overlap between the leadership of the sections and the PCI's town councilors: 27 of the 32 nonurban section secretaries were councilors and well over one-fourth of the members of the section directorates (*Comitati direttivi* or CD's)[28] were councilors. One section leader summed up the importance of the council in the section's overall activity and the way it affected other aspects of section life: "Our local strength is based on our role in the commune. . . . You ask why we have not undertaken any cultural activity. It is because we are so busy with our work in the commune."[29]

In the urban sections, work in governmental institutions was far less important; leaders rarely cited initiatives in the city council as important. This is not surprising since the work of an urban section in its immediate neighborhood is seldom directly reflected in city council matters. But the inattention toward political institutional activity was found not only with respect to the city council but also to the *consiglii di zona*, decentralized councils whose members were chosen by neighborhood party organizations.[30] Despite the fact that the federation was placing considerable emphasis on these *consiglii* as the sites for new

[28] The organizational structure within all PCI sections consists of the CD made up of anywhere from 3 to 25 members and a section secretary, all elected by the section membership at the section's congress.

[29] Interview #12 (suburban).

[30] The councils were instituted in Milan after 1967 with the strong backing of the PCI federation and city councilors. On the history of the councils see Centro Studi Lombardo, *Decentramento urbano: burocrazia o partecipazione* (Milan: Centro Studi Lombardo, 1970) and *Decentramento urbano e partecipazione sociale* (Milan: Centro Studi Lombardo, 1968). For the PCI position see "Tavola Rotonda: Partito di massa, democrazia e decentramento," *Rinascita* (January 8, 1971), pp. 7-10.

opportunities for alliance-building by the sections, few base-level leaders cited work in the zone councils as important.[31] Furthermore, in contrast to the nonurban sections, none of the members appointed to these councils by the various sections were section secretaries and only a few were prominent in the section CD. Undoubtedly one reason for the lack of interest in these councils was that they did not, as yet, have decisional power; they could only recommend policies to the city council. More important, however, was the urban section leaders' attitude that all governmental action was distant from the day-to-day needs of the people in their neighborhoods. As one leader told me: "Our major initiatives must be in the neighborhoods, on local issues among the masses. The councils are fine . . . but we don't have much time for them. To beat the DC we must work with the people."[32]

The differences between urban and nonurban sections in their attention to work in governmental institutions was not reflected in the amount of time and energy devoted to electoral campaigns.[33] Electoral periods, whether for national or administrative elections, were a high point of activity and participation in all sections. When asked what their most important initiative in the past year had been, the leaders of 37 of the 41 sample sections cited the election campaign of 1970. Furthermore, all the respondents stated that enthusiasm and active participation by the membership were higher during the campaign than at almost any other time. On the average, about 20 percent of members took a real part in the campaign, a figure which can be compared with the approximately 10 percent who participated in day-to-day section affairs and the roughly 15 per cent who attended even such important section functions as the annual congress. One urban leader's response to a query about electoral activity and participation sums up the attitude reflected in most answers: "It's sad to say it. I wish it were like that every day. The section becomes alive with movement and activity, and we see members

[31] Only two of the nine urban section secretaries noted their sections' work in the councils as one of the important areas of section initiative.

[32] Interview #1 (urban).

[33] There were no elections during the year covered by my observations of party activity. All discussions of election activity, therefore, refer to campaigns in other years, particularly to the one for the regional and administrative elections of 1970.

who usually only appear at membership renewal time. In those periods [elections] the party really makes its presence felt in the neighborhood."[34]

Despite important differences between sections operating in urban and nonurban environments, all the base-level units devoted considerable activity to some or all the tasks of the political alliance dimension. This finding, however, does not allow us to determine whether this activity can actually be interpreted as an attempt to build alliances or whether, on the other hand, it merely serves to permit the sections to accentuate the differences between the PCI and other parties. To determine which of these is the case we need to look at the content of political alliance activity, at how the sections related to the PSI and the DC.

In relations with the PSI, there are significant differences in both attitude and behavior between the three section groups. First, although none of the respondents were particularly positive in their evaluation of the PSI, hostility toward the Socialists was far higher in the nonurban—especially the peripheral—sections than in the urban ones. In both of the former groups leaders often expressed bitterness and disappointment toward the Socialists for their attempt to reunify with the Partito Socialista Democratico Italiano (PSDI) between 1966 and 1969. The attempt was seen as a betrayal of the long-standing political and social ties between the PCI and PSI; this feeling of betrayal was particularly strong in the peripheral sections. Urban leaders, in contrast, were far milder in their critique of the PSI, intensity of feeling being replaced by indifference.

The source of these marked differences in attitude appeared to lie in the differing character of contacts between the PSI and PCI in the three environments. In the city the indifference was born of lack of contact. The urban leaders noted that they had little contact with the Socialists in their neighborhoods both because the city sections of the PSI functioned almost exclusively during electoral periods and because there were no real opportunities for regular cooperation such as those afforded by the town council in the nonurban environments. In the suburban and the peripheral environments, on the other hand, the greater intensity of feeling was the result of the greater amount of contact between the two parties and of the resultant

[34] Interview #11 (suburban).

276

expectations about how the Socialists would, and should, be-have.[35]

It appeared that the smaller the environment and the greater its social stability, the more intense were the social and political relationships between the Communist leaders and their Socialist counterparts. From the interviews it was clear that the section leaders in the peripheral sections felt a much greater per-sonal, as well as political, bond with the leaders of the Socialist sections than did the leaders of the suburban sections. Further-more, the attempt at Socialist reunification had had more direct institutional consequences (less cooperation in the town council and in jointly run local organizations) in the outlying sections than in the hinterland. One incident, recounted by the secretary of a peripheral section, graphically illustrated both the intensity of relations between the two parties and the importance of the institutional context in which those relations could be played out. According to the Communist leader, at the time of the reunifica-tion attempt the PSI in his town sought to embarrass the PCI by calling for a public audit of the accounts of the cooperative and *circolo* which the two parties ran jointly but which the Commu-nists dominated. After much maneuvering, a public meeting of the members of the cooperative was held at which the PCI forced the PSI leaders to admit that there had been no wrongdoing. The Socialist participants in the cooperative council then quit and at the time of the interview had not yet returned to take back the posts which the PCI was now prepared to let them have.[36] While the details may have been dramatized, the story gives the flavor of PCI-PSI relations in the small towns; a political split affected much of the social life in the Left subculture. In the larger towns no such incidents were cited. The temporary division between the PCI and PSI had apparently been confined to the political sphere.

One might expect from the preceding that actual cooperation between Communists and Socialists woud have been difficult in the two nonurban settings, but this was not the case. Rather,

[35] Only 4 of the urban sections reported frequent or occasional contacts with PSI sections, as contrasted with 12 of the suburban and 15 of the peripheral sections.

[36] Interview #50 (peripheral). The basic facts of the incident were con-firmed in an interview with the provincial head of the Associazione Provin-ciale dei Circoli Cooperativi.

strategically determined alliance priorities appeared to override local sentiments. Two indicators of Communist willingness can be cited, both of them based on data drawn from the province as a whole rather than from the sample alone. First, in towns with fewer than 5,000 inhabitants, local elections are decided, not with proportional representation, but rather with a system which gives the list with the greatest number of votes a clear majority in the town council. The formation of coalition lists is therefore of great importance when the outcome of the election is uncertain; in cases in which a party is a sure winner, even if all the other parties in the town were to form a coalition, however, the incentives work in the opposite direction; to form a coalition is to unnecessarily accede seats on the town council to another party. When we look at Communist list formation in the province, we find that in all but 9 of 104 communes with fewer than 5,000 inhabitants in which elections were held in 1970, the PCI and the PSI formed joint lists.[37] Furthermore, in all 12 of the towns in which the PCI was sure of a majority on the council even without the Socialist voters,[38] joint lists were still formed. In these 12 cases the PCI had given up positions in the council and *giunta* in order to form a coalition with the Socialists. A second measure which applies to all the communes of the province is less clear-cut but also of interest. Jointly, the PSI and the PCI controlled 39 town governments after the local elections of 1970. In 21 of these the Communists had the mayoralty; but in the other 18 the mayor was a member of the PSI. In 17 of these 18 towns, the PCI had a significantly higher percentage of the vote than the Socialists[39] and therefore seems to have made a concession in giving the PSI the mayoralty. It is impossible to know the conditions of local bargaining in these towns and we cannot therefore say with certainty in how many of these 17 cases the PCI was displaying good faith toward the Socialists, rather than offering them the mayor's post to prevent them from forming a

---

[37] These and the subsequent figures are drawn from the reports of the Provincial Prefect. They were made available to me through the good graces of officials in the provincial administration. It should be noted that if figures of this type could be obtained for a wide number of provinces, we might be able to develop a good index of PCI-PSI cooperation and its variations in different areas and at different times.

[38] Based on the election results of the 1968 general elections. At that time the Socialists were united, and I have treated that vote as one bloc.

[39] Based on the 1968 elections.

278

government with other parties.[40] But it is likely that, in at least some of these instances, an agreement on the mayor was made in order to encourage further cooperation.[41] These figures clearly indicate that despite sometimes strong antagonisms toward the Socialists, the Communist sections operating in environments in which an opportunity to form coalitions with the PSI existed, did so. General strategic directives overruled local particularisms of PCI-PSI relations.

While relations with the Socialists were complex and varied considerably between the three environments, those with the Christian Democrats were rather simple. Instances of cooperation between the PCI and DC were extremely rare. In only four towns in the province, all of them extremly small, were the DC and the PCI jointly in the local *giunta*;[42] in the remainder, whether governed by the Left or by the DC in coalition with other parties, little accommodation was found. In all of the interviews conducted with the leaders of sections in "red" towns, the respondents said relations with the DC were cordial but restrained. In the towns in which the PCI was in the distinct minority, the pattern of relations resembled closely Stern's description, of DC-PCI relations in the "white" regions:[43] the local *giunta* listened with haughty indulgence to the Communist councilors until they were ready to come to a vote, the outcome of which was certain from the beginning. Debate in the council was of symbolic value but had no real prospect of altering anyone's opinion. It was simply more politic for the DC to treat the PCI with benign indifference than to make political martyrs of the Communist councilors. It should be noted that in the urban environment even the

---

[40] Six of these 17 towns had populations over 5,000 and thus used proportional representation. In 3 of these the PSI had the option of forming a *giunta* with the DC or with the DC and PSDI. In these the structure of the situation would suggest that the PCI had to give the Socialists the mayorality in order to prevent being excluded from the *giunta*, but we cannot know if this was, in fact, a viable threat in the local context.

[41] It is probable that the PCI federation had a role in reaching agreements on the mayor in some of these towns. I know that in some of the big cities in the province (Sesto San Giovanni and Cinisello Balsamo) the PCI and PSI reached an accord through bargaining at the federation level.

[42] According to a federation official, in each of these cases the coalition came about after the local DC had split along the lines of the Left *versus* Center and Right, and the PCI had immediately stepped in and offered to form a new government, along with the PSI, in which the dissident Catholics would have a prominent place.

[43] See Alan Stern, "Local Political Elites," and his chapter in this volume.

279

minimal opportunities for PCI-DC contact afforded by participation in a town council were not present and the urban leaders reported virtually no interaction with their Catholic counterparts. The absence of a relevant institutional context in the city made establishment of ties to the DC almost impossible.[44]

What preliminary conclusions can we draw from this examination of the sections' implementation of the tasks of the political alliance dimension? First, the use of governmental institutions to attempt to advance party positions was confined almost exclusively to the nonurban environments where local governmental affairs have a prominent place in the life of the community; in the city, where distance from government is great, apathy prevailed. Second, implementation of the electoral task was a major priority in all of the sections, and election campaigns were universally a high point in member participation and section activity. The influence of the character of the environment in which the section had to operate seemed minimal in the performance of this task, perhaps because it required little interaction with other political forces and because elections had an inherent mobilizing effect on PCI members. Third, important differences between section groups again emerged with respect to the character of the sections' relations with the PSI and the DC. In the nonurban environments, the social structure of the community tended to increase the potential for and actual antagonism between Communists and Socialists but, at the same time, also created opportunities for real cooperation between the two parties. In the city, in contrast, sentiments about the Socialists were milder, but cooperation was almost nonexistent. Finally, we found that despite the strategic priority of developing cooperative relations with the DC, sections in none of the environments were able to do so.

One point would appear to emerge most clearly from these data. No matter what the environment, political relationships between the PCI and the targets of the political alliance dimension of the strategy are relatively static. Where links already exist, they are maintained; where such links are absent, neither the attitudes of the section leaders nor the actual levels of communication with the leaderships of other parties would suggest great

[44] Seven of the 9 urban sections reported they rarely or never had contacts with local DC sections; this was true of 8 of the 14 suburban and 10 of the 18 peripheral sections. All of the sections in the latter two groups, however, had frequent contacts with the DC through the town council.

possibility for change. This finding clearly highlights the importance of the social alliance dimension of the strategy. If the sections operating in the various environments are unable to create pressure on the static political relationships through the development of a coalition of social forces pressing for change, then the Communists' overall strategic prospects are not likely to improve, at least not through grass-roots activity.

The Social Alliance Dimension

How much effort do the sections devote to implementing the tasks of the social alliance dimension, i.e., information, mobilization, and institutionalization? To what degree do those activities represent an attempt to extend the party's influence to new social forces and to create pressure on the political sphere?

To escape its position of strategic inferiority, the PCI must generate social alliances broad and strong enough to make clear to the PSI and the DC that a governmental alliance including the Communists is necessary. An initial sense of the degree to which the sections undertake the activities necessary to build these social alliances can be gained by examining the figures reported in Table 1. The data for the information and mobilization tasks

TABLE 1. AVERAGE NUMBER OF SOCIAL ALLIANCE DIMENSION ACTIVITIES PER SECTION*

	Urban (N = 9)	Suburban (N = 14)	Peripheral (N = 18)
A. INFORMATION TASK	12.3(9)†	21.2(14)	10.6(16)
B. MOBILIZATION TASK			
1) Public Assemblies	3.9(7)	6.6(13)	4.0(17)
2) Section-Sponsored Demonstrations	0.4(3)	0.1(1)	0.0(0)
3) Picketing	1.3(5)	2.1(11)	1.3(5)
4) Festival di *L'Unità*	0.7(6)	1.2(14)	1.0(15)
5) Total Mobilization	6.3	10.0	6.3
C. TOTAL (MOBILIZATION AND INFORMATION)	18.6	31.2	16.7
D. INSTITUTIONAL TASK			
1) *Circoli*	2	12	17
2) Anti-Fascist Committees	7	12	9
3) Cultural Centers	2	3	1
4) Special Interest Organizations	7	10	3
5) Number with no ties	2	0	0

*The figures cover the period July 1970–June 1971.
†The number of sections undertaking at least one of the activities is listed in parentheses.

show the average number of individual initiatives of various sorts undertaken by the three groups of sample sections; those for institutionalization, the number of sections in each group with formal ties to different types of organizations.[45]

The figures in Table 1 suggest that, overall, section performance of the tasks is fairly good,[46] though perhaps not as intense in the urban and the peripheral sections as the party might like. The sections within each group undertook an average of one information or mobilization initiative at least once every three weeks (see Row C). This level of activity would seem rather high given what we know about the operations of the grass-roots organizations of other political parties in advanced industrial societies.[47] In addition, all but two of the forty-two sample sections had formal ties with at least one mass organization and often with more than one.

This general impression, however, is certainly not adequate if we want to understand how well the sections meet the standards of performance which the strategy establishes for the social alliance dimension. First, it hides the obvious differences between the sections operating in the different environments: the subur-

[45] These data, covering the period from July 1970 to June 1971, were compiled by putting together information gathered from the interviews and observations with the schedule of section affairs, *Vita di Base*, which was published daily on the Milan page of *L'Unità*. I have counted as individual initiatives each section activity requiring the planned participation of one or more members. I have already indicated that many activities served multiple functions falling under different tasks and even dimensions. They have been classified, however, solely under the dimension and task which was most prominent. Thus an anti-Fascist demonstration, for instance, might serve to reinforce the enthusiasm and participation of section members, but its primary function was to mobilize the general public and to build social alliances and thus it would be classified under the mobilization task of the social alliance dimension. For a more detailed discussion of the system of activity classification see my "Continuity and Change," Chapter 7.

[46] In evaluating these data it should be recalled that there was no election campaign during the year covered. Thus none of the activities reported were directly election-related. The large number of initiatives, therefore, suggests that characterization of the PCI as an "electoral" or "catch-all" party is inaccurate.

[47] For a direct comparison of the base level activity of the PCI and DC, see Gianfranco Poggi, et al., *L'Organizzazione partitica del PCI e della DC* (Bologna: Società Editrice Il Mulino, 1968). Giorgio Galli, a frequent critic of the PCI, has written the following about the party: "In general, the crisis of traditional participation becomes more acute; and since it becomes so less in the PCI than in the other parties, the key to the [PCI's] system, that is, voluntary activism, still reigns." "Il PCI revisitato," in *Il Mulino* (1971) (Bologna: Società Editrice Il Mulino, 1971).

ban sections, for instance, undertook many more activities than either of the other two groups. An examination of these differences is required. Second, the numerical data do not tell us anything about the *targets* of the activities. If the PCI is to use social alliance activity to generate pressure for political change, it must not only maintain the hegemony over the Left subculture which it established after the Second World War but also must build links from that subcultural base to social forces which have formerly been unwilling to lend their support to Communist initiatives. This need to maintain existent subcultural strength while developing new social alliances suggests an analytical distinction between the targets of section initiatives. We will want to examine to what degree sections operating in different environments not only direct their activities toward those social forces already within the socialist subculture but also toward groups outside that relatively secure social base. In analyzing section performance of the three tasks of the social alliance dimension, this distinction is central.

The information task is the easiest for the sections to carry out. Successful performance does not require the sections to organize nonparty members, nor does it depend on the sections' capacity to make the targets accept the party positions as legitimate. Rather, all that is required is that a few members distribute various types of party propaganda to individuals who need themselves do nothing more than passively accept the party materials. The relative simplicity of the task is obvious when we realize that the activities falling in this category include such things as leafleting a supermarket and distributing *L'Unità*. The relative ease of the information task might lead us to expect similar performance by sections operating in different types of environments; local factors would seem less likely to play an important role when the task is simple and requires little from nonparty members. When we look at the data reported in Table 1 and at some of the results of the interviewing, however, it is clear that this is not the case; there are significant variations both in the amount of information task activity undertaken by the section groups and in the character of that activity.

The differences between section groups in the amount of activity devoted to the information task are immediately obvious from the data in Table 1, A. First, the suburban sections undertook an average of almost twice as many such activities as the sections in

283

either of the other two environments. Second, a comparison of the urban and the peripheral groups shows that the sections in the city not only averaged more individual information initiatives but also that all the urban sections undertook at least one such activity; among the peripheral sections, two did not do anything to spread party positions through the distribution of propaganda. These limited findings are suggestive in two ways. On the one hand, they indicate that the similarities between the two non-urban groups in performance of the tasks of the political alliance dimension may not carry over to the development of social alliances. On the other hand, the relatively greater effort by the urban than the peripheral sections in disseminating party materials may be a first indication that, as the urban leaders argued was the case, their low level of political alliance activity is compensated for by a more intensive attempt to cultivate new social allies.

Both these points are confirmed when we look at the character of the information initiatives undertaken by the three section groups, that is, when we examine what kinds of information they are disseminating. In both the urban and the suburban sections, the interview respondents said that a large number of information initiatives were devoted to trying to make salient a particular social problem at the national or local level and to clarification of the alternative offered by the PCI. One leader, for instance, showed me a series of leaflets distributed by his section which discussed the failure of the government's housing policy and the approach the PCI would pursue. The propaganda materials I collected in the city and suburban sections confirmed this general impression. In the peripheral sections, on the other hand, the descriptions of section propaganda offered by the respondents and the materials I collected presented a different picture. Rarely was the propaganda an attempt to elaborate the PCI's position on an issue in any detail. Rather, it tended simply to denounce governmental policy and call generically for support of the Communists. In addition, much more of the peripheral propaganda was what might be termed "celebratory," that is, proclaiming some major event in the history of the Communist movement or the PCI, (e.g., Lenin's birthday, a PCI anniversary), than was the case in the other two groups.

These differences in the character of section propaganda may be indicative of a difference in the kinds of targets toward which

284

the sections' social alliance work is directed. The type of information disseminated by the peripheral sections appeared to be directed toward reinforcing the feelings of people who were at least somewhat sympathetic to the PCI. The propaganda of the urban and the suburban sections, on the other hand, while certainly also serving to reinforce those already sympathetic, was more adapted to developing new party supporters by demonstrating that the PCI was not only a generic opposition but, in the party's own words, *un partito di governo*,[48] and therefore worthy of the support of anyone seeking substantive social reform. Thus, even this brief survey of the sections' performance of the information task suggests that rather than the two adaptive styles (urban and nonurban) which were indicated by the data on performance of the tasks of the political alliance dimension, we may be seeing three styles, each representing a particular adjustment to the character of the environment in which the sections must operate. As we look at the other two tasks of the social alliance dimension, these three styles will emerge with increasing clarity.

Effective section performance of *the mobilization task* is critical to the success of the PCI's strategy. Without mobilizing sectors of the mass public around themes singled out by the party for their political value, it is difficult to imagine that sufficient pressure for change can be brought to bear on the existing political alignments. At the same time, the task is an especially difficult one for the sections to carry out. It requires considerable organization of nonparty members for any individual initiative to succeed, and the difficulty of such organization is increased by the fact that participation by the targets implies far greater commitment than was necessary for the information task. Furthermore, mobilization of the mass public is likely to increase the intensity of opposition to the PCI by those already hostile to the party. Given the Communist's desire to reduce any possibility of further isolation, such polarization is to be avoided. Thus, carrying out

[48] Since the Second World War the PCI has consistently sought to present itself as a party of governance, that is, as a party which not only reacts critically to the proposals and actions of others but which also seeks to develop and carry out a positive, substantive program. Such an image is critical to the success of the Communist strategy both because it encourages people to support the party in order to advance their pursuit of specific governmental policies and because it may enhance those who unreservedly oppose the PCI at least to accept the party as a legitimate actor in the political system.

285

the mobilization task involves considerable tensions and difficulties for the sections and raises the issues of how much activity sections in different environments devote to mobilization and how they seek to avoid the potential polarizing effects of such activity.

Looking first at the total amount of mobilization activity undertaken by the sections (Table 1, Row B-5), we find differences between the three groups similar to those observed for the information task: the suburban sections made considerably more initiatives than either the urban or the peripheral sections and the latter two groups were identical in their output. Thus, it again appears that the suburban sections are more dynamic and that, at least at first glance, the units operating in the urban and the small town environments are quite similar.

Before examining this general picture in greater detail, two observations about the overall level of mobilization activity are necessary. First, while there are marked differences in the amount of such activity undertaken by the sections in each group, the ratio between mobilization and information activities for each group is rather similar. The sections consistently undertook almost twice as many initiatives intended to inform nonparty members as to mobilize them. This finding suggests two mutually reinforcing interpretations. First, the lesser amount of mobilization activity in all groups may simply be the result of the greater difficulty associated with carrying out such activities. Second, it may indicate the avoidance by all sections of activities which will lead to sharp polarization.

In evaluating the character of the activity, the seemingly simple distinctions between the suburban and the other two section groups become more complex. In particular, the similarities between the urban and the peripheral sections become weaker and, for purposes of analysis, the sections seem to divide into three, rather than two, types. Two characteristics of the sections' mobilization activities show this most clearly. First, both the urban and the suburban sections seem to have been somewhat more willing to undertake initiatives which could have had some polarizing effect but which, at the same time, were most likely to create pressure on the political system. Second, and closely related, more of the activities of the peripheral sections appear to have been directed primarily toward party sympathizers than was the case for the other two groups. These two characteristics can be

286

examined by looking at some examples of specific mobilization activities drawn from Table 1 and the interviews.

The *festival di L'Unità* is a section-sponsored fair, usually lasting for several days, which has the explicit purpose of raising funds to support both the section and the PCI press. It is a distinctly social occasion held outdoors during the summer months with food, music, and dancing. The political content is generally confined to exhibits of posters expounding party positions and a public speech by a party official. The festival is open to all and, when possible, is held in a place not directly associated with the PCI and to which people of all political persuasions will feel free to come. Despite these ecumenical intentions, however, many section leaders and federation officials told me that the majority of those who attended were Communist sympathizers or people who felt an affinity to the Left. More than one section secretary indicated that the festival was the major event of the year for those members who otherwise had little contact with the section and that it was one of the few times that they had contact with the membership of the PSI. Thus, the festival clearly has no polarizing effect and is directed primarily toward those who already feel some affinity to the PCI.

As is evident in Table 1, Row B-4, festivals were of differing importance in the profile of mobilization activities of the various section groups. All of the suburban and peripheral sections held at least one festival in the year covered by the data; in contrast, only six of the nine urban sections did so.[49] Furthermore, the festivals comprised a far larger proportion of the total mobilization activities in the peripheral than in the suburban sections. This latter difference is of considerable import because the leaders in all sections in which festivals were held indicated that preparation of the annual fairs was one of the most intense periods of member activity and participation, rivaled only by election campaigns. Thus it appears that the peripheral sections devoted a larger portion of their mobilizational work to social activities aimed at those already sympathetic to the party than was the case for the urban or the peripheral sections.

Similar differences in the character of the mobilizational work of the section groups appear when we look at the themes of the public assemblies they sponsored. In the peripheral sections, the

[49] This finding is particularly noteworthy because there was considerable pressure from the federation on the sections to hold festivals.

large majority of such assemblies were concerned with what I have previously termed "celebratory" themes; that is, they were intended to commemorate a major PCI or Communist movement anniversary. Only rarely were they called as a party response to a national or international event. Furthermore, section leaders indicated that these latter assemblies tended to discuss the general themes of the PCI's history and strategy rather than specific aspects of the party's program. From these observations it would appear that the peripheral sections tend to carry out mobilizational initiatives appealing primarily to those already sympathetic to the PCI; assemblies concerned with celebratory or very general national issues would seem to have little likelihood of expanding the party's social support.

In the urban, and especially the peripheral sections, the themes covered in public assemblies were somewhat different. One found fewer celebrations of party traditions and more concern with highlighting particular reform issues and with attempting to clarify the differences between the national or local government's response to those issues and the position advocated by the Communists. One urban section,[50] for instance, reported that it had held five public assemblies during the year covered by my study: three of these had been concerned with specific party reform proposals (health, transportation, reform in the *meridione*), one with a general discussion of the *via italiana* and only one with a celebratory theme (the PCI's fiftieth anniversary). This pattern was common to both the urban and the suburban sections, but in the latter the larger number of public assemblies meant that a lower percentage were devoted to themes with little or no appeal beyond Communist sympathizers. A comparison between the city and hinterland sections and those on the periphery, therefore, again suggests that the latter were far less concerned with the expansion of the PCI's base of social support beyond the limits of the Left subculture.

Neither festivals nor public assemblies are likely to polarize public opinion. But demonstrations and picketing are somewhat different. Though formally legitimate, they are a good deal more likely to arouse strong and contrasting sentiments, especially when the theme of the initiative is itself controversial. Thus, an examination of the number and type of such activities undertaken

[50] Interview #5 (urban).

by the section groups should reveal a good deal about the general commitment of party sections to such activity and about the differences in commitment of sections operating in different context.

When we look at the number of demonstration and picketing activities for the section groups reported in Table 1, Rows 2 and 3, two points are immediately apparent. First, there are too few such initiatives to warrant extensive comparison between the groups. The only two contrasts worth mentioning are the higher number of picketing initiatives by the suburban sections (a further indication of their generally higher level of activity) and the extremely low number of peripheral sections engaging in either type of activity (perhaps a further sign of their social and subcultural orientation).

Second, the extremely low number of these initiatives in any of the section groups is itself a matter of interest, suggesting there may be some general factor or tendency at work. It appears that the sections in all environments were unwilling and/or unable to undertake the type of initiatives which would be likely to create the social pressure which the party deems necessary if its strategy is to succeed but which also are most likely to have a polarizing effect on the public. Rather, they seem more inclined to do the kind of work, indicated by assemblies and festivals, which is fairly normal in any liberal democratic system. This finding suggests that the previously discussed tension between the party's desire to expand its base of social support and to create mass pressure for political change is resolved in favor of the former: intense and more controversial forms of mobilization are curtailed, replaced by forms that will permit the party to extend its image of legitimacy.[51]

[51] In this connection it is interesting to note that in recent years more intensive forms of social mobilization, such as massive street demonstrations, have been spearheaded by the partly unified trade union movement usually, but not always, with the support of the Communists. These demonstrations have often been in favor of reforms similar to those proposed by the PCI. In some ways this is an excellent development for the party because mass pressure for political change is exerted but the Communists can avoid direct responsibility for the actions. Thus the party's position is enhanced with fewer of the negative effects which might result if it were leading the demonstrations itself. These advantages, however, are present only to the degree that the demonstrations and resultant disruption do not become so great that the union movement, and the Left as a whole, become isolated.

289

The institutionalization task refers to the sections' participation in organized social groups ranging from basically social and cultural organizations such as the *circoli* to groups with a particular economic interest to pursue through political action. The degree to which the PCI sections can develop a role for themselves in the various groups will have a great deal to do with the degree of "presence" which the party achieves in any locality. The data on task performance reported in Table 1-D are broken down in terms of the type of organizations with which the sections had contacts. Two of these types, *circoli*[52] and cultural centers, were almost exclusively for people already within the Left subculture; subcultural identification was both their *raison d'être* and their principal attraction. The other two organizational types, interest groups and anti-Fascist committees, on the other hand, were intended to appeal across subcultural lines on the basis of a particular interest or value. When we examine the data in light of this distinction, significant differences between the section groups are apparent. First, far fewer of the urban sections had contacts with subcultural organizations than was the case for the sections in the other groups: whereas almost every suburban and peripheral section was affiliated with a *circolo*, only two of the nine sections in the city had such an affiliation. The explanation of this difference is rather simple. The social changes which had taken place in the city in the postwar period had almost destroyed the structure of *circoli* developed during the previous decades. Thus the urban sections had little opportunity to affiliate with such organizations. The consequences of a lack of ties to *circoli* were also clear. Most urban leaders complained of the isolation of the party from the social life of the city and of the inability of their sections to offer the kinds of social incentives which would make participation in the PCI more pleasurable. They often openly contrasted their situation with what they viewed as the advantages of the sections in the hinterland and beyond. A federation official charged with responsibility for the city organization

---

[52] The *circoli* were subcultural organizations with a bar, pinball machines, a television set, and often a *bocce* court as well as a large room for meetings. Their function was almost entirely recreational though they usually had *L'Unità* on the tables. In the small towns, and sometimes in the large ones, the local *circolo* was the major place to go and have a drink for anyone who was willing, in even the most casual way, to be identified with the Left. Often the *circolo* housed the office of the PCI section and was the place where major party meetings were held.

summed up the basic problem: "Many of the city sections just can't get a grip on their environment. They aren't linked to the social tissue of the community the way the sections outside the city are."[53]

It should be noted that many of the nonurban leaders were somewhat less sanguine about the role of the *circolo* for their section. Although they recognized its critical importance in establishing a link to their membership and to the subculture as a whole, they also indicated that the administrative tasks which accompanied participation in a *circolo* could become so burdensome that other aspects of the sections' work would suffer. This complaint was particularly common in the peripheral sections. Despite this problem, however, there is no question that the absence of contacts with *circoli* was a severe handicap for the urban sections.

If the number of sections having contacts with subcultural organizations differentiated the urban sections from the others, contacts (and the lack thereof) with cross-cutting organizations was the principal difference between the peripheral sections and those in the city and suburbs. While well over half of the latter two types had affiliations with anti-Fascist committees,[54] only half of the peripheral sections did. Similarly, more than half of the sections in the city and suburbs had contacts with special interest organizations;[55] only 3 of the 18 sections in the peripheral environments had such contacts. This finding clearly confirms the impression of the differences between the three groups developed previously. Again we see that the peripheral sections were far less concerned with the development of contacts which extend beyond the realm of the PCI's traditional allies.

In order to begin to develop some hypotheses explaining the patterns of social alliance task performance which we have found for the three section groups, a brief summary of the principal findings is necessary. Three patterns have been highlighted:

1. All the section groups placed a greater emphasis on those

[53] Interview #59 (federation).

[54] These committees were the PCI's institutional response to the rise in neo-Fascist agitation in the late 1960s, and were aimed at an extremely broad constituency similar in outline to that which had supported the Resistance twenty-five years earlier.

[55] Such organizations included the association of artisans, the association of shopkeepers, and local tenant groups.

291

activities (propaganda distribution, public assemblies, festivals) which are unlikely to increase tensions between the PCI and its opponents than on initiatives (picketing, demonstrations) likely to polarize public opinion. Widespread party legitimacy appeared to take precedence over intense mass pressure on political alignments.

2. Sections operating in suburban environments were far more active than those in either the city or the periphery. The suburban sections had almost twice as many information and mobilization activities as those in the other two groups and they had a wider spread of institutional contacts and affiliations. From the point of view of the amount of social alliance activity, the urban and the peripheral sections were rather similar.

3. Such similarities, however, were not evident when we examined the character, rather than the amount, of activity. The peripheral sections appeared to concentrate primarily on strengthening their ties with those already sympathetic to the party. The themes of their informational and assembly activities, the relative importance assigned to festivals, the groups with which they maintained institutional contacts all illustrated this point. The urban, and especially the suburban, sections, on the other hand, showed a more balanced approach, undertaking a number of activities directed both at sympathizers and at those who were not already part of the Left subculture. This pattern was most evident for the suburban sections which, while taking numerous initiatives directed primarily toward sympathizers, also undertook activities with a broader scope of targets. In the urban sections this pattern was also found but in a weaker form; particularly noteworthy was the fact that the urban sections appeared to have far weaker contacts with the traditional subculture (note the fewer festivals and ties to *circoli*).

How can these patterns of performance of the tasks of the social alliance dimension be explained? To the degree that they are similar, i.e., the tendency to promote more activities unlikely to polarize, the explanation may well lie in the character of the party strategy itself. The PCI's strategy assumes the possibility that it can come to power within the institutional framework of a liberal democracy. The ultimate goal of the strategy, therefore, involves a change in the political alignments among national political parties and necessarily leads to a concern about the party's electoral position and an awareness, deeply grounded in the

292

country's twentieth-century political history, of the need to protect the system from the threat of institutional change from the
right. This complex of concerns pushes toward what we might
call a conservative approach to social mobilization, that is, one
which is always keenly aware of the dangers inherent in social
and political polarization. At the same time, the PCI recognizes
that the political changes it seeks cannot be attained if the party
is unable to bridge traditional class and religious cleavages
through aggressive mobilization which will make salient critical
social issues and will develop strong pressure for change. In the
face of the obvious tension between these two strategic needs, the
data presented on section performance suggest that the former
concerns have the upper hand, perhaps because both historical
experience and the inherent conservatism of a political institution
as deeply embedded in the Italian polity as the PCI give primacy
to caution over risk-taking when a choice between the two seems
necessary.

Beyond the somewhat "conservative" orientation common to
the sections' social alliance activities, however, we also need to
explain the rather significant differences in their task performance. To do so it appears to me necessary to examine the interaction between strategic priorities as translated into section tasks
and the characteristics of the local environments in which the
sections operate. I will not attempt here to elaborate systematically such an explanation nor to develop the theoretical framework on which it might be based. Rather, I will merely sketch out
some of the factors which appear most important in explaining
the patterns observed for each of the section groups.

Looking first at the urban sections, it appears that the pattern
of low activity accompanied by considerable attention devoted
to expanding the party's base of support can be linked primarily
to the isolation of these sections from the environment in which
they operate. We have noted earlier that the character of politics
in the city means that the sections have poor contacts with other
political forces in their neighborhoods. They also are far more
socially isolated than the sections in the other two groups. This
isolation is most dramatically evidenced by the fact that only two
of the nine sections were linked to a *circolo*; the remainder were
without any institutionalized subcultural support and had to rely
solely on the sections' own resources to attract members and
sympathizers.

293

Three ties between this isolation and the pattern of social alliance activities in the urban sections can be suggested. First, the absence of subcultural support may make it difficult for these sections to generate the level of member participation necessary to carry out an intensive and wide-ranging round of initiatives. The isolated section simply cannot produce sufficient incentives to attract as much participation as is desired. The urban sections do, in fact, have the poorest rates of member participation. Second, isolation may create difficulties in identifying issues which will be even minimally effective in mobilizing the mass public, leading to discouragement among the active members about the possibilities for effective social alliance-building. Third, the sections' isolation may lead them to be somewhat less concerned with consolidating their minimal subcultural ties and thus to be more willing to devote their limited resources to attracting new allies. Having no easily identifiable subcultural constituency, in other words, encourages initiatives which have a broader, less differentiated, group of targets.

This analysis suggests that the urban sections are basically caught in a vicious circle in which their isolation leads to low participation, poor issue development, and a relatively low number of social alliance activities, all of which can be expected to lead to even greater isolation. At the same time, however, the sections' response to this situation involves at least some attempt to break out of the circle by undertaking activities that will expand the party's base of support.

For the sections in the periphery the situation is different. There one can suggest that the observed pattern of social alliance activities results from two factors: the static nature of the political and social environment in the peripheral towns and the strongly institutionalized subculture—itself clearly related to the relatively slow rate of political and social change. On the one hand, the power of the subcultural institutions means that beyond administering the *circoli* and undertaking a few celebratory activities the sections need do little to maintain the loyalty of those sympathetic to the PCI. Already existent social allies are relatively secure. On the other hand, the static character of the environment, reflected both in a lesser degree of urgency about the issues which are at the center of the PCI's reform program and in the domineering role played by the subcultures of the Left and the Catholics, means that the potential for effective

294

initiatives to expand the scope of the party's social alliances is low. As a result, the sections devote little attention to building new social alliances. Tied to a strong subculture, they are unchallenged and unchallenging.[56]

Finally, the suburban environment and sections display an amalgam of the strong points we have seen in the other two groups. In contrast to the periphery, the suburban environment is dynamic, creating opportunities for the sections to seek to build new alliances around the pressing social problems created by rapid change. At the same time, change has not destroyed the subcultural institutions and thus these sections continue to enjoy the benefits of better participation and contact with the environment which these institutions afford. As a result, the suburban sections can exploit their alliance opportunities, seeking to expand the party's base of social support, while also having sufficient resources to undertake the activities necessary to maintain their subcultural strength in the face of social change. In other words, in contrast to the urban sections, the suburban ones have the resources they require; in contrast to the peripheral sections, they have the opportunities effectively to utilize those resources. Thus we find sections with a high level of activity directed both at maintaining old alliances and building new ones.

The foregoing hypotheses are intended as starting points for a causal analysis of the differences in social alliance task performance in various section groups. In examining some of the activities of the sections falling within the reinforcement dimension, we shall be able to see if some of the problems of member participation which I have alluded to do, in fact, occur.

The Reinforcement Dimension

How much of the section's activity is devoted to reinforcement relative to the other dimensions previously discussed? To what degree is participation, or lack of it, an important factor in explaining overall section performance?

The reinforcement dimension includes activities designed explicitly to maintain and expand the party's membership, to increase member participation in party affairs, and to educate the

---

[56] One would assume that a mirror image of the pattern found in the PCI sections would be found for DC organizations. Thus the static relationship between the two sides is self-reinforcing.

membership about party strategy and specific policy positions. With the exception of recruitment,[57] all these activities are directed solely at members, and it is evident that they form a central part of the party's overall strategic perspective. Without a strong organization, effective performance of the tasks of the other dimensions would be impossible. Furthermore, organizational strength is itself one of the criteria used by the party to measure its strategic success. At the same time, many reinforcement activities are extremely tedious and time-consuming, requiring door-to-door solicitations. Furthermore, reinforcement often has little payoff in terms of increasing the sections' actual capacity to perform political and social alliance-building activities. Growth of membership, for instance, did not appear from my interviews to be linked in any direct manner to increased member activism.

Despite the difficulties of these activities, however, all of the sections devoted considerable attention to them. As is indicated in Table 2-A, both the urban and suburban sections undertook

TABLE 2. Reinforcement Dimension Activities*

	Urban	Suburban	Peripheral
A. Totals per Section Group			
	25.8	25.1	10.2
B. Comparison with Social Alliance Dimension			
Reinforcement	25.8	25.1	10.2
Social Alliance	18.6	31.3	16.7

*For the year July 1970–June 1971.

an average of more than two such activities per month; in the peripheral sections the average was not quite one per month. When we compare these data with those for social alliance dimension activity (Table 2-B) we see that the reinforcement work is considerable: in the urban sections there are more reinforcement initiatives than social alliance ones and in the suburban sections the relationship is only mildly in the other direction. The

[57] From my interviews and observations it appeared that the sections undertook few initiatives explicitly designed to recruit new members. Rather, they generally relied on their activities and their general "presence" to create a few recruits each year.

296

actual attention directed toward the internal development of the organization cannot be fully appreciated without taking into account the high expenditure of section resources (man-hours of work) which many of the activities require.

How is this overall situation to be explained? Why does a party which is so critically concerned with alliances and with maintaining and expanding contacts with the mass public spend so much time and energy on organizational reinforcement, especially when such reinforcement often has little immediate payoff in alliance terms?[58] Three factors explaining this general picture would seem of particular importance. First, the national and federation leadership placed a great emphasis on the performance of these tasks and especially on the maintenance of membership. Each year sections were continually pressed by federation officials to reach 100 percent of the previous year's membership, and the standings of the sections relative to this goal were published in L'Unità at least monthly throughout the year. Membership, in other words, was one of the clearest ways the performance of the sections in all strategic dimensions was measured by the federations and was considered a major indicator of the success of the party's policies. The section leaders had absorbed this perspective and the priorities which it implied: when asked how well their section was functioning, well over half of the respondents used success or failure in reaching 100 percent of the previous year's membership as the first criterion of judgment. The stress both party officials and base-level leaders placed on membership maintenance as a primary measure of organizational performance should not be surprising. Not only is the concept of a mass party a central tenet of the PCI's theory but the complexity of the strategy and the difficulty of translating other kinds of strategic activity into "hard" measures encourages a reliance on simple if superficial indicators of performance.

This point serves to introduce a second factor which seemed to contribute to the emphasis on reinforcement: the nature of the leadership of the party sections. Most of the leaders were workers—72 percent of the section secretaries could be classified as working class[59]—and they often had difficulty translating the

---

[58] The considerable activity the sections still devote to reinforcement suggests once more that a characterization of the PCI as a "catch-all" or "electoral" party is inadequate.

[59] By this I mean that they were blue-collar wage workers.

basic concepts of party strategy into concrete activities. In the interviews the section leaders repeatedly expressed their frustration in trying to develop an initiative at the local level which would be an adequate expression of the party's strategic perspective and national policies. Often they admitted that they themselves did not fully understand the tactical twists and turns of the party's national leadership. Confronted with these complexities and with their difficulty in dealing with them, administrative tasks, though boring, were the easiest outlet for the activists' desire to contribute to the party's success. If they could not develop effective initiatives in their towns or neighborhoods on local problems, they could at least make sure that the party remained strong and that it continued to have a "diffuse presence" through its mass membership.

A third factor contributing to the stress on reinforcement was the poor participation of the party membership in section affairs. Interviews and observation indicated that only about 10 percent of the members of most sections made any contribution to section initiatives during a nonelection year. There were, of course, occasions (the festivals, for instance) when participation rose markedly and the average attendance at section assemblies was usually between 15 and 20 percent, but otherwise the burden of running the section fell on the few (*pochi ma buoni*) who were willing to devote two or three evenings a week to party affairs. In the face of such member apathy, it is not surprising that reinforcement tasks were considered of such importance. If the party organization was weak, it would be impossible to take other initiatives. Since most section leaders tended to define party strength primarily in membership terms, they tended to respond to low activity by making reinforcement their highest priority, hoping as well to take political and social alliance initiatives but unwilling to take the chance that such activities would generate new active support for the section. The leaders felt it was "safer" to do what they always had done, hoping to wrench a little more activism from the established membership, and at the same time assuring that they would at least meet the membership maintenance criterion.

These three factors, when combined with the explicit role given to reinforcement in the PCI's overall strategic perspective, would appear to account for the emphasis on internally directed activities common to all the sections. But, as I have already indicated, there were significant differences between the three section groups both in the amount of reinforcement work and in the levels of member participation. An analysis of these differences tends to confirm the tentative hypotheses about the character of section adaptation to environmental conditions which were developed at the close of the discussion of the social alliance dimension.

Two major differences between the groups can be identified. First, in absolute (total number of reinforcement activities) and especially in relative (compared to the number of social alliance activities) terms, there was a declining importance of reinforcement as we move from the urban to the peripheral environment (see Table 2, A & B). In the urban sections reinforcement activities accounted for 58.1 percent of the combined social and reinforcement total, in the suburban sections for 44.5 percent, and in the peripheral units for 37.9 percent. As we move from city to periphery, in other words, there is decreasingly explicit attention devoted to reinforcing the party's organization.

How is this pattern to be explained? To discover the answer we need to return to some of the findings already presented. I have noted that the urban sections are both politically and socially far more isolated from their environments than the sections of either of the other groups. These latter have, above all else, the support structure provided by their links with *circoli*. The differences in the degree of isolation of the sections can be expected to have at least two consequences for the level of member participation and, indirectly, for the performance of the reinforcement tasks. On the one hand, the isolation will lead to a lower percentage of members who take an active part in the initiatives of the section. Fewer members will develop the close social ties to the section which can serve as an incentive to make the considerable sacrifices required of an activist. Conversely, more members could be expected to be so removed from the life of the section that only considerable efforts on the part of the activists could assure their continued loyalty to the party. Putting this hypothetical relationship another way, we are suggesting that the weaker the sections' subcultural support, the fewer will be the activists and the greater the effort (both absolutely and relative to the number of active members) necessary to maintain and educate the sections' membership.

Data collected through the interviews and observation bear

299

out these hypotheses. As reported in Table 3, the urban sections had a lower percentage of members who were active on a regular basis and a higher percentage who were total nonparticipants than was the case in either of the other two groups. Furthermore, while the nonparticipant percentage was also high in the latter, the leaders of these sections, particularly in the periphery, reported that many of the nonactive members were easily renewed each year when they came to the *circolo*. In the city, in contrast, the leaders repeatedly complained that almost all the nonpartici-

TABLE 3. Participation, 1970

	Urban		Suburban		Peripheral	
	(N)	(%)	(N)	(%)	(N)	(%)
Regularly active	36.4	8.0	51.5	11.2	22.4	11.6
Rarely active	35.2	8.9	62.8	13.5	36.6	19.1
Never active	383.3	83.1	355.3	75.3	134.3	69.3

pants required a special effort, including door-to-door solicitation, on the section's part if their memberships were to be renewed. Thus, it appeared that the urban sections had a much harder job meeting the membership maintenance priority and that they had to confront this job with fewer activists. Conversely, the peripheral sections had by far the easiest time meeting that priority.

These observations receive further confirmation when we examine the movement of membership in the three section groups in the years from 1963 to 1970. In this period the PCI as a whole and in Milan province in particular was losing members at a steady rate. As is indicated in Table 4, however, the most severe membership losses were encountered in the urban sections (24.8 percent), a figure almost double that of both the suburban and the peripheral units. What these data suggest is that in the

TABLE 4. Membership, 1963-1970

	1963	1970	1970 as % of 1963
Average urban section size	603.6	453.9	75.2
Average suburban section size	529.3	466.0	88.0
Average peripheral section size	217.2	192.1	88.4

300

city even the great effort devoted to reinforcement was not able to stem the tide of membership decline; the weakness of subcultural support and the rapid social and economic change made membership maintenance impossible. In the suburban sections, in contrast, an intensity of effort similar to that of the urban units yielded much more favorable results; a strong reinforcement effort combined with links to subcultural institutions could counteract the effects of rapid change far more adequately. Finally, in the periphery much less intense reinforcement activity still permitted the sections to do as well as those in the suburbs and much better than those in the city. Thus it appears that the similarities and differences in the number of reinforcement initiatives undertaken by the three section groups can be explained by the character of the environments in which they operate and by the effects on member participation which result therefrom.

In concluding I want to turn to an evaluation of how effectively the sections implemented the dimensions of the PCI's strategy. I have argued that Milan was an interesting locus for the study of base-level behavior both because it represented the kind of "nondominance" area in which the party strategy would have to be effectively implemented if the Communists were to escape their position of strategic inferiority and because it would allow us to see how well the party responded to the challenges presented by the social changes associated with advanced industrialization. From a general point of view, ignoring the differences we have found between section groups, it would seem fair to maintain that all sections do a fairly good job of performing a very complex and very demanding set of strategic tasks. With the single exception of the neglect of political institutions in the work of the urban sections, we have found that all units undertook a considerable number of initiatives in the various task areas and that these initiatives were usually directed not only toward old allies but also toward potential new ones traditionally beyond the reach of the Communists. We did find, however, that the activities of the social alliance dimension tended to stress expansion of the party's image of legitimacy at the expense of the kind of mobilization effort that could create significant pressure for political change. This pattern is partly a function of the extreme complexity of the social structure in a highly industrialized area and of the competitive character of politics in the province of Milan. The former may make it particularly difficult to develop the un-

301

equivocal positions around which intense mobilization can occur, while the latter makes sections extremely wary of alienating any potential allies. Complex social structure and political competitiveness, in other words, may lead the party to be more moderate in its actions than would otherwise be the case.

When we turn from this general analysis to look at the strategic performance of the individual section groups, a more articulated picture emerges. Sections implement all the dimensions of the strategy, but they adapt their behavior as a result of the character of the environment in which they operate, emphasizing some strategic tasks at the expense of others. For each of the three environments, a specific type of section can be identified. First, in the peripheral towns, we found what we might call the "enclave" type of section. It is strongly based in the socialist subculture and uses the town council to seek to advance party positions. But the peripheral sections do little to carry the battle to the enemy. The targets of most of their social alliance activities were the PCI's traditional allies and sympathizers rather than the uncommitted and the social allies of the DC. In general, these sections were rather closed in on themselves, maintaining their internal strength and ties to the subculture but rarely extending their reach despite the fact that they needed to devote few of their organizational resources to reinforcement. In the peripheral towns, therefore, it appeared that the PCI's position was secure but that there was little likelihood that local section activity would alter long-standing political alignments. The static character of the environment was reflected in the behavior of the sections themselves.

In the city we found what we might call the "embattled" type of section. Lacking the support of subcultural institutions and generally isolated from the people with whom they were to interact, these sections tried to seek out new social alliances but often found themselves having to concentrate their very limited organizational resources on section maintenance owing to their inability to elicit sufficient participation. In the urban environment it appeared that social change had created conditions in which implementation of the strategy was extremely difficult. The sections had to be primarily concerned with maintaining their limited foothold rather than with improving the party's position.

In the suburban towns we found sections that most clearly resembled the ideal set forth in the party strategy. These "combative" sections performed all the strategic tasks, usually with considerably greater intensity than in either of the other two groups. Furthermore, not only did they seek to maintain their political and social links with the party's traditional allies but they also undertook many activities intended to expand the party's base of political and social support. In the suburban environment we seemed to find the combination of factors which best permitted the conversion of strategic intentions into concrete initiatives.

Questions naturally arise at this point about the degree to which these three section types and the adaptations they represent can be expected to endure and what they suggest about the interaction between the party's strategic goals and the environments in which party units must operate. To answer these questions fully is not within the scope of this paper. By looking at the analysis of the interaction between environment and section behavior which I have tentatively advanced, however, some responses may be assayed. The data presented seem to suggest that two variables, the extent of a subcultural network in which the section can embed itself and the opportunities for alliance-building which the environment creates, are most important in explaining the different patterns observed. When the subcultural network is missing, as it is in the city, the sections do not have the organizational resources fully to implement the strategy. When the environment is stagnant, creating a low salience of reform issues and relatively polarized politics, the opportunities for effective alliance work are absent or weak.

But, as should be evident, both these variables are, in turn, related to a more general one, the character and pace of social change. The answer to the two questions I have posed, therefore, lies in an evaluation of the likely future pattern of social change in the province of Milan. And from this point of view it would appear that the future is not necessarily bleak for the PCI in the province and in industrialized areas in general. While there is little question that the conditions producing the "enclave" type of section are going to disappear, it would seem that the most probable path of evolution is not toward the urban but rather toward the suburban type of environment. In Milan, growth in recent

303

years has been much more rapid outside the city than within it and there is little reason to believe that this trend will change. If this is the case, and if the party is able to assure that despite social change in the present peripheral towns, its subcultural bases are preserved, we can expect to see an increase in the number of combative sections. And, to the degree that the Milanese pattern of development is likely to be repeated in other competitive areas of Italy, the prospects for the PCI as measured by its ability to implement its strategy would appear positive.

VIII.

Left-Wing Unity at the Grass Roots: Picardy and Languedoc

DENIS LACORNE

Scholars have often treated French political parties as homogeneous entities. Relying on official declarations and writings of national party leaders, they tend to overemphasize the decision-making process at the top and to assume that what happens in Paris adequately represents party life throughout France. The Parti Communiste Français (PCF) has been studied in this way for two fairly good reasons: until recently access to party archives has been difficult if not impossible; furthermore, the principle of democratic centralism seemed to preclude differences between branches of the party. Such an approach is misleading in that it underestimates the influence of regional factors and the autonomy of intermediate party leaders.[1] Analysis of the PCF's peripheral structures might shed some new light on the party's cohesiveness and organizational peculiarities, particularly because the future of French socialism lies in a systematic coalition strategy planned at the national level but implemented at the municipal and departmental levels as well. To understand the new alliance strategy, all three levels must be analyzed.[2]

* This study, which is based on part of my Ph.D. dissertation for Yale University, was made possible thanks to a grant from the Social Science Research Council and the American Council of Learned Societies, Foreign Area Fellowship Program. I would like to thank D. Blackmer and S. Tarrow for comments on the draft of this chapter.

[1] Pierre Grémion remarks: "The French tradition [of political science] ignores the notion of 'local government.' . . . It accepts the jurists' fallacy, i.e., the peripheral administrative apparatus of the State is nothing but an instrument of execution which is entirely subordinate to the decisions of the center." "Introduction à une étude du système politico-administratif local," *Sociologie du travail* 12 (January-March 1970): 54 and 55.

[2] On the importance of local context see the pioneering work of S. Tarrow, *Peasant Communism in Southern Italy* (New Haven and London: Yale University Press, 1967). See also, in a different context, the excellent article of J. Linz and A. de Miguel, "Within-Nation Differences and Comparisons: the Eight Spains," in R. Merrit (ed.) *Comparing Nations* (Yale University

305

In this chapter, I shall limit myself to municipal left-wing coalitions for two reasons. First, at the very moment when a large-scale strategy of left-wing unity was being developed by the Parti Socialiste (PS) and PCF leaders, left-wing coalitions won unprecedented victories in the March 1971 municipal elections.[3] Second, and perhaps more important, a municipal coalition is not an ephemeral political arrangement but one that lasts at least six years, involves a large number of participants (at least nine), and is therefore likely to affect the behavior, if not the beliefs, of the respective coalition partners.

The following analysis attempts to relate empirical findings to the current literature on coalition formation and, in some instances, it questions some of the well-established principles of coalition theory. Municipal coalitions are quite similar to what coalition theorists refer to as "governmental coalitions." They are based on a "joint use of resources by some defined set of actors [players] to achieve a common goal," and involve a potential distribution of "payoffs," that is, primarily, "the distribution of public offices among the various governing parties."[4]

To paraphrase coalition theorists, I shall deal with a specific "coalition strategy" (the so-called strategy of left-wing unity) involving two major "actors" (French Socialist and Communist municipal elites). At the same time, I shall try to determine the preconditions for a successful coalition strategy: What norms and means of enforcement are required to implement the strategy at the grass roots? What is the extent to which deviations from the norms are tolerated? Are sanctions used or not? Does the nature of the PCF "party line" resemble that of the PS? If not,

---

Press, 1966), pp. 267-319 as well as J. Linz, "Ecological Analysis and Survey Research," in Mattei Dogan and Stein Rokkan (eds.), *Quantitative Ecological Analysis in the Social Sciences* (Cambridge, Mass.: M.I.T. Press, 1969), pp. 91-131. For a reassessment of the role and power of local elites, see S. Berger, P. Gourevitch, P. Higonnet, and K. Kaiser, "The Problem of Reform in France: The Political Ideas of Local Elites," *Political Science Quarterly* 84 (September 1969): 436-460.

[3] On the March 1971 municipal election, see the special issue of *Revue française de science politique* 22 (April 1974). See also J. Hayward and V. Wright's excellent article: "The 37,708 Microcosms of an Indivisible Republic, The French Local Elections of March 1971," *Parliamentary Affairs* 24 (Autumn 1971): 284-311.

[4] The quotes are taken from E. C. Browne and M. N. Franklin, "Aspects of Coalition Payoffs in European Parliamentary Democracies," *American Political Science Review* 67 (June 1973): 453-459. Their article includes an excellent critical survey of modern coalition theory.

are conflicts likely to occur? I shall then attempt to describe the preelectoral bargaining process per se: What is the "inducement strategy" of the two parties? Who is the "initiator" of left-wing bargaining? How do Communists and Socialists communicate? What kinds of concessions are usually made? How are "payoffs" distributed? Are payoffs limited to the allocation of municipal seats or do they also involve long-term policy promises?

To answer these questions, I shall rely primarily on a series of in-depth interviews of PS and PCF peripheral elites (mayors). The interviews were conducted during the years 1971-1972 in four French departments, Aisne and Somme in Picardy and Gard and Hérault in distant Languedoc.[5]

This chapter is divided into two parts: the first attempts a definition of the coalition strategy at the center and an assessment of the nature of the respective PS and PCF "party lines"; the second examines the "practice" of the strategy at the municipal level in light of contemporary coalition theory. By way of conclusion, I shall consider whether the strategy's very success does not in the long run pose a problem for the PCF—loss of identity.

I. Preconditions for Left-Wing Unity

1.1 The Strategy of Left-Wing Unity at the National Level

Although the French drive toward left-wing unity is probably as old as French socialism itself, it assumed new importance in the late 1960s and reached a climax in June 1972 with the adop-

[5] The present analysis is based on a total of 74 interviews. Fifty percent of the respondents are Communist party members and 50 percent are Socialist party members. The two samples are exclusively made up of *elected mayors*, with the exception of large cities (10,000 inhabitants and over) where nonelected *candidats-tête-de-liste* were also interviewed. Samples were structured according to the three following categories: 1. small and predominantly rural villages (less than 1,000 inhabitants, over 30 percent of the population active in agriculture); 2. small and medium industrial towns (less than 10,000 inhabitants); 3. large regional centers (over 10,000 inhabitants).

Since left-wing coalitions are more likely to be found in fairly large or large urban centers, it was decided to underrepresent the first stratum and to overrepresent the second and third strata. About half of the above-defined Communist population and one-third of the Socialist population were interviewed. If one only considers strata 2 and 3 the representativeness of the Communist sample goes up to over two-thirds and that of the Socialist sample to nearly half of the redefined populations. On the methodological advantage of interregional comparisons, see P. Grémion and J. P. Worms, *Les Institutions régionales et la société locale* (Paris: Copédith, 1968).

tion by the PCF and the PS of a Common Governmental Program. This decision crowned nearly ten years of Communist and Socialist efforts to bring about a real alternative to the Gaullist power monopoly. The profound bipolarization of the 1973 legislative elections has clearly revealed the importance and novelty of the current restructuring of the French Left.

Mutual and reciprocal acceptance of policy concessions is probably the major precondition for a successful coalition strategy. In the case of France, these policy concessions essentially corresponded to a minimization of the ideological distance[6] which has continuously separated French socialism from French Communism since 1920.[7] On the Communist side, two major theoretical breakthroughs are worth mentioning: acceptance of the notion of a "peaceful road to socialism" and of "party pluralism."[8] Quite obviously the PCF's ideological concessions were not made independently. They followed the guidelines of the international Communist movement as expressed by the Twentieth Congress of the Soviet Communist party (CPSU) or by the 1960 world Conference of (pro-Soviet) Communist parties.[9]

On the Socialist side, the major concession, also a theoretical breakthrough, was expressed in the political resolution adopted

[6] This expression is borrowed from A. de Swaan, "An Empirical Model of Coalition Formation as an N. Person Game of Policy Distance Minimization," in Sven Groennings, E. W. Kelley, M. Leiserson (eds.), The Study of Coalition Behavior (New York: Holt, Rinehart and Winston, 1970), pp. 426, 429.

[7] The classic sources for the origin of French communism are: Annie Kriegel, Aux Origines du communisme français, 1914-1920, 2 vols. (Paris, La Haye: Mouton, 1964); R. Wohl, French Communism in the Making, 1914-1924 (Stanford, Calif.: Stanford University Press, 1966) and B. Lazitch and M. Drachkovitch, Lenin and the Comintern (Stanford, Calif.: Stanford University Press, 1972). For an excellent and concise history of this period, see J.-P. Brunet, L'Enfance du parti communiste (Paris: Presses Universitaires de France, 1972).

[8] See Tiersky, Chapter 11 in this volume as well as Chapter 8, "Où mène l'unité de la théorie et de la pratique (1962-1972)?" in his Le Mouvement communiste en France 1920-1972 (Paris: Fayard, 1973), pp. 189-219. See also Annie Kriegel, "Les Communistes français et le pouvoir," in Michelle Perrot and Annie Kriegel, Le Socialisme français et le pouvoir (Paris: Études et Documentation Internationale, 1966): pp. 95-217. For an orthodox and outstanding treatment of the recent evolution, see M. Simon, "Réflexions sur le premier bilan des conversations P.C.F.-P.S.," Cahiers du communisme (February 1971), pp. 12-23.

[9] See, for example, Waldeck Rochet, "Rapport du Comité Central au XVIIIème Congrès," Cahiers du communisme (February-March 1967), p. 63 and "Manifeste de Champigny," ibid. (January 1969), p. 136.

at the second founding Congress of the new Socialist party (held in Issy-les-Moulineaux, July 1969) which stated that "left-wing unity constitutes the *normal axis* of Socialist strategy" and explicitly rejected any alliance with Center political parties.[10] These principles were reaffirmed even more vigorously at the Epinay Congress (June 1970) and in particular in the final motion of the Congress entitled "Plan d'Action Socialiste" which stated that "a Socialist action is a *class* action"; and excluded any "compromising agreement with a political force . . . either right-wing or Center-oriented . . . which would represent capitalism."[11]

A direct consequence of the new strategy was that the PCF has ceased to be a "captive party" or a party which had no alternative but to lose since there had been no place for Communists in "third-force" winning coalitions.[12] Thanks to the Common Governmental Program, French Communists could now pretend that, instead of being a mere *force d'appoint*, they had become equal partners with the Socialists. For the Socialists, on the contrary, the new strategy meant that they no longer constituted a "pivot party,"[13] a party that could shift from a left-wing to a right-wing coalition at any moment. The "binding" nature of the Common Governmental Program has transformed the PS from a pivot party into a stable party, a reliable partner for the Communists.

1.2 The PCF "Compulsory Line"

Like any law, a party strategy, however formal and/or compulsory, is meaningful only insofar as it can be implemented at the grass roots. This requires the establishment of certain norms (the belief that the strategy chosen at the center is right or good for the base), the application of sanctions against deviations from

---

[10] The entire text of the *résolution* can be found in C. Hurtig, *De la S.F.I.O. au nouveau Parti Socialiste* (Paris: A. Colin, 1970), pp. 85-86. On the new Socialist strategy and the founding of the PS, see J. Poperen, *Histoire de la gauche française* (Paris: Fayard, 1973) and D. Motchane and J.-P. Chevènement, *Clefs pour le socialisme* (Paris: Seghers, 1973).

[11] *Bulletin socialiste*, no. 92, September 8, 1970.

[12] The most recent (and unsuccessful) attempt of a grandiose third-force strategy was that of G. Defferre—"Monsieur X"—on the verge of the 1965 presidential elections.

[13] The concepts of "captive" and "pivot" parties are taken from Sven Groennings, "Notes Toward Theories of Coalition Behavior in Multiparty Systems: Formation and Maintenance," in Groennings et al., *Coalition Behavior*, p. 451.

the norms (ultimately, exclusion from the party), and the use of a specific pedagogy related to the transmission and justification of the "orders from above." The interrelation of norms, sanctions, and pedagogical explanations constitutes what is commonly described as a "party line."

It is in the nature of a Communist party to have a "compulsory line." This results from the acceptance of the Leninist principle of "democratic centralism." Once a line has been determined at the center (hopefully after consulting the base or eventually after a majority vote), it becomes the rule, and the only rule for all members of the party, whatever their previous beliefs. A direct consequence of democratic centralism is that deviant opinion groups are not tolerated or are tolerated for only a short time before the adoption of the line.

To what extent do Communist peripheral elites follow the norms of democratic centralism? A plausible hypothesis is that public officials, particularly mayors, are not very likely to be enthusiastic about a principle that is so foreign to the daily practice of municipal administration. But Table 1 contradicts this hypothesis. For all the respondents, but one, democratic centralism has a very positive connotation.

TABLE 1. ATTITUDES OF COMMUNIST MUNICIPAL ELITES TOWARD
DEMOCRATIC CENTRALISM

Question: "Comparing the principle of democratic centralism, as it functions in the PCF, with the Socialist acceptance of party *tendances*, what would you say about democratic centralism?"

Democratic Centralism Is:	Number of Responses[a] (N = 30)	Percentage (%)
A revolutionary tool	3	7.5
A means to efficacy	18	45
True democracy	12	30
Antidemocratic	1	2.5
No answer; irrelevant answers	6	15
Total	40[b]	100

[a] Only thirty respondents are considered here, since the question was not asked in my first eight interviews.

[b] Multiple answers permitted 40 responses.

310

The most widely held belief is that democratic centralism is a means to "efficacy." The mayor of a rural city of Hérault thus proudly observed in front of his Socialist "premier adjoint": "Democratic centralism avoids the disorder (*pagaille*) which has torn apart the PS . . . it brings efficacy."

Another Communist belief is that democratic centralism leads to "true" democracy, as opposed to the apparent democracy of a party which allows the open existence of rival *tendances*. As another mayor from Hérault remarked:

> The Socialists claim that a party *tendance* is an expression of freedom. We do have the same freedom in the PCF. In our cell meetings, differences of opinion are often expressed. But once the discussion is over, we've got to find an agreement.
>
> The law of democracy is that the minority accepts the decisions of the majority. . . .
>
> As long as you care about efficacy, then *tendances* cannot exist. Take the PS and look at their opposed factions: one wonders what the hell they are doing together!

One respondent went even further when he said:

> In our case, one has first to defend his own viewpoint, then to accept the majority line. This is in our statutes. . . . We always try to enforce a decision, once it's been made. We expect that all the militants will accept it. Consider, for instance, the Garaudy affair. He was a good personal friend of mine. . . . We talked about him in the local section. What I said is that errors are permissible. But once a line is determined by a majority, then one has to accept it. Garaudy did not respect the party discipline. He should have, even if he was right, even if history was on his side . . . which I doubt. If one does not respect the party line, a party can no longer exist.

The strongest belief in the efficacy of democratic centralism was expressed by three federal leaders who identified it with the very possibility of the revolution. As one of them put it:

> Our organization is a Leninist one. It is based on factory cells. The PCF is the party of the working class. Our role is to transform the world. For this, we have a very powerful tool which the other political parties do not have: democratic centralism.

DENIS LACORNE

1.3 The PS "Indicative Line"

The Socialist respondents interpreted democratic centralism and party *tendances* differently, identifying the former with totalitarianism and the latter with true democracy. Nothing could better illustrate the noncompulsory nature of the Socialist line than the following resolution adopted by the party at the Conseil National de Bondy in October 1970, shortly before the 1971 municipal elections:

> Whenever one considers forming a coalition, one should, in the choice of partners, avoid excluding individuals who have been opposed to us in the past on ideological grounds or for various historical reasons. There is no need for the party to cut itself off from democrats [meaning Centrists and members of Parti Radical] who have clearly and consistently opposed the present regime, even if their ideology differs from ours . . . inasmuch as they challenge some of the effects of capitalism and are willing to accept the municipal program of the party.[14]

This jesuitical resolution clearly indicates that, despite what had been decided four months earlier at the Epinay Congress, there is still considerable leeway in the practical application of the line at the grass-roots level. In other words, the PS line is an "indicative line": A Socialist ought to form a left-wing coalition but can also proceed otherwise, given particular local circumstances. Although the PS has officially ceased to be a pivot party, on a practical level it still functions as a pivot party, that is, it can still form left-wing and right-wing third-force alliances. In sum, despite the affirmations of the Epinay Congress and because of the affirmations of the Conseil National de Bondy, the PS was able to claim that it had adopted a new strategy while still embracing the philosophy of the defunct Section Française de l'Internationale Ouvrière (SFIO).[15]

[14] Quoted from P. Guidoni, *Histoire du Parti Socialiste* (Paris: Tema-Action, 1973), pp. 381-382. On the discussions that preceded the adoption of this resolution, see ibid., pp. 124-136. See also Hayward and Wright, "The 37,708 Microcosms."

[15] For instance, on the verge of the 1971 municipal elections, the Socialists were involved in the formation of third-force coalitions in 35 of 193 French larger municipalities (30,000 inhabitants and over). See G. Lavau et al., "Les Stratégies du PCF et de l'UDR dans les villes de plus de 30,000 habitants," *Revue française de science politique* 22 (April 1973): 285.

1.4 Communist and Socialist Attitudes toward Left-Wing Unity

Given the nature of the PCF "compulsory" party line and that of the PS "indicative" line, one might expect to find wide differences of opinion between Socialist and Communist respondents on the question of left-wing unity. (See Table 2.)

All the Communist municipal elites agreed on its merits, whether successful or not at the grass roots. All respondents but four perceived left-wing unity as a "fundamental" or "necessary" political strategy. Over 50 percent of them considered it "the only way" to bring about a "profound" political change.

TABLE 2. ATTITUDES OF COMMUNIST AND SOCIALIST MUNICIPAL ELITES
TOWARD LEFT-WING UNITY

Question: For you personally, what is the meaning of "left-wing unity"?		
	Municipal Elites	
	PCF	PS
Types of Answers	(%)	(%)
The only way to bring about a profound political change	51	08
A fundamental/necessary strategy	33	11
An abstract ideal	11	08°
A mere electoral strategy	—	22
An impossible/unrealistic political strategy	—	46
No answer	05	05
Total	100	100
(N = 74)	(N = 37)	(N = 37)

The rows "The only way to bring about a profound political change", "A fundamental/necessary strategy", "An abstract ideal", and "A mere electoral strategy" for the PS column are bracketed together with the value 49.

°Less than four respondents.

Representative Communist descriptions of left-wing unity were: "the only way to overthrow capitalism"; "the only solution to bring about socialism." Three respondents were particularly explicit. A mayor from an industrial suburb of Somme explained that:

> For us, Communists, given the present situation, we have always considered left-wing unity as the only way to obtain a majority in Parliament and to transform the capitalistic society. This is why we are willing to work with the Socialists, despite ideological differences.

313

The bipolarization of Socialist answers contrasts with the Communist consensus. It reflects the existence of a "compulsory line" on one hand and of an "indicative line" on the other.

The gap separating Communist elites from Socialist elites is no random phenomenon limited to one single political issue but a recurrent one which concerns political questions as divergent as the definition of Socialism, belief in the existence of Socialism in the USSR or Sweden, attitude toward the Common Market, attitude toward *gauchisme*, belief in the "irreversibility" of a left-wing government. On all these issues, as my interviews revealed, 80 percent or more of the Communists answered consistently as opposed to about 40 percent of the Socialists.[16]

There are some indications that the attitudes of Communist and Socialist municipal elites are influenced by members' class origins. Communists are more likely to belong to the working class or to have working-class origins than their Socialist counterparts. Almost two-thirds of my Communist respondents had a working-class background as opposed to less than 30 percent of the Socialists; the first job of a majority of the Communists, as opposed to that of about 10 percent of the Socialists was that of a manual worker; on the average, the Communists interviewed stopped attending school at the age of thirteen while the Socialists stopped at twenty. Such a difference in social background and educational experience gives an indication why Communists are less likely to be involved in the intellectual game of *tendances* and more likely to attach themselves to a simple and uniform party line than the Socialists, especially given the anti-intellectual traditions of the French working class (*ouvrierisme*). Democratic centralism reinforces this tendency.

The principle and functioning of democratic centralism prevent the formation of heterogeneous (if not contradictory) answers by Communists, particularly when the group considered has been marked by a strong working-class subculture. On the contrary, the existence of a flexible and ambiguous Socialist "indicative line" favors the expression of heterogeneous and contra-

---

[16] For a detailed study of Communist and Socialist stereotypes, see my article, "Analyse et 'reconstruction' de stéréotypes: communistes et socialistes face au 'socialisme soviétique,'" *Revue française de science politique* 23 (December 1973): 1171-1201. On the efforts that are being made within the PCF to increase its internal democracy and modify its stereotyped language, see Michel Simon, "Le Centralisme démocratique, pourquoi, comment?" *L'Humanité*, June 22, 1973, p. 8.

dictory answers. This is particularly true of a group which has been marked by a loose middle-class subculture and where access to higher education and individual success are stressed over class solidarity, thus favoring the development of rival *tendances* (officially called *courants de pensée*).[17]

1.5 Enforcing the Party Line

The enforcement of the PS "indicative line" does not require the application of sanctions or the use of detailed explanations to justify the line, since deviations from the norm (left-wing unity) are tolerated. But what about the implementation of the PCF "compulsory line"? A significant finding is the rarity of deviance from the line at the municipal level. In the four departments observed, only five cases of Communist "insubordination" were mentioned by my respondents. All of them concerned small villages and were based on personal rivalries. Only two cases of "insubordination" persisted after federal leaders intervened.[18]

How do intermediate party leaders transmit, explain, and justify compulsory decisions that are initiated in Paris? Instead of arguing that "working-class authoritarianism," "brainwashing" (through indoctrination), or an "anticlerical imitation of the Catholic mind" are at the source of Communists' disciplined acceptance of the "line," I will emphasize the less well-known PCF "explanatory pedagogy."[19] This is the procedure through which intermediate party leaders translate a national abstract decision

[17] There are about six *tendances* within the PS:
1. a right-wing opinion group which opposes/used to oppose the strategy of left-unity (Chandernagor and Defferre before 1973);
2. the former members of the Convention des Institutions Républicaines (CIR) which was headed by Mitterrand before its merger with the PS;
3. G. Mollet's Bataille Socialiste and its Office Universitaire de Recherches Socialistes (OURS);
4. the "Savary" group (Savary was the Socialist initiator of the new united left-wing strategy);
5. the left-wing Centre d'Etudes et d'Education Socialiste (CERES) headed by J.-P. Chevènement;
6. the left-wing Etudes, Recherches et Information Socialiste (ERIS) headed by J. Poperen.
The only structured *tendances* are the Bataille Socialiste which publishes *L'Ours*, the CERES which publishes *Frontière*, and the ERIS which publishes *ERIS*.

[18] In the first case, the Communists refused to support the Socialist incumbent mayor at the second ballot of the election; in the second case, they formed a coalition with "Radicaux" against a Socialist-led coalition.

[19] The use of this expression was suggested by Annie Kriegel.

into concrete action at the grass roots. Such a pedagogy requires leadership skills as well as deep knowledge of the behavior and expectations of the rank and file. To illustrate its functioning, I shall refer to several borderline cases in which Communist party members almost refused to carry out the party "line."

CASE 1: A RURAL MUNICIPALITY OF HÉRAULT

The incumbent mayor is a Socialist who defines himself as an *anti-stalinien farouche*. Despite repeated Communist propositions, he has always refused to sign an electoral alliance with the Communists. In 1971, on the verge of municipal elections, the leaders of the local Communist cell contemplate the forming of an "anti-Socialist" municipal list including "right-wing" personalities. Contacts are established between Communist party members and Union des Démocrates pour la République (UDR) sympathizers.

Procedure: A member of the PCF federal Secretariat comes to meet the deviant Communist party members. He explains the party line and gives them a "lesson." He indicates that they should vote in favor of the hated local Socialist notable if the right-wing municipal list prevents him from being reelected on the first ballot.

Solution: The local Communists accept the explanation, withdraw their initial proposals, and form a homogeneous Communist list. Three municipal lists are confronted: the Socialist list of the incumbent mayor, the PCF list, a "right-wing" list headed by a UDR sympathizer.

Conclusion: The incumbent mayor is not challenged by a "strong" opposing municipal list and he is reelected on the first ballot.

CASE 2: AN INDUSTRIAL CONSTITUENCY OF HÉRAULT

The first ballot of the 1962 legislative elections brings some unexpected results. The Communist candidate obtains more votes (about 3,000 more votes) than the Socialist candidate, a well-known national party leader and former Deputy (Jules Moch).

316

After a dramatic meeting of the PCF federal bureau, the Communists decide to withdraw their candidate in favor of the Socialist leader. The decision is risky, mostly because the Socialist candidate has become a symbol of anticommunism. For the average Communist, Jules Moch is the former Socialist Minister of Interior who brutally repressed the 1947 Confédération Générale du Travail (CGT) strikes. (A 1947 local Communist weekly described him as "an agent of American imperialism . . . whose hands are covered with workers' blood.")

The decision was perceived by Communist federal leaders as a "breakthrough" and "a way to demonstrate the feasibility of left-wing unity." As a federal leader put it:

> We had some tough problems with the comrades. A few of them destroyed their party cards on the spot! . . . Several wives refused to meet their husbands! . . . They thought we had betrayed the party! . . . When comrade (—) arrived in the city of (—) to bring the news, the guys shouted in reply: "Treason, treason." . . . They didn't stop shouting! Two hours later, two hours of explanation, they were all convinced! When I arrived myself, they all had understood.

Conclusion: Jules Moch, the "hated Socialist," was elected without any difficulty. Over 90 percent of the Communist electorate voted in his favor. A week of official explanations had been sufficient.

CASE 3: AN INDUSTRIAL CONSTITUENCY OF AISNE

This case is almost identical to the previous one: the Communists have decided to withdraw their "best placed" candidate (at the 1967 legislative elections) in favor of the Socialist candidate. The latter is also a well-known anti-Communist. The climate is the same: the Communist "comrades" are reluctant to play the united-left game, explanations are necessary. As the involved PCF candidate explained:

> The decision was not an easy one. At the first ballot of the election, I had obtained 1,500 more votes than the Socialist candidate. However, I withdrew in his favor. [*How was it decided?*] Section delegates, from the three sections of the

317

constituency met. . . . The discussions were long. . . . They lasted for three full days. There were many problems. . . . About one-half of the party members were in favor of my withdrawal. The other half were against it. The argument of the latter was that it was useless to have one more left-wing deputy at the National Assembly since there was already a UDR majority. The PCF federation could not make a decision because the sections had not yet reached an agreement. The federation, as you might know, never decides before the sections. Finally, a slight majority was obtained in favor of the withdrawal of my candidacy (by a two-vote margin). . . . And it's only then that the federation officially announced my withdrawal.

Another version of the same events was provided by a top federal leader of the PCF federation of Aisne:

Well, in our case, we have democratic centralism. Decisions made in a party Congress must be accepted by the rank and file. This means that we have to give many explanations. For instance, with this 1967 withdrawal, we had a lot to explain. We organized a general meeting which was attended by all the party members. . . . We had to say why the withdrawal of our candidate was good for the working class. . . . We obtained a very narrow margin in favor of our thesis. After the vote, three members decided to resign from the party! The only three resignations of my whole career! Fortunately, two of them came back to the party afterwards!

Conclusion: The Socialist candidate was elected, thanks to Communist support.

What is interesting about these borderline cases is the fact that, in a crisis situation, Communist leaders insist on explaining rather than forcing a decision on the rank and file. Difficult discussions are never avoided. Federal leaders, as the three cases revealed, primarily behave as political persuaders. Their main objective is to convince the rank and file of the rightness of the party line, whatever difficulties they may encounter and however much time it may take.

My interviews confirm the fact that the threat of exclusion from the party is rarely employed by federal leaders. I was thus unable to observe any recent case of exclusion of a Communist mayor, when in contrast such cases were fairly frequent among Socialists. They usually were Socialist *têtes de liste* who had formed a municipal list with UDR party members, or organized an anti-Communist (or anti-left-wing unity) faction within a major urban PS section. (This was the case, for instance, in the cities of Amiens and Nîmes.)

On the whole, as far as left-wing unity is concerned, the Communist "explanatory pedagogy" appears to be successful, and this is probably to the credit of PCF intermediate party leaders (federal and section leaders). The word "pedagogy" is justified by the fact that the use of "official party explanations" is not a rare phenomenon limited to a specific party decision but a constant one which concerns all the aspects of the party strategy, as my interviews revealed. Most of my respondents strongly insisted on the idea that they either gave or received "explanations" and stressed the virtues of such a pedagogy.

There are, however, cases in which the "explanatory pedagogy" seems excessive and can even paralyze the very action of the party. Commenting on the PCF disapproval of the USSR occupation of Czechoslovakia, a federal leader from Somme observed: "Many old party members were opposed to the party decision. It took us nearly two months of explanations. During two full months, we didn't stop explaining. We were doing nothing but explaining. That was a tough period of explanations within the party. For two months the action of the party was paralyzed."

But, if giving explanations is not always an easy job, nothing is worse than not receiving the party explanations in time. Describing his shock at reading the first French translation of the USSR Twentieth Party Congress, an urban mayor from Hérault said:

> The Twentieth Congress was a terrible thing for us. That was an incredible shock. The catastrophe was that the first translation of the Khrushchev report had been published in *Le Monde*, not by us! We had no explanations! . . . Finally we were forced to admit the accuracy of *Le Monde's* translation, though no one had told us in advance! . . . I still remember the day when I was putting up posters which said: "Stalin is right!" . . . This Congress was a shock.

On the whole, with the exception of a few crisis situations where the information from the top is either scarce or contradictory, the PCF "compulsory line" seems to be enforced without any major difficulties. Democratic centralism does not appear to be the ruthless organizational tool with which it has often been identified. It is a rather flexible instrument, particularly once it has been put in the hands of dedicated and highly skilled inter- mediate party leaders. What counts is the explanation, that is, a pedagogy that translates the official discourse of top party lead- ers into comprehensible and justifiable language for the base. This means that a "compulsory line" is subject to a variety of in- terpretations, but to a far lesser extent than an "indicative" party line.

Implementation of a strategy of left-wing unity requires a series of preconditions:

1. a minimization of the ideological distance that has tradi- tionally separated French communism from French socialism;

2. the adoption of a "line" at the center;

3. a positive attitude toward the norms set by the center (a belief in the rightness of the strategy);

4. the adoption of measures that permit the enforcement of the strategy at the grass roots.

From the foregoing, one can logically deduce that

1. the existence of a PCF "compulsory line" greatly favors the formation of united left-wing coalitions;

2. the existence of a PS "indicative line" neither favors nor prevents the formation of left-wing coalitions;

3. sharp conflicts are likely to occur within the PS (opposing *pro* and *anti-unitaires*) and outside it (opposing Socialists to Communists).

One example will illustrate this last point. The setting is an in- dustrial city of Languedoc. The conflict opposes the Socialist mayoral candidate (a businessman and the incumbent mayor) to a Communist mayoral candidate (a trade-union leader and the head of the local Communist section). Both actors were inter- viewed in-depth. When asked whether he supported the strategy of left-wing unity, the Socialist declared himself as "very favor- able to the new strategy" but quickly added that such a strategy was not feasible in this particular city. To justify this paradox, he invoked the fact that he was "linked to the past," that he had to

320

maintain "old friends" among the incumbent municipal councilors (including several right-wingers), and that he had to preserve the traditional support of a Center-Left electorate.

His Communist counterpart gave the following description of
the negotiations that he had himself initiated:

> We had three meetings with the Socialists. . . . At the second
> meeting, we made concrete proposals, we told them: although
> we get more votes at legislative elections than you do, we'll
> leave you a majority of seats in the Municipal Council.
> We just want the positions of first and second deputy-mayor
> ("*adjoints*"). At the third meeting, they said: "No, you're ask-
> ing too much (*vous êtes trop gourmands*)." We said: "O.K., it
> doesn't matter, we'll take the positions of first and third
> deputy-mayor." Finally, they refused. They justified their deci-
> sion by claiming that "we have a special Center-oriented elec-
> torate. We have to preserve it. We cannot accept your pro-
> posals." And we learned that while they were negotiating with
> us, they were also bargaining with right-wing and Center-ori-
> ented personalities! Consequently, we formed a separate list.

This shows the pragmatic orientation of Communist decision-
makers, as well as their willingness to make concessions in order
to prevent the occurrence of third-force lists. It also shows that
Socialist decison-makers—if they assume the role of a "pivot"
party—can be involved in parallel bargaining processes, as contrasted with the Communists who have no alternative other than
to negotiate with the Socialists.

Interestingly enough, all the third-force type of municipal
alliances which I was able to observe were repetitions of old winning alliances, all established before the 1965 municipal elections.
In 1965, and even more in 1971, a "new" third-force tactic was
not likely to be successful, particularly not in a large city, because its acceptance almost always implied the disruption of the
local Socialist section and favored the establishment of rival socialist factions which would split the Socialist electorate.

In conclusion, it appears that, on the verge of the 1971 municipal elections, the Socialists did not really play the game of left-
wing unity consistently. The ambiguity of their game is reflected
in the contradictory resolutions of the Epinay Congress and the
Conseil National de Bondy. A possible explanation for this inter-

321

nal contradiction is that the new PS was not yet a well-established party and was still trying to win the support of the old SFIO *notables*.

Today one might argue that the PS line has finally become a compulsory one, particularly if one considers the large number of exclusions or resignations from the party (all of them advocates of a third-force strategy)[20] and the small number of third-force coalitions that were formed on the verge of the second ballot of the 1973 legislative elections. It remains to be seen whether this development of a compulsory line similar to that of the Communists will stand the test of the next municipal elections.

II. THE "PRACTICE" OF LEFT-WING UNITY AT THE MUNICIPAL LEVEL

By contrasting the Communist party line to the Socialist party line, I have been dealing with the most obvious difficulties that confront both partners in implementing a supposedly unified strategy of left-wing unity. The empirical data that have been used so far concern only attitudes toward left-wing unity and examples of unsuccessful left-wing coalitions.

In the present section PS and PCF coalition behavior will be examined in greater depth with a particular emphasis on the different steps that lead to the formation of a PS-PCF coalition. This involves the following questions: Who induces a bargaining process? What payoffs are sought by the respective actors? What kinds of concessions are made? Are there marked differences between PS and PCF bargaining styles? On the whole, to what extent does the PS approach to coalition-making differ from the PCF approach? The question of authority—who decides?—must be considered too. This necessitates an understanding of the degree of autonomy of the local actors and a careful analysis of the relationship between PS/PCF public officials and local or regional PS/PCF party functionaries.

2.1 The Inducement Strategy

Who makes the first step? Who is the initiator of a coalition strategy? As my interviews revealed, the initiative almost always comes from the Communists. This is owing to the fact that, in

[20] For instance the Socialist mayor of the industrial city of Villers-Cotterêts (Aisne) and the influential mayor of Abbeville (Somme) resigned on the verge of the 1973 legislative elections.

1971, the PCF was still a potential "captive party" and the PS a potential "pivot party." As explained by Sven Groennings, "A pivot party which [has] coalition options usually will not develop an inducement strategy or take the role of proposal initiator because it will contain factions advocating each of the options; therefore it will await offers." On the other hand, Groennings continues:

> A captive party which . . . can be excluded from the coalition, but which can be counted upon to support the coalition because it has no feasible alternatives, presumably will have an inducement strategy. This is an accommodative strategy characterized by its two components: a public relations effort combined with the role of initiator. . . . The purpose of the inducement strategy is to make it seem unreasonable and unjust to exclude the party from the coalition.[21]

The latter description applies well to the PCF. In most cases, Communists performed the role of proposal initiator, as early as four or five months before the elections. Whenever the Socialists were slow to answer, they publicized their proposals, stressing the importance and feasibility of left-wing coalitions and forcing their potential allies to take sides.

The major characteristic of a Socialist-Communist negotiation is its impersonal nature. The first contact is usually established through an "official letter" which suggests the opening of interparty talks, as well as a possible meeting place. If the answer is positive, the two partners meet one, two, three times—until an agreement is reached. The talks usually take place a week before the elections or between the two ballots of a municipal election. In some cases—especially when large cities are involved—they start as early as five months before the elections. Discussions are always conducted by party delegations, a fact which stresses the official nature of the debate. To avoid any favoritism, the meetings are held at the PCF local headquarters one time, at the PS headquarters the next time, or at the headquarters of a third party (either Parti Socialiste Unifié or Parti Radical). But the PCF always approaches its working-class "brother," the PS, first.[22]

---

[21] "Notes Toward Theories," in Groennings et al., *Coalition Behavior*, p. 451.

[22] In interparty meetings Communists and Socialists use the *tu* of comradeship. On the contrary, when they address themselves to members of the

For the 1971 municipal elections, the party "line" was left-wing unity at any cost. For this purpose all PCF sections and cells started (or tried to start) negotiations with the corresponding local PS organization. All my Communist respondents had therefore been involved in such negotiations. If there was no Socialist organization at the local level, then negotiations were made with *Radicaux*, PSU members, or left-wing personalities, often described as *républicains sincères, vrais démocrates* or *catholiques de gauche.* Such ideological flexibility shows that French Communists do not impose strict limits on coalition formation. Almost any actor, if he is not an anti-Communist or a Gaullist, can enter a Communist-led coalition. In organizational terms, the Communist decisional environment would be defined as "elastic." This elasticity explains why Communist party members had no problem in forming "united left-wing municipal lists," even when there were no potential Socialist partners.[23] It enables them to adapt to any local circumstances, despite the apparent uniformity of the label, *Liste d'union de la gauche.* It also enables them to cope with an apparently rigid line without too much difficulty.

But the Communists' acceptance of *vrais démocrates* and other nonparty personalities has limits. The coalition environment is elastic inasmuch as it is designed to balance a Communist majority. If Communists are to be in the minority in a coalition, they will accept subordination only to an actual Socialist majority or at least (in small cities) to well-known *personnalités de gauche,* either Socialist or Communist sympathizers.

For the Socialists, since the line is not "unity at any cost," almost any kind of coalition is permissible, with the exception of alliances with the Gaullists. Thus, nearly one-half of the Socialist mayors whom I interviewed had opted for a third-force strategy. This strategy, however, was more likely to occur in small and medium towns than in "large" regional centers. This was particularly the case in Picardy where new *pro-unitaires* federal leaders directly intervened to prevent the formation of third-force coalitions.[24] In Somme and Aisne, preliminary federal agreements

---

Radical party, they use the formal *vous* (according to a PCF federal leader in Languedoc).

[23] For an outstanding treatment of the concept of "environmental elasticity," see Robert Pagès, "L'Élasticité d'une organisation en crise de direction," *Sociologie du travail* 7 (October-December 1965): 364-382.

[24] The regional centers are Amiens (Somme); Laon, Chateau-Thierry, Hirson (Aisne). In Somme, the exception was Abbeville controlled by the "right-wing" Socialist Max Lejeune.

were signed by the respective PS and PCF secretariats. These agreements were somewhat similar in form, and provided for the establishment of united left-wing electoral lists in all the "large" urban centers, before the first ballot of the 1971 municipal elections. In Languedoc no general agreement was signed between the two partners. In both cases, the Socialist federal secretaries refused to consider the possibility of such interparty agreement.[25] But, under the initiatives of local PS and PCF section leaders, Communist-Socialist agreements were signed in five of the six "large" cities of Gard and Hérault.[26] In smaller towns and villages, over half the Socialist mayors refused to negotiate with the Communists.

Whenever this happened, Communist section leaders tried nonetheless to form "united lists" with other left-wing sympathizers. The answer of a Communist mayor from Somme gives a good illustration of this type of bargaining process:

First, the various cells of the city met. We discussed the possibility of left-wing unity. A few sectarian Communists expressed their reluctance about municipal left-wing unity. But there was a clear majority in favor of left-wing unity. Then we discussed potential candidates and themes of the electoral campaign. Finally, there was a discussion within the section with cell delegates and section leaders. At this stage, the Communist candidates were definitively chosen. . . . Then, we tried to get in touch with non-Communist personalities. We organized mixed meetings with section members and nonparty potential candidates. . . . Having selected them, we collaborated on writing campaign literature. Afterwards, we had a meeting restricted to section leaders and municipal candidates. I read them the draft of the municipal program. After a discussion and a few changes, the program was definitively accepted. Finally, we organized a public meeting, in order to present our candidates and program.

[25] It should be noted that the PS secretaries of Somme and Aisne took over their federations at the time of the creation of the PS and replaced somewhat brusquely the SFIO "Old Guard." (They are both strong advocates of the new strategy.) In Hérault and Gard, the "Old Guard" remained in power despite the repeated assaults of younger Socialists (both federal secretaries are strong anti-Communists).

[26] Montpellier, Sète, Bédarieux (Hérault); Nîmes, Alès (Gard). The major exception was Béziers where a third-force coalition was reestablished under the leadership of a Radical Deputy Mayor, Pierre Brousse.

The fact that Socialists are more likely to form coalitions with Communists in "large" cities than in small ones is probably owing to the different strategic importance attributed to each type of city. The control of a small town has very little or no importance for a party federation. On the contrary, to control a large city means a great deal not only in short-term rewards (municipal jobs, etc.) but also in long-term expectations. To win a municipal election often means to win a legislative election thereafter.[27]

United left-wing bargaining is not always easy. In the above example (a Communist stronghold), the idea of a municipal Communist majority was accepted without any discussion by the non-Communist partners. In most cases, however, the crucial part of the discussion concerns the distribution of municipal seats: Which partner will get the mayoral/*tête de liste* position? How many seats for each party involved? The whole bargain is based on power relationships. The main problem is the definition of clear "units of reference." For instance, let us assume that Communists had obtained 20 percent more votes than Socialists in the previous legislative elections. Given this "objective" criterion, they will logically demand a majority of the municipal seats, including the post of mayor. Difficulties arise when the unit of reference is a doubtful one, either because the left-wing partners obtained a similar number of votes at the previous elections, or because the past results were inconsistent. (For example, in one election, partner A gained more votes than partner B; in another election, B obtained more than A.)

This is complicated by the fact that the party loyalty of the PCF electorate is usually much greater than that of the PS electorate.[28] Under such circumstances, discussions are likely to be tough, each participant claiming his right to a majority. Solutions are diverse. In Aisne, for example, several left-wing municipal lists were made up of an equal number of Communists, Socialists, and "left-wing democrats." The *tête de liste* was the best-known left-wing personality, regardless of his party affiliation. In Gard, in one of the major cities of the department, the choice was made in favor of a Communist mayor. But in order to calm the Social-

---

[27] Eight of my respondents were thus reelected (in three cases) or elected (in five cases) in the 1973 legislative elections, among them, the mayors of two large cities of Gard (Alès and Nîmes), one large city of Hérault (Sète), and a large city of Somme (Amiens)—large meaning 10,000 inhabitants and over.

[28] See, for instance, T. Greene, "The Electorate of Nonruling Communist Parties," *Studies in Comparative Communism* 4 (July-October 1971): 76-78.

ists' anxiety (they used to control the municipality), it was decided that the Communists would not have the majority of municipal seats, which was a way of introducing a potential veto right for the Socialists.

2.2 Give-and-Take Bargaining

Municipal elections cannot be considered in isolation from cantonal and/or legislative elections, particularly when the municipality is a sizable one. A present bargain often anticipates a future bargain. Give-and-take bargaining is either past-oriented ("Since I gave you X, without any return, you'll give me Y") or future-oriented ("I give you X, and I hope that, in return, you'll give me Y"). The major characteristic is the risk involved in such bargaining. The outcome is never certain. Comparable examples of these long-term bargains can be observed in two of my four departments: Hérault and Aisne. They had the form of "I give you constituency X, but in return, you will give me city Y." The respective constituencies and cities involved were those of Sète (Hérault) and Hirson (Aisne). In both cases, the initial bargaining took place between the two ballots of the legislative elections (1962 in the case of Sète, 1967 in the case of Hirson). In both cases, the Communists withdrew their candidates in favor of the Socialist partners, though the former had gained more votes than the latter at the first ballot of these elections. In both cases the Socialist candidates were elected thanks to Communist support. At the following municipal elections (1965 for Sète, 1971 for Hirson) the Communists obtained their expected compensations: the position of *tête de liste* on the left-wing municipal lists of Sète and Hirson and the certainty of winning the municipal elections thanks to Socialist support. Needless to say, such bargains were not easily carried out and strong "resistance" was expressed by local party members and leaders.

Since the municipal bargaining process is a two-step process, it follows that (as shown by Bonnet and Schemeil in their study of large French municipalities and confirmed in this chapter) Riker's "minimum-size principle" does not apply to the formation of left-wing municipal coalitions:[29] they are almost always "larger

[29] Gilbert Bonnet and Yves Schemeil, "La Théorie des coalitions selon William Riker: Essai d'application aux élections municipales françaises de 1965 et 1971," *Revue française de science politique* 22 (April 1972): 269-274.

On the theory of coalition formation, see, among others, William Riker, *The Theory of Political Coalitions* (New Haven: Yale University Press,

than necessary to win," even in the oldest and safest Communist strongholds.[30] What is apparently a free gift to non-Communist allies actually constitutes a party resource, a bargaining capital that will be used at future cantonal, senatorial, or legislative elections.[31] For Communists, it does not even matter whether the excessively large coalition will constitute a bargaining capital or not, for it will serve a clear ideological function: to show the openness of French Communists and to reaffirm their (new) attachment to the principle of party pluralism. Finally, it should be noted that the most elaborate interparty agreements include the signing of a long-term (six-year) "contract" which details the respective responsibilities of Communist and Socialist (or non-Communist) municipal councilors with great precision, indicates the major projects to be carried out, and often prohibits the holding of "political discussions" during municipal meetings. Such long-term, constraining municipal contracts were signed in almost all the "large" cities which I was able to study.[32]

Such formality points out the novelty of PS-PCF coalitions and the caution of respective decision-makers. It also indicates a certain lack of trust between the two partners-to-be. The old feud between Socialists and Communists is far from dead. Particularly significant is the strength of Socialist anticommunism. For most Socialists interviewed, including leaders of PS-PCF coalitions, the PCF has remained a tool in the hands of a foreign country, an insincere, power-hungry partner, and an undemocratic party. A few examples illustrate these interrelated themes.

—Arguing that the PCF is completely subjugated to Moscow's *bon plaisir*, the mayor of a large working-class suburb (Aisne) said: "French Communists receive orders from Moscow. . . . The

1962), Theodore Caplow, "A Theory of Coalition in the Triad," *American Sociological Review* 21 (August 1956): 489-493, Theodore Caplow, *Two Against One, Coalitions in Triads* (Englewood Cliffs, N.J.: Prentice Hall, 1968), and William Gamson, "A Theory of Coalition Formation," *American Sociological Review* 26 (June 1961): 373-382.

For a good survey of the literature, see Jerome Chertkoff, "Sociopsychological Theories and Research on Coalition Formation," in Groennings et al., *Coalition Behavior*, pp. 297-322.

[30] See Lavau et al., "Les Stratégies du PCF," p. 284. P. Lange observes the same phenomenon in Italy in Chapter 7 in this volume.

[31] The reverse is also possible: a legislative coalition might be made in view of a forthcoming municipal election.

[32] The cities are Montpellier, Sète (Hérault); Alès, Nîmes (Gard); Hirson (Aisne); Amiens (Somme).

PCF is an Eastern party. . . . To me, Communists are not Frenchmen."

—The mayor of another large city in Aisne said, in a similar vein. "The PCF is above all the Soviet Union."[33]

—Commenting on the undemocratic nature of the PCF, a mayor from Gard indicated that the PCF resembled a military organization where "orders come from above."

—One mayor from Hérault thought that in the PCF "party members are nothing but numbers."

Convinced of the "foreign nature" of the PCF, the most anti-Communist Socialist respondents logically concluded that the strategy of left-wing unity was not feasible at the national level. According to them, if a PS-PCF coalition ever won the majority of the votes, it would be the end of the PS on one hand, of French democracy on the other.

—One respondent (Gard) thought that under such circumstances the PCF would "eat the Socialists."

—Another said: "If they [the Communists] ever came to power, they would not hesitate to establish an Eastern dictatorship against the will of the majority of the French population." (Hérault)

—One mayor from Somme developed the same idea in a shorter fashion: "The PCF. . . . It's Prague. Got it?" (Somme)

—As a respondent from the same "département" argued: "Left-wing unity will only be possible the day the PCF becomes purely French." (Somme)

Clearly such pervasive attitudes fully justify the caution of PS and PCF decision-makers as well as the establishment of formal interparty "contracts."

To sum up, the dominant trait of left-wing bargaining is the *pragmatism* expressed by the various participants, including the Communists. Though starting positions are often rigid, a compromise is usually found after two or three interparty meetings. On the Communist side, the compromise often consists of forming electoral alliances which include the so-called *républicains sincères* or *vrais démocrates*, despite the constant reaffirmation of the impossibility of any form of class collaboration. Nearly all the

[33] Seventy-seven percent of the Socialists interviewed *spontaneously* identified the PCF with "Moscow"; see my "Analyse et 'reconstruction' de stéréotypes."

united left-wing municipalities of my sample included a sub-group of *républicains sincères*.[34] In one case, the Communist compromise went to the point of accepting the loss of a municipal majority, in order to please the Socialists' demand for equality.[35] However, this pragmatism does not exclude a certain degree of formalism aimed at calming down persistent Socialist fears of Communism (a fear of being "eaten up," as several Socialists put it).

2.3 Who decides? The Communist "Collective" Approach vs. the Socialist "Individual" Approach

Who decides? Who determines the possibility of forming a left-wing coalition? Who determines the distribution of munici-pal seats? Who selects the candidates?

One might assume that the dominant actor in the decision-making process is the potential mayor (the *candidat-tête-de-liste*) or the incumbent mayor. This is certainly true in the case of a Socialist *tête de liste*: all my Socialist respondents admitted that they had performed a decisive role in negotiating or refusing to negotiate with their Communist counterpart. On the Communist side, on the contrary, the initiator of left-wing bargaining is al-most never a single individual but the executive committee of the local section or the *bureau de cellule*, in the case of a small mu-nicipality. The opposition between the Socialist individual ap-proach and the Communist collective approach to coalition for-mation reflects a crucial difference in party organization. In the case of the Communists, there is a strict differentiation of func-tions between elected public officials and party officials,[36] the former being almost always subordinate to the latter. As Jacques Duclos put it, "Elected Communist Party members should never forget that they have been elected *thanks to the Party* and thanks to the electorate's confidence in the policy of the party."[37]

[34] Interestingly enough, none of the Communist Municipal Councils ob-served were comprised of 100 percent Communist party members.

[35] This was the case of Nîmes in 1971. For more detail on the city of Nîmes, see J. Milch, Chapter 9 in this volume.

[36] S. Tarrow observes that there are greater differentiations of functions and career specializations in the PCF than in the PCI; see his Chapter 4 in this volume.

[37] J. Duclos, "Les Municipalités au service des masses laborieuses," in *Cahiers du communisme* (September 1965), pp. 91-99.

330

For the Socialists, there is not such differentiation of functions, but rather a fusion of functions (*cumul de fonctions*): about 80 percent of my Socialist respondents were self-recruited mayors/ *têtes de liste* and, at the same time, top leaders of their local party organization (usually section secretary or de facto secretary). In contrast, none of the Communists interviewed shared both types of responsibility.[38] A major effect of the Socialist fusion of functions is that personality factors are likely to be predominant, if not overwhelming, in all municipal bargaining. The fact that the control exerted by the local Socialist section is either nonexistent or purely formal explains why the outcome of a Socialist-Communist negotiation often depends on the goodwill of a single individual: the local self-recruited Socialist "notable." (An exception should be made for big cities, however.)

Duclos's statement, above, appears to be taken seriously. All my Communist respondents acknowledge that they are directed by their party and beholden to it. When asked, "Why did you decide to become a mayor?" nearly 100 percent of them answered that they had been chosen by the party, independent of their own will. For instance, the mayor of a small industrial city of Aisne said: "Well, I did not choose. When the previous mayor died in 1964— I was then the deputy-mayor—the party told me to succeed him." Another mayor from the same department observed:

> I didn't want to become a mayor. I was considered as a candidate by my political organization . . . perhaps because I was competent? I didn't choose.

One mayor from Hérault argued:

> Well, I was chosen by the party. . . . [Why?]—I don't know! Perhaps, because I had more free time than the others?

Another mayor from Hérault was much more explicit when he said,

> In the PCF, when you tell a comrade: "You will be a candidate for the party," his first answer is "NO," when in other parties such as the Socialist party, militants fight each other to be

[38] There are, of course, exceptions. One of my respondents combined the functions of deputy and mayor with that of member of the PCF Central Committee. In his case the control exerted by the local section over him is likely to be purely formal.

nominated as candidates. We do not fight for an electoral position, except a few old comrades. We are, above all, party militants. We've got to do our party work, even if we'd rather go
fishing! Sometimes it's hard to be a party candidate. . . . We
don't get any personal profit out of it! . . . It might even bring
you some problems with your own family! In any case, candidate or not, the party never leaves you without something to
do . . . or we wouldn't be party militants!

As a figurehead appointed by his party, the Communist mayor
performs only a marginal role in matters of party strategy, including municipal bargaining. The influential mayor of a large
city of Languedoc even confided that he could not describe the
Socialist-Communist talks which preceded his election, because
he had not taken part in them. This situation, however, is exceptional. Most Communist mayors are aware of pre-electoral negotiations; most of them are direct participants. But the important
point is that the negotiations are always *collective*. When a left-
wing municipal government is to be formed, the party as a whole
is engaged in the pre-electoral bargaining. To prevent any deviance from the party line, the negotiations are always conducted
by a group of "section delegates," who regularly inform the federal leaders of the progress of the local discussions. Furthermore,
whenever a "large" municipality is involved, federal leaders always directly intervene either to push the negotiations, to check
the names of the candidates, or to control the mutual concessions.
Despite this, the role of federal party leaders should not be exaggerated. The real decision-maker is the local party section and
in particular the section secretary.

2.4 Relationships between Mayor and Section

The control of the Communist section over the Communist or
Communist-led municipality is a constant one. It does not stop
with the outcome of the municipal elections but lasts as long as
the administration. The mayor-section relationships are crucial
and often ambiguous. The dominant idea is that the mayor
should always respond to the party and always relate his municipal decisions to the global policy of the party. As A. Marty has
written, "The elected party member who cuts himself off from
the party is bound to become impotent and to become a failure.

He is lost in technical matters; he forgets the 'perspective.' This fundamental failure leads him to complete municipal cretinism."[39]

The mayor-section relationships are not standardized. They vary in intensity and frequency from region to region and city to city. In a small Communist municipality, direct pressure of the cell secretary or *bureau de cellule* on the mayor is very unlikely —mostly because his power as well as the number of policy alternatives open to him are limited, and also because such a mayor is often the only (or the most) competent local Communist party member.

In a fairly large (over 5,000 inhabitants) or large (over 10,000 inhabitants) municipality, the pressure of the local section is more likely to be felt. In such communities, the mayor—like his non-Communist colleagues—is an influential and powerful individual. Policy alternatives are numerous; contracts with local industrialists involve considerable amounts of money; future elections are prepared on a day-to-day basis. In other words, the policy of the party is at stake. In such a context, the fundamental objective of the local PCF section is to prevent the formation of an independent "municipal fief" and to check the conformity of the municipal decisions with the national party line. For this purpose joint Municipal Council-party section meetings are held on a regular basis. In some cases, these meetings are frequent and formal.

Comparing a neighboring Socialist municipality with his Communist left-wing municipality, the mayor of a large industrial city of Aisne proudly said: "Take the Socialists: their party section is made up only of Socialist municipal councilors. Now, take our case. We are much more numerous. Consequently, we have to give an account of our day-to-day administration to the members of the section. Every Monday, we meet the members of the section and give a report. If the comrades do not approve of our administration, they can replace us! No doubt about that."

This type of formal relationship seems rare, however. In most cases, the control of the section over the elected party members is informal and infrequent. It consists either of a face-to-face re-

[39] A. Marty, "Les Élus municipaux communistes dans la bataille pour le pain, la démocratie et l'indépendance nationale," *Cahiers du communisme* (December 1949), p. 126.

lationship between the mayor and the section secretary, or of reciprocal telephone calls each time there is an important municipal problem or vote. As a mayor of Hérault said:

> Well, obviously one has to give an account to the party. For instance, one might want to discuss the municipal budget with the executive committee of the party section. When there is a problem of unemployment, we obviously discuss it with the leaders of the section. But there are two major risks with which a Communist mayor is confronted: the worst thing for a Communist who holds an elective office is to limit himself to his elective functions. We mayors remain, above all, party militants. The second danger for a Communist mayor is that the executive committee of the section run the municipality. This too should be avoided.

The latter danger is not always avoided and the mayor-section relationship can be a tense one. In one case, a Communist mayor accused his local party boss of making an administrative decision that normally should have been made by the mayor. As he put it to his party boss:

> After all who is the mayor? . . . It's me. . . . You've got to tell the comrades that they've chosen someone to be a mayor and I happened to be chosen! . . . Therefore I should properly be informed of what's going on here. . . . You know well enough that whatever the comrades ask me to do, I'll do it.

Despite such critical comments, the same respondent remarked later on in the interview: "The head of the party, here, is the executive committee of the section. It determines the general orientation of the municipality. Once the line is adopted by the section, it becomes the rule for all of us, municipal councilors included." He was thus living an extraordinary contradiction—a contradiction between the practice of democratic centralism and its theory.

For the Socialists, the relationship between the mayor and his party section is not likely to be tense since—in most cases—the section is, for most practical purposes, the municipal council and the section leader, the mayor. There are exceptions, however, particularly in large cities where a section is often made up of a sizable number of party members. In such context, the Socialist dominant notable (the mayor) is not able to reward *all* his followers with municipal jobs or municipal seats, and a differentiation of functions is likely to exist between party officials and public officials. Furthermore, unless he is an exceptional charismatic leader, the dominant notable will not be able to impose one of his friends at the head of the local section and to become a so-called *secrétaire par personne interposée*. Frictions between mayor and section leaders are therefore likely to occur, particularly when the "Socialist" administration of the commune is judged too apolitical by more politically-minded section leaders.

This is even more true when Socialists are in the minority of a Communist-led large municipality. In such a situation, it is inevitable that the Communists will take most of the credit for successful public achievements. Socialist section leaders will therefore try to accentuate the "Socialist side" of the coalition and put pressure on "soft" elected Socialist notables. To take only two examples: in the cities of Sète (Hérault) and Amiens (Somme), both governed by Communist-led coalitions, frictions have developed between Socialist municipal councilors and the local section (in the case of Sète) or the federal leadership (in the case of Amiens). In both cases, political cadres have criticized the actions of elected officials and accused them of being too inefficient and docile. One informant thought that "by supporting and voting for all the Communist proposals, our elected party members have become yes-men (*bénis-oui-oui*). They ruin the image of the Socialist Party."

Such frictions are difficult to suppress. In the long run they might lead to a rupture of the PS-PCF coalition, or a split within the Socialist section. In Sète, a unique solution was found: after six years of tension between PS section leaders and municipal councilors, it was decided that the young and aggressive section secretary would become a member of the Municipal Council in order to reinforce political control over Socialist public officials and to stress the distinctive character of the Socialist participation in the PS-PCF coalition by emphasizing Socialist initiatives. This solution, adopted on the verge of 1971 municipal elections has restored, so it seems, the image of the PS, but it has also brought a new malaise: Communist public officials now question the sincerity of the Socialist participants and are worried by the new aggressive style of what one of them called "the Socialist *jeunes loups*."

I have attempted to show that the Communist style of decision-

335

making differs to a certain extent from the Socialist style, the latter being more individualistic. The contrast between what was defined as an individual approach and a collective approach to decision-making should not be exaggerated, however: the pressure of political cadres is more likely to be felt by PCF public officials than by PS public officials, but it is not an exclusively Communist phenomenon. Socialist party cadres, particularly in large cities, are also likely to exert some kind of pressure on PS public officials, if only to remind them that the PS is not the PCF, after all.

2.5 Problems of Coalition Maintenance

Interparty coalitions, if they are durable, often lead to fear of absorption on the part of the smaller of the two major partners, particularly when there is a large difference in size between them. This fear of absorption is more likely to be expressed by nonelected party officials than by elected party members, the former being "inclined to be the most interested in the maintenance of purity of position for the sake of showing a distinct profile to the electorate," and the latter tending "to enjoy their functions and prestige and to become more accommodating."[40] Consequently, as was shown earlier, party cadres will, to a certain extent, contest the legitimacy of public officeholders, and try to politicize what a foreign observer might define as "daily administrative duties."

If a conflict (or at least tensions) between a Municipal Council and the local PS-PCF party section is likely to occur, it might also affect the party section itself, particularly in a party which tolerates the existence of rival "tendances" such as the PS. This is precisely what happened in three of the large cities observed (Nîmes, Alès, and Amiens) where local section leaders or incumbent mayors refused to form PS-PCF coalitions, despite the pressure of federal leaders. In all three cities, partisans of a third-force strategy were opposed to partisans of a united left-wing strategy, the latter asking for the resignation or dismissal of the former. In all three cases, after the direct intervention of federal leaders, the advocates of a third-force strategy were either dismissed or resigned in anticipation of dismissal.[41] The

---

[40] Groennings et al., *Coalition Behavior*, p. 462.

[41] It should be noted that these were not "classical" third-force strategies (i.e., "PS-Radicaux" "PS-Centristes" alliances), but "right-wing," third-force

end result was a split in all sections concerned and a considerable weakening of the local PS militant support, thus allowing the Communists to become the stronger partner in the alliance.[42]

For the PCF, the threat of an internal party split is very limited, since there is one and only one party line. The only threat that arises from the maintenance of a PS-PCF alliance is that such an alliance gives a reformist image to its policy and tends to obscure the differences between the two parties. Hence, the PCF's national leadership constantly stresses the originality and revolutionary character of the party's global strategy. They stress "mass actions" in which Communist mayors are urged to participate in demonstrations for trade unions, against the Vietnam war, in favor of civil liberties, to cite a few examples. They affirm that *tout compte fait* the PCF type organization is much superior to the Socialist one and remains the "only vanguard" of the proletariat. As Marchais puts it, the PCF is "the revolutionary party of the working-class; consequently its doctrine, its methods of struggle, and organization provide it with the means to perform the role of popular unity vanguard."[43]

CONCLUSIONS

Many of the problems confronting Communist decision-makers at the grass roots resemble those of their Socialist counterparts, despite their radically different political organizations and the existence of a "compulsory" party line on the one hand, and an "indicative" line on the other.

Communist public officials, like their Socialist opponents or allies, display a great deal of pragmatism. They are willing to negotiate and to compromise even to the point of losing a majority of seats within a municipal council. The flexibility of their bargaining vocabulary allows them to cope with a hostile "milieu" and to integrate class enemies, as long as they are defined as *républicains sincères, vrais démocrates* or *personnalités de gauche*. The normative and structural rigidity of democratic centralism

---

alliances including members of the PS, the Radical Party, "Centristes," and members of the UDR.

[42] The three cities that used to be Socialist municipalities are now headed by Communist mayors.

[43] G. Marchais, Preface to the Communist printing of the *Programme Commun de Gouvernement* (Paris: Editions Sociales, 1972), p. 45.

is considerably softened by intermediate party leaders who, instead of using sanctions or the threat of sanctions, have developed an intelligent and noncoercive instrument of policy implementation: an "explanatory pedagogy."

Such pragmatism does not mean, however, that the PCF is no longer a Leninist organization. The study of PS-PCF coalition formation and the analysis of the relationship between mayor and party section have revealed the limited autonomy of Communist grass-roots actors and the typical pyramidal structure of authority that characterizes a Bolshevik party. It is this very mixture of bourgeois pragmatism and revolutionary centralism that renders the study of the PCF so difficult, particularly when one wonders whether the PCF has really changed over the years and whether it is well integrated within the French political system. The answers vary, depending on the organizational areas under study, the historical period considered, and the type of political practice observed.

What is remarkable about a French Communist mayor is that the daily routine of municipal government and the endless pre-electoral bargains that fill his life have not impaired his belief in the rightness of the line nor his belief in the superiority of democratic centralism over all other forms of organization. The discrepancy that exists between a PCF mayor's fundamental belief (what is to be done) and his administrative actions (what is being done) might well be what most distinguishes a French Communist mayor from his Socialist counterpart.

A Liberal might claim that such a discrepancy reveals a fundamental lack of realism on the part of Communist public officials. For a Communist, on the contrary, it is a sign of realism. For example, all the PCF mayors who were asked the question, "Would you say that your administration is a left-wing administration?" answered no. A typical answer from Somme was:

> No, this is not possible, not even for a Communist municipality. This will never be possible in a capitalistic regime. We can do better than a right-wing municipality, be more open and more democratic. . . . The main difference between us and the others is our action in favor of poor districts and working-class districts, but this is all. There is no way to develop a left-wing administration (*une gestion de gauche*) when you are totally

338

dependent on the state, the prefect, and the Planning Board (*Le Plan*) for your investments and expenses.

In conclusion, the successful implementation of a unified PS-PCF strategy at the grass roots in no way seems to have threatened the identity of the PCF. The apparent rigidity of an organization based on the principle of democratic centralism does not prevent it from adapting to reformism on a short-term basis. Identity is safeguarded by the fact that the line has not changed and that belief in the superiority of the PCF type of organization is maintained. The extraordinary capacity of Communist mayors to divorce fundamental beliefs from bargaining behavior is the best guarantee for the survival of the PCF identity in an era of peaceful coexistence. As for the PS, the success of the strategy of left-wing unity does not challenge its identity, since it is, by definition a "multi-identity," as reflected in its indicative party line, the existence of party *tendances*, and the variety of its practices.

IX.

The PCF and Local Government: Continuity and Change

JEROME MILCH

In 1925, Victor Cat, the secretary of the Union of Communist Municipalities in France, characterized local government and municipal institutions as essential elements of the "political mechanisms of the capitalist state":

> Far from being the instruments of liberation for the proletariat, legislative and other [municipal] assemblies serve to guarantee the continuation of capitalist domination and, in addition to the social conservatism [which they represent], they hypocritically permit the masses to participate in the manufacture of the rods with which they are to be beaten. . . . The municipal system of bourgeois democracy is a trickery which is ten times more odious than the parliamentary system.[1]

Forty-six years later, the party's theoretical journal, *Cahiers du communisme*, described the same municipal institutions in somewhat different terms:

> In effect, the sector concerning the life of the communes includes an incalculable number of examples which demonstrate the authoritarian character of the state. But at the same time, it can be a field of the most democratic experiences, despite the constraints imposed by the state. These are the experiences which Communist municipal officials have offered for a long time now to the population of the cities and towns which they govern.[2]

Undeniably, the party's attitude toward local government has changed since the days of the "Worker-Peasant Bloc." Municipal

[1] *Le Bloc ouvrier-paysan aux elections municipales* (Paris: Librarie de l'Humanité, 1925), pp. 20-22.

[2] Georges Valbon, "La Démocratie dans la commune," *Cahiers du communisme* 47 (February 1971): 25.

340

institutions have taken on a new and more important role in the party's national strategy. At one time, local government was simply one of many arenas in which political and ideological battles were to be fought, but it has today become a particularly useful instrument with which the party can demonstrate its dedication to democratic procedures and bourgeois legality. Possibilities for significant reform, formerly dismissed as examples of utopian thinking or even of a certain "crétinisme municipale," have now been espoused by party ideologues.

These changes, however, do not obscure the lines of continuity with earlier years. Local government remains an integral part of the overall strategy of the Parti Communiste Français (PCF). Electoral alliances on the local level are still determined strictly by national party decisions.[3] The issues of former years have not been disavowed, even though previously minor and secondary themes have taken on a greater importance. In short, major changes have taken place, but they have not destroyed the links with the past.

In the following pages, we shall explore the changing attitudes of the PCF toward local government. The initial militant party line has gradually given way to a strategy aimed at attracting support and allaying suspicions among potential electoral allies. We shall consider the nature and extent of these changes by looking in detail at both the original strategical analysis of Communist leaders and the current line of the PCF. But official attitudes provide only a partial view of the relationship between the PCF and the institutions of local government. We shall, consequently, evaluate the empirical literature on the behavior of Communist militants in municipal politics, concentrating primarily on the activities of the PCF administration in the city of Nîmes. In this manner, we can help bridge the gap between attitudes and behavior and provide some indication of the extent to which strategies and tactics have filtered down to lower levels of the party.

In the final analysis, we shall consider the significance of the changes which have taken place in the approach of the PCF to local government. Are these changes merely a direct reflection of the party's national political strategy? Or are there perhaps other factors which have played a role in the establishment of the party's present attitude toward local government? Our conten-

[3] On this point, see Denis Lacorne, Chapter 8 in this volume.

tion is that changes were initiated by shifts in the party's national strategy but have been encouraged, particularly during the decade of the 1960s, by two external factors: the increasing importance of local government functions within the national political system and the changes in public expectations with regard to the performance of local public officials. The new strategy has been noticeably successful in gaining popular support, "conquering" new municipalities, and increasing public confidence in the party. These successes, in turn, have increased the price of an abrupt reversal of strategy, since the PCF has much to lose by abandoning a popular and effective policy. Certainly, it would be foolish to underestimate the possibility of change in this disciplined and hierarchical organization. The party's approach to local government is closely tied to its national strategy; if conditions dictate a more rigid and militant attitude on the national level, municipal policy will not long remain at variance. Nonetheless, party officials are likely to consider the effectiveness of their local policies in evaluating the wisdom of a shift in national strategy. The relative success which they have enjoyed on the local level suggests, at the very least, that they will hesitate before reversing their present course.

LOCAL GOVERNMENT: THE FIRST TWENTY YEARS

Between the Congress of Tours in 1920 and the advent of the Popular Front in 1934, the attitude of the PCF toward local government was entirely consonant with its evaluation of the capitalist state which it sought to overthrow. The revolutionary militance of this period was marked by frequent confrontations between communist local officials and state authorities; in 1925, for example, the party presented several female candidates on its electoral lists, even though they were neither eligible to run for office nor even permitted to vote.[4] After 1934, attitudes began to change, but policy shifts occurred gradually over a long period of time. The "new approach" became firmly entrenched only in the decade of the 1960s. Although the Popular Front constitutes the initial turning point in the evolution of the local strategy of the PCF, few changes were evident until after World War II. It

[4] François Platone, "L'Implantation municipale du Parti Communiste Français dans la Seine et sa conception de l'administration communale," *Mémoire*, Fondation Nationale des Sciences Politiques (Paris, 1967), p. 12.

342

is useful, consequently, to consider the first twenty years (1920-1940) as the period during which the original militant approach of the PCF was reflected in its outlook toward municipal government.

The principal element in the party's evaluation of local government was that "it is theoretically false to make a distinction between institutions of the state and those of the municipality."[5] "Thus," as *Cahiers du bolchevisme* explained in 1930, "all the activities of Communists in municipal institutions must be related to the actions necessary to break up [*désagréger*] the capitalist state."[6] Local problems and administrative issues were of no consequence; the proper conduct of Communist militants was to use the institutions of local government in any manner that would contribute to the destruction of the bourgeois state.

This conception of local government had several direct corollaries. In the first place, it implied that there was a single correct way to administer municipal institutions, valid for all Communist militants throughout the country. As long as the purpose of local control was solely to contribute to the party's revolutionary strategy, there could be no question of separate policies for different cities and towns. Other French political parties issued directives to local officials concerning electoral procedures; the PCF, on the other hand, maintained a clear, distinctive, and universal notion of the proper role and function of its elected local officials in day-to-day affairs. Victor Cat quoted approvingly the following plank in the platform of the old Parti Ouvrier: "In order to extend the reach of these conflicts [with the state], the workers' city governments will have to act in concert in order to formulate the same demands and take the same positions.[7] Detailed directives concerning the functions of Communist-run communes, proper procedures for handling local questions, and the correct use of local institutions to further the interests of the working class were issued before every election.[8]

A second corollary concerned the ultimate fate of communal institutions. As Victor Cat forcibly expressed in the passage

[5] Resolution of the Second Comintern Conference, quoted in "Le Parti Communiste et les collectivités locales," election pamphlet for the municipal elections of 1959 (Paris: n.d.).

[6] Pierre Semard, *Cahiers du bolchevisme* 6 (April 1930): 357.

[7] *Le Bloc ouvrier-paysan*, p. 39.

[8] See, for example, Jacques Duclos, "Programme municipale du Parti Communiste en 1935" (Paris: n.d.).

quoted above, the PCF viewed local institutions as bourgeois tricks whose major purpose was to intensify the oppression of the working class while maintaining the fiction that the workers were actually participating in the decisions that affected their lives. As such, "they must be destroyed by the revolutionary proletariat and replaced by soviets of workers' deputies."[9] The party's position on the related issue of communal autonomy was not, however, as well defined. While consistently supporting attempts to preserve and extend local freedom under the capitalist regime, the PCF tended to finesse the question of local autonomy in a socialist France. Its approach was to talk about the "false" conflict between central and local authorities in a proletarian state:

> There is no reason to fear the perpetual conflict between local and central powers, which is one of the characteristics of the pseudo-democratic bourgeoisie, because the supreme authority, that which elects the executive organs of the central power, that which is elaborated in the present [Russian] constitution, is the Congrès Panrusse des Soviets, whose delegates are chosen by the workers and peasants in their soviets and congresses.[10]

Still another corollary concerned the question of "municipal socialism." Since "they [parliamentary and municipal institutions] are identical wheels of the governmental mechanisms of the bourgeoisie,"[11] a socialist France could not be achieved peacefully by the conquest of local government. The task of Communist officials was to remind the workers of this simple truth: "This is why the workers must categorically reject the fatal notion of a certain municipal socialism, which could lead them to turn away from the inevitable necessity of the class struggle and to accept the illusion of the 'possibility' of taking power through the peaceful conquest of local government."[12] Worker control of local government could serve other purposes, but it could not change in any way the strategy for the conquest of the bourgeois state.

What then were the proper functions of local governments? As

[9] Resolution of the Second Comintern Conference, quoted in "Le Parti Communiste."

[10] Cat, *Le Bloc ouvrier-paysan*, p. 39.

[11] Resolution of the Second Comintern Conference, quoted in "Le Parti Communiste."

[12] Duclos, "Programme municipale," p. 19.

344

the party saw it, control of the communes was useful insofar as it served two major purposes: providing a forum for contact with the population and serving as a bastion of defense against the bourgeois state. The municipality was preferable to the legislature as an instrument of revolution because it was closer to the public and appeared less political.[13] Control over local governments provided the party with a forum to address the population at large and to mobilize them for revolutionary activities against the state. Similarly, the communes could serve as a place of refuge after particularly difficult struggles with the bourgeoisie.

The proper role of local government then was to serve the party's revolutionary strategy. While in power, however, Communist cities and towns were expected to "endeavor to bring some relief to the workers' misery."[14] Municipal administration was perceived as class politics and Communist officials were expected to pursue three short-range objectives: to support the struggles of the workers, ameliorate the conditions of their lives, and maintain close links between the party and the masses.

Support for the workers' struggles involved both moral and material aid. Communist municipalities were expected to defend the interests of the workers, to provide them with the physical means of continuing their struggles with their employers, and to protect them (as much as possible) from retaliation by the bourgeois state. The municipal program of the Bloc Ouvrier-Paysan stated this clearly in Section 1, Article 6: "To support politically, morally, and materially the workers and peasants in their struggles for immediate gains from the patronat."[15] Municipal employees were to be treated with particular courtesy and their demands satisfied, whatever the cost.

Ameliorating the conditions of their lives implied differentiating between segments of the population in the distribution of benefits and the imposition of costs. The socially disadvantaged (i.e., the proletariat) must be favored rather than those disadvantaged by nature (i.e., the old, the sick, etc.).[16] Day-to-day decisions had to be made in these terms, although it was recognized that there were strict limits on what local governments could accomplish. All the better, since this will "demonstrate the

[13] See Platone, "L'Implantation municipale."

[14] Maurice Thorez, *Oeuvres de Maurice Thorez*, 2d ed. (Paris: Editions Sociales, 1952), 7: 187.

[15] Cat, *Le Bloc ouvrier-paysan*, p. 56.

[16] For more details on this point, see Platone, "L'Implantation municipale."

insufficiency of reformist methods and will force the reformist chiefs to unmask themselves."[17]

Finally, local officials were encouraged to strive at all times to *maintain close contact with the masses*. This required periodic consultation with organized groups, public participation in communal affairs, and adequate information on the activities of local officials. Such procedures added to the party's prestige and corrected possible errors and oversights, while still retaining the final power of decision in the hands of party officials.

Despite these admirable and useful objectives, local officials were never to allow them to obscure the main function of local government which was to contribute to the overthrow of the bourgeois state. This would have been opportunism of the worst kind, and party officials constantly warned militants of the dangers: ·

> The Communist party wants, in the municipal councils as everywhere else, to defend the immediate demands of the working class and the working masses. It would like to make local government a base of action against the bourgeoisie, without ever becoming bogged down in a purely localist politics, detached from the revolutionary struggles.[18]

Similarly, militants were warned not to engage in "model administration": "We do not seek to win a municipality in order to work as elected officials in the general interest ('faire un travail édilitaire d'intérêt général') or to demonstrate that we are capable of administering as well as the bourgeoisie or the social-bourgeoisie."[19] Bourgeois legality was to be ignored; officials should operate "without letting themselves be stopped by the certainty that their decisions will be annulled."[20]

The dangers of opportunism were so great that Communist public officials could not be given a free hand to operate as they might wish; their activities were to be monitored closely by the party. "The elected official must not work without the party, and the party must always work with the elected official. It is the party which leads."[21] Similarly, important decisions were to be

---

[17] Cat, *Le Bloc ouvrier-paysan*, p. 56.

[18] Duclos, "Programme municipale," p. 20.

[19] Semard, *Cahiers*, p. 359.

[20] Victor Cat, "Les Socialistes ont abandonné leur programme municipale—I. Qu'est devenu la doctrine marxiste?" *L'Humanité*, March 6, 1925.

[21] This quotation comes from *Le Guide de l'élu municipal* (Paris: Amicale des Elus Communistes, 1945).

made directly by party organs: "The establishment of the municipal budget is a political act of the first importance. Hence, it must not be, in Communist municipalities, the business of the mayor and the specialists alone; it is also, and above all, the business of the party."[22]

The major objective of municipal government was to reinforce the revolutionary activities of the party. Local affairs must always remain subordinate to the system-wide objectives of the PCF; short-range goals could not be allowed to interfere with this support of party activities. Communal institutions were considered to be bourgeois and temporary; their only proper function was to help the party destroy the capitalist state.

THE NEW APPROACH

Changes in the attitude of the PCF toward local government began as early as the Popular Front era, but it was not until after the Liberation that the party began to develop the themes which today characterize its municipal strategy. Although there was some relapse during the height of the Cold War period, the rigidity of the Bloc Ouvrier-Paysan was never completely reestablished. With the advent of the Fifth Republic, the party's new approach was broadened and refined in considerably greater detail.

An increased flexibility in previously rigid positions is evident in the basic analysis of the functions and possibilities of local government. Despite the bourgeois nature of municipal institutions, the PCF now sees them as providing a "field for the most democratic experiences," providing only that they are administered by the right people. The *contrat communal* of 1971 envisions the possibility of important reforms even before a socialist state is established in France. To be sure, such progress cannot occur without a struggle: "The success of each project requires a battle of the masses against the politics of the government."[23] Similarly, the underlying problems cannot be resolved in a capitalist state: "Certainly, we are perfectly conscious of the limits imposed on our efforts both by the present reactionary politics [of the government] and by the framework of the capitalist regime itself."[24] Nonetheless, with sufficient effort, public support, and a coalition

[22] Jacques Duclos, "Les Municipalités au service des masses laborieuses," *Cahiers du communisme* 32 (July-August 1956): 69.

[23] Valbon, "La Démocratie," p. 30.

[24] Marcel Rosette, "Pourquoi un contrat communal?" *Cahiers du communisme* 47 (January 1971): 26.

of left-wing parties, important progress can be made toward improving the lot of the working masses.

The need for a universal strategy has also been modified over the years. While the PCF continues to issue directives concerning proper procedures for local officials, it has also become increasingly conscious of the need for greater flexibility in the day-to-day operations of local government. As the functions of municipal government have changed over the years, it is no longer possible for party leaders in Paris to determine, once and for all, the correct strategy to apply in every case. The nature and history of individual cities and the particular problems which they face must be taken into account: "The forms of the struggle adapt themselves according to social categories, according to the possibilities of action on the level of the neighborhood, the commune, the département, or the region."[25] A program or strategy which is appropriate for Saint-Denis may be entirely out of place in Le Havre or Arles.

The party has also become more sanguine about the ultimate fate of communal institutions. The immediate task is to utilize them for the fulfillment of social goals: "It is in this manner [by increasing participation] that a contribution can be made to the revitalization of elected assemblies, while still permitting them to work for the amelioration of the lives of the working masses."[26] But the party has also edged closer to a forthright statement of the inviolability of democratic assemblies and existing governmental institutions: "The Communist party, through political and ideological combat, will endeavor to conquer the role of avant-garde of our people, in competition with other parties of course, without substituting itself for the organs of the state, its representative institutions, and its administrations."[27]

The same kind of increased flexibility is obvious in the party's attitude toward decentralization. The PCF has been critical of the government's modest proposals for regional administration and has strongly attacked J.-J. Servan-Schreiber's more radical suggestions, but it has not opposed in principle the concept of regional government. The party's ambivalent attitude on this issue is based on some practical political considerations as well as a significant ideological concern for the integrity and primacy

[25] Valbon, "La Démocratie," p. 31.
[26] Ibid., p. 33.
[27] Rosette, "Pourquoi?" p. 27.

348

of "la nation."[28] Nonetheless, the PCF has not been reluctant to advocate greater decentralization on the municipal level. It has defended its position both in terms of increased democracy and improved efficiency: "One cannot harmoniously and rationally administer the country by decisions made at the summit."[29]

Even the relationship between party organs and local Communist officials has been modified somewhat over the years. Certainly, the party has not abdicated its role of "control" over the activities of its members in public office. Candidates are selected by the party and, once elected, remain responsible to it. Nonetheless, Communist ideologues have become increasingly aware of the need to allow more freedom to these officials and, in particular, to maintain a separation between party and local government. Thus they insisted in 1971 that "the Communist party section conducts the ideological and political battle, even in the domain of communal administration; but, during the mandate, it does not substitute itself for the municipal council directed by Communist elected officials. Such an attitude fosters a spirit of responsibility among elected officials and stimulates their initiative."[30] In practice, of course, the amount of flexibility provided to local officials depends on the particular circumstances: the size of the city, the presence of non-Communist members on the council, the "importance" of the party officials in municipal roles, etc. But even where party control remains tight, the "new approach" which takes into account the nature of specific communes and the problems which they face, allows a good deal more flexibility in the relationship between local government officials and the national party.

Shifts of emphasis and priority have also affected the attitude of the Communist party toward local government institutions. The party has never disavowed its attitude of previous years that the proper function of local government is to serve as a forum to mobilize the public and as a bastion of defense against the reactionary state; with the adoption of a new and "peaceful" national strategy, however, these functions have simply ceased to be as important as they were in the past. This decline in the revolutionary functions of the commune is evident in a recent party

[28] Peter Gourevitch, "Reforming the Napoleonic State: The Creation of Regional Government in France and Italy" (Cambridge, Mass.: West European Studies Working Paper no. 16, February 1973).

[29] Valbon, "La Démocratie," p. 27.

[30] Rosette, "Pourquoi?" p. 27.

349

attack on a political rival, the Parti Socialiste Unifié (PSU), for attempting "to transform the communes into 'centers of revolutionary struggle.' "[31] Despite the similarity with the original Communist approach to local government, the PSU strategy is labeled "reformist" and its spokesmen are characterized as "those who prattle about revolution." Such revolutionary prattle, according to party leaders, "cannot replace imagination, audacity, and a true confidence in the masses."[32] The revolutionary functions of local government have thus ceased to be important, even though they have never been formally rejected.

By contrast, what were formerly short-range and temporary objectives of Communist control have taken on a new importance with the passing years. An increasing concern for the everyday problems of life is evident: "To respond to the social needs of our times, to defend the most disadvantaged [classes], to support and organize the struggles against the politics of the regime, to engage in the organization of the social life in the city neighborhoods and rural communes, this is the meaning of "social administration in the service of the population."[33] The party has hardly become technocratically oriented, but it has unquestionably increased its interest in the problems of housing, education, and leisure.

This new interest in administrative problems has been accompanied by a redefinition of the concept of "class politics." The *contrat communal* of 1971 was introduced to Communist militants as the embodiment of the party's class orientation, even though its focus was on the interests of "all the victims of the monopolies." More often than not, *la classe ouvrière* has been replaced by *la population laborieuse*; the PCF has increasingly emphasized its concern for "all segments of the population" and, at the same time, narrowed its enemies to the "monopoly capitalists." Thus, municipal institutions are expected to function in such a way as to "defend the interests of the entire population."[34]

The broadening of interest from the working class to the "entire population" has involved more than just a rhetorical change. Issues such as fiscal responsibility and long-range planning, formerly ignored by the party, have become more important as the PCF has attempted to appeal to large segments of the middle class. Along with the older notions of "une gestion sociale et

[31] Ibid., p. 23.   [32] Ibid., p. 26.   [33] Ibid., p. 23.
[34] Valbon, "La Démocratie," p. 27.

démocratique," the *contrat communal* of 1971 included the term "moderne."

Another issue which has taken on considerably greater importance for the party has been communal democracy. Indeed, this is the major theme of the *contrat communal*, which was described by one party spokesman as "a passionate search for democracy."[35] The party's emphasis has been on the increased participation of the public in communal affairs.[36] This is not, of course, a new theme for the PCF, which has always talked about the necessity of maintaining close contacts with the public. Nonetheless, the functions of participation have changed considerably over the years. At one time, the party promoted these contacts for the specific purpose of keeping its working-class supporters informed of the activities of Communist militants. While participation still serves this purpose, there are today two additional reasons for promoting it. In the first place, it has become a major element in the party's appeal to the middle class, which has demonstrated considerable interest in local affairs. The spectacular growth of the Groupes d'Action Municipale (GAM) movement over the past eight years is striking evidence of the attractiveness of this new theme. For the PCF, the emphasis on participation serves the dual purpose of appealing to a large group of potential voters while helping to undermine the development of a troublesome and dangerous competitor.

An additional reason for promoting democracy and participation in communal life is to demonstrate to potential allies on the left, particularly the Socialists, that the PCF is committed to these values. This, in itself, has required an important change of perspective for the party. The notion of permitting local government to serve as a "model" of administrative ability and a demonstration of concern for bourgeois values was specifically rejected by party leaders. This attitude, however, has been considerably revamped. Local government control provides the party with a unique opportunity to demonstrate a concern for democracy; it is the one opportunity for a nonruling party to show how it

[35] Ibid., p. 30.

[36] Sidney Tarrow, in Chapter 4 of this volume, points out that Communist public officials in France are not nearly so active in promoting democracy and participation as their Italian counterparts. Even electoral activities are far less intense in PCF communes. From a historical perspective, however, significant changes have taken place within the PCF, and it is these changes which are of interest in this analysis.

would operate if given the reins of power. The PCF has not been reluctant to point this out:

> Finally, a not unimportant consequence, our democratic practices in communal administration permits us to give to the people an advance picture, even though partial, of the society that we shall build together in the future. How many times have we heard it said that the Communists, once in power or associated with the government, will monopolize everything: the elected assemblies, the state, the administration. But today, even with the insufficient powers which they can exercise in the municipalities, is this how the Communists operate?[37]

Thus, the PCF specifically intends its present emphasis on democracy and participation in the communes to be an example of the kind of behavior that potential allies can expect in the future.

IDEOLOGY IN PRACTICE: THE APPLICATION OF THE NEW APPROACH

These changes in the official attitude of the PCF toward the institutions of local government raise a series of questions concerning the actual behavior of party militants in public office. To what extent are the themes and directives of party leaders applied to the day-to-day affairs of local government? What happens when new problems and obstacles are encountered? Are cities governed by the PCF really different in any significant way from other French cities?

The empirical evidence on the administrative and political behavior of Communist local officials is not sufficient to provide a definitive answer to any of these questions. A thorough study of Communist local government is yet to be made, but some information is available through a few case studies, budgetary analyses, and surveys. The evidence from these studies suggests that the new approach has, to a large extent, been put into practice on the local level, although the behavior of party cadres has not been identical in every city and on all issues.

A reduction in the level of revolutionary activity is one aspect of the new approach which appears to be widely accepted by local Communist militants. François Hincker, describing the

[37] Rosette, "Pourquoi?" p. 27.

achievements of the Communist municipality of Givors, deals with the efforts of city officials to provide public housing and control land speculation, before considering the more traditional party concern for mobilizing the population against the state.[38] Political activities of this nature are not, of course, absent in PCF communities; Jean-Pierre Hoss, for example, describes the efforts of the Communist administration in Argenteuil to associate the failure to complete a civic project with the malfeasance of the central government.[39] These efforts, however, have consistently been tied to specific issues of local interest, such as an increase in the tax rate or the shortage of public facilities, and the nature of the criticism directed against the government is not significantly different in Communist municipalities than in more conservative cities.[40]

The tendency to tone down the language of class warfare is also evident in empirical research on Communist militants. Data from a study by Sidney Tarrow indicate that while Communist mayors are still more likely than other local officials to cite "assistance to particular social groups" as a rationale for pursuing civic projects, they also point more frequently to the collective benefits of their policies.[41] Sixty-four percent of the Communist mayors insist that the public interest is maximized through the projects which they pursue while only forty-seven percent of the Socialists and forty-one percent of the other mayors justify their choice in this manner.

[38] "Une municipalité dans la lutte politique: Givors," *La Nouvelle Critique*, no. 42 (March 1971): 14-18.

[39] *Communes en banlieue: Argenteuil et Bezons* (Paris: A. Colin, 1969). See esp. the picture opposite p. 113.

[40] One of the sharpest critiques of the government during the 1971 municipal elections was offered by the very conservative president of the Association des Maires de France, who said in part:

> We would have a lot to say to the Minister of Finance if he were willing to listen to us because, frequently, we must carry in his place, in the eyes of the public, the responsibility for making his decisions. Each [citizen], for example, who sees an increment in his tax bill is apt to accuse the municipal councils and the mayors of a lack of skill; the increase in his tax load is two times faster than the [increase in the] national revenue, according to our studies, and still the requirements are not satisfied. . . . The increase in the number of centimes is not a chance occurrence; we know that it was desired, calculated, and announced by the bureaucrats in the planning office.

Quoted in *Midi libre* (Nîmes), March 9, 1971.

[41] I would like to express my gratitude to Professor Tarrow for allowing me to use the data from his sample.

A second aspect of the new approach, an emphasis on the pursuit of social policies and the provision of public services, also appears to be widely accepted by Communist public officials. A comparative study of the budgets of two Paris suburbs by Jean-Claude Ducros, one governed by Communists and the other by conservatives, indicates small but consistent differences in the fiscal policies pursued by the two local administrations during the period from 1958 to 1962.[42] Villejuif, controlled by the PCF, opted to invest every available resource in the provision of new equipment for the city and borrowed heavily from the central government in order to finance these efforts. By contrast, conservative Montrouge pursued a policy of fiscal independence and consistently maintained a surplus of funds in the city treasury in order to forestall any government interference in its affairs. Differences in priorities for expenditures were also observed in the two cities; Villejuif invested primarily in educational facilities while Montrouge favored the construction of roads and housing. Moreover, Ducros noted the absence of "municipal socialism" in Villejuif,[43] but still reported a higher level of social services in that city.

These differences are not, of course, due solely to the political attitudes of local leaders; economic and social factors are certainly relevant to any analysis of output policies in municipal government. Nonetheless, other studies provide further support for the notion that Communist officials have largely applied their party's new orientation toward social policies and public services. Jean-Pierre Hoss, for example, writes that "insofar as expenses are concerned, several facts underline the 'social' character of the budgetary policies of Argenteuil, such as the significance of the resources devoted to education and social services."[44] A second comparative study of the budgets of a Communist and conservative city in the south of France, conducted during the period from 1966 to 1969, confirmed many of the results of the Paris study and discovered additional differences in fiscal policy which suggest that the "social" orientation of the PCF has been pursued with vigor by local militants.[45] Thus, the Communist administration in Nîmes has opted, to the maximum extent permitted by

[42] "Politique et finances locales," *Analyse et prevision* 2 (1966): 499-520.
[43] Ibid., p. 505.   [44] *Communes*, p. 86.

[45] J. Denis and M. Laget, "Economie urbaine et finances locales: l'exemple de Nîmes et Montpellier," *Economie Méridionale*, no. 73 (1971).

municipal law, to rely on direct taxation in balancing the budget and to minimize the use of indirect taxes and public service revenues.[46] These differences in fiscal policy cannot, of course, be generalized without further comparative study, but they do lend credence to the idea that communist officials place an increasingly strong emphasis on the pursuit of social policies and the provision of adequate public services.

This emphasis on social policies in Communist municipalities can be seen in other ways as well. Paul Thibaud suggests that PCF communal cadres have begun to conceptualize their municipal responsibilities in broader terms than the economic criteria previously employed.[47] Cultural programs, in particular, have become increasingly important. Hoss reports that "one of the greatest desires of these Communist municipalities, their ambition, is to lead the working population to interest itself in culture [and] to make it accessible to everyone."[48] Accordingly, both Argenteuil and Bezons have made impressive efforts in this direction. In Givors as well, cultural issues have taken on a profound importance for local officials; François Hincker describes the efforts of the Communist administrators of Givors to extend the benefits of high culture to the population of the city.[49]

Existing evidence also suggests a new concern among Communist public officials for "democratic proprieties" in operational procedures. Fifty percent of the Communist mayors in Tarrow's survey described their relationship with the municipal council as a collaborative effort and characterized their own role as the "spirit of the team" rather than the coach; only 19 percent of the Socialists and 21.7 percent of the other mayors in the sample had the same view of this relationship. By contrast, 23.8 percent of the Socialists and 30 percent of the nonleftist mayors considered themselves to be virtually autonomous vis-à-vis the council, while only 12.5 percent of the Communists held this view. These surveys, of course, suggest that the new attitudes of the PCF leadership have been passed down to lower-level cadres but they do not tell us whether these views have been put into practice by Communist local administrators. Nonetheless, Hoss's description of the operational procedures in the municipal administration of

---

[46] Ducros, "Politique," p. 505, also discovered at least some indication of a similar policy in Villejuif.

[47] "Le Communisme municipale," *Esprit* (October 1966).

[48] *Communes*, p. 99. [49] "Une Municipalité," p. 16.

Argenteuil reveals a strikingly regularized and democratic pattern of administration and indicates that local militants have adopted at least some democratic norms in their administrative behavior.[50]

Considerable effort has also been expended to broaden municipal government and allow for the participation of non-Communist elements in local administration. These efforts have been particularly noticeable in electoral strategy, where the local sections of the PCF, in compliance with national directives, have attempted to form coalitions with other leftist parties.[51] But the concern for broadening local government has also extended to citizen participation in communal affairs. Both Hoss and Hincker describe the efforts of Communist officials in Argenteuil, Bezons, and Givors to associate the public with local decisions.[52] The evidence in this area is, however, only partly convincing. Tarrow's data, for example, indicate that Communist public officials do not interact more frequently with private groups than mayors of other political persuasions, although they do maintain more consistent contacts with trade unions, professional groups, producers and cooperatives.[53]

A final aspect of the new approach to local government, a more flexible relationship between the local section of the PCF and the Communist municipal administration, is a difficult subject to confirm through direct empirical research, largely because the party has been reluctant to allow outsiders to probe into its internal affairs. In his article on Givors, François Hincker makes a point of distinguishing between the responsibilities of the local section and those of the municipality but does not indicate the nature and extent of any controls which might be exercised by the for-

[50] *Communes*, p. 86.

[51] For a greater elaboration of this process, see Denis Lacorne, Chapter 8 in this volume.

[52] Hoss, *Communes*, pp. 124-128, and Hincker, "Une Municipalité," p. 17.

[53] Percentage of mayors who report that they maintain contacts with:

	Trade union and professional groups	Producers and cooperatives	Cultural, educational, and civic groups	Festival, recreational, and sporting groups
PCF	51	42.9	66.7	47.6
Socialists	16	32.0	84.0	52.0
Others	8.6	38.5	81.4	60.0

mer over the latter.[54] Denis Lacorne suggests that the Communist mayor remains in close rapport with his party section, at least insofar as matters of party strategy are concerned. Moreover, larger or more significant municipalities are subject, according to Lacorne, to greater control by the local party section.[55] But Communist militants are aware of the present party line and reflect these views in their conversations. One of the mayors in Lacorne's sample, for example, points out the dangers of a municipality run by the executive committee of the section. The nature and extent of party control over the daily affairs of a Communist municipality is uncertain, but it is likely that while a Communist mayor may not be allowed to stray far from the party line, he may be given considerable leeway in determining the short-run policies of his administration.

This brief review of the data on the behavior of Communist officials in local government suggests that many aspects of the party's new approach to municipal administration have been put into practice by local militants. In certain areas, such as the emphasis on the provision of social benefits and public facilities, the evidence indicates that party cadres have made a major effort to conform to the ideological positions adopted by the central committee; in other areas, however, the evidence is less clear. A more definitive response to this problem requires continued research, but some data which might shed further light on these issues is available from a detailed case study of the municipality of Nîmes, the second largest city controlled by the PCF.[56] Nîmes is not typical of the cities governed by the PCF; less than 17 percent of its labor force is engaged in industrial occupations and only 33.9 percent can be characterized as "workers." As Table 1 indicates, these percentages are considerably different from the figures from both the traditional Communist strongholds in the "Red Belt," such as Saint-Denis, Aubervilliers, and Montreuil, and from Le Havre, the largest Communist-governed city in

---

[54] "Une Municipalité," p. 18.

[55] See Lacorne, Chapter 8 in this volume. As the size of the commune increases, however, the problems of control for the local party section become more severe.

[56] The data in this section were collected by the author between November 1970 and July 1971. More details are available in "Paris is Not France: Policy Outputs and Political Values in Two French Cities" (Ph.D. Dissertation, M.I.T., September 1973).

France. The electoral support which enabled the PCF to "conquer" this municipality came from a complex mixture of historical, economic, regional, and local factors.[57] Nîmes has been governed by the PCF only since 1965 and it is therefore impossible to contrast its present leadership with that of any previous Communist administration in the city.[58] Political leaders in Nîmes, however, are long-time party militants, and the mayor of Nîmes is a former miner.

TABLE 1. THE LABOR FORCE (from the 1968 census)

	Nîmes	Saint-Denis	Auber-villiers	Mon-treuil	Le Havre
ECONOMIC ACTIVITY					
Construction and Public Works	13.7	11.1	12.9	9.7	10.2
Industry	16.8	41.4	42.2	40.0	27.4
Transportation	8.5	6.2	5.8	4.6	18.4
Commerce	22.1	20.8	21.6	21.7	18.5
Services	14.8	9.2	8.7	10.4	12.6
Administration	22.2	11.1	8.5	13.1	11.8
SOCIO-PROFESSIONAL CATEGORIES					
"Ouvriers Qualifiés"	15.8	19.4	18.6	18.2	19.4
"Ouvriers Specialisés"	9.8	18.3	18.5	13.6	10.3
"Manoeuvres"	5.0	15.2	16.9	10.9	11.6
Total: Ouvriers	33.9	56.0	56.9	45.6	48.2

The present municipal government of Nîmes was first elected in 1965 with a majority of Communist members and a minority of PSU and dissident Socialists. In 1971 the list was expanded to include the French Socialist Party (PSF) and the Convention des Institutions Républicaines (CIR), with the PCF voluntarily ceding its majority on the council. The willingness to sacrifice its dominant position in the municipal administration was a major electoral concession by the local PCF section, but it involved no substantial change in operational procedures and generated few

[57] For more background on this issue, see J. Fauvet, A. Mendras, P. Poujol, and S. Schram, Les Paysans et la politique dans la France contemporaine, Cahiers de la Fondation Nationale des Sciences Politiques, no. 94 (Paris: A. Colin, 1958).

[58] Actually, the city did have a Communist mayor and council majority between 1945 and 1947. For a variety of reasons, however, this does not constitute a valuable period of comparison.

new difficulties for decision-making. As the minority faction on the 1965-1971 council readily admitted, the Communists never attempted to force through a decision which was not approved virtually unanimously by the council. Democratic procedures were religiously followed within the municipal administration.

The party's 1971 electoral campaign reflected the themes adopted by the national party, although the local section often went even further than the national executive in applying the new approach. With the exception of a single joint communiqué with the PSU, the local Communist list never talked about the need to support and defend the working class; instead, the terms of the electoral appeal called for "une politique au service de l'ensemble de la population." The major electoral theme was democracy in the commune; the PCF pointed with great pride to its own behavior and insisted that it had introduced a radically different approach to local government than its Socialist predecessors had used. The new set of concerns was reflected in one campaign slogan which called for the reelection of the incumbent administration on the grounds of "continuité, efficacité, et honnêteté."

The party's behavior during the period of its first mandate provides strong evidence of its acceptance and application of the new approach. Considerable effort was made to increase public participation in local affairs. Extra-municipal commissions were created to discuss issues directed to them by the local government. These commissions included both municipal council members and selected representatives of various organizations in the city. Municipal offices were established to deal with cultural issues, youth problems, and sports; these were run jointly by local government and by organized groups involved in these affairs. Formal working sessions of neighborhood groups and council members were conducted periodically to establish priorities for projects within the residential area. Moreover, local officials solicited the opinions of a wide variety of organized groups, including those which were essentially hostile to the Communist administration. Finally, major efforts were made to encourage the organization and articulation of demands by those interests which had never before entered the political arena.

Local Communist officials also appeared to understand the party's increased interest in using municipal institutions as a means to reassure potential allies and voters of its concern for democratic procedures. Bourgeois legality was strictly observed and local leaders rarely went out of their way to provoke confrontations with Gaullist prefectoral authorities.[59] Party officials claim with pride that their successful reelection campaign of 1971 was supported by people who had never before voted Communist. Although they readily admit that "it is not by means of this election that socialism will be installed in France,"[60] local officials are quick to point out that their reelection in 1971 was based on their proved abilities as able administrators and concerned democrats.

It is difficult to find much evidence of the use of municipal institutions for what were once the twin functions of local government: a forum to mobilize the public and a bastion of defense against the state. Attacks on the central government were launched from time to time by Communist officials but were invariably linked directly with the problems of the commune; the value-added tax (TVA), for example, was characterized as a *fardeau insupportable* not because it is politically and socially regressive and selectively hurts those least able to pay, but because it cripples the finances of local government. Such an attack might equally well have been launched by the archconservative leaders of neighboring Montpellier. On the few occasions that public opinion was mobilized against the state, the issues involved were always local problems of high visibility and much interest (e.g., insufficient funds to build a new school particularly needed by the city). Indeed, one of the major complaints of the PSU faction on the council was that the Communist had proved to be extremely conservative and largely unwilling to mobilize the population against the reactionary state.

The spirit in which local Communist officials responded to new difficulties reflects an increased concern for administrative matters, often at the expense of ideological positions. While the Communist section in Montpellier assailed the municipal administration for having turned over public services to private entrepreneurs, the Communist leaders of Nîmes opted for precisely the same solution when a serious problem arose in 1967 with the

[59] Interviews with several members of the prefecture of the Gard, the département in which Nîmes is located, revealed that local government officials had cooperated fully with state authorities and refrained from engaging in political controversies with them.

[60] *Midi libre* (Nîmes), March 12, 1971.

city's water system. "We didn't like to do it," said the mayor in defense of his decision, "but we are realists. We cannot be dogmatists."[61]

The major thrust of local public policy was to "favor the most disadvantaged elements in the population." Subsidies to the transportation network, which constituted nearly 4 percent of Nîmes's operational budget, could not be avoided, according to local officials, because the city's poor could not afford private means of transportation. The price of public services was maintained at an artificially low level in order to allow their widest possible use by "the working masses." Both the operational and investment budgets were consistently slanted in favor of "social" expenses, i.e., measures taken to improve the social or cultural life of the city, rather than "economic" expenses, i.e., those designed to provide for the smooth and efficient operation of the city. Special efforts were made to furnish a variety of programs and facilities in the area of education, which municipal officials characterized as the *priorité des priorités*.

The measures adopted by the Communist administration in Nîmes were quite successful with "the working masses," who expressed their approval by increasing the margin of victory for the PCF list in 1971. Direct relations with working-class groups and trade unions in the city, however, were somewhat ambiguous. The administration made a major effort to involve them in the decision-making process and expressed its support for economic demands raised by the unions in negotiations with their employers. In May 1968 city officials marched alongside workers through the streets of Nîmes. But municipal authorities have also attempted to attract industry to the city; they have established and equipped an industrial zone and offered various incentives to manufacturing interests. Fearful of acquiring a reputation for labor troubles, they have been careful not to encourage unrest among the unions. Moreover, they have been reluctant to satisfy demands leveled against them by the municipal unions; when, for example, free water and transport for municipal employees were demanded, city officials quietly but firmly refused.

In Nîmes as elsewhere, the relationship between the local party section and Communist officials in the local government has been the most difficult area to research, but available evidence indicates that there has been an increasing degree of freedom for

[61] Personal interview.

361

public officials since 1965. When first elected that year, Communist officials were thrust into roles for which they were not prepared. The national party organization sent down one of its cadres as "secretary to the mayor" in order to stay abreast of local developments. Similarly, the federation kept a close watch on the activities of public officials through its secretary, who was an assistant to the mayor. Since then, however, local officials have obtained considerably more freedom of action. According to one close observer of the Communist federation, the "municipals," those members whose primary interest is in the activities of local government, have become more influential than the "hierarchists," those who remain strongly oriented toward Paris.

To a large extent, it is precisely because local officials accepted party discipline that they have managed to obtain greater flexibility. But the complexity of local government in large cities contributes immeasurably to the difficulties faced by the party section. In order to maintain control over the daily activities of public officials, the "controllers" must absorb themselves in the nitty-gritty of local affairs. This, however, is precisely what the party would like to avoid since greater involvement in the details of administration often leads the "controllers" to identify themselves with the goals and objectives of the "controlled." The problem is immense even for a commune like Givors, with a population which is barely an eighth as large as that of Nîmes. One party official there recognized that:

> There is always a risk . . . that municipal duties will occupy all the comrades' time. Two conditions are indispensable in order to avoid [this development]: that a large number of non-Communists are associated with municipal activities and that there are numerous Communists who can divide the responsibilities among themselves.[62]

In a city as large as Nîmes, even these measures are not always adequate, and party control consists, for the most part, of a general overview of the "grand lines" of municipal strategy.

The evidence from Nîmes indicates that local Communist militants engaged in municipal activities have, to a large degree, applied the party's new approach to their daily activities. There are few vestiges of the party's previous "revolutionary" period; in-

[62] Hincker, "Une Municipalité," p. 18.

stead, local officials have absorbed the spirit of the new approach and applied it easily to new problems as well as older ones. Curiously, however, this has resulted in the loss of a distinctive *façon communiste* of administration. The party's concerns and techniques are shared by a large number of non-Communist leftist local governments today. While one may legitimately talk of a *façon gauchiste* of administration, the distinctive Communist approach no longer seems to be valid.

THE LIMITS OF CHANGE

It is far easier for the analyst to describe the changes in the attitude and behavior of the PCF than to assess their significance. The evidence presented in the previous few pages could support either of the two major alternative approaches to Communist behavior in France. By focusing on the elements of continuity in the party's new orientation toward local government, one might conclude that, in the words of Annie Kriegel, "il change, il change, et pourtant, non, rien n'est changé."[63] On the other hand, an emphasis on the considerable changes which *have* taken place in the attitude and behavior of party militants on the local level would imply that something more significant than a facelifting operation has occurred during the past two decades.

An analysis of the data on the Communist approach to local government suggests four reasons to question the significance of the changes adopted by the party. In the first place, party leaders tend to present their programs with an emphasis on continuity rather than change. Old policies are rarely if ever disavowed, even when they are no longer relevant or useful. New policies coexist with older ones; slogans are redefined to make them applicable to a new era. The very reluctance to part with old policies and themes is an indication of the importance which party leaders attach to continuity.

Secondly, not all of the changes that have been introduced have proceeded at the same rate. Some have gone considerably further than others. The party has essentially dropped its previous opposition to using the commune as a "model" of democratic behavior, but it has only slightly altered its traditional concern for party control over the activities of elected officials. Further-

[63] *Les Communistes français* (Paris: Editions du Seuil, 1968), p. 225.

more, even the new policies have their limits; significant reforms may be possible today under a bourgeois regime, but the basic problems of the commune cannot be solved until the advent of a socialist state. The same can be said for communal democracy: "The participation of the people in public affairs, as we have underlined many times, cannot occur freely and expand fully except under a socialist regime."[64]

Moreover, quite a few aspects of the PCF's approach to local government have not changed at all over the years. The party remains adamantly opposed to the *bons gestionnaires*, insisting that all decisions made by local government are political. Local issues are still carefully tied to governmental policies, and the party continues to associate the problems of the communes with the nature and policies of the state. As in the past, the PCF rejects the possibility of "municipal socialism" as absurd, unworkable, and irrelevant; it firmly maintains that local government control cannot, and will not, lead to socialism in France.

What is by far the most important element of continuity, however, concerns the nature of the relationship between the party's national and local strategies. The PCF has always considered local government to be a battlefield in the nationwide struggle for political power, one that cannot be separated from other aspects of the political system. As such, the correct strategy for local officials depends on the national situation and the objective conditions facing the party organization. During the first twenty years (1920-1940), the proper approach to local government was one which focused on the revolutionary possibilities inherent in municipal control. This approach was perfectly compatible with the party's national strategy. As the PCF came to advocate the peaceful road to socialism and to seriously seek out coalitions with other left-wing parties, its conception of local government was forced to undergo some revision. In order for it to remain a vital element in the party's strategy, it had to evolve in much the same manner as the conception and approach to parliamentary institutions. Thus, the basic element of continuity is that local government control continues to serve an instrumental purpose for the PCF, one consistent with its national strategy.

That the approach to local government is a function of the PCF's national strategy will hardly come as a surprise to any stu-

---

[64] Rosette, "Pourquoi?" p. 26.

dent of the party. It is, however, far too easy to conclude that these changes are insignificant and can be easily reversed by party leaders. For although it is clear that the changes in the party's approach were initiated by the new political strategy and reinforced by its evolution over the years, several additional factors have played a role in encouraging the changes and easing the transition from the old to the new. These factors do not serve as a barrier to prevent change, but they do make a major reversal of policy far less likely.

Two issues have become particularly salient during the decade of the 1960s, and party leaders have been quite conscious of their significance. The presentation of the *contrat communal* to party militants in *Cahiers du communisme* takes careful note of these new factors. After commenting that the concern for democracy and participation are not new additions to party ideology, Marcel Rosette offers several explanations for the increased emphasis on these themes. First:

> The municipal councils are confronted today with more numerous and complex problems. . . . In order to make the most appropriate decisions, [they] must seek out the opinions of two kinds of partners: on the one hand, the technicians and specialists of all kinds, and on the other hand, the consumers and their representatives. . . . This confrontation of opinion between elected officials, technicians, and consumers contributes the richness of collective elaboration and permits the elected assembly to make decisions [with the knowledge that it has a] thorough understanding of the issues.[65]

The party is aware that the role and responsibility of local government has increased in recent years; that it is no longer possible for part-time workers to make rational decisions on the spur of the moment; and that it is necessary to involve the public at large in the process. The additional emphasis on participation, says Rosette, is a rational and mandatory response to a new situation, assuming that the value of democracy is to be maintained.

The emphasis on the growing role of the communes and the new difficulties they face has strongly permeated the party's approach to local government. To a large extent, the PCF has attempted to foist the responsibility for the new difficulties of the

[65] Ibid., p. 24.

communes on the policies of the regime. The party has recognized, however, that some of the new difficulties are inherent in the increased role that local government is required to play in a modern industrial state. Thus, the party's position on increased autonomy and financial freedom for the communes reflects in part the need for greater flexibility to solve new problems. While it remains primarily a political position calculated to gain support for the party, it is also a rational response to a difficult situation faced by Communist municipalities.

Rosette's second explanation for the increased emphasis on participation in the communes is even more interesting:

> It is a question of the will of the masses themselves to participate in the administration of public affairs. The great struggles of May-June 1968, in underlining the extent of this sentiment, have contributed to its further development. . . . Urbanism and social housing, jobs and commerce, social and cultural *equipement*, they intend to know when and how these needs can be satisfied.[66]

In other words, two related changes in attitude by the public have encouraged the party to continue its new path: an increased expectation of practical results from local officials and an increased desire to play a direct role in the determination of the program to be followed. The party's new policy then serves not only to demonstrate a concern for democracy but also to satisfy what are perceived to be the expressed demands of the public.

In the period following the municipal elections of 1971, the party leadership concluded that the theme of communal democracy, which was recognized as a useful and important way to attract new voters from the middle classes, had to be reinforced by an increased emphasis on social projects. Democracy was an important theme for the middle classes and was not to be abandoned, but the party's traditional clientele, the working class, was more interested in concrete results than in participation. These attitudes allow the PCF to mobilize its supporters against the reactionary politics of the state,[67] but they also demand an increased emphasis on the daily problems of the workers. Thus:

[66] Ibid., p. 25.

[67] Indeed, Rosette offered one other explanation for the new emphasis on participation in communal affairs: it "leads to the organization of struggles over precise demands against the consequences of the reactionary politics of the state." Ibid., p. 26.

It is indispensable that, commune by commune, by means of a meticulous examination, Communist officials conduct studies to determine the quality and diversity of social services and indispensable public equipment. . . . Communist officials must occupy themselves with the interests of the entire population, and particularly those families whose conditions of life are the most difficult. Officials must be better acquainted with their situation and endeavor to give satisfaction to their most immediate demands.[68]

This new (post-1971) interest in the working class, however, is considerably different from the party's original approach of the 1920s and 1930s. At that time, the party's primary, and almost exclusive, interest was in the problems of the work place. Today the analysis is somewhat broader: "Housing, education, sports, health, life style, culture—men and women do not live only in the exercise of their professions; they must, for themselves and their families, unbend and amuse themselves, enrich and embellish their lives."[69] The PCF has recognized that its traditional supporters are no longer content solely with a local policy aimed at mobilizing support against the state; efforts to ameliorate the daily lives of the workers, the short-term goals of the past, have become increasingly important for the party at least partly because they have become increasingly important for the working class.

These two factors—a change in the role of local government in France and a change in public expectations vis-à-vis local officials—have helped to encourage the party's new approach to local government. It is no coincidence that the period in which these new factors have become important, the middle and late 1960s, corresponds closely to the period in which the party's new approach to local government became firmly entrenched. While it is clear that these factors did not initiate the changes in party outlook, which would have occurred in any case, they have undoubtedly helped to determine the thrust and extent of its present policy.

The PCF's local strategy has been successful insofar as it is consonant not only with the party's national strategy but with the expressed interests of the population. Public opinion polls have

[68] Marcel Rosette, "Gestion municipale au service des travailleurs," *Cahiers du communisme* 48 (July-August 1972): 34.
[69] Valbon, "La Démocratie," p. 27.

consistently demonstrated considerable support for these policies. In 1964, 44 percent of the population approved of Communist local government while only 38 percent backed the party's national program;[70] in 1968, the figures were 54 percent and 51 percent.[71] Moreover, the party's local efforts have been crowned with electoral success. Since 1959, not a single Communist local government in a town of more than 30,000 has been defeated, and the number of communes of that size controlled by the PCF has increased from 25 to 40. Only 3 percent of all French municipalities are governed by Communists, but more than 20 percent of the *grandes villes* have Communist mayors.[72] The vast majority of Communist cities are located in the Paris region where more than half of the 59 towns of over 30,000 are run by the PCF; but even in the provinces, nearly 7 percent of the cities in the same category have opted for a Communist administration. These figures, particularly the 60 percent increase between 1959 and 1971 in the number of Communist mayors of large cities, are impressive indicators of the popular success of the party's local strategy.

What this implies for the durability of the new approach, however, is considerably less clear. The PCF remains a disciplined, hierarchical organization in which local government serves a functional purpose in the national political strategy. If that strategy were to change, the party's approach to local government would change too. The developments of the past few decades ought not obscure this fundamental truth about the PCF. But if national political strategy does not change, the party may shortly be faced with a difficult strategical choice with respect to its municipal policy. The popular success on the local level has resulted largely from the increased flexibility of Communist public officials and their dedication to administrative tasks. Political cadres in Nîmes, for example, have succeeded in mobilizing electoral support by becoming efficient and concerned administrators who devote virtually all their efforts to local affairs. This support, of course, has been a major objective of Communist leaders, but the specialization of function within the party which is virtually re-

[70] These figures are from a survey by IFOP and are quoted in Thibaud, "Le Communisme."

[71] These figures, also from IFOP, are provided in "Les Français, la Politique, et le parti communiste," *Cahiers du communisme* 44 (January 1968): 32-33.

[72] Electoral figures are available in *Est et ouest*, no. 463 (March 1-15, 1971): 123.

quired by this policy has serious implications for the revolutionary potential of the PCF.

The traditional militant devotes a considerable portion of his efforts to ideological and political education, thereby increasing his fidelity to party goals and preparing him to accept radical shifts in party policy; but the militant involved in local government, particularly in large cities, can rarely afford the time for this purpose. The PCF, of course, is well aware of this difficulty and has undertaken strenuous efforts to circumvent it. But the problem may be too difficult in the long run, even for an organization with the impressive human resources of the PCF. It may eventually be forced to choose between two unpalatable alternatives: to continue the present local strategy and risk losing considerable control over party militants in public office, or to reassert its traditional concern for the continued involvement of its cadres in ideological and political education and risk losing the popular gains of the past few decades. An immediate choice is not necessary since the situation has not yet reached crisis proportions. But the growing concern of Communist leaders, as expressed in the comments of the party official in Givors cited above,[73] reflects their perception of the seriousness of the problem and the urgency with which a solution must be found.

[73] Hincker, "Une Municipalité," p. 18.

PART FOUR

Alliance Strategies

X.

The PCI's Alliance Strategy and the Case of the Middle Classes

STEPHEN HELLMAN

Introduction

Karl Marx may have predicted that capitalist society would neatly polarize into just workers and bourgeois, but he was too subtle a political analyst to ignore the fact that intermediate strata continued to exist, and thus had to be reckoned with by the workers' movement.[1] Ever since Marx, socialist theorists have scrutinized these strata—with little general agreement—hoping to distinguish friends from enemies.

Even though a Marxist analysis of class relations is supposed to provide relatively straightforward criteria for the selection of revolutionary allies, the process is really not so simple. The starting point is the so-called objective interest of a class or group: those who stand to gain most from the creation of a socialist order are the most desirable allies. But not all objectively revolutionary strata are equally important. Some may be growing in size while others stagnate or decline. Still others are more strategically located in the social structure, and some groups are simply more aggressive or combative vis-à-vis the existing system. Numerous strata exist in any society, and the tasks of the revolutionary organization are, first, to define which of them will form part of the revolutionary bloc, and then to make this bloc a reality and guide it to power.

Fieldwork in 1969 was made possible by a grant from the Foreign Area Fellowship Program, and by a supplementary grant from Yale University's Concilium on Comparative and International Studies. Research in 1973 was supported by the York University Minor Research Fund and the Fondazione Mario Einaudi, in Turin, Italy.

[1] The most famous prediction of society's polarization into just two classes is in Karl Marx and Friedrich Engels, *The Manifesto of the Communist Party* (Moscow: Foreign Languages Publishing House, 1966), pp. 52-55. But see, in contrast, Marx's *Critique of the Gotha Programme* (New York: International Publishers, 1970), p. 12.

These revolutionary tasks have proved to be extremely difficult to realize in highly industrialized societies, where traditional intermediate strata often stubbornly continue to exist as new groups develop and proliferate. Italy in particular contains a hodgepodge of social categories, only a few of which are easily defined according to the classical criteria of revolutionary potential. The Partito Comunista Italiano (PCI), aware of these difficulties, claims that it has developed a strategy which responds to Italy's peculiar conditions. The "Italian Road to Socialism" projects the peaceful transformation of Italy into a socialist society by utilizing democratic institutions to impose reforms on a recalcitrant, obtuse ruling class. The precondition for the success of this reform strategy is the construction of a broad system of alliances that cuts deeply into many social strata historically considered hostile to socialism.

This essay will examine the PCI's alliance strategy with respect to those social forces central to the strategy, but not part of traditional Marxist revolutionary alliances. These are the "productive middle strata" (*ceti medi produttivi*), petit bourgeois and capitalist candidates for the construction of socialism. An understanding of their place in the PCI's analysis provides, I feel, a much fuller understanding of the theoretical and practical intricacies of the *via italiana al socialismo*.

I. The Strategy's Background

Postwar Origins

A definitive analysis of the *via italiana* would have to dwell extensively on the PCI's history prior to and during the Second World War, but for our purposes it is sufficient to note that the strategy made an initial, incomplete appearance in the immediate postwar period. The party's definition of allies at that time was extremely broad and inclusive: everyone except monopolists, their coconspirators, and their direct collaborators qualified as potential allies of the proletariat.[2]

So inclusive a formulation may be at odds with the incisive class analysis hypothetically required of a Marxist party, but it

---

[2] Palmiro Togliatti, "Ceto medio e Emilia rossa," speech at Reggio Emilia, September 24, 1946, reprinted in *Critica marxista* 2 (July-October 1964): 102, 132-133.

374

is entirely consistent with the strategy enunciated by the PCI's new leader, Palmiro Togliatti, even prior to the war's end. This consistency flowed from two facts. First, Italy's fragmented and backward economy was totally disrupted by war, and these factors combined to blur considerably any attempt at a systematic class analysis. Second, and even more importantly, the PCI's aim was not to establish socialism immediately, but to make of Italy a "progressive democracy."[3] The party's program was consciously designed to alienate the fewest possible segments of society to enable the entire country to pull together toward postwar reconstruction and the elimination of the last residues of fascism. All parties aligned with the USSR presented similar programs in this period, but few, as we shall see, seem to have taken this program as seriously as did the PCI.

Togliatti was quite sincere when he said that the Communists wished to guarantee "the freedom of small and medium property to develop and grow without being crushed by avid, egoistic groups of plutocrats, that is, by monopoly capitalism."[4] This position represents the clearest illustration of the blend of optimism and pessimism which typified the PCI's postwar position. The optimism is quite easily explained, for the strength of the Left, and the apparent progressiveness of the Democrazia Cristiana (DC), made sweeping solutions to Italy's problems appear deceptively easy following Liberation. But we fail to understand numerous themes in the *via italiana*, particularly where the middle classes are concerned, if we forget that they have their origins in a fundamentally negative and defensive view of events. This defensiveness, or pessimism, is also quite easily explained: fascism had won an early and unequivocal victory in Italy, isolating and crushing the workers' movement. The impact of this experience on the party leadership, and its consequent effect on the party's strategy, cannot be overemphasized.

The full implications of fascism's victory were at first not appreciated by the PCI leadership. Only after much discussion did Togliatti get his colleagues to accept the view that fascism was a reactionary regime with *mass* characteristics. Previously, Mussolini had been viewed as just one more reactionary, not terribly

[3] Ibid., p. 138. See also Togliatti, "Per una costituzione democratica e progressiva," ibid., pp. 220-221.

[4] "La politica di unità nazionale dei comunisti," speech at Naples, April 11, 1944, reprinted in ibid., p. 41.

375

different from his predecessors. The acceptance of Togliatti's interpretation meant that while monopoly capitalism was still blamed for fascism's rise and success, the PCI now also accepted the unpleasant fact that many social strata had cheerfully gone along with the Fascists. Notable among these strata were numerous elements of the lower-middle and middle classes. Dropping its earlier interpretation, which held that only the declassed members of Italian society had followed Mussolini in substantial numbers, the PCI now admitted that the middle and petite bourgeoisie of the cities and countryside had been swept up in the movement.[5]

The middle strata therefore became prime targets in the Communists' postwar plans to deny any nascent reactionary movement a mass base. Right up to his death, Togliatti constantly referred to the defeat of 1922 when he wanted an example of the results of divisions between workers and *ceti medi*.[6] If the middle strata could not be drawn as protagonists into the movement for change and progress—and "progressive democracy" was largely designed to attract more moderate support—they at least should not be antagonized openly. The PCI's postwar optimism could not obscure the party's defensive, and realistic, assessment of the dangers lurking in the Italian social structure.[7]

In fact, whatever optimism the Communists did feel toward the middle classes seems largely to have been misplaced. Liberation brought an end to the often flimsy unity of the Resistance, where moderate and radical anti-Fascists had been able to cooperate only as long as a common foreign enemy was on Italian soil. The PCI understood that nationalism had largely fueled the Resistance, as its postwar slogans indicate: at the same time, it is evident that these slogans did not persuade the middle classes that either the working class or the Communist party were, as claimed, the staunchest defenders of the national interest. Another of Togliatti's arguments after the war was that changed in-

---

[5] Togliatti, "A proposito del fascismo," in Togliatti, *La via italiana al socialismo* (Rome: Editori Riuniti, 1964), pp. 12-13.

[6] Conclusions, *X Congresso del PCI: Atti e risoluzioni* (Rome: Editori Riuniti, 1963), p. 625.

[7] Two representative articles from the postwar period are Antonio Giolitti, "La politica di alleanze della classe operaia e il Fronte democratico popolare," *Rinascita* 5 (January 1948): 7-10, and Giorgio Candeloro, "Il mito della 'mediazione' e la crisi dei ceti medi," *Rinascita* 4 (June 1947): 156-158.

376

ternational conditions, highlighted by the creation of a socialist camp, were a positive sign for progressive forces. But, as his critics pointed out, the existence of peoples' democracies with wholesale policies of nationalization were hardly likely to make a wavering petit bourgeois jump into the PCI's outstretched arms.[8] In fact, the negative general example of the USSR, combined with specific events in Czechoslovakia, helped make the 1948 Italian general elections a case study in the successful exploitation of the middle strata's fear of communism. The Christian Democrats' tactics proved so effective, and the middle strata's fear proved so profound, that an absolute majority was gained by one party in the Italian Parliament for the only time in the history of the Republic.

Reemergence in 1956

Partly developed ideas about a national road to socialism remained in a state of limbo from 1948 to 1956 during the height of the Cold War. With its Eighth Congress in 1956, however, the PCI came forward with a program remarkably similar to the one it originally presented to the Constituent Assembly a decade earlier.[9] The party has never tried to hide this continuity in its strategy. On the contrary, consistency has proved to be one of the PCI's strengths. To cite one important example, commitment to its postwar formulations gave the PCI a line on which to fall back in the confusing and often floundering period which followed Khrushchev's revelations about Stalin at the Twentieth Congress of the Communist Party of the Soviet Union.

But the PCI's very consistency raises intriguing questions about the *via italiana*. Is it possible, for example, to exhume, after a decade, a program designed for a war-shattered, predominantly agricultural society and claim that it applies perfectly to a reconstructed, industrial society? The PCI's references to postwar economic development inevitably emphasize the tremendous social and economic changes Italy has undergone—but the party's basic analysis remains unaltered. In support of its position, the PCI counters that the fundamental characteristic of the Italian

[8] Livio Maitan, *Teoria e politica comunista nel dopoguerra* (Milan: Schwarz, 1959), pp. 130-131.

[9] The definitive version of the PCI's program is in *La dichiarazione programmatica e le Tesi dell'VIII Congresso del PCI* (Rome: Editori Riuniti, 1957), esp. pp. 47-54. For the program at the Constituent Assembly, see Togliatti, "Costituzione democratica," 220-222.

377

system, namely domination by monopoly capitalism, has not changed, and this in turn leaves the primary strategic choice of the party—an antimonopolistic alliance—as valid as ever.

Even if partly true, such statements draw our attention to the PCI's vague and sometimes obscurantist use of terms like "monopolies" and "monopoly state capitalism." Monopolies were singled out as the *real* enemy during fascism, and again after the war; the same diagnosis emerged in 1956, and then was re-iterated with more force than ever following the "Economic Miracle" which began in the late fifties. A revolutionary theory which supposedly rests on the analysis of a country's "objective conditions" should change significantly as those conditions alter. It should at least undergo careful reassessment. But the PCI has peremptorily reconfirmed its alliance strategy at every turn, even though the span of time described above clearly covers a wide variety of economic phases, and indeed historical epochs.[10]

The place of the *ceti medi* in the PCI's post-1956 strategy appeared to be more solid than ever. The party's analysis is worth quoting at length:

> With the aggravated subordination of the entire Italian economy to monopolistic groups and, concurrently, with the increasingly crushing control of these groups over the distribution and circulation of goods, as well as on the productive process itself, new social strata find themselves *objectively interested in a socialist transformation* of our society.
>
> In the cities as in the countryside, millions of small and medium producers see their enterprises' margins of independence and security reduced. They see them becoming subsidiary to the monopolies, geared to serve the end of maximizing the monopolies' profits. There is, therefore, an objective concordance of aims developing between the working class, which is struggling to defeat capitalism, and no longer only the proletarian and semiproletarian masses, but the bulk of agrarian smallholders and an important part of the productive middle strata in the cities. . . .
>
> While a differentiated analysis from sector to sector is still needed, the possibility of a *permanent alliance* of the working

[10] The Programmatic Declaration "reaffirms" the original postwar analysis: *Dichiarazione programmatica*, p. 39. Another assertion more than ten years after this one is the political document, *XII Congresso del PCI: Atti e risoluzioni* (Rome: Editori Riuniti, 1969), p. 783.

class with urban and rural strata of the middle classes is determined by a convergence which grows out of the historical development and the present structure of Italian capitalism. The weight of the monopolies on the economy is so suffocating that even nonmonopolistic groups of productive and commercial enterprises find it in their interest to flank and support the antimonopolistic struggle of the proletariat.[11]

The growth of the monopolies' domination appears to have reversed the rationale which makes the middle strata potential allies of the workers. After the war, to calm their fears of nationalization the *ceti medi* were assured by the PCI that socialism was *not* on the agenda. They are now objectively interested in a socialist transformation of Italy, which will provide the independence and security previously promised by "progressive democracy."

These may be unorthodox projections, but they cannot be dismissed as tactical maneuvers. The PCI's strategy since 1956 has gradually evolved in a direction which does seem to promise the middle strata a "permanent alliance" with the working class. Although it is not always clear whether one is talking about progressive democracy or some variant of socialism, the party has been firm in its insistence that small property will remain in Italy. Following the Eighth Congress, the analysis emphasized that it would be a very long time before small and medium property were called into question.[12] Since the 1960s, the claim seems, rather, to be that even a full-fledged socialist economy can and should be pluralistic and tolerate small property within the context of a controlled market. The notion that the *ceti medi* are merely tactical allies is sharply rejected, and party leaders insist that these strata are strategic allies of the working class.[13]

The PCI thus forecasts a mixed economy, largely to avoid the hypercentralization and inefficient production and distribution of consumer goods that characterizes the USSR and other socialist countries. But while the PCI defends a role for small pro-

[11] *Dichiarazione programmatica*, pp. 30-31. Emphasis added.
[12] See Togliatti's addresses to the Eighth and Ninth Congresses of the PCI, reprinted in *Nella democrazia e nella pace verso il socialismo* (Rome: Editori Riuniti, 1963), pp. 46, 148.
[13] Emilio Sereni, "Blocco storico e iniziativa politica nell'elaborazione gramsciana e nella politica del PCI," *Storia politica organizzazione nella lotta dei comunisti italiani per un nuovo blocco storico.* Quaderno no. 5 of *Critica marxista* (Supplement, 1972), pp. 14-15.

379

ducers, it is an error to claim that it favors unfettered individualistic, rather than cooperative, development in such spheres as
agriculture or commerce.[14] In fact, the party is on record since
1956 with the claim that small firms will be able to survive economically only if they band together in cooperative or associative forms.[15] Communists regularly present legislative proposals
which support the operation or creation of associative producing
and distributing units, and it uses these initiatives as proof of its
goodwill toward the intermediate strata. At the same time, the
party's intiatives and proposals do tend to be quite opportunistic.
For instance, legislative proposals usually call for benefits to entrepreneurs, peasants, or shopkeepers be they single *or* associated. And the PCI still falls back on the most generic appeals to
specific groups, e.g., "no to the supermarkets" for merchants and
shopkeepers, and "the land to those who till it" for landless
peasants.

The criticisms that this gradualist and apparently moderate
strategy would draw obviously did not escape the party leadership's attention. Togliatti always took pains to distinguish the *via
italiana* from traditional social-democratic reformism. He argued
that no reform, however important, can be seen in isolation: truly
radical changes depend not only on what the PCI achieves, but
on *how* it achieves it. Essential to the realization of any reform,
for instance, is the degree of mass mobilization behind the demand for change. Italy's socialist transformation, in this view,
will be a process which can only grow out of a mass movement
in constant battle with the existing system. This is no gradual,
piecemeal approach to socialism. On the contrary, as political
and social struggle intensifies, the movement generates ever-
more-radical demands for *further* changes. This persistent,
escalating process is what denies the ruling classes the ability
to consolidate their position or absorb reforms granted under
pressure, for it keeps them constantly off balance and restricts
their maneuvering room.[16]

---

[14] Jon Halliday, "Structural Reform in Italy—Theory and Practice," *New
Left Review* 50 (July-August 1968): 89, offers this interpretation in an
otherwise penetrating analysis of the PCI in the 1960s.

[15] *Dichiarazione programmatica*, pp. 32, 43; Togliatti, Eighth Congress
Address, p. 46, and Ninth Congress Address, pp. 141-142.

[16] Togliatti, Eighth Congress Address, p. 52; Ninth Congress Address,
p. 146; an excellent synthetic statement is his "Capitalismo e riforme di
struttura," in *Via italiana*, pp. 263-268.

These are all important qualifications, but it is clear that many serious problems remain in the PCI's alliance strategy, and these have, on occasion, given rise to extensive ideological disputes within the party. Perhaps the most significant challenge to the strategy arose in the early 1960s when the PCI was undergoing a good deal of ideological self-examination. In the face of the "Economic Miracle" and the first Center-Left coalitions, a number of Communists, especially those identified with the party's left wing (including many union leaders) began to question the PCI's mechanical application of postwar formulas to contemporary economic conditions. They argued that monopolistic expansion had wrought changes so profound in Italy that the PCI often did not grasp their full importance. In this view, Italy's economic and social structure had undergone transformations which made many of the *new* intermediate strata more important to the workers' goals than those groups traditionally singled out by the party as allies.[17] By holding to its old postwar formula, the PCI was pursuing an essentially conservative policy, lumping together everyone with a complaint against the existing state of affairs. This lack of discrimination is potentially self-defeating, for various social strata oppose the drift of contemporary capitalism for many reasons, not all of which are progressive (e.g., Poujadism in France), and many of which are contradictory. The PCI's primary responsibility was therefore seen in terms of appealing to those who are genuinely capable of forming a progressive bloc of forces for the construction of socialism.

The PCI's response to this critique presaged the way it would deal with all such attacks on its lack of precision in defining allies. The party argued that this leftist position reduces everything to a schematic worker-boss conflict, which is too sectarian and too exclusively concerned with the working class. Such an approach, in spite of its claims to be more in touch with modern developments, is thus in reality simply a return to old simplistic arguments.[18] These accusations against an orientation which relies

---

[17] The most coherent criticism is Bruno Trentin, "Le dottrine neocapitalistiche e l'ideologia delle forze dominanti nella politica economica italiana," in *Tendenze del capitalismo italiano*, 2 vols. (Rome: Editori Riuniti, 1962), 1: 141-143. This two-volume set of the proceedings of a PCI-sponsored conference held early in 1962 is an excellent source for the Communists'—and the Italian Left's—reactions to the "Economic Miracle" and the Center-Left's beginnings.

[18] See, e.g., the conclusions of Giorgio Amendola in ibid., 1: 423, 426-427.

heavily or exclusively on the working class struck, and continue to strike, sympathetic chords in the party, since so many union leaders are found among critics of the alliance strategy. In addition, the party leadership found it easy to isolate many of the critics on its left wing because they often seemed to argue that *only* developments in the most advanced sectors of society were any longer relevant to Italy. This position implicitly relegated crucial issues like the north-south division of the country to the background, or even to the dustbin.[19]

If ably handled, the PCI's response also skirted or dismissed the central point in criticisms which accuse it of casting its net too wide in the search for allies. The fundamental issue here is the distinction between *strategic* alliances and *numerical* alliances, and the PCI seems unwilling to recognize such a distinction. The internal Left, in spite of the tenor of the PCI's rebuttal, was not calling for a single-handed workers' revolution: alliances were proposed between the proletariat and white-collar workers, technicians, most employees in the service sector, elements of the traditional *petite bourgeoisie*, and, latterly, students. This is hardly an overly exclusive formula. Moreover, the most coherent critics of the party's postwar formula did not automatically exclude the traditional *ceti medi* as allies, but demanded a reexamination of these groups' potentialities under contemporary conditions. The PCI, however, has always adamantly resisted any such reexaminations.

It is tempting to write off this rigidity as proof of the PCI's inability, in spite of its claims to the contrary, to analyze the Italian economy adequately. But this is a simplistic temptation. It is more useful to understand the party leadership's inability or unwillingness to confront the flaws in its economic analysis as a reflection of the *political* motives that dictate the party's economic choices. A Marxist party's political decisions are supposed to be based on an economic analysis, but the PCI has been remarkably consistent in its reversal of these priorities. In spite of increasingly infrequent phrases about the construction of socialism, the PCI's overtures to the middle strata are based on exquisitely political (anti-Fascist) and not economic (anticapitalist) considera-

---

[19] For arguments from a leading exponent of the PCI "Left" which seem to put all the emphasis on new developments, see Lucio Magri, "Il valore e il limite delle esperienze frontiste," *Critica marxista* 3 (July-August 1965): esp. 57-63.

tions. Because of these considerations, the PCI has consistently defined *first* the bloc of forces it wishes to see established and *only then* has the party elaborated the specific strategic aims to be achieved by the bloc. The alliance strategy, and the often garbled portrayal of the monopolies' role in Italy, are both direct consequences of the PCI's commitment to the broadest possible system of alliances that can be achieved among Italy's traditional intermediate strata. The party's fear of the Left's isolation has committed it to bring together an extremely heterogeneous grouping of strata and interests. The party's economic language, as a consequence, must necessarily use terms as loose and imprecise as an "antimonopolistic alliance" which, as we will see, can sometimes lead to strange and even embarrassing situations.

II. Some Aspects of the Middle Strata's Structure and Behavior

"New" and "Old" Strata

As the debates of the early 1960s demonstrate, the PCI's claim that its strategy represents an up-to-date analysis of advanced capitalism appears particularly weak with regard to the party's view of the middle strata. Far from embarking on a specific analysis of the strata that are spawned by mature capitalist development (technical, white-collar, and research-related jobs), the PCI has simply enlarged its long-standing interpretation of the traditional middle strata to include these new groups. The primacy of the older strata is evident in the party's statistics as well as in its program. In the period between 1962 and 1971, for instance, technical and clerical employees had increased their share of the PCI's total membership, but they had risen to only 3.4 percent of all party members.[20] The broadest possible definition of the new strata in the PCI's membership—one which lumps together *all* professionals and intellectuals, students, technicians, and white-collar employees—brings us to only 5.5 percent of the membership. At the same time, as Table 1 shows, members from the traditional sectors of the urban middle classes

[20] All references to 1962 PCI membership figures in this article are drawn from PCI, *Dati sull'organizzazione del PCI* (Rome: Visigalli-Pasetti, 1964); references to 1971 statistics come from PCI, *Dati sull'organizzazione* (1972). These are the PCI's official statistics, published regularly at the time of national congresses or organizational conferences.

383

comprise a much larger proportion of the total membership than do the more modern *ceti medi*. It should also be pointed out that artisans and shopkeepers have increased their share of the total by 2.4 percent since 1962.

TABLE 1. Social Composition of PCI Membership, 1971

Social Category	Total Membership (%)	Subtotals (%)
Workers	39.51	47.51
Agricultural Wage-Earners	8.00	
Peasants*	9.69	
Artisans	4.63	17.34
Shopkeepers, Small Businessmen	3.02	
Technical and Clerical Employees	3.35	
Students	1.15	5.46
Teachers, Professionals, Intellectuals	0.96	
Housewives	12.57	
Pensioners	14.94	29.69
Others	2.18	
Total	100.00	
(N =)	(1,521,631)	

*Includes smallholders, renters, tenant-farmers, sharecroppers, etc.

Source: Sezione Centrale di Organizzazione della Direzione del PCI, *Dati sulla organizzazione del Partito* (Rome: ITER, 1972), pp. 4 and 42.

What explains the PCI's poor showing among these new strata and the slowness with which it has turned its attention to them? These are, of course, complex and heterogeneous groups which have long defied analysis.[21] But the PCI's analysis has been lax even when viewed in this context. In fact, the Parti Communiste Français (PCF), which usually is viewed as much less analyti-

[21] Much disagreement exists among contemporary Marxists, with some writers resisting the notion of "intermediate strata" altogether in favor of calling these categories "groups" or "fractions" of the *petite bourgeoisie*. See, for example, Nicos Poulantzas, "On Social Classes," *New Left Review* 78 (March-April 1973): esp. 37-43. A Marxist synthesis of various interpretations of "new intermediate strata," on the other hand, is in Marcello Lelli, *Tecnici e lotta di classe* (Bari: Laterza, 1973), pp. 58-86. A non-Marxist perspective with many of the same major points can be found in Antonio Carbonaro, *L'Italia cambia: Problemi di una società in transizione* (Florence: La Nuova Italia, 1971), Chapter 3.

384

cally acute than its Italian counterpart, appears to have faced this issue more successfully than the PCI.[22] In part because of its more schematic analyses of the past, and in part because it faces a blatantly reactionary segment of the traditional middle classes (shopkeepers), the PCF has not been distracted by the older strata in the same fashion as the PCI. Moreover, France is industrially more advanced than Italy, and there is a heavy concentration of industry in the area around Paris, which is the site of the PCF's headquarters and its greatest concentration of organizational strength. For all these reasons, the French party was probably forced to confront advanced industrial developments more rapidly than the Italian party.

The relevance of these factors becomes apparent as soon as we compare the PCI's experience to that of the PCF. Systematic efforts to analyze the new intermediate strata are beginning to appear in the PCI, and significantly these initiatives center around Turin, the home of many of Italy's industrial giants and, consequently, a center with a highly evolved and stratified work force.[23] Turin has been one of the PCI's advanced outposts from the earliest days of the party, but it is far from Rome and it cannot claim a large party organization. In fact, to find the PCI's greatest concentration of strength—and the area where it is most successful among the middle strata—we must look to central Italy's Red Belt. Because of its success in this area, the PCI has quite naturally looked to the Red Belt when it formulates its policies toward the *ceti medi*. And, in purely economic terms, the large traditional sector and the small and medium industries of

[22] See Jean Ranger, "Le Parti communiste français et les changements sociaux depuis la deuxième guerre mondiale" (Paper prepared for the conference on which this volume is based). Since the French term *"employé"* is used in a much broader sense than the Italian *tecnico* and *impiegato*, one should use extreme caution when comparing French and Italian party statistics. Still, it is revealing that PCF membership figures show 18.5 percent of the membership listed as *employés*. Figures reported in Guy Lord, "Le PCF: Structures et organisation d'une fédération départmentale" (Paper delivered at the Workshop on Communism in Western Europe, Paris, 1973), p. 11.

[23] The Piedmontese Regional Committee of the PCI is establishing the first ongoing analytical and organizational initiative in the party toward the new strata; see Comitato Regionale Piemontese del PCI, "Documento per la costruzione della commissione regionale piemontese: 'Ricerca, impiegati, tecnici,'" mimeographed (Turin, 1973). Turin also hosted a PCI conference on "Science and the Organization of Work" in 1973; the major addresses and a summary can be found in "Il Contemporaneo," *Rinascita* 30 (June 29, 1973).

the Red Belt are more representative of the Italian social structure than are the massive factories and urban concentrations of the north. But these small industries do not proliferate technical and clerical strata the way the larger firms do. Thus, to the extent that the PCI focused its attention on the Red Belt and its "typical" industrial structure, it often overlooked the growth and diversification of new social strata which accompany advanced industrial growth.

Geography and "red" traditions are not the only reasons for the PCI's tardy notice of the new strata. Throughout the 1950s and early 1960s, technical and supervisory staff were used extensively in Italy as management's agents in repressive campaigns against the organized workers' movement. This has resulted in extremely hostile feelings on both sides, and militants and leaders understandably are reluctant to accept yesterday's policeman as tomorrow's comrade-in-arms.

Finally, consistent with its attention to political rather than economic factors, the PCI has courted artisans, shopkeepers, and smallholders more actively because of the institutionally privileged position of these groups in Italian society. Because of their historic size and importance, Italian law recognizes these groups as special, and it provides them with specialized institutions and representative organs (the most important example of which would be Mutual Funds).[24] These strata are also relatively well organized, and the PCI's abilities and preferences make it most comfortable on the terrain of formally organized institutional interests. The new strata, in contrast, rarely enjoy either the special legislative status or the organized political leverage of the older, more established groups.

The foregoing helps us understand the PCI's slowness and suspicion in making overtures to the new intermediate strata. One consequence of this circumspection is a caution and subtlety in the party's initial efforts at analyzing these strata which is gen-

---

[24] Sectoral Mutual Funds (*Casse Mutue*) exist for the peasants, artisans, and merchants, among the groups we are examining here. These funds, on a provincial basis, regularly elect administrative councils which then administer state medical insurance and assistance plans. Candidates' lists follow political lines, and the PCI and PSI generally present a single list representing one of their unitary mass organizations. For a fuller discussion, see Joseph LaPalombara, *Interest Groups in Italian Politics* (Princeton: Princeton University Press, 1963), pp. 241-243.

386

erally missing in the PCI's examination of other social groups.[25] Far from lumping these modern groups together indiscriminately, the party takes pains to point out the degree to which the new strata are internally differentiated and stratified. Factors such as education, ideological predispositions, and life styles are all considered to be of great importance, and it is frankly admitted that none of these will make worker–white-collar *rapprochement* any easier.

As with the PCF, the PCI's political fortunes with the new strata have taken their most spectacular turns in relation to students and the various student movements of the country. The Italian Communists originally handled the students with much greater dispatch and sensitivity in 1968 than did their French comrades, but the courtship was brief and the relationship soon degenerated.[26] By the end of 1969, with only a few exceptions, the PCI's Federazione Giovanile Comunista Italiana (FGCI) and the student movement had disappeared from Italy's universities and secondary schools. The PCI managed to recoup its losses over the next few years, but extraparliamentary leftist groups reappeared in the schools along with PCI sections and FGCI organizations. The *extraparlamentari*, who are often extremely sectarian and dogmatic, constantly attack the "revisionist" PCI. The Communists, in turn, try to maintain a healthy, and polemical, distance from the groups.[27] While this situation has not seriously damaged the PCI's organization in the schools, one often now finds ultra-leftists outnumbering FGCI activists in medium and large cities. It is difficult to judge the long-run implications of this situation: for the first time, the PCI must accept the fact that it has nowhere near a monopoly on the youth who want to fight "the system."

Relations with other groups have not been so dramatic, but concrete evidence of improved worker–white-collar relations has been slow to appear. Even where the PCI has made significant

[25] The discussion that follows paraphrases the analysis in *Documento per la costruzione*.

[26] Luigi Longo, "Il movimento studentesco nella lotta anticapitalistica," *Rinascita* 25 (May 3, 1968): 13-16, signaled the PCI's "open phase" in its relationship with the student movement.

[27] A selection of articles which gives a contemporary history of the PCI's relationship with extraparliamentary groups and the student movement in several important cities is "Inchiesta sui gruppi estremisti," *Rinascita* 29 (February 25, 1972): 13-26.

387

headway recruiting workers into its ranks—in the wake of labor's "Hot Autumn" of 1969, which included important and often unprecedented episodes of white-collar militance—there have been no breakthroughs with nonproletarian categories in the same plants.[28]

In spite of continuing difficulties, the PCI has some reasons for optimism about its future relationship with a number of the more modern *ceti medi*. Unionization is increasing among technical and white-collar employees, and party leaders hope that this eventually will improve the PCI's poor showing. PCI leaders with experience in the factories also point favorably to the younger generations of technicians and clerks, for they find them much less prejudiced and more militant than their elders. They also point to important contract victories in the early 1970s, such as the abolition of differential pay raises for white- and blue-collar workers in key industries. The Communists, and the unions, hope that such developments will eventually force the intermediate strata to realize that they are not privileged, and must cast their lot with the workers.

Another positive factor is that, with all their problems of stratification and bourgeois values, the new intermediate strata pose many fewer theoretical problems to the construction of a socialist alliance than do the bulk of the traditional middle classes. Most of the new strata are salaried employees in the center of the productive process, and it is significant that reference is usually made to *unity* between workers, technicians, and clerks, and not simply to alliances. Whatever their problems, in other words, these groups, in theory, have a genuinely objective interest in socialism.

Ironically, so much of the PCI's attention has been spent theorizing about the continued existence of the *traditional* middle strata that the party has been extremely vague about the contours of a socialist Italy and the special status that the *new* strata might enjoy because of their place in the productive process. In fact, the party's official statements are often strangely reserved when they refer to the modern strata. Care is always taken to

[28] In Italy's largest factory, Fiat's Mirafiori plant in Turin, the PCI in 1973 had more than quadrupled its membership since 1968, passing from just over two hundred to just under a thousand. But while there are thousands of white-collar employees at Mirafiori, the PCI had only *eleven* of them in its ranks in Mirafiori's party organizations. Figures provided by the Turinese Federation of the PCI, June 1973.

underscore that not only objective location but also attitudes toward the working class must be considered when assessing
groups as potential allies: "Ideology, culture, and political orientations all play *an autonomous role* in the formation of any system of alliances."[29] This is an extremely powerful and perhaps
necessary qualification—but one will search in vain for similar
statements in the PCI's references to the traditional *ceti medi*.

If the growth of her new strata makes Italy typical of advanced
industrial societies, the continued importance of her traditional
strata makes Italy quite exceptional. The traditional *ceti medi* in
Italy depart from the presumed logic of mature capitalism: they
remain much larger than similar classes in other advanced capitalist societies, and some sectors, like commerce, actually show
signs of expansion. Because these groups are so important to the
PCI's alliance strategy, we need to examine them, and the PCI's
analysis of them, more closely.

THE RURAL MIDDLE CLASSES

Although the agricultural sector of the Italian economy is in
decline, it remains quite large, employing one-fifth of the active
population. We can see from Table 2 that by far the largest form
of land tenure is the family farm, which accounts for 86 percent
of those occupied in agriculture, and nearly 60 percent of the cultivated land. We can also see the dramatic decline of sharecropping and rental forms of tenure, which has all but eliminated
the PCI's only natural middle-class constituency in the fields.
Finally, Table 2 shows us that commercial firms, in spite of occasional PCI rhetoric to the contrary, are not "gobbling up" either
the land or the smallholders.

What these figures do not show is the full dimensions of Italy's
chronic inability to produce enough food. In 1971, Italy imported
over $2.5 billion in foodstuffs, and the total rises to over $3.25
billion when livestock is included.[30] The large farming population, and the dimensions of the agricultural crisis, make the
smallholders prime targets in the PCI's scheme of alliances. In its
appeals to small farmers, the party has set forth an extremely
large number of proposals, ranging from minor remedies for spe-

[29] Enrico Berlinguer, "Per rinnovare l'Italia, per la pace, per la liberazione
di tutti i popoli oppressi dall'imperialismo," Speech in preparation for the
XIII Congress of the PCI (Rome: Fratelli Spada, n.d.), p. 30.
[30] Banco Nacional de Comercio Exterior, *Comercio Exterior de México*
(May 1973), p. 31.

389

cific crops all the way up to projects for massive state intervention in selected primary areas of production.[31] The crisis is real enough, but the combined legacy of the sector's inefficiency plus the neglect it has suffered make it difficult to imagine how favorite PCI themes like "the revitalization of agriculture" or "persuade the youth to return to the land" can be realized. The Communists do little to clarify matters when they drag out gross statistics which show how many people have left the land over time. More useful, but so far not forthcoming, would be realistic estimates about the number of people, now or in the future, that Italy's agricultural structure could genuinely support.

TABLE 2. TYPE, NUMBER, AND EXTENSION OF ITALIAN AGRICULTURAL FIRMS IN 1961 AND 1970 (*in thousands of units*)

| | TYPE OF FIRM | | | | | | | |
| | SMALLHOLDING | | COMMERCIAL | | SHARECROP OR RENTAL | | TOTALS | |
Year	No.	Hectares	No.	Hectares	No.	Hectares	No.	Hectares
1961	3,486	13,218 $(\overline{X} = 3.8)$	330	9,160 $(\overline{X} = 27.8)$	478	4,194	4,294	26,572
1970	3,131	14,645 $(\overline{X} = 4.7)$	276	8,466 $(\overline{X} = 30.7)$	207	1,795	3,614	24,946
Net Change	−355	+1,467	−54	−694	−271	−2,399	−680	−1,626

SOURCE: ISTAT figures cited in Luigi Conte, *Aspetti storici ed attuali della questione agraria in Italia e la politicia del PCI* (Edizioni Clust: Florence, 1972), p. 42.

But even the immense technical complications pale in comparison to the *political* difficulties the PCI faces in attempting to woo small farmers. If there was ever a case where Berlinguer's dictum about "the autonomous role of ideology and political affiliation" applied—negatively—to a potential ally, it applies to Italy's smallholders. Small farmers have rarely been amenable to leftist politics, and these moderate predispositions have been reinforced in Italy by the Church's active social and political role in areas where smallholding has historically been predominant.[32] Peasant

[31] See Luigi Conte, *Aspetti storici ed attuali della questione agraria in Italia e la politica del P.C.I.* (Florence: Edizioni Clust, 1972), p. 42, for a discussion of some of the PCI's major reform proposals in agriculture.

[32] Alan Stern, Chapter 6 in this volume, discusses the background and mechanisms of the DC's legitimacy in Italy's "White Zones."

allegiance to the Church, and by extension the Democrazia Cristiana (DC), is also organizationally reinforced by an associational network which extends into every aspect of the peasants' lives. At the center of this network is the Association of Direct Cultivators (*Coldiretti*), which is notorious for its often hysterically anti-Communist and antiworker positions.[33] PCI leaders in rural areas complain that the *Coldiretti's* hold on the smallholders is so great that it can do as it wishes politically, for it inevitably manages to recuperate peasant support by delivering the goods and services on which they depend.

The PCI's decision to appeal to the smallholders in a concerted fashion, given their natural and reinforced moderatism, seriously limits the Communists' ability to maneuver on many agricultural questions. One often finds the PCI intervening to moderate demands from groups which are the party's natural agricultural allies (e.g., landless day-laborers) when these demands threaten to divide the broad rural coalition the PCI wishes to create.[34] Of course, the agricultural proletariat is sometimes intransigent, but the PCI discourages an aggressive stance which might alienate potential support from more moderate strata.

An outside observer is hard pressed to reconcile this behavior with even something as imprecise and blurred as an antimonopolist alliance. Obviously, such behavior not only has nothing to do with a class strategy in the fields, but it often runs counter to such a strategy. In light of these considerations, what is striking is not that the party has taken a basically opportunistic position on the agrarian question, but that it has done so with such an egregious lack of success. All of the evidence indicates that the PCI is extremely weak among smallholders; estimates and surveys alike rarely attribute more than 10 percent of this group's support to the Communists in elections.[35] The PCI does enjoy broader smallholding support in the Red Belt, and especially in Emilia-Romagna, but much of the smallholding peasantry here is of

[33] LaPalombara, in *Interest Groups*, discusses the *Coldiretti* and its structure of power and patronage through the 1950s.

[34] Examples from the south are cited by Sidney Tarrow, "The Political Economy of Stagnation: Communism in Southern Italy, 1960-1970," *The Journal of Politics* 34 (February 1972): 110-111.

[35] In addition to Giacomo Sani, Chapter 12 in this volume, see also Mattei Dogan, "Political Cleavage and Social Stratification in France and Italy," in Seymour Martin Lipset and Stein Rokkan (eds.), *Party Systems and Voter Alignments* (New York: The Free Press, 1967), p. 150.

sharecropping or day-laboring origin. But even this fact, and the party's extended social presence in Emilia, do not prevent the PCI-PSI (Partito Socialista Italiano) Peasant Alliance from being overwhelmed by the *Coldiretti* in provincial Mutual Fund elections. In leftist strongholds, the Peasant Alliance usually gets around 30 percent of the Mutual Fund vote; in Italy as a whole, it obtains just under 10 percent.[36] Finally, while the rural *ceti medi* still account for a significant percentage of the PCI's total membership, this proportion has declined steeply over time, from 16.3 percent in 1962 to 9.7 percent in 1971. Moreover, the bulk of the rural middle classes in the PCI are renters or sharecroppers, and not smallholders.[37]

THE COMMERCIAL MIDDLE CLASSES

The commercial and agricultural sectors of the Italian economy are similar in that both are highly fragmented and inefficient, and both are generally fiercely anti-Communist. But the commercial sector is growing. The 1971 census counted 930,000 retail commercial outlets, an increase of 100,000 in a decade; two-thirds of these outlets handle food or clothing and other dry goods; of 1.2 million commercial firms of all types, over a million employ two people or fewer.[38] Ironically, the only class of vendors among whom the PCI enjoys broad support—ambulatory vendors—declined between censuses, while all others increased.[39] The large total number and small individual size of Italy's commercial outlets make the inefficiency and built-in inflationary aspects of this sector self-explanatory.

For the PCI, the problems of the commercial sector are traceable to two fundamental causes. The *commercianti* are seen as

[36] Luigi Arbizzani, "Tradizioni socialiste e problemi attuali del movimento contadino emiliano," *Critica marxista* 8 (January-April 1970): 327.

[37] The PCI's official statistics for 1968 (*Dati sull'organizzazione*, p. 35) were the last in which smallholders were distinguished from sharecroppers, tenant farmers, and the like; in 1967, of the 12.4 percent of the PCI membership drawn from the rural *ceti medi*, 5 percent were smallholders.

[38] ISTAT (Istituto Centrale di Statistica), *Unità locali e addetti: Dati provvisori* 1, Book 1 (Rome: 1972): 1.

[39] Ambulatory outlets in commerce decreased from 156,000 to 124,700 between censuses (ibid.). PCI support is always greatest in the lowest-status groups of each social stratum; see Gianfranco Poggi, *Le preferenze politiche degli italiani* (Bologna: Società Editrice Il Mulino, 1968), Chapters 1, 2, and 3. For specific evidence about ambulatory vendors, see PCI (Fed. di Bologna), "Associazionismo e alleanze sociali," mimeographed (Bologna: PCI, 1973), p. 24.

increasingly under pressure from monopolist encroachment in the form of supermarkets and department stores. Because the largest chain stores are indeed financed by some of Italy's industrial giants like Montedison and Fiat, the party can, in this case, point its finger at monopoly capital with a good deal of accuracy. At the same time, although chain stores are rapidly expanding, they control only a tenth of the retail market, and thus it is inadequate to blame them alone.[40] The PCI does not, in fact, blame only the chain stores; it also attacks commercial wholesalers and intermediaries. These groups, irrespective of their links to large industrial or financial groups, create monopolistic or oligopolistic conditions within the commercial sector. As middlemen, they also occupy, by definition, parasitical positions in the economy as they drive prices up and line their own pockets in the process. Wholesalers, of whom there were 93,000 in 1971 (an increase of 10,000 in a decade), are the Communists' special *bête noire* of commerce along with the monopolies.[41]

The party's general defense of small shopkeepers is, on its face, persuasive. Retailers generally absorb the brunt of consumers' fury during inflationary periods, and since workers and other "popular forces" are also consumers, the PCI is extremely sensitive to the strains that are created in a proposed alliance which includes shopkeepers. The party therefore argues that consumer anger is misdirected when it strikes out at small merchants, for they are only the nearest link in the distribution chain: the really large price increases take place much closer to the point of production or importation, and it is here that reform is needed. With reason, the PCI argues that the shopkeeper who raises the price of an item by a few lire can hardly be compared to the wholesaler or importer who blithely doubles or triples the price of the original product. In response to these abuses, as in other sectors, the PCI claims that only an extensive cooperative and associative network can simultaneously rationalize the market, eliminate middlemen, guarantee the existence of the merchants, and stop the encroachment of the chain stores.

This fairly straightforward argument sidesteps several crucial

[40] Gianni DiStefano, *Ceti medi urbani nella politica del PCI: Lezioni all'Istituto Togliatti* (Rome: Salemi, 1972), p. 11. Given its status as a text for party cadres, this book is a revealing document, full of distorted statistics and fuzzy economic analyses.

[41] The figures come from ISTAT, *Unità locali.*

problems. However much the primary blame may lie with large-scale speculators, it is deceptive to argue—as the party always does in inflationary periods—that shopkeepers should not be blamed for rising prices just because a few of them are dishonest and try to exploit the situation. The question is not whether the PCI, for its own political ends, minimizes the speculative nature of shopkeepers. It is, instead, whether a distribution network with 900,000 retail outlets contributes to inflation. The answer, which the PCI avoids facing squarely, is that it obviously does. Co-operatives and associations could theoretically come to dominate the commercial sector, but as long as so many people earn their living selling necessary goods, price problems will remain. Theoretically—and not only theoretically, since the PCI attracts the more marginal elements in all social strata—the cooperatives could play a regressive role in the economy by providing marginal vendors with a toehold they otherwise would not have. Some party leaders, mindful of these problems, will admit privately that the commercial sector needs to be streamlined and that the cooperatives and the party cannot simply defend the small shopkeepers' interests. Thus far, there are few indications that the party's short-term interests have been outweighed by the more rational demands of the long run.

Some of the party's problems undoubtedly are a reflection of its weakness among shopkeepers, and its desire to increase its presence among these strata. As in the case of the smallholders, powerful ideological and organizational obstacles stand in the PCI's way. Table 1 shows that shopkeepers and small business-men together account for 3 percent of the party's total member-ship. This proportion increased by a percentage point in a dec-ade, but it is very low. In Mutual Fund elections among merchants, the Left obtains many votes from ambulatory vendors, but no one else. Even in the Red Belt, the DC-PLI (Partito Liberale Italiano) shopkeepers' association regularly and over-whelmingly outpolls the PCI-PSI organization. In the nation as a whole, it is estimated that only 15 percent of the shopkeepers, at most, vote for the PCI in general elections.[42]

THE ARTISANS AND SMALL AND MEDIUM INDUSTRIALISTS

The term "artisan" implies craftsmanship, but in modern Italy it refers to a legal classification which embraces 1.2 million small

[42] Poggi, *Preferenze politiche*, p. 47; Sani, Chapter 12 in this volume.

firms. This status is determined by a firm's characteristics, e.g., number of employees, gross sales, labor-capital ratio, and so on. In the usage of the PCI, and most other parties in Italy, "artisan plants" are those with ten or fewer employees; "small industry," equally imprecise, is generally applied to firms with between ten and a hundred employees, while "large industry" generally begins at five hundred employees.

Italy's industrial sector grew by more than 100,000 firms between censuses, and most of this growth came in construction and related industries. The trends in manufacturing industries, by far the most important branch of industry, employing 80 percent of all industrial workers, are reported in Table 3. Most notable is the fact that small plants showed the largest relative growth and continue to employ the largest proportion of the manufacturing work force.

TABLE 3. Trends in Italian Manufacturing Industries: Size of Firms and Number of Employees, 1961-1971

| | NUMBER OF PLANTS | | NUMBER OF EMPLOYEES | | PERCENT OF EMPLOYEES | |
| | | | (in thousands of units) | | 1961 | 1971 |
Size of Firm	1961	1971	1961	1971	(%)	(%)
Over 500	772	907	966.3	1229.3	21.51	23.25
100-499	4,821	5,977	970.9	1176.2	21.59	22.25
10-99	45,409	61,808	1300.1	1647.3	28.91	31.36
Under 10	557,974	559,043	1258.2	1233.9	27.99	23.34
Totals	608,976	631,408	4495.6	5286.7	100.00	100.00

Sources: For 1961: ISTAT, 4º Censimento Generale dell'Industria e Commercio (Rome, 1963), pp. 34-35. For 1971: ISTAT, Unità locali e addetti: Dati provvisori, Vol. I, Book I (Rome, 1972), p. 1.

Even a glance at the table demonstrates that small and very small firms are an integral part of Italy's industrial structure. Of 631,000 manufacturing enterprises, 99 percent have fewer than a hundred employees; these small and very small firms account for 54.5 percent of the total manufacturing work force. Such impressive figures appear to support the PCI's arguments about Italy's peculiar conditions: the evidence certainly demonstrates that small producers can survive and even expand in circumstances such as those in Italy. As we know, these circumstances also lead the PCI to argue that the smaller firms should join them in opposing the monopolies which dominate the economy.

But does the fact that the small producers exist under these circumstances really make them allies—or even potential supporters —of the workers they employ? Does it mean that *all* small producers are the workers' potential allies or supporters? Does not the proliferation or at least persistence of small industrial firms— or small commercial enterprises for that matter—suggest the need for a more careful analysis of the dynamics of Italian capitalism? The evidence increasingly suggests a very complex relationship between Italy's small and large firms: small industrial (and commercial) firms, while generally inefficient, absorb large plants' "spillover" and serve to hide a lot of structural unemployment and underemployment; many small plants are directly spawned by larger ones to simplify production and decrease labor costs. As one critic of the party's position on small producers put it, how can the PCI speak of providing autonomy for small plants when we are finding that the "logic of monopolistic development," far from trying to crush these plants out of existence, actually *needs* them?[43] Other, more thorough analyses of the symbiotic relationship between Italy's traditional and modern sectors convincingly demonstrate the political and economic untenability of championing one side against the other.[44]

The *Programmatic Declaration* spoke of the need to distinguish among the *ceti medi*. The PCI's claim that it can guarantee the autonomy and independence of small producers against the monopolies also must rest at least in part on distinctions between firms which serve larger companies and those—the presumable allies—which are in competition with the monopolies, or which have independent markets. The PCI, in the face of all the logical and factual challenges which arise, continues to repeat more forcefully than ever that *all* small producers are "conditioned" by the monopolies, and thus are equally interested in limiting monopolist expansion.[45]

---

[43] Camillo Daneo, in FIM-FIOM-UILM (Emilia-Romagna), *Convegno regionale sulle piccole e medie aziende metalmeccaniche industriali e artigiane: Atti* (Bologna: Grafiche BG, 1972), pp. 38-39.

[44] Michele Salvati, "L'origine della crisi in corso," *Quaderni piacentini* 11 (March 1972): 21-22; see also the discussion in Suzanne Berger, "The Uses of the Traditional Sector: Why the Declining Classes Survive," mimeographed (Cambridge, Mass.: The M.I.T. Press, 1972), pp. 27-31.

[45] DiStefano, *Ceti medi*, p. 27. There has of course always been, in the

Aside from these broader economic problems, the construction of an alliance with small producers must also contend with the fact that these are still "little bosses" (*padroncini*) whose firms are notorious for their poor working conditions, low pay, and repressive political atmosphere. The PCI counters with a familiar and technically correct argument, i.e., these conditions are forced by the monopolies' control of labor and material markets. But a local party leader succinctly summed up the dilemma of trying to translate this analysis into practice when she asked, "How can we tell the rank and file that Agnelli [the head of Fiat] is the *real* boss, when their own bosses are squeezing them like lemons?" With over half the industrial work force employed by people who are supposed to be their allies, this is not an abstract question.

The PCI of course does not ignore this dilemma, but while asserting that workers' rights cannot be compromised it insists that small producers must be drawn into an alliance front. Again relegating socioeconomic arguments to the sidelines, the PCI refuses to make distinctions among small producers. It lumps all small firms together in reform proposals such as demands for standardized electric rates for small and large industry or proposals for measures to facilitate credit arrangements for small firms. Typical of the PCI's desperation is the proposal that an enormous public investment be made to favor research and technological development for small industries in order to make them more viable.[46] This "structural reform" does not even specify major areas of technical and scientific inquiry. All it does, in the obvious hope of winning more support from small and very small producers, is promise that a lot of money will be spent.

In spite of their intrinsic capitalist nature, the artisans give the PCI more support than any other traditional stratum. If the Left's share of merchants' and peasants' Mutual Fund votes touches only 30 percent in the Red Belt, the national average of the PCI-dominated National Artisans' Confederation in Mutual Fund elections is 33.4 percent. In the Red Belt, the Left obtains absolute majorities: the average is 59 percent in Tuscany and 67

---

via italiana, a very strong tendency not to distinguish coexisting with the assertion that distinctions must be made among *ceti medi*. *Dichiarazione programmatica*, pp. 30-31, offers a classic example of both assertions.

[46] Claudio Sabattini's address in *Convegno regionale*, pp. 28-29, offers a good summary of the PCI's general proposals for small industry.

percent in Emilia-Romagna.[47] Broader support is not, however, so evident in the PCI's membership figures, where artisans account for a mere 4 percent of the total.

The PCI tends to dwell on the artisans and small industrialists out of a combination of strength and weakness. The party likes to play to its strong points, and it is stronger here than among *commercianti* or peasants. At the same time, because the small producers are, in a sense, in the "front lines" facing the workers, they are a potentially volatile group. Their interests are most directly and most rapidly challenged by working-class militance and this makes them more susceptible to be alienated *en masse*. Like all intermediate strata, artisans and small factory owners tend to look to the Right when they feel their interests threatened, and the Communists are very much aware of this.[48]

The party knows, then, that especially from a tactical perspective, this very obvious friction-point cannot be ignored. They may be small capitalists, but it would be foolhardy, or worse, to claim that *padroncini* and monopolists are really just birds of a feather. Even those unions most critical of the PCI's alliance strategy do not make this mistake. They make a point of negotiating contracts with small firms following a schedule, and a set of tactics, different from those used with larger enterprises. Not to make these distinctions would be to hand over to Italy's monopolies and conservative interests a united, mass political base. These are not merely the PCI's historic concerns reasserting themselves, but direct responses to the workers' isolation and backpedaling following the "Hot Autumn" of 1969.[49]

The "Hot Autumn" and Its Impact on the Alliance Strategy

An organizational tally sheet would show that the PCI gained a great deal from the "Hot Autumn." Resurgent militance enabled the party organization in the factories to halt and begin to reverse a decline that had begun more than fifteen years earlier.

---

[47] "La scelta politica del voto artigiano," *Rinascita* 27 (November 6, 1970): 8.

[48] Poggi, *Preferenze Politiche*, p. 49, shows that all elements of the *ceto medio* give increasing support to parties of the Right as they perceive a threatening economic situation.

[49] It is significant, given his earlier-cited objections in n. 17, that Bruno Trentin strongly associated himself with this *tactical* need to do everything possible to divide large from small industrialists. See his conclusions, *Convegno regionale*, pp. 104-106.

Party membership began to rise consistently for the first time in almost twenty years. Waves of new recruits resuscitated the moribund FGCI, and they brought long-awaited fresh blood to the party proper. By 1972, to cite one example, 30 percent of the members of the provincial federations' major decision-making bodies, the federal committees, were under thirty years of age.[50] Most party federations now have at least some top leaders in their early thirties, including some federal secretaries. A number of federations are now being run by people in their twenties.

The events of 1969 also provided the PCI with political benefits. A number of important reforms in which the Communists played a key role were passed, and the PSI, after a brief period of unity with the Partito Socialista Democratico Italiano (PSDI), had moved toward closer collaboration with the PCI. The Center-Left formula, originally designed to isolate and undermine the PCI, had very obviously failed on both counts.

But some successes immediately created serious difficulties for the PCI. As we have seen in the case of the artisans, it is very difficult to discuss alliances with the person one is picketing. In a period of high social tension, the PCI's legislative proposals in favor of small producers did not seem to impress the *ceti medi*. Flaws appeared in the alliance strategy even in the Red Belt, where the party enjoys its best relations with small propertied groups. Leaders in the PCI's strongest federations openly admitted that small proprietors generally aligned with the Left were defecting in large numbers to the conservative industrialists' association. The head of the PCI's Factory Commission in a Red Belt federation offered the following summary late in 1969:

> Let's understand at the outset that there is nothing to say about those with more than twenty workers, at least not in any way that can be generalized. . . . Given the kind of industry we have in Tuscany and Emilia, the issue of renewing contracts places the workers' interests and those of the artisan and small producer in direct conflict, and therefore calls the entire line into question. On an idealistic level, many are on our side, but now, with unprecedented militance reaching all the way down to firms with, say, three workers, paternalism and all sorts of other issues have come forward. Tactically, we do all we can,

[50] Bruno Bertini, "Inversione di tendenza nel reclutamento," *Rinascita* 29 (November 3, 1972): 20.

which is to minimize the damage, but still there are open breaks with the party because of the workers. . . . The fact is that this is an insoluble contradiction, and so we have to maneuver tactically.

This was only one of the contradictions which exploded in the PCI's face during and after 1969. By far the most important warning signals came from the south, in mass disturbances manipulated by Fascists, and in the general advance of the Neo-Fascist Movimento Sociale Italiano (MSI) in local and general elections. Twenty-five years after the war, the PCI's primordial specter, a mass-based Fascist party, was advancing in the Mezzogiorno at the expense of the Left as well as of the Right.[51]

The party moved quickly to correct what it felt were its shortcomings in the south, and its initial conclusions seemed to portend major clarifications, and indeed revisions, of its analysis of the *ceti medi*.[52] A surprisingly broad chorus of voices arose within the PCI and began to insist that distinctions be made between parasitical and productive middle strata.[53] The PCI had been too slow in appreciating the extent to which the reaction surging in the south was coalescing around the parasitical elements which live on patronage and privilege in the bureaucracy, among entrenched and corrupt professional groups, on building and land speculation, on absentee landownership, and on commercial price speculation.

As we know from the PCI's analysis of the commercial sector, parasitism is not a new target. What is new is that the party had, in the past, always attacked parasitism's most obvious manifestations in the same breath with which it denounced the monopolies. Because of its well-known tendency to blame everything on the monopolies, the PCI had ignored attacking large-scale manifesta-

[51] The PCI's analysis of the local elections in which the Movimento Sociale Italiano (MSI) made its first large advances, reaching increases of 10 percent and more in Sicily and Calabria, is in *Rinascita* 28 (June 18, 1971).

[52] A penetrating analysis of recent developments in the south and the PCI's policies in that area is Tarrow, "Political Economy of Stagnation," pp. 93-123.

[53] A succinct statement of the party's arguments made by the PCI's leading economist is Luciano Barca, "Alleanze e politica di riforme," in *Storia politica organizzazione*, p. 84. Those now denouncing the "parasites" included Giorgio Amendola. See his contribution to Amendola et al., *I comunisti e il Mezzogiorno* (Rome: Editori Riuniti, 1972), p. 80, and compare this with his conclusions a decade earlier in *Tendenze del capitalismo italiano* 1: 426-427.

tions of parasitism which were more indicative of backward than monopolist patterns. Only the rise of a mass reactionary threat which had very little to do with monopoly capital (indeed, most of the monopolists denounced the Fascists very strongly) jarred the Communists out of their lethargy. For a time, the PCI's denunciations of parasitism were so great that the party all but ignored the monopolies. Some critics—inside and outside the party —began to wonder whether the entire *via italiana* was being stood on its head, and asked if the new strategic goal was to align the party with the monopolies and against the parasites![54] That such an issue could be raised, even obliquely, among top party leaders gives us some idea of how intense and far-reaching have been recent economic debates in the PCI.

These developments seemed to promise some clarification of the PCI's analysis of the *ceti medi*, or at the very least a sharper definition of parasitism and, with it, the entire Italian economy. But the party quickly found that it could not push the distinction between parasitism and productivity very far without undermining a significant part of its traditional alliance strategy. The result was a quick reversion to form: political priorities again prevailed, and the PCI once more refused to make any distinctions among those strata viewed as potential allies.

Ironically, reform bills the PCI had helped push through in the offensive against parasitism were directly responsible for the party's backpedaling. An important agrarian reform, in particular, only passed with the PCI's vote: it established maximum and minimum rental rates for land cultivated by renters or sharecroppers.[55] An urban planning reform bill also passed in 1971 only because of PCI support, and this law provided for price ceilings for urban land expropriated for municipal use.[56] The PCI

[54] One such critic, a former PCI leader expelled in 1969, is Lucio Magri. See his "Italian Communism in the Sixties," *New Left Review* 66 (March-April 1971): 48. Berlinguer's statements, which were responsible for Magri's accusation, appear in *L'Unità*, July 17, 1970, p. 1. Amendola also appeared to propose a monopoly-PCI alliance in 1973 and a lively debate ensued in the pages of *Rinascita* throughout the summer.

[55] Technically, the PCI abstained on the original law (No. 11 of 1971), but then voted favorably on a subsequent revision, which became necessary because of an adverse court decision (No. 945 of 1972 is the revised reform). For a discussion of the party's position, see *Problemi del paese in Parlamento, No. 5: Agricoltura* (Rome: ITER, 1973), pp. 125-135.

[56] This law was No. 865 of 1971. The amount of land which can be expropriated, and the uses to which it can be put, are limited.

401

strongly favored both laws since they were designed to undercut urban and rural land speculation. The reason the Communists had to retreat so quickly in the face of these gains lies, of course, in the widespread reaction the reforms provoked in the *ceti medi*. In a "post-autumn" political climate which was hostile to the Left, a very efficacious campaign was waged by the Right, with the DC quickly joining, against "expropriation laws" that violated the sanctity of property. For both ideological and pragmatic reasons, large numbers of the middle strata appear to have supported the Right in the local elections of 1971 and in the general elections of 1972. Whether this shift was really so widespread is not as important as the PCI's perception of the shift: PCI leaders I interviewed in 1973 spoke constantly about recovering the middle-class votes that had been lost earlier.

The PCI had found, to its chagrin, that small-scale parasitism is either approved in principle or practiced by many of the party's ostensible allies. A PCI leader who had taken a dim view of the party's earlier frantic denunciation of parasitism illustrated the problem very clearly. Citing a parliamentary study, he showed that over a third of all agricultural rentals involve plots smaller than one hectare (2.47 acres).[57] This means that almost 300,000 small rented plots belong not to greedy land barons, but to the rural or urban *ceti medi* who use them as small investments, as a hedge against inflation, or to supplement pensions or other fixed incomes. A similar motivation underlay the *ceti medi*'s aligning with the Right in defense of urban real-estate speculation. On the one hand, they instinctively were attracted by the appeal to private property. On the other hand, even if their "rental property" consisted of only a single room or a very small apartment, they probably identified with the building societies which were the real targets of the reform.[58]

This evidence, real or perceived, of the "productive" *ceti medi*'s involvement in numerous forms of parasitism and speculation led top party strategists to conclude that overly rigid distinctions between the "advanced" and "backward" sectors of the economy are impossible. Some leaders openly confessed that the entire alliance strategy would be undermined if these distinctions

[57] Gerardo Chiaromonte, "Voto nelle campagne e strategia agraria," *Rinascita* 29 (June 2, 1972): 5.
[58] Interviews in several PCI federations, summer 1973.

were pushed too far.[59] The party's secretary-general also warned that unless the *ceti medi*'s "complex network of interests" was understood by the party, "these strata will go to the Right and the working class will have the satisfaction of having maintained its class purity," and little else; the workers will have the "honor of having a lot of enemies, and it will be isolated and defeated."[60] As Berlinguer makes clear here and elsewhere, the most serious error the PCI can commit is to choose political objectives and forms of struggle which do anything to restrict its potential alliances.[61]

The PCI proposed amendments to the agrarian reform bill, and these are indicative of the lengths to which the party will go to avoid a large-scale alienation of the *ceti medi*. The major proposals are (1) to exempt small rental properties from taxes among middle-income groups; (2) to facilitate the sale of rental properties to public development corporations; (3) to provide state subsidies to those who will not or cannot sell small rental properties so that postreform income is guaranteed at 90 percent of its prereform level.[62] This last provision appears to call for state underwriting of parasitical income, as long as that income is modest. This is an incredible reversal for a party which shortly before denounced such income so strongly, but it is apparently the only solution the PCI sees to the conflicting demands of its various constituencies.

III. The Alliance Strategy at the Local Level

How do the PCI and its personnel deal with the multitude of problems which must arise in the implementation of the alliance strategy on a local level? To answer this question, our analysis will focus on the PCI's major subnational organizational unit, the provincial federation. We shall first examine the ability of local

[59] Chiaromonte, "Riforme di struttura e direzione politica del paese," *Storia politica organizzazione*, p. 75.

[60] Enrico Berlinguer, "Per uscire dalla crisi un generale rinnovamento nei rapporti internazionali nello sviluppo economico nella difesa della legalità democratica," Address and Conclusions to the Meeting of the Central Committee and Central Control Commission of the PCI, February 7-9, 1973 (Rome: n.p., 1973). The quotation is from the conclusions, p. 65.

[61] Berlinguer, "Classe operaia e blocco sociale," *Rinascita* 28 (January 15, 1971): 16.

[62] *Problemi del paese*, pp. 17-25.

party organizations to implement the alliance strategy, and then analyze local leaders' reactions to this strategy during the "Hot Autumn."

The Ceti Medi and the Federations

Vast differences separate PCI federations in northern and central Italy, but evidence from seven federations representing a wide range of political-organizational types permits some generalizations about middle-class alliances on a local level.[63]

It is easiest to assess the alliance strategy in Italy's "White Zones," where the PCI is very weak, for in these areas the strategy comes closest to total failure. This failure is a reflection of the broader failure of the Togliattian strategy of presence by which the PCI, as a mass party, is supposed to establish itself in "every crease and fold" of Italian society. In fact, in these Catholic subcultures the PCI exists only on the margins of society and politics.[64] Communist marginality is perhaps nowhere more evident than in membership statistics for the party which show that the proportion of smallholders enrolled in the PCI in the White Zones is no greater than in other areas of Italy, even though the relative proportion of smallholders in the work force is much greater in these DC strongholds.[65]

In an atmosphere so unreceptive to the Left in general, the natural antipathy that most elements of the urban middle classes feel for the PCI is reinforced and probably even exaggerated. Substantial segments of these strata, and most of the other strata as well, have been socialized to reject the Left. The limited success the PCI achieves in these areas very much reflects this political and social isolation. Even in urban areas with extensive commercial sectors, the Communists recruit only the poorest and most marginal elements. Few in number, the *commercianti* who join

[63] Southern Italy is excluded from the analysis that follows since the research from which the material has been drawn was part of a broader study of PCI organization and behavior in the north-center. Four federations were studied in 1969. In 1973 these federations were revisited and three additional federations were studied.

[64] This is explored in this volume by Alan Stern, Chapter 6. For a more detailed discussion of the emargination of the PCI in the White Zones, see also Stephen Hellman, "Organization and Ideology in Four Italian Communist Federations" (Ph.D. dissertation, Yale University, 1973), Chapter 5.

[65] *Dati sull'organizzazione* (1968), p. 36, show that smallholders comprised 4.3 percent of the membership in Italy's "whitest" regions, while the national average was 5.0 percent.

the PCI in the three "white" federations I studied tend to come from small, family-run fruit or vegetable shops or market stalls. Informants in these areas noted that the shopkeepers who belonged to the party were all quite old. This is a result of the party's failure to recruit a significant number of merchants since the immediate postwar period. Several leaders, speaking to this point, complained that the general hostility of shopkeepers is so great toward the PCI that even when faced with economic extinction, they rebuff all attempts by Communists to approach them and discuss their problems.

Because of the age and characteristics of its own *commercianti*, the local party faces equally disappointing results when it attempts to organize initiatives among its own membership. One functionary noted that after a year and a half, a distribution cooperative among a few shopkeepers was still in the talking stage because of inertia and individualism.

The PCI fares somewhat better with artisans in areas where it is very weak. In all "white" federations studied, the party enrolled many more artisans than shopkeepers, and it also obtained a higher share of Mutual Fund votes. As in the case of the shopkeepers, however, only very small, economically marginal firms, often from the service sector, are attracted to the PCI. Occasionally one finds the owner of a larger firm in the party in these areas, but this is extremely rare and reflects proprietors who began on a small scale and kept their "special consciousness" even after they achieved moderate success. But, as several informants pointed out, even this state of affairs cannot be generalized with confidence, for successful party members, like other successful small producers, tend to join the DC-led Confederazione Generale dell'Industria Italiana (*Confindustria*). This in turn soon results in expulsion from the PCI. "Maybe this is something that works in Emilia or Tuscany," one leader said, "but it doesn't work here."

When we move from "white" federations to those where the party's strength is closer to the national average, the PCI's fortunes among the middle strata do not alter significantly. Even in areas where the party has grown markedly over time, it appears to do so as a result of a growing working class. The PCI appears quite capable of making headway among workers without simultaneously making inroads into proximate low-status groups such as shopkeepers. It is only when the party begins to edge toward

405

a third of the vote, usually in areas where it benefits from at least a "pink" tradition, that its presence among the *ceti medi* becomes more than marginal, although it remains quite limited. In areas where the DC remains the largest party, on the other hand, the PCI's presence among the middle classes often compares, in its absence, with the White Zones.

The tentative conclusion which emerges from these brief observations is that a "white" tradition does not appear to be necessary to guarantee the PCI's effective elimination from the middle strata. Rather, a "red" tradition, even of limited proportions, seems necessary to assure any substantial presence. The distinction is crucial, for it suggests that the PCI will be rejected by the middle classes almost everywhere in Italy save in areas of traditional leftist strength. This in turn leads to another conclusion, and that is that local history and tradition, and not "objective conditions," appear to be the variables which most fully explain the PCI's success or lack of success in enlisting middle-class support. The only consistent exception to this rule would be that when massive working-class concentrations develop, they appear to be capable of generating their own subculture.

The PCI is of course most favored by tradition and history in the Red Belt, the central regions of Emilia-Romagna, Tuscany, and Umbria. What concerns us here is not how the party came to be so strong in these areas, but how this domination provides the party with advantages in its wooing of the middle strata.

The most obvious benefits derive from the Communists' extensive organizational and social presence, and from the legitimacy which is a result of electoral and political domination in these areas. If the peasant in the Veneto or the Catholic parts of Lombardy and Piedmont has anticommunism bred into him, then almost the opposite is true of the ex-fieldhand or sharecropper of Emilia and Tuscany. The Communists undoubtedly exaggerate the extent to which small businessmen and artisans in the Red Belt are revolutionary former sharecroppers or ex-workers fired for their union activities during the Cold War, but it would be a mistake to dismiss this argument out of hand in "red" centers.

We have already noted that the PCI's strength among artisans attains majoritarian proportions in the Red Belt. A closer look at this phenomenon in a single province in the Red Belt provides a number of insights into the sources and nature of that strength. In the Province of Bologna, the PCI-dominated Artigianato Provinciale Bolognese (APB) enlists the formal support of 60 percent of all artisan firms in the province, and its lists obtain a whopping 79 percent of the votes for the provincial Mutual Fund.[66] In absolute terms, there are 28,000 artisan firms in Bologna, and 22,000 of them vote for, and 16,000 of them join, the APB. Yet, when we examine the PCI's membership statistics, we find that the party can claim only 5,100 artisans as full-fledged members of the PCI.[67] The PCI thus manages to enlist 18 percent of the artisans in its ranks in Bologna, while 61 percent of the artisans, who will not join the PCI, will at least vote for an organization strongly identified with the Communists.

Such great discrepancies cannot be explained by attributing support for other left-wing parties to nearly two-thirds of the artisans, for the other parties are very much junior partners in the APB and in Red Belt politics. It is more plausible to assume that Communist hegemony in areas like Bologna motivates a great number of artisans who will not join the PCI—over ten thousand in this case—to join one of its flanking organizations. Another five or six thousand Bolognese artisans will affiliate with neither group, but they nevertheless cast their Mutual Fund vote for the APB.

This evidence demonstrates the PCI's profound influence among artisans. At the same time, the evidence also suggests that Bolognese artisans are probably a cautious and far from dedicated left-wing mass of small producers. The figures above imply that quite a few of these artisans only affiliate, or vote the way they do, because of the material benefits that the party and its mass organizations provide. And, in a place like Bologna, these benefits are numerous. The PCI's control of local government, which gives it licensing and zoning powers among other perquisites, is one very obvious source of benefits. Another is the immense cooperative and distributive network controlled by the PCI in Emilia-Romagna.[68] Finally, the PCI's privileged position in the unions certainly does not hurt the very small and small

[66] Vincenzo Galetti, "Società civile e presenza del partito," *Critica marxista* 7 (January-February 1969): 127.

[67] Calculated by combining the Federations of Imola and Bologna, which together occupy the territory of the Province of Bologna, *Dati sull'organizzazione* (1968), pp. 6, 39.

[68] The extent and nature of the cooperative movement is discussed in Luciano Brunelli et al., *La presenza sociale del PCI e della DC* (Bologna: Società Editrice Il Mulino, 1968). See also Galetti, "Società civile." An

producers who are known to the local party organizations as comrades or friends.

This last point is a sensitive one, but it is an especially clear illustration of some of the costs the PCI pays in areas where it is dominant. My observations confirm those of other students of the PCI in finding that the local PCI is often drawn into labor disputes in the Red Belt, and that it then performs very much like a referee between Communist workers and Communist—or sympathetic—employers.[69] Several members of the Bolognese secretariat admitted to me that the party sometimes stepped in and mediated between the two sides. One leader said, "This of course has happened. I won't deny it for a moment. What happened? Well, we compromised, that's what happened."

The PCI's mediating behavior in disputes between "allies" is a tendency which is most common in Emilia, where the party's political and social presence is greatest. Many people inside and outside the party refer, often in joking terms, to a *via emiliana al socialismo*. But many party leaders do not find all aspects of the *via emiliana* to be a joking matter, as is evident in pointed comments directed at top Emilian leaders during the "Hot Autumn." Equally typical was the response to these criticisms by an Emilian, who said that workers ought not overemphasize the conflictual at the expense of "a general moment of unification."[70] The PCI is not immune from such attitudes and behavior in other parts of the Red Belt where its support from artisans and small industrialists is large, but the fact remains that such a stance is *characteristic* only of the region where the party is strongest and most extended as a movement. No one, after all, speaks of a *via toscana*.

The PCI's success with the commercial middle classes in the Red Belt, as we have seen, matches neither its organizational nor its electoral success with the artisans. Save for rich suburbs and isolated pockets with long-standing smallholding traditions, the PCI vote in the Red Belt is lowest in city-center commercial dis-

interesting, if negatively biased, history of the origins of the postwar movement in Emilia is in Ercole Camurani, *Dopo Stalin* (Reggio Emilia: Poligrafici S.P.A., 1968), pp. 96-110.

[69] See Alan J. Stern, "Local Political Elites and Economic Change" (Ph.D. dissertation, Yale University, 1971), Chapter 6.

[70] See the exchange between Pietro Ingrao, of the PCI National Executive, and Enrico Gualandi, secretary of the Federation of Imola, in "Ruolo e alleanze della classe operaia," *Rinascita* 26 (November 28, 1969): 13.

tricts. This electoral weakness is very obvious in provinces like Florence or Siena, where the PCI obtains more than half the vote in most cities of the province, but it hovers around a third of the vote in the capitals, which are jammed with small shops. At Bologna, the PCI is more successful, but in the historic center of the capital, which has 100,000 inhabitants, the party has dipped as low as 23 percent of the vote in local elections, which is roughly half its present strength in this city of 500,000.[71] In contrast, the DC and PLI do quite well in these concentrated commercial areas.

The PCI in the Red Belt obtains a disproportionately high, but not majoritarian, amount of support from the *commercianti*. To continue our illustration using the example of Bologna, the Left list obtains around 30 percent of the votes cast in the provincial Merchants' Mutual Fund elections. These votes break down as follows. Commercial representatives and agents, i.e., spokesmen for relatively large firms, warehouses, or agencies, cast 20 percent of their votes for the Left lists. Merchants with fixed retail outlets cast 35 percent of their votes for the Left, while those classified as ambulatory give 90 percent to the Left. Local party experts also estimate that the commercial *ceto medio* as a whole, in general elections, casts 30 percent of its vote for the PCI or PSI; 50 percent of its votes go to the parties of the Center, and 20 percent go to the PLI or MSI.[72]

The Bolognese case provides interesting insights into the limits of local power on the implementation of broader party strategy. In spite of the PCI's firm hold on all levels of power up to the region, it often lacks the legislative means to carry out its programs, or to oppose trends it feels are damaging. Party leaders often complain bitterly that the local government's licensing and zoning plan, which attempted to rationalize distribution by limiting new licenses and creating sales centers in uncongested areas, had consistently been overridden by ministerial or prefectural actions.[73] Similar interference had overridden the party's attempts to limit the growth of supermarkets. A reform has recently been

[71] Robert H. Evans, *Coexistence: Communism and Its Practice in Bologna, 1945-1965* (Notre Dame, Ind.: University of Notre Dame Press, 1967), p. 194.

[72] PCI (Fed. di Bologna), "Associazionismo e alleanze sociali," pp. 23-24.

[73] Comitato Cittadino (Fed. di Bologna), "Note e valutazioni del gruppo di lavoro per il ceto medio commerciale," mimeographed (Bologna: n.d. [1968]), pp. 9-10.

409

passed which now fixes ultimate commercial licensing authority in the hands of the municipal government, and local PCI leaders obviously view this with satisfaction, although they also realize that they now are confronted with the challenge of posing concrete alternatives to the supermarkets.

If the Bolognese party can brag about an extensive commercial cooperative and associative network which should make some of its projections easier to realize, it still has not made really substantial inroads into this stubbornly individualistic stratum. Party documents place much of the blame for this state of affairs on the shopkeepers' deeply rooted free-enterprise mentality. As a result, internal party documents often are striking in their protestations of the PCI's intention to guarantee the continued existence of merchants; at times, cooperative enterprises are implicitly denied a central role in future commercial evolution, and associative forms are mentioned only in passing.[74] Even when the question of associations is tackled in a more thorough fashion, much stress is put on the "permanent structural role" of small enterprises in all sectors of the economy, and on the entirely voluntary nature of associative forms.[75]

These emphases once again recall the *via emiliana* and the tendency to carry to an extreme the *via italiana*'s obscuring of concrete goals in favor of maintaining the unity of the movement at all costs. It is important to note that this is, in Emilia, a *general* ideological tendency. If it were present only with regard to the artisans and the party's mediation in labor disputes, one could call it a rationalization after the fact. But we also note the same tendency toward strata where the PCI is far from majoritarian, and this is especially significant for our understanding of the Emilian dynamic.

The Bolognese situation also helps us explain another peculiarly Emilian tendency, namely, the eagerness with which the party in this region wishes the PCI to become a partner in the national government. Because of the power in the hands of the Emilian party, its leaders understand very well the limits to political power in Italy short of national power. With all but state power in their hands, the leaders of the Emilian PCI are highly aware of their lack of material capabilities to resolve any of the *ceti medi's*

[74] Ibid., pp. 1-2.
[75] "Associazionismo e alleanze sociali," pp. 17-18.

basic problems, and they obviously are committed to resolving them.

Some of the national party's demands for massive state intervention in favor of technology for small industry or to fund large-scale commercial centers for merchants may appear abstract and unrealistic to outside observers, but they express deeply felt needs in areas like Emilia where a broad system of alliances happens to be neither abstract nor unrealistic. "The state is going to have to pay a political price for these groups," was the laconic comment of one Bolognese leader. Emilia's two most important Communist leaders recently zeroed in on this question in extremely precise fashion. They argue that, particularly where alliances have been successful, there is a growing awareness that their ultimate maintenance and extension can rest neither on the reflexive defense of special interests nor on generic postwar formulas, both of which, they recognize, have too long been part of the PCI's ideological baggage. Instead, the PCI must, if it is serious, provide for Italy as a whole a clear set of economic directives spelling out a developmental scheme into which an economic structure like that found in Emilia can be integrated.[76]

Of course, if this stance clearly confronts some issues, it raises others, and shows that the PCI's successes in Emilia-Romagna are far from being free of costs. Aside from the ideological "integralism" that denies the contradictions evident in the real world, and the social mediation that sometimes leaves the party astride the lower and middle strata, we also have a projected series of political costs which will be high indeed. The ideal of maintaining and expanding its middle-class alliances forces the party in Emilia to actively support proposals for such a massive infusion of state funds and such a total restructuring of economic priorities to favor the development of the middle strata that one is forced to ask, projecting his question to Italy as a whole: (1) Are such funds available, even assuming the sincerest of intentions? (2) Even if such funds were to become available, is this broad defense of the *ceti medi* really Italy's primary reform priority? One can laugh and accuse the Emilians of being narrowly provincial, but it is equally possible that only they are in a position to understand the full implications of the costs of an alliance with the middle strata.

[76] Guido Fanti and Renato Zangheri, "Classe operaia e alleanze in Emilia," in *Storia politica organizzazione*, pp. 266-267.

411

PCI Functionaries' Attitudes toward the Ceti Medi during the "Hot Autumn"

In that part of the research reported above that was carried out in 1969, four PCI federations (two in the Red Belt and two in White Zones) were visited, and almost the entire elite of these federations' apparatuses was systematically interviewed.[77] We cannot carry our scientific pretensions too far, for only thirty-four complete interviews were obtained. Nevertheless, the results of these interviews are both interesting and significant, for they clearly indicate that neither the theoretical nor the practical problems of the alliance strategy go unreflected in the leadership of the PCI's federations.

The functionaries were asked two questions which focused directly on some of the most problematic issues in the alliance strategy. The first question was open-ended and asked whether it was important to make distinctions between the various components of the intermediate strata. The issue of including artisans and small industrialists in an alliance with the PCI was explicitly pressed in an attempt to force each functionary to take a clear stand.

The question elicited a great variety of responses, many of which were difficult to classify. Seventy-five percent of the answers were relatively straightforward, and they fell into three distinct categories. Another 20 percent of the attitudes expressed were close enough to one of these three groupings to warrant their inclusion. Two answers could not be classified.

The most common response was a strongly positive defense of the PCI's strategy, but only 29 percent of the functionaries unequivocally held this position. They stressed the validity of the line, and the overriding need of the workers to have an extensive system of social alliances. Even when pressed, these leaders denied the importance of making distinctions within the *ceto medio*. Some said that worker-employer differences were problems for the unions, not the party. The following response is typical:

[77] Only full-time party leaders who occupy key *organizational* (as opposed to public or mass organization) positions in the federation hierarchies were interviewed systematically. Public officials or union leaders who hold high party posts by virtue of their location in a sphere broader than that of the party proper were excluded, in order to ensure an elite sample as comparable as possible between very strong and very weak federations.

We have resolved the conflicts [inherent in the alliance strategy] for we say, in the analysis that we are carrying forward, that small firms will have their own interests served once another pattern of development becomes the rule. Their dependence on the monopolies can become a dependence on a state which proceeds along different lines of development.

There are differences, you can always make distinctions, but in one way or another all of the *ceti medi* are dependent on the monopolies in general. . . . A democratic process of development has to be worked out in reality, in reality! and *this* is our socioeconomic reality, and it is this with which we must come to grips.

Another 12 percent of the respondents were supportive of the PCI's position, too, but they were at least mildly critical of the way the strategy was being implemented. They did not challenge the party's analysis, but they did criticize such issues as the speed with which the PCI tried to construct alliances. Some of these respondents felt the party would also have to be more courageous in the future and begin prescribing some of the things the middle strata "do not want to hear," e.g., cooperative or associative forms of economic organization.

We thus find 41 percent of the functionaries supportive of the PCI's general analysis. These responses represented the views of exactly half the functionaries in the strong federations, and a quarter of those in the weak federations. Most striking of all is the fact that all but one of the supportive responses from "red" federations came from Bologna. In other words, fourteen of thirty-four functionaries fully aligned themselves with the PCI's analysis; fully ten out of twelve Bolognesi were in this group. In spite of the small size of our sample, this is a dramatic distribution and it confirms the comment made earlier that one needs to distinguish Emilian from other Red Belt federations.

The other two types of response to the question on the *ceti medi* were each offered by 26 percent of the functionaries. One of these responses consisted of those who expressed strong doubts about the party's analysis and the likelihood of ever making common cause with the small industrialists and, in many cases, most artisans as well. These answers emphasized that any alliance with *padroncini* had to be both tactical and temporary. In the view of these leaders, the small industrialists in particular would eventually have to side with the class enemy, making the whole idea of an alliance a highly questionable one. In one leader's words,

> In spite of the fact that the discussion of alliances goes all the way back to the Programmatic Declaration of the Eighth Congress, this topic has never really been addressed very clearly, nor have the necessary distinctions within the middle strata ever been made. This is especially true as far as the small-to-medium industrialists are concerned. If you ask me, the whole thing doesn't tie together very well (*tutta la cosa si concilia male*). At most, these are *potential* allies. But you just can't bring this issue up where the class struggle in the factories is concerned: there can be no question about that. So what we try to do is win back the support of the *ceti medi* in other areas. . . .

> What I have said, at most, applies to the smallest ones. . . . The party has not spelled this out very well; for me, it only makes sense if we talk about the very smallest producers.

The response that an older functionary gave to this question suggests a sectarian attitude which was not in fact apparent in any of his other responses to several dozen questions.

> Come on, all that is just tactics. . . .

> The small industrialists are 90 percent with the monopolies. They don't feel themselves to be workers, but bosses. Since they are larger than small family firms, they have to obey the law of profits, and hence they are forced to go to the extremes that they go to. It is dog eat dog, and they often are the biggest exploiters of all. They cannot help it, it is in the nature of their position in society.

> The party's line often leads to a lot of incomprehension on the part of our proletarian comrades, who sometimes feel that we do not fight these smaller bosses enough. I say this: these guys may be comrades of ours on a political level, but they still are the class enemy.

> Listen, often these are ex-partisans and ex-workers as well. But now they are bosses. It is useless to pretend otherwise. When we come to power, they will be finished, and the best of them

414

will become managers and directors. The entrepreneur has everything to lose if he sides with us, and he knows it. It is for this reason that you don't see too many of them on our side. They can keep their houses and their cars, what do I care about that . . . but they won't exploit anyone any more.

That a quarter of the functionaries expressed their doubts clearly is proof that the most contradictory elements of the strategy have not gone unnoticed by those who are supposed to make the strategy work. The answers in this category were not overwhelmingly from any one type of federation. They were given by a third of the leaders in "white" federations, and just under a fourth of those in "red" federations. There was, on the other hand, a very marked difference between the responses of younger and older functionaries. Almost half (47 percent) of the leaders under forty years of age were doubters, while only one man over forty was. When half of one age group calls the party line into question, and only a negligible part of another group does so, a generational gulf is obvious.

The middle category of responses, which accounted for the other 26 percent of the answers, was, for apparent reasons, most difficult to classify with assurance. I have described these respondents as "conditionally supportive" of the alliance strategy toward artisans and small industrialists. All agreed that there are serious problems in the party's analysis, and most also felt that the PCI had not done enough to clarify internal contradictions in its line. At the same time, all expressed a strong measure of support for the strategy. A typical response is the following:

Alliances have to be sought on the basis of intermediate objectives, shifting the terrain from the factory to the society at large: in other words, structural reforms which also interest small firms. . . .

Contradictions are really evident when contracts have to be renewed. The workers are right to strike. But the small industrialist, who also suffers, isn't entirely to blame. We have to get reforms which would allow him to adapt and reinforce his position. But we never can back down where the workers are concerned.

These answers were clearly associated with neither the PCI's strength nor generational differences.

415

The second question directly involved some aspect of the alliance strategy too, but because it was included in a questionnaire of the "agree-disagree" variety, problems of interpretation were minimized—as was the richness of the responses. The assertion in this case tests trust of the *petite bourgeoisie* in general, rather than a specific element of the middle strata. The responses are reported in Table 4. The way the assertion is framed leaves

TABLE 4. PCI FUNCTIONARIES' REACTIONS TO ASSERTION: "THE PETITE BOURGEOISIE CANNOT BE TRUSTED IN THE EVENT OF AN HISTORICAL CRISIS," 1969

Response	Total (%)	FEDERATION TYPE		AGE GROUPS	
		"Red" (%)	"White"	Under 40 (%)	40 and Over
Agree	32	32	33	59	6
Disagree	62	68	50	35	88
Cannot Answer	6	0	17	6	6
Totals	100	100	100	100	100
(N =)	(34)	(22)	(12)	(17)	(17)

little room for tactical considerations to enter one's evaluation of it. Either one trusts the *petite bourgeoisie*, or one does not, and evidently the older leaders are much more trusting than their younger counterparts. Of course, a distrustful attitude need not imply that one does not think the alliance strategy is sound (although a trusting attitude would imply that one felt the strategy to be quite appropriate). If the PCI's historical concern with the threat of reaction has contributed to the contours of the strategy —and it obviously has—then a very good reason to desire an alliance with these groups is precisely because one does *not* trust them.

Is there, then, a relationship between attitudes on the specific issue of the small industrialists and the more general issue of trust for the *petite bourgeoisie*? There is, and, as could be expected, the strongest association is found among those who support the alliance strategy fully and those who trust the middle classes. Of fourteen respondents who fully support the strategy, twelve (86 percent) also trust the *petite bourgeoisie*. Of nine "conditional supporters," five expressed a trusting attitude (56 percent). Of nine "doubters," only three are trusting. The six functionaries who were both distrustful and doubtful on these issues relating to the alliance strategy were among the youngest in the entire sample; all were under thirty years of age in 1969.

The attitudes reported above should be understood within the context of the "Hot Autumn" or the period immediately preceding it; that climate obviously exacerbated feelings and tensions but for this very reason is important, for in a sense it "tests" the strategy when the strategy is under pressure. One also should not try to push limited findings too far, but one certainly can conclude with assurance that any profound strategic issue which divides the local party leadership to such an extent must be indicative of very serious problems in the theory and the practice of the PCI.

CONCLUSIONS

It is difficult, if not impossible, to understand the recent evolution of the *via italiana* without reference to the PCI's perceived need for middle-class support. The party's position on the *ceti medi* is important because it enables us to view recent developments in the line as neither a tactical interlude nor a radical break with the past, but as the logical outcome of the strategy's basic assumptions.

What are the changes that generate a need for such explanations? Many PCI activities since 1969 are open to various interpretations, but I think there is general agreement that the leadership has increasingly come to the conclusion that the party's aims can better be achieved in a "cool" political climate. This apparent abandonment of the more aggressive aspects of the *via italiana*, demonstrated by the Communists' willingness to moderate social conflict, has always characterized the party's behavior—especially in moments of crises.[78] Yet not only the party's behavior but the written record confirms apparently decisive departures from what has long passed as PCI orthodoxy. Most indicative of these new positions are (1) the PCI's increasingly insistent emphasis on a governing role for itself in Italy as a prelude to, not a result

[78] This aspect of the party's behavior is discussed at greater length in Alessandro Pizzorno, "Il PCI e il ruolo dell'opposizione in Italia" (Paper prepared for the conference on which this volume is based).

417

of, a series of profound structural alterations of society; (2) the PCI's explicit acceptance of the DC *en bloc* as a partner in dialogue to hasten (1).[79]

These positions and the PCI's moderate behavior could lead one to conclude that the party has finally definitively abandoned the more dynamic elements which Togliatti said distinguish the reform strategy from mere reformism.[80] At the same time, this is no takeover of the party by its right wing: the same secretary-general identified as the author of many departures since the Thirteenth Congress in 1972 helped make the Twelfth Congress, three years earlier, appear quite leftist in tenor.[81] If there has been a marked shift in the party's emphases, it clearly must be explained by the course of events, not in terms of alleged betrayals by party leaders.

These events tell us that the Communists have abandoned some of the more aggressive interpretations of their strategy because these interpretations were put to the test during and after the "Hot Autumn," and the results, in the leaders' view, were disappointing. The growth of a militant labor movement and the existence of wide-scale agitation for reforms did not expand the reform front. Instead, this front was threatened with isolation and defeat. Sharpened social contradictions did not undermine the DC's unity and threaten to split that party, as facile assumptions about the DC's interclass nature had predicted. Indeed, in the alienation of large sectors of the *ceti medi* from the Left, the PCI found itself confronted with its own "interclass" contradictions in the period following the autumn of 1969.

It is quite possible to criticize the Communist leaders' haste to jump to the above conclusions, just as it is possible to argue that they used purely numerical criteria to inform their judgments.

[79] The party's positions began to emerge officially at the Thirteenth Congress of 1972, but precongressional documents clearly foreshadowed the emphasis that would be put on a governing role for the PCI. See the articles by Sereni and Chiaromonte in *Storia politica organizzazione*; for the Congress itself and the position on the DC, see esp. Berlinguer's address, *XIII Congresso del PCI: Atti e risoluzioni* (Rome: Editori Riuniti, 1972), pp. 53-59. An excellent discussion of the major postcongressional developments is Mino Monicelli, "Falce Martello e Scudo," *L'Espresso*, October 28, 1973, pp. 10-11.

[80] For Togliatti's views, see n. 16 above. Although his argument is much more subtle and involved, this is certainly one of Magri's charges in "Italian Communism in the Sixties." For him, however, the Togliattian formula has always been intrinsically Reformist.

[81] See *XII Congresso*, pp. 768-769.

But these and other criticisms cannot change the fact that a disturbing swing to the Right did follow the "Hot Autumn." Neo-Fascist gains in the 1972 general elections appear to have been contained only because the DC moved swiftly to cover its right flank with a "law and order" campaign aimed at the Left. Moreover, the bloody destruction of Unidad Popular in Chile the following year surely must have dispelled any doubts one might still have held about the potentially destructive role the *ceti medi* and the Right can play in an experiment in parliamentary socialism. We can be sure that the PCI did not overlook this particular lesson from Chile, for while the *via italiana* may be open to many charges, underestimating reaction certainly is not one of them.

Where did this leave the PCI? A party less committed to the broadest possible construction of alliances need not interpret Italian (or Chilean) events as a signal to moderate its approach; it could just as easily conclude that the *ceti medi* must be split and act accordingly. For reasons outlined in this essay, however, the PCI could never seriously entertain this or similar options. It thus found itself confronted with the dilemma which is built into its strategy, namely, that the PCI, because it is a *Communist* party, cannot directly enlist the support of groups it has defined as essential to its ultimate goals, and it will not call these goals into question. This forced the party to select the only apparent option, to obtain middle-class support, or at least to neutralize the middle class's threat, via their major political representative and spokesman, the DC. This approach does not try to defeat the threat of reaction, but it does attempt to minimize and sidestep that threat.

But the price of avoiding that threat is extremely high, for it demands moderation in the PCI's social strategy, *de facto* collaboration with the DC, and, as a result, reforms that are likely to be colossal compromises instead of basic alterations of Italy's socioeconomic structure. And while the PCI's strategic choices attempt to minimize dangers from the Right, it is by no means certain that the party's apparent faith in the DC's ability—and its desires—to control its middle-class constituency will prove to be justified when Italy confronts her next major crisis.

XI.

Alliance Politics and Revolutionary Pretensions

RONALD TIERSKY

Shortly after the progress of international détente had begun to involve the French Left as well, Maurice Thorez recalled the alliance policy of the Parti Communiste Français (PCF) over a fifty-year existence in these words: "What a long road has been covered since 1922, since that Congress in Paris where, as a young worker, I was a delegate of the Pas-de-Calais Federation! It was then that, for the first time . . . the problems of the unity of the working class, of the united front with the Socialist party, were posed before our party. From that distant epoch we have since struggled without respite to liquidate the split, in order once again to unify all workers in a single combat front. . . ."[1] Similarly, a recent PCF commentary on the June 1972 signature of a joint program with the French Socialist party termed this watershed event a "result . . . of a fifty-year struggle for unity."[2]

To say the least, not all observers have perceived French Communist alliance policy over the last half-century as the unequivocal effort such assertions would indicate, for the Communist alliance path in France has been hardly unilinear and expressive of unambiguous designs. On the one hand, the PCF "united front" policy has sometimes meant alliance between the parties; on the other, it has sometimes meant the attempt to absorb potential allies and gain hegemony. Often, moreover, it has meant the practice of both options at the same time: the united front has

For their comments and criticisms of earlier drafts of this article, I wish to thank Professors Donald L. M. Blackmer, Annie Kriegel, and Sidney Tarrow. I wish to thank Columbia University Press for permission to use some material from my *French Communism: 1920-1972* (New York, 1974).

[1] "Unité pour la démocratie, pour le socialisme," in *Oeuvres choisis*, 3 vols. (Paris: Editions sociales, 1965-1967), 3: 329.

[2] Jean Burles et al., "De 1966 à 1972: Vers le programme commun et l'union populaire," in *Cahiers d'histoire de l'Institut Maurice Thorez* (November-December 1972), 1: 8.

been a Janus-strategy quite within the Leninist perspective on the nature of alliance politics.

In this regard the historians of French communism have still much material for study in the PCF "zigzag" since the Tours Congress, and sociologists have still much to tell us about the effects of tactical maneuvers upon the social bases of the movement as a whole and upon its various organizations. On the other hand, the attention of the political scientist interested in problems of alliance politics is drawn first of all to the very ambiguity itself in Thorez's remark, for it expresses the foundation upon which the French Communist coalition policies have been constructed over half a century, the permanent fundamental characteristic of French Communist alliance behavior: *its attempt to maintain and extend a capacity for radical—ultimately revolutionary—actions while accepting, or being obliged to work for, nonrevolutionary goals in a nonrevolutionary environment.*

The purpose of this chapter is to delineate the elements of continuity and change in the theory and practice of French Communist alliance strategy, first setting in brief perspective the legacy of the past, and then concentrating on the contradictions between alliance politics and revolutionary claims in French communism as they have evolved in the post-Stalin era of international détente.[3]

THE "GRANDS TOURNANTS": VARIATIONS ON A THEME

There are six distinguishable periods in the history of French Communist alliance practice, demarcated by the *grands tournants* that have characterized party strategy. The period from 1924 to 1934, during which the PCF was "bolshevized," was marked by increasingly sectarian and fruitless efforts to "win the masses" while shunning coalitions with other parties. During the Popular Front period, from 1934 to 1939, the major emphasis was

[3] For the detailed conceptual framework on which this chapter is based, see my *French Communism, 1920-1972* (New York: Columbia University Press, 1974), esp. Chapter 12. See also Annie Kriegel, "Les Communistes français et le pouvoir" in Michelle Perrot and Annie Kriegel, *Le Socialisme français et le pouvoir* (Paris: Etudes et documentation internationale, 1966), and Kriegel, *Les Communistes français*, 2d ed. (Paris: Editions du Seuil, 1970). The first edition was translated as *The French Communists* (Chicago: University of Chicago Press, 1972), trans. Elaine P. Halperin.

reversed, and alliance with other parties became the paramount goal. Following conclusion of the Nazi-Soviet Pact, from 1939 to 1941, the PCF was declared illegal, forced underground, and was not only without allies but almost decimated. During the fourth period, from 1941 to 1947, the French Communists were reintegrated into all aspects of French politics and society through the successive experiences of the Resistance, of national Liberation, and tripartite government. We shall review the salient aspects of French Communist alliance behavior during the first four periods, then consider how earlier patterns have changed in the two postwar periods: the Cold War, which in the French domestic context can be dated 1947 to 1962, and the present period of renewed left-wing unity.

The alliance posture of the French Communists before 1934 was only slightly influenced by the party's decline in membership (from over 100,000 after the Tours Congress to fewer than 30,000 in 1933) or its decline in parliamentary influence.[4] By 1924 the PCF-SFIO (Section Française de l'Internationale Ouvrière) membership balance of 1921 had been reversed, and during the next decade the Socialists were much the larger and more influential party. Léon Blum, Paul Faure, and other key Socialist policy-makers, who had been constrained by weakness to consider alliance with the Communists during 1921-1923, were in a better position after 1924 to look elsewhere for allies without necessarily forfeiting their own claims to mass working-class support. Thus, in the 1924 general elections, when the Communists offered an electoral alliance to the SFIO based on a hard-line proposition excluding all Radicals and Freemasons, and allowing no concessions to local situations, the SFIO leaders felt their position strong enough to form a *Cartel des gauches* with the Radicals; the ensuing electoral cooperation moved them from 67 to 104 seats in the Chamber. The Communists won 26 seats, which represented a gain of 17 over those left them in 1921, but their success was confined largely to the Paris region where 16 of the 26 were elected. By 1932-1933 the PCF had withered almost to the size of a radical sect, no longer much resembling the great

---

[4] Still, Renaud Jean, Jacques Doriot, and others argued against the "class against class" tactic on such grounds, but these were the exceptions. Cf. in particular Jean's speech in *Classe contre classe: La question française au IXe exécutif et au VIe Congrès de l'I.C.* (Paris: Editions Gît-le-Coeur, n.d.), pp. 129-135.

mass revolutionary party it had seemed at first. The Communist party electorate dropped from 1,066,000 in 1928 to 797,000 in 1932, and its parliamentary representation was reduced, because of lack of electoral allies, from 26 in 1924, to 14 in 1928, to 12 in 1932. In the labor movement, the Communist-controlled Confédération Générale du Travail Unitaire (CGTU), created in 1922, failed to challenge the predominance of the Confédération Générale du Travail (CGT), led by the Socialist Léon Jouhaux.

The various PCF tactics attempted before 1934 had failed to win either allies or converts. The Communists demanded alliance without compromise on their part, and offered membership only to those who accepted unequivocally the PCF link with the Comintern. To be sure, implementation of these policies was often confused and sometimes self-contradictory—problems provoked and aggravated by protracted conflict in the leadership during these years. During this first period, with bolshevization the dominant theme in the PCF, the party sought only alliances that would enhance its role as an instrument of revolution. Although the party continued to administer the municipalities inherited in the 1920 separation from the SFIO, during the bolshevization the party did not aspire to a significant role in national government. Constrained by its loyalty to the Comintern and faced with an environment inhospitable to Bolshevik-style penetration and mobilization, the PCF neither diversified nor enlarged during the years from 1924 to 1934: quite the contrary. The *grand tournant* of 1932-1934 transformed this situation. The PCF decided to change its behavior toward the current French regime and at the same time to broaden the dimension of the Communist movement domestically. Implicit in this new strategy was a reformulation of the party's attitude toward alliances.

The intention of the Communist Popular Front maneuver in 1934 was to move the PCF from a tactical position of dominantly hard-line, sectarian opposition to the regime to a position of broad cooperation and moderation, promoting defense of the parliamentary regime against fascism, while not relinquishing the fundamental Communist rejection of capitalist society and preserving the radical consciousness necessary for an eventual revolutionary seizure of power. The demise of the German Communist party (KPD) after the Nazi assumption of power in 1933 had shown the futility of the *Nach Hitler kommen wir* policy. As a result, the Comintern soon validated the PCF's Popular Front

423

initiatives as a way of countering the Fascist threat to the other European Communist parties and, ultimately, to the Soviet Union itself.[5]

French Communist behavior during the Popular Front period was dominantly moderate, cooperative, and alliance-oriented.[6] Within two years the 1934 anti-Fascist coalition of the PCF, the SFIO, the Radical party and other organizations led to a Communist role at the national governmental level for the first time. The PCF leadership chose not to participate in the Léon Blum government (he had hoped they would and offered participation), but nonetheless the Communist deputies voted en bloc in support of the Popular Front government and its legislative program. On the trade-union front, in March 1936 the Communist-led CGTU reunited with the CGT, and in response to the general strike of May-June 1936 the Communists called for compromise and a return to order rather than intransigence or insurrection. At all levels, in short, the Communist party reversed its "class against class" posture and in a few years forged links with a broad spectrum of non-Communist organizations. As the danger of war increased after the summer of 1936, Communist interest in broadening the soon fatally weakened Popular Front alliance became greater, and by 1937-1938 the party was proposing a "National Front" which would not only have brought Communists into the Cabinet, but would have combined the Communist party in a ruling coalition with the conservatives.

Yet Communist participation in the Popular Front had radical purposes, too. First of all, party doctrine linked the Popular Front to the long-term goal of a revolutionary outcome of the Bolshevik type. Of course, doctrinal statements do not constitute incontrovertible evidence. There is also persuasive empirical evidence that the PCF did not abandon its revolutionary goals while participating in the Popular Front. The decision not to participate actively in the Blum government, providing only parliamentary support instead, was a first step in dissociating the Com-

---

[5] The importance of the goal of protecting the Soviet Union was underlined by the fact that the PCF would have preferred a Radical-led government, as the Radicals were more inclined to active alliance with the USSR than were the Socialists, who often were pacifist as well as vehemently "anti-Soviet."

[6] In addition to Kriegel, "Communistes français" and Tiersky, *French Communism*, see Daniel Brower, *The New Jacobins: The French Communist Party and the Popular Front* (Ithaca, N.Y.: Cornell University Press, 1968).

munist party from the Socialist party. And while not in itself a radical act, the Communist decision against participation implied rejection of "the exercise of bourgeois power," to use Léon Blum's own phrase. Furthermore, the Communist leadership claimed for itself a "ministry of the masses"—essentially a severe and continuing critique of the Blum government while supporting its entire program of legislation—which set the Communist party further outside the governing alliance. This was especially significant because the Blum government had come to power in a radicalized situation—the first time the SFIO had ever participated in a government—and was perceived by the public as radical. Then the general strike which erupted just after the elections and before the actual investiture enhanced this public image despite Blum's disclaimers of revolutionary intentions. Once it became clear the Popular Front leaders were in fact not prepared to lead a revolution, as the dominant Cabinet party the SFIO's image as a revolutionary party became tarnished and the PCF, which had been reservedly cooperative yet critical, seemed by default the sole authentic revolutionary party.

Outside the arena of governmental politics, the Communists made more direct attempts to establish themselves as sole vanguard revolutionary force. In the Popular Front, rank-and-file and citizen committees, whose goal according to the PCF was to lead nonparliamentary mass action (and to develop into the soviets after the revolution!), the Communists sought to dominate or to absorb outright their allies. Alert to the danger to their own organization, the SFIO leaders intervened to prevent the committees from developing very much in either number or size. A second PCF tactic was to seek hegemony in the trade-union movement, and upon reunification of the CGT and CGTU the Communists began to seek control from within by maneuvering for key leadership positions and by zealous use of the ballot. (The rise of Communist influence in the reunified CGT was interrupted when they were excluded again from the CGT in 1939.) The third tactic in pursuit of the Soviet example was the attempt at "organic unity," a fusion of the PCF with the SFIO. Fusion was first proposed by Léon Blum in 1934-1935 at a time when the SFIO membership was about triple that of the PCF. The Communists responded coolly at first, but when the PCF became the larger party (by December 1936 it had about 280,000 members to about 250,000 in the SFIO), it began to press for a merger whose goal was "the violent overthrow of the power of the bourgeoisie and . . . installation of the dictatorship of the proletariat *through the means of soviets . . .* organized on the model of the Great Party of Lenin and Stalin."[7] Now the Socialists were not so enthusiastic, and at the end of November 1937, after two years of negotiations, the SFIO executive ended discussions, dashing PCF hopes of achieving hegemony through party alliance. However, in spite of all the various hard-line flanking maneuvers during this period, the essentially moderate character of Communist participation in the Popular Front had by 1938-1939 raised questions about the party's capacity for radical action.

The Nazi-Soviet Pact of August 1939 provided a test, and the PCF leadership chose to support the pact. As a result of this decision the party, its government representations, and its ancillaries were all divested of legality and decimated. What remained of the organization was forced underground. In Annie Kriegel's terms, the Communists were forced to operate almost entirely from "without" the polity. To put it another way, during the 1939-1941 period the French Communist presence was as "pure," in the sense of unambiguous, as it has ever been; and its illegal, clandestine organization resembled more the pre-1917 Bolshevik experience than ever before. Supporting the Nazi-Soviet Pact was an unquestionably radical act, one of almost suicidal consequences.[8] It brought the French Communist movement toward a nearly total embrace of the vanguard "proletarian internationalist" pole of behavior, a position which implied only two possible outcomes: revolution or annihilation. And given Stalin's own alliance policy, the French leaders were permitted few illusions about which was the more likely, a result they appeared willing to rationalize with the goal of "saving the first socialist country." Nonetheless, even in the midst of this imposed policy which robbed the PCF of its potential for ambiguous tacti-

[7] Thorez report to the Eighth PCF Congress (Paris, 1936), p. 128, paraphrasing the Charter, which was published in *L'Humanité*, June 8, 1935.

[8] The PCF leaders had not been informed by Stalin of the impending agreement. Their reservations for a month afterward (see Tiersky, *French Communism*, Chapter 4 and sources cited therein) indicated not only the difficulty, but also the consciousness of their choice. They could hardly have believed there was a chance of rallying allies, when the Pact meant almost certain war for France, exactly the goal all potential allies had been trying to avoid.

cal maneuvering, the French Communists made several rather desolate attempts to maintain positions in contact with the rest of France. The most apparent was the complicated reconstitution of a Communist-front parliamentary group, the *Groupe ouvrier et paysan*, during the late fall and winter of 1939-1940. This experience ended in the trial and conviction of forty-four Communist deputies between March 20 and April 3, 1940. There were also attempts at unity "at the bottom," in the rank and file of various worker and peasant organizations, and—after the armistice was signed and German occupation began—the much discussed attempts to regain legality for the party and the party newspaper *L'Humanité*. There was even a call for a French government including the Communists, efforts at once absurd and desperate. The exigencies of "proletarian internationalism" in time of war, accepted by the French Communists in 1939 in contrast to the Socialist choice in 1914, had left them allies neither among other Frenchmen nor among the supposed German partners of the Soviet government.

War and Cold War

After struggling for almost two years with the vain hope of dealing with the Nazis as had Stalin, the French Communists got a fresh start after Germany attacked the Soviet Union. Entering and eventually becoming the leading force in the metropolitan Resistance until it was absorbed by the Gaullist authorities into the Provisional Government regime, the PCF leaders pursued two immediate goals: first, to help defeat the Germans; second, to use the Liberation élan to promote French independence of American influence at the war's end. Both goals demanded the strongest, largest, and most widely allied movement possible. They were at the same time—and above all—the most effective ways in which the PCF might aid the Soviet Union and the achievement of the Eastern bloc.

As many participants and historians have asserted, during the Resistance and Liberation the Communists in France began once again to maneuver toward hegemony. But these efforts, which in the most optimistic Communist appraisal might possibly have led to an "advanced" or "people's democracy" regime, were pursued only to the extent that they did not conflict with the more important and overriding aims of Soviet policy, which is to say not very far. Nonetheless, besides the usual agitated manipulation of revolutionary doctrine characteristic of periods in which the dominant tactic is cooperation and moderation, these limited endeavors toward a Soviet-style power structure were the primary manifestation of the vanguard role during 1943-1946. The dominant facets in the composite Communist visage at this time were rather the roles of government party and popular tribune in their most participatory forms. And moreover, the paradox of unprecedented ministerial participation in General de Gaulle's Provisional Government was that, precisely in reestablishing French communism as a legal and mass movement with Cabinet representation, all of the inherent tensions between the minimum and maximum perspectives were exacerbated.

In 1943-1944 the question of a possible Communist insurrectionary attempt was posed quite clearly, and the Gaullists especially suspected the PCF might seek to use its strong positions in the *Forces Françaises de l'Intérieur* (FFI), the Departmental Liberation Committees, and the paramilitary Patriotic Militias to rise against the Provisional Government (created June 3, 1944). However, despite whatever possibility for success might have existed (and there persists a minor though vigorous debate on this point, even among Communists), the PCF leadership accepted the tacit understanding at Yalta which implied restraining the French party's goals in order to avoid placing into question the agreement which facilitated the emergence of Communist regimes in Eastern Europe. And, in any case, as François Billoux, a leading French Communist and several times minister, wrote: "It would certainly have been possible, here and there, to establish (revolutionary) islands in the general enthusiasm of the Liberation. But what would have become of them? First, a battle from city to city, from region to region, according to the state of mind of the population. Thereafter, the American troops would not long have tolerated such a situation."[9]

Maurice Thorez, who had deserted his military post October 4,

---

[9] *Quand nous étions ministres* (Paris: Editions Sociales, 1972), p. 60. Jacques Duclos adds the pertinent caution that many new Communists, who had joined the movement on the basis of the Resistance effort, would not have acquiesced in an insurrection for a Soviet-style takeover and regime. See his *Mémoires*, 6 vols. (Paris: Fayard, 1970), 3, Book 2: 303. On the other hand, failure to attempt an insurrection created a lasting and bitter disappointment for others: "We really believed, in 1944, that we were going to take power. But the chance was missed, as always." A Communist Resistance militant, cited in Jacques Doyen, *Les Soldats blancs de Ho Chi Minh* (Paris: Fayard, 1973), p. 342.

1939, and spent the war years in the Soviet Union, returned to French soil on November 27, 1944. In his first public speech he intimated that the Gaullist order to disband the militias would not be resisted any longer, as it had been for two months before his arrival. Thereupon it was evident there would be no bid to take power on the basis of the "dual power" situations which existed in the militias, the local and departmental liberation committees, and the Conseil Nationale de la Résistance (CNR) on the one hand, and on the other hand, the regular army and the Provisional Government institutions.

Increasing Communist ministerial participation—from two portfolios of April 4, 1944, in the de Gaulle government at Algiers to five ministers in the Ramadier government of January 22, 1947, the first of the Fourth Republic—does not reflect uniformly increasing Communist influence. In fact, in terms of the fundamental choices in domestic and foreign policy, the PCF was much less influential after the middle of 1946 than before.

In the two Constituent Assembly elections and the first election to the Fourth Republic Assembly, a tripartite PCF-SFIO-Mouvement Républicain Populaire (MRP) domination of the political spectrum was consistently reaffirmed. And the Communists, the strongest party in terms of membership, organizational capacity, and vote, participated in all the governments up to their ouster in May 1947—with the single exception of the one-month homogeneous SFIO government of Léon Blum in December 1946, when the PCF and MRP leaderships agreed on mutual nonparticipation as the only solution to a Cabinet crisis. Like the Communist participations in Italy, Belgium, and Finland, PCF administration of ministerial responsibility in terms of policy was generally vigorous, efficient, and certainly nonrevolutionary. The party supported the CNR program, and, partly in order not to prejudice the Communist claim to a unique future role, even opposed those who wanted to make the CNR program more radical —particularly regarding the question of nationalization. Moreover, Communist ministers voluntarily refrained from publicly attacking General de Gaulle's tendency to ignore the CNR and its program. "Produce, Produce, Produce!" was the slogan of the Tenth Congress (June 1945), and the PCF policy of broad political and economic cooperation implied unabashedly the calculation that only a rapid and peaceful recovery to economic independence might achieve political and military independence

429

from the United States. Thus, for example, simultaneously with Communist ministerial efforts to produce social and economic welfare measures, the Communist leadership in the reunified CGT counseled moderate wage demands. It was extraordinary that under the PCF Minister of Labor, Ambroize Croizat, not a single strike occurred while General de Gaulle remained head of the government.[10]

At the same time, the Communists saw their attempts to produce an "advanced" set of political institutions (i.e., closer to the formal Soviet governmental institutions) reduced to impotence, a power shift nowhere more evident than in the set of two drafts and referendums to choose a constitution for the Fourth Republic. The first draft constitution, which proposed a unicameral legislature with a virtually powerless president and strict governmental responsibility to Parliament, was the result of a temporary PCF-SFIO agreement against both the MRP and Gaullist positions. The first draft was a great Communist victory both in terms of alliance politics and policy outcomes: in fact, it was the maximum the PCF leadership could realistically have hoped to obtain. As the strongest party, and particularly given the proposal for a proportional representation electoral law, the PCF would have had the maximum possible influence in this kind of postwar French regime.[11] The rejection of the first draft constitution on May 5, 1946 (53 percent—47 percent)—the first time the French people had ever refused a referendum proposal —incited the internal balance within the SFIO leadership to shift against alliance with the Communists on the constitutional question. The second draft constitution, essentially reflecting an SFIO-MRP alliance, reincorporated an upper house (called the Council of the Republic) and in other ways reversed positions

[10] Noted by de Gaulle himself. *The Complete War Memoirs of Charles de Gaulle* (New York: Simon and Schuster, 1967), p. 782.

[11] The official PCF constitution proposition is "Texte intégral de la proposition de loi constitutionelle des deputés communistes à l'Assemblée Nationale constituante" (Algiers: Editions Liberté, 1944). The text of the first draft constitution can be found in Maurice Duverger, *Constitutions et documents politiques*, 5th ed. (Paris: Presses universitaires de France, 1968), pp. 124-137.

The October 21, 1945, Constituent Assembly elections gave the PCF and its allies 159 seats, the MRP 150 seats, and the SFIO 139 seats. Together these three parties had won about three-fourths of the vote and four-fifths of the seats. The potential influence of the PCF is thus evident, as is the reason why a return to PR is a crucial demand in the Communist program today.

430

in the first draft that were favorable to the Communists. It was adopted October 13, 1946, by a very weak majority of 10.6 million votes to 9.5 million votes, with 5 million abstentions. And what is more, the PCF leaders were even obliged to call for a yes vote on the second draft, because a Gaullist movement (the Gaullist Union) had been formed which threatened defeat and the possibility of a third draft. A third proposal might well have been based on the executive-dominated regime set out by de Gaulle in his famous Bayeux speech, an institutional framework which would have been the *least* favorable to Communist positions.[12]

However, despite the persistent limits on French Communist action and the general weakening of its influence during 1945 and 1946, the PCF continued to stick doggedly to the policy of coalition among the parties and broad alliance throughout the polity. Still, unlike the Italian Communist situation, in which historical, sociological, and political factors all seemed to render necessary an alliance with the Christian Democrats as well as the Socialists, in France the PCF attempted several times to attract the SFIO into a two-party alliance which would have had a majority alone.[13] But the Socialists refused to cut themselves off from the MRP and they did not in any case wish to isolate themselves in alliance with a party still claiming a future monopoly of political power as its historically necessary destiny. Given this, the PCF leaders continued to support the tripartite solution in government, and even became progressively more defensive of it as the danger of exclusion and isolation became more apparent in late 1946 and early 1947.

All this notwithstanding, Communist participation in the 1943-1947 alliances, as during the Popular Front, was ambivalent in certain secondary respects which reflected once again the simultaneous pursuit of conventional alliance politics and revolutionary hegemonic goals. In three separate arenas, the PCF attempted implicitly to maneuver alliance and cooperation into

[12] See Donald L. M. Blackmer, Chapter 1 in this volume, for an analysis of the PCI stake in the postwar Italian constitution, which, in establishing the party's legality for the first time durably, was to become a much more important reference than the Fourth Republic constitution for the PCF.

[13] Thus, the *main tendue*, or "outstretched hand" to the Catholic workers, first announced by Maurice Thorez in April 1936, never assumed the strategic importance which the postwar PCI leadership was to place on its overtures to the DC and the Catholic mass base. The PCF leaders in 1945-1946 even used the clerical issue as a weapon to try to separate the SFIO from alliance with the MRP.

unipolar or single-force constellations in which Communist participation would be the dominant force.

First, early in the Resistance period, the Communists sought to make the Front Nationale (FN), their own organization, into the center of all the resistance movements. Failing this they joined the CNR upon its creation, and at the end of 1944 attempted to gain a predominant power in the post-Liberation and post-CNR Resistance organization through a proposed merger of the Mouvement de Libération National (MLN) and the FN. They succeeded in obtaining only a minority split in the MLN, however, as the majority refused to go further than joint action with the Communists. Second, this failure to fuse the Resistance into a single postwar political force under Communist influence was matched by another failure to merge the PCF and SFIO themselves, in a scenario which had much in common with that of 1935-1937. And finally, also repeating the Popular Front experience, the Communist and Socialist trade-union forces were reunited in the CGT. Beginning with the clandestine Perreux agreement of April 17, 1943, the Communists were accepted back into the CGT, and by the April 1946 Congress had achieved undisputed control of the confederation as a whole through their domination of the seven largest affiliated federations. This sole success in terms of promoting hegemonic intentions was moreover to endure only until the onset of the Cold War in 1947-1948. Within a year after the creation of the Fourth Republic, it was to be demonstrated that even its moderate policies and its evident submission to constraints imposed by the postwar division of Europe could not prevent the French Communist movement from suffering the consequences of its origins in the revolutionary vanguard role as defined by the Russian Bolsheviks. And acceptance of these consequences was proof of radical intentions whose continued existence had once again been placed in doubt by the practice of alliance and governmental participation during the 1941-1947 period.

During the Cold War the crucial element determining the nature and limits of French Communist alliance policy, and the movement as a whole, was the near-complete exclusion and isolation forced upon the PCF as a secondary effect of the East-West schism at the international level. In the spring of 1947, the French Communists, like the Communists in Italy, Belgium, and

Luxembourg, were excluded from the national government in spite of their avowed policy of continued Cabinet participation. On the one hand, in purely national terms the strategy of continued long-term alliance with other forces, given the political and military configuration in Europe, was perceived as the best hope for consolidating and even further extending the organizational gains of recent years, while working toward—and waiting for—a period more favorable to new Communist initiatives in the Western European countries. On the other hand, and more importantly, it seemed that the dominant Soviet foreign policy goals of protecting the Eastern bloc consolidation and hindering the consolidation of an Atlantic Alliance demanded a continued Communist presence in Western governments. Thus, given the complex set of objectives and limits in PCF policy, in June 1945 Maurice Thorez affirmed: "We consider the prolonged maintenance in office of a government of broad democratic and national unity as the happiest prospect for our country."[14] This was also the most positive *Communist* prospect, to be sure. Furthermore, on November 18, 1946, in a celebrated interview in the London *Times*, Thorez even spoke for the first time of a "national" road to socialism: "The progress of democracy . . . permits the consideration . . . of other roads than that followed by the Russian Communists. In any case, the road is necessarily different for each country. We have always considered and declared that the French people, rich in a glorious tradition, would find its own way."

One can debate endlessly over the importance of such declarations and ponder also the fact that after their exclusion from the Cabinet on May 5, 1947, the French Communist leaders sought until September to reintegrate, to resume a role of government party despite their decreasing influence and increasing rank-and-file pressures for a more aggressive policy. But, however one may speculate upon the long-term effects of a hypothetical continuation of tripartism, the French Communist agreement to accept the Cominform and the "Zdhanov line" in September-October 1947 was the symbol of a decision to resume an alliance posture emphasizing the radical-exterior dimension of Communist opposition, in which never-abated proposals for alliance and governmental participation fell victim to an unworkable combination

[14] Cited in the official party history, *Histoire du parti communiste français* (*manuel*) (Paris: Editions Sociales, 1964), p. 461.

433

of the outstretched hand and the closed fist. The PCF still professed alliance "at the top" to the Socialists: but whereas before the Communists offered to accept the SFIO commitment to the MRP and others as part of a moderate coalition compromise, now they demanded that the Socialists move toward them, in effect to choose one of the "two camps." The corollary to this hard-line, aggressive alliance offer—since the French Socialists had already chosen the Western camp de facto—was a resignation to the role of political pariah, the ghetto existence characteristic to varying degrees of all Communist movements "trapped" in the West during the Cold War.[15] Thus, in a judicious explanation of the ineffectiveness and immobility of the PCF during the Cold War, it is as important to emphasize the externally imposed exclusion and isolation of the movement as to restate more conventional critiques of the Communist refusal to abandon unacceptable conceptions, particularly given the Popular Front and Tripartite precedents. In the situation of Cold War, exclusion and the ideological hard line were two sides of the same coin.

The extent of the exclusion and isolation imposed on the Communists can be quickly indicated.[16] After the disintegration of tripartism among the parties, and in particular the SFIO's acceptance of the "third-force" option, which is to say a coalition of parties "in between" the PCF and the Gaullist RPF, unity in the trade-union movement did not long survive. The CGT split once more, this time however resulting in a Communist-dominated majority organization and a Socialist-oriented minority, the CGT-Force Ouvrière (FO). But thereafter, in spite of its new position as the largest and potentially most influential union, the CGT was able to do very little to aid the PCF in finding allies or even to achieve cooperation with other forces in the labor movement. Aside from a brief period of ad hoc joint action with the Confédération Française des Travailleurs Chrétiens (CFTC) during a severe and somewhat unexpected strike in 1953, Communist syndicalists failed to achieve any national alliance with other unions.

In Parliament the PCF was equally excluded and isolated. The Communists were excluded *a priori* from possible government

---

[15] See Blackmer, Chapter 1 in this volume on the Italian situation, in which the Nenni Socialists maintained a limited alliance with the PCI for about a decade.

[16] For a detailed analysis see Tiersky, *French Communism*, Chapter 7.

coalitions, despite voting the investitures of Pierre Mendès-France (1954) and Guy Mollet (1956), and despite voting several important, and a host of minor, bills under various governments. Furthermore, the impossibility of forming electoral alliances reduced the PCF parliamentary delegations as well,[17] and the Communists were excluded from positions of authority in the Senate and Assembly committees almost entirely. For example, after holding six presidencies of committees in both the upper and lower chambers in 1946-1947, they have not held another since, despite representing from one-fourth to one-fifth of the electorate. Similar statistics result from an examination of the situation in regional and local governmental structures, and in the naming of representatives to European organizations.[18]

This near-complete exclusion and isolation of the PCF in the centers of political participation had two major results: First, within governmental bodies the Communists were motivated to use extreme though largely ineffectual means of action—such as the most violent kinds of parliamentary obstructionism. The classic instance of this was the attempt to block a series of "antisabotage" bills in March 1950. And the blockage of former points of institutional access also encouraged violent forms of extraparliamentary action, such as the great strike waves of 1947-1948 and the bloody demonstrations in 1952 against NATO, touched off by the arrival of General Ridgway in Paris to replace General Eisenhower as Supreme Commander. Second, with tactical gains constrained to isolated acts of almost purely symbolic significance, the perpetual "struggle for unity" of the PCF came to focus almost entirely in the ancillary organizations of the movement, and in particular the Mouvement de la Paix, or Peace Movement.

The Peace Movement was a loose, supposedly nonpartisan association of groups from different countries working "for peace." Although its origins were not Communist in France, the

[17] The controversial change in the electoral law for 1951, introducing the *apparentements*, helped reduce the Communist delegation from 27 percent of the seats in 1946 (with 28.6 percent of the vote) to 16 percent in 1951 (with 25.6 percent of the vote). The Fourth Republic PR system was then abandoned for the single constituency, double-ballot electoral law of 1958: with 18.9 percent of the vote the PCF won only 10 seats, about 2 percent of the total. To be sure, the lack of second-ballot alliance possibilities was compounded by the nearly 7 percent drop in the Communist electorate.

[18] Representatives of the PCI have been elected to sit in the European Parliament since 1969. PCF representatives were chosen by the National Assembly for the first time in May 1973.

435

PCF was able to pack the French Peace Movement quickly, without causing the organization to split. Though a minor victory, this had some importance since it was only in such associations for peace, or against the wars in Indochina and Algeria, that the Communists were able to surmount their ghetto existence during the Cold War. At one point (November 1949) the Cominform even voted a resolution calling on the European Communist parties to make the Peace Movement the focus of their entire activity.[19] Nonetheless, despite furious activity around the "peace issue" during the period roughly from 1948 to 1954, which was related to more identifiable Communist campaigns against the "Marshallization of France" and American imperialism through the NATO alliance, few tangible benefits beyond a limited contact with potential allies were achieved through the Peace Movement. This was not surprising for an organization whose major weapon was the public petition.

In sum, the French Communists during the Cold War were obliged by the international orientation of the movement to pursue an unworkable alliance orientation toward other parties. They failed almost totally, as the situation implied, although the party retained most of its electorate (26.1 percent in 1946; 25.7 percent in 1956; 18.9 percent in 1958; 21.7 percent in 1962). Trapped in the contradiction of vanguard internationalism as they conceived it and the exigencies of political alliance with other French parties, the Communist predicament was typified in that curious moment in February 1949 when—at the height of the Peace Movement's activity—Maurice Thorez chose to reaffirm what the PCF's attitude would be, should conditions in Europe be transformed: "If . . . the Soviet Army . . . should be brought to pursue the aggressors onto our soil, could the workers and people of France act . . . otherwise than did . . . the people of Poland, or Rumania, or Yugoslavia?"[20]

By 1958—their action conceived within the terms of an international calculation which accorded only marginal attention to the long-prophesied socialist revolution in France—the French Communists had arrived at an unmistakable strategic and tactical impasse in which the party organization itself had entered a deep crisis. At the leadership level the serious illness of Maurice

[19] See Marshall D. Shulman, *Stalin's Foreign Policy Reappraised* (New York: Atheneum, 1969), p. 132.

[20] *L'Humanité*, February 23, 1949, p. 1.

Thorez,[21] the Lecoeur and Marty-Tillon affairs, the death of Stalin, and finally the general crisis of the international movement which followed the Khrushchev "secret speech" and the repression of rebellion in Hungary, all had contributed to a weakening of its coherence and initiatives. At the rank-and-file and militant level, the signs of crisis were even more openly evident: membership had declined from approximately 750,000—800,000 in 1946-1947 to about 225,000 in 1959-1960. Party cells were often not meeting regularly and the level of militant activity —in particular propaganda and press—had become both less stable and less vigorous. Thus when the Fourth Republic fell, the PCF not only was unable to make capital out of the situation, but, on the contrary, saw its positions further weakened by the resurrection of Gaullism.

The Period of Détente

How have the tensions between French Communist alliance politics and revolutionary claims, between the roles of government party and radical organization, evolved in the period of détente that has now characterized international politics for over a decade?

Broadly speaking, a combination of three factors worked decisively to transform the situation of near-complete exclusion and isolation of communism in France during the Cold War. On the most general level, attenuation of the Cold War internationally after 1956—more markedly so after the Cuban Missile Crisis in 1962 and the Partial Test-Ban Treaty in 1963—had the secondary effect of altering non-Communist perceptions of Communists in many national situations, permitting and even encouraging certain forms of alliance where sufficient common interest and will existed. Secondly, as the Fifth Republic regime took unexpected forms under the influence of Gaullism, the resignation of the French Socialists and some centrists from the original Gaullist coalition of 1958-1959 had the result of providing potential partners for the French Communists though, to be sure, few observers at that point foresaw dramatic developments in relations with the PCF, given both the tenuousness of détente and the bitter his-

---

[21] Stricken by a cerebral hemorrhage on October 10, 1950, Thorez was removed to the Soviet Union for convalescence. He returned to France on April 10, 1953, thirty-five days after the death of Stalin. His absence contributed to the internal maneuvering in the Lecoeur and Marty-Tillon affairs.

437

tory of relations between Bolshevism and Social Democracy. Third, under the double influence of de-Stalinization in Soviet doctrine and practice, and of major threats to PCF electoral and organizational positions domestically, the French Communists moved themselves to undertake certain long-awaited transformations of doctrine, program, and practice attached to the vanguard role and the Communist model of socialist society.[22] Moreover, after 1965 it began to appear that this process of change would include a not-negligible degree of detachment of French Communist goal priorities from the Soviet foreign policy interest, adding some credibility to the idea of a "French road to socialism" and a specifically "French" socialist future which the PCF leadership no longer proposed to mold along the Soviet example.

In the long run, it is quite possible that persistence of these three elements would in any case have eventually drawn French Communists and Socialists into some form of renewed cooperation surpassing purely electoral partnership. However, beginning with the presidential elections of 1965 an unexpected catalyst was added which brought about a deeper alliance more quickly than had been expected, as well as constructing it around a more extremist point of axis: this was the emergence of the radicalizing and centripetal leadership of François Mitterrand and his allies in the non-Communist Left. And paradoxically, in addition to cooperating with the Communist strategy by promoting a Communist-Socialist governmental alliance, the Mitterrand leadership of the Socialist party since 1971 has in another sense made the Communist position more difficult. For in adopting an active rather than passive stance to the dilemmas of alliance with the PCF (as opposed to the SFIO leadership in 1936 and 1945), and in developing the theme of workers' self-administration—*autogestion*—as the basis of an idiosyncratic program for socialist society, the new PS (and on the trade-union level the new Confédération Française Démocratique du Travail [CFDT] in relation to the CGT) for the first time since Tours seems today to be able to define itself in relation to the PCF in other than negative

[22] On the influence of political competition and setbacks on PCF doctrine and practice toward the end of the 1950s, see the analysis developed by Thomas H. Greene, "Adoptive Change and Political Competition." (Paper presented to the Conference on French and Italian Communism, October 1972.)

438

terms, and to mobilize rank-and-file support not only *against* Communist positions but *for* Socialist positions, however vague the concept of *autogestion* remains.

French Communist alliance policy in the period of détente remains a product of the two broad considerations which have perpetually dictated the constants of PCF action: (1) the limits deriving from the French Communist link with the Soviet Communist party and the international Communist movement—and, therefore, the general climate of East-West relations, and (2) the lack of any realistic prospect of a classic revolutionary possibility in France itself. While the latter element is a strong motivation toward alliance politics within the legitimized norms of the party system—a dangerous option for a would-be revolutionary organization in an established parliamentary situation—the former element historically has determined the practicability of PCF alliance politics, including both the periods of successful coalition (1934-1938; 1941-1947; 1962-present), and the periods of non-alliance (1928-1933; 1939-1941; 1947-1962).

The emergence of international "peaceful coexistence" and national strategies of "peaceful transition to socialism" opened a new possible path of advance for nonruling Communist parties in parliamentary situations: The former contradiction between alliance politics and revolutionary goals—expressed in the fact that alliances had been possible only on the basis of nonrevolutionary goals—was now given an at least theoretically plausible manner of resolution. In other words, *because of* the Soviet policy of de-Stalinization, and *in spite of* the Soviet policy of détente and partial cooperation with the Western powers, nonruling Communist parties were now in theory "free" to seek alliances to promote their own maximum national goals within the framework of parliamentary politics. Since the bolshevization of the Comintern, this was the first time such freedom had existed.

In the case of the French Communist party, the rapprochement of Communists and Socialists and the development of an at least prospectively radical governmental alliance was begun with electoral cooperation, and developed through negotiation of program proposals. Specifically, since the renewal of contacts between Communists and Socialists, French Communist policy has been based on the effort to obtain a joint program with the Socialists, the "common program" tactic being considered the only

439

realistic means of attaining the party's strategic goals. Let us now consider how these strategic goals have been defined in the past and how they are defined now.

Before the development of the peaceful transition to socialism strategy, the goal structure of the PCF was composed of two elements, corresponding, to use the classic terms, to the "minimum" and "maximum" programs. On the one hand, the maximum program was a totalist conception of a revolutionary society constructed from the finality of implementing the Soviet example in France. In the early postwar years, however, the maximum perspective was rendered somewhat less specific by the emergence of modified Soviet regimes in Eastern Europe, although, to be sure, its essential characteristics remained. On the other hand, the party also espoused a minimum program, which amounted to a nonsystemized collection of reform proposals. In the context of the peaceful transition strategy, there are two new elements: (1) the proposed model of socialist society itself, the maximum goal, has been revised; (2) the strategy of linking the minimum and maximum programs has been changed by replacing the Soviet example of the proletarian dictatorship with an "advanced democracy," a program of broad and democratic alliance which is to be the specifically "French" transition stage between capitalism and socialism. It is this transition program which the Communists and Socialists have negotiated since 1967.

It is crucial to understand that the role of the program in French Communist strategy today is such that "the content of the program and its function are tightly linked,"[23] which is to say that the blueprint for the transition society—and even in some respects the socialist society itself—has been negotiated as a function of the strategic necessity of alliance with the Socialists. Strategic realists, the French Communist leaders demonstrate an awareness that *both* a radical program *and* a durable political alliance are necessary to even a marginal chance of realizing their long-range goals. Their tactical problem, in this perspective, has thus been to obtain an alliance with the Socialist party without fail, but also without compromising away too much of their own program, both medium and long term. Pursuit of this double goal was therefore the key to French Communist policy in the

[23] PCF historian Roger Martelli in *Cahiers d'histoire de l'Institut Maurice Thorez* (November-December 1972), 1: 116.

1967-1972 negotiations with the Socialists and remains so in the continuing confrontation of ideas and programs.

The face-to-face interparty negotiations before the general elections of March 1967 were the first direct Communist–non-Communist contacts in France in almost two decades. Previous to this, the French Communist escape from Cold War exclusion and isolation had taken various and sometimes rather bizarre forms. First came certain unilateral Communist doctrinal revisions and program proposals. Second came acceptance by the non-Communist Left of electoral cooperation with the Communists. Third came a series of very unusual maneuvers in which the PCF succeeded in being accepted as a direct, public, and "physical" partner, rather than an unofficial, semiclandestine partner.

In terms first of doctrinal revisions, one may note briefly that the essential of these had to do with reformulation of the PCF definition of its role as revolutionary vanguard, in the direction of rejecting certain aspects of the Soviet and East European experiences as inapplicable to France. The core of this redefinition, in addition to the idea of a peaceful transformation of society, was a fitful acceptance of what has become known as the "plural parties" or multiparty thesis, in contrast to the doctrine of a necessarily single-party regime: By the time of the Fifteenth Congress (1959), the French Communists had proposed an alliance of left-wing parties during the "restoration and renovation of French democracy"[24] and in the "march toward socialism"; at the Sixteenth Congress (1961) the alliance proposed was described as extending to "the realization of socialism"; and finally, at the Seventeenth Congress (1964), the new general secretary, Waldeck Rochet, went to great lengths to insist that the alliance would be valid "not only for today but for tomorrow." This appeared to be a declaration that even long-term cooperation with the Communist party was now without danger to a competitive multiparty regime.

Nonetheless, despite an extensive debate during 1964-1967 as to whether or not the French Communists had "really changed," few observers went so far as to claim the Communists had

[24] Referring to a "restoration" of democracy after the Gaullist coup of May 1958, and a "renovation" of the deficiencies in the Fourth Republic regime.

441

adopted a liberal conception of politics. And indeed, in the negotiations of 1969-1970, one of the central ambiguities in the PCF acceptance of a multiparty socialist regime was underlined in the discussion of the limits within which an "alternation in power" would be possible in the new society. However this may be, the French Communist doctrinal reformulations of the early 1960s indicated that the time was past when the party—its situation of "splendid isolation" tending to reinforce in the public eye the ascetic and self-assured character of its revolutionary claims—could avoid debating in earnest its pretensions to a unique role in history.

After 1947-1948, as indicated above, the exclusion of the French Communists from institutions of government, and even from most informal political participation with non-Communists, was extraordinarily far-reaching. And in terms of political alliances, not until the end of 1966 did the French Communists succeed in reestablishing and legitimizing open contact with other parties on the national level. In his report to the 1959 Congress, for example, Maurice Thorez noted that in March 1958, faced with the total refusal of Mollet and the SFIO leadership since 1956 even to reply to Communist alliance offers, the PCF had tried to open discussions with the newly created Union des Forces democratiques (UFD), a disparate left-wing group organized around opposition to the Algerian war and led by Daniel Mayer, Pierre Mendès-France, and François Mitterrand. However, despite the fact that some of its leaders were favorable to an understanding with the Communists, and despite the deliberately (and controversially) modulated PCF position on Algeria, the Communists could not obtain even "a meeting" with the UFD leaders.[25]

In the summer of 1960, a group of well-known personalities of the non-Communist Left organized a "judicial colloquium" to debate problems of individual liberties and the Algerian question. A Communist lawyer, Jules Borker, and several other Communist parliamentarians and legal experts were invited to attend. The significance of this development in ending the Communist isolation was to be revealed progressively over the next five years.

In addition to participating directly and voting a series of unanimous resolutions with potential allies at this series of meet-

[25] *Cahiers du communisme* (July-August 1959), p. 53.

442

ings, the Communists established a liaison with various non-Communist forces through Borker, who became one of three permanent secretaries of the continuing Colloquium.[26] Although the non-Communist Left, and in particular the SFIO under Mollet, refused the Communists direct and open contacts for six more years, from 1960 forward Borker played the role of a clandestine go-between. In 1965 his role became crucial in the events which led to Communist support of François Mitterrand's candidacy in the presidential elections, because Mitterrand's Socialist and Radical allies refused to allow him to deal directly and formally with the Communist leaders, and it was only through the indirect contacts established through Mitterrand advisers Charles Hernu and Roland Dumas on the one hand, and Jules Borker on the other, that Communist support was negotiated. And even once Communist support was assured, the presidential candidate Mitterrand was obliged to forgo a formal meeting at this point— turning down an explicit invitation from Waldeck Rochet, relayed through Borker, for a "face to face contact."[27] Finally, it was only at the October—November 1966 meetings to negotiate the electoral agreement of December 20, 1966, that the Communists made "physical contact" in open and formal alliance meetings with non-Communist partners.

Given this background of isolation and mistrust of the Communists, the hesitant and fitful consolidation of a Socialist-Communist alliance becomes more comprehensible. The first real Communist–non-Communist electoral cooperation on the national level since the beginning of the Cold War occurred in 1962.[28] First, the PCF rejection of the Gaullist referendum of October 28, 1962 (on the mode of presidential election) gave them

[26] The most important resolution of the little-known but important "Colloques juridiques de Royaumont" of June 30-July 2, 1960, was one advocating self-determination for the Algerian people. See *Le Jacobin* (monthly of the Club des Jacobins) of July 1960 for a report on the colloquium.

[27] On this incident and on Borker's role generally in 1965, the most nearly complete public record is in Jacques Derogy and Jean-François Kahn, *Les Secrets du ballottage* (Paris: Fayard, 1966), Chapter 8.

[28] In 1959 the PCF unilaterally withdrew a number of candidates in the senatorial elections, and in the municipal elections the same year there was a rise in the number of joint Communist–non-Communist lists which had persisted in isolated cases throughout the Fourth Republic. An extraordinary portrait of one of the new Communist–non-Communist municipal lists in 1959 is in Edgar Morin, *Commune en France: La Métamorphose de Plodemet* (Paris: Fayard, 1967), esp. p. 187 and passim.

443

a common position with the SFIO and certain other non-Communist groups. But more important still was the openly acknowledged cooperation between Communists and Socialists for mutual second-ballot withdrawals in the legislative elections of November, accomplished nonetheless without direct negotiations for a formal agreement. This cooperation resulted in a gain of 31 seats for the PCF, 25 for the SFIO, and 8 for the Radicals. And although these gains were not particularly threatening to the Gaullists, compared with the 1958 results, they demonstrated the value of electoral cooperation with the Communists in the new situation of the Fifth Republic.

The centrist-oriented presidential candidacy of the Socialist Gaston Defferre thereafter pushed the incipient PCF-SFIO rapprochement out of the political focal point of the French Left for the next two years. As opposed to the mutual withdrawals in 1962, Defferre's strategy was to leave the Communists no choice but to support him without a quid pro quo. However, Defferre was unable to cement the SFIO-Radical-MRP alliance upon which he had hoped to base his presidential candidacy, and his failure condemned as well his policy toward the PCF, which foresaw ultimately the absorption of the Communist rank and file into a broadly social-democratic "catch-all" party.[29] Upon Defferre's political collapse in the spring and summer of 1965, the sudden emergence of François Mitterrand and the Fédération de la Gauche Démocrate et Socialiste (FGDS) in the presidential elections of 1965 reintroduced alliance with the PCF as the dominant electoral option of the non-Communist Left.[30]

Mitterrand's unexpectedly strong showing on the second ballot (44.5 percent against 55.5 percent for De Gaulle) was due in large measure to vigorous Communist support, although the centrist candidacy of Jean Lecanuet, with almost 16 percent of the first-ballot vote, was necessary for the Left to oblige General de Gaulle to endure a run-off ballot. Furthermore, it was between July and September 1965—from the time Mitterrand began to

[29] On the Defferrist initiative of 1963-1965, see esp. Jean Poperen, *La Gauche française: Le Nouvel Âge, 1958-1965* (Paris: Fayard, 1972) and Frank L. Wilson, *The French Democratic Left, 1963-1969* (Stanford, Calif.: Stanford University Press, 1971).

[30] The FGDS comprised the SFIO, the Radical party, and the Convention of Republican Institutions, a collection of political clubs. It was called a "small federation" (i.e., without the MRP) as opposed to the "grand federation" Defferre had hoped to organize.

organize his candidacy to the moment the Communists announced their decision to support it—that Jules Borker, Charles Hernu, and Roland Dumas promoted the delicate clandestine negotiations, which many times seemed at the point of definitive rupture.

After a series of inconclusive doctrinal "debates" during the spring of 1966, conducted through the impersonal means of the PCF and SFIO newspaper editorial columns, the Communists finally succeeded in achieving face-to-face discussions with the non-Communist Left during the fall. The result was the agreement of December 20, 1966, relative to cooperation in the general elections of March 1967. The narrow victory of the Gaullist coalition in 1967—it retained only 245 seats in a chamber of 487—was thereupon a strong motivation for the FGDS leaders to accept the Communist demand to discuss a full-scale joint governmental program.[31] The negotiations begun after the March 1967 elections culminated in the first of the three crucial Communist–non-Communist program documents which have marked the incorporation of the French Communists in an alliance with realistic hopes of governing France.[32]

The Three Communist–Non-Communist Negotiations

In fashioning the "Joint Declaration" of February 24, 1968, the Communists negotiated with a heterogeneous political grouping in the FGDS, including the non-Marxist Radicals, the leaders of various political clubs, and the ambivalently Marxist SFIO Socialists. Thus the PCF was obliged to settle for much less than a "maximum" statement of intentions, and furthermore, the FGDS leadership stipulated that the document also list the numerous areas of disagreement, some of them of fundamental importance. In fact, the Joint Declaration makes no mention at all of either socialism or revolution, though it incorporates a list of far-reaching constitutional revisions (many of which later appeared also in the 1972 Common Program), a proposal to eliminate the *force*

[31] However, the substantial bloc of centrist PDM deputies (41) in 1967, neither Gaullist nor allied to the Left, meant that the near-reversal of the Gaullist majority did not imply a Left government at that point.

[32] From December 1963, the Communist leadership had attempted to impose the signature of a joint program as a precondition to electoral cooperation, but both in the presidential elections of 1965 and the legislative elections of 1967 this demand was finessed when it threatened to compromise the movement toward alliance as a whole.

445

de frappe, and a program of nationalizations whose extent was the subject of commentary texts explaining differences in position.[33] Very different policies were indicated also in the area of European and foreign policy: in particular, whereas the FGDS called for an expanded, deepened, and "democratized" political-economic European structure, the PCF position proposed a dissolution of the two blocs and the creation of a "great Europe" (i.e., including the COMECON countries). In terms of a hypothetical coalition government, these differences would place into question both the Common Market and the goal of an ultimate political union.

However, despite the large discrepancies between the Joint Declaration and the PCF's own program, hindsight suggests that the French Communists had now achieved the most important and difficult step forward toward a joint program—the first one. Furthermore, the timing of the negotiations and publication of the document were tactically fortuitous, because had the Joint Declaration not preceded the "events of May," the strains of this period might have broken the trend toward alliance much more severely. In the Joint Declaration the potential outlines of a left-wing government program had been drawn solidly enough—despite the large and dangerous gaps—that, particularly given the 1967 electoral results, a Cabinet including the Communists was rendered unavoidably a matter of first-priority consideration among the leaders of the non-Communist Left. Moreover, the very existence of the Joint Declaration posed the question of a definitive commitment in the latters' own program and strategy with increased urgency. Comparatively speaking, it was at this point that the French Communist alliance strategy became more potent than that of the Partito Comunista Italiano (PCI), de-

[33] Among the most significant constitutional changes were the abolition of Article 16, authorizing emergency powers for the president; the revision of Article 11 so as to prevent referendums from assuming the character of a "plebiscite"; the expansion of legislative competence (Article 34); the tightening of governmental responsibility before the Assembly (Article 49); the creation of a Supreme Court (Articles 56-63); automatic dissolution in the case of a successful motion of censure; reduction of the presidential mandate to five years. In terms of nationalizations, the FGDS proposed only commercial banks and the armament and space industries, while the PCF list added savings banks, insurance companies, and "key de facto monopolies"—such as the electronics and aeronautics industries, air transport companies, those automobile works not already nationalized, and the chemical and steel industries.

446

spite the PCF's slower and more reluctant de-Stalinization. In contrast to the PCI, the PCF now had obtained a tentative commitment to govern together from a group of allies whose electoral clienteles were such that a coalition including the Communists had majoritarian possibilities.[34]

The events of May 1968 in France and August 1968 in Czechoslovakia caused both a temporary hardening in Communist-Socialist relations and the self-dissolution of the FGDS. But this "hibernation" of the tendency toward consolidation of the non-Communist Left and Communist-Socialist alliance did not last long, and its minimum duration is all the more demonstrative of dominant tendencies in French politics when one considers the extremely bitter sentiments provoked in the French Left by these events. In addition, the "surprise and reprobation" expressed by the PCF at the invasion of Czechoslovakia—an open condemnation of Soviet action maintained consistently in spite of later acceptance of the "normalization"—was a sign that French Communist independence of action had widened considerably from earlier times. This was evidence that the PCF rejection of "certain regrettable features" of the Soviet experience implied a doctrinal decision of real consequence.

Considerations of space prevent giving details of the Communist-Socialist alliance renewal after the crises of spring and summer 1968. In brief, two factors intervened, the first of which was electoral disaster. In the general legislative elections of June 1968 and the presidential elections of June 1969, it was demonstrated that, on the one hand, the independent and Center electorates were not yet willing to trust Communist governmental participation, especially in a crisis situation with the possibility of a radical outcome; and that, on the other hand, the Center-Left option as attempted again in the Defferre presidential candidacy in 1969 was now almost totally impotent. Gaston Defferre in fact won only 5 percent of the first-ballot vote as against 21.5 percent for the PCF candidate Jacques Duclos. Second, and in a sense drawing the consequences of this result, the SFIO leader-

[34] Even supposing a broad alliance with the different Italian Socialist groupings, the PCI would require some Christian Democratic support or defections to be able to construct a majority alliance. Thus, besides the important factor of the greater power of regional and local governments in Italy as compared with France, the unlikelihood of building a national majority in the present circumstances seems to indicate why the PCI presently stresses the regional level in its strategy much more than the PCF.

447

ship began a serious renewal at the uppermost levels, expressed in the July 1969 replacement of First Secretary Guy Mollet by Alain Savary, and symbolized in the taking of a new title for the organization: Parti Socialiste (PS). This transformation of personnel was accompanied by the publication of a new "Socialist Plan of Action" for the following decade, a radicalized program for the medium-term which was based to a great extent on the Joint Declaration of February 1968 and the strategic alliance with the Communists implied therein.[35]

On December 18, 1969, the Socialist party leadership under Savary agreed to reopen program discussions with the Communists, this time without including either the Radicals or the clubs. After almost a year of tepid and difficult negotiations, a "First Summary" was rendered public on December 22, 1970. This second Communist-Socialist program document was, however, qualitatively different from the Joint Declaration in that it directly broached the question of alliance toward the installation of a socialist regime in France. This was quite significant in that the Communist success in achieving discussions on a program in 1967, and the Joint Declaration text itself, had led many observers to conclude that a "revisionist" point of no return had been reached, since perhaps the least arguable characteristics of French social democracy since the war had been its lukewarm radicalism and vigorous anticommunism. The SFIO radicalization of 1969 and the "First Summary" negotiations therefore had the effect of providing the first empirical indications in many years that the French Communists had—in spite of their strategic and organizational frustrations—preserved nonetheless a credible maximalist perspective, redefined as it had become during the previous decade.[36] And furthermore, it was clear that the combination of Communist persistence, a powerless opposition role, the lack of any other majority combination and an organizational rejuvenation had drawn the Socialists to commit themselves more and more deeply to the Communist alliance option, however many hesitations remained.

Still, in spite of this important difference between the First

[35] Published in the *Bulletin socialiste*, no. 92 (September 8, 1970).

[36] In terms of this redefinition of the maximum perspective, André Laurens and Thierry Pfister remark that the last time the French Communists went into the streets as "authentic commandos" was in the violent anti-Ridgway, anti-NATO demonstrations in 1952. They point out this was the last open manifestation of a possible "apparatus of 'civil war.'" See *Les Nouveaux Communistes* (Paris: Stock, 1973), p. 135.

Summary and the Joint Declaration negotiations—as well as some convergence in specific policy areas (in particular a Socialist agreement to nationalize, in addition to the Joint Declaration list, certain "key sectors of industry which determine economic development," and a Communist agreement that the "democratization of the public sector" might take "diverse forms" and be undertaken "progressively")—serious political and philosophical differences still divided the program proposals and leaderships.[37] In foreign policy certain disagreements remained fundamental although, as throughout the post-1962 evolution, the Communist leadership stated that it would not seek to make France's withdrawal from the Atlantic Alliance or dissolution of the Common Market a condition of a joint program (a rather gratuitous assertion). Furthermore, despite its declared acceptance of a competitive party regime in socialist society, the PCF leadership had failed to convince both its potential allies and a majority of public opinion that its statements did not guard a broad ambiguity regarding civil and political liberties, and especially regarding the possibility of an "alternation in power" between a left-wing socialist coalition and any other political grouping: In effect, the Communists now admitted the legitimacy of competition between socialist parties in socialist society but appeared to exclude nonsocialist parties from this hypothetical framework. The Savary leadership, hesitant and presiding over a situation in rapid flux within the Socialist party, thus presented the First Summary document to the rank and file without much fanfare. This contrasted sharply with a formal "ratification" of the statement by the PCF Central Committee, as if it were a major agreement.

The Socialist Party Congress of June 1971 at Epiney followed the First Summary by six months. At this crucial meeting the renewal and radicalization of the Socialist leadership was deepened through fusion with the Convention des Institutions Républicaines (CIR) and the election of its president, François Mitterrand, as first secretary to replace Savary. A corollary of this action was a decisive commitment of the PS to the "left-wing unity" strategy rather than the Center-Left option as a matter of Party principle.

Thereupon, key events rapidly ensued. On October 9, 1971, the PCF Central Committee published a formal and complete "pro-

[37] See the First Summary text, "Premier bilan," *Le Monde*, December 24, 1970, p. 10.

449

gram for an advanced democracy,"[38] and on December 19, the PS Executive Committee made public a program proposal of its own, which was amended and adopted March 12, 1972, by the PS Congress at Suresnes.[39] Then, on March 22 the PCF and PS leaderships agreed in principle to negotiate a joint program for the March 1973 general elections. Immediately, however, the two parties were split by a tactical dispute regarding the Pompidou referendum on enlarging the Common Market, called for April 23. The PCF opposed it outright, while the PS, in favor of the proposal but considering the referendum a plebiscite, called for abstention.[40] Despite this disagreement, on April 27, 1972, negotiations began toward a joint program, even though the potential foreign policy dilemma of a left-wing government had been once again underlined with force. The dispatch with which the Mitterrand Socialists resumed negotiations was a proof they were sincerely interested in a governmental alliance for the 1973 elections. This was significant in that Mitterrand had often been accused of playing a double game regarding the Communists, allegedly seeking to stall the momentum in order to attempt a more careful and self-interested strategy built around a Mitterrand presidential candidacy in 1976 and a joint program only for the succeeding elections. As president, this argument suggested, he could control the coalition more than as prime minister.

In any case, after only two months of intensive meetings, from April 27 to June 26, the *Programme commun de gouvernement*, or Common Program, was announced. On July 12, 1972, it was formally signed not only by the PCF and PS leaderships, but also by a dissident wing of the Radical party, calling itself the "Movement of Left-wing Radicals."

Continuity and Change

A preliminary remark is necessary: In the foregoing analysis, and in particular with reference to the discussion of pre-1956

---

[38] *Programme pour un gouvernement démocratique d'union populaire* (Paris: Éditions Sociales, 1971).

[39] *Programme de gouvernement du Parti socialiste* (Paris: Flammarion, 1972).

[40] The referendum passed only weakly, 36 percent to 17 percent, with a 47 percent level of abstentions, including some blank or void ballots. This poor result, in addition to constituting a blow to the prestige of President Pompidou in European circles, also soon added to speculation as to the chances of a Gaullist defeat in the coming elections.

French Communist practice, some may have concluded that the guiding interpretation of French communism was informed by what is now an "outdated" view of relations between Communist parties, and in particular of the influence of Soviet policy and the Soviet example on other parties. In considering such a criticism, and its homologue today—i.e., that the PCF has totally changed —it is appropriate to recall Zbigniew Brzezinski's caution in *The Soviet Bloc* against "the temptation to see now the earlier period in the light of all the conflicts that have recently surfaced. Just as formerly there was a tendency to be skeptical about the proposition that the Communist camp is not homogeneous, today there is an inclination to push back in time the different conflicts that are now so apparent."[41] One ought to approach the problem of delineating elements of continuity and change in French communism similarly, neither insisting that today must be seen as necessarily a continuation of yesterday, nor implying that yesterday ought to be rewritten *de rigueur* as a reflection of today.[42]

Although the PCF–PS-dissident Radical coalition did not come very close to winning the elections of March 1973,[43] the joint program tactic as the practical implementation of the peaceful transition to socialism remains the focal point of French Communist strategy—for lack of any feasible alternative, one is tempted to add. With no realistic prospect of revolution in the generally accepted sense of the term, and given that the office of president— now the defining institution in the regime—appears beyond their reach for many years to come, the major Communist hope is for a parliamentary coalition which would halt and reverse the trend toward complete de facto presidentialism. Such a coalition would thereby permit the implementation of certain radical changes, which in the most optimistic Communist predictions might there-

[41] *The Soviet Bloc: Unity and Conflict* (Cambridge, Mass.: Harvard University Press, 1967), p. xii.

[42] Moreover, it is significant that Donald Blackmer and Sidney Tarrow in this volume have insisted upon the wartime and Liberation periods as the decisive moment in the formation of postwar Italian communism, in contrast to the broader development of French communism in the prewar period. To the extent this distinction is valid, the analyst of French communism must be all the more alert to durable features of the pre-1939 experience.

[43] The Left alliance as a whole won slightly less than 42 percent of the first ballot vote (not counting the 3.3 percent won by the PSU and several *gauchiste* organizations who refused the Common Program alliance) and 174 of 490 seats in all. The Communists elected 73 deputies, the Socialists 89, and the dissident Radicals 12.

451

after snowball into an irreversible and thoroughgoing transformation of society. In the present situation, then, what are the major elements of continuity and change in the perennial contradiction between French Communist alliance politics and revolutionary aspirations?

First, the general PCF dilemma, which is the dilemma of all the Western European Communist parties, continues unabated: How can the party preserve a radical mentality and make both credible and effective its ambitions after a half-century of non-revolution, in a domestic situation in which the tendency to technocratic solutions more and more blunts the impact of radical proposals, and in an international situation in which the modal East-West political conflict is a stabilizing rather than destabilizing factor? Furthermore, as Donald Blackmer argues with relation to the PCI, this general dilemma is complicated by the organizational maintenance goals which the party must pursue for immediate and long-range policy purposes, but which at the same time encourage leadership caution, bureaucratization, and the danger of permanent inertia. Can the PCF surmount these contradictions? Despite certain appearances, I remain convinced there is no easy judgment to be made in this regard. A prudent conclusion is that, whereas it seems impossible to demonstrate in any statistically measurable manner that the French Communist mentality remains capable of transforming its environment, yet the party's origins, the radical tactical reversals in its past, its present program, and contemporary alliance patterns on the French left all incline one to believe that it may still be a directing force in producing quite radical changes in French politics and society. Beyond this however, the present character of Soviet foreign policy, and the apparent unlikelihood of a radical reversal in it similar to 1939 or 1947, poses a question whose answer submits to no possibility of *a priori* verification: In both 1939 and 1947 it was the internationalist dimension of French communism, its link with Soviet communism, which provoked the radical tactical reversals of policy. Has this international dimension of French Communist policy priorities—and, specifically, the identification with Soviet goals even when the latter prejudiced the national PCF organization and national goals—been a necessary condition to preservation of the radical capacities of the movement? Soviet foreign policy, having formed French communism

452

and obliged its rises and falls in the past, may now be obliging it to a complete deradicalization. In my judgment, this is not yet evident however, and may not necessarily follow in any case.[44]

A second dilemma arises paradoxically from the very success of French Communist alliance policy: In the past, the failure of French communism to make a revolution could be explained and justified by invoking the international demands on the movement, and the hostility of French socialism toward its *frère ennemi*. In the present period of international détente and domestic left-wing alliance, therefore, the very openness of the situation challenges the claims of the PCF vanguard role more directly than any previous event. Never before de-Stalinization of the international movement has the French Communist party been at liberty to formulate a strategy whose overriding goal is to begin a *national* social and economic transformation. And never previously has the party enjoyed an alliance with partners also espousing such a goal.

A third dilemma is that this new situation, which the Communists not surprisingly present as a lessening of the previous tension between political alliance and radical goals, has not been achieved without compromises in establishing the joint program. And in this regard, the contradictions in French communism are at some points deeper than ever.[45]

French Communist doctrine now asserts that the Soviet and East European examples of power takeover are unnecessary, and in any case impossible in "the specific conditions of France." As a result, the classic Popular Front-style patterns of hard-soft ambivalence in Communist alliance behavior may not be attempted consciously again. In particular, the acceptance of political pluralism is an accomplished fact to the extent the party leadership recognizes the PCF is not likely ever to be strong enough to achieve its goals alone. This recognition is further prodded by the fact that the party's very access to, and participation in the crucial power arenas is contingent upon durable alliance—that the loyal practice of alliance is, unlike the Bolshevik experience, the most effective way to promote and legitimate its own pro-

[44] I consider this question more deeply in "The PCF and Détente," *Journal of International Affairs* 28:2 (October 1974).

[45] The problems of implementing even a compromise program are further underlined by the experience of the Allende Popular Unity coalition in Chile.

453

gram. In this regard, one notes that after the electoral defeat of March 1973, the new general secretary, Georges Marchais, spoke optimistically nonetheless of a future Left government and of Communist participation, implicitly admitting the justification of public reluctance to accept the recent PCF evolution at face value:

> We will keep our promises. The USSR is the USSR, Hungary is Hungary, Czechoslovakia is Czechoslovakia, and France is France. The road we have chosen is different. . . . What is more, the Communist party is aware that it cannot travel this road alone, that a policy of unity is necessary. And the fact that it is with the Socialists and left-wing Radicals is the best guarantee that it will respect democratic liberties.[46]

With rejection of the single-party goal and with recognition of alliance as a necessity in the long run, the French Communist aspiration to a unique vanguard role is now more dependent on the self-definitions of its allies than ever before: If its allies are not credible, the party's vanguard claims themselves are implicated.

Despite the oversimplification, one may conceive the negotiation of a joint PCF-PS program in three stages between 1967 and 1972 as based upon the post-1956 deradicalization of the Communist political program and the more recent radicalization of the Socialist economic program: This broadly defined quid pro quo in effect responded to each party's most profound critique of the other's past commitments. Despite the many convergences in policy and attitude, however, it is clear that serious questions remain to be clarified in both positions. The cohesiveness of the Left coalition remains at the present uncertain, as the Communist-Socialist polemics since the March 1973 elections would suggest. Above all there is uncertainty as to how firmly these alliance commitments would resist the pressures of an actual government experience.

In sum, although for the first time the French Communists have succeeded in striking a potential majority alliance coalition with the avowed goal of transcending the capitalist structures of society, even in the case of a future Left electoral victory the tensions opposing the roles of government party and revolutionary

[46] In a speech of April 27, 1973, cited in *Le Monde*, April 29-30, 1973, p. 5.

vanguard will likely remain far from resolution. In the terms of their own logic, the Communists will resolve their ambivalent position in society and embrace the established order only when they are prepared to say that a socialist society has been attained. Yet they continue to describe this society in terms sufficiently different even from those of their partners that the gap between given ends and available means—the distance between French Communist alliance politics and revolutionary aspirations—remains apparently unbridgeable. However, even while taking full account of the broad Communist participation in, and in this sense de facto legitimation of, the established order, we are not yet justified in concluding that Communist ambitions for a radical transformation of society are irrelevant.

The long-awaited qualitative revision of the PCF vanguard conception is not yet achieved, although a point of no return may have already been passed. Without a continued evolution in doctrine and practice—which would paradoxically at once further legitimate the Communist strategy and further transform its program—the alliance tactic and the entire peaceful transition to socialism strategy implies the capacity not to resolve, but only to force a new configuration in the fundamental dilemma of the Communist relation to the rest of French society. Yet to dismiss the possibility of such a further change is to ignore certain tendencies of a post-Cold War era whose decisive international and national mutations we may be living today. Ultimately, it may not be entirely futile to hope that the left-wing reconciliation in France marks a general tendency toward transcendence both of the *société bloquée* and of Europe divided against itself.

XII.

Mass-Level Response to Party Strategy: The Italian Electorate and the Communist Party

GIACOMO SANI

Many discussions of party strategies focus quite properly on elites at both the national and local level. In the generation, application, and evaluation of strategies and tactics, party elites play a crucial role. But focusing exclusively on the elite of a party is unsatisfactory because implementing strategy involves other factors. Moreover, when the strategy involves mobilizing broad social groups, the relevant factors multiply rapidly. Leaders and activists of one party must not only consider the probable response by comparable leaders of other parties, but also determine at what segments of the population to aim. To assess whether, and to what extent, a given strategy of social mobilization has worked, is to ask questions about both those who initiated the strategy and those who responded to it. It is precisely to this type of problem that this chapter will address itself. Since 1944 the Partito Comunista Italiano (PCI) has attempted to become a significant force in Italian political life by adopting a strategy that relies at the mass level on broadening the party's base of support to include diverse social groups and at the elite level on pursuing alliances with other political forces to ease its access to local, and eventually national, government positions. The purpose of this chapter is to explore the response of the Italian electorate to the strategy of the PCI within the context of mass politics in contemporary Italian society.

The collection and analysis of the data reported in this paper were made possible by grants from the Ford Foundation and the National Science Foundation. The assistance of the Polimetrics Laboratory and the Computer Center of the Ohio State University is gratefully acknowledged. A number of friends and colleagues provided valuable criticisms and comments on an earlier draft of this paper: Herbert Asher, Sam Barnes, Donald Blackmer, Richard Hofstetter, Robert Putnam, Bradley Richardson, Ken Town, Loren Waldman, and Douglas Wertman.

After a brief overview of electoral trends in the 1946-1972 period, and of PCI strategy, I attempt to assess the party's success in terms of electoral support, popular acceptance, and political image. Finally, I propose an interpretation of both the successes and the limitations of the strategy by stressing the role of two mass-level constraints: political communication networks and popular conceptions of politics.

Throughout the chapter I rely primarily on two national surveys of the Italian electorate conducted shortly after the 1968 and 1972 elections.[1] Although these data provide answers to some questions about the political orientations of the electorate, national data are not fully adequate for problems dealing with specific narrow segments of the population, particularly when it would be desirable to make separate reference to different geopolitical subdivisions. This limitation, and others relative to the use of survey data in the Italian context, which will be discussed later, impose some oversimplification on the analysis, and limit the number and kinds of questions the chapter can address.

Trends in Popular Support for the PCI—1946-1972

When the votes of the 1972 parliamentary election were counted, the PCI reemerged, more solidly than ever, as the second largest party in the country. The returns showed that the PCI had been able to deal effectively with the threat generated on its left by the Manifesto group and others, and that it had been able to absorb the loss of strength in Parliament caused by the defection of the six members of the Lower House in 1969. In short, the election

---

[1] The 1968 survey was conducted by Samuel H. Barnes and the 1972 study jointly by the author and Barnes. Both surveys utilized a stratified random sample of electors. The interviews lasted from an hour to an hour and a half. In 1968 they were conducted by trained interviewers employed by CISER of Rome, and in 1972 by Fieldwork s.r.l. of Milan. A number of findings from the 1968 study are reported in, Samuel H. Barnes, "Left, Right and the Italian Voter," *Comparative Political Studies* 4 (July 1971): 157-176; "The Legacy of Fascism," *Comparative Political Studies* 5 (April 1972): 41-58; "Public Opinion and Political Preference in France and Italy," *Midwest Journal of Political Science* 15 (November 1971): 643-660; "Religion and Class in Italian Electoral Behavior," in Richard Rose (ed.), *Comparative Electoral Behavior: An Introduction* (New York: Free Press, 1973). Giacomo Sani, "Determinants of Party Preference in Italy: Toward the Integration of Complementary Models," *American Journal of Political Science* 18 (1974): 315-329.

overwhelmingly reconfirmed the PCI's hegemony in the Italian Left.

The 1972 election was hardly a great victory for the party and, indeed, in roughly one-third of the provinces the PCI suffered some losses. But the mean size of gains and losses in percent of the popular vote at the provincial level was very small (respectively 1.0 percent and 1.25 percent), and thus the departure from the 1968 outcome was minimal. The PCI had managed to do again what it had done before: hold onto its position and improve it marginally. In the twenty-six years of postwar electoral history, no other Italian party has been able to compile a similar record of constant, if small, gains and an overall consolidation of its support. In 1946 the PCI had obtained less than 19 percent of the vote; by 1972 its lists of candidates for the Lower House had attracted a sizable 27.2 percent of the electorate. (See Table 1.)

TABLE 1. PERCENT OF THE POPULAR VOTE FOR DIFFERENT PARTIES IN THE ELECTIONS FOR THE LOWER HOUSE, 1946-1972

	1946	1948	1953	1958	1963	1968	1972
PCI	18.9	(31.0)	22.6	22.7	25.3	26.9	27.2
PSIUP	—	—	—	—	—	4.5	1.9
PSI	20.7	(31.0)	12.7	14.2	13.8	14.5	9.6
PSDI		7.1	4.5	4.5	6.1		5.1
PRI	4.4	2.5	1.6	1.4	1.4	2.0	2.9
DC	35.2	48.5	40.1	42.4	38.3	39.1	38.8
PLI	6.8	3.8	3.0	3.5	7.0	5.8	3.9
PDIUM/PNM	2.8	2.8	6.9	4.8	1.7	1.3	8.7
MSI	—	2.0	5.8	4.8	5.1	4.5	
Others	11.2	2.3	2.8	1.7	1.3	1.4	1.9

Furthermore, analysis of the returns at the provincial level shows that this pattern of growth is not the result of aggregating the data at the national level. As the correlations for five pairs of adjacent elections show, there is a great deal of continuity in the PCI strength over time in the different areas of the country.[2]

[2] The sources for the aggregate data used in the correlations are as follows: for the period 1946-1963, V. Capecchi, V. Polacchini, G. Galli, G. Sivini, *Il comportamento elettorale in Italia* (Bologna: Società Editrice Il Mulino, 1968). For the period 1968-1972 the data were drawn from a study directed by Giovanni Sartori, sponsored by the *Consiglio Nazionale delle Ricerche*, and conducted by researchers affiliated with the Department of

(See Table 2.) Overall support for the party is not due to massive surges and declines in different areas that somehow compensate each other and leave a small positive balance, but to a pattern of slow, if uneven, growth across the nation. We gain a better appreciation of this continuity if we look at the degree of correspondence of the support for the PCI in 1946 and in 1972

TABLE 2. LINEAR CORRELATIONS BETWEEN PERCENT OF POPULAR VOTE FOR THE PCI IN 88 PROVINCES FOR PAIRS OF ADJACENT ELECTIONS

1946-1953	1953-1958	1958-1963	1963-1968	1968-1972
.839	.979	.986	.984	.991

in the different provinces. As the scatterplot of Figure 1 shows, over these twenty-six years the PCI has gained strength in all the 88 provinces considered, with a mean gain close to 9 percent. However, in spite of dramatic jumps in a number of units, the relative strength and weakness of its position in the different areas has not changed in a profoundly significant manner when one considers that the two points are separated by 5 national elections twenty-six years apart. The correlation between percent vote for the PCI in 1946 and in 1972 for the 88 provinces is still a remarkably high .894. The reason for this continuity, of course, is the fact that the gains of the PCI have not been uniformly higher in the areas where the party was originally weak. Strong gains in the south are compensated by very small rates of penetration in the Catholic northeast. At the same time, the percentage of

Social and Political Science of the University of Florence, and the Carlo Cattaneo Research Institute of Bologna. Some of the findings are reported in Giacomo Sani, "Alcuni dati sul ricambio della dirigenza politica in Italia," *Rassegna italiana di sociologia* 8, no. 1 (January-March 1967): 126-142; Gianfranco Bettin, "Partito e comunità locale," *Rassegna italiana di sociologia* 10, no. 4 (October-December 1969): 651-678; Gianfranco Bettin, *Partito e comunità locale* (Bologna: Società Editrice Il Mulino, 1970); Giacomo Sani, "Profilo dei dirigenti di partito," *Rassegna italiana di sociologia* 13, no. 1 (January-March 1972): 117-148; Giorgio Galli, *Il difficile governo* (Bologna: Il Mulino, 1972); Giacomo Sani, "La professionalizzazione dei dirigenti di partito," *Rivista italiana di scienza politica* 2, no. 2 (August 1972): 303-333; Giorgio Galli, "L'influenza della organizzazione partitica sul voto," *Rassegna italiana di sociologia* 13, no. 1 (January-March 1972): 149-169.

459

FIG. 1. PERCENT OF THE POPULAR VOTE FOR THE PCI IN 88 PROVINCES IN THE ELECTIONS OF 1946 AND 1972

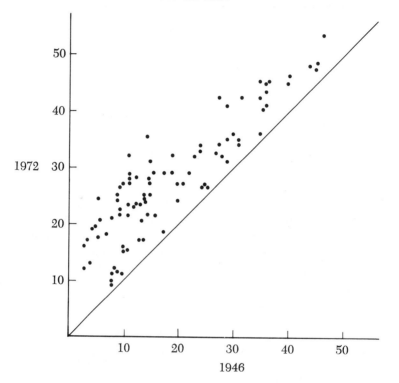

growth in the Red Belt has been very close to the national average. (See Table 3.) The noticeable increase of support for the party in the south, on which most observers have focused their attention since it represents the most obvious change, has tended to obscure the fact that growth has occurred elsewhere as well, although at lower rates.

Impressive as this performance looks, it should not be overestimated: it falls considerably short of the party's aspirations, and for good reasons. Forced into the role of permanent opposition by the distribution of political forces and by the cleavages of the party system, the PCI's hope to enter the national decision-making arena rests almost exclusively on the possibility of gaining enough strength in the country and in Parliament, to be able

460

to force the other parties, and primarily the Democrazia Cristiana party (DC), to come to terms with it. Since this is unlikely to occur as long as other viable alternatives exist for the DC, the extension of the party's support in the different regions, and in the country as a whole, assumes a critical importance. Seen in this light, the penetration so far achieved by the party is obviously still inadequate. Furthermore, the flattened-out shape of the rate of increase in the last ten years, far from being a reassuring sign of consolidation, can appear, rather, as a symptom of a basic

TABLE 3. Mean Increase in Percent of the Popular Vote for the PCI in the Period 1946-1972 in Five Geo-Political Areas[*]

Northwest	Northeast	Red Belt	Continental South	Islands
3.5	3.5	8.9	13.6	13.8

[*]The five subdivisions correspond to the grouping of provinces used in the volume, *Il Comportamento Elettorale in Italia* (Bologna: Società Editrice Il Mulino, 1968).

weakness, i.e., as proof of the party's inability to reach out beyond a sizable but still narrow circle of support. The question, then, for the party and for political observers as well, is: has the PCI effort to gain a broader base of popular support lost momentum? Is the semistasis of the 1963-1972 period essentially a consolidation that precedes a new step forward, or is it, rather, the beginning of a period of stagnation, and perhaps even decline? And, in any case, what factors account for the success and the limitations of the PCI's appeal to the electorate?

The Forward Strategy: The PCI as a Catch-All Party

As several able observers and students of the PCI have noted, the programmatic efforts made by the Italian Communist leaders in attacking the problem of access to power have been marked by considerable originality of conceptions and sophisticated intellectual analysis, that have made the party somewhat unique among the nonruling Communist parties.[3] From Antonio Gramsci to

[3] For insightful analyses of the Italian Communist party in the post-World War II era, see Sidney Tarrow, *Peasant Communism in Southern Italy* (New Haven and London: Yale University Press, 1967); Donald L. M. Blackmer,

Palmiro Togliatti, from Enrico Berlinguer to Bruno Trentin, there is a tradition of assessing current situations and outlining alternative routes of action in which social theory, history, and political ideology are closely interwoven, indeed at times in such a manner to make the identification of single elements a difficult enterprise. Observers and protagonists do concur, however, on the fact that the PCI strategy has been based on an explicit rejection of a narrow conception of the party, and has emphasized the desirability of a wide network of alliances with broad social groups.

The key elements of what was to become the dominant theme of the PCI domestic strategy for the whole postwar period were already present in a series of speeches made by Togliatti toward the end of World War II.[4] In planning the reconstruction and the expansion of the party while half of the country was still in German hands, the Communist leader argued for the creation of a party "of a new type." "We will no longer be," he said, "a small, restricted association of propagandists for the general ideas of communism . . . [but rather] a mass, popular party, solidly based on the working class, but also able to absorb all the productive energies coming to us from all sectors, the intellectuals, the young people, the women."[5] The design was even more explicitly outlined in a 1947 statement by the party's chief organizational expert, Pietro Secchia, who said: "The social composition of the party shows that we are the party of the working class, but we are not sufficiently the party of the people. . . . We have not succeeded yet in penetrating in all the strata of the working population and particularly among the urban and rural middle classes, the farmers, the technicians, the professionals and the intellectuals."[6] To be sure, Secchia was talking about the membership of the party, but the message made even more sense when applied to the whole electorate, as a number of official statements make abundantly clear.

If the electoral defeat of the Popular Front in the decisive par-

---

Unity in Diversity: Italian Communism and the Communist World (Cambridge, Mass., and London: The M.I.T. Press, 1968).

[4] Palmiro Togliatti, "La politica di unità nazionale dei comunisti" (Naples, April 1944); "Per la libertà d'Italia, per la creazione di un vero regime democratico" (Rome, July 1944); "Avanti verso la democrazia" (Rome, September 1944); "I compiti del partito nella situazione attuale" (Florence, October 1944).

[5] "Libertà."

[6] Il partito della rinascita (Rome: UESISA, 1947), p. 33.

liamentary elections of 1948 shattered the hope of playing an important role in national politics in the short run, it did not alter in any fundamental sense the party strategy and, in fact, it probably reinforced it. For what the 1948 elections explicitly confirmed to the Communist leadership was the fact that a sizable segment of the working class, and a large majority of other social groups, constituted a more or less solid support for the only other mass party, the DC. In short, in 1948 the DC emerged as the primary antagonist of the PCI, and the latter's fundamental, overriding problem became that of detaching the Catholic masses from their "reactionary" leaders. As students of the PCI have pointed out, in the views of the PCI leadership this could be accomplished by "demonstrating to a portion of the DC membership and its electorate that they had a greater community of interests with the Communists than with the intransigent right wing of their own party."[7] In this effort to bring about a gradual erosion of popular support for the DC, an important, intermediary role was assigned to the Socialists. In the words of Donald Blackmer, "If the Socialists continued to collaborate with the Communists and to fight for basic economic and social reforms inside a coalition of the Center-Left, it could serve as an instrument for splitting the Christian Democrats, softening the prejudices of anticommunism, and ultimately allowing the Communists to move from sterile opposition to participation in a reform coalition. . . . Under the right circumstances, then, the Socialists could serve to break the ice, eroding away the political and psychological barriers that had so firmly blocked the way to further Communist progresses."[8]

In the south, where the PCI concentrated its efforts for a good portion of the 1950s, one finds the same interpretation of the *via italiana al socialismo* at the center of the policy focus of the Committees for the Land, of the Committees for the Rebirth of the South, and eventually of the Peasant Alliance. That the implementation of the strategy in the south ultimately resulted in the demobilization of the peasants, as Sidney Tarrow has aptly shown, only reconfirms the fundamental nature of the PCI posture, as one in which issues pregnant with revolutionary import are soft-pedaled in order to make the party acceptable to an ever wider circle of different social groups.[9]

[7] Blackmer, *Unity in Diversity*, p. 220.
[8] Ibid., p. 231.
[9] Tarrow, *Peasant Communism*, pp. 343-368.

Despite the appearance of criticism from the left wing of the party, and more recently from small splinter groups operating outside the party and on its left, there is little indication that the overall design has changed in recent years; power is still sought by broadening the party's base. Twenty years after his early pronouncements, Togliatti confirmed his original conception, stating, "At the head of the battle there must be the working class guided by its revolutionary vanguard; in the course of the same battle, the front of the advance toward socialism must gradually extend itself to new social groups, and from them must come an even stronger socialist conscience."[10]

Whether the theoretical perspective implicit in the PCI domestic strategy represented a radical departure from standard Marxist theory can be debated. The change in perspective toward non-working-class groups was possible without renouncing Marxist theory, by revising an outdated map of society and identifying a new antagonist, in essence recognizing that in a modern, industrial, neocapitalist society, a rigid distinction between laborers and owners of the means of production is no longer a meaningful strategic tool. In such a context, the urban and rural middle classes can join the industrial working class because the real common enemy is monopolistic capitalism. In this view, there appears to be a softening of traditional class conflict by virtue of what Sidney Tarrow has called, "Togliatti's inclusive concept of groups and classes which poses alliances in additive terms."[11] Translated into an electoral strategy, this approach comes very close to defining the PCI as a "Catch-almost-all-party," since no major segment of society's productive structure is considered beyond reach.

Students of Italian communism have identified a number of problems, tensions, and dilemmas inherent in the "Forward Strategy." But it has positive implications too. The first is simply that this strategic design enlarges the target population considerably. And this, in itself, increases the probability of obtaining the support of a larger share of the electorate. Second, the fact that there are no self-imposed preclusions toward seeking the support of specific social groups means that the appeals of the party can be directed to different social strata. In essence this means that the modification of the strategy at the theoretical-

[10] *La via italiana al socialismo* (Rome: Editori Riuniti, 1964), p. 183.
[11] *Peasant Communism*, p. 116.

ideological level allows the party to seek expansion along the line of least resistance. Third, this approach enables the party to make full use of its organizational capabilities and the exploitation of favorable community traditions that would otherwise remain untapped. In short, flexibility and adaptability to different political arenas appear to be the hallmarks of a strategy designed to maximize the party's chances of deeper penetration among the electorate.

How the electorate has responded to this open and flexible posture of the Communist party is the subject of the rest of this chapter.

SOCIAL, ORGANIZATIONAL, AND CULTURAL BASES OF SUPPORT FOR THE PCI

An empirical assessment of how successful the PCI has been in translating its strategy from the theoretical-prescriptive level to that of practical implementation cannot be divorced from a discussion of the particular kind of data used, since the substantive aspects of the question, the data, and the methods of analysis are intimately related.

In dealing with contemporary mass politics in Italy, political scientists and sociologists have relied primarily on aggregate data, typically electoral statistics and census figures. While this approach has generated some massive studies and excellent analysis of trends in the postwar period, the very nature of the data used has prevented scholars from investigating a number of topics of great interest. Themes such as political socialization, policy preferences, images of parties, attitudinal configurations, and the like cannot be treated in any depth, if they can be treated at all, on the basis of information aggregated at the local, communal, or provincial level. Furthermore, even for topics like the impact of socioeconomic transformations on political preference, the suitability of aggregate data is highly questionable, in view of the well-known theoretical limitations of this methodology, and the relative weakness and problems of cross-level inferences.[12]

[12] For a thorough and up to date review of the problems of ecological inference, see Theodore Meckstroth, "Ecological Inference and the Disaggregation of Individual Decisions," in *Political Science Annual* 6 (Indianapolis: Bobbs-Merrill, forthcoming).

465

On the other hand, the recourse to survey data, which in principle would overcome these difficulties is not without its problems. And the relative paucity of studies utilizing survey data appears to reflect, over and beyond the predilections of a particular academic tradition, some well-founded reservations on the wisdom of relying on this kind of evidence in a country where the mass public seems to have a marked reluctance to make its political views known in a typical interview situation.

This trait of the Italian political culture tends to produce samples in which a sizable proportion of respondents cannot be accurately classified from the point of view of their party preference. Furthermore, there is evidence indicating that this reluctance is not spread out evenly across the political spectrum, but affects in a negative manner parties that occupy a somewhat more extreme position. This is to say that in spite of the efforts sometimes made by polling agencies to disguise the real intent of their questions, the distribution of respondents on a party-preference continuum typically underrepresents, well beyond the normal sampling error limits, the parties of the extreme Left, and, less often and to a lesser extent, those of the Right. This holds true for the few studies reported in the literature, of which the five listed in Table 4 constitute a fair sample.[13] In all five surveys the PCI voters are underrepresented; in three of them it would appear that the Partito Socialista Italiano (PSI) is stronger than the PCI; and in one of them the distortion is so pronounced that even the Partito Socialista Democratico Italiano (PSDI) appears to have more followers than the PCI. The text of the questions asked is also revealing: the underrepresentation of the PCI in the 1955 study took place in spite of a phrasing of the question in such a way as to avoid direct reference to the respondents' personal preferences. Finally, it should be noted that the apparent precision of the 1963 study is seriously misleading since the distribution reported by the polling organization and reproduced in other works, refers to male respondents only. If one were to add the other half of the sample, the percent of respondents supporting the PCI would most likely drop to less than half.

[13] The percentages for the Doxa 1955 study were recomputed on the basis of figures published by Pierpaolo Luzzatto Fegiz in *Il volto sconosciuto dell'Italia* (Milan: Giuffrè, 1957). The data relative to the Almond and Verba study are drawn from the original codebook. Distributions of political preferences resulting from the CISER study were drawn from Gianfranco Poggi, *Le preferenze politiche degli Italiani* (Bologna: Società Editrice Il Mulino, 1968).

TABLE 4. Distributions of Party Preference According to Five National Surveys Compared with the Actual Distribution of the Vote in National Elections for the Lower House

Doxa Study (1955)
(*Question:* "In the interest of Italy which party needs to be strengthened?")

	PCI	PSI	PSDI	PRI	DC	PLI	MON	MSI
Distribution of answers in the sample	10.6	15.3	12.9	2.3	37.7	5.9	8.2	7.1
Percent of vote in the 1953 elections	22.6	12.7	4.5	1.6	40.1	3.0	6.9	5.8

Almond and Verba Study (1959)
(*Question:* "For what party did you vote in the election of 1958?")

	PCI	PSI	PSDI	PRI	DC	PLI	MON	MSI
Distribution of answers in the sample	8.5	10.7	3.9	1.0	68.3	2.5	1.7	3.5
Percent of vote in the 1958 election	22.7	14.2	4.5	1.4	42.4	3.5	4.8	4.8

CISER Study (1963)
(Respondents assigned to different parties on the basis of indirect question.)

	PCI	PSI	PSDI	PRI	DC	PLI	MON	MSI
Distribution of answers by *male respondents only*	22.4	19.1	8.1	1.6	32.1	7.5	1.4	5.0
Percent of vote in the 1963 elections	25.3	13.8	6.1	1.4	38.3	7.0	1.7	5.1

Barnes Study (1968)
(*Question:* "To which of the following parties do you feel closer?")

	PCI	PSIUP	PSU	PRI	DC	PLI	MON	MSI
Distribution of answers in the sample	15.1	2.7	17.7	1.6	56.6	3.0	0.7	2.6
Percent of vote in the 1968 elections	26.9	4.5	14.5	2.0	39.1	5.8	1.3	4.5

Barnes and Sani Study (1972)
(*Question a:* "For what party did you vote in the May 1972 election?")
(*Question b:* "To what party do you habitually feel closer?")

	MAN	PCI	PSIUP	PSI	PSDI	PRI	DC	PLI	MSI-MON
Answers to Question a in the sample	0.2	21.3	1.1	12.5	4.6	2.8	50.0	2.3	5.2
Answers to Question b in the sample	0.1	21.4	1.3	11.7	4.8	2.8	50.1	2.5	5.1
Percent of vote in the 1972 election	0.7	27.2	1.9	9.6	5.1	2.9	38.8	3.9	8.7

This bias, which is particularly pronounced in the earlier studies, is more disappointing than it is puzzling. For in a society in which partisan politics has been known to cause economic, psychological, and sometimes physical damage, it is not surprising to find that the more deviant a party appears to be from the prevailing mode, the more likely it is to be underrepresented. If this interpretation is correct, the trend apparent from the 1968 and 1972 studies, although hardly conclusive, would seem to indicate that parties of the Left have become much more socially acceptable. The 1972 survey still underrepresents the PCI electorate, but the discrepancy is smaller than in any other previous study reported in the literature. Furthermore, the distribution represents answers to a straightforward question about voting in the May 1972 election, and is not a tabulation of an indirectly tapping of the respondent's general orientations. Third, the distribution of preferences for the other parties appears to be reasonably close, at least in relative terms, to the distribution of voting preferences in the population as a whole, and in the different geopolitical subdivisions.[14] In brief, while the most recent surveys are not as yet perfectly reliable tools, the marked improvement over similar undertakings of the past, and the wealth of information they provide about the mass political actor, would seem to justify their use. Needless to say, this should be done with care, with a full understanding of the limitations of the instrument used, and to corroborate plausible hypotheses rather than to provide definitive answers. With these cautions in mind, we can now turn to the questions raised at the end of the last section.

In one of the early studies of political behavior in Italy, the French social scientist Mattei Dogan, after an extensive and detailed analysis of electoral returns and census data, concluded that the PCI's claim of being the party of the industrial working class was unfounded.[15] Although Dogan's categories do not co-

[14] It is also possible to interpret the greater correspondence between sample and electorate in the last survey cited, as owing to an increasing familiarity of the Italian mass public with surveys and a lessening of fears and suspicions. If this interpretation is correct and the trend toward higher accuracy should continue, it would lead to a much more widespread acceptance of surveys as reliable tools.

[15] "La stratificazione sociale dei suffragi," in Alberto Spreafico and Joseph LaPalombara (eds.), *Elezioni e comportamento politico in Italia* (Milan: Comunità, 1963), pp. 407-474.

incide with those used later by other scholars, subsequent analyses utilizing different data by and large confirmed his estimates.[16] The 1972 survey indicates that the reality of the early 1970s is not very different from that of the 1950s. As we can see from Table 5, the six status groups in which the sample has been

TABLE 5. DISTRIBUTION OF PARTY PREFERENCES OF RESPONDENTS BELONGING TO DIFFERENT STATUS GROUPS, 1972

| | PARTY PREFERENCE | | | | | | | |
STATUS LEVEL[a]	PCI[b]	PSI	PSDI-PRI	DC	PLI	MSI	Preference not indicated	N
I. Industrialists, landowners, executives, professionals	5.0	7.6	6.1	29.7	12.2	6.1	33.3	(81)
II. White-collar workers	7.6	6.5	9.2	34.9	2.7	4.6	34.5	(261)
III. Artisans, shopkeepers, small businessmen	13.7	9.9	8.1	33.5	2.1	5.3	27.4	(284)
IV. Skilled workers	17.6	11.8	3.4	24.7	0.2	2.7	39.5	(408)
V. Small farmers	8.7	5.3	2.4	54.0	—	1.9	27.7	(206)
VI. Farm laborers and unskilled workers	25.9	6.3	3.3	27.2	1.0	2.3	34.0	(394)
VII. Status not ascertainable	10.1	8.7	2.9	39.6	0.5	3.4	34.8	(207)

[a] Status is based on the respondent's profession or on that of the head of the household.
[b] Respondents reporting voting for the *Manifesto* or the PSIUP were classified as PCI.

divided are remarkably heterogeneous in terms of party preference.[17] It is true, of course, that the percent of support received by the different parties varies from one status group to another, but no party comes close to having a monopoly of a particular

[16] For example: Poggi, *Preferenze politiche*; Lawrence E. Hazelrigg, "Religious and Class Bases of Political Conflict in Italy," *American Journal of Sociology* 75, no. 4 (January 1970): 496-511.

[17] A precise assessment of the distribution of party preferences within each status level cannot be done without making inferences about the preference of those electors—roughly one-third of the sample—who chose not to report the party they had voted for in 1972. Inspection of the data for a number of attitudinal variables suggests that this last group is composed of identifiers for all parties but that within it PCI and MSI voters are overrepresented.

469

social stratum. In short, the relation between social status and electoral behavior is weak. People belonging to lower-status groups are more likely to vote for parties of the Left, and members of higher-status groups tend to support parties of the Right, but no party has an extremely narrow social bases. As Giovanni Sartori has pointed out, the more intriguing aspect of these distributions is not "class-voting," but the remarkable extent to which there appears to be deviance from a pattern of narrow alignment between status and party preference.[18]

And it is precisely this deviance that would account for possible "catch-all" configurations of the parties' social composition profiles. If we conceptualize the ideal catch-all party as one which receives support from the different groups in proportion to their relative size in the society, the comparison of the actual profile of the Italian parties with this ideal standard proves instructive. As Figure 2 shows, the social composition profiles of the DC and PSI voters look remarkably alike, and approximate quite closely the configuration of the sample as a whole. The profile of the PCI, although somewhat more skewed toward the bottom of the social scale, is much closer to that of the other two mass parties than to any other political force. In short, only mass parties approximate configuration of the ideal catch-all party, and the PCI does not appear to be too far from reaching that goal. Although not as well balanced as the DC or the PSI, its social composition shows that the party has made inroads among professionals, white-collar workers, teachers, artisans, and small businessmen, i.e., in the social categories traditionally covered by the term "middle class."

It appears, then, that the PCI's inability to secure the support of a higher proportion of the working class has been compensated by its ability to attract members of other social groups. This suggests two conclusions and one further question. The first conclusion is that the PCI strategy of social mobilization has worked reasonably well: the party is solidly based in the working class, but it also derives considerable support from other social groups. The second conclusion is that social status alone does not determine the PCI's strength or weakness. That brings us to the question: if the success and the limits of the party's expansion cannot

[18] "From the Sociology of Politics to Political Sociology," in Seymour M. Lipset (ed.), *Politics and the Social Sciences* (New York: Oxford University Press, 1969), pp. 65-100.

470

FIG. 2. Social Composition of the Parties and of the Whole Sample

Status Levels*

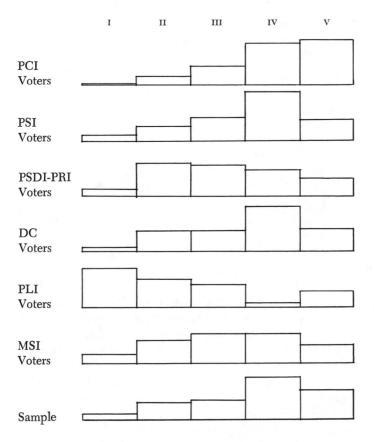

* Respondents were assigned to the status level on the basis of their profession, or the profession of the head of the household. Professions were grouped into status levels as follows:
  i. Executives, industrialists, landowners, professionals.
  ii. White-collar workers.
  iii. Artisans, shopkeepers, small businessmen.
  iv. Skilled workers and small farmers.
  v. Farm laborers and unskilled workers.

471

be accounted for in terms of social stratification, what other structural factors are involved?

Analysis of the composition of the PCI electorate in different areas of the country provides some clues. In the Red Belt area the proportion of nonworking-class respondents voting for the PCI is slightly over twice as large than in the rest of the country.[19] (See Table 6.) But the Red Belt is also the area where the

TABLE 6. PROPORTION OF "MIDDLE-CLASS" AND "WORKING-CLASS" RESPONDENTS REPORTING VOTING FOR THE PCI IN FOUR GEOGRAPHICAL AREAS*

	Industrial Northwest	Catholic Northeast	Red Belt	Center and South
Middle class	.13	.06	.22	.12
Working class	.33	.11	.43	.29

*Middle class includes respondents classified in groups I, II and III in Table 5. Working class includes respondents classified in groups IV, V and VI in the same Table.

party benefited from a strong Socialist and anticlerical tradition at the time of the reinstating of the democratic regime after the war.[20] It is also the area where the PCI has built an effective grass-roots organization which makes possible establishing and maintaining ties with wide segments of the population. This suggests that a model constructed to interpret or understand the party's electoral success must include, in addition to the social stratification component, the organizational strength of the party and the political tradition of the community. The validity of a multivariate model of this kind, originally tested on the 1968 data, is discussed elsewhere.[21] The size of the standardized coefficients reported in Figure 3 suggests the following interpreta-

[19] Given the small size of regional subsamples it was necessary to dichotomize the variable status into "middle class" and "working class." The first group includes respondents in the following professional groups: industrialists, landowners, professionals, executives, public and private white-collar personnel, teachers, merchants, shopkeepers, artisans, and technicians. The second includes respondents in the following vocations: industrial workers, service workers, small farmers, sharecroppers, farm laborers, common laborers, domestic personnel, custodians, etc.

[20] The importance of political traditions is rightly emphasized in Giorgio Galli, *Il bipartitismo imperfetto* (Bologna: Società Editrice Il Mulino, 1966).

[21] Sani, "Determinants of Party Preference"; also in *Rivista italiana di scienza politica* 3, no. 1 (April 1973): 129-143.

472

FIG. 3. Relative Influence of Three Structural Variables on Party Preference*

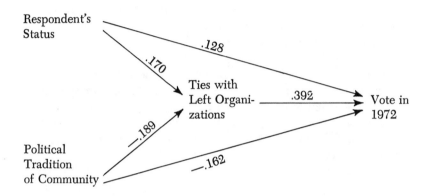

	Effects	
	Direct	*Indirect*
—Respondent's status	.128	.067
—Political tradition of Community	—.162	—.074
—Ties with Left organizations	.392	—
R	.485	

*For details on the indicators used and the scoring procedures see footnote.

tion: first, the respondent's party preference is a function of his linkage with the left-wing organizational network, the political traditions of his community, and his status;[22] and second, the first variable clearly overshadows the other two. The respondent's location in the system of social stratification of his community contributes both directly and indirectly to party preference. But once the antecedent and the intervening variables are taken into account, the direct influence of status is considerably reduced.

In sum, the reasonably well-balanced profile of the PCI, and this brief discussion of two other structural determinants of party preference in Italy suggest that in the presence of a favorable tradition and in conjunction with a strong organizational effort, the party succeeds in extending further the bases of its support both among its traditional audience and among the groups that the strategy has defined as "productive middle classes." However, even under particularly favorable conditions, after an initial rapid penetration, the PCI's growth proceeds very slowly, as if the party were facing a solid barrier that can be eroded only gradually. The nature of this barrier will be probed in the following pages.

ACCEPTANCE OF THE PCI BY THE MASS PUBLIC

It could be reasonably argued that looking at electoral support is not a very appropriate way of gauging the success of the PCI strategy and identifying its weaknesses, or, at least, that there are other aspects of the problem. For one thing, the process of obtaining outright support at the mass level is by necessity a gradual and slow one, and it is likely to be preceded by a weakening of the traditional preclusions against the party. Secondly, it can be suggested that the PCI itself did not expect an immedi-

---

[22] Ties with Left organizations were scored as follows: membership of the respondent *and* the head of the household in an organization sponsored by or close to the PCI (CGIL, ARCI, UDI, etc.), 4; membership of the respondent, 3; membership of the head of the household, 2; no ties, 1. Political tradition was operationalized by assigning to each respondent a score equal to the percentage of the popular vote received in his province of residence by the Left parties (PCI and PSIUP) in 1946. Party preference was scored taking into account the respondent's reported vote as follows: PCI-PIUP-MAN 1, PSI 2, PSDI-PRI 3, DC 4, PLI 5, MSI 6. Finally status was scored: professionals 5, white-collar workers 4, small businessmen, artisans, and farmers 3, skilled workers 2, unskilled workers and farm workers 1.

ate "conquest" of the different social groups to which it had turned, but strove rather to make itself more generally acceptable, and to acquire full political legitimacy not only at the elite level but at the mass level as well. In this light some new questions seem germane. How does the PCI fare in the eyes of the non-Communist electorate? Has its strategy helped the party become a widely accepted political force? How close does the party appear to be to those non-Communist masses whose support it seeks? Although neither the 1968 nor the 1972 study was designed specifically to answer these questions, the surveys contain several relevant items.

The first involves the notion of a Left-Right continuum. Although there never was any doubt that politicians, political observers, and the attentive section of the mass public utilize this dimension in organizing their thoughts about political matters, in Italy the question of whether the broad mass public did so remained open. The 1968 study by Barnes demonstrated conclusively that the Left-Right scale was not an abstraction invented and used by an elite, but that it was meaningful to a very large segment of the electorate.[23] Further, the data showed that there was widespread consensus on the position assigned to the parties by the respondents, and the aggregate picture obtained by summing the respondents' perceptions of the parties' location provided an ordering of the different political forces with which the competent observer had no reason to quarrel. These results were strikingly reconfirmed in the 1972 study. (See Table 7.) The mean position assigned to the parties has changed only very slightly; the ordering of the parties remains unchanged, and even the two new political groups present on the 1972 scene (Manifesto and Movimento Politico dei Lavoratori [MPL]) seemed correctly placed, in spite of the fact that they were not well known.[24] Finally, it should be added that the mean positions, and the ordering of the parties, remain essentially unaltered if instead of using the perception of the whole electorate one utilizes the judgment of party identifiers in locating their own parties.

Since this dimension appears to be remarkably stable and characterized by a substantial amount of consensus, it constitutes a

[23] Barnes, "Left, Right and the Italian Voter."
[24] Given the short life span of the MPL any assessment of the "correct" position of the party on the Left-Right scale is obviously difficult even for expert political observers.

475

first benchmark for assessing, indirectly, the acceptability of the PCI by the mass public. A look at the distribution of scores representing the perceptions of the location of the PCI, shows that the party is perceived by the electorate, and, to a somewhat lesser extent, by its own followers, as occupying an extreme position in the political spectrum. If parties are perceived as being located in a spatial dimension the collocation of a political group toward the extreme of the spectrum provides *prima facie* evidence

TABLE 7. Respondents' Placement of Political Parties on a Left-Right Scale (0-100) (Figures reported are means)

	1968		1972	
	All Respondents	*Identifiers*	*All Respondents*	*Identifiers*
Manifesto	—	—	9.4	°
PCI	12.4	17.2	17.4	20.3
PSIUP	16.8	18.0	20.7	24.4
MPL	—	—	22.5	°
PSI	32.7	33.2	33.1	35.6
PSDI			44.8	46.9
PRI	51.1	45.3	52.4	52.9
DC	55.3	55.7	55.5	55.4
PLI	72.1	71.6	65.1	58.3
MON	74.8	68.4	83.3	80.4
MSI	78.0	79.9		

°The number of identifiers for the Manifesto and MPL was too small to make the computation of the mean meaningful.

against its full acceptance by the mass public. This suspicion is reinforced when one takes into account the distribution of the respondents' self-location on the same Left-Right continuum. Two facts stand out quite clearly in Figures 4 and 5. In the first place, very little change seems to have taken place between 1968 and 1972, with the two means and standard deviations practically identical, and this provides a confirmation of the overall stability of the electorate at the aggregate level. Second, and most important, it seems that the bulk of the mass public tends to locate itself toward the center of the political spectrum. Granted that only about two-thirds of the respondents answered the question, and that the figures underestimate the true strength of the PCI, nevertheless it remains true that the bulk of the non-Communist electorate tends to locate itself at a considerable distance from

476

FIG. 4. Respondents' Self-Location on a Left-Right Continuum, 1968, 1972

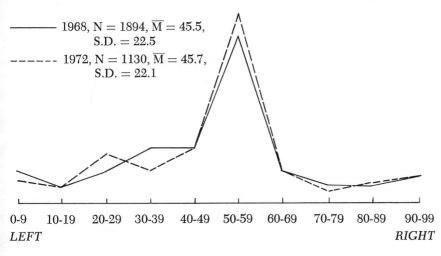

——— 1968, N = 1894, $\overline{M}$ = 45.5,
 S.D. = 22.5

------ 1972, N = 1130, $\overline{M}$ = 45.7,
 S.D. = 22.1

0-9   10-19   20-29   30-39   40-49   50-59   60-69   70-79   80-89   90-99
LEFT   RIGHT

FIG. 5. Distribution of Positions Assigned to the PCI on a Left-Right Continuum and Distribution of Self-Location of Non-Communist Voters.

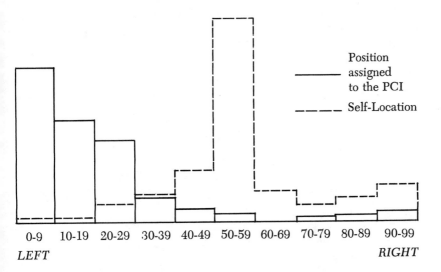

Position
——— assigned
to the PCI

— — — Self-Location

0-9   10-19   20-29   30-39   40-49   50-59   60-69   70-79   80-89   90-99
LEFT   RIGHT

what they perceive to be the position of the PCI. When we de-compose the non-Communist electorate into subgroups of iden-tifiers for the other parties, it becomes obvious that there is a con-nection between one's own perceived position and the position assigned to the PCI. This means that PSI voters see the PCI as a somewhat more moderate force than do DC voters, and that these, in turn, assign the PCI to a less extreme position than do Partito Liberali Italiano (PLI) and Movimento Sociale Italiano (MSI) followers.[25] While this is not particularly surprising, it does provide confirmation of the importance of the spatial di-mension, and also emphasizes the fact that there are noticeable differences in terms of distance from the PCI in the non-Commu-nist camp.

A second, and perhaps more direct indicator of the extent to which the PCI is accepted by the mass public, is related to what might be termed "negative party preference." In 1968 and again in 1972 the Italian respondents were asked: "Are there parties for which you would never vote in any case? Which ones?" The an-swers indicate that voters who have preclusions against one or more parties are common (over 60 percent in 1968 and over 75 percent in 1972), and this gives a general idea of the intensity of feelings associated with at least some of the parties. Even more important is the fact that the voters' objections are dispropor-tionately directed toward the MSI and the PCI. As the figures reported in Table 8 show, the PSI and DC are the targets of neg-ative party preference in few cases: 85 percent of all preclusions

TABLE 8. RELATIVE FREQUENCY WITH WHICH THE FOUR MAJOR PARTIES WERE MENTIONED AS A NONACCEPTABLE VOTING CHOICE

	1968			
PCI	PSU	DC	MSI	N*
54.7	3.8	9.8	31.7	(1675)
	1972			
PCI	PSI	DC	MSI	N*
41.9	5.1	9.2	43.8	(1210)

*In this table N does not refer to the number of respondents but to the number of mentions.

[25] For reasons of space the figures are not reported.

against the four main parties converge on the MSI and the PCI.[26] The increase in the proportion of objections against the MSI between 1968 and 1972 can possibly be attributed to the higher visibility of this neo-Fascist party and to its role in the episodes of political violence that have plagued the country since 1969. The consequence appears to have been a decrease of the percent of objections against the PCI; and this indirectly confirms the fact that the PCI gains in situations where there is a visible threat from the Right which provokes a resurgence of anti-Fascist feelings in the population. In any event, in 1972 the objections to parties identified with the Right or the Left were well balanced, a distribution that testifies to the success of the slogan "*opposti estremismi*" adopted by centrist parties in the electoral campaign.

When we move to consider where the objections to the PCI come from, we find, not surprisingly, that rates of acceptance tend to decrease as one moves away from the party in a spatial sense. (See Table 9.) The assessment of the precise rates for dif-

TABLE 9. Percent of Answers given by Identifiers with Other Parties Mentioning the PCI as a Nonacceptable Voting Alternative

	1968				
	PSU	PRI	DC	PLI	PDIUM-MSI
Percentages based on all answers	27.4	65.5	58.0	68.0	72.2
Percentages based on answers mentioning parties as unacceptable	45.6	71.0	90.3	86.0	85.1

	1972					
	PSI	PSDI	PRI	DC	PLI	MSI
Percentages based on all answers	24.5	36.4	71.4	59.7	62.0	68.2
Percentages based on answers mentioning parties as unacceptable	30.8	42.6	80.6	76.3	75.0	72.0

[26] This uneven distribution is obviously the result of some asymmetry in the distribution of negative party preferences. To put it differently, the asymmetry consists in the fact that while followers of party A find party B objectionable, the reverse does not obtain. While a full analysis of this phenomenon cannot be conducted here, it is important to point out that two distinct breaking points appear in the distribution. The asymmetry begins to operate in correspondence to the PLI and PSIUP, respectively, and becomes much more visible toward the two extremes. In short, it looks as if the two extremes accept the center but not vice versa. And this fits quite

479

ferent subgroups of non-Communist voters depends on whether we use as a base line all answers (including the D.K., N.A., refused to answer, etc.), or not. Both distributions are provided in the table and provide the elements for some intermediate estimate. Assuming that we can take the respondents' answers to this question as a sound basis for estimating their future voting behavior, it would seem that the reservoir of potential voters for the PCI is composed in large part of Socialist electors. This lends some strength to the interpretation advanced by Galli that the expansion of the PCI in the postwar period has taken place primarily at the expense of the Socialists, while the strength of the Left as a whole has remained largely unchanged.[27]

Finally, some additional evidence as to the feelings of the electorate toward the PCI is provided by a battery of items designed to tap the respondents' overall orientation toward several political "objects." These were thermometer-like scales ranging from 0 to 100, and the mean "sympathy" scores are reported in Table 10.[28] Apart from the basic identification of all respondents with their own party (in every case the score given to one's party is

TABLE 10. MEAN "SYMPATHY" SCORES TOWARD SIX GROUPS BY PARTY PREFERENCE. Scale ranges from 0 (low) to 100 (high).

POLITICAL GROUPS	PARTY PREFERENCE					
	PCI	PSI	PSDI-PRI	DC	PLI	MSI
Contestatori	28.5	17.3	19.4	16.4	16.8	21.2
PCI	88.1	47.9	28.3	18.3	14.9	17.7
Unions	79.1	64.2	55.5	50.1	43.8	35.3
Workers	91.6	88.1	85.2	80.9	70.8	76.9
PSI	52.4	81.1	57.1	35.8	34.9	30.3
DC	34.8	47.3	60.2	84.8	51.8	49.0
MSI	10.7	11.9	16.1	22.4	32.9	84.5
No. of cases on on which mean is based	(240)	(148)	(88)	(559)	(27)	(63)

well with the results obtained from the discussion of the spatial locative of the parties.

[27] Giorgio Galli (ed.), *Il comportamento elettorale in Italia* (Bologna: Società Editrice Il Mulino, 1968), p. 76.

[28] The text of the question was: "Now we would like to know what you think of certain groups and organizations that have influence in political life. Please give to each of them a score ranging from 0 (very unfavorable) to 100 (very favorable) depending on how you feel about them (50 means that you are neither favorable nor unfavorable)."

considerably higher than those given to other groups), the figures suggest a number of observations.

In the first place, the term "workers" clearly symbolizes something positive for respondents belonging to all political groups; the small differences are predictable. At the opposite end of the sympathy spectrum, we find the "protesters" ("*I Contestatori*"), and here too there is widespread consensus, but the scores run in the opposite direction. Evidently the turmoil and violence associated with the protest movement did not find much sympathy among the masses.[29]

Second, apart from these two groups, all other political "objects" involved in the evaluation elicit reactions that tend to differ sharply, and are in many cases diametrically opposed. This disagreement, which in many ways is a measure of political cleavages in the country, can be assessed in an approximate manner by looking at the range of the evaluations given by respondents with different party preferences. Here again, as in the case of negative party identification, the PCI and the MSI are the targets of most opposition and they have the highest, and almost identical, evaluation range.

Third, the mean sympathy scores change in an orderly fashion as one moves from one group of respondents to another. But it is obvious that sympathy for different parties is not reciprocal. The more moderate forces, such as the PSI and the DC, receive a higher evaluation from both the PCI and the MSI voters than the PSI and DC voters are willing to give their radical counterparts. This finding is similar to the result obtained from the data on negative party identification, and suggests that the asymmetry might be deeply embedded in the spatial ordering of the parties in the mind of the voters.

Finally, the sympathy scores received by the PCI require little comment. Apart from the Socialist respondents whose overall position appears to be one of mild neutrality, the PCI does not find much sympathy among the rest of the electorate, and indeed the scores suggest that it elicits fairly strong negative feelings.

If there is any doubt that these orientations of the electorate toward the parties are important psychological correlates of vot-

[29] This point is explored more fully in Samuel H. Barnes and Giacomo Sani, "New Politics and Old Parties in Italy" (Paper delivered at the 31st Annual Meeting of the Midwest Political Science Association, Chicago, May 1973).

ing behavior, it is easily dispelled by the addition to the regression model of party preference discussed in the preceding section of two measures: the respondents' self-location in the Left-Right scale, and the score summarizing their feelings toward the PCI. Inclusion of these two indicators makes the model much more "powerful," and increases considerably the size of the multiple correlation coefficient (.811 vs. .485). More important, as we can see from the standardized coefficients reported in Table 11, these two measures almost completely overshadow the direct

TABLE 11. REGRESSION OF PARTY PREFERENCE ON FIVE PSYCHOLOGICAL AND STRUCTURAL VARIABLES

		Beta	Sigma
Anticommunism		.444	.017
Self-location on Left-Right scale		.383	.017
Organizational ties with the Left		.128	.015
Political tradition of the community		—.052	.014
Respondents' status		.028	.014
	R	.811	

contribution of the factors analyzed earlier, and particularly that of the respondent's status.

The analysis of these data about positions on the Left-Right continuum, negative party identification, and sympathy scores, lead to the same three conclusions. First, the proportion of non-Communist respondents well disposed toward the PCI is small. Second, since the PSI constitutes the only sizable reservoir of PCI sympathizers one could say that the line of demarcation between non-Communists and anti-Communists passes through the Socialist party.[30] Third, the psychological barrier separating the PCI from the non-Communist electorate is very real, and appears to be more important than the structural determinants discussed earlier.

NEGATIVE IMAGES OF THE COMMUNIST PARTY

What accounts for the fact that a sizable proportion of the non-Communist electorate apparently has strong preclusions against,

[30] This is further confirmed by the distribution of answers to a question dealing with the participation of the PCI in a coalition government with the DC. Percent of electors approving were as follows: PSI 47.7, PSDI 25.4, PCI 14.3, DC 15.9, PLI 17.2, MSI 17.5.

482

and negative feelings toward, the PCI? In what images of the Communist party are these dispositions rooted? Although a definitive answer to these questions would require a separate study with different data bases, some tentative answers can be developed on the basis of several items contained in the 1972 survey. Four possible complementary interpretations of the negative feelings toward the PCI will be tested, albeit in a very summary fashion.

A first interpretation stressed the role played by the "ingrained Catholicism" of the Italian population. According to this view, one of the major roadblocks to the further penetration of the PCI among the masses is the strong attachments that many Italians have to the Catholic Church, plus a widely shared perception that the PCI is a strong anticlerical force. This juxtaposition has a long history, with socialism and anticlericalism being closely connected at the beginning of the era of mass politics prior to World War I. The antagonism was strongly reinforced after World War II, particularly during the 1948 electoral campaign, when the Church and its related organizations stressed the incompatibility between communism and religion. While the official position of the Church has changed considerably since then, and the PCI has behaved in a way that seems designated to minimize friction with the Catholic forces, popular perceptions of the situation may not have kept pace with these changes. In other words, it is quite possible that in the eyes of part of the electorate, the incompatibility between being a Catholic and being a Communist is still very much alive. The distribution of answers to the question "Can a good Catholic be a Communist?"—asked in June 1972 (see Table 12)—shows that the argument articulated above is not totally unfounded. The majority of electors for the DC, PLI, and MSI find this kind of preclusion toward the

TABLE 12. DISTRIBUTION OF ANSWERS TO THE QUESTION: "CAN A GOOD CATHOLIC BE A COMMUNIST?" (By party preference)

	Yes	No	N.A., D.K.
PCI	84.5	11.2	4.3
PSI	72.6	22.8	4.6
PSDI	69.1	27.3	3.6
PRI	62.8	31.4	5.7
DC	36.8	54.5	8.7
PLI	27.6	65.5	6.9
MSI	39.7	58.8	1.5

PCI still meaningful. On the other hand, for the followers of the moderate parties of the Center-Left, this secular/clerical dimension does not appear to spill over into the political dimension. If these voters object to the PCI, they do it on other grounds, as we shall see shortly. In conclusion, the "ingrained Catholicism" thesis has some merit, but it applies to only part of the non-Communist electorate.

A second interpretation is that the non-Communist electorate is basically skeptical about the PCI commitment to the maintenance of democratic institutions, and perceives the party as a potential threat to democracy. This is, of course, the theme that anti-Communist propaganda has stressed with more or less emphasis in every election, citing often the fate suffered by other countries where the Communist party has had access to power. The data available do not allow a direct test of this interpretation since the only pertinent question contained in the survey made reference to parties of the "far Left." In the political climate of 1972 this could have been understood to mean the radical, small, antiparliamentary groups operating on the left of the PCI. On the other hand, we have seen that the PCI tends to be perceived as an extremist party, and hence one could argue that it was covered by the question. To minimize the bias against the party, it is wiser to consider only the outright affirmative answers to the questions and to assume that all other answers express no objections to the PCI on this ground. Even so, we find the non-Communist electorate deeply divided with Socialists (PSI) and Liberal (PLI) respondents pulling in opposite directions (see Table 13), and approximately half of the DC, PSDI, and PRI (Partito

TABLE 13. DISTRIBUTION OF ANSWERS TO THE QUESTION: "ARE PARTIES OF THE EXTREME LEFT A THREAT TO DEMOCRACY?" (By party preference)

	Yes	No, D.K., N.A.	N
PSI	34.0	66.0	(153)
PSDI-PRI	52.3	47.7	(90)
DC	48.1	51.9	(611)
PLI-MSI	73.9	26.1	(92)

Republicano Italiano) electors rather evenly split on the issue. Like the preceding one, then, the thesis that the PCI is perceived as a threat to democracy should be accepted with the understanding that this point of view is not shared across the board but affects roughly half of the non-Communist electorate.

A third possible explanation, partly related to the second, refers to the climate of political unrest and political violence that has plagued the country since 1968. Violence was one of the most highly debated issues during the 1972 campaign, and restoring order was the single most important concern revealed by the survey.[31] Accusations and recriminations about whom to blame for the disorder and unrest have been part of the daily polemics among parties. The Left has claimed that primary responsibility for the many episodes of violence lies with right-wing groups. On the other hand, the centrist forces have stressed that both the Right and the Left during the campaign blamed each other. In this context, it does not seem unlikely that a part of the moderate electorate would perceive the PCI as heavily involved in the strife, or at least unable to restrain its own rank and file from participating in confrontations with the right-wing extremists and the police. That this image might exist is made even more likely by the survival of memories from the immediate postwar period when in some areas of the north PCI militants were engaged in forms of political strife not approved by the party's central leadership.[32] The data reported in Table 14 show that the electorate identifies the neo-Fascists and the Maoists as principal partici-

TABLE 14. Respondents' Opinion of Whether Different Groups Are Involved in Political Violence*

	Yes	No	N
a) The Neo-Fascists	86.1	13.9	1213
b) The Maoists	85.6	14.4	1120
c) The Communists	58.3	41.7	1219
d) The Socialists	22.0	78.0	1170
e) The Christian Democrats	14.9	85.1	1274

* No opinion, D.K., N.A. omitted from the table.

[31] Maintaining order in the country and stopping inflation were the first and second concern of the electorate, in that order. Together they accounted for over 78 percent of the responses to a question on the most important goals to be achieved.

[32] Evidence of the concern of the top leadership of the party for the involvement of the militants of the north in violent forms of strife is contained in several documents. See, for example, the remarks of Pietro Secchia, *Migliorare il lavoro di partito* (Rome: Società Editrice l'Unità, 1946), p. 18.

485

pants in acts of political violence. However, a sizable group of respondents perceive Communist activists as being involved as well.[33] In any event the image of the PCI, as the table indicates, differs sharply from that of the DC and the PSI. Furthermore, when asked to assign responsibility for the climate of disorder and violence a large percentage of non-Communist respondents designate as primary culprit either groups of the Left or both the Left and the Right.[34] This third hypothesis may be helpful in trying to ascertain the roots of the electorate's feelings toward the PCI.

Finally, it could be argued that the electorate perceives the PCI to be closely associated with the international Communist movement and, more specifically, that the party has maintained strong ties with the Soviet Union. In essence what this point of view challenges is the notion that there is an Italian way to socialism, that Italian communism is different, and not quite so objectionable, as other varieties of communism. To determine whether Italian electors harbor this suspicion, and how widespread it is, would require an ad hoc investigation. The survey data available provide only a weak test. It is weak and indirect because it does not give so much information on the perceived dependence of the PCI on Moscow, as on the extent to which political objects in the international arena are related in the voters' minds to internal political groups. The test consists simply of an examination of the sympathy scores utilized earlier. If it could be shown that positive feelings toward an Italian party are related in a positive or negative manner to the electors' feelings toward a foreign country, then one of the key assumptions implicit in this fourth argument could be validated.

Analysis of the sympathy scores discussed earlier, using multidimensional scaling technique, clearly demonstrates the existence of these connections. (See Figure 6.) The objects are grouped into two clusters, with the pairs of points representing the PCI and the Soviet Union and the DC and the United States very

[33] The text of the question was: "In the last few years, there have been many cases of disorder and violence of a political nature. In your opinion the persons usually involved in these events usually are . . ." followed by the name of the six groups listed in the table.

[34] To the question: "In your opinion does the principal responsibility for the disorder and violence belong to groups of the Right or groups of the Left?" the responses were as follows: Right 14.5, Left 13.9, both Right and Left 33.5, no opinion, D. K., etc. 28.1.

486

close to each other.[35] Further and more detailed analysis of the cognitive-affective maps of the Italian electorate will provide a more accurate picture. But preliminary evidence lends some plausibility to the interpretation sketched above.

How well do these four aspects account for the overall negative image of the PCI held by part of the mass public? And how much overlapping is there among these four components? Both

FIG. 6. CONFIGURATION OF POINTS REPRESENTING THE RESPONDENTS' EVALUATION OF TWELVE POLITICAL OBJECTS IN TWO DIMENSIONS

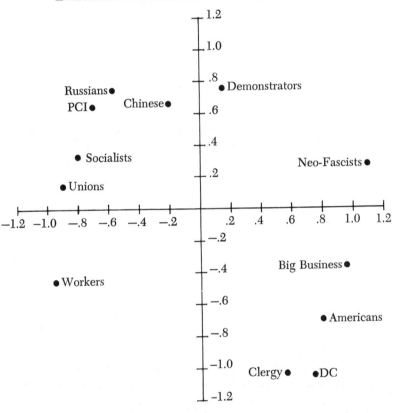

[35] The coordinates for the points representing the PCI and the USSR in a three-dimensional solution confirm the results reported in Figure 6. The coordinates in fact are: PCI: −.610, .359, .690; USSR: −.432, .393, .678. For the rationale and procedures involved in the use of this technique see J. B. Kruskal, "Non-Metric Multidimensional Scaling: A Numerical Method," in *Psychometrica* 29, no. 2 (June 1964): 115-129. I am grateful to Ken Town for his help with this part of the analysis.

487

questions are of some importance. In the first place, if the objections to the PCI reviewed in the preceding pages left a very substantial portion of the variance in anti-Communist feelings unaccounted for, one would have to conclude that there are other aspects of the electorate's orientation toward the PCI that have not been included in our model. The second question is of some relevance from the point of view of determining the size of the anti-Communist electorate. Since the reservations toward the PCI come from only a part of the mass public, a definite overlap between these partial negative images would mean that it is the same respondents who tend to share the same preclusions toward the party. On the other hand, a weak interrelationship would indicate that different groups of respondents object to the PCI on different grounds.

The appropriate evidence for both questions is reported in Table 15. It is clear that all the four components discussed are re-

TABLE 15. ZERO-ORDER CORRELATIONS BETWEEN FOUR COMPONENTS OF THE POPULAR IMAGE OF THE PCI

	(2)	(3)	(4)
(1) The extreme left is a threat to democracy	.117	−.180	.228
(2) The PCI involvement in political violence	—	−.234	.237
(3) Incompatibility between being a good Catholic and being a Communist		—	−.134
(4) Feelings toward the USSR			—

REGRESSION OF FEELINGS TOWARD THE PCI
ON FOUR COMPONENTS OF ANTICOMMUNISM

	Beta	Sigma
The extreme left as a threat to democracy	.181	.025
PCI involvement in political violence	.189	.025
Incompatibility Catholic/Communist	−.140	.025
Feelings toward the USSR	.461	.025
R	.654	

lated in a strong manner to the general measure of anticommunism, and their joint predictive power is considerable (Multiple R .654). However over 50 percent of the variance in anticommunism is still unaccounted for, and this suggests that there are other reasons for the hostility toward the PCI.[36] The inspection of the matrix of Table 15 allows us to answer the second question largely in the negative. The four items do overlap but only to a limited extent. And this means that the anti-Communist front is not a monolithic bloc. Rather, it appears that the PCI is confronting the problem of overcoming suspicions and preclusions that different segments of the population raise on different grounds.

Mass Level Constraints: Communication Networks

The identification of four components of the negative image of the PCI to be found at the mass level raises a final and fundamental question: Where does this image come from? What constraints inherent in the structure of political communication of the society affect the shaping, altering, and reinforcing of this image? And, to put it in a more general form, what mechanisms are involved in the formation and maintenance of orientations toward the Italian political parties?

These questions are not only intriguing in themselves, but they seem directly relevant to the problem of assessing a party strategy that is aimed at a broad mass public. For a strategy of this kind must eventually be translated into popular appeals and fed into channels of communication operating at the grass-roots level. The content of the strategy in itself cannot tell us very much about its effectiveness unless we can also take into account the routing of the messages and the extent to which their channeling is successful.

Unfortunately, very little attention has been paid to topics of this kind in the literature dealing with Italian politics. To date, most studies of the political behavior of the mass electorate have dealt largely with the structural antecedents of party preference, and have neglected mapping political orientations and identifying their sources. Although discussion of the impact of the mass media, primary groups, and voluntary associations is not lacking, research on the processes involved is rather scanty. The 1968 and 1972 surveys used in this chapter did not deal directly with the

[36] The most obvious possibility is that part of the moderate electorate fears the redistribution of national resources and changes in the structure of social stratification from which they now benefit.

489

topics of political communication and socialization, but they do contain enough information for a brief sketch of what appear to be the principal mechanisms involved.

Briefly, the thesis presented here is that the political orientations of Italian electors are acquired and reinforced through a number of communication stimuli coming from different sources but largely congruent and tending to reinforce each other. Although no direct evidence will be presented here, the theoretical underpinning of the proposition above is the following. Political orientations, albeit vague and generic, are absorbed rather early in life. The principal contribution is made by the immediate social environment, primarily the family and proximate members of peer groups. As life experiences become more varied and social contacts outside the family increase, other sources of information acquire significance alongside the first ones: educational institutions, mass media, membership in organizations that directly or indirectly emit politically relevant signals, and social interaction with the members of one's community.

However, not all the messages generated in this complex communication structure reach all individuals in the same manner. For as soon as some orientations are internalized and acquire stability, they begin to operate as filters or screens through which further bits of information are accepted, processed, and integrated into one's world view. These processes of selective perception, plus the different location of the actor in the social structure, and hence his different life experiences, would alone suffice to account for the different images of political objects to be found among the mass public. If we add the proposition that different clusters of individuals are likely to be exposed to different and nonoverlapping channels of communication, we come to the conclusion that individuals tend to live in a homogeneous psychological-political universe. The final argument is that because of the congruence between world view and messages received, stable rather than changing orientations are likely to result. For change could occur only if a massive dose of discordant information were to reach the individual, erode the foundations of his present attachments, and thus prepare the ground for a shift. Much less information is required to maintain an existing pattern of dispositions than to induce change. This explains why mass conversion, or even limited penetration, is hard to accomplish in a psychologically hostile environment.

Many of the propositions of this argument are diachronic in nature, and thus cannot be tested with surveys providing data about one point in time. But there are several pieces of evidence, relating to the role of the family, organizational networks, and the mass media, that corroborate the picture sketched above.

The abundant literature on political socialization accumulated in recent years indicates that the family functions as an important mechanism of transmission of political belief in many different political systems. In political systems characterized by some basic discontinuities in the nature of the political regime, such as Italy, there might be reasons to wonder whether the family plays an important role, simply because the transmission of orientations appropriate to a given political regime makes little sense in a drastically changed context. Furthermore, the cultural norms of particular societies might tend to discourage political communication within the family unit. The Italian data confirm, in part, these suspicions. The percent of respondents unable to recall their fathers' party preference is high, rates of recalled interest of fathers in politics are low, as are rates of family discussion of political matters. However, this does not necessarily mean that the family is less effective as a mechanism of political socialization. One can be socialized into apathy as well as into activism. And as the distributions of Table 16 indicate, a respondent's de-

TABLE 16. REPORTED INTEREST IN POLITICS OF RESPONDENT AND FATHER

	1968		1972	
	Father Had Some Interest	Father Had No Interest	Father Had Some Interest	Father Had No Interest
Respondent has at least "some" interest	65.2	35.4	65.4	32.7
Respondent has no interest in politics	34.8 (464)	64.6 (1066)	34.6 (589)	67.3 (1012)

gree of interest in politics is definitely related to that of his father. Furthermore, in the cases in which party preference of both parents and offspring are reported, the amount of continuity of political preference across generations is impressive. (See Table 17.) In addition, when we consider rates of continuity in

491

TABLE 17. Party Preference of Respondent and Father, 1972

Father's Party Preference	Respondent's Party Preference						
	PCI	PSI	PSDI-PRI	DC	PLI	MSI	
Communist	76.5	8.8	2.9	10.3	—	1.5	(68)
Socialist	31.8	29.4	12.4	23.2	1.6	1.6	(129)
Republican	45.5	9.1	36.3	—	9.1	—	(11)
Catholic	7.5	3.5	6.9	78.5	1.2	2.4	(173)
Liberal	—	7.1	14.3	28.6	35.7	14.3	(14)
Monarchist, MSI, U.Q., PNF, PRF	10.8	5.4	6.7	51.4	5.4	20.3	(74)

terms of broad tendencies rather than specific parties the general overall similarity of political points of view becomes even more apparent: the proportion of respondents moving far away from the political position of their fathers is exceedingly small. If people move across generation lines at all, it is by way of small, lateral moves rather than big jumps. And these results appear to be even more remarkable when we take into account the fact that for some respondents the transmission of political beliefs occurred over a period of time characterized by a drastic change of political regimes.

When we consider not family origins but the unit respondents belong to now, we find that the Italian family is substantially homogeneous in political terms, at least if we are to trust the respondents' perception of their immediate social environment. Asked whether members of their families, friends, and coworkers had the same political preference, the people interviewed replied in the manner indicated in Table 18. When we exclude from the

TABLE 18. Perceived Political Homogeneity of Family Friends and Co-workers, 1972*

	Family	Friends	Co-workers
All or almost all have the same preferences as respondent	76.4	29.6	22.4
Some have the same preference	10.6	51.4	55.7
Few or nobody	13.0	19.0	21.9
	(1357)	(1067)	(539)

*N.A., D.K. excluded.

count the "No opinion, D.K., No answers" category, it turns out that three-fourths of those who answered the question perceived their families to be politically homogeneous units. Secondly, the significance of the family as an important reference group is clearly established by data from the 1968 survey (see Table 19).

TABLE 19. IMPORTANCE ATTRIBUTED BY THE RESPONDENT TO THE OPINION OF SELECTED REFERENCE GROUPS, 1968

	Much	Some	Little	None	N
Family	71.0	18.1	6.7	4.2	(2403)
Close friends	29.1	31.5	23.8	15.6	(2353)
Colleagues and work mates	16.5	31.8	26.4	25.3	(1840)

None of the other likely reference groups listed in the table come even close to challenging the family as a mechanism of opinion formation and maintenance.

Given these two empirical premises, and the initial proposition about the influence of the environment on the stability of one's political attitudes, it follows that shifts in voting patterns should be more frequent among respondents from politically non-homogeneous families. And, as we see from Table 20, this is pre-

TABLE 20. HOMOGENEITY OF POLITICAL PREFERENCES IN THE FAMILY AND PREDISPOSITION TO CHANGE VOTE, 1972

	Voted in 1972 as in 1968, and Did Not Consider Changing	Voted in 1972 as in 1968 but Considered Changing	Voted in 1972 Differently than in 1968	N
Family mostly homogeneous	75.7	12.1	12.2	(941)
Family mostly nonhomogeneous	60.3	20.2	19.5	(282)

cisely the case. The proportion of respondents reporting that they had considered changing their vote, or that they had voted in 1972 differently from 1968, is higher among people whose family is politically less homogeneous. Although the differences are not dramatic, suggesting that other factors are involved, the trend runs in the predicted direction.

493

In sum, the data about one of the segments that constitute the individual's immediate social environment confirm the argument outlined above. Within the limits of the institutional discontinuities of the political regime, the family appears to be a significant vehicle for transmission of political preferences. It also appears to act as a reinforcer of political orientations insofar as it provides a largely homogeneous communication environment which confirms or at least does not challenge the individual's point of view.

We move now beyond primary groups to consider the impact of organizational membership. In a well-known study conducted in the late 1950s, Gabriel Almond and Sidney Verba reported much lower rates of membership in voluntary associations in Italy than in other democratic societies.[37] Ten years later, Samuel Barnes reported much higher figures and showed that organizational membership was one of the key correlates of political preference.[38] Consequently in the 1972 survey particular attention was paid to this variable, and efforts were made to determine whether the respondent and/or the head of the household was a member of a Catholic organization or of one of the organizations related to the PCI. The data show that approximately one-third of the sample had ties of this kind, and the figure most likely understates the actual extent of affiliations with leftist groups. Furthermore, a sizable proportion of people who did not belong to Catholic organizations, reported attending church regularly, a fact that from the perspective of political communication and influence is only slightly less important than straightforward organizational membership. The crucial point is that there is practically no overlap of organizational ties across these two segments of respondents. (See Table 21.) In practice, if not in principle, membership in leftist organizations and membership in Catholic organizations are mutually exclusive. Although this is neither new nor surprising, it is significant in terms of the communication structure discussed above: membership in voluntary associations in Italy is certainly not a source of cross-pressure, or of contradictory bits of political information. Insofar as they constitute another significant segment of his politically relevant social environment, organizational ties operate in a manner similar to that of the family.

[37] *The Civic Culture* (Princeton, N.J.: Princeton University Press, 1963).
[38] "Religion and Class."

494

The linkage between organizational membership and voting preferences has already been discussed with reference to left-wing organizations. Table 21 shows that the pattern holds almost as well for ties with Catholic organizations: the probability that a member of the two organizational networks will vote for a party of the "other" camp is quite small. The impact of indirect ties with the Catholic network, operationalized as frequency of

TABLE 21. Party Preference and Organizational Ties

	PCI	PSI	PSDI-PRI	DC	PLI	MSI	Party Preference Not Reported
Ties with leftist organizations	43.9	23.6	5.3	2.9	—	3.2	13.0
No organizational ties	50.0	65.3	83.0	72.5	93.5	83.9	75.4
Ties with Catholic organizations	5.8	9.0	11.7	23.8	6.5	12.9	10.3
Ties with both leftist and Catholic organizations	0.3	2.1	—	0.8	—	—	1.3
(N =)	(278)	(144)	(94)	(623)	(31)	(62)	(609)

church attendance, although not quite as pronounced, is strong enough to warrant consideration. When we look at the subsample of respondents who do not have ties with either one of the two organizational networks, we find that church attendance is a powerful discriminant, in the sense that it helps us in isolating quite well the DC voter and, to a lesser extent, the left-wing from the right-wing voter. (See Table 22.) The probability that a non-churchgoer will vote for the DC or the PCI is approximately equal. Among regular churchgoers the probability of voting DC is over ten times larger.

The mass media provide a third link between the electors and the political universe, functioning both as a source of new information and a reinforcer of political orientations. But the visibility and importance of the mass media for the informed observer can easily lead to overestimating their impact on the broad mass public. Even television, which is by far the most commonly used source of information, leaves a sizable portion of the electorate untouched. In 1968 some 40 percent of the sample claimed that they had received "no political information" from television. Four years later, 35 percent of the public reported not having followed the "*Tribuna elettorale*" program. When we consider the press, it becomes apparent that even a much smaller segment of the mass public is reached through this means. In 1972, for example, approximately one-third of the respondents had followed with some regularity newspaper accounts of the electoral campaign.

TABLE 22. Church Attendance and Party Preference, 1972
(Tabulation includes only those Respondents who do not have organizational ties with either one of the two networks)

	Church Attendance			
	At Least Once a Week	Often	Sometimes	Rarely or Never
PCI	5.4	11.4	29.7	32.3
PSI-PSDI-PRI	14.9	22.1	24.0	20.7
DC	73.8	55.1	35.5	30.7
PLI-MSI	5.9	11.4	10.8	16.3
(N =)	(374)	(140)	(121)	(130)

The paucity of rigorous studies on how political information broadcast by radio and television, and disseminated by the press, is evaluated and perceived by the mass public, prevents even limited inferences on the likely impact of this part of the communications network on the mass electorate. Two things however are fairly clear: (1) there is a close alignment between mass media sources and political forces in the country; and (2) according to a preliminary analysis of readership patterns emerging from the 1972 survey, there is a close correspondence between political preference and the political orientation of the source of the message. The percentage of respondents who, judging by what they read, expose themselves to sources of information likely to contain contradictory stimuli is rather small. Although neither one of these two facts is particularly surprising, taken together they lend some additional strength to the cognitive congruence argument.

It is appropriate to conclude this brief sketch of the structure of political communication networks with some reference to the politically apathetic segments of the mass public. Lack of interest in political matters is likely to result in limited exposure to politically relevant stimuli. Limited exposure, in turn, assumes fundamental importance from the point of view of a strategy designed to reach large masses, as a first step toward obtaining their support. For, if these politically uninterested layers of the population shut themselves off from any potential source of political communication, they become almost as hard to reach by the party's appeals as those segments of the mass public that hold a negative view of the PCI. The apathetics cannot be written off easily in the Italian context since, in spite of their declared lack of interest in political affairs, they do participate in one important respect, turning out at the polls. In light of this, the low rates of reported interest in politics signal the presence of a very difficult obstacle for the PCI, or for any other group intending to capture a share of the electorate. (See Table 23.) Given the exist-

TABLE 23. Reported Interest in Politics, 1968, 1972

	1968	1972
Very much	1.3	5.8
More or less	7.6	20.8
A little	30.1	28.9
Not at all	61.0	44.5
	(2500)	(1841)

ing attachments to some of the parties and the relative isolation in terms of political communication, this subgroup constitutes a core of "unreachables" that by its sheer inertia blocks further penetration.

The limitations of the data used in this chapter and the indirect nature of the evidence in some of the arguments make one hesitant to state the conclusions of this section in a strong form. Therefore, I offer the following summary remarks not as definitive findings but as working hypotheses.

Prevailing patterns of political communication in Italian society condition in several ways the expansion of the PCI. Political socialization, particularly the political homogeneity of the family, both benefit and harm the Communist party. On the one hand, the existence of many primary groups with a strong and consistent left-wing orientation assures a certain level of continuity of support for the party. On the other, it is precisely the same homogeneity, to be found in nuclei with different political preferences, that constitutes a roadblock to the party's penetration among wider segments of the electorate.

Patterns of organizational affiliations, and especially their non-overlapping nature, appear to function roughly in the same manner. Although this point has not been probed in the present study, it seems likely that their impact complements that of the primary groups.

In addition, the meager evidence so far analyzed on prevailing patterns of readership, and particularly the dependence on single sources of information, have the same double-edged impact. They ensure reinforcement of existing belief structures, or at least of simple positive or negative images held by the population. But this works to the advantage of all political groups, primarily of those who have more control over the mass media than does the PCI. Finally, the lack of reported interest in politics suggests that there are social segments likely to be almost completely sealed off from the stream of political communication.

Given these characteristics of the structure of political communication in Italy, and leaving aside the possibility that the PCI might not have been able to present its case effectively to the electorate, several possible alternative explanations of why the party's appeals have not been more successful suggest themselves. The first is simply that these messages never reached some segments of the population because these subgroups do not receive much political information of any kind. The second possibility is that the party's appeals never reached another portion of the electorate because this group is "plugged" into communication networks, both formal and informal, that either do not report or interpret these messages in a negative manner. The third possibility is that the messages might be received from the original source but they are screened off as unacceptable by the preexisting negative image of the source from which they come. While these exhaust the range of possibilities related to the formal or mechanical aspect of political communication, there is one further alternative: that the political stimuli emitted by the PCI reach at least part of the intended audience but are rejected because of their content. It is to this possibility that I now turn.

498

MASS-LEVEL CONSTRAINTS: POPULAR CONCEPTIONS OF POLITICS

The constraints analyzed in the preceding section dealt with the routing of political information and the possible different filters that might interrupt the flow of communication between the source and the audience. Important as they are, these constitute only one kind of barrier to the acceptance of information. For reception is only the first stage, a necessary but not sufficient condition for the effectiveness of the appeal. What we really need to look at are the conditions inherent in the nature of the message that facilitate or inhibit its acceptance.

A full exploration of this topic is a matter for linguists and psychologists. Here I simply want to suggest that large discrepancies between the linguistic and value universe of the source and that of the audience might be responsible for a further reduction of the rates of acceptance of political messages. The argument will be articulated briefly in two main propositions.

The first is simply that the language used by the professional political actors and the informed sector of the public is largely incomprehensible to the masses. Although the evidence is mostly impressionistic, there seems to be little doubt that at least the formal types of communication are forbidding to the uninitiated. Complexity of prose and abstruse terminology would seem to be the main reason for this communication gap.[39] Although this applies to political discourse in Italy in general, it is possible that the language used by the PCI is simpler and more accessible. But large differences would be surprising since party leaders and militants belong to the same universe of discourse, at least in the sense that they are obliged by the constraints of political interaction to carry on, directly or indirectly, a dialogue with the antagonist forces. In any event, anyone who has familiarity with the protocols of a large mass survey, knows how simple, unsophisticated, and naive most open-ended answers look when compared with even the most popular party documents. Given the original premise and the low level of articulation of the broad mass public, one should not be surprised to find that sheer lack of comprehension is a significant negative factor.

[39] Two recent works throw some light on the characteristics of "political language" in Italy. Vittorio Capecchi and Marino Livolsi, *La stampa quotidiana in Italia* (Milan: Bompiani, 1971); Maurizio Dardano, *Il linguaggio dei giornali Italiani* (Bari: Laterza, 1973).

The second proposition has to do with the degree of correspondence, or congruence, between the way in which social reality is interpreted by the emitting source and the canons used at the receiving end of the line. In concrete terms, at the core of the PC strategy, there is a notion of society divided into camps of mutually antagonistic interests, which is reflected in the terminology used in the party's appeals ("struggle," "victory," "defense of the workers," "class solidarity," etc.). Is this conception of politics underlying PCI strategy congruent with the way in which the mass public looks at politics? And, more specifically, does the electorate look at parties in terms of the interests they serve? In short, is the electorate likely to respond to an appeal made in "interest" terms? A general survey of the kind used here is hardly the best instrument for answering these questions. But the evidence available at this point suggests a tentative negative answer.

In the first place, if the general public, and more specifically the non-Communist electorate, looked at politics primarily in social conflict terms, there should be a definite trace of this orientation in the respondents' answers to questions about political parties and broad political tendencies. A superficial examination of answers to a question about the perceived major differences between Left and Right indicates that less than one-fifth of the respondents made explicit reference to group interest or class conflict. (See Table 24.) Even if we add to these another group of answers referring to "great principles," part of which might

TABLE 24. REFERENCES TO GROUP INTEREST OR CLASS CONFLICT IN ANSWERS TO QUESTIONS ABOUT DIFFERENCES BETWEEN LEFT AND RIGHT, AND REASONS FOR LIKING PARTY, 1968, 1972

	DIFFERENCES BETWEEN LEFT AND RIGHT		WHAT RESPONDENTS LIKE IN THEIR PARTY	
	1968	1972	1968	1972
Answers containing references to group interest or class conflict	18.4	16.5	15.3	14.5
Answers containing references to "great principles"	63.1	72.0	63.3	60.9
All other answers and no answers	18.5	11.5	21.4	24.3

have made reference to class interests, still only slightly over one-third of the electorate possesses a point of view consonant with the PCI strategy. The percent of explicit references to group interest and class conflict is very similar in answers about the respondents' reasons for liking the party they identify with. As we can see from Table 25, these references are to be found

TABLE 25. EXPLICIT REFERENCES TO GROUP INTEREST OR CLASS CONFLICT IN ANSWERS TO A QUESTION ABOUT DIFFERENCES BETWEEN LEFT AND RIGHT, 1972 (By party preference)

	PCI	PSI	PSDI-PRI	DC	PLI	MSI
Answers containing references to group interest or class conflict	40.3	32.6	18.1	6.1	6.5	11.3
Answers with reference to Great Principles	10.1	9.0	15.9	12.5	41.9	33.9
Other answers	14.7	13.4	21.3	13.9	32.3	12.9
No answer	34.9	45.0	44.7	67.5	19.3	41.9
(N =)	(278)	(144)	(94)	(623)	(31)	(62)

primarily among Communist voters; the percent of non-Communist electors sharing the basic interpretative categories is quite small.

Second, when the notion of interest is explicitly brought to their attention, a substantial majority of respondents do not identify parties as vehicles for the defense of their interests (see Table 26), ranking them third after unions and elected officials.

TABLE 26. DISTRIBUTION OF ANSWERS IN 1968, 1972 TO THE QUESTION: "TO PROTECT YOUR INTEREST ON WHICH OF THE FOLLOWING WOULD YOU COUNT MOST?"

	1968	1972
Unions and professional organizations	34.9	30.0
Elected officials	17.2	18.2
Political parties	10.6	13.2
Other answers, no opinion, no answer	36.3	38.6
(N =)	(2500)	(1841)

Surely this does not fit well with the conception of a party as spokesman for, and defender of, group interests.

Finally, a substantial majority of the people interviewed in 1972 apparently believe that "political parties serve only to create discord among the Italians." (See Table 27.) While this is suffi-

TABLE 27. Answers to the Question: "Do You Agree with the Statement that Political Parties Serve Only to Create Discord among Italians?"

Yes	No	No opinion, N.A., D.K.	
63.2	17.8	19.0	(1841)

ciently vague and generic to be interpreted in many different ways, it seems clear that parties are seen as divisive forces, and surely this must be more true of a party whose ideology stresses conflict. Perhaps not too much should be made of this evidence, but if part of the electorate yearns for social solidarity and the PCI appears to be emphasizing conflict, there can be little doubt about the lack of congruence of the two perspectives.

Additional research designed to determine conceptions of politics held by the Communist and non-Communist electorate will help provide satisfactory answers to the questions raised in this chapter. The little evidence so far available suggests as a very tentative hypothesis that PCI strategy might be ineffective with some sections of the electorate because of its erroneous assumptions about the basic components of political behavior at the mass level. Strategies imply at least two actors, and the assumptions on the part of at least one of them, as to what guides the behavior of the other. To the extent that the assumptions are incorrect, the strategy is likely to fail.

CONCLUSION

As an effort to convert large masses and harness their support, or even to win widespread acceptance, the PCI strategy has obviously not been very successful. As a guiding principle and flexible posture compatible with gradual growth, it has clearly worked.

In this chapter I have endeavored to show the reasons for the mass public's low rate of acceptance of the PCI, and I have explored the nature of some constraints at work. It has been argued that existing patterns of political communication and influence cut off and/or filter out the appeals of the party and that the conception of politics held by at least part of the non-Communist electorate is at odds with the conflict theory of politics on which the Communist strategy is based.

Under these conditions, and barring dramatic upheavals in the domestic and international scene, the most likely occurrence is gradual and limited erosion of the strength of some parties rather than massive switches. For these could occur only if large segments of the population were suddenly "disconnected" from their usual environments, exposed to new messages and appeals, and eventually refashioned for themselves new images of the political world. That this has not occurred even under the stress caused by the deep transformation of Italian society in the postwar period testifies to the power of the mechanisms involved and to the strength and durability of the electorate's cognitive maps, however simple and unsophisticated they might be. On the other hand, given the consistently high rates of geographical mobility, the increasingly high level of education of the population, altered residential patterns, changes in life style, and gradual transformation of predominant values, it is reasonable to expect that a certain amount of erosion of traditional loyalties will continue to occur. Whether the PCI will be able to benefit from such an erosion will depend, if the arguments developed in this chapter are correct, on the party's ability to extend its communication network and to make it more effective and persuasive.

XIII.

Party and Mass Organization: The Changing Relationship of PCF and CGT

GEORGE ROSS

Introduction

When the Parti Communiste Français (PCF) finally secured control over the Confédération Générale du Travail (CGT) in 1944-1945 it gained an invaluable resource for the pursuit of its political ends. The PCF's strength within the CGT has not been challenged since 1947. And, by virtue of its predominance in size and legitimacy over other unions, the CGT has been the determinant actor in French union life since.[1] At present, even after the ravages of the Cold War, CGT membership represents 65 percent of all organized workers in France, and the CGT regularly wins 60-65 percent of votes in professional elections (a good index of the CGT's following among workers who do not belong to unions). Understanding the ways in which the PCF uses the CGT as a resource will, then, provide important insights into the workings of the French Left.

In organizational terms, PCF-CGT relations have remained virtually unchanged since the immediate post-World War II period. Strong Communist infrastructures control nearly all CGT

[1] The history of the CGT, especially from the vantage point of its relations with the PCF, has not really been written. The Confederation's official history, Jean Bruhat and Marc Piolot, *La CGT: Esquisse d'une histoire* (Paris: Confédération Générale du Travail, 1966), is not very useful. Georges Lefranc's series of trade union histories (*Le Mouvement syndical sous la troisième république* (Paris: Presses Universitaires de France, 1967), *Les Expériences syndicales en France de 1939 à 1950* (Paris: Payot, 1951) and *Le Mouvement syndical en France de la Libération aux évènements de Mai-Juin 1968* (Paris: Presses Universitaires de France, 1968) help to situate problems and provide a narrative. Both Val Lorwin, *The French Labor Movement* (Cambridge, Mass.: Harvard University Press, 1954) and Henry Ehrmann, *French Labor from Popular Front to Liberation* (New York and London: Oxford University Press, 1947) stop too early to be of great help. André Barjonet, *La CGT* (Paris: Seuil, 1968) is not historical but is revealing and intelligent on political issues.

504

industrial federations and most departmental unions. PCF control over industrial federations leads to control at confederal levels of power. Communists have consistently been in a slight majority on the Bureau Confédéral (the key CGT executive organ) and on other confederal bodies. The presence of a minority of non-Communists at the CGT confederal level has little political significance. Non-Communist CGT leaders have generally been chosen to "work well" with the hegemonic PCF majority. Their most important function has been to make the CGT publicly presentable as a "mass," and not a party, organization. Almost without exception the most important CGT leaders have also been prominent PCF figures. Benoît Frachon, perhaps most notable modern French trade unionist and long-time CGT secretary-general (serving from the PCF takeover in 1945 until 1967), was for decades a member of the PCF Bureau Politique and one of the inner circle of men who actually ran the PCF. Several of Frachon's key CGT deputies were also members of the PCF Central Committee. As Georges Séguy rose to become Frachon's *dauphin* and eventual CGT secretary-general, he also joined the PCF Bureau Politique, along with Henri Krasucki (presently second in command in the CGT).[2] And the PCF Bureau Politique routinely discusses CGT and union matters (although, since PCF archives are closed, no good data exist about specific discussions).[3]

If the organizational relationship between the PCF and CGT has not changed *in form* since the early postwar period, the same cannot be said for its *content*. From 1945 until the end of the Cold War the CGT's political and trade union actions were very tightly coordinated with the unfolding of PCF political strategy. In these years the CGT was a model Marxist-Leninist "transmission belt" mass organization, marching in close cadence with the PCF in ways which will be described in the first part of this essay. By the early Fifth Republic, PCF-CGT relations had entered a new stage which took the CGT quite far away from this earlier extreme "transmission belt" stance. In this new period, the CGT

[2] On this question see Jean Ranger and Gerard Adam, "Les Liens entre le PCF et la CGT; éléments d'un débat," *Revue Française de science politique* 19 (February 1969): 182-187.

[3] The only substantive documentation of this of which I am aware came when Jacques Duclos' personal notes from 1952 Bureau Politique meetings were confiscated by the police when Duclos was arrested in June 1952 and were later leaked to the press.

acquired a substantially greater degree of autonomy as a trade union in the labor market. The second part of this chapter ("The Fifth Republic—Depoliticization?") will explore the emergence of this new CGT posture.

THE PCF AND CGT IN THE FOURTH REPUBLIC

Throughout most of the Fourth Republic, PCF-CGT relations involved strict subordination of the CGT to the PCF's political goals. In making decisions CGT leaders gave primary consideration to the party's interests. And this remained true despite the fact that the PCF's political aims changed quite dramatically at critical moments during these years. Only in the mid-1950s, when the worst of the Cold War was over, did this strict subordination come under close PCF and CGT scrutiny. Following is a brief overview of the CGT's postwar "transmission belt" period, concluding with an examination of the debates which led to a looser form of party-union collaboration in the 1960s.

A Moderate Transmission Belt—1944-1947

From Liberation to the onset of the Cold War (1944-1947) the PCF tried to carry out a political alliance strategy similar to that used in the Popular Front period. What the PCF wanted to do was to transform the Resistance coalition of reformist forces into a Left-Center Popular Front government which might initiate momentum toward basic change in France. In this context, the CGT's trade-union/labor-market functioning was quite narrowly subordinated to the PCF's political concerns. In addition, the CGT was called upon by the PCF to perform a series of more directly political tasks. Since the PCF's alliance policy dictated great CGT moderation in the period, the CGT's behavior was a model of respectability. The task of transmitting moderation did not make the CGT any less a "transmission belt," however.

The CGT's subordination to the PCF's alliance strategy was most striking in the labor market. The PCF reasoned that the success of its strategy depended upon economic reconstruction without crisis. In this context, the CGT's most important task as a trade union was to discipline the French labor force to work hard and refrain from striking. In CGT propaganda in this period, productive zeal was the workers' primary class duty, the most important way in which they could defeat capitalism. That

506

this task involved an almost total revision in the nature of the CGT's usual activity as a trade union was obvious. Nonetheless, the CGT was able to keep its troops in line; there were no major strike movements in France from Liberation until May 1947.[4] Politically, too, the postwar CGT behaved very differently from the CGT of earlier, pre-Communist, days. First of all, it consistently acted as a strong pressure group on governments, usually demanding wage concessions for its rank and file and social reforms which were part of the PCF's program. Then it attempted to use its mobilizing power to shape French politics from outside the sphere of political institutions, often doing things which the PCF itself was unable to do. Finally, on occasion it became an openly partisan political force, urging workers to support PCF positions in elections, for example.

As the post-Liberation period wore on, certain of the costs of such a strict CGT subordination to the PCF's political goals became clearer. The CGT's directly political activities progressively alienated non-Communist forces in the CGT since they occurred while PCF elements were using a great deal of organizational muscle to consolidate Communist control over the Confederation.[5] By late 1946 this had led to the crystallization of

[4] Michel Branciard, *Société Française et Lutte de Classes*, 3 vols. (Paris: Editions Ouvrières, 1967). Volume 2 provides a chronology of labor market events for this period. The PCF's *Histoire du Parti Communiste (manuel)* (Paris: Editions Sociales, 1964) and Benoît Frachon's *Au Rythme des jours*, 2 vols. (Paris: Editions Sociales, 1967-1969). Volume 1 vividly outlines the PCF/CGT "Produce, No Strike" campaign.

[5] By 1946 the PCF had come to control 21 key CGT Federations, including all of the largest and most important ones, as opposed to only 10 in 1939. Non-Communist federations had dropped from 20 in 1939 to 9 in 1946 (see Georges Lefranc, *Les Expériences syndicales*, p. 157). By 1946 the PCF had also come to control 4/5 of the CGT's departmental unions—the CGT's geographic, as opposed to industrial, organizations (descended from the old Bourses du Travail). There were many reasons for these spectacular Communist gains. The important role of PCF unionists in the Resistance was one. Another was the total disgrace faced by the anti-Communist CGT right wing (Rene Belin and the *Syndicats* group) as a result of its wartime activities. Official and unofficial post-Liberation purges eliminated hundreds of CGT rightists from union positions. Of some importance also was the fact that the CGT Center faction—the forces around Leon Jouhaux—was decapitated at critical moments. Jouhaux was held in Germany until the very end of the war, while several prominent younger centrist leaders chose to leave unionism for politics (Robert Lacoste and Christian Pineau, for example). However, the most important reason for the PCF's great progress was quite simply that there were enough Communist *cadre* in the right places at the right time to organize much of the

507

an organized anti-Communist minority, the Force Ouvrière (FO) faction (which seceded from the CGT to form an independent confederation in late 1947). Perhaps more important, the CGT's antistrike position in the labor market created a problem of defending rank-and-file material interests which the CGT was unable to solve. Wildcat strikes became ever more frequent.[6] In fact, the incident which led to the final departure of the PCF from postwar French governments followed directly from the CGT's contradictory positions. Despite CGT efforts to repress, talk down, and buy off a rank-and-file movement at Renault in April-May 1947, the strike became a mass action. First the CGT, then the PCF in government were obliged to shift their line on disciplining the labor force, leading PCF ministers in the government into a direct clash with their non-Communist colleagues.[7]

From Moderation to Confrontation: The Cold War Transmission Belt

The Cold War totally isolated the PCF. This new situation made alliance-building and political maneuvering impossible for the PCF. In fact, Cold War isolation minimized the effectiveness of Communist action through any formal institutional channels. Where avenues for action against Cold War policies remained open to the PCF, almost all fell *outside* formal political structures. The situation forced the PCF to rely on parapolitical means to act on French political life. In such new circumstances the PCF's main tools were its mass organizations, in the first in-

---

vast 1944-1946 influx of new CGT members under PCF leadership. The Resistance had greatly strengthened the PCF's infrastructure in the CGT. Thus when the growth in union membership occurred, the PCF was ready for it, especially since the PCF's organizational presence was greatest in those areas of the work force (heavy industry/mass production) where the greatest growth occurred. See Hedvig Stolvitzer, "La Scission de la CGT (1947)" (Paris: Institut d'Etudes Politiques, 1957).

[6] In January 1946 a wildcat strike occurred in the Paris press sector, fomented by anarchists within the Fédération du Livre, a union in which the PCF was weak (see Georges Lefranc, *Le Mouvement syndical . . . Mai-Juin 1968*, p. 31). In July and August 1946 a more serious wildcat emerged (particularly in various branches of the civil service) to be stifled by the CGT before they reached strike proportions.

[7] For an account of the Renault strike see Andre Tiano and Michel Rocard, *L'Expérience française du syndicalisme ouvrier* (Paris: Editions Ouvrières, 1956), pp. 136-139, also Philippe Fallachon, "Les Grèves de la Régie Renault en 1947," in *Le Mouvement Social* 21, no. 81 (October-December 1972): 111-124.

stance the CGT. Generally, then, the Cold War led to a shift in PCF strategy and, consequently, to new roles for the CGT. Yet the strict subordination of the CGT to the PCF's political goals remained.

At the Cominform meeting in October 1947 which signaled a basic strategic change for the entire international Communist movement, the PCF was advised to "rely on the masses." Relying on the masses meant, initially at least, relying on the CGT. The PCF's first Cold War analyses focused on the Marshall Plan as the main enemy. "Marshallization" (that which would follow from the implementation of the Marshall Plan in France) was seen as a form of American neocolonialism. The effects of the Marshall Plan would hit French working people economically, reducing their standard of living. The most promising line of struggle against "Marshallization" was economic. The conclusion reached by the PCF was that the CGT should resist "Marshallization" in the labor market. The CGT was thus mobilized in 1947-1948 for broad industrial confrontations in the hope that such confrontations might eventually lead to political change away from pro-American Cold War policies. The results of two major rounds of confrontation (November-December 1947 and autumn 1948) were not promising, however.[8] Workers were willing to strike. In fact, deep working-class unrest existed which the CGT was able to tap. But the CGT rank and file wanted action that might raise their living standards, not open industrial warfare with the government. Yet the latter was what the CGT had in mind. Thus the 1947-1948 strike movements saw the CGT pushing toward increasingly militant action, only to be abandoned by sectors of the trade-union rank and file when governments resorted to massive anticommunism and repression. In the process the CGT was split (between the PCF-controlled core and FO), the union rank and file was thoroughly intimidated away from direct action, union membership began to decline, and divisions between pro- and anti-Communist workers solidified.

[8] On the 1947 strikes see Benoît Frachon, "Les Grandes Grèves de novembre et décembre 1947," *Cahiers du communisme* (January 1948), pp. 7-22. On the split see Hedvig Stolvitzer, "La Scission de la CGT." The 1948 strike, which never spread beyond the coal miners, destroyed the effectiveness of miners' unions in general. It also created such deep divisions between miners' unions—between the CGT and the CFTC in particular—that unity-in-action proved impossible to achieve for a decade. Miners only returned to direct union action in the early 1960s.

The failure of relying on the masses through direct industrial action plus a shift in the Cold War toward the formation of military alliances led the PCF to change its line in early 1949. From 1949 "peace" became the watchword, with the PCF attempting to use all of its resources to unite the peace-loving French in a movement to oppose alleged United States "warmongering." With the PCF's tactical shift the CGT lost its position as *the* central agent for implementing the PCF's Cold War line. Instead, the CGT was assigned to produce a working-class core of support for the "Peace Movement." The CGT was to carry on its usual trade-union/labor-market activities, while at the same time infusing them with a strong "peace" content. In practice this proved very difficult. During the "peace period," which lasted from 1949 to 1954, the CGT was asked to convey a message to its rank and file connecting their immediate material problems with high issues of foreign policy. This message proved too subtle, controversial and, above all, too remote from real labor market experience for ordinary unionists to digest.

By 1951 the CGT had involved itself in a vicious cycle. When trouble was encountered connecting "peace" to material demands, it was dealt with by stressing peace issues to the detriment of material demands. As a result, a gap between the CGT apparatus and its rank and file developed. Since the "peace" positions were exactly those dividing the CGT politically from the other union confederations (the Confédération Française des Travailleurs Chrétiens [CFTC] and FO), peace tactics further accentuated the trade-union pluralism that had been developing apace since 1945. As political differences between unions became insuperable, trade-union unity-in-action for material struggles became impossible. For all unions ordinary trade-union actions became more and more difficult to promote. Anti-CGT hostility at all levels in the other confederations grew. Trade-union membership, including that of the CGT, continued its precipitous decline. And the French *patronat*, which had been on its chastened best behavior since 1944, returned to many of the antiunion, antilabor practices of the prewar years.[9]

[9] On the difficulties faced by the CGT and other unions in this period see François Sellier, *Stratégie de la lutte sociale* (Paris: Editions Ouvrières, 1961). On the *patronat*, Henry Ehrmann, *Organized Business in France* (Princeton: Princeton University Press, 1957) is still the best source.

A Loosening of the Reins—1954 and After

Reflection on the costs of Cold War sectarianism for both the PCF and CGT began in 1952-1953, after a series of disastrous actions led both party and trade union to the brink of organizational disaster and political repression. The Korean truce, Stalin's death, and East-West détente prodded the PCF to begin talking of peaceful coexistence, and of the possibilities for a return to a United Front-type tactic in France. At about the same moment the CGT also began to change its approach. That these shifts were connected was undeniable. More important, however, was the fact that the CGT's shift away from its preoccupation with the political issues of the Cold War meant an important loosening of the PCF's reins over the CGT.

Rumors of CGT self-criticism about "peace" and other sectarianism were rife after a series of desperate political strike actions in the spring of 1952.[10] That the rumors were true was proved in the large summer strike wave of 1953. In this important industrial movement the CGT behaved moderately and responsibly, refraining from activities that might have divided a broad front of strikers and, above all, engaging in no overtly politicizing maneuvers (in stark contrast to all of its behavior in the years immediately after 1948).[11] The CGT's shift was further hastened by open PCF criticism of the CGT leadership at the 1954 PCF Congress (criticism which was accompanied by the dropping of several important CGT leaders from the PCF Central Committee). Here the CGT's organizational behavior came under scrutiny. In the Cold War years, the CGT apparatus had come to substitute its own zeal and action for those of its rank and file, often decreeing movements from the top, then attempting to carry them out by organizational fiat without real consideration of specific and varying conditions existing at base level. The upshot of the PCF's criticism was that the CGT had better put itself back in touch with the day-to-day material problems of its supporters.

[10] See PCF, *Histoire du Parti Communiste Français* (*manuel*), pp. 535-537, Georgette Elgey, *La République des contradictions* (Paris: Fayard, 1969), p. 77, Gilles Martinet, "Le dossier du complot," in *Les Temps modernes* 9 (April 1953): 1482-1500.

[11] See Branciard, 2:84, Lefranc, *Le Mouvement syndical . . . Mai-Juin 1968*, p. 119, Jacques Toulouse, "Des Grèves d'août au gouvernement Mendès-France," *Informations sociales* (September 1, 1954), pp. 75-81.

The ultimate resolution of the CGT's Cold War identity crisis began in 1955, prompted by Maurice Thorez's "pauperization" campaign. Thorez's "pauperization" articles, when stripped of their more absurd claims about the decline in the standard of living of French workers, meant that the PCF had decided that the primary contradiction of French capitalism had ceased to be political (Cold War foreign policy) and had become economic.[12] Whereas in the later Cold War years the PCF had seen pro-American foreign policy as the main source of the oppression of French workers, from 1955 onward such oppression was seen as located in the French economy. This meant that the CGT's trade-union struggles in the labor market became struggles on the front line of battle against French capitalism and would, in themselves, be of primary political importance. Thus, after years of wandering through politics, the CGT was allowed to return to the promotion of rank-and-file material struggles. The change was symbolically consecrated at the 1955 CGT Congress when the CGT's Cold War economic programs were discarded in favor of a new "action program" which was little more than a massive list of bread-and-butter union demands.[13]

[12] Maurice Thorez's "pauperization" campaign (see "La Situation économique de la France," *Cahiers du communisme* [March 1955], p. 260 and "Nouvelles Données sur la paupérisation," *Cahiers du communisme* [July-August 1955]) was designed to confront the ideological threat of optimism about the future of French capitalism which emerged in 1954-1955. In particular, the economic reformism of Pierre Mendès-France was one of the main targets of the campaign. Thorez and the PCF feared that this new optimism might demoralize the PCF's own working-class base, hence the campaign to set workers straight about the "realities" of French capitalism. The absurdity of many of the pauperization arguments, which came at almost precisely the moment when the French economy began to grow by leaps and bounds, has often been noted.

[13] Since 1947 the broad framework of CGT economic thinking had been set out in a series of "economic programs"—mini-economic plans for the national economy and for specific industrial branches. The programs had been initiated in the "Marshallization" period as a way of publicly projecting the kinds of economic progress which might be possible were "Marshallization" and the Cold War ended. By disseminating such programs the CGT had hoped to give its militants and supporters some intelligent notions of the costs of Cold War policies to workers. By 1954-1955, however, "Marshallization" was a thing of the past. Pierre Mendès-France and the so-called New Left had begun to preach economic and social reforms which came remarkably close to some of the proposals contained in earlier CGT economic programs. Since the PCF was seriously concerned that Mendès' modernism might strike responsive chords in its own social base, and since the CGT's economic programs might have facilitated this, the CGT programs had to go. And they did at the 1955 CGT Congress.

512

Toward the 1960s

The years from Liberation in 1944 until the mid-1950s were characterized by the direct and immediate subordination of the CGT to PCF political goals. This meant not only that the CGT's broad organizational stance on political matters followed the PCF's strategic and tactical concerns. It meant also, and more importantly, that CGT activity in the labor market, *as a trade union*, was tightly coordinated to further the PCF's political ends. This was as true in the 1944-1947 period, when the PCF and CGT were both behaving with exemplary moderation in their respective spheres, as it was in the deep Cold War years, when the CGT's highly politicized stance in the labor market virtually transformed the CGT from a trade union into an agent for political agitation among workers. The break in this general pattern announced in the mid-1950s by the "pauperization" debate and the CGT's response to it, was very significant. The 1955 CGT Congress began an important reallocation of roles between the PCF and CGT. Once economic struggle in itself was held to be of primary political importance, the CGT would no longer have to engage in the inordinate politicization of union action which had marked earlier postwar years. In 1955 the PCF came to recognize the CGT's specificity as a trade union, after years of imposing profoundly political tasks on the CGT's every action.

From 1955 onward the CGT was granted much greater autonomy to develop its own industrial tactics according to the logic and dictates of conditions in the labor market. By greatly reducing its attempts to control events in the labor market in tight correspondence with its reading of the political situation, the PCF was setting up a new strategic situation both for itself and for the CGT. From this point on the CGT and PCF would both live in a more complex world. The PCF as a political party would have to adjust its actions to developments in the labor market promoted autonomously by the CGT. In turn, the CGT would have to move in the labor market without constant reference to the PCF's lines. The 1955 shift meant a new division of labor between the PCF and CGT, one whose outlines became clear in the 1960s.

The Fifth Republic—Depoliticization?

The post-Cold War soul-searching of the PCF and CGT implied a new division of labor between party and trade union. As the

513

PCF analyzed the new problems of French capitalism, as a "declining imperialism," they would primarily be economic. This meant that a diligent and militant trade unionism would, in itself, intensify the contradictions of French capitalism. The consequent depoliticization of the CGT carried the added advantage of removing the major barrier to collaboration between the CGT and other unions (a change which, in turn, might make broader labor market struggle more likely). With the CGT assigned a strictly trade-unionist identity, the PCF would function more strictly as a political party. As the PCF read things, labor-market action led by the CGT would contribute to a climate of protest in France which the PCF, as a political party, would then be able to translate into political energy favoring the success of its alliance strategy. Thus giving the CGT free rein in the labor market would not, in the PCF's eyes, create a situation in which the CGT and PCF would be working at cross purposes. Instead, the CGT in the trade-union sphere and the PCF in the political realm would pursue parallel courses, ending in change in France.

Gaullism in power after 1958 made it much easier, and much more urgent, for the PCF to occupy itself with strictly political matters. As the Algerian War came to an end, the Gaullist regime emerged as a stable regime of the Right. This meant that political groups of the non-Communist Left and Center could no longer hope to come to power via the old Fourth Republic games of coalition-building and intrigue. The Gaullist majority could be displaced only if an opposition majority formed to displace it. And there were only two plausible ways to form such an opposition. The first was the classic Cold War "third-force" route, a Center-Left coalition that excluded the Communists. The second was a United Front coalition that included the Communists. If, in the immediate aftermath of the Cold War, a third-force solution had more intrinsic appeal to non-Communists, it also stood a much smaller chance of success than a United Front. To build any viable third force the Center-Left would have had to find ways to entice political support away from the Gaullist majority on the right *and* from the Communists on the left. As the 1960s wore on the Gaullists grew stronger. And, after a temporary setback in 1958, the Communist electoral base held firm. In short, the success of Gaullism promoted a Left-Right polarization in French political life that favored the PCF's alliance aims. This success also gave the PCF its central tactical slogans. The Gaullist regime was strongly antiparliamentary. Its governments, unlike those of the Fourth Republic, were responsible directly to the president of the Republic and not to Parliament. The regime was strongly biased toward executive rather than legislative power. In the PCF's view, Gaullist rule represented a step away from democracy, a situation in which "personal power" fronted for the interests of the "monopoly caste." Hopefully, what almost all non-Gaullist forces could agree upon, then, was the need to return toward greater democracy. The PCF's central call in the Fifth Republic was, therefore, for the formation of an alliance to promote "advanced democracy" in France.

Secure Gaullist power not only raised the question of new alliances on the left and gave the PCF viable slogans with which to appeal for the kind of alliance it desired, but also shifted the activities of all opposition political parties, including the PCF, toward electoral considerations. The antiparliamentarism of the new regime, plus the solidity of the Gaullist majority in Parliament over the years, meant that any parliamentary role in day-to-day opposition to the government was minimal. This situation stood in stark contrast to that of the Fourth Republic, where shifting majorities and favorable institutions gave Parliament and parties an all-important role in defining governmental policies. The deemphasis on parliamentary action meant that opposition forces were powerless to effect significant day-to-day changes in the regime's policies. Thus opposition parties, including the PCF, focused more and more on electoral occasions and their preparation—when the task of building an alternative majority was the order of the day—and less and less on daily opposition to the regime's activities.

However, day-to-day oppositional activity did not disappear because political parties could no longer do the job adequately. Instead, the locus of such opposition tended to shift toward social organizations possessing extrapolitical power. And, for reasons having to do both with France's economic situation and with the Gaullists' conception of France's political economy, the most substantial of these extrapolitical forces, the unions, acquired a new oppositional prominence. Greater economic *dirigisme*, involving a shift toward a more structured and controlled internal market, tended to change the positions of unions, whether they liked it or not. Faced with increased European and international competition, the Gaullist regime moved full steam ahead toward a highly

515

dirigiste political economy, once the Algerian question was settled. As General de Gaulle noted in one memorable New Year's
day oration, the "Plan is everyone's business." "Operation Planning," which involved not only elaborate efforts by the regime to
sanctify French economic planning in the hearts and minds of
Frenchmen, but also attempted to implement a serious incomes
policy, became the most important domestic priority of the rulers
of the Fifth Republic.[14] In this new situation, the pursuit of purely industrial objectives by unions acquired new oppositional implications. If the government desired to hold wage raises down
to 4 percent per year, for example (as was the case from 1960 to
1965), a successful union struggle to win a 10 percent wage concession in the public sector of the economy (as occurred in the
miners' strike of 1963) not only forced an employer to back
down, but also obliged the government to modify publicly many
of its economic policies. By struggling in the labor market, then,
unions were not only engaging in conflict with employers, but
also threatening the core of the government's economic policies.

Thus it was not only PCF strategic thinking, but Gaullism as
well, that set the PCF and CGT on separate paths in the 1960s.
The new regime opened up new alliance-building possibilities for
the PCF, placing a premium on PCF behavior that would enhance its attractiveness as a political ally. The PCF's electoralism
also followed from the general "electoralization" of oppositional
politics under Gaullism. The CGT's single-minded concentration
on developing labor-market action, although the product of an
agonizing reappraisal of earlier CGT behavior, also made a great
deal of sense in itself as a response to Gaullist political economy.
Under Gaullism, extensive struggle in the labor market needed
no explicit political content to be an oppositional factor of great
importance. In itself, without any political elaboration, labor-
market action challenged the Gaullist regime. The following section will attempt to explore, in detail, the tactical development
of the CGT's new "depoliticized" role in the Fifth Republic.

New Roles? Peace and Industrial Action—1959-1963

The early years of the Fifth Republic were years of profound
crisis. As long as the Algerian War remained unsettled, business

[14] Perhaps the best introduction to this form of political economy is
Stephen S. Cohen, *Modern Capitalist Planning: The French Model* (London: Weidenfeld and Nicolson, 1969).

as usual both for political parties and trade unions was very difficult. Moreover, the 1958-1959 political crisis concluded with the
political Left, including the PCF, virtually decimated electorally
and in Parliament. This meant that the PCF's own ability to act
politically was extremely limited. It was not surprising, then, that
the CGT emerged in these years as a vastly more important body
than the PCF itself. The unusual nature of the period made it difficult to test conclusively new patterns in PCF-CGT relations.
Nonetheless, CGT behavior during these years stood in sufficiently clear contrast to its earlier "transmission belt" stance to
provide important predictors of a new CGT role.

From 1959 to its conclusion in mid-1962, the Algerian War continued to be the critical issue in French life. Threats to civil order
in France from the *colon* extreme Right in Algeria and its metropolitan allies were constant and menacing. In this context a general movement of "progressive" forces against the extreme Right
and the war itself emerged. Given the weakness of the political
Left and the fact that trade unions were, at least temporarily, the
only substantial mass organizations with the resources to mobilize protest and action, unions in general provided the main
mass backbone of anti-Fascist, antiwar activity.[15] And since the
CGT was by far the most powerful union organization, its involvement in such activity was pivotal. Because of its important
strategic position, the CGT was able to shape the broad nature
of the numerous mass demonstrations and *journées* against the
war. Thus the CGT became a very important actor in this period,
and it acted according to certain basic tactical lines. The movement had to promote the broadest possible unity of social groups
against the war. It could not be allowed to take sectarian turns
which might offend less militant groups (thus the CGT opposed
student extremism, rejected participation in illegal demonstrations, opposed draft resistance and direct aid to the Front de
Libération Nationale [FLN], etc.). At the same time, the antiwar
movement had to be brought to advocate direct negotiations with
the FLN, a position which some groups to the right of the CGT
found a bit strong.

Since the positions of the CGT on the Algerian question were
similar to those of the PCF, it was possible to see the CGT in this
period as simply a surrogate for the weakened PCF. This percep-

[15] See Pierre Belleville, "Les Syndicats sous la Ve République," *Esprit* 30
(March 1962): 381-401.

tion, although accurate in many respects, minimized the fact that the CGT acted against the war *as a trade union*, generally dealing with other trade unions and student groups to promote mobilization. The *ways* in which the CGT acted were no different from the ways in which other unions acted (the Fédération de l'Education Nationale [FEN], the CFTC and the Union Nationale des Etudiants Français [UNEF], in particular). While the CGT may have disagreed with each of these forces on specific issues (the groups disagreed with one another as well, of course) its general stance was very similar to them. In other words, although the CGT's policy positions in the antiwar movement were those of the PCF, this fact did not lead the *form* of CGT antiwar action to differ in any important ways from that of the other unions involved in the movement. In contrast, the CGT's concern for achieving unity across doctrinal divisions on the war issue dictated a moderation which was even perplexing at times. Most antiwar mobilization occurred in response to right-wing uprisings in Algeria. In such a context it often proved difficult to distinguish antiwar action as promoted by the CGT from support of the Gaullist regime (which was the immediate target of the Algerian *ultras*).[16]

In the labor market the CGT's position in these years stood in striking contrast to another "Peace Movement" period, that of the deep Cold War. In the Algerian "peace" period the CGT separated antiwar actions and day-to-day union activities with considerable care. The CGT neither abandoned labor-market struggles nor subordinated them to the demands of antiwar action. Instead, once the labor-market difficulties accompanying the change in regime had receded (the post-1958 recession connected with Gaullist economic policies made any union action difficult until 1960) the CGT went to work to promote movements for wage increases. Faced with a government determined to keep wages down, but ill-equipped to do so, especially in the public sector, the CGT began in 1960 to promote militant local struggles. These union actions, while quite unspectacular, began to pay off in the private sector, given the existence of a tight labor market. In contrast, action in the public sector was much less suc-

[16] On the PCF's antiwar positions, see Hélène Carrère d'Encausse, "Le Parti Communiste Français et le mouvement de libération nationale Algérien," in "La Poltique des puissances devant la décolonisation." (Colloquium, Fondation Nationale des Sciences Politiques, 1962.)

518

cessful. Here, the government as manager could act to freeze wages. As a result of this uneven development of industrial struggle in the private and public sector, an interesting situation emerged. Over two years (1960-1962) the conditions of public-sector workers gradually fell quite far behind those of their private sector counterparts.[17] In fact, the gap eventually became large enough to constitute an industrial time bomb under the Gaullist regime, one which finally exploded in 1963.

The miners' strike of March 1963 was one of the true turning points of the early Fifth Republic. To begin with, it showed once and for all (especially to those who had interpreted working-class defections to Gaullism in the 1958 crisis as the beginning of a trend) that French workers had not "sold out" to Gaullism. The strike also demonstrated the new political potential of certain forms of industrial action in the Fifth Republic. The government's wage freeze in the public sector was the core of its *de facto* incomes policy. The strikers' demands not only were ordinary bread-and-butter questions, then, but also drove at the heart of the government's domestic economic policies. Sensing this, the government responded accordingly, attempting to intimidate the strike by issuing requisition orders against potential strikers. The strikers' decision to defy these orders and the deep public support which this decision elicited was a major humiliation for the Gaullist regime. Indeed, all of the events involved in the miners' strike added up to an important exposé of the regime's public sector economic policies and a serious political defeat. Finally, the miners' strike offered some new evidence of the industrial stance of the CGT in the Fifth Republic.

Throughout the miners' strike the CGT played an exemplary and moderate trade-union role, doing little more than any other (non-Communist) union might have done in a comparable situation. Since the CGT controlled only a bare majority of the miners (the CFTC controlling a significant minority, with FO also a factor) questions of strike tactics dividing the unions did arise in the course of the strike. For example, initially the CGT restrained the impatience of the other miners' unions (who both wanted to push the strike in the dead of a very severe winter) in order to ensure that the strike broke out at a moment when it would have a better chance to receive strong public support. And the CGT, of all

[17] See François Sellier, "Signification économique et sociale des grèves actuelles," *Signes du temps* (July 1960), pp. 24-25.

the unions, was the most cautious about calling an unlimited strike action in the strike's early days, instead setting a 48-hour limit on its own movement. When the extensive militancy of the miners on strike plus the public support which their action received quickly became clear, the CGT changed its position. Finally, once the strike was successfully under way, the CGT blocked attempts by other unions to spread the action beyond the miners to other sectors of the work force. The strike turned into a protracted battle between the miners and the government, with the government hoping that a dissipation of the strikers' energy and their public support would allow it to limit concessions to the strikers' demands. The CGT felt that an inordinate extension of the strike might cut into public support for the miners' cause, giving the government new openings to cut its losses. Finally, the CGT felt that a major wage victory won by the miners would force up wage levels throughout the public sector much more effectively than a more generalized strike movement. The critical point about all this is that the CGT's disagreements with other miners' unions were about trade-union questions, not about politics. The CGT's cautious moderation in the miners' strike followed from trade-unionist considerations. As the majority union in the mines (and the country) the CGT became a target for the competitive efforts of other unions in situations of industrial discontent. In the miners' strike both the CFTC and FO struck more militant poses, in part out of a desire to strengthen their positions vis-à-vis the CGT. Despite this, the CGT had to make sure the miners' strike occurred in the most effective way possible; thus it tried to moderate the eagerness of the other unions. More generally, the CGT, as by far the most influential union confederation in France, had to judge the action of the miners in the light of its effects for workers in France as a whole, a judgment which also led the CGT to cautious moderation on the miners' action.[18]

Unity in Action and Broader Tactics—1963–1967

The first years of the Fifth Republic demonstrated that the CGT was determined to be a trade union and not an agency for

[18] Pierre Belleville, *Une Nouvelle Classe ouvrière* (Paris: Seuil, 1963); Philippe Bauchard and Maurice Bruzek, *Le Syndicalisme à l'épreuve* (Paris: Laffont, 1968), Chapter 1; André Gorz, "La Grève des mineurs," *Les Temps modernes* 19 (April 1963): 1837; George Ross, "Anatomy of a Strike in the Manager State," *New Politics* 2 (Spring-Summer 1963): 100-110.

political agitation. However, a trade union can behave in all sorts of different ways, on the basis of many different strategies and tactics, and still remain a trade union. What the strategy and tactics of the CGT as a trade union would be in the 1960s did not emerge clearly from the early years of the new Republic. The mid-1960s were to bring greater clarity.

The CGT after 1945 had always claimed to be interested in promoting unity-in-action, and ultimately "organic unity"—unity in one organization—with other French union confederations. The union fragmentation and pluralism which had come to exist after World War II was immensely costly in terms of any union's ability to carry out its labor market tasks. Unity was therefore quite desirable. Despite this, CGT behavior throughout the Fourth Republic had consistently made such unity impossible. For one thing, the CGT had been publicly unwilling to recognize that any other union organizations really had a right to exist. The CGT was, according to the CGT, a nonpolitical mass organization within which all French workers could find a home. Since this was true, and since the CGT had good historical grounds on which to claim that it was the most legitimate working-class mass organization, other unions came consistently to be seen in CGT eyes as run by agents of the French bourgeoisie to mislead workers away from their real home in the CGT. Thus to the CGT the CFTC became an agent of the Catholic Church while FO was the pawn of "right-wing Social Democrats" determined to split the labor movement in order to promote pro-American Cold War policies. Because the CGT held such positions vehemently, and because it was abundantly clear to other union organizations that the CGT was primarily interested in using unity-in-action as a way of penetrating their organizations and organizing away the allegiance of their rank and file, neither the CFTC nor FO was ever very interested in unity agreements.

In the early 1960s, the question of trade-union unity-in-action was radically recast. The drastic "depoliticization" of the CGT plus its new commitment to a more purely trade-unionist role were evident even to the most anti-Communist union leaders. Moreover, beginning at its 1961 Congress, the CGT leadership ceased its vituperative references to other unions. At the same time, with "peaceful coexistence" and PCF moderation in the Fifth Republic, the general effects of the Cold War years were wearing away. Finally, certain important internal changes

521

were taking place in non-Communist unions themselves. Force Ouvrière, founded and justified by the Cold War, remained exceedingly wary of the CGT. In the CFTC, however, habits and perceptions began to change fundamentally. By the late 1950s Church-oriented, "class collaborationist" CFTC leaders confronted a growing minority of militant young leaders (who originated either in the Catholic Resistance or in the postwar Jeunesse Ouvrière Catholique) with little patience for the CFTC's past behavior. By the 1960s this group had taken over the confederal leadership, leading to the CFTC's name change in 1964 (when the CFTC became the CFDT, Confédération Française Démocratique du Travail). The new CFTC-CFDT leadership was impatient for serious action in the labor market, and when such action proved extremely difficult in 1964-1965 (as a result of the Gaullist government's "stabilization plan" which loosened the labor market and led to a mild recession), CFDT thinking turned toward unity-in-action with the CGT.

After a short period of negotiation, the CGT and CFDT signed an important unity-in-action agreement in January 1966. The pact made no mention of politics at all, binding the two confederations to common labor-market action for a long list of trade-union objectives. Both organizations pledged to act together to win an amelioration of working-class buying power, living and working conditions, to defend and extend trade-union rights at the firm and plant level, to secure public guarantees of employment security and to promote a more equitable system of taxation.[19] The 1966 unity-in-action pact was, then, an important new clarification of the CGT's tactical position in the post-Cold War period. If trade-union mobilization in the labor market was in itself ultimately an important political fact, then unity-in-action with other unions for such mobilization was a logical step. The CGT inserted no political provisos into negotiations with the CFDT. It did not attempt to use the unity pact for directly political purposes. Rather it was content to work out an agreement with the CFDT that represented the highest common denominator of accord on strictly labor market objectives.

That the January 1966 CGT-CFDT pact papered over important tactical disagreements over how to proceed in the labor mar-

[19] See Gérard Adam, "L'Unité d'action CGT-CFDT," *Revue Française de science politique* 27 (June 1967): 589. For the accord see Branciard, 2:262, Frachon, 2:498.

ket was no secret. For one thing, prior to the pact the CGT and CFDT had taken quite different positions on the role of unions in economic planning and in public-sector incomes policies. The CFDT tended toward critical cooperation in the planning process and in government attempts to work out a public sector incomes policy with the ostensible aim of working to "democratize" both procedures. In contrast, the CGT was adamantly opposed to such cooperation, seeing both planning and incomes policies as ruling-class plots to entice class collaboration. The two unions also disagreed over direct action tactics, as union struggles in 1964-1965 had indicated. The CGT was concerned with promoting movements that would in turn force highly visible bargaining at the industry level in the private sector and between unions and the government at the top of each branch of the public sector. The CFDT had a much different focus. Caring much less about placing lower-level struggles in the perspective of "building" toward public higher-level confrontations, the CFDT was much more concerned with actions that would win immediate concessions wherever they occurred. It was this latter difference which caused problems between the CGT and CFDT after 1966.

In the implementation of the CGT-CFDT pact, the CGT seemed initially to get its tactical way. In 1966 and 1967 the major results of unity-in-action were a series of large, often national, one- and two-day protest strikes (with most local union efforts directed toward their preparation). In the private sector, actions and mass demonstrations were directed against industrial trade associations and the Conseil National de Patronat Français "for high-level negotiations." Analogous movements in the public sector were directed against the administration of public-sector branches. The CGT's vision of what such mobilizations ought to bring was a reenactment of the 1936 Matignon meetings. By mid-1967, however, shadows had begun to fall over CGT-CFDT collaboration. Building toward national protest movements—the CGT's tactical bias—meant deemphasizing the actual results of local movements. The CGT-CFDT "National Days of Action" were often impressive numerically and attracted a lot of attention, but they won few tangible concessions to union demands. Despite such mass mobilizations, both private- and public-sector employers remained generally intransigent. In this context, first certain CFDT federations, and then the CFDT confederal leadership, began to lose eagerness to cooperate with the CGT. By late 1967 the CFDT seemed more interested in certain other developments in the labor market. Partly as unintended consequences of the CGT-CFDT mobilizations, partly in response to an economic downturn, and partly for a variety of local factors, a series of extremely militant local strike actions began to draw the attention and energy of the CFDT. In a number of plants (such as Rhodiacéta-Besançon, Berliet-Besançon and Lyon, the Chantiers de l'Atlantique in St. Nazaire, Sud Aviation in Nantes, Saviem in Caen) local strike movements, when confronted with employer intransigence, began to take on a virulence theretofore rare in Fifth Republic labor history. In most of these movements the union rank and file, often pushed on by younger workers who bore the brunt of economic insecurity, demonstrated exceptional combativeness, leading to real violence in certain cases. And in many of these movements the CFDT took the lead, with the CGT noteworthy for its cautiousness. Such movements, plus deepening CGT-CFDT divisions, set the industrial stage for May 1968.

May-June 1968: The Political Uses of Strict Trade Unionism

By the May crisis of 1968 the outlines of CGT tactics had become clear. The shift of the CGT away from strict, almost day-to-day, subordination to the PCF's political aims toward apolitical trade unionism was complete. The CGT seemed to have taken Maurice Thorez's "pauperization" lessons to heart. Given the nature of "state monopoly capitalism" in Gaullist France there was no need to politicize labor-market/union action. It was quite sufficient for there to be serious union action. One tactical device to multiply such serious action was unity-in-action between the CGT and other unions. The retreat by the CGT from its extreme Cold War politicization made a degree of such unity possible for the first time since the beginnings of the Cold War. Experience in the mid-1960s revealed, however, that the CGT was not interested in any and all types of union action. Rather, it had quite specific tactical desiderata for the kind of union action it favored. The CGT (unlike the CFDT) was rarely interested in local union action for its own sake. Instead, the CGT saw local action as a means to build broader industrial and national mobilizations that might, in turn, lead to spectacular branch and national negotiations. One could account for this tactical bias on the part of the CGT without going beyond the sphere of trade union labor-market calculations. However, it is also hard to escape another

524

conclusion. The CGT's labor-market tactics, although apolitical and perfectly explainable without reference to political considerations, were also congruent with the PCF's very broad political aims. Labor-market mobilization of the massive public sort sought by the CGT might not only lead to major concessions from employers. It could also lead to an atmosphere of social protest against the Gaullist regime which might help the PCF's political alliance strategy. In brief, the PCF and CGT had agreed upon a new division of labor which honored the CGT's vocation as a trade union and allowed the CGT to present itself as impeccably apolitical. Yet as a trade union the CGT was faced with a broad range of possible tactical choices for its labor-market behavior. In deciding its course the CGT tended to choose those options which were compatible with the PCF's political aims, all the while retaining its apolitical credentials. That this was true was proved in May-June 1968.

It will not be necessary to review the "May Events" in any detail. Suffice it to note that the early May days of student revolt led, by mid-May, to the largest strike in French history, involving 9 million workers at its peak.[20] The strike began as a series of local wildcats around the unsatisfied trade-union demands of the 1966-1967 CGT-CFDT mobilization campaign, more often than not in exactly those areas where bitter local movements had already occurred before May 1968.[21] It took no more than two days of sprinkled, but spreading, wildcatting for the union confederations, led by the CGT, to decide to take over the promotion and direction of the strike. This meant, of course, a massive mobilization of the CGT apparatus to get people off work and keep them off. It also meant that the CGT, as the most powerful and effective French union apparatus, virtually gained control over the broad shape of the strike. This control made the CGT the central actor in the May-June crisis.

As the central actor in the crisis, the CGT undeviatingly be-

[20] See *Le Peuple* (May 15-June 15, 1968) and Lucien Rioux and René Backmann, *L'Explosion de mai* (Paris: Robert Laffont, 1968) for a chronology of the strike. See Georges Séguy, *Le Mai de la CGT* (Paris: Julliard, 1972) for a somewhat belated interpretation of the strike by the CGT's new secretary-general.

[21] The strike began in almost exactly the same geographical areas (Loire-Atlantique, southwest, Normandy, Franche-Compté) and industrial branches (aviation, motor vehicles, shipyards, metal finishing, synthetic textiles) where militant, often violent, strike actions had occurred in 1966-1967.

525

haved in accordance with the requirements of its new post-Cold War role. It remained ruthlessly trade unionist in its perspective, eschewing any direct political involvement, while orienting its trade-union activity to accord with the broad tactical options described earlier. The CGT used its directive power over the strike to push action toward the satisfaction of long-standing trade-unionist demands—in fact, those demands which had been codified in the 1966 CGT-CFDT accord. Much evidence about the early days of the strike indicates that the CGT rank and file was indeed primarily interested in the satisfaction of these demands. The CGT's insistence on the demands, given its determining power in the strike, meant that this interest was maintained and perhaps reinforced in the course of the strike. The CGT's broad tactical aim in the strike was to force spectacular, national-level negotiations of the Matignon-1936 type on the *patronat* and government.[22]

The CGT's exclusive stress on the satisfaction of material demands throughout the strike thus involved no significant departure from its earlier behavior. And there were obviously some very sound trade-unionist arguments which the CGT used to justify this behavior. The risks involved in any politicization of the strike (a course urged on the CGT from a good many quarters during the crisis) were very large. Injecting political content into the strike would almost certainly have divided the strikers between those who agreed politically and those who did not, thereby risking the unity of the strike and undermining the strike's effectiveness in winning concessions. In addition, any politicization would have seriously compromised broader public support for the strike. Ultimately, the major risk of any politicization was that, in the heated atmosphere of May-June, it would have appeared as a major step toward a Communist seizure of power. This, of course, would have been the best of all possible openings for the CGT to give to the Gaullist regime. At the very least the regime could have used such a move to restore its fortunes through anti-Communist propaganda while at the same time avoiding serious concessions to striking workers. A somewhat more remote, but still real, danger was that the regime might have used politicization as a pretext to move to break the CGT as an organization, perhaps by force.

[22] Rioux and Backmann, *L'Explosion*, pp. 78, 253; Annie Kriegel, *Les Communistes français* (Paris: Seuil, 1968), p. 244.

The CGT's line on politicizing the strike, as announced by Georges Séguy (the new secretary-general of the CGT), was that the CGT's job was "not to conduct this movement to an eventual political conclusion. For if we have a sense of the responsibilities which, by their nature, are undoubtedly ours, we have a sense equally of the responsibilities which are, in such a situation, those of the parties of the Left." The CGT was a trade union. It was the job of the political parties of the Left to do politics. The CGT had feelings about what the parties of the Left ought to do, namely to sit down and negotiate a "common program" for a Left United Front, but the CGT could do little more than urge such parties to do so. However, it is obvious that the CGT's strong apolitical stance during most of the May crisis had very great indirect political importance. By strongly controlling the strike and by insisting that its objectives be exclusively trade unionist, the CGT effectively prevented any other groups from politicizing the strike. Since some leftists did see the May crisis as an opportunity for politicizing unionists, this meant that the CGT did everything it could to sabotage their activities. The blossoming of certain forms of neosyndicalism, in particular, won the scorn of the CGT. Talk of *autogestion* (self-management) was strident, if vague, during much of the crisis, coming mainly from students, but finding an ample echo in the CFDT. Since *autogestion* talk risked fragmenting the focus of strikes and pulling them away from focus on industrial and national strike victories, the CGT's anti-workers' control vituperation knew few bounds. Such vituperation won the CGT few new friends in the student world and, more importantly, deepened the wedge between it and the CFDT.

The CGT succeeded in attaining most of its goals in the May crisis. Although neosyndicalism did attract more attention than the CGT would have wished, CGT control over the general direction and tone of the strike was never really challenged. The strike did not become politicized. Moreover, the strike did lead to the spectacular national negotiations—Matignon style—which were the central CGT objective. At the "Grenelle" talks major concessions were won from both the government and *patronat*, to be supplemented by additional concessions won in strikes continued sector by sector in the days after Grenelle.[23]

[23] Grenelle led to a large increase in the minimum wage and an alignment of the lowest agricultural salaries with the new minimum wage level.

The ultimate irony of the May-June 1968 crisis was that General de Gaulle was able to terminate the "Events" by relying in part on the predictability of the CGT's behavior. In the hysterical few days that followed the failure of Grenelle to bring an immediate end to the strike, the complete division of the political Left became clear. This set the stage for de Gaulle to recoup his fortunes. By brandishing the stick of possible repression and holding out the carrot of new legislative elections, the General put the CGT in a position where it had no choice but to end the remnants of the strike and thereby end the crisis. For the CGT not to have packed in the strike during an electoral campaign would have meant counterposing direct trade-union action to the will of the people expressed in a legitimate constitutional way, i.e., thwarting the democratic process. With the CGT deeply concerned to prove its democratic credentials, and, moreover, to prove that it was a trade union and not a political branch of the PCF, continuing the strike was unthinkable. By late June, with the strike's dissolution into an electoral campaign and with students returning home for extended vacations, all that remained of the "May Events" were handfuls of dedicated *gauchiste* cadres without audiences.

Deepening Divisions—1968-1973

The basic stance of the CGT was not changed by the "May Events." The CGT continued to define itself and act as a trade union and not a political organization, despite its ties to the PCF. Promoting struggle in the labor market was the CGT's job. Since the promotion of such struggle was obviously enhanced by trade-union unity-in-action, the CGT's desire for a *front syndical commun* with the CFDT continued to be an important tactical concern. Likewise, the CGT's preference for certain forms of labor-market action—high-level industrial or national actions, with lower-level "building" toward such actions—continued. Yet the post-May 1968 years made even such modest trade-union objectives difficult for the CGT to attain, for one important reason.

Regional differences in the minimum wage, long a *bête noire* of the unions, were also abolished. In addition, the government agreed to open up negotiations branch-by-branch in the public sector, leading the CNPF to agree to a wage increase on the order of 7.5 percent in the private sector. Finally, the government engaged itself to submit a law guaranteeing trade union rights on the plant level to parliament.

528

The CFDT, upon which unity-in-action hopes were pinned, continued to move away from the CGT. Thus in a period when the PCF was going from success to success in the political sphere—a "Common Program" with the Socialist party in 1972, a Popular Front electoral campaign in 1973—the CGT's history proved markedly different. If unity-in-action on the left in politics seemed to be the rule, unity-in-action in the labor movement was much more tenuous. Ultimately a form of united action with the CFDT was worked out, but with a very changed CFDT, newly politicized and with its own well-defined notions of trade unionism and social change in France. These changes in the CFDT left the French labor movement much more deeply pluralistic by the early 1970s.

The "May Events" left the CGT and CFDT deeply divided; indeed, contact between them ceased completely for some time. The CGT had not approved of CFDT behavior in the May crisis. As we have seen, the CGT used all of its considerable trade-union power in May-June to channel the general strike toward spectacular Matignon-type negotiations on long-standing trade-union demands. The CFDT, in contrast, proved much more open to the immediate enthusiasms of the May movement. Because the CFDT was a much more porous organization, *gauchiste* elements with ideological commitments similar to those of the May student leaders had been able to penetrate it. More important, because the CFDT was a much more decentralized organization than the CGT (lacking the strong backbone of disciplined *cadre* of the CGT and having a very different concept of the nature of the working class) the CFDT was much more receptive to the situational stimuli of the May movement. CFDT leaders and militants tended to focus much more on militant local struggles than the CGT, whose eyes were always averted upward toward national negotiations. Moreover, the CFDT began to infuse such local struggles with neosyndicalist slogans such as *autogestion*, a practice which greatly annoyed the CGT. Finally, the CFDT leadership took certain political initiatives during the latter days of the May crisis which positively infuriated the CGT. First, it supported the Charléty meeting (where the non-Communist Left moved clearly toward a third-force political stance). Later, Eugène Descamps, CFDT secretary-general, came out in favor of the political ambitions of Mendès-France. And, as a last straw, the CFDT's distinctly anti-Communist position in the June elec-

529

toral campaign brought CGT-CFDT relations to a breaking point.

Given these CGT-CFDT divisions, the pronouncements of the CGT in the immediate post-May situation were hardly surprising. While reaffirming over and over again that it wanted a *front syndical commun* with the CFDT, the CGT leadership made it quite clear that it felt that the CFDT's behavior made it an unworthy *Front* partner, at least for the time being. Feelings between the two confederations were quite bitter. Almost all of the CGT's public statements contained references to the CFDT's alleged *gauchisme* and "third forcism." Henri Krasucki, the CGT's second in command and a very skillful polemicist, made the CGT's feelings quite clear in *La Vie Ouvrière*.

> The fundamental difference between the CGT and CFDT is not new. It has always existed and it remains. It is no mystery to anyone. . . . The CGT is an organization founded on the reality of class struggle, while the CFDT is an organization founded on reformist conceptions. . . . The CFDT hopes to ameliorate capitalism without attacking the domination of monopolies over the means of production and without seriously posing the problem of political power. It is this which explains the illusions on cogestion, *autogestion* and trade-union power, etc. . . . [The CFDT] . . . values above all its anti-Communist ideas and several of its leaders are in favor of a centrist solution. . . . The differences are really there, but they manifest themselves in a concrete way, in periods of struggle, by a different orientation. We had a demonstration of it in May-June. The *gauchiste* tendencies manifested then were nothing else than a cover for this fundamental reformist position.[24]

Given persistent tactical differences about the kinds of union action called for plus the high level of mutual vituperation which prevailed between the CFDT and CGT, the CGT was obliged to forego a *front syndical commun* and act on its own for a while after May. By mid-1969 the Gaullist regime had provided it with a strong incentive to do so. Stung by May-June 1968 and the results of the 1969 regional/senate reform referendum (which led to de Gaulle's resignation and Pompidou's election), "Pompi-

[24] Henri Krasucki, *Syndicats et lutte de classes* (Paris: Editions Sociales, 1969), p. 104. This important little book is a collection of Krasucki's articles from *La Vie Ouvrière*.

530

dolisme" decided to try on a new social face. In mid-1969, the newly appointed government of Jacques Chaban-Delmas opened a major political offensive around the theme of a "new society," where coordination between diverse interests would replace class conflict. The core of Chaban's "participation" campaign restated an old Gaullist theme, *concertation* in the labor market around the goals of the national economic plan. Central to this was to be a public sector incomes policy, this time (for this was not the first attempt by the Gaullists to set up a public sector incomes policy) built around something called the "contract of progress." The *contrat du progrès* was a long-term union-management agreement which provided guaranteed annual wage raises for unions in exchange for limitations on strike action for the contract period. The government's move was a bold one. In the first instance, it hoped to establish a real public sector incomes policy, a goal which had escaped Gaullists in earlier years. Second, it hoped that success at an incomes policy in the public sector would influence wage decisions in the private sector. Third, the government hoped that the *form* of the *contrat du progrès* might serve as a new model for collective bargaining in France. The French *patronat* was notoriously backward in its attitudes toward bargaining. The model of bargaining *à l'américaine* implicit in the new approach (with recognition of the union as an *interlocuteur valable* in exchange for locking this same union into a long-term contract limiting its resort to strikes) would, if adopted, go a long way toward rationalizing labor-market conflict in France.

The CGT considered Chaban's initiative to be highly dangerous. To begin with, the CGT continued to oppose flatly the idea of a binding incomes policy, as it had throughout the 1960s. Since the CGT considered French economic planning as a device of monopolistic employers to disguise their own objectives in a "national interest" form, any incomes policy tied to the plan's objectives furthered such employers' interests. More important, the CGT saw any contractual limitation on the right to strike as a major step toward class collaboration. In the class-struggle perspective of the CGT, any agreement between workers and employers was merely a temporary truce between permanent enemies, to be called into question at any moment when the balance of forces changed. For the CGT to admit any other principle would have meant, in the CGT's eyes, granting the "monopoly caste" an immense advantage while undermining the class

531

perspectives of French workers. Thus the main labor-market effort of the CGT in the immediate aftermath of May-June 1968 was directed at blocking Chaban's refined version of "class collaboration." The task was initially a difficult one, since the CGT was acting alone and the government was proposing large wage increases in the public sector to entice the CFDT and FO to overlook the strike limiting clauses in the *contrats du progrès*. Nonetheless, the CGT went ahead. The decisive battle in the CGT's campaign was fought in 1969 and early 1970 against the contract proposed for Electricité et Gaz de France (EGF). When the CFDT and FO went ahead and signed the EGF pact, the CGT took the extraordinary step of calling a referendum of all EGF workers in January 1970, who rejected the accord. In the same year the CGT led actions on the railroads, in the mines, and on the Paris Transport System against similar contracts. In time, the CFDT was won over to opposing the antistrike clauses, and agreed, in addition, to insist with the CGT that major aspects of each public-sector contract be renegotiated on a yearly basis. In general, the CGT successfully made its point in the anti-*concertation* campaign. The antistrike clauses became a dead letter. Instead, the "contracts of progress" tended to become yearly collective bargaining sessions between unions and public-sector managers. Because these arrangements rationalized labor relations somewhat in the public sector, they represented a degree of progress for the government. However, the CGT's campaign against Chaban's reformism did play a role (together with right-wing opposition to Chaban from within the Gaullist party) in greatly limiting the edification of the "new society." By 1971 Chaban Delmas' "Modernism" was completely stymied.

Despite deep divisions between the CFDT and CGT, the absence of unity-in-action between them proved costly. Both confederations wanted extensive labor-market conflict. Separately, they were unable to promote it in the months after May-June 1968. Thus communications between the two were resumed in later 1969, without accomplishing much for a year or so. In the fall of 1970, however, serious contacts began, leading to a new unity-in-action agreement in December 1970. The new pact was simply a list of five issue areas around which the CFDT and CGT agreed to struggle in common—wages, lowering the retirement age, shortening the work week, seeking new guarantees of employment security, and expanding trade-union rights on the shop

532

level. The pact was clearly a "highest common denominator" of common concern between the CGT and CFDT. And, after two years of acrimonious exchange, it was significant. Edmond Maire, the new CFDT secretary-general, was moved to assert that "unity-in-action is inevitable from now on." But the pact was perhaps more significant for what it did not say than for what it included. Nothing at all was suggested about the tactics to be used to struggle on the five issues listed. And if one thing was clear it was that the deepest of disagreements existed between the CGT and CFDT on issues of tactics for labor-market action.

Union activity did increase in 1971 and 1972 as a result, in part, of the CGT-CFDT pact, and both unions saw this as a welcome development after 1969 and 1970, which had been two of the least active strike years of the entire Fifth Republic.[25] But unity-in-action was tenuous at best. Once again the CGT pushed the CFDT toward high level federal and national protest movements, with local actions designed to "build" toward such movements. And, as in the 1966-1967 period, the CFDT soon tired of this approach. When the CGT attempted to promote a "Journée Nationale d'Action" in June 1972, for example, the CFDT absolutely refused to go along. Edmond Maire's remarks about the CGT proposal were particularly noteworthy.

> This day of "stifling" is quite clearly destined to break down all momentum of action. At heart the CGT doesn't really believe in the effectiveness of union action. It wants to work a change in electoral majorities. This has led it to act as a "brake" on recent strikes. For the CGT everything will play itself out electorally and not in the labor movement.[26]

The CFDT, in contrast to the CGT, was much more interested in local strikes against local employers, a continuation of its own long-standing tactical bias. And in strikes such as those at the Joint Français in St. Brieuc, Pennaroya, the Nouvelles Galeries in Thionville, and Lipp in Besançon, the CFDT deepened its

[25] *Days lost in strikes, 1960-1971* (millions of days).

1960	1.0	1964	1.2	1968	150.0
1961	2.6	1965	1.0	1969	2.2
1962	1.4	1966	2.5	1970	1.7
1963	2.5	1967	4.2	1971	4.4

SOURCE: *Notes du Ministère du Travail, de l'emploi et de la population* (last issue of April every year).

[26] *Le Monde,* June 6, 1972.

growing reputation as the most militant branch of French trade unionism, a reputation respected by the French *patronat*, among others.

The CFDT's new reputation for hypermilitancy greatly bothered the CGT. Yet this reputation was well earned. Increasingly, the movements which heightened the CFDT's renown were based on "forgotten" segments of the French working class. Hypermilitant local actions were rarely undertaken in these years by the solid majority of relatively well-off French workers, those which formed the CGT's base. Rather they tended to be the work of "outsiders" in the work force, workers in backward and underprivileged regions (Brittany, Lorraine, Loire Atlantique), workers with lower-skill levels, on occasion women workers and, beginning in 1972, immigrant workers. It was clear that the CGT felt a great deal of discomfort faced with the militancy of such odd categories of workers. To cite the trade-union commentator of the 1972 *Année Politique*:

> The CGT feels it dangerous to push such local conflicts too far. The revolt of the "marginals" . . . is fragile. Immigrants and women are easily isolatable populations. The financial cost of such operations, the flanks which they open to provocations and diverse manipulations justifies its prudence to the CGT.[27]

The CFDT was much less prudent.

THE NEW CFDT AND THE "NEW" CGT —PLURALISM IN THE 1970s?

By the early 1970s the CFDT had dramatically and conclusively moved to the left. The "May Events" were probably the key factor in this change. By its 1970 Congress, the CFDT was ready to declare its acceptance of the notion of class struggle. At the core of its new class struggle strategy the CFDT placed *autogestion*, workers' control. The *autogestion* strategy addressed what the CFDT saw as the central problem for workers in advanced capitalist societies, alienation. Alienation was that condition which workers had to understand and overcome before any truly new society could be constructed. Since alienation and socialism were both about people controlling their own lives, CFDT strategy

[27] *Année politique, 1972*, p. 149.

focused on day-to-day issues of power in workers' lives, particularly power in the work place. Union tactics ought to be decentralized, with a premium placed on rank-and-file democracy in setting objectives. Working-class actions should be directed toward wresting tangible portions of power over the work situation from the employer. In the longer run the CFDT foresaw such movements laying the foundations of workers' control within capitalism, developing less alienated men through struggle and, ultimately, mobilizing workers for the political changes needed to make workers' control under socialism possible.[28]

The CFDT's politicization brought it much closer, *in form*, to the CGT (although not in content). Both union confederations claimed to be unions, not political bodies. Yet neither was willing to resign itself to being a pressure group within an economic system whose basic outlines they accepted. Instead, both saw their activities as contributions to the class struggle of workers against capitalism. Both accepted responsibilities not only to win partial victories for their supporters, but also to advance working-class consciousness for basic change. In a word, both had strategies aimed at mobilization which would transcend strict trade-union action. The politicization of the CFDT meant important change for the French labor movement. No longer was the CGT the only confederation whose union activity had goals which went beyond pure trade unionism.

The vital point of difference between the "new CFDT" and the CGT was not *form*, then, but *content*. The CFDT's new class struggle strategy was in direct and purposeful contrast to that long held by the CGT. The CGT's shaping of union tactics ultimately followed from the PCF's vision of socialism and how to get there. The CGT sought union action which would lead to broad labor-market protest. In theory, such protest would contribute to a general atmosphere of discontent with Gaullism and French capitalism which would encourage the unity and strength of the Left. Socialism, the most important victory in class struggle, would come from the political triumph of the Left, led by the PCF. Behind all of this lay the strategic thinking of the Third International and the inspiration of the Soviet model, suitably

[28] For the best short summaries of the CFDT's new positions see "Pour un socialisme democratique," in *Syndicalisme-Hebdo*, no. 1366 (November 4, 1971), and Edmond Maire's report to the 1973 CFDT Congress, *Syndicalisme-Hebdo*, special number 1436 (May 15, 1973).

edulcorated for the 1960s. The CFDT's new strategic thinking was clearly based on profoundly anti-Soviet feelings. The need to begin overcoming alienation *under* capitalism, to promote a thoroughly conscious mass mobilization *prior* to any transition to socialism and the stipulation of a decentralized, workers' control style of socialism were all determined by the CFDT's negative evaluation of the Soviet model.[29]

By 1973, then, the French trade-union situation had moved far away from the Cold War equilibrium of the 1950s. Not only had the division of labor between the PCF and CGT changed drastically, but in addition, a leftist CFDT had emerged as a militant new union force. The CFDT was pledged to the class struggle, to extensive labor-market conflict and to ultimate social change. The CFDT's difference with the CGT would not lead it to "sell out" working-class action; indeed, the contrary was true. The CFDT had clearly placed itself in a strong anticapitalist position which was difficult for the CGT to discredit as "class collaborationist," while the CFDT at the same time began to approach French workers with a vision of change which opposed that of the CGT. Whether the CGT liked it or not—and it didn't—the CFDT's radicalization created yet another element of pluralism in the French labor movement. What this will mean, only the future can tell.

CONCLUSIONS

Since Liberation there have been two basic types of PCF-CGT relationship. The first, which existed from 1944 through the mid-1950s, we have labeled the "transmission belt" type. In this earlier relationship, CGT autonomy as a trade union was greatly limited. CGT action consistently had two simultaneous reference points, the interests of its rank and file in labor-market *and* PCF political goals, the latter being determinant. In practice, the CGT's specifically unionist activities were very closely geared to the promotion of the PCF's political goals of the moment, to the point where CGT unionism became more political than unionist. This PCF-CGT practice disregarded one obvious truth, that action in the labor market did not necessarily, and would not ordinarily, move forward in one-to-one correspondence with changes in political life. It is clear that the costs of this extreme "transmis-

[29] *Syndicalisme-Hebdo*, no. 1366 (November 4, 1971), p. 6.

sion belt" relationship to the CGT were very high. Overpoliticization of the labor market by the CGT in these years contributed to division between French unions, a demoralization of the union rank and file (leading to a drastic decline in union membership), a resurgence in employer power in the labor market, and a widening gap between the CGT apparatus and its own followers.

A second type of PCF-CGT relationship—which might be called a "two-sphere" model—emerged in the 1960s. In this redefined PCF-CGT connection, the PCF and the CGT acquired clearly differentiated tasks in clearly different spheres of practice. The PCF no longer meddled openly in trade-union affairs. Instead, it stood exclusively as a political party whose main concerns were to strengthen its electoral position and engineer an alliance with parties of the non-Communist Left and Center. As we have seen, the CGT, in turn, almost totally depoliticized its actions, becoming strictly trade unionist in outlook. This new PCF-CGT relationship recognized that events in the labor market developed largely according to their own logic and could not be directly shaped according to criteria derived immediately from the political situation. It also acknowledged the possibility that developments in the labor market might well present actors in the political sphere, including the PCF, with conditions which they had neither predicted nor desired.

This change in PCF-CGT relations followed initially from processes of self-criticism internal to the two groups themselves. In essence, they decided that the CGT required a greater degree of labor-market autonomy. Neither external events, nor the CGT's acting on its own to break away from the PCF, forced the change. The CGT's new role was established by PCF strategic reevaluations, first in the declining years of the Fourth Republic, then under Gaullism. According to these reevaluations, the main contradictions of advanced French capitalism were economic. Because of this, extensive labor-market struggle, by exacerbating these contradictions, would be of political importance in itself. In the new period, then, there was no need for the CGT to be anything more than trade unionist. Indeed, politicization of the labor market would, because of its divisive effects on working-class struggles, actually minimize the CGT's effectiveness and, therefore, be counterproductive. The CGT's expanded trade-union autonomy in the 1960s brought with it an almost militantly apolitical posture. This did not mean, of course, that CGT leaders

537

refrained from making repeated suggestions to political parties—the standard theme being that political parties of the Left ought to sit down and negotiate a "Common Program" of the Left (which was, to be sure, the PCF's main objective). But it did mean that the CGT's labor-market actions were not in the least politicized by such suggestions.

In spite of this, the depoliticized CGT did not become a "mere" trade union. It continued to see itself as an actor in the class struggle in France. As a *syndicalisme de classe et de masse* the CGT retained a reference point beyond simple labor-market action, the goal of anticapitalist social change in France. In its new incarnation, the CGT's primary class duty was the promotion of labor-market conflict. Because of this ultimate commitment to the class struggle the CGT's broad tactical biases in the labor market were not totally explainable in terms of the labor market itself. At any given moment in the 1960s and early 1970s there existed a number of different and perfectly viable ways for a trade-union organization to promote the material interests of its rank and file. In choosing from among these possible options, the CGT acted to develop working-class action in a manner which not only promoted these material interests, but also advanced a strategy for change. And this strategy for change was not arbitrarily chosen by the CGT, it was that held by the PCF.

The PCF's alliance strategy for change in the Fifth Republic was basically a simple one. French capitalism—in its Gaullist manifestation as "personal power" ruling politically for a narrow "monopoly caste"—was destined to hurt large numbers of people economically, not only the working class, but peasants and significant portions of the middle class as well. The material grievances of these groups, if sensibly mobilized, could lead to an anti-Gaullist climate of social protest. It was the "new" CGT's task to contribute the core of this climate of protest by the skillful promotion of labor-market action. It was this responsibility which explained the CGT's tactical biases in the labor market. "Building" labor action toward high-level—national, if possible—and highly publicized demonstrations and confrontations made sense in purely trade-union terms (although the CFDT disagreed). Such tactics also made sense as a way of contributing to the atmosphere of social mobilization and protest which the PCF desired. The "two-sphere" division of labor between the PCF and CGT thus, on the one hand, gave the CGT incomparably greater autonomy in the labor market and, on the other, endowed the CGT's trade unionism with meaning as part of the movement for change which the PCF desired.

It was not the CGT's job to translate the results of its labor-market activities into political terms. This was the task of the PCF in the political sphere. The PCF's main goals in the Fifth Republic were to solicit an alliance of Left political forces—Communist and non-Communist—around a "Common Program" for progressive reforms, then to see such an alliance through to electoral victories. As we have noted, the political circumstances of Gaullism created a favorable environment for these goals. In addition, the climate of social protest which the CGT was to help create by assiduous labor action would also enhance the possibilities of PCF alliance-building success. It was thought that broad, cumulative social protest would tend to leave the Gaullist regime ever more exposed, an important fact in itself. Then, the very existence of such protest would also lead political forces of the non-Communist Left to perceive new political hope. Tangible evidence of the existence of a mass constituency for a political alternative to Gaullism would encourage such forces to seek out an alliance with the PCF with some urgency.

Thus the "two-sphere" division of labor between the PCF and CGT, although it stood in stark contrast with the "transmission belt" arrangement of earlier years, did not free the CGT from responsibility to the PCF. The new division of labor did acknowledge that the PCF could not hope to control the labor market through the CGT in a narrowly political way. But PCF and CGT actions in their respective spheres were meant to be complementary. That the "two-sphere" model recognized the possibility of "uneven development" between the two spheres is obvious. The May-June 1968 episode provides a good example of such conflict, where the dynamics of labor market protest were out of phase (from the PCF's point of view) with the progress of alliance politics in the political sphere, a fact which contributed greatly to the abortive conclusion of the crisis. That there would be any conflict between the CGT working in the labor market and the PCF in political life, the CGT taking a labor-market action which ran counter to the PCF's political alliance aims, for example, was extremely unlikely. Indeed, the history of the Fifth Republic to the present provides *no* evidence of any such conflict. This in itself is a good enough index that the "two-sphere" model does not mean CGT autonomy beyond clearly drawn lines. The CGT's new autonomy was not set up to challenge the PCF or to allow such a challenge. And it is most unlikely that any such challenge will occur in the future.

Despite the fact that the "two-sphere" division of labor between the PCF and CGT has not led to any change in the PCF's organizational control over the CGT (the facts of such control cited in the Introduction to this essay continue true today) it has made considerable difference in the relationships between political leaders and trade unionists within the PCF. Recognizing the functional specificity of the CGT has led to a greater recognition of the functional specificity of its leaders in the party. How CGT leaders read the labor-market situation has become a much more important datum for the PCF in its own decision-making. Likewise, the "new" CGT's leaders within high party organs undoubtedly have much more leverage to resist attempts by nonunionist PCF leaders to manipulate CGT labor-market action in accordance with strictly political considerations. In short, the "two-sphere" model has probably made CGT leaders both somewhat freer and somewhat more important within the general proceedings of the PCF.

The historical outputs of the "two-sphere" period have also led to a greatly changed general environment within which the PCF and CGT both must now act. Politically, the PCF's search for allies has made it much more tolerant of the non-Communist Left and its differences with the PCF, to the point where the PCF has recognized the likelihood and desirability of a multiparty socialism and transition to socialism. More tolerant of pluralism on the left, the PCF is now faced with a rejuvenated Socialist party. In the trade-union sphere, as we have seen, the CGT's desire for trade-union allies to promote labor-market conflict has also led it to develop a much more tolerant attitude toward other unions. The rise of a newly militant and politicized CFDT has created a lively pluralism in the labor movement as well. It is in this environment of new pluralism that the future will unfold.

XIV.

The CGIL and the PCI: From Subordination to Independent Political Force

PETER R. WEITZ

This chapter is an analysis of changes that have occurred since World War II in the Confederazione Generale Italiana del Lavoro (CGIL) which have significantly altered its relations with the Partito Comunista Italiano (PCI), the political party with which it has been most closely associated.[1] Some analysts of the Italian labor movement, and of the CGIL in particular, suggest that throughout the postwar period the CGIL has remained essentially an instrument of the PCI.[2] The type of "two-sphere" model that George Ross has used to analyze Parti Communiste

---

[1] The basic works on the Italian labor movement all treat the immediate postwar period, but only one recent volume focuses on the CGIL and the PCI in the 1960s. The basic works are Daniel Horowitz, *The Italian Labor Movement* (Cambridge, Mass.: Harvard University Press, 1963); Maurice Neufeld, *Italy* (Ithaca, N.Y.: Cornell University Press, 1961); Joseph La-Palombara, *The Italian Labor Movement—Problems and Prospects* (Ithaca, N.Y.: Cornell University Press, 1957). Sergio Turone's *Storia del sindacato in Italia 1943-69* (Bari: Laterza, 1973) is the only general up-to-date postwar history of the labor movement written by an Italian. Horowitz's book was the only general work previously available in Italian. Important but more narrowly focused recent works dealing with the CGIL's relations to the Socialist and Communist parties include: Donald L. M. Blackmer, *Unity in Diversity: Italian Communism and the Communist World* (Cambridge, Mass.: The M.I.T. Press, 1968); Cesare Pillon, *I comunisti e il sindacato* (Milan: Palazzi, 1972), which is best on the interwar years; Aldo Forbice and Paolo Favero, *I socialisti e il sindacato* (Milan: Palazzi, 1968); Gain Primo Cella et al., *La concezione sindacale della CGIL: Un sindacato per la Classe* (Rome: ACLI, 1969); and a special volume of *Quaderni di rassegna sindacale* nos. 33/34 (1972) on unions and parties (*sindacato e partiti*).

[2] Giorgio Galli, one of Italy's foremost political commentators, seems not to have changed his early postwar characterization of the CGIL as largely an instrument of the Communist party. This is reflected in numerous journalistic pieces he has written for such publications as *Panorama*, as well as in a volume for which he is principally responsible: *La presenza sociale del PCI e della DC* (Bologna: Società Editrice Il Mulino, 1968) which is summarized in Giorgio Galli and Alfonso Prandi, *Patterns of Political Participation in Italy* (New Haven, Conn.: Yale University Press, 1971).

Français (PCF)-Confédération Générale du Travail (CGT) relations in France might be instructive for these analysts of the Italian situation.

In this essay, I take issue with those scholars who believe the CGIL to be totally dominated by the PCI. Instead, I contend that the CGIL has developed not only a separate economic strategy, but also organizational and political autonomy. The CGIL is no longer strategically subordinate to the PCI in the sense that, in Ross's view, the CGT is to the PCI. The CGIL's goals are still influenced by elements of a shared but highly diffuse Communist ideology. But in developing an economic and political strategy, the CGIL is also responding to its own rank and file and to other non-Marxist labor confederations and their members. Communists in the CGIL leadership do not want to develop positions which will oppose or impede the Communist party, but they are equally unwilling to subordinate the CGIL's goals to those of the party. CGIL leaders, although neither apolitical nor nonpartisan in their personal behavior, have become increasingly nonpartisan in their roles in the labor movement.

My principal concern is to demonstrate how and why the CGIL has developed economic and political strategy independent of the PCI in recent years. I shall first briefly outline how party-union relations evolved in the immediate postwar, or Cold War, years, a period of economic reconstruction and of Communist isolation. As both labor-market and political conditions during this period constrained development of labor organizations, particularly of the CGIL, the CGIL served as a "transmission belt" for the PCI.

Next I shall discuss how the CGIL developed an economic strategy independent of the PCI during the late 1950s and 1960s. Economic boom, improved employment in the industrial northwest, and competition from other labor organizations pushed CGIL leaders to put substance into economic and organizational goals that previously had been little more than words. In increasingly close cooperation with unions (federations) in the other Italian labor confederations, the Confederazione Italiana Sindacati Lavoratori (CISL) and the Unione Italiana del Lavoro (UIL),[3] CGIL unions slowly emerged as effective *trade unions*,

[3] The Italian Confederation of Workers' Unions (CISL), has been closely linked to the Christian Democratic party and to foreign anti-Communist

representing and defending their members by improving working conditions and wages.

Finally, I shall analyze the unified and autonomous *political* strategy, the "Reform Strategy," recently developed by three Italian labor confederations, and the impact this has had on party-union ties. In this strategy, all three labor confederations have agreed on joint goals and tactics for social and economic reform on a national scale. They have taken these demands directly to the government, attempting to avoid political party mediation of their goals. This political strategy emerged as a response to a complex set of developments both in the labor movement and in the society in general.

The Immediate Postwar Period—The CGIL as a "Transmission Belt"

It was political parties, particularly the Marxist parties, and Catholic mass organizations, not trade unions, which organized the working class during the 1940s. When the Fascists were in power (1920-1944), they destroyed the independent labor organizations that had begun to develop in the early part of the twentieth century. A new labor confederation, the CGIL, was established in 1944, but it could not rally worker support without the help of political parties until the late 1950s.

The CGIL's initial weakness was a result of the political circumstances in which it was created and of subsequent tactical mistakes made by its leaders. The CGIL was a product of the same forces that allied in the Resistance, the future Communist, Socialist, and Christian Democratic parties. The unity of these political groups during the Resistance was reflected in the leadership of the new CGIL. This was to be a single nonpartisan labor

---

labor organizations. The Italian Union of Labor (UIL), is closely linked to the Social Democratic and Republican parties.

Giorgio Galli has written numerous articles and books on the Communist party. In English, see his "Italian Communism" in William E. Griffith (ed.), *Communism in Europe, Continuity, Change, and the Sino-Soviet Dispute*, Vol. I (Cambridge, Mass.: The M.I.T. Press, 1964). For a recent analysis of PCI strategy see Donald L. M. Blackmer, "Italian Communism: Strategy for the 1960's," in *Problems of Communism* 21, no. 3 (May/June 1972); Arrigo Levi, *PCI: La lunga marcia verso il potere* (Milan: Etas/Kompas, 1971); Lucio Magri, "Il PCI degli anni 60," in *Il Manifesto* 2, nos. 10-11 (1970); and, of course, chapters in this volume.

confederation, committed to the political goals of the Resistance parties and to the economic advancement of workers. In the spirit of reconstruction, workers' interests were not initially distinguished from those of the nation as a whole; all efforts were directed first toward defeating the Fascists and then toward reconstructing a democratic political system and a noncorporativistic economic system. Despite high levels of unemployment, inflation, and widespread poverty, the CGIL and the political parties, including the Communists, discouraged strikes or other forms of worker protests. The only form of economic bargaining that took place was to tie wages to increases in the cost of living.

The unified CGIL did not survive the collapse of political unity. Shortly after the Communists and Socialists were excluded from the government in 1947, the Catholic, Social Democratic, and Republican factions in the CGIL left to form independent and competing labor confederations, which still exist. The CGIL, with its roots in the Socialist and Communist parties, has remained the largest labor confederation, with membership estimated at over three million since the early 1950s.

Communists and Socialists in the CGIL never accepted the concept of an apolitical unionism which the other factions in the original CGIL, particularly the Catholic faction, sought to establish. CGIL leaders have remained committed to a concept of the CGIL as a representative of broad class interests in a struggle between employers and employees, between private capital and the worker, and ultimately between workers and the state.

The Catholic faction in the CGIL formed what became the CISL, which has had no more than two million members at any time. Rooted in a number of traditions, including Catholic social action and United States-inspired concepts of voluntaristic unionism, the CISL is the most complex Italian labor confederation to analyze.[4] In the 1950s and well into the 1960s, most CISL leaders were committed to a very restricted concept of the appropriate role for a labor organization. They sought to work as much *within* the dominant economic and social system as possible, concentrating their efforts on consensual forms of collective bargaining. Although they opposed government interference in resolvable

[4] In addition to general works on the labor movement cited in n. 1, the following volumes are helpful on the CISL: G. Candeloro, *Il movimento sindacale in Italia* (Rome: Edizione di Cultura Sociale, 1950); Giuseppe Di Vittorio et al., *I sindacati in Italia* (Bari: Laterza, 1955); Giancarlo Galli, *I cattolici e il sindacato* (Milan: Palazzi, 1969).

collective bargaining situations, CISL leaders were never really apolitical. Fervently anti-Communist, many CISL leaders were active in the parliamentary group of the Democrazia Cristiana (DC) and in the faction now called Forze Nuove.

The third and smallest confederation formed by splinter groups from the CGIL is the UIL. It has remained closest to the organization, strategy, and ideologies of the political parties to which it is linked, the Partito Socialista Italiano (PSDI) and the Republicans.

From the outset the Italian labor movement has been more genuinely pluralistic than the French. The CGIL organizes a majority of unionized workers in most economic sectors, but often only a bare majority and by no means a monolithic one. The Communist "faction" has been dominant, but there have also been strong Socialist factions. Prior to the split between the Socialist and Communist parties in 1956 the presence of factions made little difference in the CGIL but after 1956 the Socialist faction developed its own independent perspective on key issues.[5]

By 1948 the Communists and Socialists in the CGIL had dropped all pretense of trying to cooperate with other forces in the labor movement. The Marxist parties and their allies were quickly isolated by both their own strategies and external political and economic circumstances.

Isolation and repression came so soon after the creation of the CGIL that confederation leaders were not immediately able to develop a distinct and effective trade-union organization, independent of the Communist party. At the beginning they did not commit adequate resources to organizing in the factories. Until the mid-1950s they assumed that their links with the Communist party organization would assure them working-class allegiance.

The Communist party, and not the CGIL, was organizationally strong at the factory level. In 1949, 50 percent of the workers at FIAT-Mirafiori, 30 percent at Pirelli-Biccocca, and 40 percent at the RIV factory in Milan were PCI members.[6] Organizational developments in the 1960s indicate that even after the CGIL joined

---

[5] Forbice e Favero, *I socialisti*. There has been no dispassionate analysis of the contributions of the Socialist factions to CGIL strategy, but other research I have done on the CGIL in the 1960s indicates that the Socialist presence in the CGIL has not been insignificant.

[6] L. Lanzardo, *Classe operaia e partito comunista alla FIAT 1945-9* (Turin: Einaudi, 1971), p. 45. P. Bolchini, in *La Pirelli* (Rome: Samona e Savelli, 1967), confirms that the party exerted control over mass organization in the Pirelli plants.

545

the other confederations in seeking to strengthen its factory-level organization, it was not very successful.[7] Union offices were established in very few factories and, in fact, until the 1969 contracts and a 1970 Worker's Law, labor organizations did not have the guaranteed right to organize or be present in the work place. As there was relatively little collective bargaining at the plant level until the late 1960s, the major incentive to organize at this level was to secure membership and dues.

The CGIL did not ignore the factory, but its few attempts to organize at that level were vehemently and effectively opposed by management. The anti-union position of management was tacitly supported by the government, which would not intervene to protect workers' or organizers' rights. Management capitalized on the divisions among the groups seeking support, denying them the right to organize or to collect dues in the factories and prohibiting political discussions. Individuals or members of groups that did not acquiesce in management policy were harassed, transferred to undesirable jobs, laid off, or fired. The exact dimensions of this repression have not been fully studied; one to two million workers were unemployed in 1950, and during the period between 1952 and 1958 thousands of workers were fired in major industrial plants.[8] The state did not challenge these discriminatory and punitive practices engaged in by management.

Another factor which helps explain the initial failure of the CGIL to develop either factory-level organization or a collective bargaining strategy was the nature of bargaining during this period. There were no open contract negotiations. Contracts were established for national economic sectors largely through unilateral decrees of management. During most of the 1950s neither the CISL nor management would discuss contractual issues with the CGIL. The CISL decided in the early 1950s to pursue factory-level as well as national bargaining, and to develop factory

[7] The weakness of factory trade-union organizations is discussed by Tiziano Treu, *Sindacato e rappresentanze aziendali* (Bologna: Il Mulino, 1971) pp. 102-115, and by R. Aglieta et al., *I delegati operai* (Roma: Coines ed., 1970), p. 72.

[8] Diego Novelli has tried to gather data on anti-union activity for the Fiat. See his *Dossier Fiat* (Rome: Riuniti, 1970), pp. 228-229. See also Giancarlo Galli, *I Cattolici*, p. 239. Galli reports that in 1955 alone 674 CI representatives and 1,128 union activists were fired, along with thousands of other workers. See also Eugenio Guidi et al., *Movimento sindacale e contrattazione collettiva, 1945-70* (Rome: Franco Angeli, ed., 1971), p. 41; and A. Accornero, *Dalla rissa al dialogo* (Rome: E.S.I., 1967).

546

union cells to achieve this. Until after 1955, CGIL leaders did not feel there was a need for more attention to collective bargaining at either the national or the plant level.

CGIL leaders concentrated their early economic strategy on issues of national importance, such as the need for jobs. In the *Piano del lavoro* (first elaborated in 1949, and discussed by the CGIL until 1952) CGIL leaders called on the government to intervene directly to combat unemployment. This reflected a strategic commitment to the broad interests of the working class rather than exclusively to the interests of their employed members. It was not until after 1956 that CGIL leaders began to pursue, along with national economic goals, the more immediate and specific interests of its members.

In this period of isolation, CGIL leaders concentrated their economic strategy on supporting their partners, the Communist and Socialist parties. They supported the theoretical critiques and mass mobilizations against the government's economic policies, particularly acceptance of Marshall Plan aid. CGIL leaders contributed little original analysis to the Marxist critique of capitalist reconstruction; they largely followed the lead of the political parties, particularly of the PCI.

As a trade union, the CGIL was not very successful during these early years. But as a source of support for the Communist party, it fulfilled its purpose. It would have been advantageous to the party had the CGIL developed as a more effective bargaining and representative organization, but it was more important that it reinforce such other elements of party strategy as antigovernment protests and demonstrations. These conditions changed in the mid-1950s as the CGIL came under greater competitive pressure from other labor organizations and as both the CGIL and the PCI turned away from mass mobilization as a political tactic.

The CGIL in Transition

Like the CGT in France, the CGIL in the late 1950s turned to developing traditional "trade-union" functions. CGIL member unions developed a capacity to represent, particularly in collective bargaining, the immediate economic and work-place interests of their constituents. In both France and Italy, the development of independent trade-union activities was instrumental in

changing the relation between the respective labor confederations and Communist parties. In Italy these developments helped
profoundly to redefine party-labor ties.

The 1955-1956 period in Italy marked an important turning
point in the CGIL's development. It was also a period of critical
reevaluation within the Communist party. For the first time, the
two organizations confronted their relationship directly. At the
Eighth Party Congress in 1956 they formally agreed to end any
vestiges of CGIL subordination, by declaring an end to the
"transmission belt." This was a symbolic rather than a substantive
break between the two organizations. Giuseppe Di Vittorio, the
secretary-general of the CGIL, focused his comments at the Congress on the organizational weakness of the CGIL and on its need
to confront and represent more forcefully concrete member interests in the face of increasingly effective competition in the labor movement. Di Vittorio did not repudiate the political goals
shared with the PCI. He was simply calling on the CGIL to confront a number of organizational and tactical problems which
had been developing since the split in the labor movement.

A number of CGIL leaders had been aware of the weaknesses
of the CGIL in the early 1950s. Their critiques focused on the ties
between the CGIL and the political parties, and on the structure
of contract bargaining. As early as 1949, Luciano Lama (who
became secretary-general of the CGIL in 1971) had pointed out
in Rinascita that because they came from political parties, CGIL
leaders did not know how to organize and operate as trade-union
leaders. He also suggested that the existence of partisan factions
in the CGIL would prevent the development of internal democracy. Others, largely in Rinascita, focused on the fact that bargaining remained highly centralized, and that the CGIL had
done little to develop collective bargaining or a CGIL organizational presence at the local and factory level.

These problems were symbolized in the highly publicized 1955
election results for the Commissione interne (CI, Grievance or
Works Committee) at the Fiat works in Turin, in which for the
first time the CGIL did not obtain a majority of the seats on the
Committee. The CGIL did not lose its majority in many other
plants, but this highly visible loss helped to catalyze concentration on organizing and bargaining.

The commitment of CGIL leaders to strengthen their roots in
the factory and to develop collective bargaining was supported

by the Communist party leadership. In 1951, at the Seventh Party Congress, both Pietro Secchia and Luigi Longo of the party's directorate had criticized the CGIL and other mass organizations for not developing more direct ties with the rank and file, and for not paying enough attention to strengthening the one institution of worker representation in the factory, the *Commissione interne*. Longo concluded that: "The union must organize its own activities [even] in the factory."[9] Di Vittorio agreed in his reply and admitted that a major weakness of CGIL strategy lay in its obsessive fear of "corporativism" and of concentrating on factory issues. As a result, the CGIL had failed to develop a "union struggle" as opposed to broader "economic struggles."[10]

Another reason that Communist party leaders were ready publicly to concede greater autonomy to the CGIL was the importance for the party of maintaining ties with the Socialist party and Socialist activists. The formal political alliance between the Socialists and the Communists broke down in 1956. The Socialist party turned to repairing its ties with the Social Democratic faction which had split from it in the 1940s. The Socialist faction in the CGIL made no move to leave it, but Socialist faction leaders clearly expressed their desire for greater autonomy from the political parties and for greater attention to trade-union economic activities. This pressure from the Socialists in the CGIL was an added incentive to the party to loosen ties with the CGIL.

The Communist party was confronting organizational and membership problems of its own (which was a further disincentive to resisting developments in the CGIL). Independent moves by ancillary organizations like the CGIL might help to develop new and stronger ties between the organizations of the Left and the "base."

The Development of Trade-Union Activities

The development of collective bargaining and of other "trade-union" activities is a key factor in explaining changes in the labor movement and in the relations between the CGIL and the PCI in the 1960s.[11] Collective bargaining and other trade-union activi-

[9] Cesare Pillon has summarized this debate in "I comunisti e il sindacato," *Quaderni di rassegna sindacale*, nos. 33-34 (1972): 95-96.

[10] Ibid., p. 96.

[11] For analyses of the development of collective bargaining in Italy, and the role of the unions in this development, see Guidi et al., *Movimento Sindacale*, and Gino Giugni, *Il sindacato fra contratti e riforme, 1969-73* (Bari:

ties were developed by the member *unions* of the confederations rather than by the confederations themselves, thus decentralizing the labor movement and forcing the confederations to develop activities of an increasingly noncontractual nature. Union success in collective bargaining was greatly enhanced by the fact that unions in competing confederations started cooperating with each other despite continuing antagonism between the confederations. The unions' ability to develop common goals and tactics pressured the confederations, particularly leaders of the CISL, to reconsider their postwar antagonism.

There remained serious constraints to the CGIL's developing an active and decentralized collective bargaining strategy until the early 1960s. Neither management nor the other labor confederations were willing to include the CGIL and its unions in the discussion of national contracts until local activists in the CISL metalworkers union, Federazione Italiana Metalmeccanici (FIM), struck with the CGIL metalworkers union, Federazione Impiegati Operai Metallurgici (FIOM), in 1959. And until the FIM and other CISL unions opened up the possibility of joint tactics and goals, many Communist leaders in the CGIL remained only half-heartedly committed to developing collective bargaining and other trade-union activities at all. Key CISL unions acted as a catalyst to reinforce the commitment of the Socialists and some Communists in CGIL unions to develop these trade-union activities.[12]

The changes which occurred in the CISL, first in some industrial unions led by the FIM, were fundamental. They were largely the result of new leadership at the local level, produced primarily by the CISL union training school in Florence. Many leaders of the opposition to the postwar CISL leadership generation, which remained closely associated with the government and with the DC, were products of this school.[13]

An early and significant indication that the CISL leadership

De Donato, 1973). (Giugni is one of Italy's leading industrial relations experts.)

[12] Changes in the CISL, and particularly in the FIM, are analyzed by Turone, *Storia del sindacato*, and Giancarlo Galli, *I Cattolici*. See also G. P. Cella et al., *Un sindacato italiano negli anni sessanta: La FIM-CISL* (Bari: De Donato, 1972), and Tiziano Treu, *Sindacato e rappresentanza aziendale* (Bologna: Società Editrice Il Mulino, 1971).

[13] See B. De Cesaris, "La scuola CISL di Firenze negli anni '50," *Quaderni di rassegna sindacale*, no. 37 (1972): 80-94.

was uncomfortable with its pro-management identity came in 1957 when Giulio Pastore, secretary-general of the CISL, virtually forced the bulk of the FIM leadership to leave the CISL at the Turin FIAT works, accusing it of being too cozy with management. This CISL confederation move was not, however, accompanied by any overtures toward the CGIL. Then in 1958 and 1959, some local FIM provincial unions struck for common contractual goals with FIOM of the CGIL, accepting both the use of the strike and collaboration with a CGIL union. This began a new collaboration between components of the CISL and the CGIL.

CISL activitists willing to join with CGIL unions in pressing for collective agreements, and to use the strike and other forms of opposition to management in the process, slowly gained control of first the FIM in 1962, and of other CISL unions and provincial organizations later in the 1960s. By 1969, these "innovators" controlled enough votes in the CISL as a whole to seriously challenge the confederal leadership.

The militants in the CISL found willing collaborators in many CGIL industrial unions, and among Socialists throughout the CGIL. Positive results from this collaboration in bargaining came almost immediately, in the 1962 national metalwork contracts, when for the first time in the postwar period significant wage and benefit increases were won by the labor movement. This contract not only served as a model for other industrial sector contracts, it also posed a number of issues for the labor movement, two of which are relevant to our considerations. One had to do with the level and agents of collective bargaining. The other concerned the conditions for more permanent and pervasive unification of the labor movement, particularly of the confederations.

During the 1962 contract negotiations an explicit tension developed between the confederal and the union leadership over who had the right to negotiate the contract, and specifically over the right of the confederations to step in when negotiations were blocked. This issue has never been fully resolved, but the unions have pressed for complete autonomy from the confederations in collective bargaining. Some unions, particularly the metalworkers unions, were able to exclude completely the confederal leadership from the 1969 contracts. During the 1972-1973 national contract negotiations, however, the confederations again attempted to set general conditions for collective bargaining.

551

Another related question has been the decentralization of contracts. The unions with strong rank-and-file support have slowly increased the range of issues which can be finally negotiated at the plant level. First steps were taken in the 1962 contracts to allow for factory-level agreements of piece rates, job classification, and production bonuses.[14] By 1971, some 4,400 factory level agreements were in effect covering a number of wage and working condition issues.[15]

The development of factory-level bargaining, reinforced after 1968 by new forms of worker representation within the work place further democratized and decentralized the collective bargaining and representational activities of the unions, and thus of the labor movement in general.[16] Slowly but continuously during the 1960s the confederations were stripped of collective bargaining functions and were separated from the rank and file by strong union organization at the plant, local, and national level. Innovators in the CISL unions began by 1964 also to criticize the confederation leadership for its dogmatic progovernment, pro-Christian Democratic, and anti-Communist (CGIL) positions. These CISL activists were suggesting that cooperation in the labor movement should be extended to issues of national economic and political importance. These developments in the CISL provided an impetus to CGIL leaders to seek concrete terms on which their long-time goals of a unified and politically involved labor movement could be realized.

The Road to Labor Confederation Unity and Joint Political Action

Increasing union power had a decisive impact on the confederations, but it took most of the decade of the 1960s for these

---

[14] Giugni, *Il sindacato*, p. 73.   [15] Ibid., p. 90.

[16] Regular meetings of workers began to occur at the plant and shop level in 1968; they were recognized as a formal right in the 1969-1970 contracts and in the 1970 Worker Law. Worker delegates (*delegati*, similar to shop stewards) emerged independent of the old *Commissione interne* structures. The meetings and delegates have tended to replace the *Commissione interne* since 1969. Initial impetus for these new forms of worker representation came in some factories from student and intellectual groups active in some factories in 1967-1968. These outsiders formed CUB (Unified Rank-and-File Committees) which were hostile to the unions in many cases. They were quickly absorbed by the unions. Two of the first books to deal with these new forms of worker representation at the factory level are: R. Aglieta et al., *I delegati operai* (Rome: Coines, 1970), and G. Bianchi et al., *I CUB* (Rome: Coines, 1971).

changes to be reflected in the confederations. Developments outside the labor movement, too, influenced the confederations to
seek a new unified political role. Of particular importance was
the formation in 1963 of the Center-Left government, which
brought the Socialist party into the government for the first time
since 1947. The Center-Left government's impact on the labor
movement was indirect. Through a lengthy and complicated
process, it established a national agenda for social and economic
reform to help redistribute some of the benefits of the postwar
"economic miracle," but it could not achieve its goals. These
goals, articulated in a Five Year Plan in 1967, were endorsed by
most sectors of Italian society, including many CISL and CGIL
activists. The government's failure to implement the Plan provided impetus to the labor confederations to promote a mass-
action program aimed at accomplishing what the government
could not.

Initially groups in both confederations did what they could to
support the Center-Left government and its programs. The Socialists in the CGIL were committed to the *idea* of the Plan as a
blueprint of reforms, as were most activists in the CISL. But
neither the Socialists from the CGIL nor the CISL leadership
were able to significantly improve the contents of the Plan or its
chances of implementation. Their exclusion from the planning
process helped demonstrate their isolation within a Christian
Democratic Party controlled by a conservative majority to the
leaders of the CISL.

And the inability of the government then to achieve most of the
reforms outlined in the Plan reinforced the "innovators" in the
CISL who had been becoming increasingly critical of the close
ties between the CISL and the Christian Democrats as compromising to the goals of the CISL. Not only had CISL leaders been
able to exert little influence in drafting the Plan, but a document
like the Plan was politically meaningless, given the forces which
controlled the government, unless there were more vigorous and
independent support for the goals the Plan outlined.

Two types of issues separated the CISL from the CGIL during
the mid-1960s: questions of formal ties with political parties and
institutions and questions of mutually acceptable goals and tactics. The former issue caused far greater problems than the latter. The question of formal relations to political institutions has
been a cover for a deep distrust which the original generation of

553

CISL leaders have had for the Communist party and its ancillary organizations. The catchword for changes sought in confederal relations with political parties and governmental institutions has been "autonomy," which designates as "incompatible" the holding of union office while serving as a leader in a political party or as an elected official in local or national government. Both the CISL and the CGIL stated that an absolute precondition for sustained unity of action between them was clear political autonomy. The CISL has been most concerned about CGIL ties to the Communist party; the CGIL, with CISL ties not only to the Christian Democratic party but to the government, and ultimately to management and owners.

The CGIL and the PCI: Formal Ties and Personal Involvement

The CISL was not simply fabricating an issue in raising the question of autonomy. As we have already explored, the CGIL was organizationally as well as strategically very closely tied to the parties of the Left, and particularly to the Communist party, in the late 1940s and early 1950s. The CGIL developed its own organizational resources and independent economic goals during the 1950s and early 1960s, but many formal ties with the PCI and the Socialist parties remained unchanged. What were these ties, and how important were they to the CGIL and the PCI?

Two types of formal links have existed between the CGIL and political parties. Activists *within* the CGIL are clearly identified by party affiliation, and they have been organized in factions along party-membership lines; also, many CGIL activists have simultaneously held party and political office. Until recently, in their behavior outside the CGIL, CGIL activists have tended not to distinguish between "political" and "partisan" activity. The extent to which partisan loyalties have conditioned behavior within the CGIL is less clear. My argument is that Communist leaders like Giuseppe Di Vittorio in the early days of the CGIL and Luciano Lama today, while active Communist party members, have been largely nonpartisan in their role as CGIL leaders.

The factions in the CGIL are easily misinterpreted. While they are partisan in identification, they serve primarily to organize internal CGIL politics and not to transmit party directives to the CGIL. The presence of these factions has been severely criticized in recent years, both by other forces in the labor movement and by Socialists *and* Communists within the CGIL. While the factions have been formally disbanded, partisan identification still serves as the basis for promotion and occasionally for developing positions on important issues. Table 1 summarizes the relative

TABLE 1. PARTY AFFILIATION OF THE CGIL EXECUTIVE COMMITTEE

	1960 (%)	1965 (%)	1969 (%)
PCI	53	55	32
PSI	47	27	24
Other	—	4	32
PSIUP	—	14	12
	(N = 32)	(N = 22)	(N = 37)

size of the factions in the CGIL in the late 1950s and 1960s.

The internal composition of factions in the CGIL has tended to reflect existing divisions within the political parties; except in the case of the PSIUP faction, union activists have not been associated with a single group or position in the political parties. The Socialist party has itself been internally divided into a number of formal factions, based on both personal leadership and ideological position. Socialists in the CGIL are associated with a number of these factions, both "Left" and "Right." Owing partly to the fact that no single faction within the Socialist party dominates the Socialist group in the CGIL, the Socialists have been able to remain largely free of the party. They remained firmly committed to maintaining their alliance in the CGIL with the Communists despite strong pressure during the abortive reunification of the Socialist and Social Democratic parties to help form an independent "Socialist" labor confederation.[17]

The Communist party does not have formal internal factions, but during the 1960s disagreements were visible in the party over basic issues of party strategy and party organization. The Communists in the CGIL, like their Socialist colleagues, have been

[17] A group in the Socialist party, led by Giacomo Brodoloni, actually suggested at this time that a single Socialist labor confederation should be formed. This idea was immediately and soundly rejected by the Socialist faction in the CGIL. The Socialist faction in the CGIL so accurately reflects some of the divisions in the party that in 1965 it was unable to agree internally on its own leadership. Ironically, the party had to provide a "neutral" leader to lead the faction for a few years.

555

associated with many different personal and ideological positions in debates within the party. Men like Bruno Trentin, now secretary-general of the metalworkers union, the FIOM, and Sergio Garavini of the textile workers have been advocates of greater decentralization and democracy, both in the labor movement and in the party. In their writings and in their actions as labor leaders they have advocated developing alliances with non-Communist groups, largely through the unity of action strategy of the unions. These are positions on the left of the PCI. Other CGIL leaders like Agostino Novella and Luciano Lama, the past and present secretaries-general of the CGIL, are associated with the bureaucratic centralist positions of Giorgio Amendola in the party. They have been critical of the decentralization of bargaining and have been cautious in their reaction to union democratization. Yet Lama has staked his reputation on labor unity, which can be interpreted as an expression of the Communist party's social alliance strategy, a strategy most fervently supported by the left of the party.[18] As in the case of the Socialist party's relation to the Socialists in the CGIL, the fact that Communists in the CGIL are associated with a number of divergent ideological and personal groupings within the PCI helps to explain the increasing autonomy of the CGIL from the PCI.[19]

The formal ties between the CGIL and the PCI which came under severe attack by leaders of the other labor confederations included the presence of CGIL leaders in the party leadership, in elected office, and in the Soviet-dominated World Federation of Trade Unions (WFTU). Both CGIL and PCI leaders have felt that the CGIL should retain some form of presence in the WFTU and in the party leadership, but the participation of CGIL leaders in elected office became less important in recent years. Some early CGIL leaders like Giuseppe Di Vittorio played a very active and independent role in the Chamber of Deputies. But most CGIL deputies in the Chamber of Deputies (and other

[18] Blackmer in *Problems of Communism* develops the distinction between the "social" and the "political" alliance strategy.

[19] Although during the 1960s the factions were not instruments of the political parties, individuals have moved between the parties and the CGIL particularly during the 1950s. And there were, in the postwar generation of Communist leaders in the CGIL, individuals whose principal loyalty remained to the party, in both partisan and labor union activities. The presence of Communist leaders recruited from the party, and of individuals principally loyal to the party, did not impair the development of an autonomous CGIL, but it is a fact that should not be forgotten.

CGIL activists holding elected office) have had neither the time nor the inclination to pursue an active role in these institutions.[20] This fact has not been happily accepted by the Communist party leadership. Luciano Barca, one of the leaders of the Communist party group in the Chamber of Deputies, has criticized CGIL leaders for not being more active and effective in Parliament.[21]

What have CGIL activists contributed to other aspects of party activity, particularly to the PCI's electoral activity and to the leadership of the party? In a system of proportional representation with strong party organization, it is difficult to assess the contribution of individuals or of outside organizations to electoral support for a party. Few CGIL activists included on Communist party electoral lists attracted many preference votes, an indication that CGIL leaders probably drew few votes to the party. Local Chambers of Labor no doubt have occasionally supported the PCI ticket and union activists on this ticket. However, given the presence of Socialists and other non-Communist activists at almost all levels of the CGIL, since the mid-1950s partisan support by the organs of the CGIL has been very limited. Another indication that at least in recent years the direct electoral benefits of CGIL involvement in politics has been limited is the fact that electoral support for the PCI has not decreased as a result of the withdrawal of CGIL activists from electoral politics.

CGIL activists have also been present, and active, in the leadership of the Communist party. Their numerical presence is summarized in Table 2. The participation of CGIL activists in party leadership roles has been of great symbolic importance to both party and labor confederation leaders. There have also been im-

[20] A factor which confuses this issue of CGIL contributions to the substance of PCI parliamentary strategy is the lack of detailed studies of PCI parliamentary behavior. Franco Cazzola, and Galli and Prandi, have demonstrated that the PCI has pursued an activist and constructive role in the Parliament. But these observations are based on aggregate indications from final votes on pieces of legislation. What is lacking are case studies of PCI contributions to specific legislative proposals. It is only in this sort of study that we could finally determine the extent to which CGIL leaders have participated in this aspect of party parliamentary strategy. See Franco Cazzola, "Consenso e opposizione nel parlamento Italiano," *Rivista italiana di scienza politica* 2, no. 1 (1972): 71-96, and Galli and Prandi, *Patterns.* I have written in greater detail about the CGIL role in Parliament in "Labor and Politics in a Divided Movement: The Italian Case," *Industrial and Labor Relations Review* 28, no. 2 (1975).

[21] Interview with Luciano Barca, vice-president of PCI group in Chamber of Deputies, May 4, 1971.

portant substantive contributions made by CGIL activists in the PCI. This is not the place to detail the history of this contribution; it has often been subtle, and given the democratic centralist nature of the party (and the secrecy of decision-making activities of the leadership), hard to trace. But one need only think of the presence of men with the stature of Di Vittorio in the party leadership to understand the links to the agricultural and industrial workers which he, Sacchi, Romagnoli, and a few other CGIL

TABLE 2. CGIL Executive Committee Members in Party Leadership Roles (Direzione, C.C.)

1960		1965			1969		
PCI	PSI	PCI	PSI	PSIUP	PCI	PSI	PSIUP
9	8	11	7	4	10	7	6
(N = 48)		(N = 36)			(N = 50)		

leaders have provided the PCI. These men were popular leaders, with strong and visible personal followings. There have been few such communist party leaders, but many of those have come from the CGIL.

Intellectuals like Bruno Trentin of the FIOM have also made important theoretical contributions to the analysis of the role of the political Left in Italian society. In 1962, at a Conference on "Trends in Italian Capitalism,"[22] Trentin pointed out that in order to be politically effective, the Communist party and the Italian Left would have to make its concepts of needed reforms more concrete and specific. He also pointed out that the party's concentration on obtaining reforms only through government failed to take into account the economic and social importance of the private sector. Reforms should be sought in the organization of work and in the use of private capital, as well as in the allocation of public resources. In this same article, Trentin also gave a new perspective to the Gramscian goal of establishing social and political alliances with non-Communist groups in the society. He pointed out that white-collar and service-sector jobs were becoming increasingly proletarianized (not to mention more numerous in the economy) and that therefore alliances should be sought

[22] B. Trentin, "Le dottrine neocapitalistiche e l'ideologia delle forze dominanti nella politica economica italiana," in Istituto Gramsci, *Tendenze del capitalismo italiano* (Rome: Riuniti, 1962), pp. 97-144.

with these groups as well as with non-Communist working-class groups. These perspectives added new dimensions to debate over party strategy in the 1960s, as other chapters in this volume indicate.[23]

The debate on labor movement "autonomy" also focused on the role of the CGIL in the WFTU. The CISL and the UIL called on the CGIL to break all formal ties with the WFTU as well as with the Communist party. Socialists in the CGIL had been urging their Communist colleagues to leave the WFTU for many years. Many Communists in the CGIL resisted this, arguing that they wanted to concentrate on internal rather than external reform.[24] (This was similar to the CISL argument for remaining active in the DC and in Parliament.)

The Formal Break

Debate in the CGIL over what steps it should take to meet CISL demands that it break with the Communist party and the WFTU, which started in the early 1960s, was not finally resolved until 1969. The secretary-general of the CGIL, Agostino Novella, was not inclined to accept incompatibility as a step toward greater unity with the CISL. Until 1969, he and his allies in the CGIL managed to tie any CGIL action to prior moves by the CISL: If the CISL leaders were not willing to leave the Christian Democratic party, particularly the parliamentary group, the CGIL leaders would not break their ties with the Communist and Socialist parties. The Novella position prevailed in the 1965 CGIL Congress when the issue of elected office came up; this position also prevailed at a special CGIL conference at Aricia in October 1967.

The CGIL activists in favor of accepting the precondition of "incompatibility" to achieve greater unity with the other labor confederations were decisively reinforced by the acceptance of incompatibility at the 1969 CISL Congress. This Congress adopted new statutes prohibiting CISL activists from holding elected office (the CISL had already passed a statute prohibiting their activists from holding high party office).

Most CGIL leaders were prepared to leave elected office. In

[23] For a discussion of the early period of this debate, see G. Tamburrano, "Lo sviluppo del capitalismo e la crisi teorica dei comunisti italiani," *Tempi moderni*, no. 10 (1962).

[24] See Blackmer, *Unity in Diversity*, Chapter 8, for a discussion of the CGIL and the WFTU in the 1950s.

559

1966, the FIOM (metal workers union) had accepted this principle in response to similar changes in the CISL metalworkers union (the FIM). Some CGIL leaders were not happy with the provision prohibiting them from participating in party leadership. In the end, the issue was resolved by accepting the tactical imperative rather than the principle of "incompatibility" of labor leadership positions with formal office in the Communist party. As individual militants, most Communists in the CGIL accepted both the desirability and the obligation of participating in the party; they did not feel that this conditioned or adversely affected their roles in the labor movement. But for the majority of the participants in the 1969 CGIL congress the goal of unity within the labor movement warranted giving up formal participation in party leadership. Agostino Novella and some other CGIL leaders did not accept this decision and chose to remain in the Communist party leadership. Novella's successor as secretary-general of the CGIL was Luciano Lama, also a Communist, but one of the leaders of the pro-unity majority in the CGIL.[25]

The Emergence of the Reform Strategy: Unity of Action for Pension Reform

Before this dramatic affirmation of labor unity, significant progress had been made in establishing grounds for joint political action by the labor confederations. During the 1967-1969 period, the CGIL and the other labor confederations agreed on the substance of a pension system reform, and on how best to press for this reform. This helped to demonstrate that there were effective political alternatives to the close links which the confederations had maintained with the political parties.

The common pension reform strategy was developed after the final vote on the Plan, in 1967, when the weaknesses of a parliamentary strategy had been demonstrated to the labor confederations and particularly to the CISL. CISL leaders attempted to

[25] CGIL leaders accepted the tactical necessity of incompatibility, not the principle. Many explicitly hope that once unity is clearly established, they will once again be able to participate in political party leadership. One of the issues which is still being debated is the *level* of party office which is incompatible with CGIL office. Debate continues on whether or not labor activists should be allowed to participate in party Central Committees. The CISL leaders tend to argue that any labor activist should not participate in party activity, whereas CGIL leaders (backed strongly by PCI leaders) protest incompatibility to the level of shop stewards (*delegati*), sought by the CISL.

modify some of the provisions of the Plan during the final debate on the legislation, with limited success. In this process, they faced considerable opposition from within the DC. For many CISL leaders this was the final lesson needed for them to abandon a commitment to work within the Christian Democratic party for economic and social reforms.

The CGIL deputies, as members of parties on different sides of the issue, compromised by abstaining on the final vote. Some Communists in the CGIL had sought to work more closely with the planning process than the Communist party, and the Socialists in the CGIL favored the Plan as a possible instrument of control over economic and social development. The abstention in the parliamentary vote was far from an ideal solution for either group, or for the Communist party, which had to accept this break in "party discipline" to preserve harmony in the CGIL. The joint action outside Parliament for pension system reform provided all of the groups in the labor confederations with a constructive alternative to parliamentary action.

The importance of the pension reform strategy is less in the substance of the reforms sought than in the joint tactics worked out by the CISL and CGIL. For the first time, CISL confederation leaders agreed to engage in a national strike, and to adopt an opposition stance to the government. CISL confederation militancy on this issue was motivated both by rank-and-file support for the substance of the issue, mediated by the unions, and by the leadership's realization that pressure would have to be applied on the government from outside the political parties if any of the reforms outlined in the Plan, among them pension reform, were to be implemented.

The experience of jointly pressing for pension reform established important precedents for both the CGIL and CISL. First it demonstrated the willingness of the CISL leadership to work with the CGIL, and to adopt tactics, particularly strikes, which it had eschewed in the past; it also demonstrated that unified confederal positions supported by mass mobilization could achieve results: a reform was passed in 1969. Furthermore, during 1968 both confederations learned that rank-and-file involvement was possible in national reform issues. This rank-and-file involvement, not only in strikes, but also in ratifying the national agreements

561

prior to final implementation, was a manifestation of an increasing rank-and-file militancy which found outlets in the 1969 contract negotiations and in subsequent contractual and reform issues.

A New National Labor Strategy: Reforms

The year 1969 was a key one in the labor movement, both in collective bargaining and in labor's broader political role. The various developments which have been discussed above culminated in the "Hot Autumn" (*Autunno caldo*) of 1969 and the emergence of the unified confederal "Reform Strategy."[26]

Unions emerged as the principal organs of worker representation on economic and social issues at the plant and contractual level. The 1969-1970 sectoral contracts were in many ways only the final aspect of rank-and-file and union militancy which had been evident since 1967 in many sectors. The main goal of the militants was to obtain improved wages and working conditions, and to gain formal recognition of unions and new forms of worker representation at the shop level.

Many union leaders had also begun to argue, as early as 1964,[27] that even significant improvements in wages and working conditions were not enough to meet even the basic needs of workers. They linked the types of reforms discussed during the period of the Center-Left government to the concrete contractual needs of their constituents: public investment and indirect incentives had not created an adequate housing stock in areas of industrial concentration and therefore the system of public support for housing had to be revised; what housing there was, was far from places of work, and public transportation was slow and inadequate, therefore public transportation had to be improved in industrial areas; the social services of the government were in complete disarray, despite the fact that these were an important part of a worker's total income and fringe benefits package. These perspectives on the link between national social and economic reforms and more conventional aspects of collective bargaining were very congenial to many CGIL leaders who were seeking more concrete and broadly acceptable political goals. The impli-

[26] For a particularly good introduction to the "Hot Autumn" see the first chapter of Giugni, *Il sindacato.*

[27] *Dibattito sindacale,* a periodical published in Milan since 1964, has served as an outlet for this critique of CISL confederal strategy and as a forum for articles calling for new forms of political action by the labor movement.

cations of this analysis were not, however, easily accepted by many CISL leaders until 1969.

Political developments during 1968-1969 clearly indicated that there was an opportunity for new political and social forces to take initiatives for reforms. The government coalition was weakened by changes in the Christian Democratic and Unified Socialist parties. As I have already indicated, it was clear by 1968 that the reforms outlined in the Plan would not be quickly implemented, if at all. During 1968, the dominant faction in the Christian Democratic party, the *dorotei*, had begun to fall apart. This raised a question which was not new to the party and which has remained unanswered: What line would it follow in the future? The party has tried to govern with Center-Left coalitions, with Center-Right coalitions, and with minority governments since then. There remain strong pressures in the party to abandon the Center-Left formula, but brief attempts to govern with alternative forms of government have been quite unsuccessful.

The left wing of the Christian Democratic party went through a major upheaval during the 1968-1969 period. Prior to the formal break between the CISL and the party, another important collateral organization which had been a strong force on the party's left, the Associazioni Cristiane dei Lavoratori Italiani (ACLI) also broke its formal ties with the party. One of the ACLI's major leaders, Livio Labor, actually set out to create an independent quasi-political organization independent of the Christian Democrats.[28]

At the same time that the future path of the Christian Democratic government became more uncertain, the Unified Socialist party, child of the Center-Left government, collapsed. Losses sustained by the party in the 1968 elections demonstrated that the unification of the Socialists and the Social Democrats lacked the support of the electorate. During 1969, the Socialist party reemerged as an articulate reformist party willing to oppose the government.

[28] The ACLI was an important source of support for the *Forze nuove* faction in the DC, along with the CISL and Catholic youth organizations. Livio Labor's quasi-political organization, the MPL, no longer exists. It was completely unsuccessful as an electoral organization. It is interesting to note that the *Forze nuove* group in the DC have not suffered electorally as a result of the ACLI and CISL move to break their ties with the party. The reasons for this are discussed in my Ph.D. dissertation, "Paths to Power: The Changing Political Involvement of the Italian Labor Movement," M.I.T., forthcoming.

These developments in the Christian Democratic and Socialist parties increased government immobilism while encouraging labor confederation leaders to think that there was a political void into which they might step. The confederation leadership were supported in this belief by rank-and-file and union pressure, and by the example of their success in achieving a reform of the pension system. How could the confederations benefit from worker militancy and reestablish leadership in significant areas of collective action? How could the fragmentation of the political leadership be offset to achieve badly needed reforms? How could the links developing between the confederations be strengthened by more than verbal commitments? The answer was the Reform Strategy, a unified confederal commitment to seek specific national reforms and to use the range of resources available to the labor movement, including mass mobilization, to support the reform demands.

The confederations' reform strategy was launched in November 1969 with a national strike calling for changes in the public housing system and related land use legislation. The confederations called on the government to negotiate these reforms with them, and also to begin discussions on other reforms which the confederations outlined during the next few months.

The legislative goals of the strategy grew quickly and somewhat haphazardly. The two initial goals were housing and a major reform in the system of national health insurance and health-care delivery systems. Both of these issues were negotiated with the government to a point of agreement on proposed legislation. The confederations have also raised a number of other specific and general issues which have not led to legislative proposals. Inequities in the tax system, the inadequacy of public transportation, and a range of problems in the education system have all been the subject of debate and of mobilization in the labor movement.

The confederations have also developed critical positions on the government's economic policies. In 1970, the labor movement developed a two-pronged attack on the lack of economic development in southern Italy. At the national level the confederations called for a major reform in the special government "Fund for the South," and a change in the investment patterns of semipublic enterprise so that southern workers would no longer have to leave their homes to seek work. Locally, industrial unions put pressure on firms in the sectors which they organized, and particularly on large firms like Fiat and Pirelli, to make more investments in the south.[29]

The economy, in a period of expansion when the strategy was launched, has since suffered a serious downturn with investment falling off, prices rising, and unemployment increasing. In response to these developments the confederations have put pressure on the government to intervene more effectively to deal particularly with unemployment. This led, in early 1973, to the first national strike called against a government in general rather than for the reform of a particular sector.

While the Reform Strategy has not achieved some of its explicit goals, it has redefined the place of the labor movement in national politics. The confederations have emerged as important and effective spokesmen on a range of economic and social issues. While not united on all issues, since 1969 they have maintained unified positions on issues of national importance. In this process, they have established considerable independence from the political parties.

The Communist Party Reaction to the Changes in the Labor Movement

What role has the Communist party taken in stimulating or resisting these changes in the labor movement? What impact have these changes had on the party's relations with the CGIL? What are the implications of a unified and politically aggressive labor movement for the Communist party?

As I have already indicated, formal relations between the CGIL and the PCI have changed considerably. CGIL activists are no longer PCI deputies, nor do they hold local elected office. The CGIL leadership, while it has not been explicitly partisan in its national activities for many years, must be exceedingly careful not to alienate allies in the CISL and the UIL through partisan comments. This has all tended to diffuse support which the CGIL provided the PCI during the 1950s and 1960s. But have these "losses" to the party been offset by the gains which the developments in the labor movement provide?

[29] It is interesting to note that the metalworkers unions have explicitly negotiated with management for greater investments in the south. This is an unusual and innovative collective bargaining objective.

565

No clear answer can be found in statements of Communist party leaders. Reactions have been mixed, reflecting different perspectives on the labor movement and on long-term party strategy. This is the key to understanding reactions in the party to developments in the labor movement: There is no unidimensional or specifically defined theory of the role of the labor movement in party strategy to which the labor movement could be subordinated.

There is some historical consistency in the PCI's perspective on the labor movement. As the debate during the 1951 Congress indicated, the party leadership has wanted the CGIL to develop its own organizational links with the working class and to defend the short-term economic interests of its constituency. The PCI has always supported the principal of a unified labor movement. The party has rejected and criticized any tendencies toward pure "economic" or apolitical unionism. It has also realized that its own path to power depended not only on incremental increases in electoral support and in gaining power in the institutions of local and national government, i.e., a political strategy, but also on forging new alliances with non-Communist groups at all levels of society outside the formal institutions of government.

Quite clearly, the developments in the CGIL, and in the labor movement in general, have enhanced the possibilities of achieving these goals. The labor movement is now more unified, more politically militant, and organizationally better rooted in its mass membership than it has ever been in the past. This has involved the establishment of alliances between Communist and non-Communist groups in many social strata, yet it has not involved the rejection of important common goals of the CGIL and the PCI. The labor movement is reformist, but it seeks reforms basic to redefining and reallocating economic and political power in the society.

Thus, from a macroscopic perspective, the developments in the labor movement have clearly enhanced and complemented the Communist party's achievement of its own goals. But this of course is not the perspective of many party leaders, involved in the day-to-day realities of politics.

The initial response of the party leadership to the Reform Strategy was positive. In late 1969 and early 1970, the strategy represented both effective unity in the labor movement and the reassertion of some centralized control over worker militancy.

During 1967-1969 the decentralization and concentration on economic issues of the unions had begun to disturb some party leaders. In the Reform Strategy, the confederations reasserted central control over some aspects of labor activity and reconfirmed the commitment of the labor movement to political as well as to collective bargaining goals.

By late 1970, some of the weaknesses of the Reform Strategy were becoming apparent. While the labor confederations had reached formal agreement with the government on the outline of two major reforms, the future of these and other reforms was put in doubt by the emergence of increasingly effective opposition to the labor confederations, and their strategy of bypassing traditional channels of interest aggregation and of political decision-making, particularly the political parties and Parliament.

Communist party leaders began to express concern that the labor confederations had gone beyond their organizational and political resources. At a Communist party Central Committee meeting in November, party secretary Berlinguer reminded those listening that "the struggle for the reforms cannot be conducted solely by union action and using the fora available to the unions."[30] Other mass organizations must also be involved, and must be coordinated by the Communist party. Reflecting the Communist party's commitment to the major institutions of government, Berlinguer also reiterated the party position that Parliament must be the central decision-making body for all social and economic reforms.

Just a few months later, in March 1971 at another Central Committee meeting, Giorgio Amendola, one of the principal architects of the party's political strategy, reiterated the warning that the labor confederations should not presume to lead the struggle for reforms. Thus, although the party has not openly opposed the Reform Strategy, it has urged the labor confederations to draw back from confrontation on a wide range of economic and social issues and to limit demands for government action to concrete issues closely tied to collective bargaining issues.[31]

The party's seemingly cautious position vis-à-vis mass mobilization and reforms is consistent with its general political strat-

[30] L'Unità, November 14, 1970 (author's translation).

[31] For a statement of this position see Fernando Di Giulio, "Il più politico degli scioperi generali," Rinascita, no. 3 (January 19, 1973): 3. Di Giulio was then responsible for PCI relations with mass organizations.

567

egy. The PCI seeks reforms but not at the cost of economic chaos or major social disruption. Labor's strategy was to ask for action on a number of fronts, and to keep pressure on the government as long and as intensely as possible while the confederations established their own sense of priorities. This approach was far too ambitious, too poorly coordinated, and too threatening to party hegemony for the taste of many party strategists.

Communist party leaders have also questioned the costs of labor unity, particularly the rigid concepts of autonomy imposed by the CISL. As I have stated, many Communists in the CGIL were not satisfied with the formal autonomy from the party required in the process of establishing closer ties with the rest of the labor movement, but they accepted this as a tactical necessity. Men like Trentin have not suddenly stopped talking to other Communists, in person or in print. Nonetheless, some party leaders would rather have their colleagues from the CGIL talking to them in the Central Committee as well as from outside the party.

Overall, the reaction of party leaders to developments in the labor movement have been a reflection of tensions which run through the party's own strategy. Labor unity is a significant achievement, a goal which has always been important to party leaders. But labor unity has not directly reinforced party hegemony in the working class or among wage earners in other sectors. Labor unity has been achieved on the basis of agreement on issues, both contractual and of broader social importance, developed by the labor movement itself. Unity also has been achieved partly through the decentralization of the labor movement, particularly in bargaining matters. This degree of decentralization, and concentration on collective bargaining by powerful sectors of the labor movement, has made some party leaders uncomfortable. And the emergence of the labor movement as an important political force in national politics, on the left or reformist part of the political spectrum in the mind of some PCI leaders further weakens the ability of the party to coordinate and benefit from reformist impulses and their limitations. Concerns over these developments reflect different perceptions with the Communist party on the types of political and social alliances which the party should encourage on its "road to socialism." It also reflects the inherent tensions between a loosely structured alliance strategy and a more tightly controlled political strategy. And fundamentally, the developments in the labor movement

568

pose the basic question of the degree of democratization and decentralization among the various forces contributing to building a socialist alternative possible and desirable from the point of view of the major Marxist "opposition" party in Italy.

THE PRESENT AND THE FUTURE: SUMMARY AND SPECULATION

The increased independence of the labor movement from political parties and from government, particularly Parliament, reflected in the changed relations of the CGIL to the Communist party contributed to increased labor unity in the Italian social and political context. While the CGIL was close and in many ways subordinate to the Communist party in the early postwar years, Communists and Socialists in both the CGIL and in the political parties put a high priority on reunification of the labor movement. When initially conceived, the goal of labor unity no doubt was consistent with potential Communist party domination of the labor movement. It was not until well into the 1950s that the viability and success of the CISL and other non-Communist labor organizations became clear. Once a genuine pluralism was established in the labor movement, the Communists and the Socialists might have abandoned the goal of labor unity, the terms of which they could no longer dictate.

Organized by competing political parties as well as by competing labor confederations, as labor unity increased but agreement between the competing political parties did not, the labor confederations sought to increase their independence from the political parties in order to reinforce the tendencies toward unity. This posed no particular problems as long as unity measures were confined to collective bargaining; this was a realm in which the Communists and other parties had little interest. New problems arose as the labor confederations sought to develop an essentially political strategy. Socialists and most Communists in the leadership of the CGIL were genuinely committed to labor unity and to pursuing national economic and social reforms. As the opportunity to work more closely with the CISL and the UIL developed in the late 1960s, these CGIL leaders chose to accept as a condition for greater labor unity formal autonomy from the political parties. This was an instrumental decision. Whereas for CISL leaders a presence in the Christian Democratic group in Parliament had been functionally important in representing the

569

interests of their members, CGIL leaders had never seen their presence in Parliament or in the political parties in quite the same "interest group" sense. CGIL leaders were not in these institutions primarily to promote the interests of their constituents. The Communists participated in Parliament as a duty imposed by the party and they participated in the party leadership as a responsibility of Communist militants. By leaving the party leadership, Communists in the CGIL demonstrated their primary commitment to the labor movement. They resigned without renouncing either the Communist party or the importance of participation in political party activities. Communists in the CGIL remain actively involved in debates over party strategy, and committed to the broad political goals of the party.

While in the broadest sense the unity of political strategy of the labor movement is complementary to the strategy of the Communist party, in day-to-day politics tension and disagreement do exist. The labor strategy, both in its national economic and social reform goals and in its contractual aspects, is influenced by very different forces and considerations than the Communist party's concrete political strategy.

At the current time the Communist party is increasingly supporting the governing coalition. Its abstention from Parliamentary votes has, on more than one occasion in recent years, saved the government from defeat on the floor of the Chamber of Deputies. The more the party becomes involved in the government, the more it must demonstrate its ability to support the goals of other parties. One of these is labor peace. Christian Democrats, Republicans, and Social Democrats still hold the Communist party responsible for the actions of the CGIL. To these parties, labor unrest is to some extent the responsibility of the Communist party. As in fact the Communists cannot control either the CGIL, or the other labor confederations, there are increasing tensions between the Communist party and the labor movement over labor's contractual goals and particularly over use of strikes. There are also explicit disagreements on the scope of labor's political strategy. Many party leaders feel that the Reform Strategy has intruded too deeply into the realm of political party activity, not by seeking elected office, but in expressing popular demands for social and economic reforms.

Even if the labor movement retreats from some of the broader social reform goals it espoused in the early 1970s, it is unlikely to

570

abandon its concern with national policies as they affect employment, inflation, and wage levels. In this area the labor movement must respond to the short term, as well as the longer term, concern of its members. And if the experience of other European countries is relevant to speculation about Italy's future, there is every reason to believe that the national economic and political objectives of a political party increasingly involved with governing and of a unified labor movement, whose constituents must bear the immediate impact of unemployment and inflation, will not always coincide.

PART FIVE

Comparisons and Conclusions

XV.

Communism in Italy and France: Adaptation and Change

SIDNEY TARROW

What is the fate of the revolutionary party in a nonrevolutionary situation? This is the underlying question raised by the contributions to this volume. In both France and Italy, the Communist party has, for some time, maintained an uneasy position between opposition and compromise, a position to which the models of "revisionism" and "integration," derived from the earlier European social-democratic experience, do not really apply. Nor can these parties be effectively understood as variants of the "party of total opposition," a model popular during the Cold War, for they participate in numerous ways in the day-to-day life of Parliaments, local governments, and trade unions. Recent changes, documented throughout this volume, have made the dilemma even greater, with Communists launched, in France, on a joint strategy with the Socialists and, in Italy, on the path of "a great historic compromise," in the words of their present secretary-general.

In discussing how the Partito Comunista Italiano (PCI) and Parti Communiste Français (PCF) have adapted to life in an advanced capitalist system without suffering the fate of the parties of the Second International, it will soon be obvious that the term "advanced capitalist system" is an imperfect way of describing either the French or the Italian economy, for in both systems, remnants of a traditional past have been preserved alongside new characteristics which place both countries in the forefront of European neocapitalism: extensive state-run enterprises, a

I am grateful to representatives of three generations of scholars of European communism for their advice in revising earlier versions of this chapter. They are Donald Blackmer, Mario Einaudi, Luigi Graziano, Thomas Greene, Stephen Hellman, Denis Lacorne, Peter Lange, Alessandro Pizzorno, and Ronald Tiersky. Needless to say, none of these individuals is in the least responsible for errors of fact or interpretation in which I may have persisted despite their accumulated wisdom and assistance.

high level of concentration in the advanced sectors of industry, and systems of public welfare and social security which give the state tremendous leverage over civil society. As a result, the adaptation of communism in France and Italy means both more and less than an accommodation to the classical structures of a pure capitalist economy, and the "nonrevolutionary situation" to which the PCI and PCF have attempted to adapt is not the same as that which developed in Europe during the 1920s.

Moreover, what does it mean today to describe the PCI and PCF as "revolutionary parties?" Is it that they derive from the same revolutionary ferment of the period 1919-1921, that they both retain strong organizational ties with the Soviet Union, or that they claim brotherhood with the revolutionary movements of Asia or the Third World? None of these explanations is wholly convincing: nor are estimates of Communist intentions which rest on the assumption that—whatever its outward behavior—there is in a Communist party a "hidden pole . . . the pole of the constant" which, "beyond circumstantial adaptations and modifications . . . always maintains its own identity."[1] Only through the preservation and continual modernization of its revolutionary will and capacity can a Communist party remain revolutionary. An ability to transform or utilize influences from the system around it; the capacity to mobilize broad masses of the population; a leadership which does not become so thoroughly committed to order that it cannot stimulate change—it is to some of these more empirical, albeit ambiguous, indicators that we will turn in this concluding chapter.[2]

Because the PCI and the PCF have the same basic strategic problem, have they adapted to their current situation in basically similar ways? To some extent, they have. Both parties participate actively in local government, in parliamentary affairs, and in social and economic life. Both have chosen the path of alliances—political and social—as a way of overcoming permanent minority status in the electorate. And both—with some obvious variations and differential rates of change—have modified their interpretations of capitalism as a system of exploitation and appropriation.

[1] Annie Kriegel, "Communism in France," in T. J. Nossiter, A. H. Hanson and Stein Rokkan (eds.), *Imagination and Precision in the Social Sciences: Essays in Memory of Peter Nettl* (London: Faber & Faber, 1972), p. 376. See also her *Les Communistes français* (Paris: Seuil, 1968).

[2] Kriegel, "Communism in France," p. 371, seems to take a more conservative view.

Indeed, a purely doctrinal analysis of their shifts in strategy and propaganda would have to stress the similarities in their adaptation to the current historical situation, especially since the death of Thorez unleashed a series of doctrinal and tactical changes in the PCF.

But if in doctrinal matters the differences between the two parties have narrowed in recent years, their modalities of adaptation are not necessarily the same. In this chapter it will be shown that initially similar *strategies* for the achievement of socialism have diverged increasingly since 1945 as the result of factors in both the environments and internal lives of the two parties. These factors can be summarized as follows:

First, the historical heritage of each party and country, and inherent differences in their political traditions;

Second, the social, economic, and political setting that has emerged in each country since the end of World War II;

Third, the bases of support and leadership within each party and the nature of the population groupings to which they are able to appeal;

Fourth, the organizational traditions of each party, a factor which affects where decisions are made, how they are made and, to some extent, the content of the parties' policies.

After dealing with each of these factors, we will turn to our central problem: their impact on the patterns of behavior found in each party's relation to its respective political system, in particular, in the behavior of its politicians in local and national political institutions and in their strategies of alliances. In the final section, we will attempt to show how these patterns of behavior affect each party's response to major areas of change in both the international and domestic arenas.

THE INFLUENCES OF THE PAST

In comparing the differences and similarities in the development of these two Communist parties, it will be convenient to begin with a point of seemingly identical behavior and strategy: their participation in the postwar coalition governments established in each country after the Liberation. Returning from Russia, Togliatti and Thorez had brought with them essentially similar strategies. Each leader emphasized three basic goals: first, reconstruction—particularly in the factory, where Communists were told that their first duty lay in increased production; second, alliances, and especially the search for alliances between "workers of the hand and workers of the brain"; and, finally, renovation of the creaking social structures of the past.[3] As Togliatti observed in an oft-cited speech of 1944,

> We are the party of the working class. . . . But the working class has never been foreign to the national interest. . . . As a Communist party, as the party of the working class, we claim the right to participate in the construction of this new Italy, conscious of the fact that if we do not claim this right or were not able to fulfill this function now or in the future, Italy would not be reconstructed and the prospects for our country would be very grave indeed.[4]

Thorez was hardly less accommodating. As de Gaulle himself was to point out later,

> As for Thorez, while he strives to advance the interests of communism, on many occasions he will render great service to the public interest. . . . Is it simply a result of tactical decisions? I will not deny it, but it is enough for me that France will profit from it.[5]

Were these the signs of an incipient reformism in both parties, a fruit of the lessons of the past and of a growing integration into their respective political systems? In the short run, at least, it was mainly less indigenous forces that were at work. The strategy of productivity, alliances, and renovation reflected the presence of Allied armies on European soil, the immediate needs of Soviet foreign policy and the weakness of the Left as a political force more than any long-term vision of the role of a Communist party in an advanced society.

[3] The best analyses of this period for the PCI's strategy are Alessandro Pizzorno's "Le Parti communiste italien dans le système politique italien," mimeographed paper presented to the Colloque sur le communisme en France et en Italie (Paris, 1968) and Liliana Lanzardo, *Classe operaia e partito comunista alla Fiat, la Strategia della collaborazione: 1945-1949* (Turin: Einaudi, 1971). For the French party's strategic turn of this period, see Ronald Tiersky, *Le Mouvement communiste en France: 1920-1972* (Paris: Fayard, 1973), pp. 113-130.

[4] *Rinascita* (August 29, 1944), p. 4.

[5] Charles de Gaulle, *Memoires de Guerre* (Paris: Plon, 1954), 3: 782-783.

However, it would be unfair to both leaders—and to the aspirations of the masses of the population they claimed to represent—to infer that their postwar line was merely an outgrowth of Stalinist foreign policy. Certainly to Togliatti, and perhaps to Thorez as well, coming to power by electoral means seemed a real possibility in the halcyon days before 1948.[6] Everywhere, but especially where the struggle against fascism had been strongest, there were plausible domestic reasons to counsel a strategy of productivity, alliances, and renovation of the outworn structures of French and Italian society.

But the urge to participate in the building of a new society had even deeper roots. The leaders of both parties knew that the sectarian "class-against-class" strategy that had dominated their parties' strategies before 1936 had been a disaster. This was especially acute in Italy but, even in France, real success in recruiting significant numbers of new members only came in the 1930s, when the country was moving toward the Popular Front. To this experience, with its modest successes for both parties, was added the spirit of left-wing solidarity that grew up during the Resistance. Thus, there were *indigenous*, as well as international, sources for the strategies of accommodation that characterized both the PCI and the PCF after the war.

It was only after 1947—when the spirit of the Liberation had subsided and the hard line of the early Cold War had appeared —that some symptomatic differences began to appear. First, Togliatti was slower than Thorez in implementing the tactics of widespread riots and strikes ordered by the Cominform in 1947-1948.[7] Second, the PCF joined more vigorously in the anti-Tito campaign that began in 1948 and was carried on even beyond Stalin's death in 1953.[8] Third, the PCI soon began to reveal some internal

[6] For a discussion of this point, see Ernesto Ragionieri, "Il PCI nella Resistenza" (Paper delivered at the Convegno sui partiti politici nella Resistenza, Milan, November 1968) and P. A. Allum, "The Italian Communist Party since 1945: Grandeurs and Servitudes of a European Socialist Strategy," University of Reading Graduate School of Contemporary European Studies, Occasional Papers no. 2 (Reading, England, 1970), p. 11.

[7] On this point, see Thomas H. Greene, "The Communist Parties of Italy and France: A Study in Comparative Communism," *World Politics* 21 (October 1968): 4.

[8] Ibid. For views which seriously question the PCF's contribution to the Resistance, see Angelo Rossi, *A Communist Party in Action: An Account of the Organizations and Operations in France* (New Haven: Yale Univer-

traits that were nowhere evident in the PCF: in particular, a rapid numerical expansion that was not matched by the construction of a well-articulated party structure.[9]

Were these emerging differences symptomatic of anything more than temporary or accidental characteristics? There were, of course, many such factors, but there were also some deeper historical causes whose influence would become more marked as the postwar political crisis resolved itself into a number of more distinct national problems. Observers have stressed a number of similar features in the political traditions of the two countries, features which quite early influenced the paths of their Communist parties. First, with an uneven record of the extension of full citizenship to the lower classes, deep social cleavages, and strong anarchist traditions, neither country was likely to develop either consensual politics or stable liberal democracy. In addition, both countries suffered a Church-state conflict well into the twentieth century. Exacerbated in Italy by the presence of the Vatican, in France the conflict was perhaps more intense owing to a more deeply rooted and virulently anticlerical revolutionary tradition.

Second, in Italy, the still unresolved issue of unification was so pressing that the *questione politica* was tackled while the *questione sociale* was largely ignored. In France, where real political unification had come earlier, political leaders were able to confront the crises of industrialization with less concern for problems of integration. On the other hand, a structure of deep conflicts among the political class intensified France's political cleavages and led to massive ministerial instability. In Italy, so bereft was the Liberal state of modern political organization that the dominant political problem was that of *trasformismo* rendered cabinets incapable of coherent policies.

Third, in both countries industrialization had been partial and limited until after World War II, with enormous regional differences and thousands of small paternalistic firms. In this context a large-scale modern economic sector emerged whose future economic and political power was clear. In the rural sector, a tradi-

---

sity Press, 1949) and George Lichtheim, *Marxism in Modern France* (New York: Columbia University Press, 1966), pp. 59-60.

[9] See Giacomo Sani, "Le strutture organizzative del PCI e della DC," in Instituto Carlo Cattaneo, *L'Organizzazione partitica del PCI e della DC* (Bologna: Società Editrice Il Mulino, 1968), p. 49, and the party sources cited therein.

tional peasantry survived in most of the country, with pockets of rural radicalism that predated the industrial revolution. The penetration of commerce worsened the plight of the peasantry, guaranteeing support for powerful left-wing radical movements until well after World War II.

But by the end of World War I, some differences were already obvious in the social and political traditions of each country. First, France's solid democratic heritage could survive the crises of the 1920s, whereas Italy's tenuous liberal institutions could not withstand the Fascist onslaught. Second, by World War I, the French Socialist Left was predominantly republican in orientation, whereas the Italian Socialists mouthed revolutionary shibboleths that helped turn Italian politics, in Angelo Tasca's words, into "a non-stop banquet where the capital of revolution is dissipated in orgies of words."[10] Third, the French Right was both ideologically and organizationally fragmented, compared to the potentially great unifying force of the Vatican and the bloc of forces that had begun forming around it even before fascism. These historical differences greatly influenced the shape of the two new Communist parties created in France and Italy in 1920 and 1921.

The first important effect—and the most obvious one—is that France's more democratic structure allowed the PCF to grow up in the relatively liberal atmosphere of the Third Republic, while the PCI had no sooner emerged in 1921 than it was forced underground by an increasingly confident Fascist movement. Although the immediate impact must have been to turn the PCI more definitively toward conspiratorial models of party behavior, in the long run the results of Fascist repression were more complex. The PCI's absence from Italian politics for nearly twenty years saved it from appearing to sanction some of the worst periods of Stalinist brutality. Ostensibly inactive, the PCI could not be blamed for the show trials of the 1930s, the Nazi-Soviet pact, or the sudden reversals in domestic policy that accompanied these events for those Communist parties, like the French one, that retained an unbroken legal existence up to 1939. By the time the PCI returned to the Italian scene, the anti-Fascist alliance was in full swing and the Red Army was winning fantastic battles in the East. "The French Communists," writes George Lichtheim, "were

[10] Quoted in Giuseppe Fiori, *Antonio Gramsci: Life of a Revolutionary* (New York: Dutton, 1971), p. 126.

indeed not as fortunate as their Italian colleagues."[11] They would have great difficulty after the war in escaping the taint of complicity with Stalin's crimes.[12]

Second, the more moderate nature of the Section Française de l'Internationale Ouvrière (SFIO), compared to the greater influence of the Left in the Partito Socialista Italiano (PSI), also led to important constitutive differences. The sectarian current in the PSI had hastened the coming of fascism by favoring the landless rural proletariat over other depressed rural groups, thereby forcing even small landowners and sharecroppers toward the extreme Right. This maximalist orientation, however, had a benefit; it helped to keep the "centrists" in the PSI within the party when the Communist faction broke away, at Lenin's insistence, in 1921.[13] With majorities in only fifteen provinces and the support of only one chamber of labor, the PCI was born in poverty and isolation.[14]

Because the French Socialists lacked such a radical élan, the PCF was able to take away many of the SFIO's members, as well as its respected journal, *L'Humanité*, and many of its organizational resources. This left the new party with the artificial character of a loose and variegated political movement including, as Lichtheim has observed, "prewar Syndicalists and rural neophytes looking for an opportunity to manifest [their] revolutionary longings."[15] The International directed its efforts to purging the PCF of this motley character in the early 1920s. If it could hack away with bold strokes, it was partly because the new party was large and secure enough to stand considerable pruning. The PCI, a much smaller party and more leftist, suffered less from "democratic assumptions," "humanitarian illusions," and "reform-

[11] Lichtheim, *Marxism in France*, p. 53.

[12] For a biased but thoroughly documented treatment of the effects of this period on the PCF, see Rossi, *A Communist Party*.

[13] For the effects of Lenin's shortsighted attitude toward the so-called centrists in the Italian Socialist party and its disastrous consequences for the new Communist party, see Fiori, *Antonio Gramsci*, p. 144. Interestingly enough, Gramsci considered the split at Livorno a defeat, since it "detached the greater part of the Italian proletariat from the Communist International." Quoted in Fiori, p. 147.

[14] For details on this period, see John Cammett, *Antonio Gramsci and the Origins of Italian Communism* (Stanford, Calif.: Stanford University Press, 1967), Chapter 7; Paolo Spriano, *Storia del partito comunista italiano*, Vol. 1 (Turin: 1967), and Fiori, *Antonio Gramsci*.

[15] Lichtheim, *Marxism in France*, pp. 36-37.

ist errors," in the words of Boris Souvarine.[16] The party that emerged from Livorno in January 1921 under the rousing leadership of Amedeo Bordiga was sectarian and the Soviets used their influence in Italy during the 1920s mainly to neutralize the influence of the extremists who led it, and not to change its social character.

The results were soon apparent; in the PCF, the process of bolshevization brought a working-class cadre of malleable leaders into power to change what Zinoviev called "the motley social composition of the party."[17] A totally bolshevized party organization meant replacing the intellectuals by cadres of working-class derivation whose Marxism was learned within the party and who would respond more readily to directives from the International.[18] In Italy, bolshevization in the frightful conditions of the 1920s meant little more than replacing Bordiga and his friends and having the PCI toe the Soviet doctrinal line. As many of its early members began to slip away—as a result of either Fascist repression, internal polemics, or both—the PCI came more and more under the influence of its intellectuals. While these were hardly autonomous spirits in the atmosphere of the 1920s, they had a potential for independent theory that was gradually being squeezed out of the French party.

Third, the disorganization and ideological conflict within the French Right—compared to the more cohesive Right in Italy— was another feature with profound implications for the future of French and Italian communism, particularly with respect to the strategy of alliances. During the 1930s, the limits of the French party's alliance strategy were made plain because the French Right, in the face of widespread labor unrest and economic decline had temporarily collapsed. The Left—Radicals, Socialists, and Communists—could, for the first time, jointly sponsor a common program. If the moment was not ripe for revolution, it was pregnant with new possibilities for communism, as the dramatic membership increases in the PCF would soon reveal.

But perhaps because the Right was for the moment in retreat,

[16] Quoted in Robert Wohl, *French Communism in the Making: 1914-1924* (Stanford, Calif.: Stanford University Press, 1966), p. 354. For an analysis of the same period, see Annie Kriegel, *Aux origines du communisme français: 1914-1920* (Paris: Mouton, 1964).

[17] Wohl, *French Communism*, p. 277.

[18] Ibid., Chapter 12; Lichtheim, *Marxism in France*, p. 52.

583

the French Communists never conceived of the Popular Front in more than tactical terms, defining it as only "the preface to armed insurrection for the dictatorship of the proletariat."[19] For instance, the PCF chose not to participate in this government, claiming for itself instead a "ministry of the masses—essentially a severe and continuing critique of the Blum government while it was supporting its entire program of legislation."[20] At the base, the party continued to organize for the moment when it would seize power, even utilizing its traditional tactic of *noyautage* within the briefly reunited CGT in order to do so. Even at the extreme of its alliance propensity, the PCF never even posed the problem of its relation to the forces of order and tradition.

Here is a major source of the strategic differences between the two Communist parties. Although the Vatican kept in the background of Italian politics until after World War I, its potential hegemonic power on the right could be forecast. In education and culture in general, in the legal system and in the economy (where the Church had fostered some highly successful mass organizations and cooperatives)[21] and even in local administration, the Italian Church had built up a political and social presence which would stand as a bulwark against the Left after the destruction of Fascism.

From their sectarian position on the left, the maximalists in the Socialist party had failed to note that the unique position of the Church deeply affected the class configuration of Italian society. For them, there were but two actors on the Italian political scene —bourgeoisie and proletariat. It was the contribution of Antonio Gramsci to recognize the inherent popular strength of the Italian Right represented by the still unorganized forces of the Church, and to experiment tentatively with extending the concept of alliances beyond the forces of the traditional Left. As early as his *Ordine Nuovo* days, he argued in favor of contacts with left-

[19] The quotation, cited by Ronald Tiersky in Chapter 11 in this volume, is from Thorez' report to the Eighth National Congress of the PCF, pp. 133-134.

[20] Tiersky, in this volume, p. 425.

[21] For an outline discussion of these aspects of the Catholic movement in pre-Fascist Italy, see Alan Stern, Chapter 6 in this volume, and the sources cited therein. The basic source in Italian is Gabriele De Rosa, *Storia del movimento cattolico in Italia: Dalla restaurazione all'età giolittiana* (Bari: Laterza, 1966).

leaning Catholics and others. Later, in his *Alcuni temi della quistione meridionale*, he called the *"quistione vaticana"*—along with the problem of the south—one of the two major aspects of the problem of alliances for the PCI.[22] But his clearest perceptions appear in the analyses of Italian history and politics written in prison during the 1930s and published posthumously.[23] While the organizational divisions of the French Right encouraged the PCF to limit its alliance propensity, even after 1945, the strength of the Catholic subculture of the Italian Right was to lead to a much broader alliance strategy for the PCI for years to come.

The triumph of Fascism was a second source of the broader alliance perspectives that the Italian party was to develop. In France, the republican tradition had a solid foundation among both the working and middle classes, but in Italy, once the revolutionary ferment of 1919-1920 had passed, thousands of workers were easily enticed into collaboration with the Fascists, even providing, as is well known, a significant portion of the "syndicalists" in the new regime's corporate structure. The PCl was profoundly shocked when the masses of the Italian working class and peasantry swung over to Fascism. If they could be deceived once, they could be deceived again, unless the Left could establish a permanent and legitimate presence in what Gramsci called "the trenches and fortifications of bourgeois society."[24] That a position within these "trenches and fortifications" would go considerably beyond traditional alliance tactics was true in two important senses. First, it would inevitably involve the party in political relationships with organized Catholicism and, second, it implied a PCI presence within the social structures of civil society, and not simply in political alliances.[25] In contrast, the PCF would never go beyond the limited model of its "participation" in the Popular Front.

[22] "Alcuni temi della quistione meridionale" may be found in Giansiro Ferrata and Niccolo Gallo (eds.), *2000 pagine de Gramsci* (Milan: Feltrinelli, 1966) and, in a much abridged translation under the title "The Southern Question," in Antonio Gramsci, *The Modern Prince and Other Writings* (New York: International, 1957), pp. 28-51, p. 31.

[23] These are now available in a selected (and excellent) translation in Quintin Hoare and Geoffrey Nowell Smith (eds.), *Selections from the Prison Notebooks of Antonio Gramsci* (New York: International, 1971).

[24] Ibid., p. 238.

[25] These points are treated in greater detail in my "Le PCI et la société italienne," in *Sociologie du communisme en Italie*, Fondation Nationale des Sciences Politiques (Paris: A. Colin, 1974).

585

Even during the Resistance, in many ways the epitome of the PCF's engagements with other political forces, the personnel and the models of behavior developed during the 1930s continued to dominate its perspectives. For by 1941, the character of French communism had been firmly crystallized by twenty years of internal development and habitual relationships with the rest of the French political system. For the Italian party and for most of its postwar leadership, the period beginning with the Resistance movement and the constituent elections of 1946 was a *constitutive* period in its history. The dominant policy line of that period— that of a broad structure of interclass alliances—was etched deeply into its consciousness, if only because the PCI had been in limbo for most of the preceding generation, and many of its leaders had no prior political experiences upon which to draw. Hence, alliances that went much further than the traditional Communist-Socialist coalition would repeatedly emerge at the center of its postwar political ambitions.

In summary, although these historical factors were not, in any serious sense, "determining," they did predispose the PCI and the PCF to divergent paths. The PCF would enter the postwar period with a model of class struggle and of alliance politics that had been developed in Moscow and applied to France in an atmosphere of mainly economic and class struggles. It had a cadre of proletarian leaders who had been installed from the mid-1920s on in a relatively liberal atmosphere which allowed the Russians to work their will on the party with impunity. And for a variety of reasons, it has never had to test its theoretical mettle by developing an alliance posture vis-à-vis the forces of order and tradition. In contrast, the PCI entered the postwar world with its greatest trauma the memory of mass support for fascism, with a sharp appreciation of the hegemonic power of the Church, and with its only glory the interclass, national struggle for liberation from fascism. In turning from the historical to the contemporary setting of the French and Italian Communist parties, we shall see how these historical factors continue to influence their choices.

THE CONTEMPORARY SETTING

It is an old but useful adage that while Leninist parties pay homage to an essentially economic view of historical change, they respond in practice to the *political* forces around them. There is, of course, no contradiction in these two factors, as long as one believes—as a Marxist must—that fundamental political factors are, "in the final instance," but surface expressions of underlying social and economic phenomena. The problem, though, is to understand how the social and economic characteristics of an entire historical period are transformed into political factors in each country and combine with its distinctive temperament and institutions to produce a particular strategic setting for each party.

Turning first to the underlying social and economic changes which have shaped the contemporary European scene, we must first confront the notion—until recently confidently accepted by most non-Marxist writers on the subject—that the capitalist system in the West has left behind the moment when a dream of a revolutionary breakthrough could coincide with an upsurge of popular discontent. The old dream is still there, but has the powder keg not moved elsewhere, with the rise to revolutionary consciousness of the non-Western world and with the coming of the neo-capitalist welfare state in the West?

One may at least question the assumption that Europe, once in the vanguard of the revolutionary movement, must inevitably subside into a backwater of insurrectionary ambitions with little real revolutionary capacity. The explosive, if short-lived, student movement of the late 1960s would speak against this view, as may the possibly more lasting changes afoot in the trade-union movements of many European countries.[26] More fundamental still, the intensified involvement of Europe in a world network of economic and political relationships makes it questionable whether one can fairly gauge the continent's political future merely in terms of its internal social and economic arrangements. In a decade when the whole of the industrialized world can be thrown into chaos at the caprice of a few oil sheikdoms in the Middle East, it is uncertain how effective the reforms of the post-Keynesian welfare state will be in stilling dissent or in improving real living standards.

In the broadest sense, then, the contemporary setting of communism in Western Europe may be nonrevolutionary without becoming *post*-revolutionary. The increasing impoverishment of certain strata of both the traditional working class and of newer white-collar workers; the cleavages in the work force between

[26] See Chapters 13 and 14 by George Ross and Peter Weitz in this volume.

the highly skilled and the semi-skilled, or between the native born and the immigrant worker; the unresolved problems of backward regions and of the entire agricultural sector; the tensions unleashed (and still poorly understood) by the definitive loss of the colonies and of the guaranteed markets and sources of raw materials they represented: these factors and many others have rendered illusory the view of the postwar period as one in which the Left would move inexorably to the center of the political spectrum.

This may be no more than saying that there are secular swings in the global setting of the European Left that shift the strategic balance, first in favor of the revolutionary movement and then against it: but which never definitively destroy it. Historians will look back upon the late 1960s as the initiation of a cycle of radicalization, one that may have ended, or moved into a more intensive phase, with the economic and political crises of the first half of the 1970s. The same is, of course, true of the international setting. From the secure, if frightening, stalemate of the Cold War, Europe has drifted rapidly into a vortex created by an increasingly multipolar international system. The implications of this process for the PCI and PCF are still unclear, as is the very notion of a "European" interest on any of the major issues that divide the world today. As Europe gropes toward an independent path for herself, not even the old adage that "the Communist party is neither on the left nor on the right, but in the East" can go unchallenged forever.

Finally, the increased role of the state in the Western economy is another factor which makes the prospects for radical parties still remarkably unclear. After the early nationalizations of industry in Great Britain by the postwar Labour government, it was fashionable to speak of "the planned economy."[27] It was only when the enthusiasm of the early postwar proponents of the welfare state had dwindled that the more balanced phrase, "the mixed economy" began to be used, and by the time Andrew Shonfield wrote his *Modern Capitalism*, he referred only to "the balance of public and private power."[28] In other words, planning is not socialism, welfare is not equality, and the nationalization

[27] See Edward H. Carr, *The New Society* (London: Macmillan, 1951).
[28] Andrew Shonfield, *Modern Capitalism: The Changing Balance of Public and Private Power* (London: Oxford, 1965).

or control of industry does not in itself change the patterns of appropriation in a capitalist economy.

But the immensely increased power of the state in the economy does have one potential result that is far less certain. Although it is currently the core of a neocapitalist economic system, the activist state has created a new structure of functional and corporate ties that could conceivably present a hypothetical left-wing government with the instruments to turn a neocapitalist system into a quasi-Socialist one.[29] Control of the government is, of course, not equivalent to controlling the massive bureaucracies that have grown up around it. However, it is clear that a structure for control can provide a victorious radical party or coalition, much more easily than was the case under classical capitalism, with the mechanisms to bring about a Socialist transformation of the economy.

These changes—at work throughout the Western world—have particular implications for radical movements in Italy and France. We saw how the political traditions of these two countries contributed to the rise of the PCI and the PCF and helped to shape each party's historical development. The same can be said of the contemporary domestic setting. If they have survived the changes of the past thirty years with little or no loss of support, this is at least in part because they reflect living traditions of domestic dissent, traditions which, of course, cannot be separated from the evolution of each political system during the period that concerns us.

In turning to these systems as they looked after World War II, what strikes the observer are, once again, the similarities between them, similarities which relate both to the international tensions that were dividing Europe into two hostile camps after the war, and to each country's internal system of "polarized pluralism."[30] Most of all, each system was threatened on the left by an apparently irreconcilable and aggressive Communist party,

---

[29] Ibid., Part iv.

[30] Arend Lijphart, "Typologies of Democratic Systems," *Comparative Political Studies* 1 (April 1968): 13-16; Giovanni Sartori, "European Political Parties: The Case of Polarized Pluralism," in Joseph LaPalombara and Myron Wiener (eds.), *Political Parties and Political Development* (Princeton: Princeton University Press, 1966), pp. 134-177; and Gabriel Almond, "Comparative Political Systems," *The Journal of Politics* 18 (August 1956): 398-399, 407.

589

contributing to, as well as reflecting, the tensions of the Cold War that were tightening around them.[31]

It was not long, however, until important national differences began to be evident. First, among the PCI's Socialist neighbors, there persisted a verbal revolutionism and a practical subordination that were evident as early as 1948, when the two parties fielded a joint electoral slate. In France, in contrast, the SFIO soon emerged as a thoroughly reformist party with solid electoral bases of support and a sense of its own mission.[32] If the trade-union splits that took place in each country had essentially the same aim—that of isolating the Marxist Left—their results were nevertheless very different: leaving the PSI associated with the Communist-dominated Confederazione Generale Italiana del Lavoro (CGIL) in Italy, while the French Socialists were helping to form the anti-Communist Force Ouvrière (FO).

Second, the traditional fragmentation of the French Right would continue well into the 1950s, with the failure of either the Gaullist movement or the Catholic Mouvement Républicain Populaire (MRP) to emerge as a modern conservative party, and the tendency of many voters to follow incipient "flash parties" like the Poujadists.[33] If the Communists could not form a solid government of their own, neither could the Right or the Center. Indeed, SFIO-supported centrist coalitions throughout the Fourth Republic had a way of sliding imperceptibly toward the right during each Legislature, thereby condemning them to an inevitable loss of confidence in the Assembly.[34] The weakness of the Right, plus the discriminatory policies of both Center and Right (for example, the electoral reform of 1951) helped keep the PCF in a state of complacency and isolation; if the Center-Right could not form a stable government and the SFIO could not hold onto power, sooner or later, it seemed to follow, the PCF's chance would come.

For reasons that are still not entirely clear—perhaps the habits formed during the Fascist period, perhaps the network of its

[31] Joseph LaPalombara, "Political Party Systems and Crisis Governments: French and Italian Contrasts," Midwest Journal of Political Science 11 (May 1958): 117-142.

[32] Bruce Graham, French Socialism and Tripartism, 1944-1947 (Toronto: University of Toronto Press, 1965).

[33] Stanley Hoffmann, Le Mouvement Poujade (Paris: A. Colin, 1956).

[34] Duncan McRae, Parliament, Parties and Society in France, 1946-1958 (New York and London: St. Martins, 1967).

existing institutions or the social doctrine of Catholicism—the Catholic Right in Italy emerged from the war as a highly *organized* subculture. And while the initial impetus for organization was confessional, the Democrazia Cristiana (DC) could maintain an organized political presence even where religious devotion was moderate or on the decline. In contrast to the asymmetrical distribution of mass and party organizations in France—where only the Left was highly organized—postwar politics in Italy emerged as a bipolar confrontation between two organized subcultures, each of which was attempting to colonize Italian society from top to bottom. In these circumstances, the PCI had a real protagonist—one which could dominate every coalition and offer voters the fruits of governmental largesse for their support. And while the Right was no less hostile to communism in Italy than in France, between an organized Catholic subculture and an organized Marxist one, there would be a competing attempt to colonize whole sectors of Italian society and even, perhaps, an ultimate possibility of ruling together in a *repubblica conciliare*.

But the French Communists would not always be faced by a Right that was disorganized and ideologically confused. With the accession to power of Charles de Gaulle in 1958, the French Right began on the slow road toward political cohesion. If its tactics and rhetoric differed from those of the DC, this was owing not only to differences in national political cultures, but also to the Gaullists' strategic dilemma as a governmental party without a dependable majority in the electorate. This was revealed in the abortive referendum of 1969 that cast de Gaulle from power. It was this fundamental contradiction which led them, between 1958 and 1962, to institute constitutional changes that turned France into a quasi-plebiscitarian presidential democracy, with all the dangers for conflict between executive and legislature that such a system implied.

Given the conditions of the early 1960s, however, these dangers were offset by a number of immediate gains: Parliament was stripped of its ability to affect policy; the electoral strength that the Left had maintained in both local and national politics under the proportional system of the Fourth Republic was eroded by the two-ballot majority system of the Fifth; and de Gaulle succeeded in delegitimizing partisan loyalty by the politically shrewd policy of governing above the despised "régime de partis." If this transparent stratagem worked, it was not only because the French were fed up with the quarrels of the Fourth Republic; it was also because de Gaulle appealed to a persistent strain of antipartisanship that is fundamental to the ideology of the French Center and Right.[35]

There can be no greater contrast with the political culture of Italy. Here the government responded to the organized partisanship of the Left by creating a network of party and mass organizations around the Church and its Catholic Action affiliates and by turning party membership into an entry ticket for the spoils of governmental power. This served both to deideologize party membership by rendering it commonplace, and to entrench the voters into a system of stable partisan balance that has barely been altered since the 1950s. The Center-Left governments of the 1960s reinforced this balance by simply extending the trough of governmental patronage and the commercialization of partisanship that accompanied it somewhat further to the Left. In France, in contrast, the "apolitical" appeals of Gaullism—ideological as they may have been—still left unsolved the problem of the unaffiliated masses of voters who would return to the Gaullist fold in every moment of danger—as in June 1968—but who were apt to stray into casual allegiances, as in April 1973 or May 1974.[36]

These differences in the stability of partisan alignments have helped to define the balance between ambition and despair in the two Communist parties in the 1970s. In Italy, the PCI's share of the vote has grown steadily, until it now has close to 30 percent of the electorate in national elections.[37] However, the *stability* of Italian party identification places a discouraging constraint on the party's ability to expand its electoral influence much further. It may, by now, have reached such a point of saturation in the electorate that it will have to turn increasingly to political arrangements at the elite level or risk a loss of momentum and the beginnings of decline. And while it temporized with critically needed reforms—divorce, for example—the electoral stalemate experienced since 1968 has led to increasingly open evidence of

[35] Sidney Tarrow, "Partisanship and Political Exchange in French and Italian Local Politics: A Contribution to the Typology of Party Systems" (London and Beverly Hills: Sage Publications). Professional Papers in Contemporary Comparative Political Sociology. 1974.

[36] David Cameron, "Stability and Change in Patterns of French Partisanship," *Public Opinion Quarterly* 36 (Spring 1972): 19-30.

[37] See Chapter 12 by Giacomo Sani in this volume.

the PCI's willingness to cooperate with the Right for a share of public power.

In France, in contrast, Gaullist policies have succeeded in limiting the PCF to approximately 20 percent of the vote,[38] but the *fluidity* of the electorate leaves open the possibility of an ultimate breakthrough that would bring the PCF, together with hypothetical allies, into the circles of power. Hence, the urge in recent years to break out of its isolation is due, not to any internal transformation, but to the debilitating institutional reforms of the Fifth Republic—and especially the Gaullist electoral system—and to the tantalizing possibility of capturing a portion of the still footloose non-Communist electorate. With the death of de Gaulle and the increasing incapacity of his heirs to keep his house in order, this possibility appears more plausible. It is these characteristics of its political setting that explains, more than anything, the PCF's Common Program with the Socialists and the *ouverture* that the French party has proclaimed far and wide to be its goal in the 1970s.[39]

But is it merely a hand on the levers of power of the French state that the Communists seek, or something more far-reaching? This brings us to another contrast in the two countries' contemporary political settings: the different role of the state. It is traditional to regard both Italy and France as products of the Napoleonic administrative tradition, but the power and efficiency of the French state has always been immeasurably greater. Of course, the Italian bureaucracy is inflated, with power highly centralized in Rome, but each ministry is a feudal entity, and many of the state's important economic activities tend to escape their control. Even the recent process of regionalization reveals the different role of the state in each country: in the Italian case, the coming of the regions has taken place outside the framework of ordinary administration, while in France the rather modest reforms that have been passed leave the territorial organization of the state virtually unscathed.[40]

[38] Jean Ranger, "L'Evolution du vote communiste en France depuis 1945," in *Le Communisme en France*, Cahiers de la Fondation Nationale des Sciences Politiques 175 (Paris: A. Colin, 1969).

[39] See Chapter 3 in this volume by Georges Lavau for a view which is perhaps more optimistic about the internal sources of change in the PCF.

[40] For a comparison of regionalism in the two countries, see Peter Gourevitch, "Reforming the Napoleonic State: The Creation of Regional Govern-

Thus, while the state has played an important role in both post-war economies, in France control has been more complete, with the preference for growth more domineering and the politicization of the bureaucracy less thoroughgoing.[41] Under the Fifth Republic, with a ruling party that has failed to sink deep organizational roots, there has been an increased effort to use the state's power for the government's purposes, but there has also been a growing spirit of independence in the bureaucracy and an increase in the power of technocratically minded administrators. These are not progressive men, and a Popular Front coalition government would certainly have a difficult time bending them to its will. In other words, short of an actual power play, the French state is probably relatively impermeable to penetration by the Left, even assuming the Gaullists—as seems increasingly likely—are losing the grip they had during the General's lifetime.

Not so in Italy, where almost every governmental contract is announced as a personal achievement of the local *onorevole*. At the moment, the politicization of the state redounds mainly to the advantage of the DC and helps to sustain it as an organized subculture in Italian society. But it is by no means clear that the Italian bureaucracy excludes colonization from the left, as was revealed during the heyday of the Center-Left, when the state began to appear as a grabbag of patronage to be divided up and consumed by the various parties and their electorates in proportion to their strength in Parliament, in local government, and in the hundreds of semicorporate boards and commissions that run much of Italian civil society.

From this process of the division of the public purse for partisan purposes, not even the Communists have been wholly absent, at least at the local level. The Italian state lacks the cohesion, the *esprit de corps* and the apolitical tradition to avoid colonization by whatever political forces are found in the government. Thus, faced with apparent electoral stagnation and with other problems which will be made clear below, the PCI is tempted to approach its goals through alliances from above; not through the "trenches and fortifications of civil society," as Gramsci wrote,

---

ment in France and Italy" (Paper delivered at the Ninth World Congress of the International Political Science Association, Montreal, 1973).

[41] Shonfield, *Modern Capitalism*, Chapters 7 and 9.

but through a compromise with the existing political class and an attempt to transform, from within, the corporate structures of the neocapitalist state in a socialist direction.

One final contrast in the contemporary setting should be mentioned before turning to the parties themselves, to their organizations, and their bases of support and leadership. For strategic reasons, what happens in France is of more fundamental importance to the Soviet Union than what happens in Italy. If France is a second-level power, Italy is only a third-rate one; if France lies geographically at the center of the Western alliance, Italy is on its periphery. Since 1958 the French have struggled against the domination of Europe by the United States; Italy, in contrast, is ruled by a pro-American Christian Democratic party which has benefited from the fact that the essentials of its foreign policy are made in Washington. In other words, quite independent of the attitudes or the attributes of the PCF and the PCI, the role of the USSR is more important in the internal life of the French party because France is more important to the foreign policy interests of the Soviet Union than is Italy.

But the foreign policies of the two parties are intertwined with the party strategies which precede them. It was not any innately greater dependence upon the Soviet Union that led the PCF, after the war, to reflect the goals of Soviet foreign policy more completely than the PCI, but the development of a pattern of commitment and behavior and a strategic *model* in which loyalty to the Soviet Union played a more useful role. Thus, if the party tempered its attacks on Gaullism, it was not only because that party's foreign policy favored American disengagement from Europe,[42] but also because such a foreign policy was popular among the electorate. And if the PCF preferred a bipolar system with Pompidou as president to a Poher-led coalition whose outlines were unclear, this too related to the domestic strategy of the PCF, and not only to the foreign policy interest of the Soviet Union.

Similarly, the PCI's more liberal foreign policy stance has been shaped more by domestic considerations than by control by the Soviet Union. It was the development of a pattern of commitments and behavior and of a strategic model very different from that of the PCF that determined the PCI's more independent re-

[42] See Annie Kriegel's chapter in this volume for this point of view.

595

sponse to the Soviet Union's international and domestic political involvement, especially after 1956. This was a strategy that was logically inconsistent with a dependent relation on the USSR and on the Soviet model of socialism. This will emerge more clearly after we turn to the two parties' internal lives and to their relation to their respective political systems.

Sources of Support and Leadership

When scholars compare Communist parties—even nonruling ones—their attention focuses instinctively upon the Leninist organization that traditionally endows such parties with the flexibility and discipline to come to power. Less frequently have scholars studied the kinds of people who enter Communist parties, except to demonstrate how unusual they sometimes are.[43] But Communist parties like the French and Italian ones which persist for long periods of legal and legitimate political activity must, almost by definition, appeal to a broad spectrum of the population.[44] Whether they are referred to as the "exterior corona" of Communist voters in France or as the "reservoir of forces that could pour into the ranks of Communism" in Italy,[45] the characteristics of Frenchmen and Italians who identify with communism must at least condition the parties' potentialities. Even if such parties only await the right moment for launching an aggressive social strategy, the sources of support and leadership in their organizations will affect their capacity to carry out such a strategy. Hence, the social and geographic sources of the party's militants, the intensity and goals of their commitment, and their propensity to join in a potentially aggressive strategy will condition the development of a Communist party's strategic model as much as the classical outlines of its Leninist organizational model.

We have seen that the French Communist party entered the

[43] See, for example, Gabriel Almond, *The Appeals of Communism* (Princeton: Princeton University Press, 1954), Chapter 10, with respect to the American and British Communist parties after World War II, and Lucian Pye, *Guerrilla Communism in Malaya: Its Social and Political Meaning* (Princeton: Princeton University Press, 1956).

[44] Alfred Meyer, *Communism* (Ann Arbor: University of Michigan Press, 1960), pp. 185-186, and Almond, *Appeals of Communism*, p. 381.

[45] William Ascher and Sidney Tarrow, "The Stability of Communist Electorates: Evidence from a Longitudinal Analysis of French and Italian Aggregate Data," *American Journal of Political Science* (Summer, 1975).

postwar period with a cadre of leaders who had been carefully selected from among the working class during the long period of that party's legal activity and whose major formative experiences lay in the economic struggles of the 1930s. In contrast, the major formative experience for the Italian party was the interclass struggle for liberation from Fascism, a struggle in which political questions far outstripped the struggle against capitalism. Thus we might expect a less indoctrinated leadership in the PCI, a greater emphasis on political than on economic goals, and a broader basis of class recruitment than would be found in the PCF.

Empirical work on the social origins, the political goals, and the level of ideological indoctrination of the militants of these two political parties only began in the early 1950s. Even then, it was only from the imperfect materials of interviews with former Communists that Gabriel Almond and his collaborators concluded that the PCF had emerged from the Second World War with "the largest core of fully indoctrinated and dedicated militants of any of the parties of the West."[46] In contrast, wrote Almond, "with the exception of a few thousands of survivors of the fascist prisons and exile, the Italian communist party consists of an enormous mass of new, unindoctrinated or half-indoctrinated recruits."[47]

Although the depredations of the Fascist period and the human losses of the war were the primary reasons for the lack of trained cadres in the PCI, the memory of the failures of the 1920s when it had been made up of a small number of dedicated cadres, as well as the sudden opportunity offered by the Resistance, made the party willingly open its doors to thousands of new members in 1945. In contrast, the major source of cadres for the PCF continued to be the workers who had risen to political consciousness during the 1930s. Moreover, in Italy, little or no attempt would be made to resist the flow of new and untried members.[48] As a result, the PCI's membership continued to increase long after the PCF's had peaked.[49] And while the proportionately larger PCF losses from the late 1940s on almost certainly

[46] Almond, *Appeals of Communism*, p. 173.

[47] Ibid.

[48] Giordano Sivini, "Gli iscritti al PCI e alla DC: 1944-1963," in *L'Organizzazione partitica del PCI e della DC*, Istituto di Studi e Ricerche "Carlo Cattaneo" (Bologna: Il Mulino, 1968), pp. 325-336.

[49] Greene, "Communist Parties of Italy and France," p. 14.

597

skimmed off most of the "part-time" members who had joined up in the rush of enthusiasm of the Liberation, the PCI's membership, despite the loss of over 700,000 members, remained at well over one million throughout the postwar decades, a factor which made it far more difficult for the Italian party to exercise effective organizational control.

This is not to ignore the benefits of the PCI's larger membership. Both the PCI and the PCF are parties of integration which seek to make contact with a broader public through the mobilization of primary identifiers—their card-carrying members. Its greater size gives the Italian party a distinct advantage in election campaigns, and also provides it with a potentially larger group of supporters who can be mobilized on behalf of advanced social or economic aims.[50] Moreover, with a larger organization, the Italian Communists have a greater defense against potential attacks from the Right: a defense that the French party could well have used during the coup d'état of May 1958. Finally, with its large organization, the PCI has had cadres to spare for the "colonization" of poorly organized areas like the south and the Veneto,[51] a luxury that the PCF might well have used in areas of France where it is poorly organized.

But, of course, the *quality* of affiliation in the PCI has suffered as a result of its large membership and the lack of control over who joins its organizations. Almond found in the late 1940s that almost half the ex-Communists he studied in France were exposed to the classics of Leninism before joining the party, compared to only 14 percent in Italy.[52] The years after 1950 saw a further decline in the level of activity and integration in the PCI. The authors of the *Attivista di partito* even suspect, "in the case of the younger members . . . a kind of emancipation from a primary type of integration in the party."[53] The PCF, in contrast, according to Annie Kriegel, continues to "reject the plural modes which, in a western democracy, can define one's affiliation to a political ideology, giving preference instead to a single, priv-

---

[50] Ascher and Tarrow, "The Stability of Communist Electorates."

[51] The process of penetration of the south by PCI organizers after World War II is analyzed in Sidney Tarrow, *Peasant Communism in Southern Italy* (New Haven: Yale University Press, 1967), pp. 229-230.

[52] Almond, *Appeals of Communism*, pp. 100, 173, and 222.

[53] Istituto di Studi e Ricerche "Carlo Cattaneo," *L'attivista di partito* (Bologna: Il Mulino, 1967), p. 318.

ileged one: the absolute mode of the militant's engagement."[54] When a party's membership is small and well indoctrinated, as in the PCF, it is simpler to reject such "plural modes of affiliation" than when it is large and only partly indoctrinated, as in the case of the PCI.

The diffusion of the quality of membership in the PCI is, of course, increased by its socially more heterogeneous character. While about 57 percent of the PCF's membership is working class, according to a party report of 1967, about 40 percent of the PCI's members during the same period came from among urban workers.[55] At the parliamentary level, a study in the early 1960s showed that 47 percent of the French party's deputies reported working-class occupations, compared to 32 percent of the PCI deputies who reported their fathers' occupations as working class.[56] It is true that, at the level of section activists, the PCI, like the PCF, is largely working class, but this too is changing in the direction of greater social heterogeneity in the Italian party.[57] This greater heterogeneity has resulted, in part, from the legacy of the Resistance, in part from the teachings of Gramsci, but also from the persistent lack of seriousness of the PSI, which might otherwise have been expected to attract many of the middle-class Italians who affiliate with the PCI. In France, in contrast, the absence of these factors still leads to a large numerical domi-

[54] Kriegel, Les Communistes français, p. 33.

[55] The PCF figures are from Georges Marchais, "Rapport au XVIII Congrès du PCF," in Cahiers du communisme (February-March 1967), p. 273. The PCI figures are from PCI, Dati sulla organizzazione del partito (Rome: PCI, 1968), p. 37.

[56] The PCI parliamentary data are from Giovanni Sartori, et al., Il Parlamento Italiano (Naples: E.S.I., 1963), p. 89. The PCF data are from Pierre Ferrari and Herbert Maisl, Les Groupes communistes aux assemblées parlementaires italiennes et françaises (Paris: P.U.F., 1969), p. 137. But note the sharp increase in middle-class occupations among PCF deputies elected in March 1973, reported in Le Monde, March 13 and 14, 1973. I am indebted to Denis Lacorne for pointing this out to me.

[57] Data on 1,875 PCI sections show that 51.4 percent of their secretaries are workers (Dati sulla organizzazione, p. 87). On the changing character of section leaders, see the Piero Pieralli "Report to the XIV Congresso provinciale della federazione fiorentina del PCI," mimeographed (Florence: 1972), pp. 70-71. After noting that young people who just a few years earlier were condemning the party have now chosen the via maestra of the PCI, he then feels compelled to add that not all of the new youthful members are students. I am indebted to Stephen Hellman for this information.

nance of urban working-class members, despite persistent efforts to attract a broader membership.

Greater regional diversity, too, characterizes the PCI's membership. Both the PCI and the PCF have two major regional sources of support: large industrial cities and the strongholds of rural radicalism that were inherited, in France, in the Midi and around the Massif Central and, in Italy, in the Red Belt. But while both metropolitan and provincial bastions contribute heavily to PCI *membership*, PCF membership is concentrated largely in its metropolitan fortresses, with remarkably few provincial members.[58]

For instance, in the Corrèze, a traditionally radical region, the PCF has only one member for every nine voters and an organization that has only barely maintained its immediate postwar strength in the face of Gaullist penetration.[59] In contrast, in radical areas of central Italy like the province of Florence, the Italian party has one member for every three or four voters and an average of three party sections per commune.[60] It is, therefore, only slightly exaggerated to characterize PCF strength in the Massif Central as largely an institutionalized protest vote inherited from the anti-Parisian radicalism of the past, while that of the PCI in central Italy is based upon a well-organized, entrenched, and culturally self-conscious political subculture.[61]

In part, it is true, PCI strength in central Italy is also inherited from an older political tradition not unlike the left-wing tradition of central and southern France. But no iron law declared that the pre-Fascist radical voters of Emilia-Romagna and Tuscany would move into PCI organizations after the Liberation, just as no law declared that PCF organizational implantation in the Limousin or the Allier would remain comparatively limited. It

[58] Alain Savy, "Recherches sur le personnel politique en Haute-Vienne, 1945-1965" (Memoire in Political Science, Faculty of Law and Economic Sciences, University of Poitiers, October 1965).

[59] Guy Lord, "Le PCF: Structures et organisation d'une fédération départementale" (mimeographed paper presented to the Workshop on Communism in Western Europe, Paris, June 1973), p. 3. I wish to thank Professor Lord for his permission to cite these figures.

[60] The Florentine data are from *Dati sulla organizzazione*, and from the PCI federation of the province of Florence, to whose officials I wish to express my thanks.

[61] See Alan Stern, "Local Political Party Organization and Economic Change: Evidence from a Study of Four Italian Communities" (Paper delivered at the Annual Meeting of the American Political Science Association, Chicago, September 1971), pp. 3-7.

600

seems likely that the differences in historical formation and in the contemporary setting were at least contributing factors. If proportionally fewer Communist voters join the PCF in central France than in central Italy, it is in part because the PCF is more oriented toward the urban proletariat, and in part because Frenchmen are less likely to join parties than Italians.

This contrast is reflected in the changing nature of recruitment in the rural areas of both regions as a result of population migration. The PCI has managed to expand its central Italian electorate from the sharecroppers and farm workers who were the bases of its organization in the past to many other social groups, including small family farmers, artisans, shopkeepers, and other middle-class groups.[62] In France, by contrast, rural recruitment seems to be viewed more with an eye to the party's urban presence than to its rural one. Annie Kriegel says of this "work in the countryside" that it has, "in the long run, less effect in defining an agrarian policy and in adding sympathies and militants that are, properly speaking, peasant, than in keeping a lever over one of the most important sources for the renewal of *urban* working class groups during an era of great rural exodus."[63] (Emphasis added.)

That the regional diversity in the Italian party is not due merely to its inheritance of preexisting left-wing subcultures is revealed in a different way in the south. Few districts in this poor and traditional region had strong left-wing traditions, and almost nowhere was there the organized proletariat, the large-scale, mechanized agriculture, or the cultural and social bases needed for the construction of a mass party. Yet the PCI, from 1945 onward, launched a campaign to penetrate the south both organizationally and electorally that led to a doubling of the party's vote in the region between 1946 and 1958 and to a major political success in helping to force the government into an agrarian reform during 1949-1951.[64] Although the impediments to organization have not been overcome, and the party's vote in the region has shown a tendency to level off at about 25 percent of the total, the PCI has continued to expend organizational resources in the re-

[62] For a detailed analysis of the relation between social change and the sources of the PCI's electoral strength in the various Italian regions, see Istituto di Studi e Ricerche "Carlo Cattaneo," *Il comportamento elettorale in Italia* (Bologna: Il Mulino, 1968), pp. 391-394.

[63] Kriegel, *Les Communistes français*, p. 67.

[64] Tarrow, *Peasant Communism*, Chapters 7 and 11.

601

gion that could be better utilized where the chances for electoral success are greater.[65] (Much the same can be said of the PCI's attempts to gain a foothold in the Catholic Veneto, although there the results have been very modest indeed.)[66]

This insistence on organizing in weak regions illustrates a cardinal point in PCI strategy; it is not a favorable political climate or electoral mania that leads to a strong PCI organizational effort, but the urge, among the party's leaders, to be *present* in every sector of Italian politics and society. This desire has no real parallel in the more measured attempts of the PCF to penetrate nonindustrial regions. In the French party, weak regions have gotten weaker and strong ones stronger, and the leadership has shown little inclination to waste its resources on the "deserts" of conservatism in the Catholic west or the conservative east.

The real center of the French party's organizational strength is, and always has been, the urban proletarian *banlieue* surrounding Paris where most of its local governmental strength and its membership can be found.[67] Even in the 1920s, this was the industrial heartland of a centralized country, its capital and the home of the most advanced elements of the French working class. That the centralization of the French state was to find a counterpart in the tight central control in the PCF was expressed in the numerical and moral domination of the Federation of the Seine over the party. One out of four PCF members was found in the Paris region in 1926, one out of three in the 1930s, and one out of five after the Resistance, which had been largely a provincial phenomenon. By the middle of the 1960s, it was apparent that Gaullist incursions had been greatest in the provinces, for about one out of four Communist members could again be found in the Paris area.[68] It is no accident that the problems and perceptions

---

[65] The persistence of the PCI in southern Italy is also underscored by recent changes in its personnel and policies there. For some of these developments until 1972, see Tarrow, "The Political Economy of Stagnation: Communism in Southern Italy, 1960-1970," *The Journal of Politics* 34 (February 1972): 93-123. For the period after 1972 see Telesio Malaspina, "Il Compagno modello '81," *L'Espresso*, May 20, 1973, p. 9.

[66] See, in particular, Alan Stern, Chapter 6 in this volume.

[67] See the statistics on the distribution of Communist local governments in communities of more than 30,000 in population in Jerome Milch, Chapter 9 in this volume.

[68] The figures from 1926 through 1945 are estimated by Kriegel in her *Les Communistes*, p. 57. The 1960s figures are very tentative ones from *La Voie communiste* (November 1963) which fails to reveal their sources.

of the Paris region have a tremendous importance in setting the tone of the PCF's internal life.[69]

This geographic concentration also reinforces the proletarian emphasis in the PCF, for it is in regions of the greatest PCF implantation, like Paris, that the relative weight of the working class is greatest in the membership. In contrast, the regions of greatest PCI implantation produce a majority of *non*working–class members. For instance, in the four regions of the central Red Belt, the proportion of workers in the membership is only about 37 percent. In northeastern Italy, where the PCI is extremely weak, over 50 percent of the members come from the working class.[70] The PCI approaches the dimensions of an organized subculture only where it has overcome the sectarian axiom "class equals party;" the PCF is strongest where the proletariat has the greatest proportional weight within its organizations.

It is not only the greater predominance of workers in the membership or the concentration of proletarian members in the Paris region that gives the French party its special character, but the fact that this regional and occupational concentration *coincides with* the party's central organs and with the nation's government. In some ways, the PCF has simply internalized and transformed in a Leninist sense the Jacobin tradition that, in its revolutionary variant, was best symbolized by Blanqui. This can be seen in the party's lukewarm support for regional reform of any variety. The PCF says it supports the concept of the region, but it also "supports" the commune, the department, and the nation with an evenhandedness that makes it difficult to infer what a regional reform under its auspices might possibly be worth.[71]

Communism in central Italy differs fundamentally from that in the "Jacobin heartland" of the Paris region in all major respects. We have seen that the PCI is more heterogeneous sociologically there than the PCF is in the Paris region. Second, provinces and communes that it controls in the region—far from being proletarian dormitories—contain large rural and middle-class populations and cater to a greater variety of needs and

---

[69] For a rich description of PCF local strongholds in the Paris region, see Jean-Pierre Hoss, *Communes en banlieue: Argenteuil et Bezons* (Paris: A. Colin, 1969).

[70] *Dati sulla organizzazione*, p. 36.

[71] For the PCF's ambiguity on the regional question, see Peter Gourevitch, "Reforming the Napoleonic State."

interests. Third, and most important, central Italy is politically, culturally, and administratively distant from the capital and its political tradition is marked by a deep suspicion of Rome. While the left-wing political culture of Paris is Jacobin and elitist, that of Tuscany, Emilia, and the Marches is populist and autonomist. The Paris *banlieue* is the heartland of proletarian orthodoxy for the PCF, but the Italian Red Belt represents only a particular tendency in Italian communism, and one which the leadership is careful to contain within regional limits.[72]

The differences in membership size and commitment and in the social and regional diversity of the two parties are accompanied at the leadership level by a far more significant role for the intellectuals in the Italian party than in the PCF. The difference in the role of the intellectuals in the two parties is more than sociological; it has to do with the very legitimacy of intellectual work in their respective visions of the road to socialism. The French party has developed a myth of proletarian legitimacy that is far less evident in the PCI. The French Communist intellectual is forever being reminded that "intellectuals lack firmness . . . are more susceptible to bourgeois influences and . . . understand nothing of the needs for political action."[73] There are intellectuals abounding in the Parisian *haute société communiste*, but rarely do they play an important role in the party's internal life. As André Barjonet writes, "The party is proud of its sages, painters, and writers. . . . It covers them with honors, but fails to give them the smallest real responsibility in the party leadership."[74] Through the years, many intellectuals have defected, frustrated by their insulation from the mainstream of PCF policy. The party's myth of proletarian legitimacy leads those who remain to "make touching efforts to imitate the attitudes of the workers," thus vitiating whatever independent contribution they might make to the party's activities.[75]

In the PCI, in contrast, intellectuals are deeply involved in the internal life of the party, where they carry out organizational,

[72] Giorgio Galli, *Il bipartitismo imperfetto; Comunisti e democristiani in Italia* (Bologna: Il Mulino, 1966), pp. 342-347.

[73] Jean Baby, *Critique de base: Le parti communiste français entre le passé et l'avenir* (Paris: Maspero, 1960), pp. 178-179.

[74] André Barjonet, *Le Parti communiste français* (Paris: Didier, 1969), p. 139.

[75] Ibid.

formative, and public relations functions.[76] They are active in animating informal groups which organize around current problems, like the recent environmental concern. This leads to two problems. First, intellectuals tend to set the tone of activity in the PCI, which can leave working-class militants with more dreary tasks and with the impression that they are strangers in their own house. Second, PCI intellectuals have become committed to a variety of tasks, public and organizational, and may fulfill some of them very badly as a result. In particular, how can they attend to the theoretical tasks of the party when they are never freed from responsibility for the day-to-day tasks that the PCI insists that they carry out?

The important role of the intellectuals within its organization also creates great problems of ideological discipline for the PCI. This problem culminated in the formation of the Manifesto grouping in the late 1960s, but it has been common throughout the postwar period for intellectuals to use their positions in the party organization to publicize their differences with the leadership. In the PCF, in contrast, ideological dissent has had to be expressed *outside* the party's media of communications. This has the undoubted benefit of preserving at least the impression of unity to the outside world without which no Communist party feels it is being true to its proclaimed Leninist heritage.

But despite these obvious advantages for the French party, the narrower role it allocates to its intellectuals has been a liability in adapting to political life in an advanced industrial democracy. For a start, the PCF was much slower than its Italian ally in laying aside outdated doctrines like the absolute pauperization of the proletariat, which made the party an object of ridicule during the height of the European economic miracle. Second, without the leavening influence of intellectuals, internal debate became stultified and even the party's language ceased to correspond to reality. It became a "specialized, more or less hermetically sealed language of 'marxist' inspiration" which, in one critic's words, has had the effect of "profoundly isolating it from other political groups, and even from a very important

[76] See, for example, the discussion of the "ideal" section described in Balbo and Pizzorno, "Partiti, élites e 'base' in una città meridionale" in Giordano Sivini (ed.), *Partiti e partecipazione politica in Italia* (Milan: Giuffré, 1968), p. 280.

sector of the population."[77] Third, although the leadership has continued to proclaim its desire for fruitful relationships with nonproletarian groups, its myth of proletarian legitimacy and its inability to devise new intellectual approaches to potentially sympathetic social groups critically impaired the PCF's alliance strategy, at least until quite recently.

In contrast, despite the disadvantages of occasionally having to air its dirty wash in public, the PCI gains immense advantages from the strength of the intellectuals in its ranks. Intellectuals can initiate "formative activities" in order to "attract groups and individuals with particular ideological interests and political goals."[78] They can identify new issues which can appeal to both working- and middle-class voters and ease the transition from outmoded ideological positions to new ones. And they can provide the party with a capacity for internal dialogue which—despite some obvious limitations—at least holds open a prospect for the liberalization of its internal life. These characteristics of the personnel found within its organizations combine with some unusual organizational features to orient the PCI toward a strategy of broad presence in Italian society. In contrast, the more restricted support and leadership bases of the PCF combine with its organizational system to preserve a bipolar model of the political arena and a more selective policy of participation in French political institutions and society.

Organizational Problems and Strategies

Now we can begin to assess the strengths and weaknesses of the French and Italian parties' organizations. With a larger membership, and a more diverse one, the PCI has also placed a greater value upon organizational size, perhaps in the hope of achieving a Marxian transformation of quantity into quality. In contrast, the PCF has elevated its small membership into a virtue, recalling the Leninist precept that strength lies in discipline and discipline is found in a devoted cadre of pure revolutionaries. The characteristic organizational problems of each party flow from these factors, as will be seen after some basic differences in their organizations at the base are briefly outlined.

[77] Barjonet, *Le Parti communiste français*, pp. 149 and 143.
[78] Balbo and Pizzorno, "Partiti, élites e 'base.'"

First, with the enormous expansion of its membership after 1945, it soon became clear to the PCI that it could not integrate all of its new members into the confines of the classical party cell. Indeed, party cells in the factories began to suffer a dramatic crisis from the 1950s on, especially after large numbers of party militants were transferred to the trade unions.[79] Making a virtue out of necessity, the PCI began to stress the life of the section and to accept that the cell, in very many cases, existed only on paper.[80] This was particularly true in the south where, outside of a few key provinces, an effective organizational network at the base has never been established.[81] In contrast, the smaller and more homogeneous membership of the PCF could be contained within its traditional cell structure, although losses in the number of cells appear, if anything, to have been proportionally greater than the simultaneous losses in membership that the French party was suffering.[82]

Second, while neither party has been lacking in organizational problems, the Italian party's organization has shown a greater spirit of experimentation. PCF party cells, with their narrow social basis and vertical isolation, are the ideal instrument for secret or revolutionary activities. However, during times of relative social peace like most of the past thirty years, the cells are largely condemned to traditional tasks of agitation and propaganda and to internal tasks of organizational maintenance. This is certainly one of the reasons for the low level of activity at the base that has marked the PCF, with the exception of a few periods, since the war.[83]

The shift to the section as the basic capillary unit of the PCI meant—at least in theory—a greater capacity to implement a strategy of presence at the base, particularly in sections where diverse social and occupational groupings were conjoined. Wherever this condition was met, the section could engage in

[79] See Weitz, Chapter 14 in this volume.

[80] Giordano Sivini, "Struttura organizzative e partecipazione di base nel Partito comunista italiano," in Sivini (ed.), Partiti e partecipazione, pp. 141-168.

[81] Tarrow, Peasant Communism, Chapter 8.

[82] Lord, in his "Structures et organisation," p. 17, points out that several cantons in the relatively "strong" federation of Corrèze have only one or two party cells for a relatively large number of communes.

[83] Baby, Critique, Chapter 5.

ideological and cultural activities, as well as actions designed to identify issues with appeal to a variety of groups and classes.[84] In the nature of things, this is more likely to be true in smaller population centers, where a single large section unites all the party members in the district, than in either villages or large cities, where either a peasant or a predominantly working-class membership is numerically dominant within the section.[85]

Third, above the section level the two parties have responded to organizational crises in fundamentally different ways. The PCI has experimented constantly with new forms of organization, like communal committees, zonal committees, regional committees and, most recently—in strong provinces like Bologna—with sub-provincial, supra-municipal forms of organization that parallel the recent division of the province into planning districts (*comprensori*).[86] Some observers detect a growing influence of the PCI's regional leadership since the institution, in 1970, of the Italian regional governments.[87] The party's typical reaction to lethargy in any level of its organizations is to attempt to assign new tasks to that level or to experiment with a new form of organization there. In the PCF, in contrast, the dominant tendency has been to plough ahead in the same organizational furrow, perhaps for fear of exposing that the party is not the organizational monolith it claims to be.[88]

A similar contrast between organizational proliferation and conservatism can be noted in the two parties' attitudes toward their mass organizations. While the PCF has focused on a few key front organizations like the peace movement, the PCI has created, on paper at least, a myriad of loosely structured committees and movements, many of them overlapping in function or in target populations, and often succeeding each other with great rapidity. Such was the party's history in the south during the

[84] Balbo and Pizzorno, "Partiti, élites e 'base,'" p. 280.

[85] See Peter Lange, Chapter 7 in this volume for the greater staying power of the PCI organizational subculture in smaller population centers.

[86] Stephen Hellman, "Ideology and Organization in Four Italian Communist Federations" (Ph.D. dissertation, Yale University, 1973).

[87] Norman Kogan, "The Impact of the New Italian Regional Governments on the Structure of Power within the Parties" (Paper delivered at the Ninth World Congress of the International Political Science Association, Montreal, 1973).

[88] This is an inference that can be drawn from the data carefully assembled by Guy Lord ("Le PCF: Structures et organisation") on the PCF's organizational adaptation in the Corrèze. See esp. pp. 17-21 of his paper.

stormy days of the peasants' occupation of the *latifundia*. And rather than drawing in a broader public, these organizations were often dominated by the same people, wearing different hats, who animated them and came to their meetings.[89] In contrast, the only major innovation in the mass organizations created by the PCF over the last decade has been the Mouvement de Défense des Exploitants Familiaux (MODEF), an association of left-wing peasants' organizations, mainly from south of the Loire, which took a long time to germinate, and was turned into a successful mass movement of left-wing rural sympathizers after the party deliberated long and hard.[90] The contrast with the PCI-animated Alleanza Nazionale dei Contadini could not be greater: the Italian peasant movement was formed rapidly, and without much thought, from a number of regional and sectoral organizations, and has neither sunk deep roots among the peasants nor found a stable place for itself alongside the older PCI-dominated organizations of agricultural day workers (*Federbraccianti*) or sharecroppers (*Federmezzadri*).[91]

These differing approaches to party organization have led to a number of characteristic differences in the utilization and control of party militants in the two parties. First, the PCF has a simpler chain of command that poses fewer problems of communication and control than that of the PCI. For instance, when the debate in Italy on the obsolescence of the party cell began, many PCI activists were highly disoriented by what was happening. "Cadres at the base . . . who had worked intensively for years were surrounded by criticism, self-criticism, perplexity, an absence of alternatives and paralysis."[92] The party's complex and shifting organizational pyramid can also inhibit the communication of policies to the base. For instance, in Milan a party survey showed that "among the comrades there is a state of confusion and uncertainty about several fundamental aspects of the party's policies. And they are truly basic concepts, not secondary matters."[93] These problems in the chain of command have made it

[89] Tarrow, *Peasant Communism*, pp. 354-367.

[90] Yves Tavernier, "Le Mouvement de défense des exploitants familiaux," in Tavernier (ed.), *L'Univers politique des paysans* (Paris: A. Colin, 1972), pp. 467-496.

[91] *Peasant Communism*, pp. 359-364. For signs of the continuing crisis in the peasant movement, see Gerardo Chiaromonte, *Agricoltura, sviluppo economico, democrazia* (Bari: Laterza, 1973), pp. 99-101.

[92] Sivini, "Struttura organizzativa," p. 163.

[93] Ibid., p. 161.

609

more difficult for the PCI than for the PCF to keep the base in line with respect to situations like the party's attitude toward the Soviet invasion of Czechoslovakia.

The "chain of command" problem is also greater in the PCI with respect to the career patterns of its cadres. There is a relatively greater degree of career specialization in the French party, and a greater diffusion of different types of political experience in the PCI. We have already mentioned the effect of the PCF's cellular structure in isolating militants into a single kind of activity and that of the PCI's sections in exposing them to a broader range of contacts and activities. Complementing this is the French party's more specialized conception of the proper role of the militant in either organizational, elective or trade-union functions. Writing about the section secretary in the Haute-Vienne, for example, one student observes that he "is always a militant, and very rarely a public official, for it is considered that [party] activity should be much broader than the exercise of an elective function."[94] In the PCI, in contrast, militants move around a great deal between elective, organizational, and economic and social tasks and often hold several such roles simultaneously—a pattern which gives them less experience in any single branch of activities and probably makes for less party control over their behavior. When militants in the trade unions, the party apparatus, and public office have shared experiences and understand each other's problems, local or regional factions can form more easily than when each group has ties to only one kind of organization. In the PCF, in contrast, local party organizers have closer ties to higher-ups in the party hierarchy than they do with either elected officials or representatives of the mass organizations.

But the strong chain of command and high degree of specialization in the PCF are of questionable use in preparing its cadres to play an aggressive role in identifying the common problems of various social groups or in responding creatively to directives to take the initiative in particular policy areas. It also makes it more difficult than in the Italian party for cooperation to take place between public officials, party organizers, and representatives of the mass organizations in electoral campaigns. Since the latter two groups in the PCF have little experience in campaigning, they are of less use to party candidates trying to get elected

[94] Savy, "Recherches sur le personnel politique," p. 21.

610

than in Italy, where each group is likely to have had significant experience in public office.

The most interesting consequences of the organizational differences outlined above are found in combination with the differences in social and regional support bases that were dealt with earlier. At its best, the combination of a more flexible organization and a more diversified internal composition allows the PCI to present itself to the Italian public as a genuinely popular party with the creativity, the flexibility, and the internal resources to propose plausible solutions to a variety of problems. But the defects of these characteristics are also obvious. At its worst, the PCI is a slack organizational system with a heterodox social composition that can lead to a concentration on particularistic interests and on issues that are extraneous to the party's national line. When this happens in particular regions or localities, the party leadership has no choice but to impose the instruments of Leninist discipline, an outcome which, of course, contrasts grotesquely with its claim to be an internally democratic party.

The worst consequences of this combination of organizational flexibility and social diversity are found in regions where there is no solid working-class cadre to balance the influence of intellectuals, members of the middle strata, or peasants in the party's organizations. This is most obvious in the south, where the party's strength is found mainly outside the major urban centers of population. How can a historic bloc of progressive forces be built around the magnetic nerve center of the organized working class where the working class is small, poorly organized, and largely indifferent to communism? How can the resources of the "productive middle strata" be drawn upon in a region in which the middle class is more engaged in commerce than in industry, more parasitic than productive, and still infested with a nostalgia for the corporate state? And how to appeal to a peasantry that is itself internally divided between the militant agricultural workers, land-poor small farmers and tenants, and the owners of medium-sized commercial farms? In the absence of a strong working-class base, the PCI in the south has tried to attract all these social groupings simultaneously, with contradictory results for its internal life that would have been even greater had its successes been more complete. The greatest failures of the PCI strategy of alliances are still found in the south, where the doubling of the party's electoral strength during the 1950s has never

611

been matched by anything like the same degree of social or organizational strength.[95]

In contrast, the PCF has followed the logic of its bipolar class strategy in seeking a middle-class, an intellectual, and a peasant presence within its organizations *only* to the degree that they can be carefully controlled. At party conferences, a favorite topic has always been the maintenance of a "just" balance between proletarian and nonproletarian members. This creates a problem in those party-led organizations—such as the youth or student movements—where a proletarian presence can never be especially strong. As François Billoux maintained at the Eighth PCF Congress, "The organization of the union of the younger generation is not the particular business of this or that organization. . . . It is the business of the Communist party, the highest organizational form of the working class."[96] The freedom of action of the PCF's peasant organizers has been limited by the same concern. Speaking in 1963, François Clavand said that "it is the party and only the party, that can show the peasants that economic and social struggles must necessarily develop into a larger struggle against personalistic government and against the capitalist system."[97]

The problems in the organizational systems of the two Communist parties can now be briefly summarized. The greatest problems for the Italian party are the proliferation of its organizations, the dispersion of its activists' efforts in pursuit of a multitude of goals, and the party's need to maintain the sprawling organizational life it has created. The urge to be "present" brings with it the need to maintain the organizations that guarantee that presence, and this, in turn, consumes such an enormous proportion of the resources of the party's cadres that it can severely limit the time or energy they have left for aggressive, outward-looking activities.[98] Party members whose commitment is lukewarm must be stimulated to participate, conflicts between different elements in the sections must be smoothed over and, where necessary, arbitrated, comrades whose perspectives remain sectarian

[95] Tarrow, "The Political Economy of Stagnation," pp. 97-101.

[96] Quoted in Kriegel, *Les Communistes*, p. 45.

[97] Fernand Clavand, "La Situation à la campagne et les tâches du parti," in *Cahiers du communisme* 39 (November 1963): 95.

[98] Lange, for example, points out in Chapter 7 that a good deal of the time of PCI section leaders is devoted to maintenance activity of uncertain value for the party's outward looking strategy.

612

must be urged to bury their hatred of the middle class in the name of the strategy of broad unity, and gregarious middle-class militants must be cautioned lest their contacts with the bourgeois parties become too embarrassing.[99] If members are lost from among the working class or the agricultural proletariat, the losses must be made up, even if this entails an approach to social groups whose enthusiasm for communism is dubious, to say the least.

The PCF, with its more streamlined, traditional, and conventional organization, can avoid most of these problems. The French Communists remain suspicious of members whose commitment is less than total. Since the range of activities in which members are asked to participate is narrow and the membership is smaller and more committed, problems of nonparticipation are less likely to arise. Since the social basis of the party is more markedly proletarian, and is found, in particular, among the proletariat organized by the CGT, membership can more easily be maintained at its optimal level. Finally, because of the dominant myth of proletarian legitimacy at the base, and the fact that PCF intellectuals are isolated into their own cells, the potential problem of embarrassing overtures to the middle classes at the base is largely avoided. All such "outward-looking" activities are conceived as the business of the party center and not of the grassroots. Although this attitude to relations with the middle class and other potential social "allies" is beginning to change, the heritage of the past still lies heavy on the PCF.

These PCF characteristics are related to—but not identical with—the classical virtues of the Leninist party organization. But that model has its disadvantages too, especially for a party which claims to be serious about being a legitimate contender for power in a parliamentary democracy. From the evidence presented above, it is hard to escape the conclusion that, whatever else changes, the PCF is determined to maintain the organizational traits it has inherited from the past. In contrast, so much has changed in the organizational life of the Italian party that the remaining Leninist logic (as evidenced by the case of the *Manifesto*) seems increasingly out of place by comparison.

Having gone so far toward change, how much longer can the

---

[99] See Alan Stern's discussion of the "embarrassing" PCI alliances with local entrepreneurs in a central Italian town, in his "Local Party Organization," pp. 9-10.

613

PCI remain simultaneously a "party of a special type" and the truly national party that Togliatti proclaimed so long ago? And having retained so much of its classical organizational culture and characteristics, how much can the PCF actually change? These questions will be confronted as we turn to the increasingly complex relationships between the two parties and their respective political systems.

COMMUNISM IN THE POLITICAL SYSTEM

Which Communist party, the PCF or the PCI, has adapted better to the conditions of its respective political system? The question seems to us an unanswerable one, given the variety of conditions and traditions to which each party has had to adapt, and the differences in their support and leadership and in their organizational patterns and problems. If the PCF has preserved a purer Leninist heritage than the PCI (and a greater degree of fidelity to the Soviet Union) this may not be because the French Communists are more "foreign" but because the Leninist model has been more useful in Paris than in Rome. As Norman Kogan writes, "If the French Communists have a heavy Russian accent, perhaps it is because the Russian bolsheviks inherited more than just a revolutionary tradition from the French middle class."[100]

Indeed, one of the things that our analysis has shown is that the line between what is "Communist" and what is "French" or "Italian" in these two Communist parties is extremely difficult to draw. If the French party has "a heavy stress on conventional morality, a suspicion of flamboyance, individualism and lack of orthodoxy," is this so very different from the dominant values of French society?[101] Similarly, if the Italian party has an intellectual leadership and an organizational diffusion that seem to erode its "antisystem" qualities, is this so different from the other Italian parties?

From an analytical—if not from an ideological—point of view, the distinction between "system" and "antisystem" properties is of no use at all. What seems more important is the patterns of

[100] Norman Kogan, "The French Communists—and Their Italian Comrades," *Studies in Comparative Communism* 6, nos. 1 and 2 (Spring/Summer 1973): 185.

[101] Mark Kesselman, "Changes in the French Party System," *Comparative Politics* 4 (January 1972): 299.

614

commitment and behavior that each of these parties has built up over time as the result of the domestic and international, historical and contemporary, and organizational and political factors we have outlined above. These patterns of commitment could no doubt be studied in several different arenas: in the parties' ideologies, in their links to the international Communist movement, or in their cultural and ideological contributions. If we have decided to focus on their relation to their respective political systems, it is because this seems to be the most important problem of all. Before turning to the responses of the PCI and the PCF to the changes in their international and domestic environments, we shall focus on the patterns of commitment and behavior that have emerged in these two parties with respect to (a) their participation in Parliament and in local government and (b) their respective strategies and successes in attracting allies within each country. For it is the patterns of commitment and behavior built up over the past thirty years that are the best guide to each party's response to changes in its environment both in the present and in the future.

THE COMMUNIST POLITICIAN

"For almost fifty years," writes Ronald Tiersky, "the solidarity and the resilience of communism has constituted one of the essential elements of French political life."[102] This perseverance is also evident in the present Communist political elite, which has been in control of the PCF, with few changes, since 1934. Promotion through the ranks of the PCF has been slow and cautious, as is evident in the character of its present secretary-general, a man whose selection and formation were carefully programmed and controlled, notably throughout a long series of bilateral and multilateral meetings with the delegates of the other fraternal parties and, needless to say, the Soviet party too, according to Annie Kriegel.[103] Kriegel means to emphasize the international ties of the PCF, but equally important is the continuity in PCF leadership that is evident at both the national and local levels. In the last few years there has been an important infusion of new blood in the municipal and parliamentary leadership groups of

102 Tiersky, *Le Mouvement communiste*, p. 7.
103 Annie Kriegel, in this volume, Chapter 2.

615

the PCF but it remains to be seen if such changes will filter into the party apparatus.[104]

The PCI, in contrast, emerged as a practically new party in the 1940s, and its highest level of leadership consists of men whose political formation dates from the crises of the late 1930s and the 1940s. But even these relatively younger men are being hard-pressed from below; periodically since the Second World War, generational changes have occurred in the PCI which have brought younger members into positions of authority within the party. This happened during the post-1956 de-Stalinization campaign and again, in a more limited way, after the radicalization of the late 1960s, when a group of young men in their late twenties moved into the PCI's provincial organizations.[105] Such shifts have been particularly noticeable in the south, where a large number of older regional and provincial secretaries were recently replaced by younger men from the north and center.[106]

From the beginning of the postwar period, PCI politicians have shown a greater commitment to political values than their PCF counterparts. This was even evident in their early socialization and recruitment; in 1954 Almond could show that the most important resentment in the lives of the French ex-Communists he interviewed had been economic, with 47 percent having been hurt either by family economic suffering or by strikes or labor disorders. In Italy, in contrast, the largest group of ex-Communists interviewed had been hurt by Fascism or by enemy occupation.[107] The myth of proletarian legitimacy in the PCF reinforces its leaders' emphasis on the economic struggle; in fact, what remains in them of the syndicalist tradition is mainly a dislike of politics and the desire to paint themselves as simple men who serve the proletariat in the sometimes distasteful tasks of political representation. As Robert Ballanger, a long-time PCF parliamentarian, explained, "We have lived the life of the people and we continue to live it with the salary of a skilled worker . . . hav-

[104] See Jean Daniel, "PCF: Berlinguer tradotto in francese," *L'Espresso*, February 18, 1973, p. 14.

[105] Stephen Hellman, "Generational Differences in the Federal Apparatus of the Italian Communist Party: Origins and Implications" (Paper delivered at the Annual Meeting of the American Political Science Association, Washington, D.C., 1972).

[106] Malaspina, "Il Compagno modello."

[107] Almond, *Appeals of Communism*, p. 198.

ing never lived otherwise, we feel the needs of the people and we are the best equipped to express them in Parliament."[108]

The PCI's politicians are far more professionalized. For a start, they no longer subsist "with the salary of a skilled worker," nor do they cultivate an image as proletarianized as the one that Ballanger portrays. More basic, PCI politicians have developed a greater feeling for the nuances of politics and a greater passion for the political game than we can sense among their counterparts in France. This is illustrated by the greater enjoyment of politics revealed by the PCI mayors whose attitudes were reported on elsewhere in this volume.[109] It is also evident in the greater network of political contacts that Italian Communist politicians maintain, and in their greater degree of initiative in capturing resources from the state through unabashed political bartering.[110]

At the parliamentary level too, the Italian Communists have developed a greater degree of flexibility and political professionalism than their French counterparts. PCI deputies spend much of their time promoting their constituents' interests and negotiating with non-Communist politicians in the parliamentary committees that are responsible for most of the legislative output of the Italian parliament.[111] Their parliamentary group is responsible for a wide variety of bills and interpellations of interest to many occupational sectors,[112] making so many concrete proposals to serve the interests of its members' districts that PCI deputies must sometimes be reminded by the party leadership not to go overboard in the "local and particularistic nature of their action" in Parliament.[113] In recent years, there have been examples of arrangements with dubious allies for short-term legislative purposes.

In the French parliamentary arena, PCF deputies tend to focus

[108] Quoted in Ferrari and Maisl, *Les Groupes communistes*, p. 54.

[109] See Chapter 4 in this volume.

[110] Ibid.

[111] Maria Antoinetta Macciocchi, *Letters to Louis Althusser From Inside the PCI* (London: New Left Books, 1974).

[112] An article by Franco Cazzola, "Consenso e opposizione nel parlamento italiano: Il ruolo del PCI dalla I alla IV legislatura," *Rivista italiana di scienza politica* 2 (April 1972): 71-96 makes clear that the PCI engages in a high degree of "consensual" behavior for what others have called an "anti-system" party.

[113] Ferrari and Maisl, *Les Groupes communistes*, p. 101.

on a few policy areas, mainly those of direct interest to the working class. But what stands out most about their parliamentary activity is its uniformity. The bills they propose are identical in
format, concentrate mainly on problems of labor and industry,
and are seldom followed by a nuanced debate. As one writer
says, "the Communist [parliamentary] group seems to limit itself
to a minimum of interventions. It is essentially a question of making known, in strongly orthodox language . . . a rigid position
which doesn't need to be refined by several speakers."[114] The lack
of emphasis upon political skills that is indicated by these observations is undoubtedly due, in part, to the weakened role of
Parliament in the Fifth Republic; but it also reflects the pattern
of rigid and narrow partisanship that we have encountered
throughout our discussion of the PCF's adaptation to French
political life.

The achievements of the two Communist parties in the parliamentary institutions of each country diverge in much the same
way. In their study of the parliamentary groups of the PCI and
the PCF, Ferrari and Maisl have shown that, of 523 bills proposed by the PCI between 1958 and 1963, 13 percent were
adopted and an equal number were absorbed by positive votes
on similar bills proposed by other groups. The attitude of the
other parliamentary groups with respect to the Communists,
moreover,

> is not an attitude of rejection, pure and simple, nor one of hos-
> tility. . . . This is important, for, seeing the relative success it
> achieves, the latter group will not be tempted to throw itself
> into a purely demagogic activity, but will try to make its prop-
> ositions more concrete, without, however, abandoning the line
> of the party.[115]

In France, the PCF proposed a total of 93 bills in the legislative sessions between 1962 and 1967, of which only 3 percent
were adopted. This proportion is strikingly low, but under the
antiparliamentary system of the Fifth Republic, it should be remembered, it is not much lower than the proportion of adopted
bills presented by all the parliamentary groups (10 percent).
Even the UNR's bills had an adoption rate of only 14.4 percent,
in a parliamentary system in which legislation is mainly initiated

[114] Ibid., p. 186.   [115] Ibid., pp. 48-49.

by the executive.[116] The indications are, however, that the PCF was no more successful during the Fourth Republic, as was revealed by its unsuccessful attempts to support the Mendès-France government. It is small wonder, then, that the goal of many of the PCF's proposals seems to be, not their adoption, but their popularization.[117]

The benefits of the PCI's flexibility and productivity in Parliament are beyond dispute, but what are its costs? We may well ask to what extent the politically entrepreneurial Italian Communist legislators have escaped absorption into a political institution that has been described as "a tribune for electoral rallies" rather than "a qualified setting for the exploration of concrete problems and technical questions."[118] But does this absorption into an institution whose defects are all too real imply a deradicalization of the PCI's parliamentary representatives? The evidence argues against this. As Robert Putman has shown, the PCI politician is as ideologically dedicated to the defeat of Italian capitalism as we might expect his PCF comrade to be.[119] What does seem to result from PCI parliamentary participation is a commitment to procedural democracy that goes far beyond a merely rhetorical commitment to the republican constitution. But there may be something else as well: the assimilation of the habits of parliamentary petty deals and political horse-trading that is so characteristic of the Italian political elite and is the source of so many defects in Italian public life. In this sense, at least, PCI politicians in Parliament are procedurally *within* the system, although their ideological radicalism cries out against it.

The same combination of high policy productivity, commitment to the radical transformation of their society, and involvement in both the dignified and the squalid aspects of Italian democracy is typical of the PCI local elite. PCI mayors work hard to make their municipalities into model communes; they claim to do so in the hope of encouraging a radical redistribution of income from the rich to the poor. They are as committed, at the practical level, to the system of political exchange that gives Italian public life its squalid character as they are, at the norma-

[116] Ibid., p. 160.   [117] Ibid., p. 177.
[118] Bianca Avanzini, "Communisti e democristiani nel parlamento italiano: Analisi di contenuto di un campione di interventi nelle prime tre legislature," in *Rassegna italiana di sociologia* 9 (January-March 1968): 81-116.
[119] See his contribution to this volume, Chapter 5.

tive level, to the values of procedural democracy that they espouse. The typical Communist local politician is an able political activist with a wide range of contacts both in the local community and throughout the political system, contacts that he deftly utilizes to capture resources to improve the life of the people in his community. The unanswered question is the long-range commitments and entanglements which may result from a habitual recourse to such tactics. Could the PCI mayor who is well known in his district as a shrewd political entrepreneur credibly assist in an aggressive social or political strategy were the circumstances to warrant it?

There are, of course, "model" Communist-run communes in France as well, particularly in the working-class suburbs around Paris and in a patchwork of red regions in the provinces. As illustrated elsewhere in this volume, French Communist administrators have made a real effort to modernize their approach to local government. If their innovations have been more impressive in their administrative than in their political aspects, this is no doubt related to the stronger hand of the French state over local government, but also reflects the lower level of political sensitivity and flexibility we found in the PCF municipal elite. Only time can tell whether the substantial numbers of new Communist municipal officials elected in 1971 will bring a breath of fresh air to a local PCF political class that has been more notable for its efficiency than for its imagination.

The Communist local and provincial elites who govern many of Italy's communes, provinces, and regions reveal something else as well of great political importance: a degree of diversity and relative autonomy that is certainly lacking in their counterparts in France. Perhaps because there are proportionally more Communist local officials in Italy or because they administer such a variety of localities, there is a greater margin of differentiation in the Italian party's local and provincial representatives than in France. We have touched on this point briefly in discussing the "special" character of communism *all'emiliana*. It is equally evident in the increasingly autonomous policies of Communist local officials who are obliged to deal, on a day-to-day basis, with a variety of concrete problems for which the party hierarchy cannot possibly provide concrete directives. For instance, in 1973 a controversy over hunting rights pitted the Communist mayor of Bologna, Renato Zangheri, against regional officials and against the left-wing association of hunters of the province of Bologna. The issue soon blew up into a national debate reported both in the pages of *L'Unità* and in the national non-Communist press. While civic-minded, middle-class Italians were writing letters to the PCI daily calling for closer control over the massive slaughter of birds, the Communist-led association of hunters was reviling environmentalists as people who, in one man's words, "fight against the hunting of the common people but defend private hunting preserves."[120]

Nowhere in the evidence collected on the PCF either in this volume or elsewhere do we find the kind of open policy debates that have become common on the local and provincial level of the PCI in recent years. Indeed, evidence presented in this volume suggests a continued tight control over local officials' activities by the party organization, a type of control that appears to have fallen into disuse in the Italian party.[121] At the same time, however, French mayors and local councilmen appear to be less integrated into the party organization than their Italian counterparts.[122] Does this render the French party more susceptible to ideological deviation than the PCI? Probably not, for in a party like the PCF, in which the party organization is both dominant and unchanging, the contribution that local elites can make on the road to socialism is minimal indeed. In Italy, in contrast, local elites represent a basic pillar of the *via italiana al socialismo*: a strategy that is based fundamentally on the concept of the party's being present wherever decisions are being made in Italian society. It is the application of the concept of presence—as opposed to the PCF's commitment to what it sees as the interests of the proletariat—that most distinguishes the two parties' politicians in the national and local institutions in which they are active.

ALLIES AND ENEMIES

This takes us to the most general difference in the implementation of the two parties' strategies: their strategies of alliances with other parties and groups in the political system. The PCF, with its bipolar model of the class struggle, approaches potential

[120] Some aspects of this debate are reported in *Corriere della Sera* (June 1973) and *L'Unità* (June 22, 1973), p. 6.

[121] See Chapters 8 and 9 in this volume by Denis Lacorne and Jerome Milch.

[122] See Chapter 4 in this volume.

allies from a cautious and defensive posture. The PCI, for which a network of alliances is seen as central to its key notion of presence throughout Italian society, approaches potential allies with less reserve. This general contrast has many dimensions, only the most essential of which can be treated here.

First, the problem of alliances seems to be more centrally planned and directed in the French party, even during the recent period of alliance with the Socialists. Where the PCI has made a general strategic directive of the need for alliances, allowing scope to local and sectoral organizations to work autonomously at the problem, the PCF works out alliance policies at the center, changing the degree of its commitment to alliances according to the political circumstances, and leaving little scope for variation at the local level or in different sectors of the party's activity. While this can be a distinct advantage in forming electoral alliances like the one with the Socialists in 1973, it is a disadvantage in negotiating with local political or social groups, where the party cadres could profit from a greater degree of flexibility and continuity.

In the PCI's approach, the danger is a different one: that local leaders will go too far to achieve alliances with groups of dubious social or political provenance. This was obvious in the notorious Milazzo experiment in Sicily in the early 1960s, when the PCI Regional Committee entered a temporary alliance with a breakaway, and not particularly progressive, Christian Democratic faction. A similar problem has been noted in central Italy where PCI leaders have reached over backwards to bring small businessmen into relations with the party. In a small Tuscan city reported on by Alan Stern, 41 industrialists were found to be members of the PCI section. Many had been party members before going into business, but "nevertheless, the conspicuous party participation of some of the entrepreneurs and the widely discussed suspicion that many of them utilized PCI ties to bolster their fledgling businesses in matters of credit, transport, and labor relations has embarrassed the local party considerably."[123]

Despite these dangers, the local and sectoral flexibility of PCI alliance strategy is of great political use. For a start, it helps the party to adjust to the enormous regional differences of the country. In the Veneto, for example, the PCI has supported experi-

[123] Stern, "Local Party Organization."

ments in Catholic-Communist local government with the support of progressive *democristiani*, alliances that would hardly be possible in the south, where the DC is far more reactionary. Similarly, the Communist trade-union confederation, the CGIL, has gained the flexibility to bargain credibly with the other two trade-union centrals, in a process of unification that has even led the confederation to loosen its ties with the Moscow-dominated World Federation of Trade Unions.[124]

While the PCI's willingness to allow its local or sectoral leaders to experiment with new alliances can sometimes be embarrassing, the PCF has an even greater dilemma: that of convincing the public it is serious when it begins a centrally orchestrated alliance campaign. It was only shortly after the Garaudy exclusion that the PCF set off on a course of wooing teachers and other intellectuals! Much of the French public is so suspicious toward actual contacts with Communists that the party must often limit itself to hortatory statements and to pats on its own back for its policies of broad *ouverture* toward this or that putative ally. And although recent overtures to the middle classes have been more outgoing than in the past, in practice there is still something artificial about the exercise.

But one thing is clear: the PCF knows who its enemies are and identifies them publicly in uncompromising and classical language. For its commitment to proletarian legitimacy and to the bipolar class model that follows from it makes obvious who are its enemies: big monopoly capital, the profiteering commercial farmers, speculators and real estate developers, and conservatives of all kinds. In contrast, the PCI, which fears the alienation of all those social groups who contributed to the success of Fascism, has at one time or another made overtures to a remarkable array of marginal and sometimes conservative political and social groupings. While the PCF views alliances in extremely selective terms, the PCI perceives of them in additive terms, and its strategic goal makes the party unwilling to cast off the idea of a particular alliance, even where it has patently failed. This is particularly true in southern Italy, where the profusion of groups to which the party has tried to appeal—were they actually to unite—would create a very mixed bag of allies indeed. Even in central Italy, many Communist leaders are skeptical of a policy

[124] On the changes in the CGIL, see Weitz, Chapter 14 in this volume.

623

of accommodation with the middle class that has little chance of success and may even cost the party the support of more radical elements in the population.[125]

The problem of too inclusive commitments also has an effect on Communist local government in central Italy. In many of the cities that the PCI has controlled since the Liberation, its leaders have followed conservative fiscal policies designed to appeal to middle-class supporters. Moreover, because the party has been most successful in gaining control of communes with a large *rural* component in the population (this is even true of many cities of over 100,000 inhabitants that it controls), its municipal leaders have devoted fewer resources to the public services than would be true in communes with a greater population density.[126] PCF local administrations are more typically found in urbanized areas like the Paris *banlieue*, where the electorate is more uniformly working class and public expenditures can be more "social" in character.[127]

The PCF's strategy of scrutinizing every potential alliance carefully—and at the summit—has begun to pay off in recent years. Thus, Jean Ranger shows that theoretical and practical progress has been made in the party's approach to new middle-class groups, both in industry and in the professions. Especially great has been the French party's progress among teachers, many of them appreciative of its conservative stand against the *gauchistes*, and among supervisory personnel in industry, who are rapidly becoming aware of their subaltern status in the economy.[128] Similarly, Yves Tavernier has shown that the party's changing approach to the peasantry, especially through the Mouvement de Défense des Exploitants Familiaux (MODEF), has led to a certain success in employing the language and the

[125] See Stephen Hellman, Chapter 10 in this volume.

[126] Robert Fried, "Communism, Urban Budgets and the Two Italies: A Case Study in Comparative Urban Governments," *The Journal of Politics* 33 (November 1971): 1041.

[127] Jean-Claude Ducros, "Politique et finances locales," *Analyse et Prévision* 2 (1966): 499-518. Also see Jerome Milch's "Influence as Power: French Local Government Reconsidered," *British Journal of Political Science*, 4 (December, 1974) pp. 139-161.

[128] See Jean Ranger, "Le Parti communiste français et les changements sociaux depuis la deuxième guerre mondiale" (Paper delivered at the Conference on French and Italian Communism sponsored by the Planning Group on Comparative Communist Studies of American Council of Learned Societies, Dedham, Mass., October 1972).

624

demands needed to attract the support of younger farmers, a group that has always turned more naturally to the conservative Confédération Nationale des Jeunes Agriculteurs (CNJA).[129] But the hand of tradition is still strong; the PCF "seems to allocate the greatest part of its attention and its support [in the country-side] to the organization and development of its own rural cells. . . . Up to now, the Communist party has judged dangerous a peasant syndicalism that is strictly Communist and that runs the risk of isolating it from its political allies on the left in the countryside."[130]

This leads directly to the third important contrast between the alliance strategies of the two Communist parties: the tendency of the PCF to think of alliances predominantly in terms of ar-rangements with neighboring *political* groups and that of the PCI to think in terms of constructing a bloc of *social* forces. Perhaps because they have been able to assume relatively favorable rela-tions with the Socialists, the Italian Communists have moved be-yond the political idea of a Popular Front, while the PCF's long estrangement from the non-Communist Left has made the achievement of left-wing unity, despite its obvious limitations, still a cherished goal. In other words, the PCI has been able to gear itself to a strategy of social alliances because it has had strong ties with its political neighbors, while the PCF has failed to explore the terrain of social alliances so aggressively because its political isolation has been so great. Indeed, the almost total absence of any joint social goal from the "Common Program" signed between the PCF and Parti Socialiste (PS) before the 1973 election campaign testifies to the concentration of both French parties on the purely political aspect of their alliance. This lack of a firm social programmatic basis has left the alliance ex-tremely fragile, especially since the death of Pompidou has widened the potential rifts in the majority and opened new possibilities of expansion on the Left.

However, the Italian party's emphasis on broad social alliances has continued even after its relations with the PSI cooled off in the early 1960s, for there is a more basic reason for the differ-ences in the two parties' alliance policies than political contingen-cies: the strategic model of the two parties, in which permanent

[129] Yves Tavernier, "Le Mouvement de défense des exploitants familiaux," pp. 488-489.
[130] Ibid., p. 482.

social alliances play a vastly different role. Differences in organizational strength are also important: with over a million and a half members, the PCI has sufficient cadres to spare for the sometimes discouraging task of constructing bridges to nonworking-class groups; with less than one-fourth that number, the PCF must limit itself to largely hortatory directives to its cadres and to a few strategically viable organizational initiatives. Finally, the differences in the two parties' organizations play a role too: social alliances are potentially more compromising and more dangerous for a party like the PCF than for a party like the PCI. Political alliances worked out by leaders at the summit, despite their contingent and temporary nature, can be more easily controlled than social alliances implemented on a day-to-day basis by the party's cadres at the base.

Of course, the actual record of the PCI's social alliances is far less successful than the party's public line would lead one to believe. In the south, in relation to the middle class and with respect to the Catholic working class, successes have been few, with the important exception of Emilia where the PCI is almost a household word. In the meantime, the party's increasingly skilled political class has been making successful strides in the political marketplace, dealing fruitfully and making alliances with the most diverse political groups—even, at times, with representatives of the class enemy. This leads to the paradox that, while the PCI *talks* a great deal about its broad social alliances, it actually attends more to the *political* aspects of its alliance posture, if only because of the nature of its leaders' skills. In a Parliament that has actually gained in strength amid the paralysis of cabinet government and the atrophy of the bureaucracy, and in a system of local and regional councils that gives great scope to their political skill, the PCI's leaders have gained a degree of influence that continues to elude them in civil society. The reasons for this apparent paradox will become clear when we turn to the changes in the domestic and international setting to which the PCI has tried to adapt.

In contrast, the French party, with a narrower but clearer view of its priorities, wastes little time on social alliance possibilities that may not pan out, and concentrates upon its political relationships in Paris. These have thus far proved elusive, dissolving during crises like that of May 1968, and involving only a limited area of agreement during the successful periods like that of the "common program" with the Socialists. Why this should be true relates to changes in French politics, especially since 1958 and to the rather large number of strategic options that have been closed off to the PCF through the action of forces beyond its control. But it also relates to the party's organizational logic and dominant myths, factors which have persisted even in the face of the substantial ideological change described elsewhere in this volume.

PATTERNS OF CONTINUITY AND CHANGE

Thus, the French and Italian Communist parties have developed patterns of continuity that are evident in their organization and leadership, their appeals for support and alliances, and their behavior in each country's political institutions. In the PCF, we find a party which lays great stress on its continuity with the past—and on its ties to the Soviet Union—and which has built a tight and efficient organization around its bulwark in the urban working class. It is more oriented toward economic struggles than to political exchange, and its leadership reflects both of these factors, plus a cautious and conservative attitude toward external alliances and to policy innovation. The PCI, in contrast, which took form during the victorious struggle against fascism and the subsequent period of creating republican institutions, has internalized the symbols of that period in a deeper commitment to both social and political alliances and in a party organization that stresses quantity over the quality of commitment. The PCI aims to be present throughout the structures of Italian society, but its frustrations in that area—in contrast to its relative success in the parliamentary and local government arenas—have led to a steady politicization of its alliance strategy as well. Neither party shows any intention of casting aside its Leninist heritage, but the Italian party is characterized by a more flexible internal life, while the PCF maintains an organizational conservatism that inhibits its political ambitions.

In distilling these patterns of continuity and behavior from the thirty-year postwar history of both parties, we have, of course, dealt only marginally with many of the changes that have occurred during this period, some of which have formed the sub-

627

ject of the contributions to this volume. In particular, we have given less weight than some observers—for instance, Georges Lavau—to recent changes in the French party, changes whose results were evident, in particular, in the results of its electoral alliance with the Socialists in the 1973 legislative elections and in the presidential election of May 1974. But if the emphasis has been on continuity, this has not been only for convenience; it is mainly through the filter of a strategic model worked out during years of internal evolution and adaptation to its setting that a party can change. Without pretending to summarize all such changes in a few pages, we can, nevertheless, touch upon the ones that seem most important, thus illustrating our contention that the pattern of continuity outlined above continues to influence each party in a fundamental way.

Changes in the International System

The most obvious changes to which the PCI and the PCF have adjusted have taken place in the international Communist movement. When the 1956 revelations by Khrushchev fell on both nonruling parties, the PCF resisted de-Stalinization as long as possible, while the PCI—at first cautiously and then more boldly—turned the growing crisis in the Soviet camp to its own advantage.[131] Is this a sign of greater Soviet "control" over the PCF? It seems more likely that it resulted from a lesser disposition in the French party, and a greater one in the PCI, to use the situation to institute changes in its position in national life. This was evident both in the PCI's reshuffling of its cadres to remove the best-known Stalinists from positions of power and in Togliatti's expansion of Khrushchev's call for "national roads to socialism"—by which the Russian leader meant only a greater degree of economic differentiation in Eastern Europe—into a doctrine applicable to the nonruling parties' strategies for assuming power. Indeed, even the Italian party's strategy of seeking a broad range of domestic alliances was supported, in Togliatti's reading, by the new doctrine. As Blackmer writes, "Greater autonomy of individual parties, in short, would allow each in its own way to

[131] See Donald L. M. Blackmer, *Unity in Diversity: Italian Communism and the Communist World* (Cambridge, Mass., and London: The M.I.T. Press, 1968).

pursue alliances with non-Communist forces, just as the PCI had done with the Italian Socialists."[132]

Some scholars have argued that the PCF's more orthodox reaction to the changes in the socialist world was the result of a greater degree of policy control on the part of Moscow. Our interpretation is somewhat different; although one can scarcely deny the great importance of the PCF to the Soviet Union's global strategy, the link between the two parties is more organic and less explicit than is often supposed. The PCF responds to the Soviet Union's signals in international affairs to the degree that it does mainly because the Soviet path to socialism was an integral part of the French party's internal development. This responsiveness is not determined merely by adulation of Stalin and of the great Soviet party (the majority of the Italian party's cadres retain an instinctive loyalty to Stalinism, too), but by the PCF's dependence for its guiding myths, its organizational system, and its major policy goals upon the maintenance of an organic link to the Soviet Union.

The domestic events which took place in each country during the 1960s helped to increase the differences in the responses of the two parties to the USSR even further. If the Fourth Republic provided a relatively comfortable—if isolated—oppositional position for the PCF, the early years of the Fifth threatened it with electoral extinction. This increased the utility of the Soviet link for the French party, if only as a source of hope and sustenance. But at the same time, in Italy, the opening to the Left and the economic miracle—also discouraging to the Left—were leading the PCI "to take the *via Italiana*, which had been in the mid-fifties little more than a propaganda slogan, a good deal more seriously."[133] This led the Italians to launch a persistent critique of life in the Soviet Union, of the way the international movement was being run, and, more and more, of the way that the increasingly tense confrontation with the Chinese was being handled. By the late 1960s, the French and Italian parties would differ on this important question, not only in their conclusions, but in the

[132] Donald L. M. Blackmer, "The International Strategy of the Italian Communist Party," in Blackmer and Kriegel, *The International Role of the Communist Parties of Italy and France* (Cambridge, Mass.: Center for International Affairs, Harvard University, 1975), p. 10.

[133] Ibid., pp. 14-15.

basis of the arguments they would make. For example, in May 1969, *Rinascita* published the following statement about the Sino-Soviet rift:

> The fundamental problem remains the problem of internationalism. . . . Mutual accusations of the abandonment of socialism, or of underground collusion with the imperialists, do not help the process of clarification, and becomes an ideological veil that disguises the real . . . problems.

On the same day, the PCF *Bureau Politique* published a very different kind of statement on the same issue:

> The adventurist, chauvinist and anti-Soviet policies of the group around Mao Tse Tung, their repeated violations of frontiers, their systematic attacks against the CP-USSR and other Communist parties, all cause great damage to the cause of socialism.[134]

The same differences in the two parties' reactions were evident in their policies on the Common Market. "Although sharing the basic Soviet appraisal of the Market's disastrous economic consequences for Western Europe," writes Blackmer, "the PCI from the outset expressed cautious sympathy for the general principle of economic integration and tended to place relatively more emphasis on the objective economic roots of the union than on its purely political-military character."[135] The PCF, in contrast, remained committed to its original view that the Market was subservient to NATO and to the United States. The same was true of the two parties' reactions to the Czechoslovakian problem: the PCF backing down after a ritual criticism of the Soviet Union and the PCI responding with a categorical denunciation that crystallized the position it had been developing since 1956 that "sovereignty is an inalienable right. For us," wrote *l'Unità* in 1971, "this is not an abstract interpretation but a value which we cannot renounce."[136]

On all three issues—the Sino-Soviet split, the Czech events, and the EEC—the Italian party has responded in terms of an approach which "strongly emphasized the virtue of active partici-

[134] Both quotations can be found in *Politique aujourd'hui* (June 1969), pp. 34-35.

[135] Blackmer, "International Strategy," p. 19.

[136] Ibid., p. 15. It should be noted that Marchais, during a recent visit to Moscow, also spoke of the PCF's "sovereignty," but in a far less controversial context.

630

pation and influence from within as opposed to passive criticism or sterile denunciation" from outside.[137] "We must always be present," said *l'Unità* in 1971 with respect to the EEC, "not in the illusion that our presence in itself can change the situation, but in order to struggle to take advantage of the ever new contradictions that spring from the very process of integration."[138] PCI policy on Europe, therefore, is an exact parallel of the party's domestic strategy, a strategy which has made the notion of presence its central component.

Although there have been changes in the French party's international positions over the past few years, mainly in connection with its effort to establish the grounds for an alliance with the Socialists, much of its original conservatism on international issues remains. Some think this is due to continued Soviet control over the major aspects of PCF foreign policy (François Mitterrand confided to a French journalist that when the Common Program between his party and the Communists was being discussed, the latter group telephoned Moscow frequently for instructions).[139] However, PCF subservience to the USSR's foreign policy interest appears to go farther than would be necessary if the issues were only international. In supporting a variety of Moscow's initiatives—both within and outside of the Soviet Union—the PCF also supports its own tight and disciplined organizational system, its vision of the behavior required of the authentic party of the working class, and, it should be added, its leaders' cynicism about the importance of certain "bourgeois" values. For example, its comment on the publication of Solzhenitsyn's *Gulag Archipelago* in 1973 was symptomatic of far more than of its loyalty to the Soviet Union:

> Now the facts that serve as the basis of this book have been known for a long, long time and have been condemned by the Communist party of the Soviet Union itself. . . . The only new element that we find in this book is that Solzhenitsyn reveals himself here as a declared enemy of socialism itself.[140]

The experience of the Italian party's leaders with dictatorship, and the greater viability of their experience within parliamentary institutions have given them a greater appreciation of the impor-

---

[137] Ibid., p. 20.
[138] Quoted in "International Strategy," p. 21.
[139] Quoted in Kogan, "The French Communists," p. 195.
[140] "Soljenitsyne se disqualifie," *Le Monde*, January 20-21, 1974, p. 6.

tance of such values, whether or not one wishes to call them "bourgeois." Their increasingly detached position vis-à-vis the Soviet Union has led to political gains for the PCI among intellectuals and other Italians that seem to far outweigh the cost of incurring the wrath of those who retain the memories and emotional attachments of earlier years. On the issues of China, of dissent in Eastern Europe, and of the lack of freedom in the Soviet Union, the PCI's positions are now inseparable from the character of its domestic organization and support base, its participation in parliamentary and local institutions, and its strategic model for arriving at socialism in an advanced society.

But if all these things are true, ought we to expect, in the not too distant future, a dissolution of the Italian party's remaining ties with the Soviet Union? This would be assuming too much: first, because its identification with international communism remains a critical element in the PCI's internal cohesion; second, because—particularly since its organizational system allows for much diversity of opinion—the PCI needs to maintain the claim of the unity and effectiveness to make difficult decisions. As Blackmer writes, "Could it continue to make that claim if it cut itself off from the Soviet party that represents the continuity and force of that political tradition?"[141] "The more its domestic politics and programs come to resemble those of other groups," concludes Blackmer, "the more important it may be that it continue to offer a distinctly different international perspective and a different understanding of the nature and role of a political party."[142] As long as the PCI lacks concrete prospects for participation in an Italian government, the concern with its internal unity and with its differentiation from the other parties in the political system will probably continue to outweigh the possible advantages for the PCI of a completely neutral stance in foreign affairs. But this raises the question of the domestic prospects of the PCI, and it is to the changes in the domestic power balance of the two Communist parties that we should now turn.

CHANGES IN THE DOMESTIC POWER BALANCE

In discussing the political traditions of Italy and France, we pointed to three substantial differences: first, the stronger demo-

[141] Blackmer, "International Strategy," p. 29.
[142] Ibid., p. 29.

632

cratic fabric of France; second, the more reformist character of SFIO; and, third, the more cohesive character of the Italian Right. It is a measure of the degree of the domestic change each country has undergone since 1945 that, in each of these areas, the position is somewhat reversed, vis-à-vis what was true thirty years ago. Although no one would call Italy a successful pluralistic democracy, with the fall of Greece to the colonels and the shift of France to a presidential regime, it was the only Mediterranean country which retained a pure parliamentary system. In France, the restrictions on parliamentary freedom, the tight control of the press and media, and the majoritarian two-ballot electoral system limit severely the representative character of the regime. Recent threats from the Right in Italy have been much greater, especially since the decline of the French *ultras* in the early 1960s, yet the freedom of action of the Italian Left has, if anything, grown, just as the Left in France was being deprived by the Gaullist constitution of much of its institutional basis of support. And, if the threat from the Right has been political in Italy and constitutional in France, the response of the two Communist parties has been exactly the reverse: the PCF responding to a constitutional threat with a political alliance which recalls the Popular Front, and the PCI responding to a political threat by wrapping itself in the republican constitution and calling for a renewal of the anti-Fascist coalition. Each party responds to the threat from the Right in terms of its own strategic model and in the light of the patterns of continuity that it has developed over the years.

Second, if the PSI in the turbulent years before fascism was in sectarian hands, while the SFIO was so reformist that it lost most of its radical members to the PCF, that position has now been reversed. From its tentative collaboration in the Center-Left experiments of the early 1960s, the PSI has plummeted headlong into a series of governments which have disappointed not only the radical hopes of their Socialist participants but even the moderate hopes of American supporters. And from its uncompromising anticommunism in the 1950s, the SFIO under François Mitterrand has been transformed into a new *Parti socialiste* which has taken substantial steps toward the policy positions of the Communists and away from the *tiers force* strategy it had hoped to develop earlier.

The contrast in strategy can be extended even further left: if

633

the PCI reacted to the rightward flight of its Socialist neighbors with the greatest moderation—seeming at times to be attempting to leapfrog over the PSI in its overtures to the Christian Democracy—the PCF has made few real compromises with the PS, for the simple reason that it has been the Socialists who have made the most important shifts toward the positions of the Communists, rather than vice versa. Thus, the PCF-PS entente was not destroyed by the Communist *non* in the referendum on the European Community. On the contrary, the Communist *non* clarified the points the Communists regarded as nonnegotiable and just what price the Socialists would have to pay if they wanted to reach an agreement.[143] But this contingent factor, which illustrates the limited nature of the French Communists' commitment to alliances, also suggests the possibly tactical character of the Socialists' reconversion—with the exception of a radical fringe—to Marxism; if the Socialists ended up more eager for an agreement than the Communists, it was not because they have fallen into the position of subservience that the PSI occupied vis-à-vis the PCI in the 1950s, but, rather, that they were anxious to form an alliance, whether it be with the Communists or anyone else.[144] Given the continued suspicion of many Socialist voters that the PCF, once in the government, "would use any means to stay there," and the new perspectives opened up by Pompidou's death, one may therefore be skeptical of the permanence of the Communist-Socialist alliance in France.[145]

In contrast, each Italian Socialist move to the right has been met on the part of the PCI by an attempt to propose an even more alluring prospect to the Christian Democrats than the PSI could offer. With the fall of the Center-Right government of Giulio Andreotti and the return to the formula of the Center-Left in July 1973, Berlinguer went further than ever before in offering the DC a Communist partnership in government. In what would later be called his "great historical compromise" speech, Berlinguer said,

> In Italy, to transform the society in a socialist sense, it would not be enough for the Left to arrive at 51 percent of the vote.

[143] See Kriegel's contribution to this volume, Chapter 2.
[144] Ibid., pp. 81-82.
[145] SOFRES (Société Française d'Enquêtes par Sondages), "l'Image du parti communiste," pamphlet (Paris, 1971).

It would be a majority that would be far too weak. What would be necessary would also be the agreement of the masses represented by the DC.[146]

When Luigi Longo, heir to Togliatti and Berlinguer's predecessor as party secretary, rebaptized the concept from "historical compromise" to the more traditional term "historical bloc," it was clear that an issue had been joined in the PCI.[147] Once again, while the circumstances differ in each country, it is the strategic model of each party which seems the surest guide to its reactions: the PCF responding to the leftist overtures of the French Socialists with only modest doctrinal changes and the PCI responding to the centrist march of the PSI with even more energetic appeals to the Christian Democracy, attempting to shift that party's axis to the left.

Third, if the traditional Right in France has been ideologically and organizationally disunited, and the Italian Right has been held together by the hegemonic power of the Church, this too has changed. For the first time during the 1960s, there developed a majority political current on the French Right, one which not even the departure of Pompidou could completely disrupt. It is mainly this—added to the willingness of the Parti socialiste to move to the left—which has convinced the PCF of the need to strike a political bargain with the non-Communist Left. Isolation is only palatable when revolution is on the agenda or when—as during the Fourth Republic—the rest of the political system is in disarray. If the Gaullists and the rest of the Center and Right can remain united behind Giscard, the chances for continuation of the PCF-PS alliance are, therefore, good.

Does this mean that the French and Italian Right are now united in presenting a bold front of opposition to communism? The reality is, in fact, somewhat more complex. The Catholic Right in Italy has a highly *organized* subculture that helps to protect the party's sources of electoral strength from eroding even where religious devotion tends to decline. But the colonization by the DC and its affiliates of every corner of Italian society was always somewhat artificial, and its social presence has tended to

[146] Sandro Parone, "Berlinguer: Cara DC," *Panorama*, October 25, 1973, p. 43.

[147] Guido Quaranta, "I compromessi sposi," *Panorama*, November 8, 1973, p. 41.

635

recede as its militants leave, become old and prosperous, and the threat from international communism recedes. Indeed, the emerging pattern is for the DC social presence to survive only where its control of the state and its financial resources enable it to take on the characteristics of a political machine. Everywhere else, the picture for the DC has been one of increasing factionalism, parochialism, and internal ideological conflict that is in some ways greater than the conflict between the party and the rest of the political system. And as the conflicts within Italy's ruling party have increased, the temptation on the part of the PCI to attempt to stimulate a schism in the DC's ranks by appealing to left-wing Catholics has grown proportionally. The decline in the cohesion of the Italian Right combines with the changes evident in Italian socialism and with the enhanced freedom of action for the Left in Italian parliamentary institutions to encourage the continuation of the PCI's basic strategic model: a model of presence within, and transformation of, the structures of Italian society on the basis of a system of alliances involving the Socialists, the Catholic Left, and the variety of regional and social alliances that the party has cultivated over the past thirty years.

But how plausible is the PCI's hope for an ever-expanding structure of alliances reaching to the left-wing of the Christian Democratic party? Because the Christian Democracy has based its strength, at least in part, on a "natural" subculture of religious devotion, it has deep roots in all social classes and in all regions of the country. This suggests that unless Italian society undergoes a rapid secularization that destroys the traditional bases of DC support, the PCI—despite its attempts at an opening to the Church—will find it very difficult to expand into the Catholic electorate. Berlinguer himself has pointed out that the DC's losses in voters do not necessarily redound to the benefit of the PCI—indeed, in certain regions Catholic losses have been translated into gains for the extreme Right—throwing the Communists into great confusion. On the other hand, the outcome of the divorce referendum suggests a greater secularization of Italian society than the PCI had supposed.

But the DC does not seem likely to disintegrate under the influence of PCI allurements to its left-wing. What a "great historical compromise" can mean then, is a call for a political deal between the Communists and the Christian Democrats at the level of the political elite—a strategy which could clearly lead to a shelving of the PCI's social goals to the benefit of its political ones. Such a policy would not represent any basic change in the PCI's practical approach to Italian politics, but only the apotheosis of its failure to establish that position in the "trenches and fortifications" of Italian civil society that follows from its most basic theoretical commitments. Only a large scale political change—as in the regional elections of 1975, for example—could bring about a shift in partisan alignments and give the *compromesso storico* a concrete social content.

What has happened to frustrate the PCI's strategy of social presence and social alliances while its political leaders have made such strides in carving out a broad political presence? The basic problem has been a failure to keep pace theoretically with the social and economic changes of the postwar world. Initially it was the Italian party that seemed to be adapting more rapidly to the integration of the working class, the rise in mass consumption, and the rise of a whole number of issues that can best be summarized under the rubric of "quality of life." While Maurice Thorez was still insisting, in the early 1960s, that the worker under advanced capitalism would never escape from the plague of "total immiseration," the PCI was organizing a series of meetings on the changes in Italian capitalism, and on their implications for the party's strategy. And while the PCI was adjusting its strategy to the demands of an economy in which a backward south persisted alongside a booming Industrial Triangle, the PCF continued to regard French capitalism as an undifferentiated phenomenon, ignoring secondary contradictions, like the regional one, in favor of a predominant emphasis upon the primary contradiction between capital and labor.

But, paradoxically, the PCI's adaptation to the changes in the Italian economy may have been premature, for its major strategic lines were set during the 1940s, when the weight of the elements of tradition in Italian society were far more important than they are today. The basic problem was the party's strategy of alliances. It was couched in terms that would appeal to a backward peasantry which was soon to become far more modern, and to a middle class that was based primarily on artisans and shopkeepers, rather than on the technicians and white-collar workers of today, and it was based on a regional cleavage that has been declining somewhat in importance. The same factors are evident in the PCI's original approach to the Church. Clerical power was a patently "traditional" motif when Gramsci first raised the issue of coming to terms with *"la quistione cattolica,"* and even in 1945 the PCI seems to have assumed that, in the Church, it was dealing with a residue of the past. But the cultural and economic staying power of organized Catholicism in Italy has been enormous—even in Catholic regions like Lombardy and the Veneto that can hardly be considered underdeveloped. As a result, the Church is not an exception to Italy's modernization but a fundamental part of it.

This is not to suggest that the Italian party has been unaware of the need to revise its theoretical analysis of Italian society. Its frequent theoretical conferences and the pages of its publications are full of the most searching *critica* and *autocritica* along many of the lines outlined above. But its practical political activities continue along much the same path that was started in the late 1940s, and its recent stress on a political compromise with the forces of political Catholicism suggest an even greater substitution of the political for the social, and of the elite for the base, than has been true in the past. In other words, the PCI continues to talk the language of social alliances and broad social presence that spring from its original strategic model, but its instincts have grown to be far more short term and far more political.

The changes we have described on the French political scene do not appear to have brought about a basic change in the outlook of the PCF either. The PCF has undoubtedly made a large number of programmatic changes—and these should not be underrated in their future impact on its policies and organization. Similarly, the party's local and national representatives are increasingly younger and more modern, and, in its approach to the public, it has adopted a highly successful tone of quiet competence and sweet reason. But it is hard to discern any real change in the underlying strategic model of the French party, just as it is difficult yet to see any real change in its fidelity to the Soviet Union or its internal life. Such changes are always possible and should not be excluded, but they are discouraged by the undoubted benefits that the traditional approach has given the French party. As the *Nouvel Observateur* asks, in commenting on the changes in the procedure of the PCF Central Committee under Georges Marchais:

Above and beyond the formal liberty of debate established and even expanded under Marchais, when will we see a delegate get up at a Central Committee meeting and say plainly, "As for me, I don't agree . . ."?[148]

In one important area, there has been a limited change in the PCF, but one which may have great implications for its future strategy: the French party, belatedly it is true, has begun a serious analysis of the changes in French capitalism. In contrast to the PCI, it can respond to these changes in terms of economic structures whose future shape has already become clear, to social classes whose configuration has already changed, and to a popular culture that is already largely secularized. A primary example is the party's approach to the middle class. Unlike the Italian party, which concentrated from the first on artisans, tradesmen, and small shopkeepers, the PCF, after a failure to penetrate the traditional middle class, has begun with an analysis —a slow and tortuous one, it is true—of the role of the *new* middle classes in the French economy, especially the technicians and white-collar workers who help to man its most important sectors.

But these social groups are also the natural terrain for the expansion of the new and dynamic Parti socialiste, and the PCF— with no other route opened up for it by its traditions or by its domestic possibilities than a popular front with the Socialists— faces a dilemma in approaching such groups. On the one hand, if it succeeds in organizing among them, it will endanger its alliance with the Socialists; on the other, if it fails to do so, these members of the new middle class will gravitate elsewhere. It is this dilemma that underlies the PCF's recent overtures to the middle strata, overtures which have, so far, taken place more at an ideological than an organizational level.

Moreover, to engage seriously in a policy of practical alliances with the middle class and other nonproletarian groups the PCF will have to open up its internal life, transcend the myth of proletarian hegemony that has sustained it, and take active positions on a host of issues that it has consciously ignored in the past. More than anything else, the PCF must liquidate the image of its internal life as a somber, well-drilled barracks room of the revolution, an image, it should be added, that is due as much to the

[148] Marcelle Padovani, "Les 'quatre erreurs' du PCF," *Le Nouvel Observateur*, March 26, 1973, p. 31.

639

self-image projected by the party as to the ill will of its opponents. One cannot escape the suspicion that this, the fundamental change that would be necessary to make the PCF an acceptable governmental alternative, has not yet occurred, despite all the changes in program and in propaganda that have taken place over the past decade.

List of Contributors

DONALD L. M. BLACKMER is Professor of Political Science and Associate Dean of the School of Humanities and Social Science at M.I.T. He is the author of *Unity in Diversity: Italian Communism and the Communist World* (1968) and co-author of *The International Role of the Communist Parties of Italy and France* (1975).

STEPHEN HELLMAN is Associate Professor of Political Science at York University, Toronto. He has written numerous articles on the PCI and on the Italian left in general, and is the translator of Maria Antonietta Macchiocchi's *Letters from Inside the Italian Communist Party to Louis Althusser* (1973).

ANNIE J. KRIEGEL is Professor of Political Sociology at the University of Paris-X-Nanterre. She is the author of *Aux origines du communisme français* (Paris, 1964); *The French Communists: Profile of a People* (Paris, 1968; Chicago, 1972); and *Communisme au miroir français* (Paris, 1974).

DENIS LACORNE teaches Social Science at the University of California at Irvine. He has taught at the University of Quebec at Montreal and at the University of California at La Jolla. He has written articles on French politics for the *Revue Française de Science Politique* and in *Comparative Politics.*

PETER LANGE is Associate Professor of Government and Coordinator of the Seminar on the State and Capitalism at the Center for European Studies at Harvard. He has published in *Foreign Policy*, in *Il Mulino*, and is a contributor to Bailer (ed.), *Radicalism in the Contemporary Age* (1977) and is presently working on a study of the evolution and current strategy and organization of the Italian Communist Party.

GEORGES LAVAU is Professor of Political Sociology at the Institute of Political Studies, Paris, and has been director of the Centre d'Étude de la Vie Politique Française and editor of the *Revue Française de Science Politique*. He was a contributor to *Le Communisme en France* (1970) and has written numerous articles on French political parties.

641

JEROME MILCH is Assistant Professor in Science, Technology and Society and in Business and Public Administration at Cornell. He has written several articles on French local government and is currently at work on a comparative study of the politics of technological decision-making.

ROBERT D. PUTNAM is Professor of Political Science and Research Scientist at the Institute of Public Policy Studies at the University of Michigan. He is the author of *The Beliefs of Politicians* (1973) and of *The Comparative Study of Political Elites* (1975). He is currently working on a longitudinal study of the institutionalization of the Italian regions.

GEORGE ROSS is Associate Professor of Sociology at Brandeis. He is the author of *The Nationalization of Steel* (London, 1965) plus several articles and a forthcoming manuscript on the French labor movement. He is also a contributor to *The Nation, New Politics*, and other reviews.

GIACOMO SANI is Professor of Political Science at Ohio State University and has taught extensively in Italy. He is the author of *Gruppi professionali, struttura burocratica e tensioni organizzative* (1965), co-author of *L'organizzazione del PCI e della DC* (1970) and has published articles on Italian voting behavior in Italy and America.

ALAN STERN is Associate Professor of Political Science at the University of North Carolina at Chapel Hill. He has published articles on Italian local politics in both Italy and America and is currently working on the application of psychoanalysis to studies of political socialization.

SIDNEY TARROW is Professor of Government at Cornell. His published work includes *Peasant Communism in Southern Italy* (1967) and *Between Center and Periphery: Grassroots Politicians in Italy and France* (1977). He is a co-author of *Sociologie du communisme italien* (Paris, 1975) and of *Territorial Politics in Industrial States* (to be published).

RONALD TIERSKY is Assistant Professor of Political Science at Amherst College. He is the author of *French Communism, 1920-1972* (1974) and has also published in *Problems of Communism*.

PETER R. WEITZ is Coordinator for European Programs for the German Marshall Fund of the U.S. in Washington. He is author of "Labor and Politics in a Divided Movement: the Italian Case," *Industrial and Labor Relations Review* (1975) and is currently completing a study of postwar changes in the political involvement of the Italian labor movement.

642

Index

ACLI (Associazioni Cristiane dei Lavoratori Italiani), 51, 56, 247, 249, 250, 253, 255, 563

Algerian war, *see* foreign policy (PCF)

alliance strategy (PCF), 108, 155, 538-539, 612, 621-627, 633
  and emphasis on popular participation, 351-352, 359, 366. *See also* local government
  in Fifth Republic, 76-77, 83, 437-450, 538-539
  implementation at local level, 154-155, 156-157, 169, 316-318, 320-321, 322-332, 336-337, 356, 358, 613, 622
  and May 1968, *see* left-wing extremism
  and middle classes, 101-102, 108, 350, 366, 385, 612, 613, 623, 624-625, 639-640
  municipal elites and left-wing unity, 313-314
  in prewar period, 421-427, 579, 583-584, 585-586. *See also* popular front
  in Resistance through Cold War period, 427-437, 506
  See also Common Program

alliance strategy (PCI), 32-34, 55-56, 63, 155, 190, 263-267, 382-383, 462, 464, 594-595, 611, 621-627, 633-635, 636-638
  attitudes of party functionaries, 412-417
  and Catholics, *see* Catholics; Catholic Church; DC
  concept of "presence" in civil society, 36, 161, 404, 621, 636
  fear of isolation, 26, 27, 30, 49, 293, 383, 403
  and hot autumn, 398-403
  impact of Chilean coup, 419
  impact of Fascist experience, 27,

151, 215n, 375-376, 579, 585-586
  immediate postwar period, *see* participation in government
  implementation at local level, 154-157, 239-240, 265-268, 273-295, 403-411, 619-620, 622-624
  and middle classes, *see* middle classes
  obstacles to electoral expansion, 262-263, 497-503, 592, 636
  organizational prerequisites of, 58-59, 606
  and Resistance, *see* Resistance
  and South, *see* South
  Svolta di Salerno, see Togliatti

Althusser, Louis, 137

Amendola, Giorgio, 66, 401n, 556, 567

Andreotti, Giulio, 634

army, PCF attitude toward, 95

Badoglio, Pietro, 27, 41

Ballanger, Robert, 616-617

Barca, Luciano, 557

Berlinguer, Enrico, 263n, 418, 462, 567, 636
  and "historic compromise," 264n, 575, 634-635
  and models of socialism, 60
  and PCI alliance strategy, 266n, 390, 403

Bertrand, Mireille, 134

Bidault, Georges, 126

Billoux, François, 100n, 108n, 116, 126-127, 428, 612

Blum, Léon, 97, 100, 119n, 422, 424-425, 429, 584. *See also* popular front, 1934-1939

Bordiga, Amedeo, 26, 583

Borker, Jules, 442, 443, 445

Brodoloni, Giacomo, 555n

Casanova, Laurent, 73

643

Library of Congress Cataloging in Publication Data

Main entry under title:
Communism in Italy and France.

    Partito Comunista d'Italia—Addresses, essays, lectures. 2. Parti Communiste français—Addresses, essays, lectures. I. Blackmer, Donald L. M.
II. Tarrow, Sidney G.
JN5657.C63C65   329.9'45   74-25612
ISBN 0-691-08724-5